The Most Popular Plays
of the
American Theatre

BOOKS AND PLAYS BY STANLEY RICHARDS

BOOKS:

GREAT MUSICALS OF THE AMERICAN THEATRE: VOLUME ONE
GREAT MUSICALS OF THE AMERICAN THEATRE: VOLUME TWO
GREAT ROCK MUSICALS
AMERICA ON STAGE: TEN GREAT PLAYS OF AMERICAN HISTORY
THE TONY WINNERS
BEST PLAYS OF THE SIXTIES
TWENTY ONE-ACT PLAYS
BEST MYSTERY AND SUSPENSE PLAYS OF THE MODERN THEATRE
10 CLASSIC MYSTERY AND SUSPENSE PLAYS OF THE MODERN THEATRE
MODERN SHORT COMEDIES FROM BROADWAY AND LONDON
BEST SHORT PLAYS OF THE WORLD THEATRE: 1968–1973
BEST SHORT PLAYS OF THE WORLD THEATRE: 1958–1967
THE BEST SHORT PLAYS 1979
THE BEST SHORT PLAYS 1978
THE BEST SHORT PLAYS 1977
THE BEST SHORT PLAYS 1976
THE BEST SHORT PLAYS 1975
THE BEST SHORT PLAYS 1974
THE BEST SHORT PLAYS 1973
THE BEST SHORT PLAYS 1972
THE BEST SHORT PLAYS 1971
THE BEST SHORT PLAYS 1970
THE BEST SHORT PLAYS 1969
THE BEST SHORT PLAYS 1968
CANADA ON STAGE

PLAYS:

THROUGH A GLASS, DARKLY
AUGUST HEAT
SUN DECK
TUNNEL OF LOVE
JOURNEY TO BAHIA
O DISTANT LAND
MOOD PIECE
MR. BELL'S CREATION
THE PROUD AGE
ONCE TO EVERY BOY
HALF-HOUR, PLEASE
KNOW YOUR NEIGHBOR
GIN AND BITTERNESS
THE HILLS OF BATAAN
DISTRICT OF COLUMBIA

The Most

Popular Plays of the American Theatre

TEN OF BROADWAY'S LONGEST-RUNNING PLAYS

EDITED, WITH AN INTRODUCTION AND NOTES BY

STANLEY RICHARDS

STEIN AND DAY/*Publishers*/New York

First published in 1979

Copyright © 1979 by Stanley Richards
All rights reserved
Designed by David Miller
Printed in the United States of America
Stein and Day/*Publishers*/Scarborough House
Briarcliff Manor, N.Y. 10510

Library of Congress Cataloging in Publication Data

Main entry under title:

The most popular plays of the American theatre.

CONTENTS: Lindsay, H., and Crouse, R. Life with father.—Kirkland, J. Tobacco Road.—Nichols, A. Abie's Irish rose. [etc.]
1. American drama—20th century. I. Richards, Stanley, 1918-
PS634.M66   812'.5'08   79-65112
ISBN: 0-8128-2682-5

for
CAROL FEINSTEIN

CONTENTS

*Photographs from original productions
between pages 287–289*

INTRODUCTION

In the Broadway theatre, a long run is defined as a play (or musical) that runs for at least 500 consecutive performances. A production that attains 1,000 or more performances gains entry into the theatre's golden circle of most popular attractions. Ten of the latter are represented in these pages. Of the reigning circle, three—*Born Yesterday, The Voice of the Turtle,* and *Lightnin'*—for reasons best known to their rights' holders, were unavailable for reprint. But, happily, they were supplanted by those next in line and whose popularity was equally established during their lengthy New York engagements.

The overall champion among plays, of course, is *Life With Father,* with its record-breaking 3,224 performances. Yet, it is a musical, *Fiddler on the Roof,* with its 3,242 performances that bears the crown of Broadway's all-time record holder. (From this vantage point, it may soon be displaced by another durable musical, *Grease.*) But since this collection is devoted only to plays the concentration therefore is on the non-musical theatre.

Of the top twelve achievers, nine are comedies, one a seriocomic study, and two suspense tales. This, then, must be taken as a reflection of the tastes and demands of the majority of playgoers with its distinct predilection for amusing, rather than cerebral or heavy, entertainment. There is hardly a potent drama in sight, though Tennessee Williams' *A Streetcar Named Desire* approaches closely with its total of 855 performances.

The combined number of performances given by the plays in this collection is slightly over 19,000. This figure represents their original Broadway engagements and does not include touring companies, revivals, stock, regional, and subsequent community and amateur theatre showings that undoubtedly reached another awesome sum.

There are a number of theories as to what makes plays run for 500 or more performances on Broadway, yet the most apparent of all remains audience acceptance and response. Surely, one cannot credit the drama critics, for, with the exception of several plays, their notices were at most friendly rather than eloquent and, in two cases (as pointed out in the individual prefaces), they were almost downright disdainful or begrudging. Nevertheless, while critics may endorse a play, it is the public who keeps it running.

Nor can an author's reputation be given as the reason for a play's

9

marathon performance. (As a matter of pure fact, when *Barefoot in the Park* opened in 1963, Neil Simon was scarcely the household name or influential writer he is today.) As Abe Laufe observed in his admirable treatise *Anatomy of a Hit*: "An author's reputation might logically explain a play's popularity, but if reputation means recognition from critics, then the list of authors who have written long-running plays presents some curious omissions. Eugene O'Neill heads the list of prize-winning American dramatists with four Pulitzer Prizes, one Critics' Circle Award, and the Nobel Prize for literature. Robert E. Sherwood ranks second with four Pulitzer Prizes, one for biography and three for drama. Yet not one play written by O'Neill or Sherwood ever reached the five-hundred-performance record." These are just two of many distinguished American dramatists who never achieved that mark. Nor, it may be added, did any of the contributors to this collection ever duplicate the records established with these properties.

By the same token, neither can theatrical longevity be attributed to name stars. Valuable as they may have been at the time of their openings, all of the plays in this volume survived the eventual loss of their original leads and carried prosperously through with an assortment of replacements.

What remains then are the plays themselves, with their abundant appeal to vast audiences. Their popularity in their specific times in theatrical history remained steadfast. Their deliverance of entertainment to theatre-goers was indelibly recorded and whether one agrees or disagrees with their values today, the plays contained herein are, without question, ten of the most popular plays of the commercial theatre.

STANLEY RICHARDS

CLARENCE DAY'S

Life With Father

MADE INTO A PLAY BY
HOWARD LINDSAY
AND RUSSEL CROUSE

HOWARD LINDSAY
AND RUSSEL CROUSE

The all-time champion among nonmusical shows is *Life With Father*, whose enormous popularity brought it a record-breaking run of 3,224 performances, and no current (or future) Broadway dramatic production even looms as a possible contender to usurp its throne as New York's longest-running play. Its appeal was not limited to Broadway, for the comedy played in more than two hundred cities in the United States and Canada as well as in various other parts of the world, some theretofore only remotely familiar with American period mores.

What made *Life With Father* so very special? According to Brooks Atkinson of *The New York Times*: "Sooner or later every one will have to see it. For the late Clarence Day's vastly amusing sketches of his despotic parent have now been translated into a perfect comedy by Howard Lindsay and Russel Crouse and must be reckoned an authentic part of our American folklore. They were as genuine as that when they first appeared in *The New Yorker*, and later between covers in book form. In the form of a narrative drama of family life, Mr. Lindsay and Mr. Crouse have now pulled that immortal saga together, wonderfully preserving the humanity as well as the fantastic humor. . . . The dialogue is sparkling, the story is shrewdly told, and the acting is a treasury of appreciative humor. Life with father may have been trying at black moments on Madison Avenue, but it is overpoweringly funny in the theatre. It is also enchanting, for *Life With Father* is a darlin' play."

In his tribute to *The Making of the American Theatre*, Howard Taubman observed: "*Life With Father* ran for seven and a half years on Broadway to break every record and to become not only a warm memory for millions of theatregoers but a shining example of the theatre's unpredictability. Who would have guessed that this family comedy, neither sexy nor sophisticated, would flourish so famously?" The fact that *Life With Father* did not receive either of the two major dramatic awards (the Pulitzer Prize or the New York Drama Critics' Circle Award) also surprised not only the public but a number of the critics who felt that it fully deserved more recognition. But its recognition was unequivocally fulfilled when it toppled all previous long-run records, establishing it as America's favorite comedy.

13

Life With Father was not the only Lindsay and Crouse collaboration. In twenty-eight years, beginning in 1934, they teamed on a variety of other plays and musicals. Their partnership was remarkably happy as well as longevous. Both admitted they themselves could not tell which line was whose when a play was completed, so closely did they work together. Their method has often been described. First, they talked over their ideas for a show at great length. Then Crouse began typing while his partner paced the room. Both continued talking. In three or four months, after Lindsay (at his estimate) had paced off 5,000 miles and Crouse had typed out 150 pages, another play was born.

Shortly before his death, Lindsay recalled how they had gotten involved with *Life With Father*. He initially encountered the sketches in *The New Yorker* in the 1930s, and developed an affinity for them while reading them aloud to his actress–wife, Dorothy Stickney. But it took several years before it evolved as a play, and there were problems. The producer who held the stage rights had assigned another playwright to the project, and only when the latter's version proved unsatisfactory did the Lindsay–Crouse team receive the go-ahead signal.

Although Lindsay also costarred as Father Day, playing opposite Miss Stickney as Vinnie, it was never his intention to appear in the comedy. Actually, when it was being prepared for its Broadway premiere, the plan was to find a major star for box-office insurance. When no one proved available (either because of a lack of enthusiasm or a prior commitment) he reluctantly took on the assignment. (He played the Victorian autocrat of the breakfast table so long and convincingly that Miss Stickney said he adopted the make-up and character in his private life ever after.)

Howard Lindsay (1889–1968) was born in Waterford, New York, but grew up in Boston. He was educated at the Boston Latin School and studied at Harvard for one year, then almost immediately turned his attention to the theatre. In 1909, he obtained his first role in the touring company of *Polly of the Circus*. From then until he entered the Army during World War I, he played on the road, in silent movies, tent shows, burlesque and vaudeville, and as a member of Margaret Anglin's repertory company. He also doubled on occasion as director.

He scored his first major success in 1921 as director of *Dulcy*, a comedy by George S. Kaufman and Marc Connelly, starring Lynn Fontanne. While still acting and directing, he began to write in collaboration with Bertrand Robinson. These plays included the popular *Tommy* and *Your Uncle Dudley*. He also dramatized the Edward Hope novel, *She Loves Me Not*, a leading success in 1933.

The collaborative life with Crouse came about in 1934 when they were both hired separately to hastily revise the script of a new Cole Porter shipboard musical, which resulted in *Anything Goes*, with Ethel Merman, William Gaxton, and Victor Moore at the helm. Thereafter, except for one play, *A Slight Case of Murder*, written with Damon Runyon in 1935,

Lindsay never collaborated with any other writer but Crouse. Together they turned out *Red, Hot and Blue!*; *Hooray for What!*; *Strip for Action*; *State of the Union* (winner of the Pulitzer Prize, 1946); *Life With Mother* (the sequel to *Life With Father*); *Call Me Madam*; *Remains to Be Seen*; *The Prescott Proposals*; *The Great Sebastians*; *Happy Hunting*; *Tall Story*; *The Sound of Music*; and *Mr. President*.

Russel Crouse (1893–1966) was born in Findlay, Ohio, the son of a newspaper publisher. He spent several years as a reporter on Cincinnati and Kansas papers, and, after duty with the Navy in World War I, worked on several New York dailies, including the *New York Evening Post*, writing a humorous column, "Left at the Post." He also served as press representative for the Theatre Guild for five years. Prior to his teaming with Lindsay, he wrote the books for two Broadway musicals: *The Gang's All Here* and (with Corey Ford) *Hold Your Horses*, a vehicle for comedian Joe Cook. Then, in 1934, came that consequential event, his first collaboration with Lindsay. . . .

As producers, the pair also presented a number of successful Broadway plays including Joseph Kesselring's *Arsenic and Old Lace*, John Patrick's *The Hasty Heart*, and Sidney Kingsley's *Detective Story*.

A film version of *Life With Father* (with William Powell, Irene Dunne, and Elizabeth Taylor) was released in 1947.

LIFE WITH FATHER was first produced at the Empire Theatre, New York, on November 8, 1939, by Oscar Serlin. The cast was as follows:

ANNIE	*Katherine Bard*
VINNIE	*Dorothy Stickney*
CLARENCE	*John Drew Devereaux*
JOHN	*Richard Simon*
WHITNEY	*Raymond Roe*
HARLAN	*Larry Robinson*
FATHER	*Howard Lindsay*
MARGARET	*Dorothy Bernard*
CORA	*Ruth Hammond*
MARY	*Teresa Wright*
THE REVEREND DR. LLOYD	*Richard Sterling*
DELIA	*Portia Morrow*
NORA	*Nellie Burt*
DR. HUMPHREYS	*A. H. Van Buren*
DR. SOMERS	*John C. King*
MAGGIE	*Timothy Kearse*

Directed by Bretaigne Windust
Setting and Costumes by Stewart Chaney

Time: Late in the 1880s. The entire action takes place in the Morning Room of the Day home on Madison Avenue.

ACT ONE

Scene 1: Breakfast time. An early summer morning.
Scene 2: Tea time. The same day.

ACT TWO
Scene 1: Sunday, after church. A week later.
Scene 2: Breakfast time. Two days later. (During Scene 2 the curtain is lowered to denote a lapse of three hours.)

ACT THREE

Scene 1: Mid-afternoon. A month later.
Scene 2: Breakfast time. The next morning.

ACT ONE

The morning room of the Day home at 420 Madison Avenue. In the custom of the Victorian period, this was the room where the family gathered for breakfast, and because it was often the most comfortable room in the house, it served also as a living room for the family and their intimates.

There is a large arch in the center of the upstage wall of the room, through which we can see the hall and the stairs leading to the second floor, and below them the rail of the stairwell leading to the basement. The room can be closed off from the hall by sliding doors in the archway. The front door of the house, which is stage right, can't be seen, but frequently is heard to slam.

In the morning room the sunshine streams through the large window at the right which looks out on Madison Avenue. The room itself is furnished with the somewhat less than comfortable furniture of the period, which is the late 1880s. The general color scheme in drapes and upholstery is green. Below the window is a large comfortable chair where FATHER *generally sits to read his paper. Right of center is the table which serves as a living room table, with its proper table cover and fruit bowl; but now, expanded by extra leaves, it is doing service as a breakfast table. Against the back wall, either side of the arch, are two console tables which are used by the maid as serving tables. Left of center is a sofa, with a table just above its right end holding a lamp, framed photographs, and other ornaments. In the left wall is a fireplace, its mantel draped with a lambrequin. On the mantel are a clock and other ornaments, and above the mantel is a large mirror in a Victorian frame. The room is cluttered with the minutiae of the period, including the inevitable rubber plant, and looking down from the walls are the Day ancestors in painted portraits. The room has the warm quality that comes only from having been lived in by a family which enjoys each other's company—a family of considerable means.*

As the curtain rises, ANNIE, *the new maid, a young Irish girl, is finishing setting the table for breakfast. After an uncertain look at the result she crosses over to her tray on the console table.* VINNIE *comes down the stairs and into the room.* VINNIE *is a charming, lovable, and spirited woman of forty. She has a lively mind which darts quickly away from any practical matter. She has red hair.*

ANNIE: Good morning, ma'am.

VINNIE: Good morning, Annie. How are you getting along?

ANNIE: All right, ma'am, I hope.

VINNIE: Now, don't be worried just because this is your first day. Everything's going to be all right—but I do hope nothing goes wrong. [*Goes to the table*] Now, let's see, is the table all set? [ANNIE *follows her*] The cream and the sugar go down at this end.

ANNIE: [*Placing them where* VINNIE *has indicated*] I thought in the center, ma'am; everyone could reach them easier.

VINNIE: Mr. Day sits here.

ANNIE: [*Gets a tray of napkins, neatly rolled and in their rings, from the console table*] I didn't know where to place the napkins, ma'am.

VINNIE: You can tell which go where by the rings. [*Takes them from the tray and puts them down as she goes around the table.* ANNIE *follows her*] This one belongs to Whitney—it has his initial on it, "W"; that one with the little dog on it is Harlan's, of course. He's the baby. This "J" is for John and the "C" is for Clarence. This narrow plain one is mine. And this is Mr. Day's. It's just like mine—except that it got bent one morning. And that reminds me—always be sure Mr. Day's coffee is piping hot.

ANNIE: Ah, your man has coffee instead of tea of a morning?

VINNIE: We all have coffee except the two youngest boys. They have their milk. And, Annie, always speak of my husband as Mr. Day.

ANNIE: I will that.

VINNIE: [*Correcting her*] "Yes, ma'am," Annie.

ANNIE: Yes, ma'am.

VINNIE: And if Mr. Day speaks to you, just say: "Yes, sir." Don't be nervous—you'll get used to him.

> [CLARENCE, *the eldest son, about seventeen, comes down the stairs and into the room. He is a manly, serious, good-looking boy. Because he is starting in at Yale next year, he thinks he is grown-up. He is redheaded*]

CLARENCE: Good morning, Mother. [*He kisses her*]

VINNIE: Good morning, Clarence.

CLARENCE: Did you sleep well, Mother?

VINNIE: Yes, thank you, dear. [CLARENCE *goes to* FATHER's *chair and picks up the morning paper. To* ANNIE] We always start with fruit, except the two young boys, who have porridge.

> [ANNIE *brings the fruit and porridge to the table.* CLARENCE, *looking at the paper, makes a whistling sound*]

CLARENCE: Jiminy! Another wreck on the New Haven. That always disturbs the market. Father won't like that.

VINNIE: I do wish that New Haven would stop having wrecks. If they knew how it upset you father—[*Sees that* CLARENCE's *coat has been torn and mended*] My soul and body, Clarence, what's happened to your coat?

CLARENCE: I tore it. Margaret mended it for me.

VINNIE: It looks terrible. Why don't you wear your blue suit?

CLARENCE: That looks worse than this one. You know, I burnt that hole in it.

VINNIE: Oh, yes—well, you can't go around looking like that. I'll have to speak to your father. Oh, dear!

[JOHN, *who is about fifteen, comes down the stairs and into the room.* JOHN *is gangly and a little overgrown. He is red-headed*]

JOHN: Good morning, Mother. [*He kisses her*]

VINNIE: Good morning, John.

JOHN: [*To* CLARENCE] Who won?

CLARENCE: I haven't looked yet.

JOHN: Let me see. [*He tries to take the paper away from* CLARENCE]

CLARENCE: Be careful!

VINNIE: Boys, don't wrinkle that paper before your father's looked at it.

CLARENCE: [*To* JOHN] Yes!

[VINNIE *turns to* ANNIE]

VINNIE: You'd better get things started. We want everything ready when Mr. Day comes down. [ANNIE *exits*] Clarence, right after breakfast I want you and John to move the small bureau from my room into yours.

CLARENCE: What for? Is somebody coming to visit us?

JOHN: Who's coming?

VINNIE: I haven't said anyone was coming. And don't you say anything about it. I want it to be a surprise.

CLARENCE: Oh! Father doesn't know yet?

VINNIE: No. And I'd better speak to him about a new suit for you before he finds out he's being surprised by visitors.

[ANNIE *enters with a tray on which are two glasses of milk, which she puts at* HARLAN's *and* WHITNEY's *places at the table.* WHITNEY *comes down the stairs and rushes into the room. He is about thirteen. Suiting his age, he is a lively active boy. He is red-headed*]

WHITNEY: Morning. [*He kisses his mother quickly, then runs to* CLARENCE *and* JOHN] Who won?

JOHN: The Giants, 7 to 3. Buck Ewing hit a home run.

WHITNEY: Let me see!

[HARLAN *comes sliding down the banister. He enters the room, runs to his mother, and kisses her.* HARLAN *is a roly-poly, lovable, good-natured youngster of six. He is red-headed*]

VINNIE: How's your finger, darling?

HARLAN: It itches.

VINNIE: [*Kissing the finger*] That's a sign it's getting better. Now don't scratch it. Sit down, boys. Get in your chair, darling. [*The boys move to the table and take their places.* CLARENCE *puts the newspaper beside his*

father's plate. JOHN *stands waiting to place* VINNIE's *chair when she sits*]
Now, Annie, watch Mr. Day, and as soon as he finishes his fruit— [*Leaves
the admonition hanging in mid-air as the sound of* FATHER's *voice booms
from upstairs*]

FATHER'S VOICE: Vinnie! Vinnie!

[*All eyes turn toward the staircase.* VINNIE *rushes to the foot of the
stairs, speaking as she goes*]

VINNIE: What's the matter, Clare?

FATHER'S VOICE: Where's my necktie?

VINNIE: Which necktie?

FATHER'S VOICE: The one I gave you yesterday.

VINNIE: It isn't pressed yet. I forgot to give it to Margaret.

FATHER'S VOICE: I told you distinctly I wanted to wear that necktie today.

VINNIE: You've got plenty of neckties. Put on another one right away and
come down to breakfast.

FATHER'S VOICE: Oh, damn! Damnation!

[VINNIE *goes to her place at the table.* JOHN *places her chair for her,
then sits.* WHITNEY *has started eating*]

CLARENCE: Whitney!

VINNIE: Wait for your father, Whitney.

WHITNEY: Oh, and I'm in a hurry! John, can I borrow your glove today? I'm
going to pitch.

JOHN: If I don't play myself.

WHITNEY: Look, if you need it, we're playing in that big field at the corner of
Fifty-seventh and Madison.

VINNIE: 'Way up there!

WHITNEY: They're building a house on that vacant lot on Fiftieth Street.

VINNIE: My! My! Here we move to Forty-eighth Street just to get out of the
city!

WHITNEY: Can't I start breakfast, Mother? I promised to be there by eight
o'clock.

VINNIE: After breakfast, Whitney, you have to study your catechism.

WHITNEY: Mother, can't I do that this afternoon?

VINNIE: Whitney, you have to learn five questions every morning before you
leave the house.

WHITNEY: Aw, Mother—

VINNIE: You weren't very sure of yourself when I heard you last night.

WHITNEY: I know them now.

VINNIE: Let's see. [WHITNEY *rises and faces his mother*] "What is your
name?"

WHITNEY: Whitney Benjamin.

VINNIE: "Who gave you this name?"

WHITNEY: "My sponsors in baptism, wherein I was made a member of Christ, the child of God and an inheritor of the Kingdom of Heaven." Mother, if I hadn't been baptized wouldn't I have a name?

VINNIE: Not in the sight of the Church. "What did your sponsors then do for you?"

WHITNEY: "They did promise and vow three things in my name—"

> [FATHER *makes his appearance on the stairway and comes down into the room.* FATHER *is in his forties, distinguished in appearance, with great charm and vitality, extremely well dressed in a conservative way. He is red-headed*]

FATHER: [*Heartily*] Good morning, boys. [*They rise and answer him*] Good morning, Vinnie. [*He goes to her and kisses her*] Have a good night?

VINNIE: Yes, thank you, Clare.

FATHER: Good! Sit down, boys.

> [*The doorbell rings and a postman's whistle is heard*]

VINNIE: That's the doorbell, Annie. [ANNIE *exits*] Clare, that new suit looks very nice.

FATHER: Too damn tight! [*He sits in his place at the head of the table*] What's the matter with those fellows over in London! I wrote them a year ago they were making my clothes too tight!

VINNIE: You've put on a little weight, Clare.

FATHER: I weigh just the same as I always have. [*Attacks his orange. The boys dive into their breakfasts.* ANNIE *enters with the mail, starts to take it to* VINNIE. FATHER *sees her*] What's that? The mail? That goes to me.

> [ANNIE *gives the mail to* FATHER *and exits with her tray*]

VINNIE: Well, Clarence has just managed to tear the only decent suit of clothes he has.

FATHER: [*Looking through the mail*] Here's one for you, Vinnie. John, hand that to your mother. [*He passes the letter on*]

VINNIE: Clare dear, I'm sorry, but I'm afraid Clarence is going to have to have a new suit of clothes.

FATHER: Vinnie, Clarence has to learn not to be so hard on his clothes.

CLARENCE: Father, I thought—

FATHER: Clarence, when you start in Yale in the fall, I'm going to set aside a thousand dollars just to outfit you, but you'll get no new clothes this summer.

CLARENCE: Can't I have one of your old suits cut down for me?

FATHER: Every suit I own still has plenty of wear in it. I wear my clothes until they're worn out.

VINNIE: Well, if you want your clothes worn out, Clarence can wear them out much faster than you can.

CLARENCE: Yes, and, Father, you don't get a chance to wear them out. Every time you get a new batch of clothes, Mother sends the old ones to the missionary barrel. I guess I'm just as good as any old missionary.

[ANNIE *returns with a platter of bacon and eggs and a pot of coffee*]

VINNIE: Clarence, before you compare yourself to a missionary, remember the sacrifices they make.

FATHER: [*Chuckling*] I don't know, Vinnie, I think my clothes would look better on Clarence than on some Hottentot. [*To* CLARENCE] Have that black suit of mine cut down to fit you before your mother.gets her hands on it.

[ANNIE *clears the fruit*]

CLARENCE: Thank you, Father. [*To* JOHN] One of Father's suits! Thank you, sir!

FATHER: Whitney, don't eat so fast.

WHITNEY: Well, Father, I'm going to pitch today and I promised to get there early, but before I go I have to study my catechism.

FATHER: What do you bother with that for?

VINNIE: [*With spirit*] Because if he doesn't know his catechism he can't be confirmed!

WHITNEY: [*Pleading*] But I'm going to pitch today.

FATHER: Vinnie, Whitney's going to pitch today and he can be confirmed any old time.

VINNIE: Clare, sometimes it seems to me that you don't care whether your children get to Heaven or not.

FATHER: Oh, Whitney'll get to Heaven all right. [*To* WHITNEY] I'll be there before you are, Whitney; I'll see that you get in.

VINNIE: What makes you so sure they'll let you in?

FATHER: Well, if they don't I'll certainly raise a devil of a row.

[ANNIE *is at* FATHER's *side with the platter of bacon and eggs, ready to serve him, and draws back at this astounding declaration, raising the platter*]

VINNIE: [*With shocked awe*] Clare, I do hope you'll behave when you get to Heaven.

[FATHER *has turned to serve himself from the platter, but* ANNIE, *not yet recovered from the picture of* FATHER *raising a row at the gates of Heaven, is holding it too high for him*]

FATHER: [*Storming*] Vinnie, how many times have I asked you not to engage a maid who doesn't even know how to serve properly?

VINNIE: Clare, can't you see she's new and doing her best?

FATHER: How can I serve myself when she's holding that platter over my head?

VINNIE: Annie, why don't you hold it lower?.

[ANNIE *lowers the platter.* FATHER *serves himself, but goes on talking*]

FATHER: Where'd she come from anyway? What became of the one we had yesterday? I don't see why you can't keep a maid.

VINNIE: Oh, you don't!

FATHER: All I want is service. [ANNIE *serves the others nervously. So far as* FATHER *is concerned, however, the storm has passed, and he turns genially to* WHITNEY] Whitney, when we get to Heaven we'll organize a baseball team of our own. [*The boys laugh*]

VINNIE: It would be just like you to try to run things up there.

FATHER: Well, from all I've heard about Heaven, it seems to be a pretty unbusinesslike place. They could probably use a good man like me. [*Stamps on the floor three times. It is his traditional signal to summon* MARGARET, *the cook, from the kitchen below*]

VINNIE: What do you want Margaret for? What's wrong?

[ANNIE *has reached the sideboard and is sniffling audibly*]

FATHER: [*Distracted*] What's that damn noise?

VINNIE: Shhh—it's Annie.

FATHER: Annie? Who's Annie?

VINNIE: The maid. [ANNIE, *seeing that she has attracted attention, hurries out into the hall where she can't be seen or heard*] Clare, aren't you ashamed of yourself?

FATHER: [*Surprised*] What have I done now?

VINNIE: You made her cry—speaking to her the way you did.

FATHER: I never said a word to her—I was addressing myself to you.

VINNIE: I do wish you'd be more careful. It's hard enough to keep a maid— and the uniforms just fit this one.

[MARGARET, *the cook, a small Irishwoman of about fifty, hurries into the room*]

MARGARET: What's wanting?

FATHER: Margaret, this bacon is good. [MARGARET *beams and gestures deprecatingly*] It's *good.* It's done just right!

MARGARET: Yes, sir!

[*She smiles and exits.* ANNIE *returns, recovered, and starts serving the coffee.* VINNIE *has opened her letter and glanced through it*]

VINNIE: Clare, this letter gives me a good idea. I've decided that next winter I won't give a series of dinners.

FATHER: I should hope not.

VINNIE: I'll give a big musicale instead.

FATHER: You'll give a what?

VINNIE: A musicale.

FATHER: [*Peremptorily*] Vinnie, I won't have my peaceful home turned into a Roman arena with a lot of hairy fiddlers prancing about.

VINNIE: I didn't say a word about hairy fiddlers. Mrs. Spiller has written me about this lovely young girl who will come for very little.

FATHER: What instrument does this inexpensive paragon play?

VINNIE: She doesn't play, Clare, she whistles.

FATHER: Whistles? Good God!

VINNIE: She whistles sixteen different pieces. All for twenty-five dollars.

FATHER: [*Stormily*] I won't pay twenty-five dollars to any human peanut stand. [*He tastes his coffee, grimaces, and again stamps three times on the floor*]

VINNIE: Clare, I can arrange this so it won't cost you a penny. If I invite fifty people and charge them fifty cents apiece, there's the twenty-five dollars right there!

FATHER: You can't invite people to your own house and charge them admission.

VINNIE: I can if the money's for the missionary fund.

FATHER: Then where will you get the twenty-five dollars to pay that poor girl for her whistling?

VINNIE: Now, Clare, let's not cross that bridge until we come to it.

FATHER: And if we do cross it, it will cost me twenty-five dollars. Vinnie, I'm putting my foot down about this musicale, just as I've had to put my foot down about your keeping this house full of visiting relatives. Why can't we live here by ourselves in peace and comfort?

[MARGARET *comes dashing into the room*]

MARGARET: What's wanting?

FATHER: [*Sternly*] Margaret, what is this? [*He holds up his coffee cup and points at it*]

MARGARET: It's coffee, sir.

FATHER: It is not coffee! You couldn't possibly take water and coffee beans and arrive at that! It's slops, that's what it is—slops! Take it away! Take it away, I tell you!

[MARGARET *takes* FATHER's *cup and dashes out.* ANNIE *starts to take* VINNIE's *cup*]

VINNIE: Leave my coffee there, Annie! It's perfectly all right!

[ANNIE *leaves the room*]

FATHER: [*Angrily*] It is not! I swear I can't imagine how she concocts such an atrocity. I come down to this table every morning hungry—

VINNIE: Well, if you're hungry, Clare, why aren't you eating your breakfast?

FATHER: What?

VINNIE: If you're hungry, why aren't you eating your breakfast?

FATHER: [*Thrown out of bounds*] I am. [*He takes a mouthful of bacon and munches it happily, his eyes falling on* HARLAN] Harlan, how's that finger? Come over here and let me see it. [HARLAN *goes to his father's side. He shows his finger*] Well, that's healing nicely. Now don't pick that scab or it will leave a scar, and we don't want scars on our fingers, do we? [*He chuckles*] I guess you'll remember after this that cats don't like to be hugged. It's all right to stroke them, but don't squeeze them. Now go back and finish your oatmeal.

HARLAN: I don't like oatmeal.

FATHER: [*Kindly*] It's good for you. Go back and eat it.

HARLAN: But I don't like it.

FATHER: [*Quietly, but firmly*] I'll tell you what you like and what you don't like. You're not old enough to know about such things. You've no business not to like oatmeal. It's good.

HARLAN: I hate it.

FATHER: [*Firmly, but not quietly*] That's enough! We won't discuss it! Eat that oatmeal at once!

   [*In contrast to* HARLAN, WHITNEY *has been eating his oatmeal at a terrific rate of speed. He pauses and puts down his spoon*]

WHITNEY: I've finished *my* oatmeal. May I be excused?

FATHER: Yes, Whitney, you may go. [WHITNEY *slides off his chair and hurries to the stairs*] Pitch a good game.

VINNIE: Whitney!

WHITNEY: I'm going upstairs to study my catechism.

VINNIE: Oh, that's all right. Run along.

WHITNEY: [*On the way up*] Harlan, you'd better hurry up and finish your oatmeal if you want to go with me.

   [*Throughout breakfast* FATHER *has been opening and glancing through his mail. He has just reached one letter, however, that bewilders him*]

FATHER: I don't understand why I'm always getting damn fool letters like this!

VINNIE: What is it, Clare?

FATHER: "Dear Friend Day: We are assigning you the exclusive rights for Staten Island for selling the Gem Home Popper for popcorn—"

CLARENCE: I think that's for me, Father.

FATHER: Then why isn't it addressed to Clarence Day, Jr.? [*He looks at the envelope*] Oh, it is. Well, I'm sorry. I didn't mean to open your mail.

   [MARGARET *returns and slips a cup of coffee to the table beside* FATHER]

VINNIE: I wouldn't get mixed up in that, Clarence. People like popcorn, but they won't go all the way to Staten Island to buy it.

[FATHER has picked up the paper and is reading it. He drinks his coffee absentmindedly]

FATHER: Chauncey Depew's having another birthday.

VINNIE: How nice.

FATHER: He's always having birthdays. Two or three a year. Damn! Another wreck on the New Haven!

VINNIE: Yes. Oh, that reminds me. Mrs. Bailey dropped in yesterday.

FATHER: Was she in the wreck?

VINNIE: No. But she was born in New Haven. Clarence, you're having tea with Edith Bailey Thursday afternoon.

CLARENCE: Oh, Mother, do I have to?

JOHN: [Singing] "I like coffee, I like tea. I like the girls and the girls like me."

CLARENCE: Well, the girls don't like me and I don't like them.

VINNIE: Edith Bailey's a very nice girl, isn't she, Clare?

FATHER: Edith Bailey? Don't like her. Don't blame Clarence.

[FATHER goes to his chair by the window and sits down with his newspaper and a cigar. The others rise. HARLAN runs upstairs. ANNIE starts clearing the table and exits with the tray of dishes a little later. VINNIE speaks in a guarded tone to the two boys]

VINNIE: Clarence, you and John go upstairs and do—what I asked you to.

JOHN: You said the small bureau, Mother?

VINNIE: Shh! Run along.

[The boys go upstairs, somewhat unwillingly. MARGARET enters]

MARGARET: If you please, ma'am, there's a package been delivered with a dollar due on it. Some kitchen knives.

VINNIE: Oh, yes, those knives from Lewis & Conger's. [She gets her purse from the drawer in the console table and gives MARGARET a dollar] Here, give this dollar to the man, Margaret.

FATHER: Make a memorandum of that, Vinnie. One dollar and whatever it was for.

VINNIE: [Looking into purse] Clare, dear, I'm afraid I'm going to need some more money.

FATHER: What for?

VINNIE: You were complaining of the coffee this morning. Well, that nice French drip coffee pot is broken—and you know how it got broken.

FATHER: [Taking out his wallet] Never mind that, Vinnie. As I remember, the coffee pot cost five dollars and something. Here's six dollars. [He gives her six dollars] And when you get it, enter the exact amount in the ledger downstairs.

VINNIE: Thank you, Clare.

FATHER: We can't go on month after month having the household accounts in such a mess.

VINNIE: [*She sits on the arm of* FATHER's *chair*] No, and I've thought of a system that will make my bookkeeping perfect.

FATHER: I'm certainly relieved to hear that. What is it?

VINNIE: Well, Clare dear, you never make half the fuss over how much I've spent as you do over my not being able to remember what I've spent it for.

FATHER: Exactly. This house must be run on a business basis. That's why I insist on your keeping books.

VINNIE: That's the whole point, Clare. All we have to do is open charge accounts everywhere and the stores will do my bookkeeping for me.

FATHER: Wait a minute, Vinnie—

VINNIE: Then when the bills come in you'd know exactly where your money had gone.

FATHER: I certainly would. Vinnie, I get enough bills as it is.

VINNIE: Yes, and those bills always help. They show you just where I spent the money. Now if we had charge accounts everywhere—

FATHER: Now, Vinnie, I don't know about that.

VINNIE: Clare dear, don't you hate those arguments we have every month? I certainly do. Not to have those I should think would be worth something to you.

FATHER: Well, I'll open an account at Lewis & Conger's—and one at Mc-Creery's to start with—we'll see how it works out. [*He shakes his head doubtfully. Her victory gained,* VINNIE *moves away*]

VINNIE: Thank you, Clare. Oh—the rector's coming to tea today.

FATHER: The rector? I'm glad you warned me. I'll go to the club. Don't expect me home until dinner time.

VINNIE: I do wish you'd take a little more interest in the church. [*Goes behind* FATHER's *chair and looks down at him with concern*]

FATHER: Vinnie, getting me into Heaven's your job. If there's anything wrong with my ticket when I get there, you can fix it up. Everybody loves you so much—I'm sure God must, too.

VINNIE: I'll do my best, Clare. It wouldn't be Heaven without you.

FATHER: If you're there, Vinnie, I'll manage to get in some way, even if I have to climb the fence.

JOHN: [*From upstairs*] Mother, we've moved it. Is there anything else?

FATHER: What's being moved?

VINNIE: Never mind, Clare. I'll come right up, John. [*She goes to the arch, stops. Looks back at* FATHER] Oh, Clare, it's eight thirty. You don't want to be late at the office.

FATHER: Plenty of time. [VINNIE *looks nervously toward the door, then goes upstairs.* FATHER *returns to his newspaper.* VINNIE *has barely disappeared when something in the paper arouses* FATHER's *indignation*] Oh, God!

[VINNIE *comes running downstairs*]

VINNIE: What's the matter, Clare? What's wrong?

FATHER: Why did God make so many damn fools and Democrats?

VINNIE: [*Relieved*] Oh, politics. [*She goes upstairs again*]

FATHER: [*Shouting after her*] Yes, but it's taking the bread out of our mouths. It's robbery, that's what it is, highway robbery! Honest Hugh Grant! Honest! Bah! A fine mayor you've turned out to be. [FATHER *launches into a vigorous denunciation of Mayor Hugh Grant, addressing that gentleman as though he were present in the room, called up on the Day carpet to listen to* FATHER's *opinion of Tammany's latest attack on his pocketbook*] If you can't run this city without raising taxes every five minutes, you'd better get out and let someone who can. Let me tell you, sir, that the real-estate owners of New York City are not going to tolerate these conditions any longer. Tell me this—are these increased taxes going into public improvements or are they going into graft—answer me that, honestly, if you can, Mr. Honest Hugh Grant. You can't! I thought so. Bah! [ANNIE *enters with her tray. Hearing* FATHER *talking, she curtsies and backs into the hall, as if uncertain whether to intrude on* FATHER *and the Mayor.* VINNIE *comes downstairs*] If you don't stop your plundering of the pocketbooks of the good citizens of New York, we're going to throw you and your boodle Board of Aldermen out of office.

VINNIE: Annie, why aren't you clearing the table?

ANNIE: Mr. Day's got a visitor.

FATHER: I'm warning you for the last time.

VINNIE: Oh, nonsense, he's just reading his paper, Annie. Clear the table.

[VINNIE *goes off through the arch.* ANNIE *comes in timidly and starts to clear the table*]

FATHER: [*Still lecturing Mayor Grant*] We pay you a good round sum to watch after our interests, and all we get is inefficiency! [ANNIE *looks around trying to see the Mayor and, finding the room empty, assumes* FATHER's *remarks are directed at her*] I know you're a nincompoop and I strongly suspect you of being a scalawag. [ANNIE *stands petrified.* WHITNEY *comes downstairs*] It's graft—that's what it is—Tammany graft—and if you're not getting it, somebody else is.

WHITNEY: [*To* FATHER] Where's John? Do you know where John is?

FATHER: Dick Croker's running this town and you're just his cat's-paw.

[VINNIE *comes in from downstairs and* HARLAN *comes down from upstairs.* FATHER *goes on talking. The others carry on their conversation simultaneously, ignoring* FATHER *and his imaginary visitor*]

HARLAN: Mother, where's John?

VINNIE: He's upstairs, dear.

FATHER: And as for you, Richard Croker—don't think, just because you're hiding behind these minions you've put in public office, that you're going to escape your legal responsibilities.

WHITNEY: [*Calling upstairs*] John, I'm going to take your glove!

JOHN: [*From upstairs*] Don't you lose it! And don't let anybody else have it either!

VINNIE: Annie, you should have cleared the table long ago.

[ANNIE *loads her tray feverishly, eager to escape*]

FATHER: [*Rising and slamming down the paper in his chair*] Legal responsibilities—by gad, sir, I mean *criminal* responsibilities.

[*The boys start toward the front door*]

VINNIE: [*Starting upstairs*] Now you watch Harlan, Whitney. Don't let him be anywhere the ball can hit him. Do what Whitney says, Harlan. And don't be late for lunch.

[FATHER *has reached the arch on his way out of the room, where he pauses for a final shot at Mayor Grant*]

FATHER: Don't forget what happened to William Marcy Tweed—and if you put our taxes up once more, we'll put you in jail!

[*He goes out of the archway to the left. A few seconds later he is seen passing the arch toward the outer door wearing his square derby and carrying his stick and gloves. The door is heard to slam loudly.* ANNIE *seizes her tray of dishes and runs out of the arch to the left toward the basement stairs. A second later there is a scream from* ANNIE *and a tremendous crash.* JOHN *and* CLARENCE *come rushing down and look over the rail of the stairs below.* VINNIE *follows them almost immediately*]

VINNIE: What is it? What happened?

CLARENCE: The maid fell downstairs.

VINNIE: I don't wonder, with your father getting her so upset. Why couldn't she have finished with the table before she fell downstairs?

JOHN: I don't think she hurt herself.

VINNIE: And today of all days! Boys, will you finish the table? And, Clarence, don't leave the house until I talk to you. [*She goes downstairs*]

[*During the following scene* CLARENCE *and* JOHN *remove* VINNIE's *best breakfast tablecloth and cram it carelessly into the drawer of the console table, then take out the extra leaves from the table, push it together, and replace the livingroom table cover and the bowl of fruit*]

JOHN: What do you suppose Mother wants to talk to you about?

CLARENCE: Oh, probably about Edith Bailey.

JOHN: What do you talk about when you have tea alone with a girl?

CLARENCE: We don't talk about anything. I say: "Isn't it a nice day?" and she says: "Yes," and I say: "I think it's a little warmer than yesterday," and she says: "Yes, I like warm weather, don't you?" and I say: "Yes," and then we wait for the tea to come in. And then she says: "How many lumps?" and I say: "Two, thank you," and she says: "You must have a sweet tooth," and I can't say: "Yes" and I can't say: "No," so we just sit there and look at each other for half an hour. Then I say: "Well, it's time I was going," and she says: "Must you?" and I say: "I've enjoyed seeing you very much," and she says: "You must come again," and I say: "I will," and get out.

JOHN: [*Shaking his head*] Some fellows like girls.

CLARENCE: I don't.

JOHN: And did you ever notice fellows, when they get sweet on a girl—the silly things a girl can make them do? And they don't even seem to know they're acting silly.

CLARENCE: Well, not for Yours Truly!

[VINNIE *returns from downstairs*]

VINNIE: I declare I don't see how anyone could be so clumsy.

CLARENCE: Did she hurt herself?

VINNIE: No, she's not hurt—she's just hysterical! She doesn't make sense. Your father may have raised his voice; and if she doesn't know how to hold a platter properly, she deserved it—but I know he didn't threaten to put her in jail. Oh, well! Clarence, I want you to move your things into the front room. You'll have to sleep with the other boys for a night or two.

CLARENCE: You haven't told us who's coming.

VINNIE: [*Happily*] Cousin Cora. Isn't that nice?

CLARENCE: It's not nice for me. I can't get any sleep in there with those children.

JOHN: Wait'll Father finds out she's here! There'll be a rumpus.

VINNIE: John, don't criticize your father. He's very hospitable after he gets used to the idea.

[*The doorbell rings.* JOHN *and* VINNIE *go to the window*]

JOHN: Yes, it's Cousin Cora. Look, there's somebody with her.

VINNIE: [*Looking out*] She wrote me she was bringing a friend of hers. They're both going to stay here. [*A limping* ANNIE *passes through the hall*] Finish with the room, boys.

CLARENCE: Do I have to sleep with the other boys and have tea with Edith Bailey all in the same week?

VINNIE: Yes, and you'd better take your father's suit to the tailor's right away, so it will be ready by Thursday.

[VINNIE *goes down the hall to greet* CORA *and* MARY. CLARENCE *hurries off, carrying the table leaves*]

VINNIE'S VOICE: [*in the hall*] Cora, dear—

CORA'S VOICE: Cousin Vinnie, I'm so glad to see you! This is Mary Skinner.

VINNIE'S VOICE: Ed Skinner's daughter! I'm so glad to see you. Leave your bags in the hall and come right upstairs.

[VINNIE *enters, going toward the stairs.* CORA *follows her, but, seeing* JOHN, *enters the room and goes to him.* MARY *follows* CORA *in timidly.* CORA *is an attractive country cousin of about thirty.* MARY *is a refreshingly pretty small-town girl of sixteen*]

CORA: [*Seeing John*] Well, Clarence, it's so good to see you!

VINNIE: [*Coming into the room*] Oh, no, that's John.

CORA: John! Why, how you've grown! You'll be a man before your mother! [*She laughs herself at this time-worn quip*] John, this is Mary Skinner. [*They exchange greetings*] Vinnie, I have so much to tell you. We wrote you Aunt Carrie broke her hip. That was the night Robert Ingersoll lectured. Of course she couldn't get there; and it was a good thing for Mr. Ingersoll she didn't. [CLARENCE *enters*] And Grandpa Ebbetts hasn't been at all well.

CLARENCE: How do you do, Cousin Cora? I'm glad to see you.

CORA: This can't be Clarence!

VINNIE: Yes, it is.

CORA: My goodness, every time I see you boys you've grown another foot. Let's see—you're going to St. Paul's now, aren't you?

CLARENCE: [*With pained dignity*] St. Paul's! I was through with St. Paul's long ago. I'm starting in Yale this fall.

MARY: Yale!

CORA: Oh, Mary, this is Clarence—Mary Skinner. [MARY *smiles, and* CLARENCE, *the woman-hater, nods politely and walks away*] This is Mary's first trip to New York. She was so excited when she saw a horse-car.

VINNIE: We'll have to show Mary around. I'll tell you—I'll have Mr. Day take us all to Delmonico's for dinner tonight.

MARY: Delmonico's!

CORA: Oh, that's marvelous! Think of that, Mary—Delmonico's! And Cousin Clare's such a wonderful host.

VINNIE: I know you girls want to freshen up. So come upstairs. Clarence, I'll let the girls use your room now, and when they've finished you can move, and bring up their bags. They're out in the hall. [*Starts upstairs with* CORA] I've given you girls Clarence's room, but he didn't know about it until this morning and he hasn't moved out yet.

[VINNIE *and* CORA *disappear upstairs.* MARY *follows more slowly and on the second step stops and looks back.* CLARENCE *has gone into the hall with his back toward* MARY *and stares morosely in the direction of their luggage*]

CLARENCE: John, get their old bags.

[JOHN *disappears toward the front door. The voices of* VINNIE *and* CORA *have trailed off into the upper reaches of the house.* CLARENCE *turns to scowl in their direction and finds himself looking full into the face of* MARY]

MARY: Cora didn't tell me about you. I never met a Yale man before.

[*She gives him a devastating smile and with an audible whinny of girlish excitement she runs upstairs.* CLARENCE *stares after her a few seconds, then turns toward the audience with a look of "What happened to me just then?" Suddenly, however, his face breaks into a smile which indicates that, whatever has happened, he likes it*]

CURTAIN

SCENE TWO

The same day. Tea time.

VINNIE *and the* RECTOR *are having tea.* THE REVEREND DR. LLOYD *is a plump, bustling man, very good-hearted and pleasant.* VINNIE *and* DR. LLOYD *have one strong point in common: their devotion to the Church and its ritual.* VINNIE's *devotion comes from her natural piety;* DR. LLOYD's *is a little more professional.*

At rise, DR. LLOYD *is seated with a cup of tea.* VINNIE *is also seated and* WHITNEY *is standing next to her, stiffly erect in the manner of a boy reciting.* HARLAN *is seated next to his mother, watching* WHITNEY's *performance.*

WHITNEY: [*reciting*] "—to worship Him, to give Him thanks; to put my whole trust in Him, to call upon Him—" [*He hesitates*]

VINNIE: [*Prompting*]. "—to honor—"

WHITNEY: "—to honor His Holy Name and His word and to serve Him truly all the days of my life."

DR. LLOYD: "What is thy duty toward thy neighbor?"

WHITNEY: Whew! [*He pulls himself together and makes a brave start*] "My duty toward my neighbor is to love him as myself, and to do to all men as I would they should do unto me; to love, honor, and succor my father and my mother; to honor and obey—"

VINNIE: "—civil authorities."

WHITNEY: "—civil authorities. To—to—to—"

VINNIE: [*To* DR. LLOYD] He really knows it.

WHITNEY: I know most of the others.

DR. LLOYD: Well, he's done very well for so young a boy. I'm sure if he applies himself between now and Sunday I could hear him again—with the others.

VINNIE: There, Whitney, you'll have to study very hard if you want Dr. Lloyd to send your name in to Bishop Potter next Sunday. I must confess to you, Dr. Lloyd, it's really my fault. Instead of hearing Whitney say his catechism this morning I let him play baseball.

WHITNEY: We won, too; 35 to 27.

DR. LLOYD: That's splendid, my child. I'm glad your side won. But winning over your catechism is a richer and fuller victory.

WHITNEY: Can I go now?

VINNIE: Yes, darling. Thank Dr. Lloyd for hearing you and run along.

WHITNEY: Thank you, Dr. Lloyd.

DR. LLOYD: Not at all, my little man.

[WHITNEY *starts out, turns back, takes a piece of cake and runs out*]

VINNIE: Little Harlan is very apt at learning things by heart.

HARLAN: [*Scrambling to his feet*] I can spell Constantinople. Want to hear me? [DR. LLOYD *smiles his assent*] C-o-ennaconny—annaconny—sissaconny—tan-tan-tee—and a nople and a pople and a Constantinople!

DR. LLOYD: Very well done, my child.

VINNIE: [*Handing him a cake from the tea tray*] That's nice, darling. This is what you get for saying it so well.

[HARLAN *quickly looks at the cake and back to* DR. LLOYD]

HARLAN: Want me to say it again for you?

VINNIE: No, darling. One cake is enough. You run along and play with Whitney.

HARLAN: I can spell "huckleberry pie."

VINNIE: Run along, dear.

[HARLAN *goes out, skipping in rhythm to his recitation*]

HARLAN: H-a-huckle—b-a-buckle—h-a-huck-le-high. H-a-huckle—b-a-buckle—huckleberry pie!

DR. LLOYD: [*Amused*] You and Mr. Day must be very proud of your children. [VINNIE *beams*] I was hoping I'd find Mr. Day at home this afternoon.

VINNIE: [*Evasively*] Well, he's usually home from the office by this time.

DR. LLOYD: Perhaps he's gone for a gallop in the park—it's such a fine day. He's very fond of horseback riding, I believe.

VINNIE: Oh, yes.

DR. LLOYD: Tell me—has he ever been thrown from a horse?

VINNIE: Oh, no! No horse would throw Mr. Day.

DR. LLOYD: I've wondered. I thought he might have had an accident. I notice he never kneels in church.

VINNIE: Oh, that's no accident! But I don't want you to think he doesn't pray. He does. Why, sometimes you can hear him pray all over the house. But he never kneels.

DR. LLOYD: Never kneels! Dear me! I was hoping to have the opportunity to tell you and Mr. Day about our plans for the new edifice.

VINNIE: I'm so glad we're going to have a new church.

DR. LLOYD: I'm happy to announce that we're now ready to proceed. The only thing left to do is raise the money.

VINNIE: No one should hesitate about contributing to that.

[*The front door slams*]

DR. LLOYD: Perhaps that's Mr. Day now.

VINNIE: Oh, no, I hardly think so. [FATHER *appears in the archway*] Why, it is!

FATHER: Oh, damn! I forgot.

VINNIE: Clare, you're just in time. Dr. Lloyd's here for tea.

FATHER: I'll be right in. [*He disappears the other side of the archway*]

VINNIE: I'll send for some fresh tea. [*She goes to the bell-pull and rings for the maid*]

DR. LLOYD: Now we can tell Mr. Day about our plans for the new edifice.

VINNIE: [*Knowing her man*] After he's had his tea.

[FATHER *comes back into the room.* DR. LLOYD *rises*]

FATHER: How are you, Dr. Lloyd?

[CLARENCE *comes down the stairs and eagerly looks around for* MARY]

CLARENCE: Oh, it was Father.

DR. LLOYD: Very well, thank you. [*They shake hands*]

CLARENCE: [*To* VINNIE] They're not back yet?

VINNIE: No! Clarence, no!

[CLARENCE *turns, disappointed, and goes back upstairs*]

DR. LLOYD: It's a great pleasure to have a visit with you, Mr. Day. Except for a fleeting glimpse on the Sabbath, I don't see much of you.

[FATHER *grunts and sits down.* DELIA, *a new maid, enters*]

DELIA: Yes, ma'am.

VINNIE: Some fresh tea and a cup for Mr. Day. [DELIA *exits and* VINNIE *hurries down to the tea table to start the conversation*] Well, Clare, did you have a busy day at the office?

FATHER: Damn busy.

VINNIE: Clare!

FATHER: Very busy day. Tired out.

VINNIE: I've ordered some fresh tea. [*To* DR. LLOYD] Poor Clare, he must work very hard. He always comes home tired. Although how a man can get tired just sitting at his desk all day, I don't know. I suppose Wall Street is just as much a mystery to you as it is to me, Dr. Lloyd.

DR. LLOYD: No, no, it's all very clear to me. My mind often goes to the businessman. The picture I'm most fond of is when I envision him at the close of the day's work. There he sits—this hard-headed man of affairs— surrounded by the ledgers that he has been studying closely and harshly for hours. I see him pausing in his toil—and by chance he raises his eyes and looks out of the window at the light in God's sky and it comes over him that money and ledgers are dross. [FATHER *stares at* DR. LLOYD *with some amazement*] He realizes that all those figures of profit and loss are without importance or consequence—vanity and dust. And I see this troubled man bow his head and with streaming eyes resolve to devote his life to far higher things.

FATHER: Well, I'll be damned!

[*At this moment* DELIA *returns with the fresh tea for* FATHER]

VINNIE: Here's your tea, Clare.

[FATHER *notices the new maid*]

FATHER: Who's this?

VINNIE: [*Quickly*] The new maid.

FATHER: Where's the one we had this morning?

VINNIE: Never mind, Clare.

FATHER: The one we had this morning was prettier. [DELIA, *with a slight resentment, exits.* FATHER *attacks the tea and cake with relish*] Vinnie, these cakes are good.

DR. LLOYD: Delicious!

VINNIE: Dr. Lloyd wants to tell us about the plans for the new edifice.

FATHER: The new what?

VINNIE: The new church—Clare, you knew we were planning to build a new church.

DR. LLOYD: Of course, we're going to have to raise a large sum of money.

FATHER: [*Alive to the danger*] Well, personally, I'm against the church hop-skipping-and-jumping all over the town. And it so happens that during the last year I've suffered heavy losses in the market—damned heavy losses—

VINNIE: Clare!

FATHER:—so any contribution I make will have to be a small one.

VINNIE: But, Clare, for so worthy a cause!

FATHER: And if your Finance Committee thinks it's too small they can blame the rascals that are running the New Haven Railroad!

DR. LLOYD: The amount everyone is to subscribe has already been decided.

FATHER: [*bristling*] Who decided it?

DR. LLOYD: After considerable thought we've found a formula which we believe is fair and equitable. It apportions the burden lightly on those least able to carry it and justly on those whose shoulders we know are stronger. We've voted that our supporting members should each contribute a sum equal to the cost of their pews.

[FATHER's *jaw drops*]

FATHER: I paid five thousand dollars for my pew!

VINNIE: Yes, Clare. That makes our contribution five thousand dollars.

FATHER: That's robbery! Do you know what that pew is worth today? Three thousand dollars. That's what the last one sold for. I've taken a dead loss of two thousand dollars on that pew already. Frank Baggs sold me that pew when the market was at its peak. He knew when to get out. [*He turns to* VINNIE] And I'm warning you now that if the market ever goes up I'm going to unload that pew.

VINNIE: Clarence Day! How can you speak of the Lord's temple as though it were something to be bought and sold on Wall Street!

FATHER: Vinnie, this is a matter of dollars and cents, and that's something you don't know anything about!

VINNIE: Your talking of religion in the terms of dollars and cents seems to me pretty close to blasphemy.

DR. LLOYD: [*Soothingly*] Now, Mrs. Day, your husband is a businessman and he has a practical approach toward this problem. We've had to be practical about it, too—we have all the facts and figures.

FATHER: Oh, really! What's the new piece of property going to cost you?

DR. LLOYD: I think the figure I've heard mentioned is eighty-five thousand dollars—or was it a hundred and eighty-five thousand dollars?

FATHER: What's the property worth where we are now?

DR. LLOYD: Well, there's quite a difference of opinion about that.

FATHER: How much do you have to raise to build the new church?

DR. LLOYD: Now, I've seen those figures—let me see—I know it depends somewhat upon the amount of the mortgage.

FATHER: Mortgage, eh? What are the terms of the amortization?

DR. LLOYD: Amortization? That's not a word I'm familiar with.

FATHER: It all seems pretty vague and unsound to me. I certainly wouldn't let any customer of mine invest on what I've heard.

[*The doorbell rings*]

DR. LLOYD: We've given it a great deal of thought. I don't see how you can call it vague.

[DELIA *passes along the hall toward the front door*]

FATHER: Dr. Lloyd, you preach that some day we'll all have to answer to God.

DR. LLOYD: We shall indeed!

FATHER: Well, I hope God doesn't ask you any question with figures in them.

[CORA's *voice is heard in the hall, thanking* DELIA. VINNIE *goes to the arch just in time to meet* CORA *and* MARY *as they enter, heavily laden with packages, which they put down.* FATHER *and* DR. LLOYD *rise*]

CORA: Oh, Vinnie, what a day! We've been to every shop in town and—[*She sees* FATHER] Cousin Clare!

FATHER: [*Cordially*] Cora, what are you doing in New York?

CORA: We're just passing through on our way to Springfield.

FATHER: We?

[CLARENCE *comes downstairs into the room with eyes only for* MARY]

VINNIE: Oh, Dr. Lloyd, this is my favorite cousin, Miss Cartwright, and her friend, Mary Skinner. [*They exchange mutual how-do-you-do's*]

DR. LLOYD: This seems to be a family reunion. I'll just run along.

FATHER: [*Promptly*] Good-by, Dr. Lloyd.

DR. LLOYD: Good-by, Miss Cartwright. Good-by, Miss—er—

VINNIE: Clarence, you haven't said how-do-you-do to Dr. Lloyd.

CLARENCE: Good-by, Dr. Lloyd.

VINNIE: [*To* DR. LLOYD] I'll go to the door with you.

[DR. LLOYD *and* VINNIE *go out, talking*]

FATHER: Cora, you're as welcome as the flowers in May! Have some tea with us. [*To* DELIA] Bring some fresh tea—and some more of those cakes.

CORA: Oh, we've had tea! We were so tired shopping we had tea downtown.

[*With a gesture* FATHER *countermands his order to* DELIA, *who removes the tea table and exits*]

MARY: At the Fifth Avenue Hotel.

FATHER: At the Fifth Avenue Hotel, eh? Who'd you say this pretty little girl was?

CORA: She's Ed Skinner's daughter. Well, Mary, at last you've met Mr. Day. I've told Mary so much about you, Cousin Clare, that she's just been dying to meet you.

FATHER: Well, sit down! Sit down! Even if you have had tea you can stop and visit for a while. As a matter of fact, why don't you both stay to dinner?

[VINNIE *enters just in time to hear this and cuts in quickly*]

VINNIE: That's all arranged, Clare. Cora and Mary are going to have dinner with us.

FATHER: That's fine! That's fine!

CORA: Cousin Clare, I don't know how to thank you and Vinnie for your hospitality.

MARY: Yes, Mr. Day.

FATHER: Well, you'll just have to take pot luck.

CORA: No, I mean—

[VINNIE *speaks quickly to postpone the revelation that* FATHER *has house guests*]

VINNIE: Clare, did you know the girls are going to visit Aunt Judith in Springfield for a whole month?

FATHER: That's fine. How long are you going to be in New York, Cora?

CORA: All week.

FATHER: Splendid. We'll hope to see something of you, eh, Vinnie?

[CORA *looks bewildered and is about to speak*]

VINNIE: Did you find anything you wanted in the shops?

CORA: Just everything.

VINNIE: I want to see what you got.

CORA: I just can't want to show you. [*She goes coyly to* FATHER] But I'm afraid some of the packages can't be opened in front of Cousin Clare.

FATHER: Shall I leave the room? [*Laughs at his own joke*]

CORA: Clarence, do you mind taking the packages up to our room—or should I say your room? [*To* FATHER] Wasn't it nice of Clarence to give up his room to us for a whole week?

FATHER: [*With a sudden drop in temperature*] Vinnie!

VINNIE: Come on, Cora, I just can't wait to see what's in those packages.

[CORA, MARY, *and* VINNIE *start out.* CLARENCE *is gathering up the packages*]

FATHER: [*Ominously*] Vinnie, I wish to speak to you before you go upstairs.

VINNIE: I'll be down in just a minute, Clare.

FATHER: I wish to speak to you now!

[*The girls have disappeared upstairs*]

VINNIE: I'll be up in just a minute, Cora.

[*We hear a faint "All right" from upstairs*]

FATHER: [*His voice is low but stern*] Are those two women encamped in this house?

VINNIE: Now, Clare!

FATHER: [*Much louder*] Answer me, Vinnie!

VINNIE: Just a minute—control yourself, Clare.

[VINNIE, *sensing the coming storm hurries to the sliding doors.* CLARENCE *has reached the hall with his packages and he, too, has recognized the danger signal and as* VINNIE *closes one door he closes the other, leaving himself out in the hall and* FATHER *and* VINNIE *facing each other in the room*]

VINNIE: [*Persuasively*] Now, Clare, you know you've always liked Cora.

FATHER: [*exploding*] What has that got to do with her planking herself down in my house and bringing hordes of strangers with her?

VINNIE: [*reproachfully*] How can you call that sweet little girl a horde of strangers?

FATHER: Why don't they go to a hotel? New York is full of hotels built for the express purpose of housing such nuisances.

VINNIE: Clare! Two girls alone in a hotel! Who knows what might happen to them?

FATHER: All right. Then put 'em on the next train. If they want to roam—the damned gypsies—lend 'em a hand! Keep 'em roaming!

VINNIE: What have we got a home for if we can't show a little hospitality?

FATHER: I didn't buy this home to show hospitality—I bought it for my own comfort!

VINNIE: Well, how much are they going to interfere with your comfort living in that little room of Clarence's?

FATHER: The trouble is, damn it, they don't live there. They live in the bathroom! Every time I want to take my bath it's full of giggling females—washing their hair. From the time they take, you'd think it was the seven Sutherland Sisters. I tell you, I won't have it! Send 'em to a hotel. I'll pay the bill gladly, but get them out of here!

[CLARENCE *puts his head through the sliding door*]

CLARENCE: Father, I'm afraid they can hear you upstairs.

FATHER: Then keep those doors closed!

VINNIE: [*With decision*] Clarence, you open those doors—open them all the way!

[CLARENCE *does so*]

VINNIE: [*To* FATHER, *lowering her voice, but maintaining her spirit*] Now, Clare, you behave yourself! [FATHER *glares at her angrily*] They're here and they're going to stay here.

FATHER: That's enough, Vinnie! I want no more of this argument. [*He goes to his chair by the window, muttering*] Damnation!

CLARENCE: [*To* VINNIE] Mother, Cousin Cora's waiting for you.

FATHER: What I don't understand is why this swarm of locusts always descends on us without any warning. [*He sits down.* VINNIE *looks at him; then, convinced of her victory, she goes upstairs*] Damn! Damnation! Damn! [*He follows her upstairs with his eyes; he remembers he is very fond of her*] Vinnie! Dear Vinnie! [*He remembers he is very angry at her*] Damn!

CLARENCE: Father, can't I go along with the rest of you to Delmonico's tonight?

FATHER: What's that? Delmonico's?

CLARENCE: You're taking Mother, Cora, and Mary to Delmonico's for dinner.

FATHER: [*Exploding*] Oh, God! [*At this sound from* FATHER, VINNIE *comes flying downstairs again*] I won't have it. I won't have it. [FATHER *stamps angrily across the room*]

VINNIE: [*On the way down*] Clarence, the doors!

FATHER: I won't stand it, by God! I won't stand it!

[VINNIE *and* CLARENCE *hurriedly close the sliding doors again*]

VINNIE: Clare! What's the matter now?

FATHER: [*With the calm of anger that has turned to ice*] Do I understand that I can't have dinner in my own home?

VINNIE: It'll do us both good to get out of this house. You need a little change. It'll make you feel better.

FATHER: I have a home to have dinner in. Any time I can't have dinner at home this house is for sale!

VINNIE: Well, you can't have dinner here tonight because it isn't ordered.

FATHER: Let me tell you I'm ready to sell this place this very minute if I can't live here in peace. And we can all go and sit under a palm tree and live on breadfruit and pickles.

VINNIE: But, Clare, Cora and Mary want to see something of New York.

FATHER: Oh, that's it! Well, that's no affair of mine! I am not a guide to Chinatown and the Bowery. [*Drawing himself up, he stalks out, throwing open the sliding doors. As he reaches the foot of the stairs,* MARY *comes tripping down*]

MARY: I love your house, Mr. Day. I could just live here forever. [FATHER *utters a bark of disgust and continues on upstairs.* MARY *comes into the room a little wide-eyed*] Cora's waiting for you, Mrs. Day.

VINNIE: Oh, yes, I'll run right up. [*She goes upstairs*]

CLARENCE: I'm glad you like our house.

MARY: Oh, yes, I like it very much. I like green.

CLARENCE: I like green myself. [*She looks up at his red hair*]

MARY: Red's my favorite color.

[*Embarrassed,* CLARENCE *suddenly hears himself talking about something he has never thought about*]

CLARENCE: It's an interesting thing about colors. Red's a nice color in a house, too; but outside, too much red would be bad. I mean, for instance, if all the trees and the grass were red. Outside, green is the best color.

MARY: [*Impressed*] That's right! I've never thought of it that way—but when you do think of it, it's quite a thought! I'll bet you'll make your mark at Yale.

CLARENCE: [*Pleased, but modest*] Oh!

[*The outer door is heard to slam*]

MARY: My mother wants me to go to college. Do you believe in girls going to college.

CLARENCE: I guess it's all right if they want to waste that much time—before they get married, I mean.

[JOHN *comes in, bringing* The Youth's Companion]

JOHN: Oh, hello! Look! A new *Youth's Companion!*

[*They say* "Hello" *to him*]

CLARENCE: [*From a mature height*] John enjoys The Youth's Companion. [JOHN *sits right down and starts to read.* CLARENCE *is worried by this.*] John! [JOHN *looks at him nonplussed.* CLARENCE *glances toward* MARY. JOHN *remembers his manners and stands.* CLARENCE *speaks formally to* MARY] Won't you sit down?

MARY: Oh, thank you! [*She sits.* JOHN *sits down again quickly and dives back into* The Youth's Companion. CLARENCE *sits beside* MARY]

CLARENCE: As I was saying—I think it's all right for a girl to go to college if she goes to a girls' college.

MARY: Well, Mother wants me to go to Ohio Wesleyan—because it's Methodist. [*Then almost as a confession*] You see, we're Methodists.

CLARENCE: Oh, that's too bad! I don't mean it's too bad that you're a Methodist. Anybody's got a right to be anything they want. But what I mean is—we're Episcopalians.

MARY: Yes, I know. I've known ever since I saw your minister—and his collar. [*She looks pretty sad for a minute and then her face brightens*] Oh, I just remembered—my father was an Episcopalian. He was baptized an Episcopalian. He was an Episcopalian right up to the time he married my mother. *She* was the Methodist. [MARY's *tone would have surprised her mother—and even* MARY, *if she had been listening*]

CLARENCE: I'll bet your father's a nice man.

MARY: Yes, he is. He owns the livery stable.

CLARENCE: He does? Well, then you must like horses.

MARY: Oh, I love horses! [*They are happily united again in their common love of horses*]

CLARENCE: They're my favorite animal. Father and I both think there's nothing like a horse!

[FATHER *comes down the stairs and into the room. The children all stand*]

MARY: Oh, Mr. Day, I'm having such a lovely time here!

FATHER: Clarence is keeping you entertained, eh?

MARY: Oh, yes, sir. We've been talking about everything—colors and horses and religion.

FATHER: Oh! [*To* JOHN] Has the evening paper come yet?

JOHN: No, sir.

FATHER: What are you reading?

JOHN: *The Youth's Companion*, sir.

[WHITNEY *and* HARLAN *enter from the hall,* WHITNEY *carrying a small box*]

WHITNEY: Look what we've got!

FATHER: What is it?

WHITNEY: Tiddle-dy-winks. We put our money together and bought it.

FATHER: That's a nice game. Do you know how to play it?

WHITNEY: I've played it lots of times.

HARLAN: Show me how to play it.

FATHER: Here, I'll show you. [*Opens the box and arranges the glass and disks*]

MARY: [*Hopefully to* CLARENCE] Are you going out to dinner with us to-night?

CLARENCE: [*Looking at* FATHER] I don't know yet—but it's beginning to look as though I might.

FATHER: It's easy, Harlan. You press down like this and snap the little fellow into the glass. Now watch me. [*He snaps it and it goes off the table*] The table isn't quite large enough. You boys better play it on the floor.

WHITNEY: Come on, Harlan, I'll take the reds, and you take the yellows.

FATHER: John, have you practiced your piano today?

JOHN: I was going to practice this evening.

FATHER: Better do it now. Music is a delight in the home.

[JOHN *exits, passing* CORA *and* VINNIE *as they enter, coming downstairs*]

VINNIE: Clare, what do you think Cora just told me? She and Clyde are going to be married this fall!

FATHER: Oh, you finally landed him, eh? [*Everybody laughs*] Well, he's a very lucky man. Cora, being married is the only way to live.

CORA: If we can be half as happy as you and Cousin Vinnie—

VINNIE: [*Who has gone to the children*] Boys, shouldn't you be playing that on the table?

WHITNEY: The table isn't big enough. Father told us to play on the floor.

VINNIE: My soul and body! Look at your hands! Delia will have your supper ready in a few minutes. Go wash your hands right away and come back and show Mother they're clean.

[*The boys pick up the tiddle-dy-winks and depart reluctantly. From the next room we hear* JOHN *playing "The Happy Farmer"*]

FATHER: [*Sitting down on the sofa with* MARY] Vinnie, this young lady looks about the same age you were when I came out to Pleasantville to rescue you.

VINNIE: Rescue me! You came out there to talk me into marrying you.

FATHER: It worked out just the same. I saved you from spending the rest of your life in that one-horse town.

VINNIE: Cora, the other day I came across a tintype of Clare taken in Pleasantville. I want to show it to you. You'll see who needed rescuing. [*She goes to the table and starts to rummage around in its drawer*]

FATHER: There isn't time for that, Vinnie. If we're going to Delmonico's for dinner hadn't we all better be getting ready? It's after six now.

CORA: Gracious! I'll have to start. If I'm going to dine in public with a prominent citizen like you, Cousin Clare—I'll have to look my best. [*She goes to the arch*]

MARY: I've changed already.

CORA: Yes, I know, but I'm afraid I'll have to ask you to come along and hook me up, Mary.

MARY: Of course.

CORA: It won't take a minute and then you can come right back.

[FATHER *rises.* MARY *crosses in front of* FATHER *and starts toward the hall, then turns and looks back at him*]

MARY: Mr. Day, were you always an Episcopalian?

FATHER: What?

MARY: Were you always an Episcopalian?

FATHER: I've always gone to the Episcopal church, yes.

MARY: But you weren't baptized a Methodist or anything, were you? You were baptized an Episcopalian?

FATHER: Come to think of it, I don't believe I was ever baptized at all.

MARY: Oh!

VINNIE: Clare, that's not very funny, joking about a subject like that.

FATHER: I'm not joking—I remember now—I never was baptized.

VINNIE: Clare, that's ridiculous, everyone's baptized.

FATHER: [*Sitting down complacently*] Well, I'm not.

VINNIE: Why, no one would keep a little baby from being baptized.

FATHER: You know Father and Mother—free-thinkers, both of them—believed their children should decide those things for themselves.

VINNIE: But, Clare—

FATHER: I remember when I was ten or twelve years old, Mother said I ought to give some thought to it. I suppose I thought about it, but I never got around to having it done to me.

[*The shock to* VINNIE *is as great as if* FATHER *had calmly announced himself guilty of murder. She walks to* FATHER *staring at him in horror.* CORA *and* MARY, *sensing the coming battle, withdraw to the neutral shelter of the hall*]

VINNIE: Clare, do you know what you're saying?

FATHER: I'm saying I've never been baptized.

VINNIE: [*In a sudden panic*] Then something has to be done about it right away.

FATHER: [*Not the least concerned*] Now, Vinnie, don't get excited over nothing.

VINNIE: Nothing! [*Then, as only a woman can ask such a question*] Clare, why haven't you ever told me?

FATHER: What difference does it make?

VINNIE: [*The panic returning*] I've never heard of anyone who wasn't baptized. Even the savages in darkest Africa—

FATHER: It's all right for savages and children. But if an oversight was made in my case it's too late to correct it now.

VINNIE: But if you're not baptized you're not a Christian!

FATHER: [*Rising in wrath*] Why, confound it, of course I'm a Christian! A damn good Christian, too! [FATHER'S *voice tells* CLARENCE *a major engagement has begun. He hurriedly springs to the sliding doors and closes them, removing himself,* MARY, *and* CORA *from the scene of action*] A lot better Christian than those psalm-singing donkeys in church!

VINNIE: You can't be if you won't be baptized.

FATHER: I won't be baptized and I will be a Christian! I beg to inform you I'll be a Christian in my own way.

VINNIE: Clare, don't you want to meet us all in Heaven?

FATHER: Of course! And I'm going to!

VINNIE: But you can't go to Heaven if you're not baptized!

FATHER: That's a lot of folderol!

VINNIE: Clarence Day, don't you blaspheme like that! You're coming to church with me before you go to the office in the morning and be baptized then and there!

FATHER: Vinnie, don't be ridiculous! If you think I'm going to stand there and have some minister splash water on me at my age, you're mistaken!

VINNIE: But, Clare—

FATHER: That's enough of this, Vinnie. I'm hungry. [*Draws himself up and starts for the door. He does not realize that he and* VINNIE *are now engaged in a battle to the death*] I'm dressing for dinner. [*Throws open the doors, revealing* WHITNEY *and* HARLAN, *who obviously have been eavesdropping and have heard the awful revelation of* FATHER'S *paganism.* FATHER *stalks past them upstairs. The two boys come down into the room staring at their mother, who has been standing, too shocked at* FATHER'S *callous impiety to speak or move*]

WHITNEY: Mother, if Father hasn't been baptized he hasn't any name. In the sight of the Church he hasn't any name.

VINNIE: That's right! [*To herself*] Maybe we're not even married!

[*This awful thought takes possession of* VINNIE. *Her eyes turn slowly toward the children and she suddenly realizes their doubtful status. Her hand goes to her mouth to cover a quick gasp of horror as the curtain falls*]

CURTAIN

ACT TWO

SCENE ONE

The same.
   The following Sunday. After Church.
   The stage is empty as the curtain rises. VINNIE *comes into the archway from the street door, dressed in her Sunday best, carrying her prayer book, hymnal, and a cold indignation. As soon as she is in the room,* FATHER *passes across the hall in his Sunday cutaway and silk hat, carrying gloves and cane.* VINNIE *looks over her shoulder at him as he disappears.* CORA, WHITNEY, *and* HARLAN *come into the room,* CORA *glancing after* FATHER *and then toward* VINNIE. *All three walk as though the sound of a footfall might cause an explosion, and speak in subdued tones.*

HARLAN: Cousin Cora, will you play a game of tiddle-dy-winks with me before you go?

CORA: I'm going to be busy packing until it's time to leave.

WHITNEY: We can't play games on Sunday.

[*We hear the door close and* JOHN *enters and looks into the room apprehensively*]

CORA: John, where are Clarence and Mary?

JOHN: They dropped behind—'way behind! [*He goes upstairs.* WHITNEY *takes* HARLAN's *hat from him and starts toward the arch*]

VINNIE: Whitney, don't hang up your hat. I want you to go over to Sherry's for the ice-cream for dinner. Tell Mr. Sherry strawberry—if he has it. And take Harlan with you.

WHITNEY: All right, Mother. [*He and* HARLAN, *trained in the good manners of the period, bow and exit*]

CORA: Oh, Vinnie, I hate to leave. We've had such a lovely week.

VINNIE: [*Voice quivers in a tone of scandalized apology*] Cora, what must you think of Clare, making such a scene on his way out of church today?

CORA: Cousin Clare probably thinks that you put the rector up to preaching that sermon.

VINNIE: [*Tone changes from apology to self-defense with overtones of guilt*] Well, I had to go to see Dr. Lloyd to find out whether we were really married. The sermon on baptism was his own idea. If Clare just hadn't *shouted* so—now the whole congregation knows he's never been baptized! But he's going to be, Cora—you mark my words—he's going to be! I just couldn't go to Heaven without Clare. Why, I get lonesome for him when I go to Ohio.

> [FATHER *enters holding his watch. He's also holding his temper. He speaks quietly*]

FATHER: Vinnie, I went to the dining room and the table isn't set for dinner yet.

VINNIE: We're having dinner late today.

FATHER: Why can't I have my meals on time?

VINNIE: The girls' train leaves at one-thirty. Their cab's coming at one o'clock.

FATHER: Cab? The horse cars go right past our door.

VINNIE: They have those heavy bags.

FATHER: Clarence and John could have gone along to carry their bags. Cabs are just a waste of money. Why didn't we have an early dinner?

VINNIE: There wasn't time for an early dinner and church, too.

FATHER: As far as I'm concerned this would have been a good day to miss church.

VINNIE: [*Spiritedly*] I wish we had!

FATHER: [*Flaring*] I'll bet you put him up to preaching that sermon!

VINNIE: I've never been so mortified in all my life! You stamping up the aisle roaring your head off at the top of your voice!

FATHER: That Lloyd needn't preach at me as though I were some damn criminal! I wanted him to know it, and as far as I'm concerned the whole congregation can know it, too!

VINNIE: They certainly know it now!

FATHER: That suits me!

VINNIE: [*Pleading*] Clare, you don't seem to understand what the church is for.

FATHER: [*Laying down a new Commandment*] Vinnie, if there's one place the church should leave alone, it's a man's soul!

VINNIE: Clare, dear, don't you believe what it says in the Bible?

FATHER: A man has to use his common sense about the Bible, Vinnie, if he has any. For instance, you'd be in a pretty fix if I gave all my money to the poor.

VINNIE: Well, that's just silly!

FATHER: Speaking of money—where are this month's bills?

VINNIE: Clare, it isn't fair to go over the household accounts while you're hungry.

FATHER: Where are those bills, Vinnie?

VINNIE: They're downstairs on your desk. [FATHER *exits almost eagerly. Figures are something he understands better than he does women*] Of all times! [*To* CORA] It's awfully hard on a woman to love a man like Clare so much.

CORA: Yes, men can be aggravating. Clyde gets me so provoked! We kept company for six years, but the minute he proposed—the moment I said "Yes"—he began to take me for granted.

VINNIE: You have to expect that, Cora. I don't believe Clare has come right out and told me he loves me since we've been married. Of course I know he does, because I keep reminding him of it. You have to keep reminding them, Cora.

[*The door slams*]

CORA: That must be Mary and Clarence. [*There's a moment's pause. The two women look toward the hall—then at each other with a knowing sort of smile.* CORA *rises, goes up to the arch, peeks out—then faces front and innocently asks*] Is that you, Mary?

MARY: [*Dashing in*] Yes!

[CLARENCE *crosses the arch to hang up his hat*]

CORA: We have to change our clothes and finish our packing. [*Goes upstairs*]

[CLARENCE *returns as* MARY *starts up the stairs*]

MARY: [*To* CLARENCE] It won't take me long.

CLARENCE: Can I help you pack?

VINNIE: [*Shocked*] Clarence! [MARY *runs upstairs.* CLARENCE *drifts into the living room, somewhat abashed.* VINNIE *collects her hat and gloves, starts out, stops to look at* CLARENCE, *then comes down to him*] Clarence, why didn't you kneel in church today?

CLARENCE: What, Mother?

VINNIE: Why didn't you kneel in church today?

CLARENCE: [*Troubled*] I just couldn't.

VINNIE: Has it anything to do with Mary? I know she's a Methodist.

CLARENCE: Oh, no, Mother! Methodists kneel. Mary told me. They don't get up and down so much, but they stay down longer.

VINNIE: If it's because your father doesn't kneel—you must remember he wasn't brought up to kneel in church. But you were—you always have—and, Clarence, you want to, don't you?

CLARENCE: Oh, yes! I wanted to today! I started to—you saw me start—but I just couldn't.

VINNIE: Is that suit of your father's too tight for you?

CLARENCE: No, it's not too *tight*. It fits fine. But it *is* the suit. Very peculiar things have happened to me since I started to wear it. I haven't been myself since I put it on.

VINNIE: In what way, Clarence? How do you mean?

[CLARENCE *pauses, then blurts out his problem*]

CLARENCE: Mother, I can't seem to make these clothes do anything Father wouldn't do!

VINNIE: That's nonsense, Clarence—and not to kneel in church is a sacrilege.

CLARENCE: But making Father's trousers kneel seemed more of a sacrilege.

VINNIE: Clarence!

CLARENCE: No! Remember the first time I wore this? It was at Dora Wakefield's party for Mary. Do you know what happened? We were playing musical chairs and Dora Wakefield sat down suddenly right in my lap. I jumped up so fast she almost got hurt.

VINNIE: But it was all perfectly innocent.

CLARENCE: It wasn't that Dora was sitting on my lap—she was sitting on Father's trousers. Mother, I've got to have a suit of my own.

[CLARENCE's *metaphysical problem is one that* VINNIE *can't cope with at this particular minute*]

VINNIE: My soul and body! Clarence, you have a talk with your father about it. I'm sure if you approach him the right way—you know—tactfully—he'll see—

[MARY *comes downstairs and hesitates at the arch*]

MARY: Oh, excuse me.

VINNIE: Gracious! Have you finished your packing?

MARY: Practically. I never put my comb and brush in until I'm ready to close my bag.

VINNIE: I must see Margaret about your box lunch for the train. I'll leave you two together. Remember, it's Sunday. [*She goes downstairs*]

CLARENCE: I was hoping we could have a few minutes together before you left.

MARY: [*Not to admit her eagerness*] Cora had so much to do I wanted to get out of her way.

CLARENCE: Well, didn't you want to see me?

MARY: [*Self-consciously*] I did want to tell you how much I've enjoyed our friendship.

CLARENCE: You're going to write me when you get to Springfield, aren't you?

MARY: Of course, if you write me first.

CLARENCE: But you'll have something to write about—your trip—and Aunt Judith—and how things are in Springfield. You write me as soon as you get there.

MARY: Maybe I'll be too busy. Maybe I won't have time. [*She sits on the sofa*]

CLARENCE: [*With the authority of* FATHER's *trousers*] You find the time! Let's not have any nonsense about that! You'll write me first—and you'll do it right away, the first day! [*Sits beside her*]

MARY: How do you know I'll take orders from you?

CLARENCE: I'll show you. [*He takes a quick glance toward the hall*] Give me your hand!

MARY: Why should I?

CLARENCE: Give me your hand, confound it!

[MARY *gives it to him*]

MARY: What do you want with my hand?

CLARENCE: I just wanted it. [*Holding her hand, he melts a little and smiles at her. She melts, too. Their hands, clasped together, are resting on* CLARENCE's *knee and they relax happily*] What are you thinking about?

MARY: I was just thinking.

CLARENCE: About what?

MARY: Well, when we were talking about writing each other I was hoping you'd write me first because that would mean you liked me.

CLARENCE: [*With the logic of the male*] What's writing first got to do with my liking you?

MARY: Oh, you *do* like me?

CLARENCE: Of course I do. I like you better than any girl I ever met.

MARY: [*With the logic of the female*] But you don't like me well enough to write first?

CLARENCE: I don't see how one thing's got anything to do with the other.

MARY: But a girl can't write first—because she's a *girl*.

CLARENCE: That doesn't make sense. If a girl has something to write about and a fellow hasn't, there's no reason why she shouldn't write first.

MARY: [*Starting a flanking movement*] You know, the first few days I was here you'd do anything for me and then you changed. You used to be a lot of fun—and then all of a sudden you turned into an old sober-sides.

CLARENCE: When did I?

MARY: The first time I noticed it was when we walked home from Dora Wakefield's party. My, you were on your dignity! You've been that way ever since. You even dress like an old sober-sides. [CLARENCE's *face changes as* FATHER's *pants rise to haunt him. Then he notices that their clasped hands are resting on these very pants, and he lifts them off. Agony obviously is setting in.* MARY *sees the expression on his face*] What's the matter?

CLARENCE: I just happened to remember something.

MARY: What? [CLARENCE *doesn't answer, but his face does*] Oh, I know. This is the last time we'll be together. [*She puts her hand on his shoulder. He draws away*]

CLARENCE: Mary, please!

MARY: But, Clarence! We'll see each other in a month. And we'll be writing each other, too. I hope we will. [*She gets up*] Oh, Clarence, please write me first, because it will show me how much you like me. Please! I'll show you how much I like you! [*She throws herself on his lap and buries her head on his shoulder.* CLARENCE *stiffens in agony*]

CLARENCE: [*Hoarsely*] Get up! Get up! [*She pulls back her head and looks at him, then springs from his lap and runs away, covering her face and sobbing.* CLARENCE *goes to her*] Don't do that, Mary! Please don't do that!

MARY: Now you'll think I'm just a bold and forward girl.

CLARENCE: Oh, no!

MARY: Yes, you will—you'll think I'm bold!

CLARENCE: Oh, no—it's not that.

MARY: [*Hopefully*] Was it because it's Sunday?

CLARENCE: [*In despair*] No, it would be the same any day—[*He is about to explain, but* MARY *flares*]

MARY: Oh, it's just because you didn't want me sitting on your lap.

CLARENCE: It was nice of you to do it.

MARY: It was nice of me! So you told me to get up! You just couldn't bear to have me sit there. Well, you needn't write me first. You needn't write me any letters at all, because I'll tear them up without opening them! [FATHER *enters the archway, a sheath of bills in his hand and his account book under his arm*] I guess I know now you don't like me! I never want to see you again. I—I—

[*She breaks and starts to run toward the stairs. At the sight of* FATHER *she stops, but only for a gasp, then continues on upstairs, unable to control her sobs.* CLARENCE, *who has been standing in unhappy indecision, turns to follow her, but stops short at the sight of* FATHER, *who is standing in the arch looking at him with some amazement.* FATHER *looks from* CLARENCE *toward the vanished* MARY, *then back to* CLARENCE]

FATHER: Clarence, that young girl is crying—she's in tears. What's the meaning of this?

CLARENCE: I'm sorry, Father, it's all my fault.

FATHER: Nonsense! What's that girl trying to do to you?

CLARENCE: What? No, she wasn't—it was—I—how long have you been here?

FATHER: Well, whatever the quarrel was about, Clarence, I'm glad you held your own. Where's your mother?

CLARENCE: [*Desperately*] I have to have a new suit of clothes—you've *got* to give me the money for it.

[FATHER's *account book reaches the table with a sharp bang as he stares at* CLARENCE *in astonishment*]

FATHER: Young man, do you realize you're addressing your father?

[CLARENCE *wilts miserably and sinks into a chair*]

CLARENCE: I'm sorry, Father—I apologize—but you don't know how important this is to me. [CLARENCE's *tone of misery gives* FATHER *pause*]

FATHER: A suit of clothes is so—? Now, why should a—? [*Something dawns on* FATHER *and he looks up in the direction in which* MARY *has disappeared, then looks back at* CLARENCE] Has your need for a suit of clothes anything to do with that young lady?

CLARENCE: Yes, Father.

FATHER: Why, Clarence! [*Suddenly realizes that women have come into* CLARENCE's *emotional life and there comes a yearning to protect this inexperienced and defenseless member of his own sex*] This comes as quite a shock to me.

CLARENCE: What does, Father?

FATHER: Your being so grown up! Still, I might have known that if you're going to college this fall—yes, you're at an age when you'll be meeting girls. Clarence, there are things about women that I think you ought to know! [*He goes up and closes the doors, then comes down and sits beside* CLARENCE, *hesitating for a moment before he speaks*] Yes, I think it's better for you to hear this from me than to have to learn it for yourself. Clarence, women aren't the angels that you think they are! Well, now— first, let me explain this to you. You see, Clarence, we men have to run this world and it's not an easy job. It takes work, and it takes thinking. A man has to be sure of his facts and figures. He has to reason things out. Now, you take a woman—a woman thinks—no I'm wrong right there—a woman doesn't think at all! She gets stirred up! And she gets stirred up over the damnedest things! Now, I love my wife just as much as any man, but that doesn't mean I should stand for a lot of folderol! By God! I won't stand for it! [*Looks around toward the spot where he had his last clash with* VINNIE]

CLARENCE: Stand for what, Father?

FATHER: [*To himself*] That's the one thing I will not submit myself to. [*Has ceased explaining women to* CLARENCE *and is now explaining himself*] Clarence, if a man thinks a certain thing is the wrong thing to do he shouldn't do it. If he thinks a thing is right he should do it. Now that has nothing to do with whether he loves his wife or not.

CLARENCE: Who says it has, Father?

FATHER: They do!

CLARENCE: Who, sir?

FATHER: Women! They get stirred up and then they try to get you stirred up, too. If you can keep reason and logic in the argument, a man can hold his own, of course. But if they can *switch* you—pretty soon the argument's about whether you love them or not. I swear I don't know how they do it! Don't you let 'em, Clarence! Don't you let 'em!

CLARENCE: I see what you mean so far, Father. If you don't watch yourself, love can make you do a lot of things you don't want to do.

FATHER: Exactly!

CLARENCE: But if you do watch out and know just how to handle women—

FATHER: Then you'll be all right. All a man has to do is be firm. You know how sometimes I have to be firm with your mother. Just now about this month's household accounts—

CLARENCE: Yes, but what can you do when they cry?

FATHER: [*He gives this a moment's thought*] Well, that's quite a question. You just have to make them understand that what you're doing is for their good.

CLARENCE: I see.

FATHER: [*Rising*] Now, Clarence, you know all about women. [*Goes to the table and sits down in front of his account book, opening it.* CLARENCE *rises and looks at him*]

CLARENCE: But, Father—

FATHER: Yes, Clarence.

CLARENCE: I thought you were going to tell me about—

FATHER: About what?

CLARENCE: About women.

[FATHER *realizes with some shock that* CLARENCE *expected him to be more specific*]

FATHER: Clarence, there are some things gentlemen don't discuss! I've told you all you need to know. The thing for you to remember is—be firm! [CLARENCE *turns away. There is a knock at the sliding doors*] Yes, come in.

[MARY *opens the doors*]

MARY: Excuse me!

[MARY *enters.* FATHER *turns his attention to the household accounts.* MARY *goes to the couch and picks up her handkerchief and continues around the couch.* CLARENCE *crosses to meet her above the couch, determined to be firm.* MARY *passes him without a glance.* CLARENCE *wilts, then again assuming firmness, turns up into the arch in an attempt to quail* MARY *with a look.* MARY *marches upstairs ignoring him.* CLARENCE *turns back into the room defeated. He looks down at his clothes unhappily, then decides to be firm with his father. He straightens up and steps toward him. At this moment* FATHER, *staring at a bill, emits his cry of rage*]

FATHER: Oh, God!

[CLARENCE *retreats.* FATHER *rises and holds the bill in question between thumb and forefinger as though it were too repulsive to touch.* VINNIE *comes rushing down the stairs*]

VINNIE: What's the matter, Clare? What's wrong?

FATHER: I will *not* send this person a check!

> [VINNIE *looks at it*]

VINNIE: Why, Clare, that's the only hat I've bought since March and it was reduced from forty dollars.

FATHER: I don't question your buying the hat or what you paid for it, but the person from whom you bought it—this Mademoiselle Mimi—isn't fit to be in the hat business or any other.

VINNIE: I never went there before, but it's a very nice place and I don't see why you object to it.

FATHER: [*Exasperated*] I object to it because this confounded person doesn't put her name on her bills! Mimi what? Mimi O'Brien? Mimi Jones? Mimi Weinstein?

VINNIE: How do I know? It's just Mimi.

FATHER: It isn't just Mimi. She must have some other name, damn it! Now, I wouldn't make a check payable to Charley or to Jimmy, and I won't make out a check payable to Mimi. Find out what her last name is, and I'll pay her the money.

VINNIE: All right. All right. [*She starts out*]

FATHER: Just a minute, Vinnie, that isn't all.

VINNIE: But Cora will be leaving any minute, Clare, and it isn't polite for me—

FATHER: Never mind Cora. Sit down. [CLARENCE *goes into the hall, looks upstairs, wanders up and down the hall restlessly.* VINNIE *reluctantly sits down opposite* FATHER *at the table*] Vinnie, you know I like to live well, and I want my family to live well. But this house must be run on a business basis. I must know how much money I'm spending and what for. For instance, if you recall, two weeks ago I gave you six dollars to buy a new coffee pot—

VINNIE: Yes, because you broke the old one. You threw it right on the floor.

FATHER: I'm not talking about that. I'm simply endeavoring—

VINNIE: But it was so silly to break that nice coffee pot, Clare, and there was nothing the matter with the coffee that morning. It was made just the same as always.

FATHER: It was not! It was made in a damned barbaric manner!

VINNIE: I couldn't get another imported one. That little shop has stopped selling them. They said the tariff wouldn't let them. And that's your fault, Clare, because you're always voting to raise the tariff.

FATHER: The tariff protects America against cheap foreign labor. [*He sounds as though he is quoting*] Now I find that—

VINNIE: The tariff does nothing but put up the prices and that's hard on everybody, especially the farmer. [*She sounds as though she is quoting back*]

FATHER: [*Annoyed*] I wish to God you wouldn't talk about matters you don't know a damn thing about!

VINNIE: I do too know about them. Miss Gulick says every intelligent woman should have some opinion—

FATHER: Who, may I ask, is Miss Gulick?

VINNIE: Why, she's that current-events woman I told you about and the tickets are a dollar every Tuesday.

FATHER: Do you mean to tell me that a pack of idle-minded females pay a dollar apiece to hear another female gabble about the events of the day? Listen to me if you want to know anything about the events of the day!

VINNIE: But you get so excited, Clare, and besides, Miss Gulick says that our President, whom you're always belittling, prays to God for guidance and—

FATHER: [*Having had enough of Miss Gulick*] Vinnie, what happened to that six dollars?

VINNIE: What six dollars?

FATHER: I gave you six dollars to buy a new coffee pot and now I find that you apparently got one at Lewis & Conger's and charged it. Here's their bill: "One coffee pot—five dollars."

VINNIE: So you owe me a dollar and you can hand it right over. [*She holds out her hand for it*]

FATHER: I'll do nothing of the kind! What did you do with that six dollars?

VINNIE: Why, Clare, I can't tell you now, dear. Why didn't you ask me at the time?

FATHER: Oh, my God!

VINNIE: Wait a moment! I spent four dollars and a half for that new umbrella I told you I wanted and you said I didn't need, but I did, very much.

[FATHER *takes his pencil and writes in the account book*]

FATHER: Now we're getting somewhere. One umbrella—four dollars and a half.

VINNIE: And that must have been the week I paid Mrs. Tobin for two extra days' washing.

FATHER: [*Entering the item*] Mrs. Tobin.

VINNIE: So that was two dollars more.

FATHER: Two dollars.

VINNIE: That makes six dollars and fifty cents. And that's another fifty cents you owe me.

FATHER: I don't owe you anything. [*Stung by* VINNIE's *tactics into a determination to pin her butterfly mind down*] What you owe me is an explanation of where my money's gone! We're going over this account book item by item. [*Starts to sort the bills for the purposes of cross-examination, but the butterfly takes wing again*]

VINNIE: I do the very best I can to keep down expenses. And you know yourself that Cousin Phoebe spends twice as much as we do.

FATHER: Damn Cousin Phoebe!—I don't wish to be told how she throws her money around.

VINNIE: Oh, Clare, how can you? And I thought you were so fond of Cousin Phoebe.

FATHER: All right, I am fond of Cousin Phoebe, but I can get along without hearing so much about her.

VINNIE: You talk about your own relatives enough.

FATHER: [*Hurt*] That's not fair, Vinnie. When I talk about my relatives I criticize them.

VINNIE: If I can't even speak of Cousin Phoebe—

FATHER: You can speak of her all you want to—but I won't have Cousin Phoebe or anyone else dictating to me how to run my house. Now this month's total—

VINNIE: [*Righteously*] I didn't say a word about her dictating, Clare—she isn't that kind!

FATHER: [*Dazed*] I don't know what you said, now. You never stick to the point. I endeavor to show you how to run this house on a business basis and you wind up by jibbering and jabbering about everything under the sun. If you'll just explain to me—

[*Finally cornered,* VINNIE *realizes the time has come for tears. Quietly she turns them on*]

VINNIE: I don't know what you expect of me. I tire myself out chasing up and down those stairs all day long—trying to look after your comfort—to bring up our children—I do the mending and the marketing and as if that isn't enough, you want me to be an expert bookkeeper, too.

FATHER: [*Touched where* VINNIE *has hoped to touch him*] Vinnie, I want to be reasonable; but can't you understand?—I'm doing all this for your own good. [VINNIE *rises with a moan.* FATHER *sighs with resignation*] I suppose I'll have to go ahead just paying the bills and hoping I've got money enough in the bank to meet them. But it's all very discouraging.

VINNIE: I'll try to do better, Clare.

[FATHER *looks up into her tearful face and melts*]

FATHER: That's all I'm asking. [*She goes to him and puts her arm around his shoulder*] I'll go down and make out the checks and sign them. [VINNIE *doesn't seem entirely consoled, so he attempts a lighter note to cheer her up*] Oh, Vinnie, maybe I haven't any right to sign those checks, since in the sight of the Lord I haven't any name at all. Do you suppose the bank will feel that way about it too—or do you think they'll take a chance? [*He should not have said this*]

VINNIE: That's right! Clare, to make those checks good you'll have to be baptized right away.

FATHER: [*Retreating angrily*] Vinnie, the bank doesn't care whether I've been baptized or not!

VINNIE: Well, I care! And no matter what Dr. Lloyd says, I'm not sure we're really married.

FATHER: Damn it, Vinnie, we have four children! If we're not married now we never will be!

VINNIE: Oh, Clare, don't you see how serious this is? You've got to do something about it.

FATHER: Well, just now I've got to do something about these damn bills you've run up. [*Sternly*] I'm going downstairs.

VINNIE: Not before you give me that dollar and a half!

FATHER: What dollar and a half?

VINNIE: The dollar and a half you owe me!

FATHER: [*Thoroughly enraged*] I don't owe you any dollar and a half! I gave you money to buy a coffee pot for me and somehow it turned into an umbrella for you.

VINNIE: Clarence Day, what kind of a man are you? Quibbling about a dollar and a half when your immortal soul is in danger! And what's more—

FATHER: All right. All right. All right. [*He takes the dollar and a half from his change purse and gives it to her*]

VINNIE: [*Smiling*] Thank you, Clare.

[VINNIE *turns and leaves the room. Her progress upstairs is a one-woman march of triumph.* FATHER *puts his purse back, gathers up his papers and his dignity, and starts out.* CLARENCE *waylays him in the arch*]

CLARENCE: Father—you never did tell me—can I have a new suit of clothes?

FATHER: No, Clarence! I'm sorry, but I have to be firm with you, too!

[*He stalks off.* JOHN *comes down the stairs carrying a traveling bag, which he takes out toward the front door. He returns empty-handed and starts up the stairs again*]

CLARENCE: John, come here a minute.

JOHN: [*Coming into the room*] What do you want?

CLARENCE: John, have you got any money you could lend me?

JOHN: With this week's allowance, I'll have about three dollars.

CLARENCE: That's no good. I've got to have enough to buy a new suit of clothes.

JOHN: Why don't you earn some money? That's what I'm going to do. I'm going to buy a bicycle—one of those new low kind, with both wheels the same size—you know, a safety.

CLARENCE: How are you going to earn that much money?

JOHN: I've got a job practically. Look, I found this ad in the paper. [*He hands* CLARENCE *a clipping from his pocket*]

CLARENCE: [*Reading*] "Wanted, an energetic young man to handle household necessity that sells on sight. Liberal commissions. Apply 312 West Fourteenth Street, Tuesday from eight to twelve." Listen, John, let me have that job.

JOHN: Why should I give you my job? They're hard to get.

CLARENCE: But I've got to have a new suit of clothes.

JOHN: Maybe I could get a job for both of us. [*The doorbell rings*] I'll tell you what I'll do, I'll ask the man.

FATHER: [*Hurrying to the foot of the stairs*] Vinnie! Cora! The cab's here. Hurry up! [*Goes through the arch toward the front door*]

CLARENCE: John, we've both got to get down there early Tuesday—the first thing.

JOHN: Oh, no you don't—I'm going alone. But I'll put in a good word with the boss about you.

FATHER: [*Off*] They'll be right out. Vinnie! Cora! [*He comes back to the foot of the stairs and calls up*] Are you coming? The cab's waiting!

VINNIE: [*From upstairs*] We heard you, Clare. We'll be down in a minute.

[FATHER *comes into the room*]

FATHER: John, go upstairs and hurry them down.

[JOHN *goes upstairs.* FATHER *crosses to the window and looks out, then consults his watch*]

FATHER: What's the matter with those women? Don't they know cabs cost money? Clarence, go see what's causing this infernal delay!

[CLARENCE *goes out to the hall*]

CLARENCE: Here they come, Father.

[MARY *comes sedately downstairs. She passes* CLARENCE *without a glance and goes to* FATHER]

MARY: Good-by, Mr. Day. I can't tell you how much I appreciate your hospitality.

FATHER: Not at all! Not at all!

[VINNIE *and* CORA *appear at top of stairs and come down.* JOHN *follows with the bags and takes them out*]

CORA: Good-by, Clarence. [*She starts into the room*]

FATHER: Cora, we can say good-by to you on the sidewalk.

VINNIE: There's no hurry. Their train doesn't go until one-thirty.

FATHER: Cabs cost money. If they have any waiting to do they ought to do it at the Grand Central Depot. They've got a waiting room there just *for* that.

VINNIE: [*To* MARY] If there's one thing Mr. Day can't stand it's to keep a cab waiting.

CORA: It's been so nice seeing you again, Clarence. [*She kisses him*]

[MARGARET *enters with a box of lunch*]

MARGARET: Here's the lunch.

FATHER: All right. All right. Give it to me. Let's get started.

[MARGARET *gives it to him and exits*]

CORA: Where's John?

FATHER: He's outside. Come on. [*Leads the way.* CORA *and* VINNIE *follow.* MARY *starts*]

CLARENCE: Mary, aren't you going even to shake hands with me?

MARY: I don't think I'd better. You may remember that when I get too close to you you feel contaminated. [*Starts out.* CLARENCE *follows her*]

CLARENCE: Mary! [*She stops in the arch. He goes to her*] You're going to write me, aren't you?

MARY: Are you going to write first?

CLARENCE: [*Resolutely*] No, Mary. There are times when a man has to be firm.

[JOHN *enters*]

JOHN: Mary, Mother says you'd better hurry out before Father starts yelling. It's Sunday.

MARY: Good-by, John. I'm very happy to have made *your* acquaintance.

[*She walks out. We hear the door close.* JOHN *goes out.* CLARENCE *takes a step toward the door, stops, suffers a moment, then turns to the writing desk, takes paper and pen and ink to the table, and sits down to write a letter*]

CLARENCE: [*Writing*] Dear Mary—

CURTAIN

SCENE TWO

The same.

Two days later. The breakfast table.

HARLAN *and* WHITNEY *are at the table, ready to start breakfast.* CLARENCE *is near the window reading the paper. The places of* JOHN *and* VINNIE *and* FATHER *are empty.* NORA, *a new maid, is serving the fruit and cereal.* NORA *is heavily built and along toward middle age. The doorbell rings and we hear the postman's whistle.* CLARENCE *drops the paper and looks out the window toward the door.* NORA *starts toward the arch.*

CLARENCE: Never mind, Nora. It's the postman. I'll go. [*He runs out through the arch*]

WHITNEY: [*To* NORA] You forgot the sugar. It goes here between me and Father.

[CLARENCE *comes back with three or four letters which he sorts ea-*

gerly. Then his face falls in utter dejection. FATHER *comes down the stairs*]

FATHER: Good morning, boys! John late? [*He shouts*] John! John! Hurry down to your breakfast.

CLARENCE: John had his breakfast early, Father, and went out to see about something.

FATHER: See about what?

CLARENCE: John and I thought we'd work this summer and earn some money.

FATHER: Good! Sit down, boys. [*Goes to his chair*]

CLARENCE: We saw an ad in the paper and John went down to see about it.

FATHER: Why didn't you go, too?

CLARENCE: I was expecting an answer to a letter I wrote, but it didn't come. Here's the mail. [*He seems depressed*]

FATHER: [*Sitting*] What kind of work is this you're planning to do?

CLARENCE: Sort of salesman, the ad said.

FATHER: Um-hum. Well, work never hurt anybody. It's good for them. But if you're going to work, work hard. King Solomon had the right idea about work. "Whatever thy hand findeth to do," Solomon said, "do thy damnedest!" Where's your mother?

NORA: If you please, sir, Mrs. Day doesn't want any breakfast. She isn't feeling well, so she went back upstairs to lie down again.

FATHER: [*Uneasily*] Now, why does your mother do that to me? She knows it just upsets my day when she doesn't come down to breakfast. Clarence, go tell your mother I'll be up to see her before I start for the office.

CLARENCE: Yes, sir. [*He goes upstairs*]

HARLAN: What's the matter with Mother?

FATHER: There's nothing the matter with your mother. Perfectly healthy woman. She gets an ache or a twinge and instead of being firm about it, she just gives in to it. [*The postman whistles. Then the doorbell rings.* NORA *answers it*] Boys, after breakfast you find out what your mother wants you to do today. Whitney, you take care of Harlan.

[NORA *comes back with a special-delivery letter*]

NORA: It's a special delivery. [*She hands it to* FATHER, *who tears it open at once.* CLARENCE *comes rushing down the stairs*]

CLARENCE: Was that the postman again?

WHITNEY: It was a special delivery.

CLARENCE: Yes? Where is it?

WHITNEY: It was for Father.

CLARENCE: [*Again disappointed*] Oh— [*He sits at the table*]

[FATHER *has opened the letter and is reading it. Bewildered, he turns it over and looks at the signature*]

FATHER: I don't understand this at all. Here's a letter from some woman I never even heard of.

[FATHER *tackles the letter again.* CLARENCE *sees the envelope, picks it up, looks at the postmark, worried*]

CLARENCE: Father!

FATHER: Oh, God!

CLARENCE: What is it, Father?

FATHER: This is the damnedest nonsense I ever read! As far as I can make out this woman claims that she sat on my lap and I didn't like it. [CLARENCE *begins to turn red.* FATHER *goes on reading a little further and then holds the letter over in front of* CLARENCE] Can you make out what that word is? [CLARENCE *begins feverishly to read as much as possible, but* FATHER *cuts in*] No, that word right there. [*He points*]

CLARENCE: It looks like—"curiosity."

[FATHER *withdraws the letter,* CLARENCE's *eyes following it hungrily*]

FATHER: [*Reads*] "I only opened your letter as a matter of curiosity." [*Breaking off reading aloud as he turns the page*]

CLARENCE: Yes? Go on.

FATHER: Why, this gets worse and worse! It just turns into a lot of sentimental lovey-dovey mush. [*Crushes the letter, stalks across the room, and throws it into the fireplace.* CLARENCE *watching him with dismay*] Is this someone's idea of a practical joke? Why must I be the butt—

[VINNIE *comes hurrying down the stairs. Her hair is down in two braids over her shoulders. She is wearing a lacy combing jacket over her corset cover, and a striped petticoat*]

VINNIE: What's the matter, Clare? What's wrong?

FATHER: [*Going to her*] Nothing wrong—just a damn fool letter. How are you, Vinnie?

VINNIE: [*Weakly*] I don't feel well. I thought you needed me, but if you don't I'll go back to bed.

FATHER: No, now that you're here, sit down with us. [*He moves out her chair*] Get some food in your stomach. Do you good.

VINNIE: [*Protesting*] I don't feel like eating anything, Clare.

[NORA *enters with a tray of bacon and eggs, stops at the serving table*]

FATHER: [*Heartily*] That's all the more reason why you should eat. Build up your strength! [*He forces* VINNIE *into her chair and turns to speak to* NORA, *who has her back to him*] Here— [*Then to* CLARENCE] What's this one's name?

CLARENCE: Nora.

FATHER: Nora! Give Mrs. Day some of the bacon and eggs.

VINNIE: No, Clare! [NORA, *however, has gone to* VINNIE's *side with the platter*] No, take it away, Nora. I don't even want to smell it.

[*The maid retreats, and serves* FATHER; *then* CLARENCE; *then serves coffee and exits*]

FATHER: Vinnie, it's just weak to give in to an ailment. Any disease can be cured by firmness. What you need is strength of character.

VINNIE: I don't know why you object to my complaining a little. I notice when you have a headache you yell and groan and swear enough.

FATHER: Of course I yell! That's to prove to the headache that I'm stronger than it is. I can usually swear it right out of my system.

VINNIE: This isn't a headache. I think I've caught some kind of a germ. There's a lot of sickness around. Several of my friends have had to send for the doctor. I may have the same thing.

FATHER: I'll bet this is all your imagination, Vinnie. You hear of a lot of other people having some disease and then you get scared and think you have it yourself. So you go to bed and send for the doctor. The doctor—all poppycock!

VINNIE: I didn't say anything about my sending for the doctor.

FATHER: I should hope not. Doctors think they know a damn lot, but they don't.

VINNIE: But Clare, dear, when people are seriously ill you have to do something.

FATHER: Certainly you have to do something! Cheer 'em up—that's the way to cure 'em!

VINNIE: [*With slight irony*] How would you go about cheering them up?

FATHER: I? I'd tell 'em—bah! [VINNIE, *out of exasperation and weakness, begins to cry.* FATHER *looks at her amazed*] What have I done now?

VINNIE: Oh, Clare—hush up! [*She moves from the table to the sofa, where she tries to control her crying.* HARLAN *slides out of his chair and runs over to her*] Harlan dear, keep away from Mother. You might catch what she's got. Whitney, if you've finished your breakfast—

WHITNEY: [*Rising*] Yes, Mother.

VINNIE: I promised Mrs. Whitehead to send over Margaret's recipe for floating-island pudding. Margaret has it all written out. And take Harlan with you.

WHITNEY: All right, Mother. I hope you feel better.

[WHITNEY *and* HARLAN *exit.* FATHER *goes over and sits beside* VINNIE *on the sofa*]

FATHER: Vinnie. [*Contritely*] I didn't mean to upset you. I was just trying to help. [*He pats her hand*] When you take to your bed I have a damned lonely time around here. So when I see you getting it into your head that you're sick, I want to do something about it. [*He continues to pat her hand vigorously with what he thinks is reassurance*] Just because some of your friends have given in to this is no reason why you should imagine you're sick, Vinnie.

VINNIE: [*Snatching her hand away*] Oh, stop, Clare!—get out of this house and go to your office!

[FATHER *is a little bewildered and somewhat indignant at this rebuff to his tenderness. He gets up and goes out into the hall, comes back with his hat and stick, and marches out of the house, slamming the door.* VINNIE *rises and starts toward the stairs*]

CLARENCE: I'm sorry you're not feeling well, Mother.

VINNIE: Oh, I'll be all right, Clarence. Remember last fall I had a touch of this and I was all right the next morning.

CLARENCE: Are you sure you don't want the doctor?

VINNIE: Oh, no. I really don't need him—and besides doctors worry your father. I don't want him to be upset.

CLARENCE: Is there anything I can do for you?

VINNIE: Ask Margaret to send me up a cup of tea. I'll try to drink it. I'm going back to bed.

CLARENCE: Do you mind if John and I go out today or will you need us?

VINNIE: You run right along. I just want to be left alone.

[*She exits up the stairs.* CLARENCE *starts for the fireplace eager to retrieve Mary's letter.* NORA *enters. He stops*]

CLARENCE: Oh!—Nora—will you take a cup of tea up to Mrs. Day in her room?

NORA: Yes, sir. [*Exits*]

[CLARENCE *hurries around the table, gets the crumpled letter, and starts to read it feverishly. He reads quickly to the end, then draws a deep, happy breath. The door slams. He puts the letter in his pocket.* JOHN *enters, carrying two heavy packages*]

CLARENCE: Did you get the job?

JOHN: Yes, for both of us. Look, I've got it with me.

CLARENCE: What is it?

JOHN: Medicine.

CLARENCE: [*Dismayed*] Medicine! You took a job for us to go out and sell medicine!

JOHN: But it's wonderful medicine. [*Gets a bottle out of the package and reads from the label*] "Bartlett's Beneficent Balm—A Boon to Mankind." Look what it cures! [*He hands the bottle to* CLARENCE]

CLARENCE: [*Reading*] "A sovereign cure for colds, coughs, catarrh, asthma, quinsy, and sore throat; poor digestion, summer complaint, colic, dyspepsia, heartburn, and shortness of breath; lumbago, rheumatism, heart disease, giddiness, and women's complaints; nervous prostration, St. Vitus' dance, jaundice, and la grippe; proud flesh, pink eye, seasickness, and pimples." [*As* CLARENCE *has read off the list he has become more and more impressed*]

JOHN: See?

CLARENCE: Say, that sounds all right!

JOHN: It's made "from a secret formula known only to Dr. Bartlett."

CLARENCE: He must be quite a doctor!

JOHN: [*Enthusiastically*] It sells for a dollar a bottle and we get twenty-five cents commission on every bottle.

CLARENCE: Well, where does he want us to sell it?

JOHN: He's given us the territory of all Manhattan Island.

CLARENCE: That's bully! Anybody that's sick at all ought to need a bottle of this. Let's start by calling on friends of Father and Mother.

JOHN: That's a good idea. But wait a minute. Suppose they ask us if we use it at our house?

CLARENCE: [*A little worried*] Oh, yes. It would be better if we could say we did.

JOHN: But we can't because we haven't had it here long enough.

> [NORA *enters with a tray with a cup of tea. She goes to the table and puts the sugar bowl and cream pitcher on it*]

CLARENCE: Is that the tea for Mrs. Day?

NORA: Yes.

> [*The suspicion of a good idea dawns on* CLARENCE]

CLARENCE: I'll take it up to her. You needn't bother.

NORA: Thank you. Take it up right away while it's hot. [*She exits.* CLARENCE *watches her out*]

CLARENCE: [*Eyeing* JOHN] Mother wasn't feeling well this morning.

JOHN: What was the matter with her?

CLARENCE: I don't know—she was just complaining.

JOHN: [*Getting the idea immediately and consulting the bottle*] Well, it says here it's good for women's complaints. [*They look at each other.* CLARENCE *opens the bottle and smells its contents.* JOHN *leans over and takes a sniff, too. Then he nods to* CLARENCE, *who quickly reaches for a spoon and measures out a teaspoonful, which he puts into the tea.* JOHN, *wanting to be sure* MOTHER *has enough to cure her, pours still more into the tea from the bottle as the curtain falls*]

> [*The curtain remains down for a few seconds to denote a lapse of three hours. When the curtain rises again, the breakfast things have been cleared and the room is in order.* HARLAN *is kneeling on* FATHER'S *chair looking out the window as if watching for someone.* MARGARET *comes down from upstairs*]

MARGARET: Has your father come yet?

HARLAN: Not yet.

> [NORA *enters from downstairs with a steaming tea-kettle and a towel and meets* MARGARET *in the hall*]

MARGARET: Hurry that upstairs. The doctor's waiting for it. I've got to go out.

NORA: Where are you going?

MARGARET: I have to go and get the minister.

[NORA *goes upstairs*]

HARLAN: There's a cab coming up the street.

MARGARET: Well, I hope it's him, poor man—but a cab doesn't sound like your father. [*She hurries downstairs*]

[HARLAN *sees something through the window, then rushes to the stairwell and shouts down to* MARGARET]

HARLAN: Yes, it's Father. Whitney got him all right. [*Runs back to the window. The front door slams and* FATHER *crosses the arch and hurries upstairs.* WHITNEY *comes into the room*] What took you so long?

WHITNEY: Long? I wasn't long. I went right down on the elevated and got Father right away and we came all the way back in a *cab*.

HARLAN: I thought you were never coming.

WHITNEY: Well, the horse didn't go very fast at first. The cabby whipped him and swore at him and still he wouldn't gallop. Then Father spoke to the horse personally—How is Mother?

HARLAN: I don't know. The doctor's up there now.

WHITNEY: Well, she'd better be good and sick or Father may be mad at me for getting him up here—'specially in a cab.

[FATHER *comes down the stairs muttering to himself*]

FATHER: [*Indignantly*] Well, huh!—It seems to me I ought to be shown a little consideration. I guess I've got some feelings, too!

WHITNEY: [*Hopefully*] Mother's awfully sick, isn't she?

FATHER: How do I know? I wasn't allowed to stay in the same room with her.

WHITNEY: Did the doctor put you out?

FATHER: No, it was your mother, damn it! [*He goes out and hangs up his hat and stick, then returns.* FATHER *may be annoyed, but he is also worried*] You boys keep quiet around here today.

WHITNEY: She must be pretty sick.

FATHER: She must be, Whitney! I don't know! Nobody ever tells me anything in this house. Not a damn thing!

[DR. HUMPHREYS *comes down the stairs. He's the family-doctor type of the period, with just enough whiskers to make him impressive. He carries his satchel*]

DR. HUMPHREYS: Mrs. Day is quieter now.

FATHER: How sick is she? What's the matter with her?

DR. HUMPHREYS: She's a pretty sick woman, Mr. Day. I had given her a sedative just before you came—and after you left the room I had to give her another. Have you a telephone?

FATHER: A telephone! No—I don't believe in them. Why?

DR. HUMPHREYS: Well, it would only have saved me a few steps. I'll be back in ten minutes. [*He turns to go*]

FATHER: Wait a minute—I think I'm entitled to know what's the matter with my wife.

    [DR. HUMPHREYS *turns back*]

DR. HUMPHREYS: What did Mrs. Day have for breakfast this morning?

FATHER: She didn't eat anything—not a thing.

DR. HUMPHREYS: Are you sure?

FATHER: I tried to get her to eat something, but she wouldn't.

DR. HUMPHREYS: [*Almost to himself*] I can't understand it.

FATHER: Understand what?

DR. HUMPHREYS: These violent attacks of nausea. It's almost as though she were poisoned.

FATHER: Poisoned!

DR. HUMPHREYS: I'll try not to be gone more than ten or fifteen minutes. [*He exits*]

FATHER: [*Trying to reassure himself*] Damn doctors! They never know what's the matter with anybody. Well, he'd better get your mother well, and damn soon or he'll hear from me.

WHITNEY: Mother's going to get well, isn't she?

    [FATHER *looks at* WHITNEY *sharply as though he is a little angry at anyone even raising the question*]

FATHER: Of course she's going to get well!

HARLAN: [*Running to* FATHER] I hope she gets well soon. When Mamma stays in bed it's lonesome.

FATHER: Yes, it is, Harlan. It's lonesome. [*He looks around the room and finds it pretty empty*] What were you boys supposed to do today?

WHITNEY: I was to learn the rest of my catechism.

FATHER: Well, if that's what your mother wanted you to do, you'd better do it.

WHITNEY: I know it—I think.

FATHER: You'd better be sure.

WHITNEY: I can't be sure unless somebody hears me. Will you hear me?

FATHER: [*With sudden willingness to be useful*] All right. I'll hear you, Whitney.

    [WHITNEY *goes to the mantel and gets* VINNIE's *prayer book.* FATHER *sits on the sofa.* HARLAN *climbs up beside him*]

HARLAN: If Mamma's still sick will you read to me tonight?

FATHER: Of course I'll read to you.

    [WHITNEY *opens the prayer book and hands it to* FATHER]

WHITNEY: Here it is, Father. Just the end of it. Mother knows I know the rest. Look, start here. [*He points*]

FATHER: All right. [*Reading*] "How many parts are there in a Sacrament?"

WHITNEY: [*Reciting*] "Two; the outward visible sign, and the inward spiritual grace."

[FATHER *nods in approval*]

FATHER: "What is the outward visible sign or form in Baptism?"

WHITNEY: "Water; wherein the person is baptized, in the name of the Father, and of the Son, and of the Holy Ghost." You haven't been baptized, Father, have you?

FATHER: [*Ignoring it*] "What is the inward and spiritual grace?"

WHITNEY: If you don't have to be baptized, why do I have to be confirmed?

FATHER: [*Ignoring this even more*] "What is the inward and spiritual grace?"

WHITNEY: "A death unto sin, and a new birth unto righteousness; for being by nature born in sin, and the children of wrath, we are hereby made the children of grace." Is that why you get mad so much Father—because you're a child of wrath?

FATHER: Whitney, mind your manners! You're not supposed to ask questions of your elders! "What is required of persons to be baptized?"

WHITNEY: "Repentance, whereby—whereby—" [*He pauses*]

FATHER: [*Quickly shutting the book and handing it to* WHITNEY] You don't know it well enough, Whitney. You'd better study it some more.

WHITNEY: Now?

FATHER: [*Softening*] No, you don't have to do it now. Let's see, now, what can we do?

WHITNEY: Well, I was working with my tool chest out in the back yard. [*Edges toward the arch*]

FATHER: Better not do any hammering with your mother sick upstairs. You'd better stay here.

WHITNEY: I wasn't hammering—I was doing wood-carving.

FATHER: Well, Harlan—how about you? Shall we play some tiddle-dy-winks?

HARLAN: [*Edging toward* WHITNEY] I was helping Whitney.

FATHER: Oh—all right. [*The boys go out.* FATHER *goes to the stairwell*] Boys, don't do any shouting. We all have to be very quiet around here. [*He stands in the hall and looks up toward* VINNIE, *worried. Then he tiptoes across the room and stares gloomily out of the window. Then he tiptoes back into the hall and goes to the rail of the basement stairs, and calls quietly*] Margaret! [*There is no answer, and he raises his voice a little*] Margaret! [*There is still no answer and he lets loose*] Margaret! Why don't you answer when you hear me calling?

[*At this moment* MARGARET, *hat on, appears in the arch from the right, having come through the front door*]

MARGARET: Sh—sh—

> [FATHER *turns quickly and sees* MARGARET]

FATHER: Oh, there you are!

MARGARET: [*Reprovingly*] We must all be quiet, Mr. Day—Mrs. Day is very sick.

FATHER: [*Testily*] I know she's sick. That's what I wanted you for. You go up and wait outside her door in case she needs anything. [MARGARET *starts upstairs*] And what were you doing out of the house, anyway?

MARGARET: I was sent for the minister!

FATHER: [*Startled*] The minister!

MARGARET: Yes, he'll be right in. He's paying off the cab. [MARGARET *continues upstairs*]

> [*The door slams.* THE REVEREND DR. LLOYD *appears in the archway and meets* FATHER *in the hall*]

DR. LLOYD: I was deeply shocked to hear of Mrs. Day's illness. I hope I can be of some service. Will you take me up to her?

FATHER: [*With a trace of hostility*] She's resting now. She can't be disturbed.

DR. LLOYD: But I've been summoned.

FATHER: The doctor will be back in a few minutes and we'll see what he has to say about it. You'd better come in and wait.

DR. LLOYD: Thank you. [*Comes into the room.* FATHER *follows him reluctantly*] Mrs. Day has been a tower of strength in the parish. Everyone liked her so much. Yes, she was a fine woman.

FATHER: I wish to God you wouldn't talk about Mrs. Day as if she were dead.

> [NORA *comes down the stairs and looks into the room*]

NORA: Is the doctor back yet?

FATHER: No. Does she need him?

NORA: She's kinda restless. She's talking in her sleep and twisting and turning. [*She goes downstairs*]

> [FATHER *looks up toward* VINNIE'S *room, worried, then looks angrily toward the front door*]

FATHER: That doctor said he'd be right back. [*He goes to the window*]

MARGARET: [*Coming downstairs*] Here comes the doctor. I was watching for him out the window. [*She goes to the front door. A moment later* DR. HUMPHREYS *enters*]

FATHER: Well, Doctor—seems to me that was a pretty long ten minutes.

DR. HUMPHREYS: [*Indignantly*] See here, Mr. Day, if I'm to be responsible for Mrs. Day's health, I must be allowed to handle this case in my own way.

FATHER: Well, you can't handle it if you're out of the house.

DR. HUMPHREYS: [*Flaring*] I left this house because—[DR. SOMERS, *an impos-ing medical figure, enters and stops at* DR. HUMPHREYS' *side*] This is Dr. Somers.

DR. SOMERS: How do you do?

DR. HUMPHREYS: I felt that Mrs. Day's condition warranted my getting Dr. Somers here as soon as possible for consultation. I hope that meets with your approval.

FATHER: [*A little awed*] Why, yes, of course. Anything that can be done.

DR. HUMPHREYS: Upstairs, Doctor! [*The two doctors go upstairs.* FATHER *turns back into the room, obviously shaken*]

DR. LLOYD: Mrs. Day is in good hands now, Mr. Day. There's nothing you and I can do at the moment to help.

[*After a moment's consideration* FATHER *decides there is something that can be done to help. He goes to* DR. LLOYD. FATHER *indicates the seat in front of the table to* DR. LLOYD *and they both sit*]

FATHER: Dr. Lloyd, there's something that's troubling Mrs. Day's mind. I think you know what I refer to.

DR. LLOYD: Yes—you mean the fact that you've never been baptized.

FATHER: I gathered you knew about it from your sermon last Sunday. [*Looks at him a second with indignant memory*] But let's not get angry. I think something had better be done about it.

DR. LLOYD: Yes, Mr. Day.

FATHER: When the doctors get through up there I want you to talk to Mrs. Day. I want you to tell her something.

DR. LLOYD: [*Eagerly*] Yes, I'll be glad to.

FATHER: You're just the man to do it! She shouldn't be upset about this—I want you to tell her that my being baptized would just be a lot of damn nonsense.]

[*This isn't what* DR. LLOYD *has expected and it is hardly his idea of how to help* MRS. DAY]

DR. LLOYD: But, Mr. Day!

FATHER: No, she'd take your word on a thing like that—and we've got to do everything we can to help her now.

DR. LLOYD: [*Rising*] But baptism is one of the sacraments of the Church—

FATHER: [*Rising*] You're her minister and you're supposed to bring her comfort and peace of mind.

DR. LLOYD: But the solution is so simple. It would take only your consent to be baptized.

FATHER: That's out of the question! And I'm surprised that a grown man like you should suggest such a thing.

DR. LLOYD: If you're really concerned about Mrs. Day's peace of mind, don't you think—

FATHER: Now see here—if you're just going to keep her stirred up about this, I'm not going to let you see her at all. [*He turns away.* DR. LLOYD *follows him*]

DR. LLOYD: Now, Mr. Day, as you said, we must do everything we can—

[*The doctors come downstairs.* FATHER *sees them*]

FATHER: Well, Doctor, how is she? What have you decided?

DR. HUMPHREYS: We've just left Mrs. Day. Is there a room we could use for our consultation?

FATHER: Of course. [MARGARET *starts downstairs*] Margaret, you go back upstairs! I don't want Mrs. Day left alone!

MARGARET: I have to do something for the doctor. I'll go back up as soon as I get it started.

FATHER: Well, hurry. And, Margaret, show these gentlemen downstairs to the billiard room.

MARGARET: Yes, sir. This way, Doctor—downstairs. [*Exits, followed by* DR. SOMMERS. FATHER *delays* DR. HUMPHREYS]

FATHER: Dr. Humphreys, you know now, don't you—this isn't serious, is it?

DR. HUMPHREYS: After we've had our consultation we'll talk to you, Mr. Day.

FATHER: But surely you must—

DR. HUMPHREYS: Just rest assured that Dr. Somers will do everything that is humanly possible.

FATHER: Why, you don't mean—

DR. HUMPHREYS: We'll try not to be long. [*Exits.* FATHER *turns and looks at* DR. LLOYD. *He is obviously frightened*]

FATHER: This Dr. Somers—I've heard his name often—he's very well thought of, isn't he?

DR. LLOYD: Oh, yes indeed.

FATHER: If Vinnie's really—if anyone could help her, he could—don't you think?

DR. LLOYD: A very fine physician. But there's a greater Help, ever present in the hour of need. Let us turn to Him in prayer. Let us kneel and pray. [FATHER *looks at him, straightens, then walks to the other side of the room*] Let us kneel and pray. [FATHER *finally bows his head.* DR. LLOYD *looks at him and, not kneeling himself, raises his head and speaks simply in prayer*] Oh, Lord, look down from Heaven—behold, visit, and relieve this Thy servant who is grieved with sickness, and extend to her Thy accustomed goodness. We know she has sinned against Thee in thought, word, and deed. Have mercy on her. O Lord, have mercy on this miserable sinner. Forgive her—

FATHER: She's not a miserable sinner and you know it! [*Then* FATHER *speaks directly to the Deity*] O God! You know Vinnie's not a miserable sinner. She's a damn fine woman! She shouldn't be made to suffer. It's got to stop, I tell You, it's got to stop!

[VINNIE *appears on the stairway in her nightgown*]

VINNIE: What's the matter, Clare? What's wrong?

FATHER: [*Not hearing her*] Have mercy, I say, Have mercy, damn it!

VINNIE: What's the matter Clare? What's wrong?

[FATHER *turns, sees* VINNIE, *and rushes to her*]

FATHER: Vinnie, what are you doing down here? You shouldn't be out of bed. You get right back upstairs. [*He now has his arms around her*]

VINNIE: Oh, Clare, I heard you call. Do you need me?

FATHER: [*Deeply moved*] Vinnie—I know now how much I need you. Get well, Vinnie. I'll be baptized. I promise. I'll be baptized.

VINNIE: You will? Oh, Clare!

FATHER: I'll do anything. We'll go to Europe, just we two—you won't have to worry about the children or the household accounts—[VINNIE *faints against* FATHER's *shoulder*] Vinnie! [*He stoops to lift her*]

DR. LLOYD: I'll get the doctor. But don't worry, Mr. Day—she'll be all right now. [FATHER *lifts* VINNIE *up in his arms*] Bless you for what you've done, Mr. Day.

FATHER: What did I do?

DR. LLOYD: You promised to be baptized!

FATHER: [*Aghast*] I did? [*With horror* FATHER *realizes he has been betrayed—and by himself*] OH, GOD!

CURTAIN

ACT THREE

SCENE ONE

The same.
   A month later. Mid-afternoon.
   VINNIE *is seated on the sofa embroidering petit point.* MARGARET *enters, as usual uncomfortable at being upstairs.*

MARGARET: You wanted to speak to me, ma'am?

VINNIE: Yes, Margaret, about tomorrow morning's breakfast—we must plan it very carefully.

MARGARET: [*Puzzled*] Mr. Day hasn't complained to me about his breakfasts lately. As a matter of fact, I've been blessing my luck!

VINNIE: Oh, no, it's not that. But tomorrow morning I'd like something for his breakfast that would surprise him.

MARGARET: [*Doubtfully*] Surprising Mr. Day is always a bit of a risk, ma'am. My motto with him has always been "Let well enough alone."

VINNIE: But if we think of something he especially likes, Margaret—what would you say to kippers?

MARGARET: Well, I've served him kippers, but I don't recall his ever saying he liked them.

VINNIE: He's never said he didn't like them, has he?

MARGARET: They've never got a stamp on the floor out of him one way or the other.

VINNIE: If Mr. Day doesn't say he doesn't like a thing you can assume that he does. Let's take a chance on kippers, Margaret.

MARGARET: Very well, ma'am. [*She starts out*]

VINNIE: [*Innocently*] And, Margaret, you'd better have enough breakfast for two extra places.

MARGARET: [*Knowingly*] Oh—so that's it! We're going to have company again.

VINNIE: Yes, my cousin, Miss Cartwright, and her friend are coming back from Springfield. I'm afraid they'll get here just about breakfast time.

MARGARET: Well, in that case I'd better make some of my Sunday morning hot biscuits, too.

VINNIE: Yes. We *know* Mr. Day likes those.

MARGARET: I've been getting him to church with them for the last fifteen years. [*The door slams.* MARGARET *goes to the arch and looks*] Oh, it's Mr. Clarence, ma'am. [*Goes off downstairs and* CLARENCE *enters with a large package*]

CLARENCE: Here it is, Mother. [*He puts it on the table*]

VINNIE: Oh, it was still in the store! They hadn't sold it! I'm so thrilled. Didn't you admire it, Clarence? [*She hurries over to the table*]

CLARENCE: Well, it's unusual.

VINNIE: [*Unwrapping the package*] You know, I saw this down there the day before I got sick. I was walking through the bric-a-brac section and it caught my eye. I was so tempted to buy it! And all the time I lay ill I just couldn't get it out of my head. I can't understand how it could stay in the store all this time without somebody snatching it up. [*She takes it out of the box. It is a large china pug dog*] Isn't that the darlingest thing you ever saw! It does need a ribbon, though. I've got the very thing somewhere. Oh, yes, I know. [*Goes to the side table and gets a red ribbon out of the drawer*]

CLARENCE: Isn't John home yet?

VINNIE: I haven't seen him. Why?

CLARENCE: Well, you know we've been working and John went down to collect our money.

VINNIE: That's fine. [*She ties the ribbon around the dog's neck*] Oh, Clarence, I have a secret for just the two of us; who do you think is coming to visit us tomorrow?—Cousin Cora and Mary.

CLARENCE: Yes, I know.

VINNIE: How did you know?

CLARENCE: I happened to get a letter.

[JOHN *enters, carrying two packages of medicine*]

VINNIE: John, did you ever see anything so sweet?

JOHN: What is it?

VINNIE: It's a pug dog. Your father would never let me have a real one, but he can't object to one made of china. This ribbon needs pressing. I'll take it down and have Margaret do it right away. [*Exits with the beribboned pug dog*]

CLARENCE: What did you bring home more medicine for? [*Then, with sudden fright*] Dr. Bartlett paid us off, didn't he?

JOHN: Oh, yes!

CLARENCE: [*Heaving a great sigh of relief*] You had me scared for a minute. When I went down to McCreery's to get that pug dog for Mother, I ordered the daisiest suit you ever saw. Dr. Bartlett owed us sixteen dollars apiece, and the suit was only fifteen. Wasn't that lucky? Come on, give me my money.

JOHN: Clarence, Dr. Bartlett paid us off in medicine.

CLARENCE: You let him pay us off with that old Beneficent Balm!

JOHN: Well, he thanked us, too, for our services to mankind.

CLARENCE: [*In agony*] But my suit!

JOHN: You'll just have to wait for your suit.

CLARENCE: I can't wait! I've got to have it tomorrow—and besides they're making the alterations. I've got to pay for it this afternoon! Fifteen dollars!

JOHN: [*Helpfully*] Why don't you offer them fifteen bottles of medicine?

[CLARENCE *gives it a little desperate thought*]

CLARENCE: They wouldn't take it. McCreery's don't sell medicine.

[JOHN *is by the window and looks out*]

JOHN: That's too bad. Here comes Father.

CLARENCE: I'll have to brace him for that fifteen dollars. I hate to do it, but I've got to—that's all—I've got to.

JOHN: I'm not going to be here when you do. I'd better hide this somewhere, anyway. [*Takes the packages and hurries upstairs. The door slams.* FATHER *enters and looks into the room*]

CLARENCE: Good afternoon, sir.

FATHER: How's your mother, Clarence? Where is she?

CLARENCE: She's all right. She's downstairs with Margaret. Oh, Father—

[FATHER *goes off down the hall and we hear him calling downstairs*]

FATHER: Vinnie! Vinnie! I'm home. [*Comes back into the room, carrying his newspaper*]

CLARENCE: Father, Mother will be well enough to go to church with us next Sunday.

FATHER: That's fine, Clarence. That's fine.

CLARENCE: Father, have you noticed that I haven't been kneeling down in church lately?

FATHER: Clarence, don't let your mother catch you at it.

CLARENCE: Then I've got to have a new suit of clothes right away!

FATHER: [*After a puzzled look*] Clarence, you're not even making sense!

CLARENCE: But a fellow doesn't feel right in cut-down clothes—especially your clothes. That's why I can't kneel down in church—I can't do anything in them you wouldn't do.

FATHER: Well, that's a damn good thing! If my old clothes make you behave yourself I don't think you ought to wear anything else.

CLARENCE: [*Desperately*] *Oh, no!* You're you and I'm me! I want to be myself! Besides, you're older and there are things I've got to do that I wouldn't do at your age.

FATHER: Clarence, you should never do anything I wouldn't do.

CLARENCE: Oh, yes,—look, for instance: Suppose I should want to kneel down in front of a girl?

FATHER: Why in Heaven's name should you want to do a thing like that?

CLARENCE: Well, I've got to get married *sometime*. I've got to propose to a girl *sometime*.

FATHER: [*Exasperated*] Before you're married, you'll be earning your own clothes, I hope. Don't get the idea into your head I'm going to support you and a wife, too. Besides, at your age, Clarence—

CLARENCE: [*Hastily*] Oh, I'm not going to be married right away, but for fifteen dollars I can get a good suit of clothes.

FATHER: [*Bewildered and irrritated*] Clarence! [*He stares at him. At this second,* VINNIE *comes through the arch*] Why, you're beginning to talk as crazy as your mother. [*He sees her*] Oh, hello, Vinnie. How're you feeling today?

VINNIE: I'm fine, Clare. [*They kiss*] You don't have to hurry home from the office every day like this.

[CLARENCE *throws himself in the chair by the window, sick with disappointment*]

FATHER: Business the way it is, no use going to the office at all.

VINNIE: But you haven't been to your club for weeks.

FATHER: Can't stand the damn place. You do look better, Vinnie. What did you do today? [*Drops on the sofa.* VINNIE *stands behind the sofa. Her chatter does not succeed in diverting* FATHER *from his newspaper*]

VINNIE: I took a long walk and dropped in to call on old Mrs. Whitehead.

FATHER: Well, that's fine.

VINNIE: And, Clare, it was the most fortunate thing that ever happened. I've got wonderful news for you! Who do you think was there? Mr. Morley!

FATHER: [*Not placing him*] Morley?

VINNIE: You remember—that nice young minister who substituted for Dr. Lloyd one Sunday?

FATHER: Oh, yes! Bright young fellow, preached a good sensible sermon.

VINNIE: It was the only time I ever saw you put five dollars in the plate!

FATHER: Ought to be more ministers like him. I could get along with that young man without any trouble at all.

VINNIE: Well, Clare, his parish is in Audubon—you know, 'way up above Harlem.

FATHER: Is that so?

VINNIE: Isn't that wonderful? Nobody knows you up there. You'll be perfectly safe!

FATHER: Safe? Vinnie, what the devil are you talking about?

VINNIE: I've been all over everything with Mr. Morley and he's agreed to baptize you.

FATHER: Oh, he has—the young whippersnapper! Damn nice of him!

VINNIE: We can go up there any morning, Clare—we don't even have to make an appointment.

FATHER: Vinnie, you're just making a lot of plans for nothing. Who said I was going to be baptized at all?

VINNIE: [*Aghast*] Why, Clare! *You* did!

FATHER: Now, Vinnie!—

VINNIE: You gave me your promise—your Sacred Promise. You stood right on that spot and said: "I'll be baptized. I promise—I'll be baptized."

FATHER: What if I did?

VINNIE: [*Amazed, she comes down and faces him*] Aren't you a man of your word?

FATHER: [*Rising*] Vinnie, that was under entirely different circumstances. We all thought you were dying, so naturally I said that to make you feel better. As a matter of fact, the doctor told me that's what cured you. So it seems to me pretty ungrateful of you to press this matter any further.

VINNIE: Clarence Day, you gave me your Sacred Promise!

FATHER: [*Getting annoyed*] Vinnie, you were sick when I said that. Now you're well again.

> [MARGARET *enters with the pug dog, which now has the freshly pressed ribbon tied around its neck. She puts it on the table*]

MARGARET: Is that all right, Mrs. Day?

VINNIE: [*Dismissingly*] That's fine, Margaret, thank you. [MARGARET *exits*] My being well has nothing to do with it. You gave me your word! You gave the Lord your word. If you had seen how eager Mr. Morley was to bring you into the fold. [FATHER, *trying to escape, has been moving toward the arch when suddenly the pug dog catches his eye and he stares at it fascinated*] And you're going to march yourself up to his church some morning before you go to the office and be christened. If you think for one minute that I'm going to—

FATHER: What in the name of Heaven is that?

VINNIE: If you think I'm going to let you add the sin of breaking your Solemn and Sacred Promise—

FATHER: I demand to know what that repulsive object is!

VINNIE: [*Exasperated in her turn*] It's perfectly plain what it is—it's a pug dog!

FATHER: What's it doing in this house?

VINNIE: [*Defiantly*] I wanted it and I bought it.

FATHER: You spent good money for that?

VINNIE: Clare, we're not talking about that! We're talking about you. Don't try to change the subject!

FATHER: How much did you pay for that atrocity?

VINNIE: I don't know. I sent Clarence down for it. Listen to me, Clare—

FATHER: Clarence, what did you pay for that?

CLARENCE: I didn't pay anything. I charged it.

FATHER: [*Looking at* VINNIE] Charged it! I might have known. [*To* CLARENCE] How much was it?

CLARENCE: Fifteen dollars.

FATHER: Fifteen dollars for that eyesore?

VINNIE: [*To the rescue of the pug dog*] Don't you call that lovely work of art an eyesore! That will look beautiful sitting on a red cushion by the fireplace in the parlor.

FATHER: If that sits in the parlor, I won't! Furthermore, I don't even want it in the same house with me. Get it out of here! [*He starts for the stairs*]

VINNIE: You're just using that for an excuse. You're not going to get out of this room until you set a date for your baptism.

> [FATHER *turns at the foot of the stairs*]

FATHER: I'll tell you one thing! I'll never be baptized while that hideous monstrosity is in this house. [*He stalks upstairs*]

VINNIE: [*Calling after him*] All right! [*She goes to the pug dog*] All right! It goes back this afternoon and he's christened first thing in the morning.

CLARENCE: But, Mother—

VINNIE: Clarence, you heard him say that he'd be baptized as soon as I got this pug dog out of the house. You hurry right back to McCreery's with it—and be sure they credit us with fifteen dollars.

[*The fifteen dollars rings a bell in* CLARENCE's *mind*]

CLARENCE: Oh, say, Mother, while I was at McCreery's, I happened to see a suit I would like very much and the suit was only fifteen dollars.

VINNIE: [*Regretfully*] Well, Clarence, I think your suit will have to wait until after I get your father christened.

CLARENCE: [*Hopefully*] No. I meant that since the suit cost just the same as the pug dog, if I exchanged the pug dog for the suit—

VINNIE: Why, yes! Then your suit wouldn't cost Father anything! Why, how bright of you, Clarence, to think of that!

CLARENCE: [*Quickly*] I'd better start right away before McCreery's closes. [*They have collected the box, wrapper, and tissue paper*]

VINNIE: Yes. Let's see. If we're going to take your father all the way up to Audubon—Clarence, you stop at Ryerson & Brown's on your way back and tell them to have a cab here at eight o'clock tomorrow morning.

CLARENCE: Mother, a cab! Do you think you ought to do that?

VINNIE: Well, we can't walk to Audubon.

CLARENCE: [*Warningly*] But you know what a cab does to Father!

VINNIE: This is an important occasion.

CLARENCE: [*With a shrug*] All right! A brougham or a Victoria?

VINNIE: Get one of their best cabs—the kind they use at funerals.

CLARENCE: Those cost two dollars an hour! And if Father gets mad—

VINNIE: Well, if your father starts to argue in the morning, you remember—

CLARENCE: [*Remembering his suit*] Oh, he agreed to it! We both heard him!

[VINNIE *has removed the ribbon and is about to put the pug dog back in the box*]

VINNIE: [*Regretfully*] I did have my heart set on this. [*An idea comes to her.*] Still—if they didn't sell him in all that time, he might be safe there for a few more weeks. [*She gives the dog a reassuring pat and puts him in the box. She begins to sing "Sweet Marie" happily.* FATHER *comes down the stairs.* CLARENCE *takes his hat and the box and goes happily and quickly out.* FATHER *watches him*] I hope you notice that Clarence is returning the pug dog.

FATHER: That's a sign you're getting your faculties back. [VINNIE *is singing quietly to herself in a satisfied way*] Good to hear you singing again, Vinnie. [*Suddenly remembering something*] Oh!—on my way uptown I stopped in at Tiffany's and bought you a little something. Thought you might like it. [*He takes out of his pocket a small ring box and holds it out to her. She takes it*]

VINNIE: Oh, Clare. [*She opens it eagerly*] What a beautiful ring! [*She takes the ring out, puts it on her finger, and admires it*]

FATHER: Glad if it pleases you. [*He settles down to his newspaper on the sofa*]

VINNIE: I don't know how to thank you. [*She kisses him*]

FATHER: It's thanks enough for me to have you up and around again. When you're sick, Vinnie, this house is like a tomb. There's no excitement.

VINNIE: [*Sitting beside him*] Clare, this is the loveliest ring you ever bought me. Now that I have this, you needn't buy me any more rings.

FATHER: Well, if you don't want any more.

VINNIE: What I'd really like now is a nice diamond necklace.

FATHER: [*Alarmed*] Vinnie, do you know how much a diamond necklace costs?

VINNIE: I know, Clare, but don't you see?—your giving me this ring shows that I mean a little something to you. Now, a diamond necklace—

FATHER: Good God, if you don't know by this time how I feel about you! We've been married for twenty years and I've loved you every minute of it.

VINNIE: What did you say? [*Her eyes well with tears at* FATHER's *definite statement of his love*]

FATHER: I said we'd been married twenty years and I've loved you every minute of it. But if I have to buy out jewelry stores to prove it—if I haven't shown it to you in my words and actions, I might as well— [*He turns and sees* VINNIE *dabbing her eyes and speaks with resignation*] What have I done now?

VINNIE: It's all right, Clare—I'm just so happy.

FATHER: Happy!

VINNIE: You said you loved me! And this beautiful ring—that's something else I didn't expect. Oh, Clare, I love surprises. [*She nestles against him*]

FATHER: That's another thing I can't understand about you, Vinnie. Now, *I* like to know what to expect. Then I'm prepared to meet it.

VINNIE: [*Putting her head on his shoulder*] Yes, I know. But, Clare, life would be pretty dull if we always knew what was coming.

FATHER: Well, it's certainly not dull around here. In this house you never know what's going to hit you tomorrow.

VINNIE: [*To herself*] Tomorrow! [*She starts to sing,* FATHER *listening to her happily*]
"Every daisy in the dell,
  Knows my secret, knows it well,

And yet I dare not tell,
Sweet Marie!"

CURTAIN

SCENE TWO

The same.
    The next morning. Breakfast. All the family except JOHN *and* VINNIE *are at the table and in good spirits.*

JOHN: [*Entering*] Mother says she'll be right down. [*He sits at the table*]
    [MAGGIE, *the new maid, enters with a plate of hot biscuits and serves* FATHER. As FATHER *takes a biscuit, he glances up at her and shows some little surprise*]

FATHER: Who are you? What's your name?

MAGGIE: Margaret, sir.

FATHER: Can't be Margaret. We've got one Margaret in the house.

MAGGIE: At home they call me Maggie, sir.

FATHER: [*Genially*] All right, Maggie. [MAGGIE *continues serving the biscuits*] Boys, if her name's Margaret, that's a good sign. Maybe she'll stay awhile. You know, boys, your mother used to be just the same about cooks as she is about maids. Never could keep them for some reason. Well, one day about fifteen years ago—yes, it was right after you were born, John—my, you were a homely baby. [*They all laugh at* JOHN's *expense*] I came home that night all tired out and what did I find?—no dinner, because the cook had left. Well, I decided I'd had just about enough of that, so I just marched over to the employment agency on Sixth Avenue and said to the woman in charge: "Where do you keep the cooks?" She tried to hold me up with a lot of red-tape folderol, but I just walked into the room where the girls were waiting, looked 'em over, saw Margaret, pointed at her, and said: "I'll take that one." I walked her home, she cooked dinner that night, and she's been cooking for us ever since. Damn good cook, too. [*He stamps on the floor three times*]
    [VINNIE *comes down the stairs dressed in white. Somehow she almost has the appearance of a bride going to her wedding*]

VINNIE: Good morning, Clare. Good morning, boys.
    [*The boys and* FATHER *rise.* VINNIE *takes her bonnet and gloves and lays them on the chair below the fireplace.* FATHER *goes to* VINNIE's *chair and holds it out for her, glancing at her holiday appearance.* VINNIE *sits*]

FATHER: Sit down, boys. [*As* FATHER *returns to his own chair, he notices that all of the boys are dressed in their Sunday best*] Everyone's dressed up this morning. What's on the program for this fine day?

[VINNIE, *who always postpones crises in the hope some miracle will aid her, postpones this one*]

VINNIE: Well, this afternoon May Lewis's mother is giving a party for everyone in May's dancing class. Harlan's going to that.

HARLAN: I don't want to go, Mamma.

VINNIE: Why, Harlan, don't you want to go to a party and get ice cream and cake?

HARLAN: May Lewis always tries to kiss me.

[*This is greeted with family laughter*]

FATHER: [*Genially*] When you get a little older, you won't object to girls wanting to kiss you, will he, Clarence?

[MARGARET *comes hurrying in*]

MARGARET: What's wanting?

FATHER: Margaret, these kippers are good. [MARGARET *makes her usual deprecatory gesture toward him*] Haven't had kippers for a long time. I'm glad you remembered I like them.

MARGARET: Yes, sir.

[MARGARET *and* VINNIE *exchange knowing looks.* MARGARET *goes out happy*]

FATHER: What's got into Margaret this morning? Hot biscuits, too!

VINNIE: She knows you're fond of them. [*The doorbell rings.* MAGGIE *goes to answer it.* VINNIE *stirs nervously in her chair*] Who can that be? It can't be the mail man because he's been here.

FATHER: [*With sly humor*] Clarence has been getting a good many special deliveries lately. Is that business deal going through, Clarence?

[*The family has a laugh at* CLARENCE. MAGGIE *comes back into the arch with a suit box*]

MAGGIE: This is for you, Mr. Day. Where shall I put it?

CLARENCE: [*Hastily*] Oh, that's for me, I think. Take it upstairs, Maggie.

FATHER: Wait a minute, Maggie bring it here. Let's see it.

[CLARENCE *takes the box from* MAGGIE, *who exits. He holds it toward his father*]

CLARENCE: See, it's for me, Father—Clarence Day, Jr.

FATHER: Let me look. Why, that's from McCreery's and it's marked "Charge." What is it?

VINNIE: It's all right, Clare. It's nothing for you to worry about.

FATHER: Well, at least I think I should know what's being charged to me. What is it?

VINNIE: Now, Clare, stop your fussing. It's a new suit of clothes for Clarence and it's not costing you a penny.

FATHER: It's marked "Charge fifteen dollars"—it's costing me fifteen dollars. And I told Clarence—

VINNIE: Clare, can't you take my word it isn't costing you a penny?

FATHER: I'd like to have you explain why it isn't.

VINNIE: [*Triumphantly*] Because Clarence took the pug dog back and got the suit instead.

FATHER: Of course, and they'll charge me fifteen dollars for the suit.

VINNIE: Nonsense, Clare. We gave them the pug dog for the suit. Don't you see?

FATHER: Then they'll charge me fifteen dollars for the pug dog.

VINNIE: But, Clare, they can't! We haven't got the pug dog. We sent that back.

FATHER: [*Bewildered, but not convinced*] Now wait a minute, Vinnie. There's something wrong with your reasoning.

VINNIE: I'm surprised, Clare, and you're supposed to be so good at figures. Why, it's perfectly clear to me.

FATHER: Vinnie! They're going to charge me for one thing or the other.

VINNIE: Don't you let them!

[FATHER *gets up and throws his napkin on the table*]

FATHER: Well, McCreery's aren't giving away suits and they aren't giving away pug dogs. [*He walks over to the window in his irritation*] Can't you get it through your—[*Looking out the window*] Oh, God!

VINNIE: What is it, Clare? What's wrong?

FATHER: Don't anybody answer the door.

VINNIE: Who is it? Who's coming?

FATHER: Those damn women are back!

WHITNEY: What women?

FATHER: Cora and that little idiot. [CLARENCE *dashes madly up the stairs clutching the box containing his new suit*] They're moving in on us again, bag and baggage! [*The doorbell rings*] Don't let them in!

VINNIE: Clarence Day, as if we could turn our own relatives away!

FATHER: Tell them to get back in that cab and drive right on to Ohio. If they're extravagant enough to take cabs when horse cars run right by our door—

[MAGGIE *crosses the hall to answer the doorbell*]

VINNIE: Now, Clare—you be quiet and behave yourself. They're here and there's nothing you can do about it. [*She starts toward the hall*]

FATHER: [*Shouting after her*] Well, why do they always pounce on us without warning?—the damn gypsies!

VINNIE: [*From the arch*] Shhh!—Clare! [*Then in her best welcoming tone*] Cora! Mary! It's so nice to have you back again.

CORA: How are you, Vinnie? We've been so worried about you.

VINNIE: Oh, I'm fine now!

> [CORA *and* MARY *and* VINNIE *enter and* CORA *sweeps right down into the room*]

CORA: Hello, Harlan! Whitney! Well, Cousin Clare. Here we are again! [*Kisses* FATHER *on the cheek. He draws back sternly.* MARY *looks quickly around the room for* CLARENCE, *then greets and is greeted by the other boys*] And John! Where's Clarence?

MARY: Yes, where is Clarence?

VINNIE: John, go find Clarence and tell him that Cora and Mary are here.

JOHN: Yes, Mother. [*Goes upstairs*]

VINNIE: You got here just in time to have breakfast with us.

CORA: We had breakfast at the depot.

VINNIE: Well, as a matter of fact, we'd just finished.

FATHER: [*With cold dignity*] I haven't finished my breakfast!

VINNIE: Well, then sit down, Clare. [*To* CORA *and* MARY] Margaret gave us kippers this morning and Clare's so fond of kippers. Why don't we all sit down? [*Indicates the empty places and the girls sit.* FATHER *resumes his chair and breakfast in stony silence.* MAGGIE *has come into the room to await orders*] Maggie, clear those things away. [*She indicates the dishes in front of the girls, and* MAGGIE *removes them.* FATHER *takes a letter from his stack of morning mail and opens it*] Clare, don't let your kippers get cold. [*To* CORA] Now—tell us all about Springfield.

CORA: We had a wonderful month—but tell us about you, Cousin Vinnie. You must have had a terrible time.

VINNIE: Yes, I was pretty sick, but I'm all right again now.

CORA: What was it?

VINNIE: Well, the doctors don't know exactly, but they did say this—that they'd never seen anything like it before, whatever it was.

CORA: You certainly look well enough now. Doesn't she, Clare?

> [*Whatever is in the letter* FATHER *has been reading comes to him as a shock*]

FATHER: Oh, God!

VINNIE: What's the matter, Clare? What's wrong?

FATHER: John! John!

> [JOHN *is seen halfway up the stairs with the girls' bags. He comes running down the stairs, going to* FATHER]

JOHN: Yes, Father?

FATHER: Have you been going around this town selling medicine?

JOHN: [*A little frightened*] Yes, Father.

FATHER: Dog medicine?

JOHN: [*Indignantly*] No, Father, not dog medicine!

FATHER: It must have been dog medicine!

JOHN: It wasn't dog medicine, Father—

FATHER: This letter from Mrs. Spraque says you sold her a bottle of this medicine and that her little boy gave some of it to their dog and it killed him! Now she wants ten dollars from me for a new dog.

JOHN: Well, he shouldn't have given it to a dog. It's for humans! Why, it's Bartlett's Beneficent Balm—"Made from a secret formula"!

FATHER: Have you been going around among our friends and neighbors selling some damned Dr. Munyon patent nostrum?

JOHN: But it's good medicine, Father. I can prove it by Mother.

FATHER: Vinnie, what do you know about this?

VINNIE: Nothing, Clare, but I'm sure that John—

JOHN: No, I mean that day Mother—

FATHER: That's enough! You're going to every house where you sold a bottle of that concoction and buy it all back.

JOHN: [*Dismayed*] But it's a dollar a bottle!

FATHER: I don't care how much it is. How many bottles did you sell?

JOHN: A hundred and twenty-eight.

FATHER: [*Roaring*] A hundred and twenty-eight!

VINNIE: Clare, I always told you John would make a good businessman.

FATHER: [*Calmly*] Young man, I'll give you the money to buy it back—a hundred and twenty-eight dollars. And ten more for Mrs. Sprague. That's a hundred and thirty-eight dollars. But it's coming out of your allowance! That means you'll not get another penny until that hundred and thirty-eight dollars is all paid up.

[JOHN *starts toward the hall, counting on his fingers, then turns and addresses his father in dismay*]

JOHN: I'll be twenty-one years old!

[FATHER *glares at him.* JOHN *turns and goes on up the stairs, with the bags*]

VINNIE: [*Persuasively*] Clare, you know you've always encouraged the boys to earn their own money.

FATHER: Vinnie, I'll handle this. [*There is a pause. He buries himself in his newspaper*]

CORA: [*Breaking through the constraint*] Of course, Aunt Judith sent her love to all of you—

VINNIE: I haven't seen Judith for years. You'd think living so close to Springfield—maybe I could run up there before the summer's over.

CORA: Oh, she'll be leaving for Pleasantville any day now. Grandpa Ebbetts has been failing very fast and that's why I have to hurry back.

VINNIE: Hurry back? Well, you and Mary can stay with us a few days at least.

CORA: No, I hate to break the news to you, Vinnie, but we can't even stay overnight. We're leaving on the five o'clock train this afternoon.

VINNIE: [*Disappointed*] Oh, what a pity!

[FATHER *lowers the paper*]

FATHER: [*Heartily*] Well, Cora, it certainly is good to see you again. [*To* MARY] Young lady, I think you've been enjoying yourself—you look prettier than ever.

[MARY *laughs and blushes*]

WHITNEY: I'll bet Clarence will think so.

[*The doorbell rings.* MAGGIE *crosses to answer it*]

FATHER: That can't be another special delivery for Clarence. [*To* MARY *slyly*] While you were in Springfield our postman was kept pretty busy. Sure you girls don't want any breakfast?

MARY: No, thank you. [*Rises and goes to the arch and stands looking upstairs, watching for* CLARENCE]

CORA: Oh, no, thank you, Cousin Clare, we've had our breakfast.

FATHER: At least you ought to have a cup of coffee with us. Vinnie, you might have thought to order some coffee for the girls.

CORA: No, no, thank you, Cousin Clare.

[MAGGIE *appears again in the arch*]

MAGGIE: It's the cab, ma'am. [*Exits*]

FATHER: The cab! What cab?

VINNIE: The cab that's to take us to Audubon.

FATHER: Who's going to Audubon?

VINNIE: We all are. Cora, the most wonderful thing has happened!

CORA: What, Cousin Vinnie?

VINNIE: [*Happily*] Clare's going to be baptized this morning.

FATHER: [*Not believing his ears*] Vinnie—what are you saying?

VINNIE: [*With determination*] I'm saying you're going to be baptized this morning!

FATHER: I am not going to be baptized this morning or any other morning!

VINNIE: You promised yesterday that as soon as I sent that pug dog back you'd be baptized.

FATHER: I promised no such thing!

VINNIE: You certainly did!

FATHER: I never said anything remotely like that!

VINNIE: Clarence was right here and heard it. You ask him!

FATHER: Clarence be damned! I know what I said! I don't remember exactly, but it wasn't that!

VINNIE: Well, I remember. That's why I ordered the cab!

FATHER: [*Suddenly remembering*] The cab! Oh, my God, that cab! [*He rises and glares out the window at the cab, then turns back and speaks peremptorily*] Vinnie! You send that right back!

VINNIE: I'll do nothing of the kind. I'm going to see that you get to Heaven.

FATHER: I can't go to Heaven in a cab!

VINNIE: Well, you can start in a cab! I'm not sure whether they'll ever let you into Heaven or not, but I know they won't unless you're baptized.

FATHER: They can't keep me out of Heaven on a technicality.

VINNIE: Clare, stop quibbling! You might as well face it—you've got to make your peace with God.

FATHER: I never had any trouble with God until you stirred Him up!

[MARY *is tired of waiting for* CLARENCE *and chooses this moment to interrupt*]

MARY: Mrs. Day?

[VINNIE *answers her quickly, as if expecting* MARY *to supply her with an added argument*]

VINNIE: Yes, Mary?

MARY: Where do you suppose Clarence is?

FATHER: You keep out of this, young lady! If it hadn't been for you, no one would have known whether I was baptized or not. [MARY *breaks into tears*] Damn! Damnation!

VINNIE: Harlan! Whitney! Get your Sunday hats. [*Calls upstairs*] John! Clarence!

[HARLAN *and* WHITNEY *start out, but stop as* FATHER *speaks*]

FATHER: [*Blazing with new fire*] Vinnie, are you mad? Was it your plan that my own children should witness this indignity?

VINNIE: Why, Clare, they'll be proud of you!

FATHER: I suppose Harlan is to be my godfather! [*With determination*] Vinnie, it's no use. I can't go through with this thing and I won't. That's final.

VINNIE: Why, Clare dear, if you feel that way about it—

FATHER: I do!

VINNIE: —the children don't have to go.

[JOHN *enters*]

JOHN: Yes, Mother?

[FATHER *sees* JOHN *and an avenue of escape opens up*]

FATHER: Oh, John! Vinnie, I can't do anything like that this morning. I've got to take John down to the office and give him the money to buy back that medicine. [*To* JOHN] When I think of you going around this town selling dog medicine!—

JOHN: [*Insistently*] It wasn't dog medicine, Father.

FATHER: John, we're starting downtown this minute!

VINNIE: You're doing no such thing! You gave me your Sacred Promise that day I almost died—

JOHN: Yes, and she would have died if we hadn't given her some of that medicine. That proves it's good medicine!

FATHER: [*Aghast*] You gave your Mother some of that dog medicine!

VINNIE: Oh, no, John, you didn't! [*Sinks weakly into the chair below the fireplace*]

JOHN: Yes, we did, Mother. We put some in your tea that morning.

FATHER: You did what? Without her knowing it? Do you realize you might have killed your Mother? You did kill Mrs. Sprague's dog. [*After a solemn pause*] John, you've done a very serious thing. I'll have to give considerable thought as to how you're going to be punished for this.

VINNIE: But, Clare—

FATHER: No, Vinnie. When I think of that day—with the house full of doctors—why, Cora, we even sent for the minister. Why, we might have lost you! [*He goes to* VINNIE, *really moved, and puts his hand on her shoulder*] It's all right now, Vinnie, thank God. You're well again. But what I went through that afternoon—the way I felt—I'll never forget it.

VINNIE: Don't talk that way, Clare. You've forgotten it already.

FATHER: What do you mean?

VINNIE: That was the day you gave me your Sacred Promise.

FATHER: But I wouldn't have promised if I hadn't thought you were dying— and you wouldn't have almost died if John hadn't given you that medicine. Don't you see? The whole thing's illegal!

VINNIE: Suppose I had died! It wouldn't make any difference to you. You don't care whether we meet in Heaven or not—you don't care whether you ever see me and the children again. [*She almost succeeds in crying.* HARLAN *and* WHITNEY *go to her in sympathy, putting their arms around her*]

FATHER: [*Distressed*] Now, Vinnie, you're not being fair to me.

VINNIE: It's all right, Clare. If you don't love us enough there's nothing we can do about it.

[*Hurt,* FATHER *walks away to the other side of the room*]

FATHER: That's got nothing to do with it! I love my family as much as any man. There's nothing within reason I wouldn't do for you, and you know it! All these years I've struggled and worked just to prove—[*He has reached the window and looks out*] There's that damn cab! Vinnie, you're not well enough to go all the way up to Audubon.

VINNIE: [*Perkily*] I'm well enough if we ride.

FATHER: But that trip would take all morning. And those cabs cost a dollar an hour.

VINNIE: [*With smug complacence*] That's one of their best cabs. That costs two dollars an hour.

[FATHER *stares at her a second, horrified—then explodes*]

FATHER: Then why aren't you ready? Get your hat on! Damn! Damnation! Amen! [*Exits for his hat and stick.* VINNIE *is stunned for a moment by this sudden surrender, then hastily puts on her bonnet*]

WHITNEY: Let's watch them start! Come on, Cousin Cora, let's watch them start!

CORA: I wouldn't miss it!

[WHITNEY, HARLAN, *and* CORA *hurry out.* VINNIE *starts, but* JOHN *stops her in the arch*]

JOHN: [*Contritely*] Mother, I didn't mean to almost kill you.

VINNIE: Now, don't you worry about what your father said. [*Tenderly*] It's all right, dear. [*She kisses him*] It worked out fine!

[*She exits.* JOHN *looks upstairs, then at* MARY, *who has gone to the window*]

JOHN: Mary! Here comes Clarence!

[JOHN *exits.* MARY *sits in* FATHER'S *chair.* CLARENCE *comes down the stairs in his new suit. He goes into the room and right to* MARY. *Without saying a word he kneels in front of her. They both are starry-eyed*]

[FATHER, *with hat and stick, comes into the arch on his way out. He sees* CLARENCE *kneeling at* MARY'S *feet*]

FATHER: *Oh, God!*

[CLARENCE *springs up in embarrassment.* VINNIE *re-enters hurriedly*]

VINNIE: What's the matter? What's wrong?

CLARENCE: Nothing's wrong, Mother. [*Then, for want of something to say:*] Going to the office, Father?

FATHER: No! I'm going to be baptized, damn it!

[*He slams his hat on angrily and stalks out.* VINNIE *gives a triumphant nod and follows him. The curtain starts down, and as it falls,* CLARENCE *again kneels at* MARY'S *feet*]

CURTAIN

Tobacco Road

JACK KIRKLAND

From the Novel by
ERSKINE CALDWELL

JACK KIRKLAND
AND
ERSKINE CALDWELL

While *Tobacco Road* may never have won any awards or made any "ten best" lists, no history of the American theater can be considered complete without mention of it. Ranking second among the longest-running Broadway plays, the curtain rose for 3,182 consecutive performances. Something of a theatrical feat, for the opening night notices were far from encouraging. Only Percy Hammond of the *New York Herald Tribune* commended it: "It is a vividly authentic, minor and squalid tragedy, lighted in the right spots with glowing and honest humor." Brooks Atkinson declared in *The New York Times* that the Jack Kirkland dramatization of Erskine Caldwell's novel was "clumsy and rudderless." Several months after the opening, however, he viewed it somewhat differently in an article by terming it "the one play of the season that has enriched our knowledge of the American people. In his stage adaptation of the novel, Jack Kirkland has preserved Mr. Caldwell's demoniac genius, which makes this rambling sketch of the Georgia cracker's degeneration horrible and comic, foul and tragic."

More than a quarter of a century later, Mr. Atkinson was to offer further thoughts about the play in his book *Broadway*: "*Tobacco Road* was a genuine folkplay that substituted brutal truth for the bucolic charm of the genre . . . and theatregoers who kept it on the stage for almost eight years must also have been startled by the bleakness, ignorance, and shiftlessness of a part of Georgia they hardly knew about."

It was widely contended that the success of the play derived from its scandal value, the vulgarity and profanity of its language, and its reputation for obscenity. Yet, while it may have attracted curiosity and thrill seekers for a while, it also drew regular theater patrons, for no production could survive for that length of time on the merely curious. It even garnered support from sociologists and reformers, bringing the play to the attention of a wide variety of theatregoers.

Years later, Kirkland recalled: "I had a hunch after that first night at the Masque that the show would click. It left me all in a heap. I felt it was an American classic, and I think it will live to be recognized as such."

Today, historians of the drama, undoubtedly impressed with the lengthy run, now regard this dramatic narrative about the poverty and degradation of the backroads of the South and the inability of the Lesters to make adjustments to economic changes as a naturalistic drama with social awareness.

Tobacco Road, which originally starred Henry Hull and later James Barton, had four New York revivals, toured the country for many years (it was banned in Chicago and one or two other cities), and was staged several times in London.

Jack Kirkland (1902–69) was born in St. Louis, Missouri. He attended Columbia University and worked on a number of newspapers (including the New York *Daily News*) before turning to playwriting.

Frankie and Johnnie, his first play to reach the stage, was produced in 1928. This was followed by *Tobacco Road* in 1933. According to a newspaper account, his initial interest in the property came from his being ill in bed for several days. A friend lent him a copy of the book to pass the time. Impressed by its stage potentials, he negotiated for the rights, then went off to Mallorca to work on the dramatization.

His next theatrical venture was *Tortilla Flat,* adapted from John Steinbeck's novel. Subsequent plays were *I Must Love Someone* (coauthor with Leyla Georgie); and the stage adaptations of Mary Lasswell's *Suds in Your Eyes,* Caldwell's *Georgia Boy,* and Nelson Algren's *The Man With the Golden Arm.*

An eminent American author, Erskine Caldwell was born in Georgia in 1903. After studying at the University of Virginia, he published two novelettes in 1930, *The Bastard* and *Poor Fool,* but his first fame was to come in 1932 with *Tobacco Road.* Like his next novel, *God's Little Acre* (1933), it showed a rich sense of folk humor and indignation at social inequities.

Thereafter, Caldwell published more than two dozen volumes of novels, short stories, documentary books (several in collaboration with his second wife, Margaret Bourke-White, the noted photographer), and travel experiences.

A film version of *Tobacco Road,* released in 1941, was directed by John Ford and starred Charley Grapewin as Jeeter Lester.

TOBACCO ROAD was first produced at the Masque Theatre, New York, on December 4, 1933, by Anthony Brown. The cast was as follows:

DUDE LESTER	*Sam Byrd*
JEETER LESTER	*Henry Hull*
ADA LESTER	*Margaret Wycherly*
ELLIE MAY	*Ruth Hunter*
GRANDMA LESTER	*Patricia Quinn*
LOV BENSEY	*Dean Jagger*
HENRY PEABODY	*Ashley Cooper*
SISTER BESSIE RICE	*Maude Odell*
PEARL	*Reneice Rehan*
CAPTAIN TIM	*Lamar King*
GEORGE PAYNE	*Edwin Walter*

Directed by Anthony Brown
Setting by Robert Redington Sharpe

The entire action of the play takes place at the farm of Jeeter Lester, situated on a tobacco road in the back country of Georgia.

ACT ONE

Late afternoon.

ACT TWO

Next morning.

ACT THREE

Dawn, the following day.

ACT ONE

TIME: *The 1920s.*

PLACE: *The back country, Georgia—thirty miles or so from Augusta. It is a famished, desolate land, once given over to the profitable raising of tobacco, then turned into small cotton plantations, which have been so intensively and stupidly cultivated as to exhaust the soil. Poverty, want, squalor, degeneracy, pitiful helplessness and grotesque, tragic lusts have stamped a lost, outpaced people with the mark of inevitable end. Unequipped to face a changing economic program, bound up in traditions, ties, and prejudices, they unknowingly face extinction. It is a passing scene, contemporary and fast fading, hurling the lie at nature's mercy and challenging a god who reputedly looks after his own. Grim humor pervades all, stalking side by side with tragedy on the last short mile which leads to complete, eventual elimination. The pride and hope of a once aggressive group, pioneers in a great new world, thus meet ironic conclusion. The world moves on, unmindful of their ghosts.*

SCENE: *The squalid shack of* JEETER LESTER, *where live his wife, his mother, and two children, last of a multiple brood and last of many generations of deep Georgia crackers. Left stage, angled to curtain line, is the front of the cracked and bleeding house. A small porch, one step up from the yard, projects beyond the building front. Rear, running parallel with the curtain line and disappearing—left, behind the house, and, right, behind a clump of bushes—is the immediate section of the Tobacco Road. Center stage, from road rear to foots, is a sandy yard. Right center stage is a leafless chinaberry tree, under which is a broken, weatherworn bench. Downstage from this, to within two feet of the curtain line, is a well structure, behind which, masking right stage to curtain, is a broken corn crib. A sprawling, broken log fence separates the yard from the road, beyond which fields of sedge brush stretch away in the distance.*

AT RISE: JEETER, *dressed in dirty, torn overalls and dark shirt, an old, battered hat on his head, and heavy, worn boots on his feet, is sitting on the edge of the porch, trying vainly to patch a rotted inner tube. He is really concentrating on his work, but that does not hinder an almost constant run of chatter, most of it a complaining monotone. Standing in the yard and hurling a ball, which he retrieves on the rebound, against the side of the house, upstage beyond the porch, is* DUDE, *last son of* JEETER *to remain at home.* DUDE *is just sixteen, dirty, skinny, and not too bright. He is dressed like his father in dirty overalls and a shirt. Underfeeding has had its effect on both* JEETER *and* DUDE. *They are scrawny and emaciated.* DUDE *continues thump-*

ing the ball against the house and catching it on the rebound in spite of the fact that the old boards aren't capable of much resistance. The ball hits the house several times before JEETER *complains.*

JEETER: Stop chunkin' that ball against that there old house, Dude. You've clear about got all the weatherboards knocked off already. [DUDE, *ignoring him, throws the ball three more times*] Don't you never do what I tell you? Quit chunkin' that ball at them there weatherboards. The durned old house is going to pitch over and fall on the ground one of these days if you don't stop doing that.

DUDE: [*Casually*] Aw, go to hell, you dried-up old clod. Nobody asked you nothin'. [*Throws ball again*]

JEETER: [*An edge of supplication in his voice*] Now, Dude, is that a way to treat your old pa? You ought to sort of help me out instead of always doing something contrary. You ought to be helping me fix up this old inner tube instead of chunking that ball at that old house all the time.

DUDE: That there old inner tube ain't going to stay fixed noway. You might just as well quit tryin'.

JEETER: Maybe you're right. Maybe I ought to try filling the tires with cotton hulls and drivin' on them that way. A man told me that was the way to do it.

DUDE: [*Between throwing the ball*] That old automobile ain't no good. It ain't got no horn on it no more and there ain't no sense drivin' an automobile unless you got a horn.

JEETER: It had one of the prettiest horns in the country when it was new.

DUDE: Well, it ain't got no horn now, and it don't hardly run neither.

JEETER: It used to be one of the prettiest runnin' and prettiest soundin' automobiles you ever saw. I used to put you children in it and let you blow the horn all you liked.

DUDE: That was so long ago it ain't doing me no good now.

JEETER: That old automobile is just about the last of my goods. It looks like a man can't have any goods no more.

DUDE: [*Suddenly—fierce*] Some day I'm going to have me a new automobile. I'm going to have me a new automobile and a new horn on it and I'm going to ride through the country just a raisin' of hell. [GRANDMA LESTER, *an old, bent hag in ragged, black clothes comes around the far corner of the house just as* DUDE *throws his ball with particular viciousness, almost striking her. In fright, she drops to her knees and begins crawling downstage toward the porch.* DUDE *catches the ball on the rebound and prepares to hurl it again*] Look out of the way, old woman, or I'll knock your head off. [DUDE *hurls the ball against the house just above the old woman as she crawls, whimpering, along the ground in the direction of the porch steps. He takes savage delight in her fears. She moves painfully and slowly and he has time for two throws before she reaches the comparative safety of the steps, under which she crawls*]

JEETER: Now, Dude, is that a way to act toward your old grandma? You got her scared half to death.

DUDE: Aw, shut up. You wish she was dead just as much as anybody, even if she is your own ma.

JEETER: Now, Dude . . . I never wished no harm to nobody.

DUDE: You're a dirty old liar. You don't even give her nothing to eat.

JEETER: I don't give her nothing because there ain't nothing.

DUDE: Even when there is you don't give it to her. You needn't go telling me you don't want her dead.

JEETER: Now, Dude, is that a way to talk? It don't seem to me like that's a way a son should talk to his father.

DUDE: Then keep your mouth out of it when nobody's asked you nothing. [DUDE *throws the ball against the house, beginning his game again.* JEETER *resumes work on the inner tube, sitting on the patch.* GRANDMA *comes slowly from under the edge of the porch, rises and starts cautiously to move around* DUDE *in the direction of the Tobacco Road. She is carrying an old gunny sack*]

DUDE: [*Seeing the old woman and stopping*] Where you going now? There ain't no use you picking up firewood today. There ain't going to be anything to eat. [*The* OLD WOMAN *shuffles on toward right rear hole in the log fence.* DUDE *looks after her, the spirit of hurt in his heart and mind*] You better run, old woman, I'm going to chunk this ball at you. [*He holds ball to throw. She sees his gesture, moves more quickly, stumbles, falls, gets up*] Look out now, I'm going to hit you in the head—I'm going to hit you in the head. [GRANDMA *stumbles again in her hurry, but this time doesn't rise, continuing her exit on hands and knees.* DUDE *is on the point of throwing the ball at her, when his eye catches the torn cover and checks him. He looks at the ball more closely*] Goddam, just look at that ball. Just look at what that old house done to that ball.

JEETER: [*Wiggling on tube to make the patch stick*] Let me see it here. [DUDE *hands him the ball. He looks at it and shakes his head*] Yes, sir, it's plumb wore out.

DUDE: [*Taking back the ball, holding it up, and looking at it*] It ain't even round no more. That old house just about ruined it for good. [*Sits on ground, inspecting ball*]

JEETER: Looks like about everything around here is wore out. Seems like the Lord just ain't with us no more at all.

DUDE: I'm going down to Fuller tomorrow and steal me a new ball. That's what I'm going to do.

JEETER: Stealing is powerful sinful, Dude. I wouldn't want you doing that. I guess stealing is about the most sinful thing a man can do.

DUDE: Go on, you old liar. You're always stealing something if you can find it.

JEETER: Now, Dude! Maybe I have been a powerful sinner in my time, but ain't nobody never been sorrier than me when he's done something against the Lord.

DUDE: You're always praying and shouting after you been stealing something, but that ain't never stopped you from doing it. I'd like to hear you tell me of one time when it stopped you. Just tell me. [*Pauses while* JEETER *fiddles with inner tube*] You just won't tell me—that's what.

JEETER: [*Avoiding the issue, pulls at the patch, which comes off in his hand*] Just look at that old inner tube. . . . [*Inspects it for an instant, tosses it aside*] Well, I guess there ain't no use trying to fix that no more. Looks to me like I got to figure some other way of getting a load of wood down to Augusta. [*Yawns, stretches*] I got to do some thinking about that. [*Lies back on porch, tilting his hat over his eyes.* DUDE *continues to pound ball on rock*] I know what I'm going to do. I'm going down to Fuller one of these days and borrow me a mule. I expect I could take a load of wood to Augusta almost every day that way.

DUDE: [*Laughs*] Ho! Ho! Ain't nobody going to loan you a mule. You can't even get seed-cotton and guano to plant a crop with.

JEETER: Never you mind now. That way I could do about everything I wanted. When I wasn't hauling wood I could cultivate the fields. That's what a man ought to be doing anyway. When February comes like this and the ground gets right for plowing a man ought to be planting in the ground and growing things. That's what the Lord intended a man should do. But he can't do much without a mule to plow with. [*Nods his head, sits up*] Yes, sir, that's what I'm going to do. I'm going down to Fuller or maybe even McCoy one of these days and borrow me a mule. [*Lies down on his back again, tilting hat over his eyes*] I got to do some thinking about that.

> [DUDE *makes no comment, concentrating on pounding the ball back into shape. Hits it twice on the ground*]

DUDE: Goddam that old house! This ball never will get round no more.

> [*Enter* ADA *through doorway on to the porch and taking in* JEETER'S *recumbent form with a quick, irritated glance.* ADA *is a thin, gaunt, pellagra-ridden woman. Her shapeless dress is dirty and ragged. She was never a beauty, and pellagra and forty years of living with* JEETER *have not helped to improve her appearance. Her hair is a stringy, colorless gray-brown. She shambles rather than walks, and leans against anything strong enough to bear her weight. An inevitable snuff stick protrudes from her lips. She speaks when* DUDE *stops pounding the ball to inspect it again*]

ADA: What are you doing laying down there on the porch, Jeeter Lester? Ain't you going to haul no wood to Augusta?

JEETER: [*Pushing back hat and sitting up. Even in that short time he has fallen asleep. He regards his wife vaguely*] What's that?

ADA: When you going to haul some wood to Augusta?

JEETER: [*Sinking back*] I'm aiming to take a load over there tomorrow or the next day.

DUDE: The hell he is, Ma. He's just trying to lie out of it.

JEETER: Now, Dude.

ADA: You're just lazy, that's what's wrong with you. If you wasn't lazy you could haul a load every day, and I'd have me some snuff when I wanted it most.

JEETER: I ain't no durn wood-chopper. I'm a farmer. The wood-choppers hauling wood to Augusta ain't got no farming to take up their time like I has. Why, I expect I'm going to grow near about fifty bales of cotton this year.

ADA: That's the way you talk every year about this time, but you don't never get started.

JEETER: This year I'm going to get at it. Dude and me'll burn the broom sedge off the fields one of these days and it won't take long then to put in a crop.

ADA: I been listening to you talk like that so long I don't believe nothing you say now. It's a big old whopping lie.

JEETER: Now leave me be, Ada. I'm going to start in the morning. Soon as I get all the fields burned off I'll go borrow me some mules. I wouldn't be surprised if me and Dude growed more than fifty bales of cotton this year, if I can get me some seed-cotton and guano.

DUDE: Who's going to give you seed-cotton and guano this year any more than they did last year or the year before, or the year before that?

JEETER: God is aiming to provide for me. I'm getting ready right now to receive His bounty.

ADA: You just lay there and see! Even the children has got more sense than you has. Didn't they go off and work in the mills as soon as they was big enough? If I wasn't so old I'd go up there right now and make me some money myself, just like you ought to be doing.

JEETER: [*Intensely—sitting bolt upright*] It's wicked, you saying that, Ada. City ways ain't God-given. It wasn't intended for a man with the smell of the land in him to live in a mill in Augusta.

ADA: It's a whole lot better to live in the mills than it is to stay out here on the Tobacco Road and starve to death.

DUDE: Cuss the hell out of him, Ma.

JEETER: [*Sadly. Again lying down*] The Lord sends me every misery He can think of just to try my soul. He must be aiming to do something powerful big for me because He sure tests me hard. I reckon He figures if I can put up with my own people I can stand to fight back at the devil.

ADA: Humph! If He don't hurry up and do something about it, it will be too late. My poor stomach gives me a powerful pain all day long when I ain't got the snuff to calm it.

JEETER: [*Without moving*] Yes, I reckon you women folks is about near as hungry as I is. I sure feel right sorry for you women folks. [*Pulls hat over his eyes and dozes off again*]

> [*Enter* ELLIE MAY *right on Tobacco Road.* ELLIE MAY *is eighteen, and not unattractive as to figure. Her eyes are good; her hair is brown. The outstanding feature, however, is a slit lip, red and fiery, the opening running from about the center of the lip to the left side of her nose. When she speaks, which is seldom, she has the garbled pronunciation and nasal emphasis of those afflicted with a harelip. She is barefoot and hatless, and her light cotton dress is old, rumpled, and streaked with dirt. She comes forward shyly, like a frightened doe, her eyes watching the three other people. She only comes in as far as the chinaberry tree, half edging behind it*]

ADA: You talk like an old fool. . . . Where you been there, Ellie May?

ELLIE MAY: No place, Ma.

ADA: [*Eagerly*] You didn't maybe go to see Pearl, did you?

ELLIE MAY: No, Ma.

ADA: [*More to herself than to anyone*] I declare I don't know what's got into that girl. I ain't see hide nor hair of her since she and Lov got married.

DUDE: [*With deliberate cruelty*] Why should Pearl want to see you?

ADA: She loves her old ma, that's why.

DUDE: Well, she ain't been back, has she?

ADA: Pearl is different. There ain't one of the whole seventeen she's like.

DUDE: [*Pointedly—leering*] She sure ain't like the rest of us, all right. . . . What was you doing, Ma, horsing around some man besides that old fool over there?

ADA: You ain't no right talking like that to your old ma, Dude Lester. The Lord will strike you dead one of these days.

DUDE: I ain't afraid of the Lord. He ain't never done nothing for me one way or the other. . . .

ADA: If you was a good son, you wouldn't be saying things like that. You'd be helping to get rations and snuff for your old ma. I declare to goodness I don't know when I've had enough to eat. It's getting so if I had a stylish dress to be buried in I'd like to lie down right now and die.

DUDE: [*With vicious humor*] You ain't never going to get a new dress to die in. You're going to die and be buried in just what you got on. They're going to bury you in that same old dress.

ADA: Now, Dude, don't start fooling with your old ma like that.

> [JEETER *is aroused and straightens up sleepily.* ELLIE MAY *moves a step*

nearer the porch, but is still close to the chinaberry tree. DUDE *gets to his feet, leering with joy at the effect of his cruel tormenting.* ADA *steps down from the porch, but one hand still holds the upright*]

DUDE: I ain't fooling. I guess I know . . . Yeh, and they're going to bury pa just like he is, too. They're going to lay you in the corn crib and then they're going to bury you both just like you is.

JEETER: [*Plaintively*] What are you saying, Dude? You're always saying that when you know how I feel about it. They ain't going to lay me in no corn crib. Lov swore to me he'd dig a hole and put me right in it.

DUDE: What do I care what Lov promised? I know what they're going to do.

ADA: Make him say they ain't, Jeeter.

JEETER: Dude, you can't let them do that. My pa was laid in the corn crib before they buried him and the rats ate off half his face. You can't let them do that to me.

DUDE: What you so worried about? You'll be dead, anyhow.

JEETER: My old pa was dead and I know he minded.

DUDE: There ain't no rats in that old corn crib no more. There ain't been no corn in there for five years. They've all gone away.

JEETER: They'll come back, when they know I'm layin' there. They got it in good and heavy for me because there ain't been no corn in that old crib all this time. They'll just be waitin' to come back when I'm dead and eat off me when I can't do nothing to keep 'em away.

DUDE: What do I care about that?

ADA: You're the only boy left to see your old ma is buried in a stylish dress. You got to swear to me, Dude.

DUDE: [*Getting up*] I ain't going to swear to nothing.

JEETER: [*Coming forward a few steps*] Now, Dude, boy——

DUDE: Aw, go to hell. What do I care about you? [*Turns—starts to chant*] You're going to die and get laid in the corn crib—you're going to die and get laid in the corn crib.

JEETER: [*Threateningly*] You shut up, Dude Lester. You shut up your mouth.

DUDE: [*Continuing chant, walking toward gate*] You're going to die and get laid in the corn crib—you're going to die, etc.

  [JEETER *rushes at* DUDE]

JEETER: [*Striking weakly at* DUDE's *back*] Shut up. You hear me—shut up!

DUDE: [*Turning—blocking blows easily*] What you trying to do, you old fool? Get away from me. [*Pushes* JEETER, *who stumbles back, falling*] You keep away from me when I tell you. [*Turns—breaks again into chant*] You're going to die and get laid in the corn crib . . . etc. [*Exits*]

ADA: [*Plaintively*] Dude, you come back here. You can't go off like that without making a promise to your old ma.

[ADA *is answered only by* DUDE'S *grim chant, diminishing in the distance.* JEETER *gets up, goes back to the porch and sits, abstractedly picking up the inner tube and working on it.* ADA *is at the bench*]

JEETER: [*After a pause*] I reckon Dude is about the worst child of the whole lot. Seems like a boy would have the proper respect for his old pa.

ADA: I know Lizzie Belle'd help me get a stylish dress if I could find out where she is at. She used to love her old ma a heap. Clara might help some, too. She used to tell me how pretty I looked when I combed my hair mornings and put on a clean apron. I don't know if the others would want to help none or not. It's been such a long time since I saw the rest of them I've just about forgot what they was like. Seems like I can't recall their names even.

JEETER: Lizzie Belle might be making a lot of money over in the mills. Maybe if I was to find her and ask her about it, she might come sometime and bring us a little money. I know Bailey would. Bailey was just about the best of all the boys.

ADA: Reckon any of the children is dead?

JEETER: Some, I reckon. . . . But Tom ain't dead. I know that for sure. I ain't got around to doing it yet, but one of these days I'm going over to Burke County and see him. Everybody in Fuller tells me he's hauling cross ties out of the camp by the wagon load day and night. From what people say about him he's a powerful rich man now. He sure ought to give me some money.

ADA: When you see Tom tell him that his old ma would like to see him. You tell him that I said he was near about the best of the whole seventeen. Clara and Lizzie Belle was about the best, I reckon, but Tom and Bailey led the boys when it came to being good children. You tell Tom I said he was the best and maybe he'll send me some money for a stylish dress.

JEETER: Pearl is the prettiest. Ain't none of the other gals got pretty yellow hair like she has. Nor them pale blue eyes, neither.

ADA: Pearl is my real favorite. But I wish she'd come to see me sometime. What do you think makes her stay away since she got married, Jeeter?

JEETER: There never was no telling what Pearl was going to do. You was much like her yourself in that respect when you was twelve or thirteen.

ADA: Do you think she's happily married to Lov?

JEETER: Happy? I don't know anything about that. When a gal is mated to a man that's all there is to it.

ADA: Maybe she should've gone off to Augusta like the others done, even if she was scared. That's where a pretty girl ought to be. She ought to be where there's pretty clothes and shoes to wear and windows to look at.

JEETER: I don't agree to that. People that's born on the land should stay on the land. The Lord intended such. I made her go to live with Lov because that was the best thing for her to do.

ADA: Humph! Well, it might be she's satisfied. Maybe she don't care about seeing her old ma right now. When girls is satisfied they sometimes don't like to talk about their husbands any more than they do when they ain't satisfied.

JEETER: Pearl don't talk none anyway. Reckon she talks to Lov, Ada?

ADA: When girls sleep in the bed with their husbands they usually talk to them, I've discovered.

JEETER: By God and by Jesus you was certainly in no hurry to talk to me even then.

ADA: I'll go down to see her one of these days if she don't come to see me. You go see Lov, too. It's time you done that.

JEETER: Don't bother me about that now. I got to figure out some way to plant me a crop this year. [*Leans against upright*] I got to do some thinking about that right away.

[JEETER *pulls hat over his eyes and promptly goes to sleep.* ADA *shakes her head.* ELLIE MAY *starts out gate, but* ADA *sees her*]

ADA: Ellie May! Hey you, Ellie May! You come inside and fix up the beds. They ain't been made all day and somebody's got to do something around here.

[ELLIE MAY *turns and reluctantly starts toward house, when* DUDE *enters excitedly from right and comes to right of porch*]

DUDE: Hey, Lov's coming! Lov's coming down the road.

[ELLIE MAY *crosses to right end of fence; looks down road*]

JEETER: [*Drowsily*] What?

ADA: [*Kicks* JEETER] Wake up, you old fool—Lov's coming. Maybe he wants to talk about Pearl.

JEETER: What do I care about that now? By God, woman, can't you see I'm thinking?

DUDE: He's toting a croker sack that's got something in it.

JEETER: [*Suddenly wide awake*] A croker sack! [*Rises*] What does it look like is in that croker sack, Dude?

DUDE: He's just coming over the ridge now and I couldn't make out. But nobody carries a sack that ain't got nothing good in it.

[JEETER *runs to the fence and looks over it down the road.* ELLIE MAY *also goes to the fence, but as far right stage from the others as possible. Enter* GRANDMA LESTER *with a sackful of twigs which she drags along the ground. She does not even glance at the others, who are gazing in the opposite direction down the road, but crosses to the porch, releases the sack, and sits, pressing her hands to her side in pain and swaying back and forth*]

JEETER: [*Peering over fence*] By God and by Jesus, that's Lov all right. Do you think them's turnips he's toting, Dude? Do you think them's turnips in that croker sack?

DUDE: It's something all right.

JEETER: [*Delighted*] By God and by Jesus, I just been waiting to have me some turnips.

ADA: If them's turnips do you reckon he'll let me have some?

JEETER: I'll mention it when I talk to him, but I don't know how he'll take it. He must have paid a good stiff price if they's winter turnips.

DUDE: Lov ain't giving away nothing he paid a good stiff price for.

JEETER: I ain't concerning myself about that. Lov and me think a heap of each other.

DUDE: If he don't give you none, is you going to try and steal some?

JEETER: [*Admonishingly*] Now, Dude! Stealing is about the most sinful thing a man can do. The Lord don't have no truck with stealing. [ELLIE MAY *giggles foolishly.* JEETER *turns to her*] Get away from that fence, Ellie May. Lov ain't likely to come in here at all if he sees that face of yours.

> [ELLIE MAY *giggles foolishly again and moves behind chinaberry tree, from where she peeks.* GRANDMA LESTER *shuffles downstage and flattens herself against the corner of the porch nearest the curtain line.* JEETER *and* DUDE *stretch far over the fence to watch* LOV's *approach*]

ADA: Is he near about here, Jeeter?

JEETER: Near about. He's just about here now.

ADA: Is them turnips?

JEETER: By God, if they ain't, I sure is doing a hell of a lot of stretching for nothing.

> [JEETER *gives his full attention to the approaching man for a second, then turns and motions to the others*]

JEETER: Get away from that fence—all of you. Come on, sit down. Act unconcerned.

> [JEETER *goes to side of house;* ADA *to the well;* DUDE *sits on fence. Enter* LOV BENSEY. LOV *is a man about thirty, dressed in coal-grimed overalls and wearing a dirty, floppy hat. When he removes the hat to wipe the sweat from his face a shock of unruly hair is seen rising above a sunburned face. He is not unattractive in his dull, slow way, and his body shows the result of hard work and a reasonable amount of food. He is not a big man, but he is stronger and better nourished than either* DUDE *or* JEETER. *He carries a partly filled gunny sack over his shoulder. Caution and suspicion mark his every move in dealing with the the Lesters, and this is in evidence now as he comes into the scene*]

JEETER: [*Hiding his eagerness by trying to be casual*] Hi there, Lov.

LOV: Hi. [*He moves on beyond them toward center stage*]

JEETER: Ain't seen you in a long time.

LOV: No. [*He stops near the gate, and shifts bag*]

JEETER: You must be plumb wore out toting that croker sack. Come in off the Tobacco Road and rest yourself.

LOV: I ain't tired.

JEETER: You must of come a far piece off if you come from down Fuller way.

LOV: Umm.

JEETER: Come inside and get yourself a drink.

LOV: I ain't thirsty.

JEETER: [*With calculated amiability*] We was just talking about you, Lov. We ain't seen you since a way long the first of the winter. How is you and Pearl getting on down there at the coal chute?

ADA: [*A trace of anxiety*] Pearl—is she all right?

LOV: Humph! [*He glances suspiciously at all of them*] I want to talk to you, Jeeter.

JEETER: Sure. Come inside the yard and sit down. No use toting that croker sack while you're talking. [LOV *repeats his glance of suspicion, but comes hesitatingly inside and drops the sack against fence near gate. He stands in front of it, guarding it.* JEETER *tries to make his voice casual, but every eye on the stage is on that sack, giving the lie to their pretended indifference*] What you got in that croker sack, Lov? [*Innocently, as* LOV *doesn't answer*] I heard it said that some people has got turnips this year. [LOV's *eyes narrow with suspicion and he backs even more protectively against the sack*]

LOV: [*Shrewdly*] It's Pearl I want to talk to you about.

ADA: She ain't sick, is she?

LOV: [*Suddenly angry*] By God, she's something! [*He lets himself to ground, sitting beside turnips and gripping neck of sack*]

JEETER: [*Archly*] Why don't you go over on the porch? That ain't no place to sit.

LOV: I'll sit right where I is.

JEETER: [*Agreeably*] What you got to say to me, Lov? You must have a heap to say, toting that sack all this way to do it.

LOV: I sure has. You got to go talk to Pearl. That's what I got to say.

JEETER: What's that gal up to? I never could understand her. What's she done now?

LOV: It's just like she done ever since she went down to live with me at the chute, only I'm getting pretty durn tired of it by this time. All the niggers make fun of me because of the way she treats me.

JEETER: Pearl is just like her ma. Her ma used to do the queerest things in her time.

ADA: [*Sharply*] Is you treating her right?

LOV: That ain't got a goddam thing to do with it. She's married to me, ain't she?

JEETER: You got leave of the county. I remember that all right.

LOV: Then why the hell don't she act like she ought to? Every time I want to have her around, she runs off in the broom sedge. She won't talk to me, neither, and she won't cook nothing I want to eat.

JEETER: Great day in the morning, now what do you think makes her do that?

LOV: I don't know and I don't care. But I call it a hell of a business.

JEETER: About the cooking you is just about right. But when it comes to not talking I don't see no harm in that. Ada, there, didn't used to talk neither, but, by God and by Jesus, now you can't make her shut up.

LOV: [*Stubbornly*] I want Pearl to talk to me. I want her to ask me if my back is sore when I come home from the chute, or if it's going to rain, or when I is going to get a hair cut. There's a hell of a lot of things she could ask me about, but she don't talk at all.

JEETER: Maybe you don't try the right way to make her.

LOV: I tried kicking her and I tried pouring water on her and chunking rocks and sticks at her, but it don't do no good. She cries a lot when she's hurt, but, by God, I don't call that talking.

ADA: Don't you dare hurt her, Lov Bensey.

LOV: You keep out of this. I guess I know my rights. [*He pauses, looking belligerently from* ADA *to* JEETER] And they is something else she don't do neither.

JEETER: For one little gal they sure is a heap of things she don't do. What else don't she do, Lov?

LOV: She don't sleep in the bed with me, that's what. [*Viciously to* ADA] And what you got to say about that?

JEETER: [*Much more interested*] Now that's something. By God and by Jesus, that's something.

LOV: [*Turning back to* JEETER] She ain't never slept in the bed. It's a durn pallet on the floor she sleeps on every night. Now what I say is, what the hell is the sense in me marrying a wife if I don't get none of the benefits?

ADA: If you don't like what she's doing, you send her right home and get yourself another girl. Her old ma will look after her.

LOV: No. I ain't going to do that neither. I want Pearl. She's about the prettiest piece in the whole country and I want her.

JEETER: You give her time and she'll get in the bed.

LOV: By God. I already give her enough time. Right now I feel like I got to have me a woman. [*He looks at* ELLIE MAY. ELLIE MAY *catches his glance and giggles. She begins the wriggling movement, which at the right time brings her near* LOV]

JEETER: I know how you feel, Lov. When the time to plow and put seed in the ground comes along a man feels just like that. Even at this day and age I could do with a little of that myself.

LOV: Well, then, you go down and talk to her. You tell her to stop sleeping on that durn pallet and get in the bed—and tell her to talk to me, too, by God.

JEETER: I might do that if I felt you was ready and willing to do something for me in return.

LOV: [*Suspiciously*] What do you mean by that, Jeeter?

JEETER: [*Unable longer to restrain himself*] By God and by Jesus, Lov, what you got in that croker sack? I been looking at it ever since you been here and I sure got to know.

LOV: I don't see what that's got to do with it?

JEETER: What is they, I tell you!

LOV: [*After a short pause for emphasis and a hard, proud glance around*] Turnips, by God.

> [*His announcement causes a noticeable reaction on everyone. Their bodies stiffen and lean forward and a look of greed appears in their faces. But wisely they refrain from taking any actual steps forward. Instinctively they wait for JEETER to see it through. Only ELLIE MAY forgets her hunger in the sharpening force of passion brought on by proximity to LOV, and continues her sex-conscious wriggling*]

JEETER: [*Keyed up, but holding himself in*] Turnips! Where'd you get turnips, Lov?

LOV: Wouldn't you like to know?

JEETER: Turnips is about the thing I want most of all right now. I could just about eat me a whole croker sackful between now and sundown.

LOV: Well, don't look to me to give you none because I ain't.

JEETER: That's a mean thing to say, Lov. It's a whopping mean thing to say to Pearl's old pa.

LOV: To hell with that. I had to pay fifty cents for this many in a sack and I had to walk clear to the other side of Fuller to fetch them.

JEETER: I was thinking maybe you and me could fix up some sort of trade. I could go down to your house and tell Pearl she's got to sleep in the bed, and you could give me some of them—

LOV: No, by God. You're Pearl's daddy, and you ought to make her behave for nothing.

JEETER: By God and by Jesus, Lov, you oughtn't to talk to me like that. I just got to have me some turnips. I ain't had a good turnip since a year ago this spring. All the turnips I raised this year has got them damn-blasted green-gutted worms in them.

LOV: I don't see what that's got to do with Pearl one way or another. I gave you seven dollars when she came to live with me and that's enough.

JEETER: Maybe it was then, but it ain't now. We is about starved around here. What God made turnip-worms for I can't make out. It appears to me like He just naturally has got it in good and heavy for a poor man. I worked all the fall last year digging up a patch of ground to grow turnips in, and when they're getting about big enough to pull up and eat, along come them damn-blasted green-gutted worms and bore clear to the middle of them.

[LOV *is entirely indifferent to* JEETER's *plea. Cruelly he takes a turnip from the sack and takes a big bite. Chewing the bite to the agony of the starving Lesters, he points the stub of the turnip at the wriggling* ELLIE MAY, *sitting on the ground near the bench and looking at him with avid eyes. She giggles*]

LOV: Now if Pearl was anything like Ellie May there, she wouldn't act like she does. You go down and tell her to act like Ellie May.

JEETER: Is you in mind then to make a trade with them turnips?

LOV: [*Eating*] I ain't trading turnips with nobody.

JEETER: That's a hell of a thing to say, Lov. I'm wanting turnips God himself knows how bad.

LOV: Go over to Fuller and buy yourself some, then. I went over there to get mine.

JEETER: Now, Lov, you know I ain't got a penny to my name. You got a good job down there at the chute and it pays you a heap of money.

LOV: I don't make but a dollar a day. House rent takes up near about all that and eating the rest of it.

JEETER: Makes no difference. You don't want to sit there and let me starve, do you?

LOV: I can't help it if you do. The Lord looks at us with equal favor, they say. He gives me mine and if you don't get yours you better go talk to Him about it.

DUDE: You give him hell, Lov. If he wasn't so durn lazy he'd do something instead of cussing about it all the time. He's the laziest son-of-a-bitch I ever seen.

JEETER: My children all blame me because God sees fit to make me poverty-ridden, Lov. They and their ma is all the time cussing me because we ain't got nothing to eat. It ain't my fault that Captain John shut down on giving us rations and snuff, and then went away and died.

LOV: [*Indifferently*] It ain't my fault neither.

JEETER: I worked all my life for Captain John, Lov. I worked harder than any four of his niggers in the field; then the first thing I knowed he came down here one morning and says he can't be letting me get no more rations and snuff at the store. After that he sells all the mules and goes up to Augusta to live. He said there wasn't no use trying to run a farm no more—fifty plows or one plow. He told me I could stay on the land as long as I liked, but that ain't doing me no good. Ain't no work I can find to do for hire and I can't raise a crop of my own because I ain't got no mule and I ain't got no credit. [LOV's *attention turns from* JEETER *to* ELLIE

MAY, *whose wriggling movement is bringing her inch by inch closer to him*] That's what I'm wanting to do powerful strong right now—raise me a crop. When the winter goes and when it gets time to burn off the broom sedge in the fields, I sort of want to cry. I reckon it is the smell of that sedge smoke this time of year near about drives me crazy. Then pretty soon all the other farmers start plowing. That's what's the worst. When the smell of that new earth turning over behind the plows strikes me, I get all weak and shaky. It's in my nature—burning broom sedge and plowing in the ground this time of year. I did it for near about fifty years, and my pa and his pa before him was the same kind of men. Us Lesters sure like to stir up the earth and make plants grow in it. The land has got a powerful hold on me, Lov.

> [LOV *is giving his full attention to* ELLIE MAY *now, a half-eaten turnip arrested on its way to his mouth.* ELLIE MAY *leans back until she rests on the ground and continues her wriggling and squealing.* LOV *begins to edge toward her.* DUDE *watches them closely*]

DUDE: Hey, Pa.

JEETER: Shut up, Dude. It didn't always used to be like it is now, neither, Lov. I can remember a short time back when all the merchants in Fuller was tickled to give me credit. Then all of a sudden Captain John went away and pretty soon the sheriff comes and takes away near about every durn piece of goods I possessed. He took every durn thing I had, excepting that old automobile and the cow. He said the cow wasn't no good because she wouldn't take no freshening, and the automobile wasn't no good neither. I reckon he was right, too, because the automobile won't run no more and the cow died.

DUDE: [*Throwing a broken piece of weather-boarding at* JEETER] Hey, you.

JEETER: [*Angrily*] What you want, Dude? What's the matter with you— chunking weather-boarding at me like that?

DUDE: Ellie May's horsing. That's horsing from way back yonder, hey, Pa?

JEETER: [*Giving the action conscious attention for the first time*] By God and by Jesus, Lov, has you been paying attention to what I was saying? You ain't answered me about them turnips yet.

DUDE: Lov ain't thinking about no turnips. He's wanting to hang up with Ellie May. Look at her straining for him. She's liable to bust a gut if she don't look out.

> [*It's* JEETER's *turn now to be indifferent to conversation. He watches while* LOV *creeps several yards from the turnip sack up to* ELLIE MAY *and awkwardly begins to fondle her. Their backs meet and rub together in a primitive love gesture.*
> *Slowly and silently,* JEETER *puts aside the inner tube which he has been holding and vaguely trying to fix and gets to his feet. Inch by inch he begins edging toward the sack.* LOV *has worked his way around*

in back of ELLIE MAY *and his hands are around her, stroking her arms and legs.*

JEETER *moves closer and closer to the sack, unseen by* LOV. *Only* ADA *and* GRANDMA LESTER *notice him.* DUDE *is too occupied watching* LOV *and* ELLIE MAY.]

By God, Lov ain't never got that close before. He said he wouldn't never get close enough to Ellie May to touch her with a stick. But he ain't paying no mind to that now. I bet he don't even know she's got a slit-lip on her. If he does know it, he don't give a good goddam.

[*And now* JEETER *makes his play. In one swift lunge he crosses the intervening distance and grabs up the sack.* LOV *sees him, turns swiftly, and reaches for him, but misses. He starts to rise as* JEETER *backs a step away, but* ELLIE MAY *grabs his leg, tripping him up. Before he can shake her off,* ADA *hurries from the well, picking up a stick on the way.* GRANDMA LESTER *totters from her place, also brandishing a stick. The two* OLD WOMEN *move down on* LOV *to help* ELLIE MAY]

LOV: Drop them turnips, Jeeter! Drop them turnips. [ELLIE MAY, *quicker than* LOV, *practically leaps on top of him, holding him down. They roll and struggle. To* ELLIE MAY] Get off me, you. Get off me. [LOV *struggles to rise.* ADA *and* GRANDMA *slap and jab at him with their sticks*]

JEETER: [*At the gate*] You tell Pearl I said be good to you, Lov. I'll be down to see about that first thing in the morning. [*He exits, running*]

LOV: Goddam you! [LOV, *by dint of great effort, throws off the women, literally hurling* ELLIE MAY *to the ground and dashes to the gate. He stops there, looking down the road, trying to spy* JEETER]

DUDE: Ain't no use trying to catch pa. He's run off in the brush and there ain't nobody can catch pa when he runs off in the brush.

[LOV *realizes the truth of* DUDE's *statement, and, winded and panting, leans against the fence, making no effort to run.* ELLIE MAY *lies on the ground, also breathing hard, but her eyes still are on* LOV]

ADA: Go on back to Ellie May, Lov. Don't be scared of her. You might even get to like her and let Pearl come back here to me.

[LOV *doesn't answer, pulling a huge colored handkerchief from his pocket and wiping his streaming face.* DUDE *moves to the fence, center*]

DUDE: How many scoops-full does that No. 17 freight engine empty at the chute every morning, Lov? Looks to me like them freight engines takes on twice as much coal as the passenger ones does. [LOV *pays no attention.* ADA *goes back to the porch.* GRANDMA LESTER *picks up her sack of twigs, and, groaning, goes into the house*] Why don't the firemen blow the whistles more than they do, Lov? If I was a fireman I'd pull the whistle cord near about all the time. [DUDE *makes noise like locomotive whistle.* LOV *turns from the fence, goes back into the yard, recovers his hat, glances at* ELLIE MAY, *who lies sprawled on the ground. Then he turns and starts off.* DUDE *follows* LOV *to the gate.* LOV *finishes adjusting his overalls and crosses to the gate,* DUDE *following*] When is you going to buy yourself an automobile, Lov? You make a heap of money at the chute. You ought to get one that has got a great big horn on it. [*Repeats locomotive sound. Ecstatically*] Whistles and horns sure make a pretty sound.

[*Ignoring* DUDE, LOV *exits through the gate and down the road*] I reckon Lov don't feel much like talking today.

ADA: Dude, you run right out in the brush and find your pa before he eats up all them turnips. [DUDE *starts*] See you bring some of them back to your old ma, too. [*Exit* DUDE. ADA *watches him through the gate, then calls*] Ellie May . . . Ellie May!

ELLIE MAY: [*Looking up—blinking*] Yes, Ma.

ADA: You get inside the house and fix up them beds like I told you a long time ago. [ELLIE MAY *stretches and yawns, showing no disposition to move*] I declare to goodness there ain't nobody around here got gumption enough to do anything. Now you get inside the house and do like I tell you. Do you hear me? Come on.

ELLIE MAY: [*Slowly getting to her feet*] All right—I'm a coming.

[*Enter* HENRY PEABODY, *a man who, except for his voice and slight differences in his dress, might well be* JEETER. HENRY *is very excited. He doesn't come into the yard, but hangs over the fence.* ELLIE MAY *promptly sits again*]

PEABODY: Hey you, Ada. Is Jeeter home?

ADA: [*Shaking her head negatively*] He went out into the brush a little while back. I'm expecting him pretty soon, but I ain't certain.

PEABODY: You tell him I was here.

ADA: What's got you so excited, Henry Peabody? I ain't seen you hurry like that since you was a boy.

PEABODY: I ain't got time to tell you about it now, but you tell Jeeter I been here and I'll stop again on my way home.

[*Enter* SISTER BESSIE RICE, *a rather portly woman of about forty. She is dressed in a faded apron and wears a sunbonnet over her large, round face.* BESSIE *is one of the brood of itinerant women preachers peculiar to certain sections of the deep South. She owes allegiance to no church, and her creed and method of divine teaching are entirely her own. She is loud and sure of voice, and is generally accepted at her own value by the God-fearing innocents among whom she moves. She enters by way of the gate, coming inside the yard, and takes off her sunbonnet, fanning herself, as she gives her greeting*]

BESSIE: Good evening, Brother Henry—good evening, Sister Ada. The Lord's blessing be with you.

PEABODY: Good evening, Sister Bessie.... Well, I got to be rushing off. [*Starts off*]

BESSIE: What's hurrying you, Brother Henry? You been sinning against the Lord?

PEABODY: No, praise God, but I got to hurry. [*Exits*]

BESSIE: [*Calling after him*] I'm coming down to your house for preaching and praying one of these days, Brother Henry. [*There is no answer and she turns to* ADA] Now what do you suppose that Henry Peabody's been up to? I bet he's been a powerful wicked man here of late to hurry off like that. Looks like the devil's got into him sure.

ADA: Come inside, Bessie. I reckon Jeeter will be right glad to see you.

BESSIE: I'll be right pleased to, Sister. I reckon I walked near about three miles getting here. [*Walks to the porch, stands for a second*]

ADA: Set down.

BESSIE: Has you got a chair, Sister? My poor back's so weary it feels like it's mighty near breaking in half.

ADA: H'mm. [*She exits into house.* BESSIE, *looking around and fanning herself, sees* ELLIE MAY. ELLIE MAY *giggles*]

BESSIE: How is you, child? God be with you. [*She goes onto the porch singing the hymn "Shall We Gather at the River." Midway in the song* ADA *returns from the house dragging an old rocking chair which she thumps down.* BESSIE *abruptly stops singing. To* ADA] Bless you, Sister. [*She sits, rocking back and forth, fanning herself.* ADA *stands on the ground, leaning against the porch upright, chewing on her snuff stick*] Where is Jeeter at this time of day, Sister Ada? Has that man been up to something sinful again?

ADA: He's out in the broom sedge, eating up turnips he stole from Lov a while back.

BESSIE: Lord, O Lord, he's been stealing again. Jeeter's a powerful sinful man. Ain't no sin like stealing.... Was they good eating winter turnips, Sister?

ADA: I reckon.

BESSIE: Lord forgive us our sins, and particularly forgive Jeeter.... Is he coming back with any of them turnips, Ada?

ADA: I told Dude to fetch him before he eats them all up. Maybe he will and maybe he won't.

BESSIE: Dude will do right by the Lord. Dude's a mighty fine boy, Sister.

ADA: Humph.

BESSIE: We got to be careful against delivering him to the Hardshell Baptists, though. They're sinful people. They don't know the working of the Lord like I does.

ADA: What do you call your religion, Sister Bessie? You ain't never said what name you called it.

BESSIE: It ain't got no name. I generally just call it "Holy." It's just me and God. God talks to me in prayer and I answer him back. I get most things done that way.

ADA: I want you to say a prayer for Pearl before you go away, Bessie. I reckon Lov's mad about Jeeter stealing his turnips and he might beat Pearl more than he ought to.

BESSIE: I'll be right happy to say a prayer for Pearl. But she ought to pray for herself, too. That sometimes helps a lot with the Lord.

ADA: Pearl don't talk to nobody except me—not even the Lord. I reckon what praying's done for her has got to be done by somebody else.

BESSIE: I'll mention that to the Lord and see if he'll let loose her tongue. There's sin someplace in her or she'd talk like everybody else. The Lord didn't intend for a woman not to talk.

ADA: Ellie May don't talk much, either. But that's because of her lip. It sounds funny when she talks.

BESSIE: There's been a powerful lot of sinning among you Lesters, or Ellie May wouldn't have that lip. One way or another I reckon you Lesters is about the most sinful people in the country. [*They are interrupted by the offstage sound of* JEETER *and* DUDE *quarreling*]

DUDE: [*Offstage*] You ain't the only one that likes turnips. I ain't had no more to eat this week than you has.

JEETER: [*Offstage*] You had five already.

DUDE: Give me some more. Do you hear me?

JEETER: You don't need no more.

DUDE: I'll wham you!

> [*At this point* JEETER *comes running to the gate. He has his pockets filled with turnips.* DUDE *is right on his heels and catches him in the gate, throws one arm around him from behind and holds him as he extracts turnips from his pockets with his right hand*]

JEETER: [*Trying to free himself*] Stop that, Dude, you stop that!

DUDE: [*Laughing at him*] Ho! Ho! You can't hurt nobody. You're as weak as an old cat. [*Pushes* JEETER *who falls on the ground near the corner of the house.* DUDE *crosses to right of gate eating a turnip*]

JEETER: [*Lying on ground*] Now that's all you're going to git. [*Picks himself up*]

BESSIE: [*Oracularly*] You been sinning again, Jeeter Lester.

JEETER: [*Seeing* BESSIE *for the first time*] Sister Bessie! The good Lord be praised. [*He rushes to the porch*] I knowed God would send His angel to take away my sins. You come just at the right time.

BESSIE: The Lord always knows the right time. I was at home sweeping out the kitchen when He come to me and said, "Sister Bessie, Jeeter Lester is doing something evil. You go to his house and pray for him right now before it's too late." I looked right back at the Lord and said, "Lord, Jeeter Lester is a powerful sinful man, but I'll pray for him until the devil goes clear back to hell." That's what I told Him and here I is.

JEETER: [*Dancing ecstatically in front of* BESSIE's *chair on the porch*] I knowed the good Lord wouldn't let me slip and fall in the devil's hands. I knowed it! I knowed it!

BESSIE: Ain't you going to give me a turnip, Jeeter? I ain't had so much to eat lately. Times is hard for the good and bad alike.

JEETER: Sure, Bessie. [JEETER *selects several of the largest, gives them to* BESSIE. *Turns to* ADA] Here you is, Ada. [*Gives her some. As others get theirs,* GRANDMA *enters, comes to* JEETER, *and starts pulling at his coat. To* BESSIE] I wish I had something to give you to take home, Sister. When I had plenty, I used to give Brother Rice a whole armful of chickens and potatoes at a time. Now I ain't got nothing but a handful of turnips, but I ain't ashamed of them. The Lord growed them and His doings is good enough for me.

BESSIE: [*With full mouth*] Praise be the Lord.

JEETER *and* ADA: Amen, Sister! Amen.

BESSIE: [*Finishing her turnip with a sigh*] I feel the call of the Lord. Let's have a little prayer. [BESSIE *gets up and crosses to the center of the yard,* JEETER *following, as does* ADA *and* GRANDMA LESTER, *who groans as she moves.* ELLIE MAY *and* DUDE *sit on the porch, eating the turnips and watching*] Some people make an objection to kneeling down and having prayer out of doors. They say, "Sister Bessie, can't we go in the house and pray just as good?" And do you know what I do? I say, "Brothers and Sisters, I ain't ashamed to pray out here in the open. I want folks passing along the road to know that I'm on God's side. It's the old devil that's always whispering about going in the house out of sight." That's what I tell them. That's the way I stick up for the Lord.

JEETER: Praise the Lord.

BESSIE: Let's get ready to pray. [*They all kneel*] Sister Ada, is you still suffering from pleurisy?

ADA: All the time.

[JEETER *and* ADA *bow their heads and close their eyes, but* GRANDMA LESTER *stares straight ahead, her eyes open, her head raised a bit.* BESSIE *nods to* ADA, *then prays*]

BESSIE: Dear God, here I is again to offer a little prayer for sinful people. Jeeter Lester and his family want me to pray for them again. The last time helped a whole lot, but Jeeter let the devil get hold of him today and he went and done a powerful sinful thing. He stole all of Lov's turnips. They're just about all et up now, so it's too late to take them back. That's why we want to pray for Jeeter. You ought to make him stop stealing like he does. I never seen a more stealing man in all my days. Jeeter wants to quit, but it seems like the devil gets hold of him almost as soon as we get through praying for him. You ain't going to let the old devil tell You what to do, is You? The Lord ought to tell the devil what he should do. . . . And Sister Ada has got the pleurisy again. You ought to do something for her this time sure enough. The last time didn't help none too much. If You'll make her well of it she'll quit the devil for all time. Won't you, Sister Ada?

ADA: Yes, Lord.

BESSIE: And old Mother Lester has got a misery in her sides. She's in pain all the time with it. She's kneeling down right now, but she can't do it many more times. . . . You ought to bless Ellie May, too. Ellie May has got that slit in her lip that makes her an awful sight to look at. [ELLIE MAY *buries her face in her hands.* DUDE *looks at her and grins*]

JEETER: Don't forget to pray for Pearl, Sister Bessie. Pearl needs praying for something awful.

BESSIE: I was just going to do that. Sister Ada told me to pray Lov wouldn't beat her too hard because of them turnips you stole.

JEETER: It ain't that. It's what Pearl's done herself.

BESSIE: What has Pearl done sinful, Brother Jeeter?

JEETER: That was what Lov spoke to me about today. He says Pearl won't talk to him and she won't let him touch her. When night comes she gets down and sleeps on a durn pallet on the floor, and Lov has got to sleep in the bed by himself. That's a pretty bad thing for a wife to do, and God ought to make her quit it.

BESSIE: Brother Jeeter, little girls like Pearl don't know how to live married lives like we grown-up women do. So maybe if I was to talk to her myself instead of getting God to do it, she would change her ways. I expect I know more about what to tell her than He does, because I been a married woman up to the past summer when my former husband died. I expect I know all about it. God wouldn't know what to tell her.

JEETER: Well, you can talk to her, but maybe if you asked God about it He might help some, too. Maybe He's run across gals like that before, though I don't believe there's another durn gal in the whole country who's as contrary-minded about sleeping in the bed as Pearl is.

[DUDE *stands up and takes his ball from his pocket*]

BESSIE: Maybe it wouldn't hurt none if I was to mention it.

JEETER: That's right. You speak to the Lord about it, too. Both of you together ought to get something done. [DUDE *hurls the ball against the house and catches it.* JEETER *speaks angrily*] Quit chunking that there ball against that old house, Dude. Don't you see Sister Bessie's praying. I declare I wish you had more sense.

DUDE: Aw, go to hell.

BESSIE: Now, Dude . . . [*Waits until he stops*] Now, Lord, I've got something special to pray about. I don't ask favors unless they is things I want pretty bad, so this time I'm asking for a favor for Pearl. I want You to make her stop sleeping on a pallet on the floor while Brother Lov has to sleep by himself in the bed. I was a good wife to my former husband. I never slept on no pallet on the floor. Sister Ada here don't do nothing like that. And when I marry another man, I ain't going to do that neither. I'm going to get in bed just as big as my new husband does. So You tell Pearl to quit doing that.

JEETER: What was that you was saying, Sister Bessie? Didn't I hear you say you was going to marry yourself a new husband?

BESSIE: Well, I ain't made up my mind yet. I been looking around some, though.

JEETER: Now if it wasn't for Ada there. . . .

BESSIE: [*Giggling*] You hush up, Brother Jeeter. How'd you know I'd take you anyway? You're pretty old, ain't you?

JEETER: Maybe I is and maybe I ain't, but if I is I ain't too old for that.

ADA: [*Stiffly*] I reckon you'd better finish up the prayer. You ain't done like I asked you about Pearl yet.

BESSIE: So I ain't. . . . Please, Lord, Sister Ada wants me to ask You not to let Lov beat up Pearl too much. And I guess that's about all . . . Save us from the devil and——

JEETER: Hey, wait a minute. You clear forgot to say a little prayer for Dude. You left Dude out all around.

DUDE: No, sir, not me, you don't. I don't want no praying.

[BESSIE *jumps up and runs to* DUDE. *Clutching him by the arm she starts dragging him back to the praying circle*]

BESSIE: Come on, Dude. Come and kneel with me.

DUDE: [*Angrily*] I don't want to do that. I don't want no praying for me.

[BESSIE *puts one arm around his waist, holding him very close, and with her free hand strokes his shoulder*]

BESSIE: [*Tenderly*] I got to pray for you, Dude. The Lord didn't leave you out no more than He did Ellie May. [*She kneels, but keeps his legs encircled in her arms*] Come on now. All of us has got to have prayer some time or another. [DUDE *finds the pressure of her arms on his legs quite stimulating and exciting, and he begins giggling and squirming*]

JEETER: Quit that jumping up and down, Dude. What ails you?

[DUDE *puts his arms around her neck and begins rubbing her as she is rubbing him*]

BESSIE: You kneel down beside me and let me pray for you. You'll do that, won't you, Dude?

DUDE: [*Snickering*] Hell, I don't give a damn if I do. [*He kneels, continuing to keep his arms about her, and she keeps her arms around him*]

BESSIE: I knowed you would want me to pray for you, Dude. It will help you get shed of your sins like Jeeter did. [*Closes her eyes, lifts her head*] Dear God, I'm asking You to save Brother Dude from the devil and make a place for him in heaven. That's all. Amen.

JEETER: Praise the Lord, but that was a durn short prayer for a sinner like Dude. [*He gets to his feet.* BESSIE *and* DUDE *continue to hold each other*]

BESSIE: [*Smiling fondly at* DUDE] Dude don't need no more praying for. He's just a boy, and he's not sinful like us grown-ups is.

JEETER: Well, maybe you're right. But I sort of recollect the Bible says a son shouldn't cuss his ma and pa like he does other people.

BESSIE: [*Stroking* DUDE's *hair*] Dude won't do that again. He's a fine boy, Dude is. He would make a handsome preacher, too. He's mighty like my former husband in his younger days. [*She and* DUDE *stop kneeling, but sit on the ground and continue to hold each other*]

JEETER: Dude's about sixteen years old now. That makes him two years younger than Ellie May. He'll be getting a wife pretty soon, I reckon. All my other male children married early in life, just like the gals done. If it wasn't for Ellie May's lip she'd been married as quick as any. Men here around Fuller all want to marry gals about eleven or twelve years old, like Pearl was. Ada, there, was just turning twelve when I married her.

BESSIE: The Lord intended all of us should be mated. He made us that way. My former husband was just like the Lord in that respect. They both believed in the same thing when it came to mating.

JEETER: I reckon the Lord did intend for us all to get mated, but He didn't take into account a woman with a slit in her mouth like Ellie May's got.

BESSIE: The Lord's ways is wise, Jeeter.

JEETER: Well, maybe, but I don't believe He done the right thing by her when He opened up her lip. That's the only contrary thing I ever said about the Lord, but it's the truth. What use is a slit like that for? You can't spit through it, and you can't whistle through it, now can you? It was just meanness on His part when He done that—just durn meanness.

BESSIE: You shouldn't talk about the Lord like that. He knows what He done it for. He had the best reason in the world for doing it.

JEETER: What reason?

BESSIE: Maybe I ought not to say it, Jeeter.

JEETER: You sure ought to tell me if you tell anybody. I'm her pa.

BESSIE: He done that to save her pure body from you, Brother Jeeter.

JEETER: From me?

BESSIE: [*Nodding*] He knowed she would be safe in this house when He made her like that. He knowed that you was once a powerful sinner, and that you might be again.

JEETER: That's the truth. I used to be a powerful sinful man in my time. I reckon at one time I was the most powerful sinful man in the whole country. Now you take them Peabody children over across the field. I reckon near about all of them is half mine, one way or another.

BESSIE: You wait till I finish accusing you, Jeeter, before you start lying out of it.

JEETER: Praise God, I ain't lying out of it. I just now told you how powerful sinful I once was.

BESSIE: Don't think the Lord didn't know about it.

JEETER: [*Chuckles; crossing to well*] Henry Peabody didn't know nothing about it, though.

ADA: Humph.

JEETER: [*Turns left; really noticing* BESSIE's *and* DUDE's *goings on*] Say, Sister Bessie, what in hell is you and Dude doing? You and him has been squatting there, hugging and rubbing of the other, for near about half an hour. [BESSIE *manages as much of a blush as she is capable of*]

BESSIE: [*Removing* DUDE's *arm from around her waist, trying to rise*] The Lord was speaking to me. [DUDE *replaces his arm about her waist*] He was telling me I ought to marry a new husband.

JEETER: He didn't tell you to marry Dude, did he?

BESSIE: Dude would make a fine preacher. He would be just about as good as my former husband was, maybe better. He is just suitable for preaching and living with me. Ain't you, Dude?

DUDE: [*Quickly*] You want me to go home with you now? [*Takes a step toward her*]

BESSIE: Not now, Dude. I'll have to ask the Lord if you'll do. [*Crosses left of* DUDE] He's sometimes particular about his male preachers, especially if they is going to marry women preachers. I got to pray over it first—[*With a knowing glance at* DUDE]—and Dude, you pray over it, too.

DUDE: [*Giggles in embarrassment*] Aw, like hell I will. [*Crosses to left of gate*]

JEETER: [*Crossing to* DUDE] What's the matter with you, Dude? Didn't you hear Sister Bessie tell you to pray over that? You is the luckiest man alive. What's the matter with you, anyway? Great day in the morning, if you ain't the goddamdest boy I ever heard tell of!

[*Enter* HENRY PEABODY. *He comes running to the gate*]

PEABODY: Hey, you, Jeeter—Jeeter.

JEETER: [*Crosses to* PEABODY] What's the matter, Henry?

PEABODY: Didn't Ada tell you nothing?

JEETER: She didn't tell me nothing.

PEABODY: Didn't she tell you I was here before?

JEETER: [*Impatiently*] No. What is it you've got to say?

PEABODY: It's big news, Jeeter.

JEETER: Well, start telling it. It ain't going to do me no good keeping it to yourself.

PEABODY: [*Impressively*] Captain John's coming back.

JEETER: [*Shocked*] Captain John! Captain John's dead.

PEABODY: Well, not Captain John, but his boy is.

JEETER: He is! [*Turning on* ADA] Do you hear that, Ada? Captain John's coming back!

ADA: He didn't say Captain John. He said Captain John's boy.

JEETER: That don't make no difference. Captain Tim is Captain John's boy, ain't he? [*To* PEABODY] He figures on giving credit to the farmers again, don't he?

PEABODY: I reckon so. That's what everybody thinks. He's down in Fuller now, but he'll be around about here tomorrow.

JEETER: God be praised. I knowed the Lord was aiming to provide. [*To* ADA] Well, what has you got to say now, woman? Didn't I tell you I was going to plant me a crop this year? [*To* DUDE, *as* ADA *shrugs and doesn't answer*] Hey, you, Dude. Get out in the fields and start burning off that broom sedge. You go to the far side and I'll go to the near. We're going to burn off all the fields this year. We're going to grow us the biggest crop you ever seen.

PEABODY: Well, I got to be going, Jeeter. I reckon I'll burn off my own fields now myself.

[JEETER *nods and he exits*]

JEETER: Good-by, Henry . . . Now you go in that house, Ada, and fix us something to eat. We're going to be hungry when we come back.

ADA: There ain't nothing to fix.

JEETER: You're the contrariest woman I ever seen. By God and by Jesus, if you ain't. You do like I tell you and quit saying all them damn fool things. . . . Come on, Dude, Captain John's boy has got to see we is all ready when he comes around tomorrow. Hurry up now . . . come on.

[JEETER *climbs over fence, left, in his hurry, exiting down the Tobacco Road.* DUDE *gives a hungry glance at* BESSIE, *then hurries to the gate and exits.* BESSIE *runs to fence and calls after* DUDE]

BESSIE: Hey, you, Dude. Don't you forget. You pray like I told you and I'll be back here in the morning and let you know. [*Turns to* ADA *with a benevolent smile*] Something tells me the Lord is going to like Dude a whole lot.

CURTAIN

ACT TWO

SCENE: *Same as Act One.*
   TIME: *The following day.*
   AT RISE: *It is still early morning and the amber glow of dawning day haunts the scene. Slowly, as time passes, the light comes on fuller and brighter until full day has arrived. As the curtain rises, no one is seen, the rotting house enjoying the dawn in solitude. In a moment, however,* BESSIE *enters swiftly through the gate, crosses to the porch, and hammers loudly on the door with her fists.*

BESSIE: Dude.... Hey, you, Dude.... Dude! [*She waits impatiently a few seconds, glancing first to the upstage corner of the house, then to the window downstage of the porch. Then she flings open the door and yells inside*] Where is you, Dude?

   [JEETER, *yawning and scratching, sticks his head out of the window and rubs his mouth with the back of his hand before speaking. He is still sleepy but is wearing, already, his tattered hat, although the rest of his body is, apparently, as naked as a blue jay*]

JEETER: What you want with Dude this time of day, Bessie?

BESSIE: Never you mind. I want Dude.... Hey, you, Dude. [*She exits through the door, calling*] Dude.... You, Dude. [JEETER *draws back from the window, looking inside, as* BESSIE'S *voice continues, off*] Where is you, Dude? ...

   [*For an instant the stage is empty. Then* DUDE *enters left down Tobacco Road and crosses yard to the well, where he draws up water and drinks. He pays no attention to* BESSIE'S *occasionally repeated cry for him. Enter* JEETER *through the house door. He is getting into his overalls, and is carrying his shirt, also socks and shoes in his hands. He sees* DUDE]

JEETER: Hey, you, Dude, where you been? Bessie's been looking all over for you. [DUDE *doesn't answer, continuing to drink water.* JEETER *drops shoes and socks and slips into overalls*] She just about tore up every bed in the house. Why don't you tell her where you is?

DUDE: Aw, to hell with her. [*Drinks*]

JEETER: [*Dressing*] By God and by Jesus, I never seen a woman so anxious to see anybody. I reckon she wants to get married to you after all. [*Glances up as* DUDE *doesn't answer*] Is you thinking about getting yourself married to her if that's what she wants?

DUDE: Aw, what do I want to do that for?

JEETER: You sure looked like you was set on doing that yesterday—all that hugging and rubbing of the other. What do you think about that now, Dude?

DUDE: Aw, hell, it don't always look the same to a man in the morning.

BESSIE: [*Off*] Dude! . . . Hey, you, Dude.

JEETER: Listen to her yelling. She must of gone clear through to the backyard by this time. Why don't you answer her, Dude? Where was you when she went looking in the bed for you? Where was you anyway?

DUDE: Out in the fields.

JEETER: [*Excitedly*] What about them fields? Is they finished burning?

DUDE: [*Nodding*] Most. Them to the north is still burning some.

JEETER: I is sure glad to hear that. We want to be ready to start the plowing and planting when Captain John's boy comes around today.

BESSIE: [*Off*] Dude . . . Where is you, Dude? [BESSIE *enters around upstage corner of house, sees* DUDE] There you is! [*Crosses swiftly to him. He glances at her, but keeps his back to her as she comes up*] Didn't you hear me call you? [*Affectionately—putting her arms around his waist from the rear*] Don't you know I been looking for you, Dude boy? [*Her arms tighten in a sudden and sharp squeeze that causes the water to slosh from the bucket he is holding*]

DUDE: Hey, now look what you made me go and do.

BESSIE: Now that ain't nothing, Dude. Ain't you glad to see me? [*She presses him closer*] Don't that make you feel good?

DUDE: [*Grinning*] H'mm. [*He puts down the bucket, turns and embraces her. Their posture is awkward and amusing. On the steps,* JEETER *continues to pick his feet and slowly put on shoes and socks, the while he watches the amorous couple*]

JEETER: You must be figuring on getting married after all, Bessie.

[BESSIE *starts to smooth down* DUDE'S *wet hair.* ADA *appears in doorway,* ELLIE MAY *at window*]

BESSIE: [*Confidentially—nodding affirmatively*] The Lord told me to do it. I asked Him about it last night and He said, "Sister Bessie, Dude Lester is the man I want you to wed. Get up early in the morning and go to the Lester place and marry Dude the first thing." That's what He said, so I got out of bed and ran up here as fast as I could, because the Lord don't like to be kept waiting. [BESSIE *affectionately regards* DUDE, *who grins self-consciously*]

JEETER: You hear what the Lord told Sister Bessie. What do you think of doing that now, Dude?

DUDE: Shucks! I don't know.

JEETER: What's ailing you? Ain't you man enough?

DUDE: Maybe I is, and maybe I ain't.

BESSIE: There ain't nothing to be scared of, Dude. You'll like being married to me because I know how to treat men fine.

> [DUDE *hesitates*. ADA *moves forward from doorway and rests against the porch upright*. GRANDMA LESTER *appears around the upstage corner of the house but keeps crouched and hidden so as not to attract attention*]

JEETER: Well, is you going to do it, Dude?

DUDE: [*Self-consciously*] Aw, hell, what do I want to go marry her for? [DUDE *pulls ball out of his pocket and throws it against house.* BESSIE *glances swiftly at* DUDE'S *averted face, then plays her trump card. She turns to* JEETER]

BESSIE: [*Wisely to* JEETER] Do you know what I is going to do, Jeeter?

JEETER: What?

BESSIE: I is going to buy me a new automobile. [*The effect of this on all of them is electric.* JEETER *comes quickly to his feet, and* DUDE *stops throwing ball with sudden awed interest*]

JEETER: A new automobile? A sure enough brand-new automobile?

BESSIE: [*Nodding*] A brand-new one. [BESSIE *shakes her head emphatically.* DUDE *looks at her wide-eyed and unbelieving*]

JEETER: Is you got money?

BESSIE: [*Proudly*] Eight hundred dollars.

JEETER: Eight hundred dollars! Where did you get all that money, Bessie?

BESSIE: [*Nodding*] My former husband had that in insurance and when he died I got it and put it in the bank.

JEETER: That sure is a heap of money. I didn't think there was that much real money in the whole country.

ADA: You ain't going to spend all that on a new automobile, is you?

BESSIE: [*Nodding*] Dude and me wants the best there is. Don't we, Dude? [DUDE *can only look at her wide-eyed*]

ADA: It don't seem right to me. It seems to me like if you wanted to do right you'd give some of that money to Dude's old ma and pa. We could sure use it for snuff and food.

BESSIE: No, Sister Ada, the Lord didn't intend for it to be used like that. He intended I should use it to carry on the preaching and the praying. That's what I'm buying the new automobile for, so Dude and me can drive around when we take a notion to go somewheres in the Lord's work.

JEETER: Sister Bessie's right, Ada. There ain't nothing like working for the Lord. It don't make no difference to us about that money noway. Captain John's boy, Captain Tim, is back now and I'll get all the credit I need.

ADA: Humph. You is sure mighty highhanded with something you ain't got yet.

JEETER: Never you mind about her, Bessie. When you going to buy that new automobile?

BESSIE: I'm going over to Fuller and get it right now. [*Glances at* DUDE *eagerly*] That is, if Dude and me gets married.

JEETER: What do you say to that now, Dude? Will you be wanting to marry Sister Bessie and ride around the country preaching and praying in a new automobile?

DUDE: Will it have a horn on it?

BESSIE: I reckon it will. Don't all new automobiles have horns?

DUDE: Can I drive it?

BESSIE: That's what I'm buying it for.

DUDE: Can I drive it all the time?

BESSIE: Sure, Dude. I don't know how to drive an automobile.

DUDE: Then why the hell not?

BESSIE: [*Joyfully hugging him and trying to kiss him*] Oh, Dude! [DUDE *escapes from her embrace and begins to put on his shoes*]

ADA: When is you and Dude going to do all this riding around and preaching and praying? Is you going to get married before or after?

BESSIE: Before. We'll walk over to Fuller right now and buy the new automobile and then get married.

JEETER: Is you going to get leave of the county, or is you just going to live along without it?

BESSIE: I'm going to get the license for marrying.

JEETER: That costs about two dollars. Is you got two dollars? Dude ain't— Dude ain't got nothing.

BESSIE: I ain't asking Dude for one penny of money. I'll attend to that part myself. I've got eight hundred dollars in the bank and a few more besides. Dude and me won't have nothing to worry about. Will we, Dude?

DUDE: [*Impatiently*] Naw. Come on. We ain't got no time to lose. [DUDE *starts to walk away, while* BESSIE *is delayed arranging her hair, walking more slowly to the gate*]

ADA: You'll have to make Dude wash his feet every once in a while, Bessie, because if you don't he'll dirty up the quilts. Sometimes he don't wash himself all winter long, and the quilts get that dirty you don't know how to go about the cleaning of them.

BESSIE: [*Pleasantly to* DUDE, *who is waiting at gate*] Is you like that, Dude?

DUDE: [*Impatiently*] If we is going to buy that new automobile, let's buy it.

ADA: Dude is just careless like his pa. I had the hardest time learning him to wear his socks in the bed, because it was the only way I could keep the quilts clean. Dude is just going on the way his pa done, so maybe you'd better make him wear his socks, too.

BESSIE: That's all right. Me and Dude'll know how to get along fine. [*Exit* DUDE. *Exit* BESSIE]

ADA: [*Calling after* BESSIE *and* DUDE] If you get down around where Pearl lives, I wish you'd tell her that her ma sure would like to see her again.

> [JEETER, ADA, *and* ELLIE MAY *move to fence to look after* DUDE *and* BESSIE. *Even* GRANDMA LESTER *looks from behind the trunk of the chinaberry tree*]

JEETER: [*Shakes his head emphatically*] That Dude is the luckiest man alive. [*Directly to others*] Now, ain't he? . . . He's going to get a brand-new car to ride around in and he's going to get married all at the same time. There's not many men get all that in the same day, I tell you. There ain't nobody else that I know of between here and the river who has got a brand-new automobile. And there ain't many men who has a wife as fine-looking as Sister Bessie is, neither. Bessie makes a fine woman for a man— any man, I don't care where you find him. She might be just a little bit more than Dude can take care of, though. Now if it was me, there wouldn't be no question of it. I'd please Sister Bessie coming and going right from the start, and keep it up clear to the end.

ADA: [*In disgust*] Huh!

JEETER: [*Speaks now to* ELLIE MAY] Now you, Ellie May, it's time you was finding yourself a man. All my other children has got married. It's your time next. It was your time a long while ago, but I make allowances for you on account of your face. I know it's harder for you to mate up than it is for anybody else, but you ought to get out and find yourself a man to marry right away. It ain't going to get you nowhere fooling around with Lov like you was doing, because he's married already. He might have married you if it wasn't for the way you looked, but don't show your face too much and it won't stop the boys from getting after you. [*He pauses, and to his amazement* ELLIE MAY *bursts into heartbroken sobs, hiding her face in her hands*] What's the matter? What's the matter with you, Ellie May? [*Still sobbing,* ELLIE MAY *runs to the gate and exits down the road.* JEETER *turns helplessly to* ADA] Now I never seen the likes of that before. I wonder what I said to make her carry on like that? [JEETER *sits on porch*] I declare to goodness I don't know what gets into women folks sometimes. There ain't never no way to figure them out. [*Starts to lie down, but* ADA *is in the way*] By God and by Jesus, woman, can't you move over when a man wants to lay down?

ADA: Ain't you going to take no wood to Augusta today?

JEETER: Are you going to start that talk again? Ain't I told you Captain Tim is coming and I'm going to plant me a crop. I've got to save my strength for that.

ADA: Humph! There ain't a bite in the house, and nobody never saved their strength by not eating.

JEETER: Never mind that now. Captain Tim will fix that. Anyhow, I couldn't make that old automobile go even if I wanted to.

ADA: Do you reckon Dude and Bessie will let you take a load in their new car?

JEETER: I ain't aiming to carry no more wood to Augusta. But I sure is going to take a ride in that new car. I reckon I'll be riding clear over into Burke County one of these days to see Tom.

ADA: If you see him you might mention that his old ma sure would like a stylish dress to die in. I know he won't stand back with his money for a little thing like that.

JEETER: I'll mention it, but I don't know how he'll take it. I expect he's got a raft of children to provide for.

ADA: Reckon he has got some children?

JEETER: Maybe some.

ADA: I sure would like to see them. I know I must have a whole heap of grandchildren somewhere. I'm bound to have, with all them boys and girls off from home.

JEETER: Clara has got a raft of children, I bet. She was always talking about having them. And they say over in Fuller that Lizzie Belle has got a lot of them, too. I don't know how other folks know more about such things than I do. Looks like I ought to be the one who knows most about my own children. [*Enter* LOV, *who stands just inside gate, panting heavily and looking at* ADA *and* JEETER. JEETER *glances up and sees* LOV, *whose heaving chest and haunted eyes make him believe* LOV *has come for revenge for stealing the turnips*] Lov, by God! [*He springs to his feet and darts for the downstage corner of the well*]

LOV: [*Through quick breathing*] Never mind running, Jeeter, I ain't going to hurt you.

JEETER: [*At corner of house, still ready to run*] Ain't you peeved about me stealing them turnips yesterday?

LOV: [*Wearily*] I don't care about that no more.

JEETER: What's the matter with you, Lov? You look like you run all the way here. What's wrong with you, anyway? [LOV *doesn't answer and sits*] Is you sick? [LOV *nods negatively*]

ADA: [*Higher note—stepping forward*] It's Pearl! That's what it is—it's Pearl! [LOV *looks at her and nods. She comes forward hysterically*]

JEETER: What's the matter with her, Lov?

LOV: She run off.

ADA: No! She didn't! She wouldn't have done that without seeing her ma first.

LOV: [*Coming forward—shaking head*] She just run off.

JEETER: How do you know, Lov? Maybe she's just hiding in the woods someplace.

LOV: [*Shakes his head*] Jones Peabody saw her walking along the road to Augusta this morning.

ADA: Augusta!

LOV: He said he stopped and asked her where she was going, but she wouldn't talk to him. She just kept on going.

ADA: [*Fiercely to* LOV] You done something to her. Don't tell me you didn't!

LOV: No, I didn't, Ada. I woke up early this morning and looked at her down on that pallet on the floor and I just couldn't stand it no longer. I got down and hugged her in my arms. I wasn't going to hurt her. I just wanted to hold her for a minute. But she got loose from me and I ain't seen her since.

  [ADA *rocks, heartbroken, on the porch*]

JEETER: Well, I figured that she was going to run off to Augusta one of these days, only she was always afraid before.

LOV: Jones Peabody said she acted like she was about scared to death this morning. [*Desperately*] I got to get her back, Jeeter. I just got to get her back.

JEETER: Ain't much use you figuring on that. All them girls went off all of a sudden. Lizzie Belle up and went to Augusta just like that. [*He snaps his fingers*]

LOV: Ain't there something I can do, Jeeter?

JEETER: About the best thing you can do, Lov, is let her be.

LOV: If I was to go up to Augusta and find her, do you reckon she'd let me bring her back home to stay? . . . Reckon she would, Jeeter?

JEETER: I wouldn't recommend that. You'll lose your time down there at the chute while you was looking for her, and if you was to bring her back she'd run off again twice as quick.

LOV: She might get hurt up there.

JEETER: Lizzie Belle and Clara took care of themselves all right, didn't they?

LOV: Pearl ain't like them.

JEETER: In many ways she ain't, but in many she is, too. She wasn't never satisfied living down here on the Tobacco Road. She's just like Lizzie Belle and Clara and the other gals in that respect. I can't call all their names right now, but it was every durn one of them, anyhow. They all wanted stylish clothes.

LOV: Pearl never said nothing to me about wanting stylish clothes. She never said anything to me at all.

JEETER: It's just like I said. They're like their ma. Ada there ain't satisfied neither, but she can't do nothing about it. I broke her of wanting to run off, but them gals was more than I could take care of. There was too durn many of them for one man to break. They just up and went.

LOV: [*Thinking aloud*] I sort of hate to lose her, for some reason or another. All them long yellow curls hanging down her back always made me hate the time when she would grow up and be old.

JEETER: That sure ain't no lie. Pearl had the prettiest yellow hair of any gal I ever saw. I wish Ada had been that pretty. Even when Ada was a young gal she was that durn ugly it was a sin. I reckon I ain't never seen an uglier woman in the whole country.

LOV: I been the lonesomest man in the whole country for the longest time, Jeeter. Ain't there something you can do to get her back again?

JEETER: I might try something, but it wouldn't do no good. One way or another I've said about everything I can to that girl, but she won't even answer me. She won't talk to nobody but her ma. It wouldn't do no good for me to do anything, even if you could find her.

LOV: Ada, will you? . . . [*Sees hopelessness of help from* ADA. *Abjectly*] Well, I've got to get back to the chute. That morning freight will be coming along pretty soon now and it always empties all the scoops. They raise hell if they ain't filled up again. [*Turns; crosses to gate; leans against post*]

JEETER: I sure am glad you wasn't riled about the turnips, Lov. I meant to go down first thing this morning and talk to you about that, but Dude and Bessie went off to get married and I forgot all about it. Did you hear about that, Lov? Dude and Bessie went off to Fuller to get married and buy them a new automobile all at the same time. Now ain't that something! [LOV *nods*]

LOV: If you happen to see or hear anything about Pearl, you let me know. [LOV *exits down road left*]

JEETER: [*Turning back to* ADA, *who still sits on the porch, staring blankly into space*] Lov sure is a funny one. He just can't think about anything but Pearl. It looks to me like he wouldn't want a gal that won't stay in the bed with him. I don't understand him at all. I don't understand Pearl, for that matter, neither. I'd of bet almost anything she would have come up here and told us good-by before running off. But it's like I always said. Coming or going, you can't never tell about women. [*Looks at* ADA, *hoping she'll talk to him. Crosses closer to her, but her eyes stare straight ahead. Finally he hits her gently with the back of his hand*] That's all right, Ada. [*He crosses to fence, left, climbs it, glances back at her*] If Captain John's boy comes along, you tell him I'll be back soon. I'm going out to look at them fields.

> [JEETER *exits,* ADA *sits staring ahead, her eyes holding a depth of suffering. Suddenly there is an offstage cry from* JEETER *and she turns to look toward the gate*]

JEETER: [*Off—calling*] Ada—Ada! [*Lower, but still off*] Come on, child—come on. [*He appears at the edge of the gate, pulling someone after him.* ADA, *eyes wide with wonder, stands up*] Come on—there ain't nothing to be afraid of. Your old pa ain't going to hurt you. [*He pulls* PEARL *through the gate*] Look, Ada—look what I found hiding in the broom sedge.

ADA: [*Lifts her hands, palms turned up, toward her daughter*] Pearl!

PEARL: Ma!! [*Pulling away from* JEETER, PEARL *rushes across stage and flings herself, sobbing, into her mother's arms.* JEETER, *eager and alive with excitement and admiration, comes up to the two women.* PEARL *is a beautiful child. She looks at least sixteen, in spite of the fact that she is much less than that, and is almost as tall as* ADA. *She is barefoot, and wears only a shabby, dark gray calico dress. Her hair hangs down over her shoulders like a cloud of spun gold.* ADA *soothes her*]

ADA: There, now—there, now, don't cry. You got your old ma again.

JEETER: [*Prancing around* PEARL] Now ain't that somethin'! I was just turning to go across the fields when I saw that yellow head of hers moving in the broom sedge and there she was. If she hadn't stumbled I never would of caught her. Ain't she pretty! She's about the prettiest piece in the whole country. . . .

ADA: Go away, Jeeter.

JEETER: [*Who hasn't the slightest intention of going away*] Ain't she growed some in the past year, though? She's most a grown woman by now. [*Moves* PEARL's *dress the better to see her figure*] By God and by Jesus if she ain't.

ADA: [*Sharply—slapping* JEETER's *hand away*] Stop that, Jeeter.

JEETER: What for? She is, ain't she? Look how white and gold she looks with that yellow hair hanging down her back. . . . What are you standing there crying for, Pearl? Why didn't you go on to Augusta like you started to anyway? Was you scared? Was that it, Pearl?

ADA: She wanted to see her old ma first. [*To* PEARL] That was it, wasn't it, child? [PEARL *nods, her head still on her mother's shoulder, and* ADA *speaks to* JEETER] There, you see that, Jeeter. Now you go on away like I tell you. She ain't going to talk none while you're here.

JEETER: I got to speak to her about Lov first. Now that she ain't run away she'll have to begin treating him right.

ADA: Hush up, Jeeter. Maybe she ain't going to go back and live with Lov at all. Just because she didn't go all the way to Augusta, don't mean she's going to stay with Lov again.

JEETER: What's that? Now you wait a minute. That ain't right. When a gal is mated up with a man she's got to live with him.

ADA: Mind your own business, Jeeter.

JEETER: I is minding my own business. I'm minding my business and Lov's business, too. A gal's got no right to act like Pearl's been acting. No, sir. I

say Pearl has got to go back and live in the house with Lov and let him
have his rights with her.

ADA: [*Angrily*] Now you listen to me, Jeeter Lester. You keep out of this. If I
says so Pearl can do just like she wants. You ain't got the right to tell her
what she's got to do.

JEETER: What! Who you talking to, anyway? I'm her pa, ain't I?

ADA: No, you ain't.

JEETER: What?

ADA: That's what.

JEETER: By God and by Jesus! Do you know what you're saying, woman?

ADA: I sure do. You ain't her pa. You never was and never will be.

JEETER: [*Lightly amazed*] Well, by damn—now what do you think of that?

ADA: Whatever made you think you was, anyway? Do you think a lazy old
fool like you could be the daddy of a gal like Pearl?

JEETER: [*Without rancor*] Well, I thought about that now and then. She
didn't look to me like none of the Lesters I ever heard of.

ADA: There ain't no Lester in her. Her real pa wouldn't have no truck with
any of you.

JEETER: It wasn't that Henry Peabody down the road, was it?

ADA: [*With disgust*] No.

JEETER: I didn't think it was. He couldn't have a pretty piece like Pearl for a
child any more than I could. Who was it, Ada?

ADA: Nobody you ever knew. He came from South Carolina and was on his
way to Texas.

JEETER: H'mm. I don't remember nobody like that. I must of been in Fuller,
or even maybe in Augusta at the time.

ADA: You was down seeing Captain John about a mule to plow with.

JEETER: By God and by Jesus, I remember now. I remember that old mule
just like I remember that old cow I used to have. Remember that old
mule, Ada?

ADA: I reckon.

JEETER: It was the last one I ever got off Captain John. Pretty soon after that
he moved up to Augusta and I ain't heard a word from him since, until
just now when his boy is coming back. [*To* PEARL] Did you hear about
that, Pearl? Captain John's boy is coming back this morning and I'm
going to plant me a crop this year sure.

ADA: Pearl ain't interested in that now.

JEETER: [*Indignantly*] Well, she ought to be. Everybody ought to be when
they's been born and raised on the land like I was. Captain John was and
Captain John's boy that comes after him is interested just as much, you'll
find out. You can't keep nobody like Captain John or me away from the
land forever.

ADA: Shut up, Jeeter. Can't you see Pearl is all wore out? If Jones Peabody saw her on the road to Augusta she must of walked about ten miles this morning to get here. [*To* PEARL] Is you hungry, Pearl? [PEARL *shakes her head affirmatively*]

JEETER: [*Watching the girl with disapproval*] Now what's the sense to all that shaking of your head? [*Mimics her*] What's the meaning of all that? It's plain to see you ain't no child of mine all right. Coming and going us Lesters has always talked about as much as anybody in the whole country. Can't you speak up?

ADA: Quit your nagging, Jeeter. You know what she means all right. She's hungry. You get busy and find her something to eat.

JEETER: Ain't you got no sense at all, Ada? How can I get her something to eat when there ain't even nothing for myself.

ADA: You got something yesterday from Lov when *you* was hungry.

JEETER: Is you aiming to make me steal again, woman? [ADA *shrugs*] Well, if you is I ain't. The Lord's a wise old somebody. He's watching around the corner every minute for just such as that. You can't fool Him about stealing. . . . Besides there ain't nothing between here and Fuller to steal noway.

ADA: I heard tell Morgan Prior bought hisself a sack of corn meal down to McCoy the other day.

JEETER: Corn meal! I ain't et corn meal since— [*Checks himself*] No, sir! Maybe he did and maybe he didn't, but I ain't going near Morgan Prior's house no matter what the circumstance. I promised the Lord—

ADA: [*Shrewdly*] They say he's got some bacon and fat back, too.

JEETER: Woman, you is a sinner in the eyes of God! . . . [*Whistles*] Morgan Prior must be a powerful rich man to have all that to eat. Maybe if I went down there and asked him he might let me borrow some for a little while.

ADA: Humph! I don't build no hopes on that. Morgan Prior ain't going to let you borrow nothing.

JEETER: I don't see why he oughtn't. The Lord says the rich should share their bounty with the poor. You come along with me, Ada, and we'll see if Morgan Prior is ready to do like the Lord says.

ADA: Me? What do you want me for?

JEETER: Don't you know nothing, woman? If I want to borrow me something from Morgan Prior somebody's got to talk to him at the front door, while I go around to the back, don't they? [*A full, belligerent pause*] Now, hurry up. Morgan Prior might be out early plowing the fields and it would be an almighty temptation and a sin if we borrowed something when he wasn't at home.

ADA: You go get my old hairbrush first. Pearl ain't brushed her hair this morning.

JEETER: [*Eagerly*] Is she going to do that?

ADA: [*With an abrupt nod*] While I'm gone off.

> [JEETER *exits quickly into house*]

PEARL: [*Gripping* ADA] Oh, Ma, don't go off from me.

ADA: [*Comforting her*] There now. You don't need to worry no more. Your old ma's looking out for you from now on. You don't have to go back and live with Lov no matter what Jeeter says.

PEARL: I don't never want to go back!

ADA: You don't have to. But one of these days you got to go down to Augusta to live. I've made up my mind to that.

PEARL: I'm scared, Ma.

> [JEETER *enters with hairbrush*]

JEETER: [*Eagerly*] Here you is, Ada. Great day, we ought to see something now! Lov says there ain't a prettier piece in the whole country than Pearl when she's brushing her hair and I'm inclined to agree with him.

ADA: [*Snatching brush*] Go along, Jeeter. Don't think you're going to stay around here all day watching Pearl.

JEETER: Lord, Ada, don't get so peeved. I ain't doing nothing.

ADA: No, and you never would if I didn't make you. Hurry up now. You go along. I'll catch up with you down the road.

JEETER: Well— [*Reluctantly crossing to gate*] Pearl, if Captain John's boy comes here, you tell him I won't be gone long. You tell him I got a little business down the way and to wait right here for me. [*Exits*]

ADA: Now you listen to me, honey. There ain't no sense you being scared about going off to Augusta. All my other gals went there or someplace else to live and they don't regret it.

PEARL: [*Fervently*] I want to stay here with you.

ADA: Never mind that. I ain't going to be here long. One of these days I'm going to die.

PEARL: No—no, you ain't!

ADA: That's all right, honey. It don't matter—only sometimes I do wish I had me a stylish dress to be buried in.

PEARL: I'll get you a stylish dress, Ma. Honest I will.

ADA: Don't you care about me. You got to look out for yourself. You got to have a hat to put on and shoes and dresses to wear like the gals in Augusta.

PEARL: I don't want none.

ADA: Sure you do. You don't want to stay here like your old ma, raising a raft of children and no snuff to calm you when there ain't nothing to eat. None of my other children was as pretty as you, or as smart, neither, when you want to talk, and if they can do it you can do it.

> [JEETER *appears on Tobacco Road*]

JEETER: Hey, you, Ada. Is you coming or ain't you?

ADA: I heard you, I'm coming. [*Gets up. Speaks to* PEARL] Now, honey, you just think about that while I'm gone. And don't fret none. I won't be off long. [*Enter* GRANDMA LESTER *from around house, as* ADA *crosses to gate*] Hey, you, old woman. You go out in the broom sedge and pick up some sticks for the fire. We might be wanting to cook around here pretty soon now. [*To* PEARL] Fix up your hair now, honey.

> [ADA *exits and* GRANDMA LESTER *hurries to the porch and pulls her old croker sack from beneath it.* PEARL *watches her. Straightening up, the old woman looks long at* PEARL. *Hobbling forward she tries to touch the girl's hair, but* PEARL *backs away from her.* GRANDMA LESTER *stops, her eyes reflecting her deep hurt and disappointment. For a moment more she gazes at the girl, then turns and shuffles off.* PEARL *stands looking after her, and when the* OLD WOMAN *has quite gone, she goes to the well and dips her brush in the bucket. She has taken a stroke or two with the brush when she suddenly stops and listens. The audience hears nothing, but she does. Moving quickly in back of the well, she drops to her knees, listening and waiting. Presently* HENRY PEABODY *enters down the road, running. He glances inside the yard, sees nothing, and then comes through the gate to the porch. Pushing open the door he calls inside*]

PEABODY: Jeeter—hey, you, Jeeter—Ada.... Aw, to hell with them. [*No answer and he comes down from the porch and goes to upstage corner of the house; he glances around. Seeing nothing, then, he moves quickly to the gate and exits. Slowly and cautiously* PEARL *now comes around from behind the well, runs to the road to see if* PEABODY *has gone, then comes back to the porch and sits, her back to the gate, brushing her hair. She is so preoccupied she does not hear* LOV *enter quietly on the Tobacco Road. He sees her. He pauses. He moves silently through the gate across the yard on the balls of his feet and stands in back of her, watching. Suddenly he reaches down and takes her hand firmly as it makes a stroke with the brush. She leaps to her feet, panic-stricken, to run off, but his hold is too strong and he pulls her back*]

LOV: [*Pleading*] Don't run off, Pearl. I ain't going to hurt you. [*She won't answer or look at him*] If you only wouldn't run away, I'd leave hold of you now and just watch you brush your hair again. I'd rather see you do that than anything I can think of. There ain't nobody got pretty hair like you. I used to sit on the porch and watch through the window when you was combing and brushing it and I just couldn't keep my eyes off it. Will you promise you won't run off again if I leave you go? [*Pause as he waits for her to answer*] Won't you talk to me? Won't you say nothing to me at all? You don't know how I been missing you since you run off. I didn't mean nothing by what I done this morning. It's just that you won't stay in the bed with me or talk to me. Sometimes I just shake all over, for wanting to squeeze you so hard. I keep on thinking how pretty your eyes is early in the morning. They's pretty any time of the day, but early in the morning they's the prettiest things a man could ever want to look at. Won't you come back again sometime? You won't even have to stay in the bed with me. Will you come back if I do that, Pearl? [*He waits, but still there is no answer*] Remember that last pretty I got for you? I can remember like it was yesterday. They was green beads on a long string and when you put them around your neck I swear to God if it didn't make you about the prettiest girl I ever heard tell about. [*Pitiful enthusiasm*] I tell you what . . . one of these days we'll ride up to Augusta and buy you a hat—and a stylish dress, too. Would you like to do that? Maybe Dude and Bessie will take us in the new automobile they're buying today. Did you know about that, Pearl? Dude and Bessie is getting married and is buying a new automobile. [*Not a flicker of interest shows in* PEARL'S *impassive expression.* LOV *has a dream*] A new automobile! That's what we'll get one of these days, and we'll ride all over the whole country faster than that old No. 7 passenger ever thought of going— [*In the excitement stimulated by imagination,* LOV *has released his hold on* PEARL'S *wrist and she has sprung clear of him. His pleading, broken cry falls on unhearing ears. Swiftly—much more swiftly than his clumsiness will permit him to follow—she steps away from the porch, whirls, and dashes to the gate*] Pearl! [*Just as* PEARL *reaches the gate,* ADA *appears and the girl throws herself into her mother's arms*]

PEARL: Ma! Ma! [ADA *says nothing, but over* PEARL'S *shoulder her eyes fasten malevolently on the innocent* LOV. *Appearances are against him, he knows it, and he is so emotionally upset his sense of guilt gains upper hand. For a full pause they regard each other*]

LOV: [*Pitifully apologetic*] I didn't do nothing, Ada. We was just talking. I didn't hurt her none. [ADA *pushes* PEARL *behind her, picks up stick, and advances grimly and silently on him. He takes an involuntary step back*] I just wanted her to come back and live in the house with me. [ADA *comes up to him, her fury blazing in her eyes. The stick falls across* LOV'S *hunched shoulders. He stands his ground, but lowers his head and raises his arms to protect himself.* PEARL *is thrilled*] Don't do that, Ada—don't do that! [*Her answer is to strike him again. Enter* JEETER, *carrying a couple of small packages. His eyes light up as he sees the action*]

JEETER: Great day in the morning, will you look at that! What you beating Lov for, Ada? What's he done to make you beat him like that?

LOV: I ain't done nothing, Jeeter— [*He is stopped by a whack*]

JEETER: By God and by Jesus, maybe you ain't, but you sure is getting a beating for it just the same. I don't remember when I ever seen such a good, round beating as you is getting right this minute.

[LOV *gives ground slowly, so that* ADA *misses now and again*]

LOV: I tell you I ain't done nothing!

JEETER: That don't stand to reason to me. In my experience I found that people usually get what's coming to them in this world or the next and it looks to me like right now you is getting yours in this.

LOV: I swear to God I ain't, Jeeter.

JEETER: Do you hear that, Ada? Lov says he ain't done nothing. What have you got to say about that?

ADA: Shut up.

JEETER: By God, woman, don't talk like that. Put down that stick, do you hear me? You has already done one whopping big sin today. You ought to be mighty sorry to do another. [LOV *manages to grab* ADA's *stick and stop the attack.* JEETER *nods approval*] I'm glad to see you do that, Lov. That was no way for Ada to treat you. But what did you do to her anyway to make her keep hitting you with that old stick all the time?

LOV: I only wanted Pearl to come back and live with me.

ADA: [*Holding* PEARL] Pearl ain't never going back and live with you. There ain't no use you trying to make her, either. She's going to Augusta just like she set out to do this morning and nothing you do can stop her.

LOV: I'm her husband, ain't I? I can stop her and by God I will!

ADA: [*Belligerently*] You just try it.

JEETER: There ain't no sense you trying to carry your point, Lov. Ada's made up her mind Pearl's going to Augusta and there ain't nothing I know can change it.

LOV: You can't be letting Pearl do that. It ain't right.

JEETER: Right or wrong ain't got nothing to do with it where Ada is concerned. Just a little while ago she made me borrow something when Morgan Prior wasn't at the house. That's about the biggest sin a woman can make a man do, but she don't care none. There ain't no use talking to her about right or wrong.

LOV: Augusta ain't no place for a girl as pretty as she is.

JEETER: I sure would like to stand in her way, but I ain't got no more right than that— [*Snaps his fingers characteristically*] Ada's the one you got to talk to, about that.

LOV: Ada's her ma, but you're her pa, ain't you?

JEETER: By God and by Jesus, no! Ada there was horsing around big as you please with some man while I was down borrowing me a mule one time. That don't make me her pa no more than you is.

LOV: You took care of her until she was married to me. That's the same thing.

JEETER: No, it ain't. The Lord don't take no recognition of that. The Lord is a wise old somebody. He said His flesh is His flesh. That don't make no provision for Ada horsing around while I'm down borrowing me a mule.

[*Enter* ELLIE MAY, *who hides bashfully behind tree when she sees* LOV]

ADA: You might just as well go away, Lov. I ain't lettin' Pearl go back with you no matter how much you talk, less'n she wants to.... And I don't reckon she wants to.

LOV: Pearl—won't you come back? [PEARL *shrinks farther back.* LOV *glances pleadingly at* ADA] Ada— [LOV *glances helplessly from* ADA *to* PEARL, *then lowers his head and reaches down to pick up his hat, which has fallen off. He dusts it off on his knee and is starting away when* JEETER *stops him*]

JEETER: Hold on there, Lov. No sense you going off without a gal just because Pearl don't want to go with you. Why don't you take Ellie May there? [ELLIE MAY, *behind her chinaberry tree, giggles and puts her arm over her mouth to hide the torn lip.* LOV *glances from* JEETER *to* ELLIE MAY, *then back to* JEETER *again. Without a word he pulls his hat tighter and again starts off.* JEETER *takes a step forward as he sees* LOV'S *indifference.* LOV *takes another step and* JEETER *follows*] Ellie May's got to get a man somewhere. When me and Ada's dead and gone there won't be nobody to watch after her. The niggers would haul off and come here by the dozen. The niggers would get her in no time if she was here by herself. [ELLIE MAY *sets up her giggling and wriggling again and* LOV *once more regards her objectively and solemnly*]

LOV: [*Looking away from* ELLIE MAY. *He speaks stubbornly*] I want Pearl.

JEETER: [*Exasperated*] By God and by Jesus, you know you ain't going to get Pearl, so what's the sense going on talking about that? Now Ellie May there's got a lot of—

LOV: Ellie May's got that ugly-looking face.

> [ELLIE MAY, *standing in* LOV'S *path, giggles and squirms.* LOV *looks at her hard as* JEETER *continues*]

JEETER: You and her was hugging and rubbing of each other to beat all hell just yesterday. Wouldn't you like to do that some more?

LOV: [*Still looking hard at* ELLIE MAY] No, by God! I want Pearl or nothing. [*He moves past her and exits.* JEETER *shakes his head as he watches* LOV *disappear down the road*]

JEETER: [*Chiefly to* ADA] Now that's something I can't understand at all. It looks to me when a man loses one gal he'd be thankful to get another— hey, stop that! What you doing there, Ellie May?

> [*His sentence has been broken by* ELLIE MAY'S *attack on* PEARL. *She pushes* PEARL *to the ground, picks up the stick* ADA *dropped after beating* LOV, *and belabors her pretty sister furiously.* JEETER *steps forward to stop her, but he is slower than the infuriated* ADA, *who grabs the stick away from* ELLIE MAY *and starts beating her in turn.* ELLIE MAY *fights back for a moment.* GRANDMA LESTER *enters furtively and goes behind the chinaberry tree where she observes scene*]

ADA: [*Swinging stick sharply*] I'll show you—I'll show you. [ELLIE MAY *gives up the unequal fight and flees through the gate and left down road.* PEARL *gets up and seeks protection behind her mother]* Don't you worry none, Pearl. She won't do that no more. *[She starts dusting off* PEARL'S *dress]*

JEETER: *[Shaking his head]* Great day in the morning! I never seen such beating one of the other as I seen here today. What do you suppose Ellie May done that for, Ada? *[*ADA *shoots him a baleful glance, but the disdainful reply she is forming is checked by the sudden muffled blast of a motor car horn. All of them look up. The horn, louder, sounds again.* JEETER'S *face lights up]* That's Dude! That's Dude and Bessie in that new automobile. *[*JEETER *goes through gate, works to center stage, and looks down the road.* ADA *crosses to fence and looks. Even* PEARL *is moved by sudden interest and goes to the fence.*

Only GRANDMA LESTER *comes further in, taking her place downstage of the well, where she huddles, listening and waiting]* Here they come! Just look at them! It's a brand-new automobile, all right—just look at that shiny black paint! Great day in the morning! Just look at them coming yonder! *[The horn sounds again—closer.* JEETER *speaks with pride]* Listen to Dude blow that horn. Don't he blow it pretty, though?

> *[*ELLIE MAY *enters left and flashes down the Tobacco Road on a dead run, exiting right to meet the car]*

ADA: Ain't that the prettiest sight to see, Pearl? Look at that dust flying up behind. It makes it look like a big black chariot, running away from a cyclone.

> *[The horn sounds again, to the same rhythm of an engineer blowing a locomotive whistle]*

JEETER: That's Dude driving it and blowing the horn, too. *[Mounting excitement]* Hi, there, Dude! Hi, Bessie. *[Swinging down from the fence, he runs through gate and exits down road toward car. The horn continues to sound.* ADA, PEARL, *and* GRANDMA LESTER *wait, watching. We hear* JEETER *returning before we see him]* By God, Bessie, I been seeing you come a far piece off in that new automobile. *[*BESSIE *and* JEETER *enter]* In all my days I never seen a finer looking machine. Is it real brand new?

BESSIE: *[Vigorously and proudly]* I paid the whole eight hundred dollars for it.

> *[The horn sounds]*

JEETER: *[Listens to* DUDE, *then speaks]* By God and by Jesus, it sure does make me feel happy again to know there's such a handsome automobile around. Don't you reckon you could take me for a little trip, Bessie? I sure would like to go off in it for a piece.

BESSIE: *[Looking pretentiously at marriage license she carries]* I reckon when Dude and me gets back you can go riding.

JEETER: Where is you and Dude going to, Bessie?

BESSIE: *[Proudly]* We're going to ride around like married folks.

ADA: Did you and Dude get married in Fuller?

BESSIE: Not all the way. I got leave of the county, however. It cost two dollars to do that little bit. [*Waves license at them*] There's the paper to show it.

ADA: Ain't you going to get a preacher?

BESSIE: I is not! Ain't I a preacher of the gospel? I'm going to do it myself. Ain't no Hardshell Baptist going to fool with us.

JEETER: I knowed you would do it the right way. You sure is a fine woman preacher, Sister Bessie. [DUDE *blows horn again.* JEETER *smiles complacently*] That there old Dude sure does like fooling around with that there old horn.

BESSIE: [*A bit peeved*] He's been doing that about every minute all the way up from Fuller. Looks to me like he'd want to stop now that we is about to do the rest of the marrying.

ADA: Did you and Dude have any trouble getting leave from the county?

BESSIE: None to speak of. At first the man said Dude was too young and that I'd have to get the consent of his ma and pa. I told him the Lord said for me to marry Dude, but he told me that didn't make no difference. So I started praying right then and there, and pretty soon the man said if I would just stop he'd do anything I wanted.

JEETER: You sure is a powerful pray-er, all right, Sister Bessie. You is about the best pray-er and Dude is about the best automobile driver in the country. Coming and going that makes you just about equal. [*Enter* DUDE *lugging, with quite some noise, a torn-off, dented fender.* JEETER *whirls to look at him*] Great day, Dude, what you got there? Ain't that a fender off your new car?

DUDE: [*Dropping fender without concern*] Uh-huh.

JEETER: Now how did that happen? Did you run into something?

DUDE: We was coming back from Fuller and I was looking out at a big turpentine still, and then the first thing I knowed we was smashed smack bang into the back of a two-horse wagon.

JEETER: Didn't hurt the running of the automobile, though, did it?

DUDE: Naw. It runs like it was brand new yet. The horn wasn't hurt none at all. It blows just as pretty as it did at the start.

JEETER: [*Nodding in agreement*] Don't pay no attention to it, Bessie. Just leave it be and you'll never know that machine was any different than when you got it.

BESSIE: That's right. I ain't letting it worry me none, because it wasn't Dude's fault. He was looking at the big turpentive still alongside the road, when the wagon got in our way. The nigger driving it ought to have had enough sense to move over.

JEETER: Was you blowing the horn then, Dude?

DUDE: Not right then I wasn't. I was busy looking at that big still. I never saw one that big nowhere. It was most as big as a corn-liquor still, only it wasn't so shiny-looking.

BESSIE: [*Bending down and wiping dust from fender with her skirt*] It's a shame to get the new car smashed up so soon, however. It was brand new not more than an hour ago.

DUDE: It was that damn nigger. If he hadn't been asleep on the wagon it wouldn't have happened at all. He was plumb asleep till it woke him up and threw him out in the ditch.

JEETER: He didn't get hurt much, did he?

DUDE: I don't know about that. The wagon turned over on him and mashed him some. His eyes was wide open all the time, but I couldn't make him say nothing. He looked like he was dead.

JEETER: Niggers will get killed. Looks like there just ain't no way to stop it.

[DUDE *takes out ball and hurls it against house*]

ADA: When is you and Dude going to go on with the marrying?

BESSIE: [*Turning from fender and resuming her aggressive manner*] Right this minute. [*Smooths her skirt. Unrolls license again*] Come on, Dude.

DUDE: [*Turning impatiently with ball in hand*] What do you want to do now?

BESSIE: Marry us.

DUDE: Didn't you get that all done at the courthouse in Fuller?

BESSIE: [*Still extending his end of license*] That wasn't all. We got to get married in the sight of the Lord.

DUDE: Humph! [*Throws ball again*]

JEETER: By God and by Jesus, Dude, stop chunking that ball against that old house and do what Bessie tells you.

DUDE: I want to take a ride.

BESSIE: We got plenty of time to ride around after we is married.

DUDE: Will we go then?

BESSIE: Yes, Dude.

DUDE: Is you sure?

BESSIE: Sure, Dude.

DUDE: What the hell, then. Then what do I do?

BESSIE: [*Extending license*] You hold your end of the license while I pray. [DUDE *gingerly takes one end of license, and* BESSIE *the other.* BESSIE *lowers her head and closes her eyes for several seconds of silent prayer, while* DUDE *looks down on her with a slight, rather perplexed frown. Presently* BESSIE *lifts her head, but her eyes are still closed as she intones*] I marry us man and wife. So be it. That's all, God. Amen. [*She opens her eyes and smiles gently up at* DUDE]

DUDE: [*Pulling away*] Come on.

BESSIE: I got to pray now. You kneel down on the ground while I make a little prayer. [BESSIE *and others all kneel and* DUDE *reluctantly follows, still watching her with his expression of bored annoyance. Praying*] Dear God, Dude and me is married now. We is wife and husband. Dude, he is an innocent young boy, unused to the sinful ways of the country, and I am a woman preacher of the gospel. You ought to make Dude a preacher, too, and let us use our new automobile in taking trips to pray for sinners. You ought to learn him how to be a fine preacher so we can make all the goats into sheep. That's all this time. We're in a hurry now. Save us from the devil and make a place for us in heaven. Amen. [*She opens her eyes and smiles brightly at* DUDE]

JEETER: [*Jumping up*] Bless the Lord, that was one of the prettiest marriages I ever seen. Dude sure got hisself good and wed, didn't he, Ada?

ADA: HUMPH!

JEETER: [*Goes to* BESSIE *and kisses her*] Praise God, Sister Bessie, that Dude is a lucky man. I'd sure like to be in his place right now.

BESSIE: [*Laughing coyly*] Be still, you old sinner.

JEETER: [*To* DUDE] Yes, sir, Dude, boy. You sure is lucky to get a fine woman like Bessie.

DUDE: [*Shaking him off*] Aw, shut up, you old fool.

[BESSIE *raps on the porch and* JEETER *turns to look at her*]

JEETER: What you knocking on the porch for, Bessie? [*She raps again and* JEETER's *face clears*] Great day! Now, why didn't I think of that? . . . You, Dude—can't you see how bad Sister Bessie wants to go into the house?

DUDE: What for?

JEETER: Never mind what for. [*He starts pushing* DUDE]

BESSIE: [*Taking* DUDE's *arm*] Just for now. Come on, Dude.

DUDE: You said we was going for a ride.

BESSIE: We can go after a little while.

JEETER: [*Pushing him harder*] What's the matter with you, Dude? Go on in with Sister Bessie.

[*Slowly and grudgingly* DUDE *allows himself to be shoved and pulled on to the porch. At the door he pauses*]

DUDE: This is a hell of a time to be going indoors.

[BESSIE *and* DUDE *exit into the house, the door closing.* JEETER *stands almost center stage, his eyes shining with excitement.* ELLIE MAY *crosses quickly to the window and draws herself up on her toes, her fingers on the sill, as she tries to look into the house.* JEETER *crosses to window and pulls* ELLIE MAY *away*]

JEETER: You got no business trying to see inside. Sister Bessie and Dude is married. [*Shoving* ELLIE MAY *aside, he promptly pulls himself up on the sill to see.* ELLIE MAY *suddenly turns and crosses swiftly toward porch, where* ADA *leans against an upright.* PEARL *stands on the ground at the edge of the porch near her mother*]

ELLIE MAY: [*Passing* PEARL] Come on around to the back.

[PEARL *hesitates for an instant, then joins her, and the two girls exit around upstage corner of house.* JEETER *hasn't much success seeing into the window, and he suddenly stops trying and scampers around the upstage corner of the house. He returns almost immediately with a chopping block on which he climbs to see into the room. A smile of approval beams on his weathered face*]

JEETER: Sister Bessie sure is a finelooking woman, ain't she, Dude?

BESSIE: [*Appearing at window*] Get away from there, Jeeter Lester.

JEETER: What's the matter, Bessie? I ain't done nothing.

BESSIE: Never you mind. You get away from there.

JEETER: Now don't get peeved, Bessie. This time of year puts a queer feeling into a man. I feel that way every late February and early March. No matter how many children a man's got, he always wants to get more.

BESSIE: That don't matter. I don't want to have nothing to do with you. You is an old sinner.

JEETER: [*Complacently*] Yes, I reckon I is. I reckon I is one of the biggest sinners in the whole country. [*Suddenly changes and roars*] But, by God and by Jesus, woman—what's a man going to do!

[DUDE *comes up to window and starts pushing at* JEETER *as enter* CAPTAIN TIM *and* GEORGE PAYNE]

DUDE: Get away from there, you old fool, or I'll wham you one.

TIM: [*Amused*] Well, Jeeter, what's all the excitement?

JEETER: [*Turning on block*] Captain John's boy!—Captain Tim!

[JEETER *steps from the block and runs swiftly to meet* TIM *at the gate, almost frantic with excitement.* ADA *stands on the porch, eyeing the strangers impassively and sucking on her snuff brush. The old* GRAND-MOTHER *peers out from behind the protecting well.* TIM *extends his hand as* JEETER *comes running up*]

TIM: How are you, Jeeter, how are you?

JEETER: [*Eagerly*] Captain Tim, I sure is glad to see you!

TIM: Jeeter, this is Mr. Payne, from Augusta.

PAYNE: How do you do, Mr. Lester?

JEETER: Morning, sir.

TIM: [*Seeing* ADA *on porch*] That's Ada, isn't it? Good morning, Ada.

ADA: [*Coldly*] Morning.

TIM: [*Indicating* DUDE] I don't recognize the boy, Jeeter. Which one is he?

JEETER: That's Dude.

TIM: Oh, yes, I remember Dude now. [*To* DUDE] Hello there, Dude. Do you remember me?

DUDE: [*Impudently*] Naw! [*Giggles self-consciously*]

JEETER: That there next to Dude is Sister Bessie. They just married themselves before you came.

PAYNE: Married *themselves?*

JEETER: Sister Bessie is a woman preacher and she done it.

PAYNE: [*Dubiously*] I see.

TIM: [*To* DUDE] Well, congratulations, Dude. Congratulations, Sister Bessie.
[*To* JEETER] Is Dude the only one of your children left, Jeeter?

JEETER: Ellie May and Pearl is around someplace.

TIM: [*Looking about*] Well, the place hasn't changed much. What keeps it
from falling down, Jeeter?

JEETER: Praise God, Captain Tim, I don't know. I expect it will one of these
days. . . . Now you come on the porch and sit down. . . . Dude, you bring
some chairs out here.

PAYNE: Don't bother. I'm afraid we won't be able to stay very long.

JEETER: Ain't no bother at all. Could you do with a drink of water, Captain
Tim?

TIM: Thanks, Jeeter.

> [PAYNE *crosses up left, glancing about the property and inspecting the*
> *house*]

JEETER: [*Crossing to well for water*] Dude, you go do what I told you.
[*While* JEETER *is getting the water,* PAYNE *glances around curiously. His*
eyes meet TIM's *and he shakes his head to suggest his reaction to the*
surroundings. DUDE *pulls a chair on to the porch*] Here you is. [*Crossing*
to TIM *with dipper of water*]

TIM: Much obliged. [*Drinks*]

JEETER: I sure is glad to see you back, Captain. I knowed you couldn't stay
away from the land any more than your Daddy could. Maybe city ways is
all right for a short time, but when they start cleaning off the fields and
burning the broom sedge, a man ain't happy unless he can be seeing it
and be doing it, too.

TIM: You must be getting pretty old, Jeeter. I'd think you'd be tired of it by
this time.

JEETER: No, sir. I is ready to do just as big a day's work as the next one. Ada
there is always saying I is lazy, but there ain't no truth in that when it
comes to planting a crop.

TIM: [*Going to well and putting cup down*] How have crops been lately?

JEETER: Praise God there ain't been none in seven years. We just ain't been
able to get credit down here on the Tobacco Road. Ain't nobody got no
money. By God and by Jesus, I is glad you came back to provide that
again.

TIM: [*Turning—surprised*] What?

JEETER: Yes, sir, Captain Tim. I was just telling Ada a short time back that the Lord was aiming to take care of me out of His bounty. I wasn't thinking about you at the time, but soon as I heard you was here again Dude and me set to burning off the fields. Them north fields is burning some right this minute.

TIM: [*After a glance at* PAYNE] Well, I don't know how that idea got around. I'm sure sorry, but I'm—well, Jeeter, I'm afraid I can't help you. I'm in pretty much the same fix you are.

JEETER: [*Unbelieving*] What's that, Captain Tim?

TIM: [*Turning to* PAYNE] You'd better tell him, Payne.

PAYNE: Well, you see, Mr. Lester, I'm from the bank in Augusta. We're down here to collect money, not lend it.

JEETER: You mean I can't have no credit to grow me a crop this year?

PAYNE: I'm afraid not.

JEETER: But I just got to have credit. Me and my folks is starving out here on the Tobacco Road.

PAYNE: Well, then you ought to be glad we came. We're ready to help you to get away from here to where you have a chance of making a living.

JEETER: I don't want to get away from here. If you mean go off and work in the mills, I say, by God and by Jesus, no!—I ain't going to do it.

PAYNE: But if you're really starving——

JEETER: That ain't got nothing to do with it. Captain John said I could live here as long as I wanted. He said he couldn't give me credit at the stores in Fuller no more, but he told me I could stay here and live until I died. You know that, Captain Tim.

TIM: Yes, Jeeter, I remember, and that was all right as long as the land was ours. But it's not any more. I had to borrow money on every farm we owned around here and now I can't pay it back. Like your granddaddy used to own the land and Captain John took it over, the bank's doing it with me.

JEETER: [*Heatedly*] I don't understand that. This was my daddy's place and his daddy's before him, and I don't know how many Lesters before that. There wasn't nothing here in the whole country before they came. They made that road out there hauling tobacco kegs fifteen miles down the ridge to the river. Now I don't own it and you don't own it and it belongs to a durn bank that ain't never had nothing to do with it even.

TIM: That's the way things just seem to happen, Jeeter.

JEETER: Praise God, it ain't the way things just happen. It's the rich folks in Augusta that's doing it. They don't work none, but they get all the money us farmers make. One time I borrowed me three hundred dollars from a loan company there to grow a crop and when I gave them interest and payments and every other durn thing they could think of I didn't make but seven dollars the whole year working every day. By God, that ain't right, I tell you. God won't stand for such cheating much longer. He ain't so liking of the rich people as they think He is. God, He likes the poor.

PAYNE: Now, Mr. Lester. We don't want to be hard on you old farmers, but we're going to try putting this whole section under scientific cultivation and there wouldn't be any use for you.

JEETER: Why not? If you is going to grow things on the land, why can't I stay right here and do it, too? I'd work for you just like I did for Captain John and no nigger ever worked harder than that.

PAYNE: I'm afraid that's impossible.

DUDE: What did I tell you, you old fool? Nobody ain't going to give you nothing.

JEETER: You shut up, Dude Lester! You shut up and get away from here. Captain Tim ain't going to let them send me away. Is you, Captain Tim?

PAYNE: Be reasonable, Mr. Lester. You've proved you can't get along here. Why don't you move your family up to Augusta or across the river in South Carolina where the mills are?

JEETER: No! By God and by Jesus, no! That's one thing I ain't never going to do. Them durn cotton mills is for the women folks to work in. I say it's a hell of a job for a man to spend his time winding strings on spools.

PAYNE: It shouldn't be any harder than trying to grow a crop here. Even if you do get one, you can't make enough out of it to live on.

JEETER: I don't care. God made the land, but you don't see Him building no durn cotton mills.

PAYNE: That hasn't anything to do with it. You old farmers are all the same. You don't realize that times have changed.

JEETER: That's no concern of mine. I is ready to look after my own like the Bible says, but that don't include no goddam mill! [*Turning to* TIM] Please, Captain Tim, don't let them make me do that. I'm like to die pretty soon now, anyway, but up there I'd go before my time. You ain't going to let them do that to me, is you?

TIM: Lord, Jeeter, what can I do? That's up to Mr. Payne now. [*Turning to* PAYNE] How about it, Payne? Couldn't you do something for this man?

PAYNE: I'm sorry, Mr. Harmon, but if we made an exception for one we'd have to for all of them. Of course, if he could pay rent——

JEETER: Rent! No use asking that. I couldn't pay no rent. Praise God, I hasn't even got money to buy food with.

TIM: What about your children? Couldn't one of them help you?

JEETER: I don't know where none of them is except Tom—— [*A sudden idea*] By God and by Jesus—Tom!

TIM: I remember Tom. What's Tom doing?

JEETER: They say down in Fuller he's a powerful rich man now. They tell me he hauls all the ties for the railroad. [*Turns to* PAYNE] How much money would you be wanting for rent, mister?

PAYNE: Well—this place ought to be worth a hundred dollars a year.

JEETER: That's a heap of money, but Tom ought to be ready to help out his old pa at a time like this. When would you be wanting that hundred dollars?

PAYNE: We ought to be starting back early tomorrow.

JEETER: I got time for that. Tom's only over in Burke County. [*Turns and calls*] Hey, you, Dude. You and Bessie get in that new automobile and ride over and see Tom. You tell him his old pa has got to have a hundred dollars. Don't lose no time about doing it neither.

DUDE: [*Jumping off porch—eager for a ride*] Come on, Bessie. We is going for a ride. [BESSIE *hesitates, glancing back into the house*]

JEETER: You hurry up there, Bessie. Ain't no time to be thinking about going in the house now.

> [*With a last disappointed glance,* BESSIE *comes down off the porch.* DUDE *moves ahead of her to the gate*]

TIM: Don't you think you ought to go and speak to Tom yourself, Jeeter?

JEETER: He might not like that so much. He might have changed some since he was a boy. He'll talk to Dude and Bessie, though. [BESSIE *and* DUDE *disappear down the road, and* JEETER *runs to the gate to call after them*] Hey, you, Dude. You tell Tom his old pa needs that money powerful bad. You tell him we ain't got anything to eat here, either, and his ma needs snuff to calm her stomach with. [*Turns back to* TIM] Tom was just about the best of all the boys. I reckon Bailey was the best, but Tom was good, too. He always said he was going to make a heap of money. [*The horn sounds off in* DUDE'S *inimitable manner.* JEETER *speaks proudly*] That's Dude doing that. Don't he blow the horn pretty, though? Just listen to it. [*The horn sounds again, somewhat fainter, and* JEETER *again smiles with pride at* TIM] That's Dude. [*He is listening again as the curtain falls*]

CURTAIN

ACT THREE

SCENE: *The same.*

TIME: *Dawn the following morning.*

AT RISE: JEETER, *shoeless, is discovered asleep on the porch, his back against one of the uprights, head slumped forward on his chest. Again the early sun spreads its soft golden glow, soon to become a fierce white glare as the morning advances.* JEETER *awakens abruptly, as one does who all night has tried to fight off sleep, and crosses swiftly to the gate, where he gazes off right stage down the empty, silent road. Disappointed, he comes back into the yard to the well, where he performs his casual morning ablutions, using, as always, his shirt for a towel. Fingers through his hair serve as a comb for his scraggly hair; his hat goes back on his head. He is ready for the day. Again he crosses to the road, where his anxious gaze once more sweeps the horizon right for a glimpse of* DUDE *and* BESSIE. ADA *appears on the porch, pressing her sides to ease the early morning pains of a body that sleep can no longer refresh.*

ADA: Is they coming yet?

JEETER: No. [*Comes inside to porch where he sits and starts putting on shoes*] By God and by Jesus, I don't understand that. They been gone long enough to go to Burke County and back three times over.

ADA: It's that Bessie. She ain't going to hurry none just because you want her to.

JEETER: They must of seen Tom all right if they been gone this long. Maybe he made them stay all night. Do you think he done that, Ada?

ADA: Maybe he did and maybe he didn't. But if he asked them, you can bet that Bessie stayed all right. She ain't going to come home as long as there is any other place to go.

JEETER: What is you so peeved at Bessie for? She's a fine woman preacher.

ADA: She's a old hussy, that's what she is.

JEETER: Now what makes you say that? Sister Bessie is——

ADA: Don't tell me what she is. I know. Walking around here so uppity because she bought herself that new automobile. Why didn't she buy us some rations and snuff instead of spending all that money. That's what a good woman preacher would have done.

JEETER: She wants that new automobile to carry on the preaching and the praying. Women preachers ain't like the rest of us. They is got the Lord's work to do.

ADA: Humph. Looks to me like the Lord's work would be done better if she bought Dude's Ma a stylish dress. The Lord would understand that.

JEETER: [*Suddenly and impatiently*] Say, when is we going to eat this morning, anyway? Ain't there none of that meal left we borrowed from Morgan Prior yesterday?

ADA: [*Crossly*] There's some meal all right, but there ain't no kindling wood. Ellie May's ready to cook it as soon as she gets some.

JEETER: You tell Ma Lester to go get it then.

ADA: Ma Lester ain't here.

JEETER: Where is she?

ADA: I don't know. She didn't sleep in the bed last night.

JEETER: H'mm. Maybe she went out in the broom sedge yesterday and couldn't get back. Maybe she even died out there.

ADA: Maybe. She ain't never stayed away before.

JEETER: I'll go out and look around one of these days. . . . Well, you tell Ellie May to go out and get some wood. I sure got to have my chicory before long. . . .

ADA: [Calling inside house] Ellie May—Ellie May!

ELLIE MAY: [Off—in house] What you want, Ma?

ADA: You go out in the fields and get some sticks for the fire.

ELLIE MAY: [Off] Oh, make that old woman go.

ADA: She ain't here.

ELLIE MAY: [Complaining] Well, where is she?

ADA: She's likely dead. You go on do like I tell you.

[ELLIE MAY enters yawning and scratching her head]

ELLIE MAY: Why don't you make Pearl go? She don't never do nothing.

ADA: Never you mind now. I got other things for Pearl to do.

ELLIE MAY: Aw, gee!

JEETER: You hurry up. I is near about dying for my chicory.

ELLIE MAY: [Complaining] Can't I even get me a drink of water?

JEETER: All right, you get you some water, then get along. But keep away from the north fields. They might be burning some yet. That's probably what happened to your old grandma. The fire come up on her and she couldn't get away from it. [He is filled with sudden energy, gets up, crosses to the road, and looks down it, shakes his head. ELLIE MAY drinks leisurely from the water dipper] By God and by Jesus, they ought to be back with that money before this. First thing you know Captain Tim and that man will be along here looking for it.

ADA: [Calling into house—ignoring JEETER] Pearl—Pearl, git up, honey. Come out here and freshen up. We'll be having something to eat pretty soon now. Bring that old brush with you, too. I want to pretty up your hair.

[ELLIE MAY hears ADA and takes the dipper slowly down from her mouth. She looks at ADA, her face livid with unspoken rage. Suddenly she flings the dipper at ADA, the water spilling. JEETER, coming through the gate, regards ELLIE MAY with anger]

JEETER: Great day in the morning, what's the meaning of all that!

[ELLIE MAY, disregarding JEETER, looks at her mother with blazing eyes, her breath coming hard. ADA returns the look with level coldness. ELLIE MAY's throat contracts with half-stifled sobs and she turns and rushes to the gate. She starts down the Tobacco Road left when something she sees offstage stops her. For an instant she is rigid, then, with the first pronounced sob, she turns, and exits right, running down *the road.* JEETER *follows* ELLIE MAY *with a puzzled glance, then turns to* ADA]

JEETER: Now if that ain't the durndest gal. What do you suppose made her turn around like that for? [*He answers his own curiosity by crossing to the road and looking off left. He turns back with some surprise*] It's Lov coming down the road.

ADA: Don't you let him come in here.

JEETER: What the hell, woman. He ain't going to do no harm. He looks too durned tired.

ADA: He ain't going to have Pearl.

JEETER: Who said he was. I just said he was coming down the road.

ADA: [*Calling inside*] Pearl, Lov's coming. Stay where you is and get ready to run case he starts trying to get at you. [ADA *shuts the door and stands with her back to it*]

JEETER: Great day, he's toting something again. Now whatever could be in that anyway? I bet you one thing, by God—it ain't turnips! [*Twitching with eagerness, he comes inside the yard and takes his familiar place, hanging over the fence, his back to the audience, straining to see down the road*] Whatever he's got, I sure could use some, even if I can't see it. I certainly is happy Lov and me is friends about this time.

ADA: Humph! The only way you'll ever get anything from him is stealing it.

JEETER: No, sir! The Lord forgave me for that before and I ain't going to risk his wrath again.

ADA: Humph.

JEETER: [*Again stretching over fence to peer down the road*] Now, Ada, don't be too hard on Lov and I might be able to prevail on him to give us a little something.

ADA: Then he better keep away from Pearl. [JEETER *waves her quiet and turns back to the fence, but he restrains his eagerness, as he did in the first act, so that* LOV *will not be frightened off.* LOV *enters disconsolately, carrying a small flour sack, the bottom of which bulges somewhat from an object the size of a brick*]

JEETER: [*Casually*] Hi, there, Lov. [LOV *stops*]

LOV: [*After a pause*] I want to talk to you, Jeeter.

JEETER: Sure, Lov. Come inside and rest yourself. [LOV *slowly comes through the gate*] What you got in that sack, Lov? What you got there anyway?

LOV: [*After a significant pause and a glance from* JEETER *to* ADA *and back to* JEETER. *Knowing the bombshell effect of his words*] Salt pork.

JEETER: [*Electrified*] Salt pork! Lord a'mighty! I ain't had salt pork since the Lord himself knows how long. Is you going to give me some of that, Lov? I sure could do with a small piece about this time.

LOV: Take it. [*He holds sack to the astounded* JEETER]

JEETER: [*Unbelieving*] Take it? You mean take it all?

LOV: I bought it for that.

JEETER: [*Taking sack*] Great day in the morning, I never heard of such bounty! [*Turns*] Did you hear that, Ada? Lov has give me all this salt pork.

ADA: [*Coldly*] What does he want for it?

JEETER: He don't want nothing for it. Lov just give it to me, that's all.

ADA: Ask him.

JEETER: [*Doubtfully*] Well, now. . . . What have you got to say about that, Lov? Is you after something from me in return for this salt pork?

LOV: I want to talk to you about Pearl.

ADA: That's just what I thought. Well, you ain't going to have her back. No use you trying to talk Jeeter into it, neither. He ain't got nothing to say about it. You give him back that salt pork, Jeeter.

JEETER: Now, Ada, there ain't no sense in being hasty about this matter. What you say is right, but there can't be no harm in talking about it.

ADA: You just want to hold on to that salt pork.

JEETER: Now, Ada——

LOV: [*With sudden desperation*] I got to have Pearl back, Jeeter, no matter what you said yesterday. I just got to have her back.

JEETER: Now, Lov, we talked all about that before. I told you——

LOV: I don't care what you told me. Maybe you ain't Pearl's real pa, but you got the right of her.

JEETER: I wish I could agree with you on that matter, Lov, but it ain't right in the eyes of God.

LOV: I'll pay you, Jeeter. I'll give you a dollar every week out of the money I make at the chute.

JEETER: [*Whistles*] That's a heap of money, Lov, and coming and going I might have considered it a short time back. But I ain't going to need money bad enough now to make me fly against the wrath of the Lord. Dude and Bessie is over with Tom right this minute and he'll be sending me all the money I want for my needs.

LOV: I'll give you two dollars.

JEETER: Two dollars a week! Now, Lov Bensey, you quit tempting me.

LOV: [*With sudden fury*] By God, I want my wife!

> [ADA *plants her back more firmly against the door and the movement tells* LOV *where* PEARL *is. He takes a few steps to the edge of the porch.* ADA's *arms raise to cover the door*]

ADA: You come any closer, and I'll call to her to run off.

> [LOV, *checked by the threat, stops, his sudden anger cooling*]

LOV: [*Defeated*] No, don't do that. [JEETER *takes this opportunity to hide the sack behind the well.* LOV *slowly turns to* JEETER] Jeeter, I don't see how I can make it more than two dollars every week. But that's a heap of money.

JEETER: Praise God, I know it, Lov.

ADA: Get out of here, Lov Bensey—get out!

[LOV *slowly turns and crosses to the gate;* JEETER *keeps himself in front of the well to lessen any chance of* LOV *seeing and remembering the salt pork.* LOV *exits left.* JEETER *waits until* LOV *has gone, then runs to the fence and looks after him*]

JEETER: He's gone all right. He's gone and forgot that salt pork, too. [*Running back to the well, he picks up the sack and takes out the pork*] Now ain't that something! That must be near about two pounds. Lov sure is a generous provider. [*Crosses to* ADA] There you is, Ada. You fix up some of this with the corn meal when Ellie May comes back with the kindling. [ADA *takes the sack. She has moved away from the door on* LOV's *exit and is in her usual position, leaning against an upright*] Now what do you think's happened to Ellie May, anyway? What's happened to Dude and Bessie for that matter? By God and by Jesus, they ought to be back with that money before this.

ADA: What is you going to do with that money, Jeeter?

JEETER: [*Pausing with foot half raised to put on other shoe. He is outraged*] What is I going to do? Is you crazy, woman! I got to give it to that man with Captain Tim.

ADA: Humph! That don't make no sense to me.

JEETER: Great day in the morning, you *is* crazy! That money's going to keep me my land, ain't it? That money's going to let me stay here and raise a crop. By God and by Jesus, what do you mean there ain't no sense in that?

ADA: You give the money to that man and what has you got left? Nothing! You ain't got no seed cotton to plant in the fields, you ain't got nothing to eat and you ain't no better off than you was before.

JEETER: I ain't aiming to be better off. I'm aiming to keep my land.

ADA: You're an old fool, Jeeter Lester. With that money we could get us a place to live up in Augusta. Maybe we could even buy us an automobile like Bessie's. [*Wisely*] You wouldn't have to worry none about being laid in the corn crib when you die neither. Ain't no telling what's going to happen if you stay here.

JEETER: Shut up! You just say that to scare me into doing what you want. Well, I ain't going to be laid in no corn crib, and I ain't going to work in no cotton mill neither.

ADA: Maybe you wouldn't have to work none up there. [*Glances toward door*] Maybe Ellie May and Pearl could do that. Pearl would like that a lot. She wouldn't be scared of going if her old ma went.

JEETER: You ain't thinking about my wants when you talk like that. It's Pearl you is thinking about. Well, you can take her if that's what you want, and leave me here alone. I was born here on the land, and by God and by Jesus that's where I'll die.

ADA: [*Fiercely*] I hope you do. I hope you die and they lay you in the corn crib and the rats eat off your face just like they done your pa.

JEETER: [*Rising—threatening and furious, raising his shoe to strike her*] Goddam you, woman! [*The horn, sounded in* DUDE's *inimitable style, checks* JEETER's *descending blow. Radiance replaces black fury in his face as he hears it again*] Here they is. That's them, all right. That's Dude blowing that old horn. [PEARL *and* ELLIE MAY *enter on to porch. Hobbling because of the one shoe,* JEETER *crosses to the gate, where he stops and starts to pull on his shoe, while the horn continues its bleat.* JEETER's *shoe goes on with difficulty. Once or twice he starts off with it half on, but is so impeded that he stops and works on it again. The horn stops.* JEETER, *giving up the job of putting on the shoe while standing, plumps to the ground, puts it on, and gets through the gate, starting down the road right, when* BESSIE *enters*] Here you is, Bessie. I been waiting all night and day for you and Dude to come back. Where you been anyway?

BESSIE: [*Proudly*] In Augusta.

JEETER: Augusta! Didn't you go see Tom?

BESSIE: We saw Tom first. Then we rode up to Augusta and had us a honeymoon.

JEETER: Honeymoon? What the hell is that?

BESSIE: A honeymoon is when two people is married and they get in the bed together.

JEETER: Where did you do that?

BESSIE: [*Proudly*] At a hotel.

JEETER: Great day in the morning! Didn't that take a heap of money?

BESSIE: It took two bits.

JEETER: Hear that, Ada? Dude and Bessie stayed at a hotel in Augusta.

ADA: [*Dourly*] Did they bring us anything back?

BESSIE: I didn't have no money left to do that. That two bits was the last piece of money I had.

ADA: Humph! Looks to me like you might have brought some snuff back to Dude's old ma instead of wasting money like that.

[*Enter* DUDE *carrying broken headlight*]

JEETER: Now, Ada, you let Bessie alone. [*Sees* DUDE] Here you is, Dude. Bessie just told us about staying all night in Augusta—— [*Sees headlight*] Great day, just look at that old headlight. What done that?

DUDE: A goddam old pine tree. That's what.

JEETER: [*Inspecting light*] H'mm. Was you looking where you was going?

DUDE: I just looked back once and there it was—smack in front of me.

JEETER: Well, it don't look like it's going to be much good no more.

DUDE: If I had me an ax, I'd have chopped that tree down right then and there.

JEETER: I wouldn't concern myself much about it. One headlight is plenty to drive with.

DUDE: Oh, to hell with it. [*He drops light on ground, crosses to gate*] It's just the way that pine tree got in front of me, that's all.

JEETER: Looks like they will do that sometimes. Hey, Dude. Where is the money Tom sent me?

DUDE: Tom didn't send you no money. Why the hell did you think he would anyway? [*Exits*]

JEETER: Hey, Dude—— [*Turning back to* BESSIE] Dude's lying, ain't he, Bessie?

BESSIE: [*Nodding*] Tom ain't at all like he used to be, Jeeter.

JEETER: [*Desperately*] Now, Bessie—don't fool with me. Give me the money.

BESSIE: There ain't no money, Jeeter. Tom just didn't send any—that's all.

JEETER: You is crazy, woman. He did send it. Tom wouldn't do that to me.

BESSIE: Yes, he did, Jeeter. He's a wicked man, Tom is.

JEETER: No, sir, I don't believe it. You is got the money and I want it. Give it to me, hear me—give it to me.

BESSIE: I ain't got it, Jeeter.

JEETER: You is a liar. That's what you is—an old liar. Tom did send it. [*Enter* DUDE *rolling an auto wheel.* JEETER *rushes over to him inside the gate and grabs him*] Dude, give me that money—hear me, give me that money.

DUDE: [*Shaking him off*] Didn't I tell you once! There ain't no money. Now get away from me and shut up! [*Bends over wheel, his back half to* BESSIE]

JEETER: No. Tom wouldn't do that. He was my special boy. You just didn't go see him.

DUDE: We saw him all right. We saw him and he said to tell you to go to hell. [BESSIE *grabs him by the neck and shakes him so that the wheel falls to the ground.* DUDE *is furious*] Damn you, turn loose of me! [*Shakes free*] What the hell you doing?

BESSIE: You shouldn't have told Jeeter that. That's a wicked thing to say.

DUDE: I didn't say it—Tom said it. And you keep off me. I didn't do nothing to you.

BESSIE: Praise the Lord, you won't be fit to preach a sermon next Sunday if you cuss like that. Good folks don't want to have God send them sermons by cussing preachers.

DUDE: All right, I won't cuss no more. But don't you go jumping on my neck no more neither. [*He picks up wheel and rolls it against fence near the other broken pieces of the automobile, and sits.* JEETER *sits on fence, staring blankly ahead.* PEARL *and* ELLIE MAY *exit into the house*]

ADA: What does Tom look like now? Has he changed much?

BESSIE: He looks a lot like Jeeter. There ain't much resemblance in him and you.

ADA: Humph! There was a time when I'd have declared it was the other way around.

BESSIE: Maybe one time, but now he looks more like Jeeter than Jeeter does hisself.

ADA: What did he say when you told him you and Dude was married?

BESSIE: He didn't say nothing much. Looked to me like he didn't care one way or the other.

DUDE: [*Over his shoulder from where he sits, back to audience, appraising the damaged parts*] Tom said she used to be a two-bit slut when he knowed her. [*With a bound* BESSIE *is on his neck again, choking him. He jerks away from her quickly and pushes his hand at her face, getting up, threatening*] Goddam you! You keep off me.

BESSIE: [*Tenderly as she backs off*] Now, Dude, you promised me you wasn't going to cuss no more.

DUDE: Then, by God, quit choking me. I'm getting damned sick and tired of you doing that.

BESSIE: You shouldn't talk like that about the woman you is mated to.

DUDE: Well, that's what Tom said. He told it right to you and you didn't do nothing. Why didn't you do something to him if he was telling a lie?

BESSIE: Tom is a wicked man. The Lord punishes wicked men like that.

DUDE: Well, then, you let the Lord punish me and keep your hands off my neck. [DUDE *pulls wheel down and begins trying to straighten spokes by pulling on them with his hands and pounding them with a hand-sized rock*]

ADA: Did Tom say he had any children?

BESSIE: He didn't mention it if he had. He didn't seem to want to talk very much, not even when I told him you and Jeeter didn't have meal nor meat in the house.

DUDE: [*Looking up from his work*] He just said he didn't give a damn and went on driving his team of ox.

ADA: [*Briskly—pleased*] Well, I reckon we better be getting ready to go off, Jeeter.

JEETER: What?—— [*Snapped back from his stunned silence*] No, I ain't going, I tell you.

ADA: [*Exasperated*] Tom didn't send you no money. How you going to stay here?

JEETER: By God, I'm going to stay, that's all.

[ADA, *realizing the uselessness of arguing with him, turns and exits into the house.* BESSIE *turns to* DUDE *and watches him work*]

BESSIE: Do you reckon you'll ever get that wheel straight again, Dude?

DUDE: [*Crossly*] I'm trying, ain't I?

JEETER: [*Abstractedly, pointing to wheel*] What done that?

DUDE: Remember that old pine tree that busted the headlight?

JEETER: Um.

DUDE: Well, I was backing away from that and some durn fool left a pile of cross ties right where I'd run smack into them.

JEETER: [*Easily*] Well, now what do you think?

DUDE: It busted the back of the car in, too.

BESSIE: It looks like everything's trying to ruin my new automobile. Ain't nothing like it was when I paid eight hundred dollars for it in Fuller just yesterday.

JEETER: It ain't hurt the running of it none, though, has it? It runs good yet.

BESSIE: I reckon so, but it makes a powerful lot of noise when it's running up hill—and down hill, too.

DUDE: That's because we was running it without oil. The man at the gasoline station said something was burned out inside.

JEETER: That's a pity.

DUDE: It runs pretty good, though, even if it does make all that racket.

JEETER: Some automobiles is like that. [*Jumps down from fence, suddenly his old self again*] By God and by Jesus, now why didn't I think of that before. Quit pounding on that old wheel, Dude. You come with me.

DUDE: [*Still sitting*] What you want to do now? I done enough running around for one morning.

JEETER: You get up from there and do like I say. You and me is going to start hauling wood to Augusta right this minute.

DUDE: You're just an old fool. That old machine of yours can't carry no wood to Augusta.

JEETER: No, but that there new one can. You come on.

DUDE: What do I want to haul wood to Augusta for?

JEETER: So I can get me some money for the bank—that's what for.

DUDE: You ain't going to get no hundred dollars for no load of wood, or nothing else like it.

JEETER: I can get a couple of dollars maybe, and every day doing that I can get me more than a hundred.

BESSIE: You stop right where you is, Jeeter. You ain't going to use my new automobile for no such purpose.

JEETER: Now, Bessie, ain't I always shared what I had with you and your former husband? You ain't going to see me lose my land, is you?

BESSIE: That ain't no concern of mine. Hauling wood in my new machine would punch holes in the seat and the top just like it done to your old one.

JEETER: I won't let it hurt it none.

BESSIE: It's already broke up enough. I ain't going to let you do it.

JEETER: Now, Bessie——

BESSIE: You can't have it and that's all.

JEETER: [*With heat*] That's a hell of a way to act toward me. You ain't got the mercy of the Lord in you. I say you is a hell of a woman preacher.

BESSIE: [*Angrily*] You shut up cussing at me, Jeeter Lester!

JEETER: I won't. You is an old bitch, that's what you is. You is an old bitch!

BESSIE: [*With equal fury*] You is an old bitch, too! You is an old son-of-a-bitch. All you Lesters is sons-of-bitches!

> [DUDE *looks up, amused*]

JEETER: [*Coming up to her threateningly*] Get off my land! If I can't borrow me that automobile, you get off my land.

BESSIE: It ain't your land. It's the bank's land and *you* got to get off it.

JEETER: It's the old Lester place, and I ain't going to get off it while I'm alive. But durned if I can't run you off—— [*Enter* PEARL *from house with small, blackened pot*] Now git!—You hear me, gi——

> [JEETER *sees* PEARL, *who has hesitated on the porch at sight of the quarrel, and suddenly stops his tirade, the hand raised to strike* BESSIE *halted in midair.* PEARL *comes down from the porch and crosses to the well,* JEETER'S *eyes following her and his hand slowly lowering to his side. The fury in his eyes dies to a strange, puzzled, contemplative expression.* DUDE, *who has been amused by the quarrel, a smile wreathing his face, follows his father's glance curiously, but without enlightenment.* BESSIE *glances from* JEETER *to* PEARL *and back to* JEETER *again, a frown wrinkling her forehead*]

BESSIE: What's the matter with you, you old fool? Has you lost your mind?

JEETER: [*Suddenly turning away from regarding* PEARL *at the well, smiling at* BESSIE, *and moving away a few steps*] Ain't no sense you and me fighting, Bessie. You and me always thought a heap of each other. You can stay here just as long as you has a mind to.

BESSIE: H'mm. [*Suspicious and uncompromising*] You ain't going to have the use of my new automobile to haul wood to Augusta.

JEETER: I gave up thinking about that a long time back. Don't concern yourself about that no more. However, I might be wanting you and Dude to take a little trip for me pretty soon now. Will you do that?

BESSIE: [*Suspiciously*] Maybe. What you want us to do?

JEETER: Never you mind. It won't be far.

BESSIE: Well, if it ain't far.

JEETER: It won't hardly take no time. [*Crosses to* DUDE] How is you getting on there, Dude?

DUDE: [*Back trying to straighten spokes*] Maybe it will be all right. It don't much matter if all the spokes ain't straight.

JEETER: Umm. [*Out of the corner of his eye* JEETER *watches* PEARL, *who, having filled the kettle, crosses back from well to house and exits.* JEETER *leaves his place at the fence and nonchalantly ambles to the porch and leans, taking out his knife and whittling on a piece of broken weatherboarding. Although he tries to appear at ease, his tenseness is apparent, and occasional swift glances at the door reveal his real interest*]

DUDE: [*Hitting at spokes with a stone harder than before*] This is a hell of a job.

JEETER: Don't worry too much about that. The wheels of my old machine wasn't straight much after the first few days and it didn't hurt the running of it hardly any.

BESSIE: I don't like my new car busted up like that though. [*Indicating headlight*] Look there, Dude. There ain't hardly a piece of glass left in that headlight.

DUDE: Don't I know it. Goddam it, can't you let me be? Can't you see I'm trying to fix this old wheel?

BESSIE: Now, Dude, is that a way to talk? Good folks don't want to go and hear a Sunday sermon by a cussing preacher. I thought you wasn't going to swear no more.

DUDE: Then don't be always poking around. Go sit down someplace.

[*Enter* PEARL *with pan.* JEETER *watches her sharply as she crosses to well*]

JEETER: [*Pretending interest*] When's Dude going to start being a preacher, Bessie? [*Follows* PEARL *slowly to well*]

BESSIE: He's going to preach a little short sermon next Sunday. I is already telling him what to say when he preaches.

JEETER: Dude might make a fine man preacher at that under your direction, although I never thought he had right good sense. I used to think he was going to stay on the land like I always done, but I reckon he'll be better off riding around the country preaching and praying with you. [*Edges forward a bit as* PEARL *fills her bucket and starts back to door. With a spring,* JEETER *is at* PEARL'S *side and grabs her firmly by the wrist. The bucket falls—the girl's cry rings out, as she makes a desperate effort to pull away and run*]

PEARL: Ma!

[BESSIE *and* DUDE *whirl around to look*]

JEETER: Hey, Dude—you and Bessie ride down to the chute and get Lov. Tell him I got Pearl for him.

[*The door flies open and an infuriated* ADA *takes in the scene. She rushes down on* JEETER *and begins hitting at him furiously*]

ADA: You let her be—you let her be!

JEETER: [*Pushing off* ADA *with his free hand*] Hurry up there, Dude. You tell Lov if he's still ready to pay that two dollars a week I'll make Pearl go back and live with him.

BESSIE: Jeeter, that ain't the right thing to do.

JEETER: [*Fighting off* ADA] Maybe it wasn't right before, but it sure is now. You get the hell out of here!

DUDE: [*Grabbing* BESSIE] Come on. [DUDE *half pulls* BESSIE *through gate*]

ADA: [*Clawing at* JEETER *and yelling at* DUDE] Don't you go, Dude—don't you go!

JEETER: Go on, Dude. You do like I tell you.

[DUDE *and* BESSIE *exit right.* ADA *strikes at* JEETER, *but when she sees* DUDE *and* BESSIE *exit, she suddenly stops her attack and runs after them*]

ADA: Don't go, Dude. Wait! Wait!

[ADA *exits.* PEARL *continues to scratch and fight against* JEETER, *her gasping sobs the only sound she utters.* JEETER *holds her, but looks off in direction the others have gone. For an instant there is silence, broken only by* PEARL's *sobs. Then the sound of an engine starting up and the blare of a horn come from the road below, and hard on this rings out the high shriek of a woman in agony. Again the scream cuts the silence, and even* PEARL's *sobs are hushed, as she and* JEETER *listen. Suddenly she again struggles to free herself in a frenzy of effort to be with her mother, but* JEETER's *hold does not relax. Nothing is spoken, no voice is heard, for a full pause. Then, on hands and knees, crawling along the Tobacco Road and whimpering like a hurt puppy, comes* ADA. PEARL's *struggles cease and she stands horrified, still in* JEETER's *grasp, as* ADA *continues forward. At the gate her strength deserts her, and she sinks to her side, now dragging herself along by her arms alone, until she is in the yard*]

PEARL: Ma! . . . Let me go, goddam you—let me go!

[*But* JEETER *holds fast,* DUDE *and* BESSIE *come running up to fence outside, followed by* ELLIE MAY. DUDE *leans over the fence, looking at his mother. There is no grief in his voice, only calm explanation.* JEETER *holds* PEARL, *who stands transfixed*]

DUDE: We was backing on to the road and she got in the way. I guess the wheels ran over her.

[ADA *makes a last movement forward and a stifled groan comes from her crushed, racked body as she props herself on her arm. A sob escapes* PEARL *and she tries to pull away from* JEETER]

ADA: Let her go, Jeeter. Let her come to me.

JEETER: Praise God, I'd like to do that for you, Ada, but she'll run away.

ADA: Just let her come close to me, that's all.

> [JEETER *yields several steps, so that* PEARL, *kneeling, can reach out her hand to touch* ADA. ELLIE MAY *enters and stands outside the fence*]

PEARL: [*Kneeling—touching her mother—sobbing*] Ma! Ma! Don't die. You can't, Ma—you can't!

ADA: That's all right, Pearl. I was going pretty soon now anyway. [*Glances around as best she can*] I wish I had that stylish dress to be buried in, though. Reckon you can get me one, Jeeter?

JEETER: I sure would like to promise you that, Ada, but it ain't likely.

PEARL: I'll get you one, Ma. I'll get you one.

ADA: [*Matter-of-factly, without either self-pity or bitterness*] Never mind, honey. I never really thought I'd get it. It would have sort of pleased me, though. [*Pauses, looks at* PEARL, *then* JEETER] Let her go, Jeeter. I never asked for nothing before, but now I'm going to die.

JEETER: I sure would like to, Ada, but I'm going to die pretty soon myself now. I feel it inside me. But I got to die on the land. Don't you understand? If I don't hold on to her for Lov I won't be able to do that.

ADA: Please, Jeeter, don't make her go back.

JEETER: Praise God, Ada, I got to.

ADA: All my life I been working for you. I picked cotton in the fields and turned over the furrows. I took care of your house and raised your children, and now when I'm going to die you won't even do what I want you to.

JEETER: My concern is with the living. The dead has to look out for themselves.

ADA: You're a sinful man, Jeeter Lester. You're a sinful man, and you're going to hell. [*Holds out arm to* PEARL] Come here, child. Just put your arm around me so I can sit up.

> [JEETER *allows* PEARL *to come close enough to* ADA, *so that her free arm goes around her mother, and* JEETER's *hand works close to* ADA's *mouth. Suddenly* ADA *leans forward the few necessary inches and her teeth sink into* JEETER's *hand. With a smothered exclamation* JEETER *jerks back his hand, releasing* PEARL. *With flashing quickness the girl is on her feet. A dash carries her through the gate before* JEETER *recovers from the shock of his pain. Pausing,* PEARL *looks back at her mother, propped on her arm in the yard*]

PEARL: Good-by, Ma.

> [JEETER *springs forward toward her, but with a last wave of her hand,* PEARL *flashes down the road and is gone.* JEETER *reaches the fence, makes to run after her, then stops, realizing the hopelessness of over-taking the girl.* ADA, *holding herself up with her last strength, sees his defeat. A low laugh escapes her and she rolls forward on her face and*

is dead. JEETER *slowly turns and comes back inside. He stops to look down at* ADA *for a moment and then crosses to the porch where he sits. His hand doesn't hurt much now, but he continues to hold it.* LOV *enters*]

DUDE: Hi, there, Lov. Jeeter was looking for you, but I guess it's too late now. Pearl's done gone.

LOV: [*After a pause, indicating* ADA] What's the matter with her?

DUDE: Me and Bessie run over her in the new automobile a while back.

LOV: Is she hurt bad?

DUDE: Looks like she's dead.

[LOV *comes inside, kneels down, looks at* ADA. *Then goes up to* JEETER]

LOV: Ada's dead, Jeeter.

[JEETER *nods, half dazed. Crossing to* ADA, *he stands over her for a long pause. At last he speaks.*]

JEETER: Lov, you and Dude go out in the fields and find the best place to bury her. Make a deep hole—Ada would like that. . . . Bessie, you do some praying, too. It would please Ada a whole lot.

BESSIE: Praise the Lord, I'll be glad to, Brother Jeeter.

[LOV, DUDE, *and* BESSIE *exit.* ELLIE MAY *moves forward tentatively and* JEETER *notices her*]

JEETER: Ellie May, you better go down to Lov's house and fix it up for him. He'll be coming home to supper tonight and you cook him what he wants. Be nice to him and maybe he'll let you stay. He'll be wanting a woman pretty bad now.

[ELLIE MAY, *frantic with delight, drops her sticks and crosses on a run down the road. Just before she exits, she stops and looks back*]

ELLIE MAY: Good-by, Pa.

[JEETER *nods.* ELLIE MAY *exits, running.* JEETER *looks down at* ADA]

JEETER: You shouldn't have done that, Ada. One way and another it didn't do anybody much good except maybe Pearl.

[*For a brief second* JEETER *looks down at* ADA, *then he crosses to the porch and sits. He bends down slowly, takes a pinch of the earth between his fingers and rubs it into dust. He sits back, leaning against the upright, and tilts his hat forward over his eyes. It is the same posture he has assumed so many times before when he has suddenly and unexpectedly fallen asleep. For a moment he continues abstractedly to rub the dirt between his fingers. Then all movement ceases. Seconds of somber silence pass. A rotten shingle falls from the sagging porch, and the curtain falls slowly*]

CURTAIN

Abie's Irish Rose

ANNE NICHOLS

ANNE NICHOLS

The phenomenon that was *Abie's Irish Rose* has never been duplicated in the American theatre. A ragbag of a play populated with an assortment of stereotypes, replete with low-grade vaudeville humor and peppered with comic dialects, it nevertheless ran for 2,327 performances in New York, a record that was not to be topped until a decade later by *Tobacco Road.*

Surely, it wasn't the critics who propelled it to its fantastic success and popularity. Although the notices were far from favorable they were not quite as lethal as historians have led us to believe. *The New York Times* critic, William B. Chase, for example, wrote that some scenes "sagged," but he noted that the audience had "laughed uproariously" and indicated that a long run was a possibility.

As Howard Taubman reflected in *The Making of the American Theatre:* "Were standards lower in the twenties? They must have been. How else can we explain the records *Abie's Irish Rose* piled up—the performances by road and stock companies and the total audiences of 11,000,000 which paid $22,000,000 for the privilege of laughing and rejoicing as love conquered all for a Jewish boy and an Irish girl?"

The comedy, which ran for five years on Broadway and for more than twenty years on the road, brought author Anne Nichols millions of dollars in royalties. But it took weeks for the show to catch on. Miss Nichols had mortgaged her home to get the play produced and the public's apathy at first gave it a shaky start. To keep it going, the actors took a pay cut, and tickets were sold at reduced rates. Then, miracle of miracles, suddenly *Abie's Irish Rose* was a hit. Everybody made fun of the play. Yet everybody went to see it.

Its Broadway closing in 1927 was not the end of *Abie.* There were two revivals in New York, in 1937 and 1954, two film versions, in 1928 and 1946, a radio show in 1942, and innumerable touring productions well into the 1940s. "It is more than a play," its author once observed. "It has never stopped playing somewhere." Quite true, for in addition to regaling American audiences for years it was played in practically every country in the world and in many languages.

What gave *Abie's Irish Rose* its immense popularity and longevity? Miss Nichols ascribed its success to its message—"the spirit of tolerance." More likely though, it prospered because audiences enjoyed the jokes, however hackneyed, the situations, and the characters who were instantly familiar and typical. They had been exposed to similar characters in vaudeville (then in its heyday), in revues, and in burlesque in the 1920s.

The temper of the times had begun to change, however, and the subsequent New York revivals met with little public support and with strong opposition from religious leaders and a younger generation manifesting a growing resentment toward ethnic caricature. Today, its main distinction is that it held the title of Broadway's longest running play for fourteen years, and however we may judge it now it always shall remain in the annals of the theatre as one of America's most popular plays.

Born in Dales Mill, Georgia, Anne Nichols left home at an early age and came to New York to pursue her desire to become an actress. She worked in choruses, played small roles, and toured in vaudeville with Fiske O'Hara. But she soon discovered that her talent lay in writing for the theatre rather than in acting and she went on to become successful as a collaborator and as an individual playwright. "People think *Abie's Irish Rose* is the only thing I ever did," Miss Nichols often complained. She then would point out that her works included dozens of vaudeville sketches and some twenty plays with titles like *Just Married, Heart's Desire, Linger Longer Letty,* and *Pre-Honeymoon.* But it was still that sentimental comedy about the young lovers and their warring families (shades of *Romeo and Juliet!*) that made her and kept her famous for the remainder of her life.

After a prolonged illness, Miss Nichols died in 1966 at the age of seventy-five.

ABIE'S IRISH ROSE was first produced at the Fulton Theatre, New York, on May 23, 1922, by Anne Nichols. The cast was as follows:

MRS. ISAAC COHEN	*Mathilde Cottrelly*
ISAAC COHEN	*Bernard Borcey*
DR. JACOB SAMUELS	*Howard Lang*
SOLOMON LEVY	*Alfred Wiseman*
ABRAHAM LEVY	*Robert B. Williams*
ROSE MARY MURPHY	*Marie Carroll*
PATRICK MURPHY	*John Cope*
FATHER WHALEN	*Harry Bradley*
FLOWER GIRL	*Dorothy Grau*

Directed by Laurence Marston

BRIDESMAIDS   *Eveyln Nicholas, Alma Wall, Leslie Rice, Mary Wall, Kathleen Bolton, Martha Haworth*

ACT ONE

Solomon Levy's apartment, New York.

ACT TWO

The same. One week later.

ACT THREE

Abie and Rose Mary's apartment, New York. Christmas Eve, one year later.

ACT ONE

SCENE: *The home of a New York business man, a prosperous one. The living room is comfortably furnished, without particular effort made to follow any special period, both as to architecture and decoration. The ensemble is rich in appearance and denotes very good taste.*

There are glass doors in the right and left walls, and two arches right and left center in the back wall. There are glass double doors in these arches, opening off; the draperies on these doors cut off the view beyond when the doors are closed. In the right center hall is a stairway leading to the upper part of the house; and the main entrance is off right. Beyond the left center arch is the conservatory. There is a window up right.

At right center is a davenport with a library table behind it; a stand above the right door and a table above the window; a hat tree in the hall together with a large lamp; a table and a chair up center; a table and two chairs in the room up left center; a table up left; a chair below left door; a table and two chairs left center; a heavy chandelier hangs from the ceiling. The chandelier is very ornate of the New York gas and electricity combined period.

In Act Two the room is decorated with orange trees in upper right and left corners. These are about eight feet high, with real oranges. There are smaller trees, poppies and other California flowers placed on the tables to give the room an atmosphere of California. Ribbons are attached to the chandelier and carried to the four corners of the room. The ribbons are orange in color with a small vine entwined around them, preferably bridal wreath or smilax. The left corner table has been removed and the chairs pushed aside. The left center doors are closed.

As the curtain goes up COHEN *is on the davenport. He has the funny part of the evening paper which he is reading with evident enjoyment.* MRS. COHEN *and* RABBI *are seated at table.*

COHEN *laughs.* MRS. COHEN *gives him a look and continues speech.*

MRS. COHEN: Yes, sir, I says to Isaac, says I, "Isaac call the doctor, I know ven I god a differend pain. Ven my indegestive tablets don't voik, I know how I veel!" [COHEN *laughing uproariously at the funny paper. The* RABBI *looks at him.* MRS. COHEN *is furious at this interruption. Continues with her monologue*] So Isaac he calls the doctor. [COHEN *laughs again, which interrupts* MRS. COHEN. *She looks at him then at the* RABBI] Such a foolishness! [*She gives* COHEN *another look which he doesn't see, so interested in his paper is he, then she turns back again to the* RABBI] Vhere was I?

165

RABBI: [*Impatiently*] Isaac had just called the doctor.

MRS. COHEN: Oh, yess! Und de doctor came und— [COHEN *laughs again.* MRS. COHEN *stops, looks at* COHEN *furiously.* COHEN *takes paper down from his face*] Will you stop dot laughin at nodings!

COHEN: [*Laughs to himself, vaguely hearing her, then it penetrates that he has been spoken to. There is a deep silence. He looks up.* MRS. COHEN *is looking daggers at him. The* RABBI *is trying not to laugh*] Huh? Vot? You speak to me, Mama?

MRS. COHEN: Such a foolishness! Laughing at nodings!

COHEN: [*Hurt*] Mama. I was laughing at Maggy and Jiggs. Such a vife!

MRS. COHEN: [*Sore now and ready for an argument*] Oh, so you voss laughing at the vife?

COHEN: No. No, I'm keeping up with Maggy and Jiggs. [*He picks up the paper again. His face beams as he starts to read. Reading*—"What a man— What a man, just like me."] Mama, listen. "You big walrus why don'd you go into some pizzness, instead of loafing all day; ged oud of my sight." Dod's Maggy vot she says. Und Jiggs he says, vid de cigar in his mout and his hands on his hips, "Vell" says Jiggs, "Maggy" dods the wife from Jiggs. "Vell," says Jiggs, "Maggy you soitantly kin tink of disagreeable tings." [COHEN *laughs. The* RABBI *is also interested*]

MRS. COHEN: [*Rises, with her face all set for a fight. Her mouth gathered together into a little knot*] Is dod funny?

COHEN: Vait a minute! [*Laughs*] Und Jiggs goes oud for a pizzness!

RABBI: Is that the one, Isaac, where he goes into business with Mr. Duem?

COHEN: [*Laughing uproariously*] Yess, und meets all the pretty girls. [*Crossing to* MRS. COHEN; *shows her paper and nudges her*] Und Maggy catches him making lofe to the stenographer. [*Laughing, goes back to davenport; sits*] Ain't that funny, Mama?

MRS. COHEN: [*Now thoroughly disgusted with both of them*] I'm dying with laughing! [RABBI *laughing at the thought of it.* MRS. COHEN *sits.* COHEN *looks at her; stops laughing, then picks up his paper, turns it over and looks at another page.* MRS. COHEN *looks at him satisfied she will not be interrupted again. The* RABBI *yawns behind his hand*] Vot vass I talking aboud?

RABBI: Your operation!

MRS. COHEN: Oh, yes, Where vas I—in the hospital?

RABBI: Oh, no. Isaac had just called the doctor.

MRS. COHEN: Und the doctor he came. Und I said—"good evening, Doctor." Und the doctor he say "good evening"—and—

RABBI: And did he diagnose the case as appendicitis?

MRS. COHEN: Like that. Didn't he, Isaac? [*There is a pause, then* COHEN *looks up*]

COHEN: Oh yes, sure, Mama. [*He turns back—then*]

RABBI: And did he operate immediately?

MRS. COHEN: No, he didn't want to.

RABBI: Didn't want to?

MRS. COHEN: He didn't want to. Did he, Isaac? [*Pause*] *Did he, Isaac?!!!!?*

COHEN: No.—No. [*Pause*] Didn't want to what, Mama?

MRS. COHEN: Didn't want to operate.

COHEN: Oh, the doctor . No. [*He turns back again to paper*]

RABBI: I sympathize with you, Mrs. Cohen.

MRS. COHEN: I tell you, Doctor Samuels, it is the woman what silently suffers.

COHEN: Yes, Mama—you were silent with the ether, but you haven't been silent ever since.

MRS. COHEN: Oh, I don't talk so much.

COHEN: Yes, you do, Mama. Always you talk about ether.

MRS. COHEN: I didn't say a word about the ether.

COHEN: But, Mama—

MRS. COHEN: Ssh—Isaac!!!

COHEN: All right, noo—

RABBI: I wonder what is keeping our good host.

MRS. COHEN: He went to find Sarah—someone called him on the phone, and Sarah couldn't hear the message. He's waiting for it to ring any minute. Poor Solomon.

COHEN: See. Why do you say "poor Solomon," Mama? He ain't poor.

MRS. COHEN: Papa—always you—argue—

COHEN: But, Mama. Poor is arem and arem is poor. If he ain't arem how can he be poor—

MRS. COHEN: But why should you always argue— *Shweig Shtill!*

RABBI: You know—we three might help Solomon—

MRS. COHEN: How?

RABBI: Have you ever tried concentration?

COHEN: Concentration?

RABBI: I mean, keep quiet—not talk.

COHEN: Mama did vonce, but it didn't agree vid her.

RABBI: I mean to concentrate, to think!

MRS. COHEN: All I can think of vos dod operation.

RABBI: If we three concentrate, think, all together, that we want that telephone to ring again and relieve Solomon's mind about Abie it might result successfully.

COHEN: If it does, I'll concentrate on a million dollars.

MRS. COHEN: Let's try. It don't cost nothink!

RABBI: Very well! Now for one minute think hard that you want *that* telephone to ring.

[*All sit thinking. Fifteen seconds pass; the clock strikes one, all sit up nervously.* COHEN *assumes a pose of "The Thinker."* MRS. COHEN *looks at the time*]

MRS. COHEN: How early it iss of late!

RABBI: Concentrate, *my friends! Concentrate!*

[COHEN *repeats "Thinker" pose. All sit again quietly. The doorbell rings violently.* SOLOMON *enters. He is a good natured man with a round Jewish face. Hard work has made him older than his years, but hard luck has only softened his nature. He is a prosperous business man now, but still wears his comfortable old clothes of his other years. He is not stingy, but having known the want of things in days gone by he wastes nothing extravagantly*]

SOLOMON: Vos dod the phone? [*Sees the* RABBI]

MRS. COHEN: No. Mr. Levy, dot vas the doorbell.

SOLOMON: [*To* MRS. COHEN] Thank you. Hello, Doctor Samuels; glad to see you! Eggscuse me blease! Sarah can't hear a void over the phone and she can'd hear the doorpell any more—keeps me busy running my servants' errands. [*Doorbell rings again*] Hello, Isaac. [*He exits quickly*]

MRS. COHEN: Why he don't discharge Sarah is more than I could learn.

COHEN: Poor Solomon! He's worried about Abie. [*This is to the* RABBI] He vosn't to the store all day!

MRS. COHEN: Sowin' his vild oats!

RABBI: Nonsense. I know his son Abie as well as I know his father, and if Abie has been away from the store all day, he has had a very good reason, you'll see.

MRS. COHEN: Dod's *vod you say!* [*She squints her eye knowingly. The telephone rings,* SOLOMON *rushes in like mad*] Yess, dod vos the phone dod time, Solomon. [*She says this in a most sympathetic manner as much as to say "poor thing, I pity you."*]

SOLOMON: [*Grabs the telephone, picking it up*] Thank God! [*He has the receiver off the hook by this time*] Hello! Who iss it? Yes vot? Me! Yes, it's me! Who am me? Say who am you? What number? I don't know the number! I didn't get the phone to call myself! Oh, Abie wishes to speak vid his fadder? Pud him on! [*To* RABBI] Abie. [SOLOMON *laughs at others.* MRS. COHEN *makes a knowing face at* COHEN, *they are all interested.* SOLOMON *seems very angry at the telephone*] Hello! Iss dod you? Oh, it iss? Vell you—you—loafer! V-here have you been all tay and vot iss it? I've a good notion to—Vot? Huh? A vod vid you? You vont to bring a lady home to dinner? [*He turns to* COHEN *and winks, belying his bad humor. In a whisper, as though* ABIE *could hear*] He vonts to bring a lady home to dinner! [*Then back to the telephone again*]

COHEN: [*To* SOLOMON, *who with his eyes warns of* MRS. COHEN's *presence*] Oy, I can't wait! [*Turns around, sees* MRS. COHEN—*and is squelched*]

SOLOMON: Vot, I didn't heard you—say it twice! Oh, she's a very sweet girl? Oh, I vill, vill I? [*He turns to them again*] He says I'll like her! She's a sveet girl. [*Then immediately back into telephone*] Jewish? [*He smiles and turns to them again*] He says, vait till I see her! [*Then back in the telephone again*] You little goniff—I smell a mices! Sure! I'll tell Sarah. Goodbye, Abie, goodbye. [*He hangs up receiver. They all sit waiting for him to tell them everything*] Ha, ha, peoples, my Abie's got a girl. Maybe the good Rabbi will soon officiate at a wedding. Eh?

COHEN: Is she Hebrew?

SOLOMON: Of course. Hebrew. Jewish Hebrew. [*He is delighted. He nudges* COHEN] Abie says, vait till I see her! [*Turns to* RABBI] Doctor Samuels— "Lieber Freund"— Maybe we'll all be goin' to a vedding soon! Yes!

COHEN: Solomon, why are you trying to get Abie married? He's happy.

MRS. COHEN: You mean to say he wouldn't be happy if he was married?

COHEN: Mama, can't I talk at all?

RABBI: Oh, Isaac didn't mean to infer he isn't happy. He is happy, aren't you, Isaac?

COHEN: Perfectly.

SOLOMON: No, it isn't the idea that I want my Abie married exactly, but I want his grandchildren.

COHEN: You don't want him to get married. But you want him to have children. Mama, listen to that.

MRS. COHEN: Isaac, you don't know what Solomon means.

COHEN: Sure, I do, he—

MRS. COHEN: You don't understand a word he says—

COHEN: Concentrate, Mama, concentrate.

SOLOMON: Yes, Isaac. I want grandchildren—dozens of them.

COHEN: Right away you talk wholesale.

SOLOMON: You see before my Abie was born, Rebecca and I we always used to plan for him. I wanted him to be a politician. Rebecca says, "No, Solomon. I want my boy—our son—to stay close by his father."

COHEN: And he certainly has.

SOLOMON: Yes.

RABBI: Yes, I don't know what your business would have done without him.

SOLOMON: Neither do I. But don't tell him I said so.

MRS. COHEN: Why don't you take him into the firm?

RABBI: Right. Solomon Levy and Son—that wouldn't sound bad at all.

SOLOMON: *That's* just exactly what I am going to do. When he's married— not before.

RABBI: Why must you wait until he's married?

SOLOMON: Did you ever see any of Abie's girls?

RABBI: No.

SOLOMON: Not one Jewish and my Abie is not going to marry anyone but a Jewish girl if I can help it.

COHEN: Maybe you won't be able to help it.

SOLOMON: Who said it, not be able to help it? Let him try and you'll see how I could help it.

MRS. COHEN: Are you sure that this new girl is the right one?

SOLOMON: Didn't he say wait till I see her? Oh, what a relief when I'll see that son of mine safely married. I must tell Sarah dinner for three—

MRS. COHEN: [*Rises and starts to go*] Ve must be going.

SOLOMON: Den please come back later and take a look at her.

MRS. COHEN: If ve can, ve vill.

COHEN: Vhy can't we, Mama? [*Rises*]

MRS. COHEN: [*To* COHEN] Because I'm awfully tired and you ought to go to bed early.

COHEN: [*Crestfallen*] See—she's tired, and I got to go to bed early. [*Going out through hall followed by* MRS. COHEN]

RABBI: [*Starting for the door*] I'll drop in later, Solomon.

SOLOMON: Goodbye, peoples, goodbye, and don't forget. When my Abie says a thing you can build a bank on it. [*To photograph on table*] Abele, Boyele meiner.

> [SOLOMON *takes out cigarette paper, puts in two pinches of tobacco, singing "Masseltof" as he reaches left center door, moistens cigarette, causes discord in song, and exits.* ABIE *enters the room from right center cautiously looking about, then he beckons to* ROSE MARY *who enters after him. They are both nervous and frightened.* ABIE *looks upstairs, listens a moment, then comes down to door left, opens it, listens, then closes it carefully, not making any noise. He goes to door right and repeats business, then back to arch*]

ABIE: Well, the coast is clear.

ROSE MARY: Oh, Abie, I'm so frightened!

ABIE: With a perfectly good husband to protect you?

ROSE MARY: Oh, I forgot!

ABIE: [*Takes her in his arms*] You haven't been married long enough yet to be used to it. Let's see— [*Looks at his watch*] Just one hour and thirty-three minutes. Do you realize, young lady, you are no longer Rose Mary Murphy? You are Mrs. Abraham Levy.

ROSE MARY: Mrs. Abraham Levy! Glory be to God!

ABIE: Isn't it wonderful?

ROSE MARY: Abie, we will both be disowned.

ABIE: Well, that's better than being separated for the rest of our lives, isn't it?

ROSE MARY: [*Hesitating over it*] Yes.

ABIE: Why do you say it that way?

ROSE MARY: I am not so sure that they won't try to separate us.

ABIE: Oh, yes, try. But we're not going to let them. Are we?

ROSE MARY: No.

ABIE: [*Takes her in his arms*] We were married good and tight by a nice Methodist minister.

ROSE MARY: "Till death do us part."

ABIE: [*Breaks embrace and takes her hands*] Oh, that reminds me, why did you refuse to say "I do" to the obey me?

ROSE MARY: [*With a slight brogue, smiling*] Shure—I'm that Irish!

ABIE: I didn't balk when he said "repeat after me, With all my worldly goods I thee endow." You know it's fifty-fifty.

ROSE MARY: To be sure it is. Faith, you haven't any worldly goods and your father is liable to disown you when he finds out you haven't married a nice little Jewish girl.

ABIE: So is your father, when he finds out you haven't married a nice little Irish boy.

ROSE MARY: [*With true Irish foresight*] That would be fifty-fifty.

ABIE: You know, Rose Mary, I was just thinking.

ROSE MARY: You are liable to have to do a whole lot of thinking, so you had better get into practice. [*Sits on davenport. He sits with her*]

ABIE: No, in all seriousness, Rose Mary, you know I'm sure Father will be crazy about you.

ROSE MARY: [*Lapsing into brogue*] He might be crazy about me all right, but when he hears about "me religion" he'll be crazier.

ABIE: Silly, isn't it, to be so narrow-minded. Well, he can't any more than tell us to go, can he?

ROSE MARY: But Abie—you work for your father!

ABIE: Yep! [*Sighing*] And if you don't make a hit with him, I'm liable to lose my job. I should worry. I'll find another.

ROSE MARY: And if you lost your job I'll have to do my own housework, and learn to cook.

ABIE: You can fry eggs, can't you?

ROSE MARY: I can, but I can't turn them over.

ABIE: [*With his arm around her*] I'll turn them over for you. [*She cuddles close to him, forgetting for an instant what is coming*]

ROSE MARY: Oh, Abie! Will you always be willing to do so much for me?

ABIE: Always!

ROSE MARY: Abie!

ABIE: Yes, dear?

ROSE MARY: Wouldn't it be wonderful if our fathers would take our marriage nicely!

ABIE: Wonderful!

ROSE MARY Then we wouldn't have to worry about a thing. You could go on with your job—and—

ABIE: Now, you stop worrying about that, dear. I'm sure Father will fall in love with you as I did, on first sight.

ROSE MARY: Abie, you're a dear! You know sometimes [*Lapsing into brogue*] I think you've a bit of Irish tucked away in you somewhere. Faith, I believe you're half Irish.

ABIE: [*Right back to her with a brogue*] To be sure Mavourneen, my better half is Irish.

ROSE MARY: [*Laughing*] And my better half is Jewish.

ABIE: What could be sweeter? [*Kiss. In embrace,* SOLOMON *sings off left*] That's Father!

ROSE MARY: [*Frightened. Both rise*] Oh, Abie!

ABIE: Don't weaken, dear! And no matter what he says, remember he's a peach when you get under his skin.

ROSE MARY: I hope it isn't a long way under.

　　　[SOLOMON *enters. He sees* ABIE—*does not see* ROSE MARY, *who is standing back of* ABIE. SOLOMON *singing* "Oi—oi—"]

ABIE: [*Trying to be casual*] Hello, Dad.

SOLOMON: Vell? [*Stopping short*] You loafer! Vhere hafe you peen all afternoon?

ABIE: Away. [*Crosses to* SOLOMON. ROSE MARY *follows close behind, unseen by* SOLOMON]

SOLOMON: Is dod an excuse— Away?

ABIE: Certainly not, but—

SOLOMON: [*Not letting him get a word in edgeways*] Und de pizzness! Pi! Such a day! Vid everybody esking for you.

ABIE: Missed me, eh, Dad?

SOLOMON: [*Angrily*] Loafer! [*On word "Loafer"* ROSE MARY *quickly sneaks to arch and watches the two from behind draperies.* ABIE *tries to find* ROSE MARY *with hands behind him*] Nobody vants me to vait on dem. It's "Vhere is Abraham, Mr. Levy? Vhere you son iss, Mr. Levy? No tank you, Mr. Levy. I'll vait for your son, Mr. Levy, he knows eggsactly vot I vant, Mr. Levy." All tay long! Abie, I'm not going to stand for this nonsense—

ABIE: [*With a winning smile*] Now, Dad—

SOLOMON:]*Holds* ABIE *off, and looks at him fondly, then he hugs him to him*] Abie—Boyele meiner—

    [ROSE MARY *enters laughing; comes down center.* SOLOMON *sees* ROSE MARY, *who has been standing watching this scene intently. He looks at her first as if he cannot believe his eyes—drops* ABIE *and steps back. Her smile fades*]

ABIE: Dad—this—is the lady I just phoned you about. [*Looking at* ROSE MARY —*then back again at his father. Taking* ROSE MARY *by the hand and leading her to his father*] Dad, I want you to meet a very dear friend of mine!

SOLOMON: [*Looks at* ROSE MARY *skeptically*] Who's de name blease?

ABIE: [*Ignoring the question*] I met her just before the Armistice was signed!

SOLOMON: [*Not at all friendly*] Iss dod so?

ROSE MARY: Yes, in France!!

    [ABIE *and* ROSE MARY *do not know what to say*]

SOLOMON: A trained nurse, dod's a pizzness!

ROSE MARY: Well, I wasn't exactly a trained nurse.

SOLOMON: [*Looking at her skeptically*] No? Well, I had a trained nurse vonce and she wasn't eggsactly von either.

ABIE: [*Trying to break the tenseness of the situation*] She was an entertainer, Dad. You know, keeping the boys' minds off the war. Making it easier for them, you know!

SOLOMON: Yes, I know. [*Looking at* ROSE MARY'S *prettiness and believing it*]

ROSE MARY: I used to sing for the boys in back of the lines.

SOLOMON: Oy—an actress!

ROSE MARY: Mercy, no!

ABIE: [*Impatiently*] Dad!

SOLOMON: Vell, you introduced me *vonce* to an actress. And believe me *dod* girl could act. Her name was O'Brien! Oi! Vod a name! [ABIE *backs up a step.* ABIE *and* ROSE MARY *exchange glances.* ROSE MARY *crosses to davenport*] I tought you vos an actress, too, by the dress.

ROSE MARY: [*Trying to laugh*] You think this dress is loud?

SOLOMON: It's not so quiet—und there ain'd much of id. [*He motions with his hands that the dress is short*] Maybe it shrunk!

ABIE: Of course, it didn't shrink. All the girls are wearing their dresses short this year, Dad.

SOLOMON: Iss dod so? Well, boy, your mudder always wore long dresses. [*Looking skeptically at* ROSE MARY'S *legs*]

ABIE: I'll bet if Mother were alive today she would be wearing short dresses, too.

ROSE MARY: [*Steps toward him*] It's much more sanitary, Mr. Levy. Long skirts trailing along the ground get full of microbes.

SOLOMON: The microbes would have some high jump to make dod hem.

[*She turns away*]

ABIE: [*Who is dreadfully ill at ease*] Never mind, Rose.

SOLOMON: [*Suspiciously*] Rose? Rose vot?

ROSE MARY: Rose Mary.

SOLOMON: [*Closing up like a clam toward her*] Dot's vot I thought.

ABIE: You thought what!

SOLOMON: Ven my son goes vid a girl, dot girl must speak the English language like a Jewess.

ABIE: Father!

SOLOMON: [*Sternly*] Still!!! [*Crossing to* ROSE MARY] I have nodings against you. I like Rose. I like the name of Rose. *Mary* might have been a grand old name, but I don't like it.

ROSE MARY: My name was good enough for my mother, sure it's good enough for me.

ABIE: Of course it is!

SOLOMON: Vell, tell me, vhere did you learn does Irish expressions? Sure!

ROSE MARY: [*Very proudly*] From my father.

SOLOMON: [*Now highly suspicious*] Hah! Iss dod so?

ABIE: [*Interrupting hastily*] Why yes, Dad. He was once an actor.

SOLOMON: *So?* Vell vot is *his* name? Is it Mary, too?

ROSE MARY: My father's name Mary?

SOLOMON: You just said your name vos Rose *Mary*.

ABIE: [*Interrupting hastily again*] His name is Solomon!

SOLOMON: Oh! Your name is Rose Mary Solomon?

ROSE MARY: [*Very indignant*] Certainly not!

SOLOMON: [*Quickly*] Oh, your father's *first* name is Solomon?

ABIE: [*Quickly*] Yes!

[ROSE MARY *looks at him—he is too fast for her—she gasps, so quickly has* ABIE *retorted*]

SOLOMON: Oh! Well, Solomon vhot?

ROSE MARY: Murphy—

[SOLOMON *looks at her quickly;* ABIE *interrupts and finishes before* ROSE MARY *knows exactly what he is doing*]

ABIE: [*Quickly*] Miss Murpheski.

SOLOMON: Murpheski! Say, dod's a fine nize name! Now there you are. [ROSE MARY *is so taken back by this interruption of* ABIE's *she is speechless*] At first I thought you vouldn't have a name like dod. You don'd look id!

ABIE: No, she doesn't, does she?

SOLOMON: [*Looking at* ROSE MARY] Faces are very deceiving! [*Smiling benignly for the first time on* ROSE MARY] Take off your coad, Miss Murpheski! [*He turns to* ABIE *very reprovingly*] Abie, I'm surprised at your inhospitality! Honest! [*He turns back to* ROSE MARY, *takes her wrap, looks at the material very closely, putting his glasses on to do so*] You buy fine materials, Miss Murpheski.

ROSE MARY: Thank you.

SOLOMON: Noo, Abe, voss shtaistie vie a laimener goilem. Hang it up. [*Gives coat to* ABIE. ABIE *takes coat to hall, hangs it up and returns*] Sit down, Miss Murpheski. Ay, ay, ay! [*Sitting on davenport*] Dod's some ring you are varing, yes? [*Breathes on ring.* ABIE, *standing behind davenport, makes motions over* SOLOMON's *shoulder to* ROSE MARY]

ROSE MARY: Yes, my father gave me that.

SOLOMON: Oh, your papa! [*After* ROSE MARY *has seated herself he settles himself back contentedly for a chat*] So you and Abie have known each odder a long time, eh?

ROSE MARY: Oh, yes. We met in France! Your son's a wonderful hero, Mr. Levy, do you realize that?

SOLOMON: Ain'd he my son? How could he be anything else? [SOLOMON *smiles on him proudly*]

ABIE: With such a father, eh! Dad? [ABIE *is kidding, but* SOLOMON *hasn't that kind of a sense of humor*]

SOLOMON: Dod's vhat I *say!*—You know every time dot— [*He turns to* ROSE MARY, *rising, offering his hand*] Oi! I'm pleased to meet you, Miss Murpheski!

[*This comes as a surprise to* ROSE MARY. SOLOMON *goes to* ABIE]

ROSE MARY: Thank you.

SOLOMON: Abie, ve must esk Miss Murpheski to stay to supper, yes?

ABIE: I phoned you that she would stay to dinner.

SOLOMON: Oh, yes, dod's so.

ROSE MARY: I don't want to be any trouble.

SOLOMON: *Nod* at all! Miss Murpheski. Eggscuse me, I'll speak to Sarah. Murpheski! Abele boyele meiner! Murpheski!

[*He exits, leaving* ROSE MARY *and* ABIE *together.* ROSE MARY *turns to* ABIE *furiously*]

ROSE MARY: [*Rises*] Murpheski!

ABIE: Rose Mary, I just had to do it. I saw that he wasn't even going to give himself a chance to like you.

ROSE MARY: I don't want him to like me! Murpheski! Oh, Shades of St. Patrick!

ABIE: [*Trying to calm her*] Rose Mary, dear—

ROSE MARY: He even objects to my first name. First thing I know you'll be calling me Rebecca!

ABIE: Ssh! He'll hear you.

ROSE MARY: I want him to hear me! I was never so insulted in my life. Sure, Murphy's my grand name—I don't know why you had to tack "ski" on to it. [*Crying*]

ABIE: I know, dear, but if I had told him your name was Murphy we wouldn't have had a chance. It's our happiness *I'm* fighting for!

ROSE MARY: But he'll have to know some day that I'm Irish!

ABIE: I have a grand idea.

ROSE MARY: If it's anything like the last few you've sprung on me, please don't tell me. [*Sits on davenport*]

ABIE: [*Slight pause—then sits beside her*] Listen! You love me, don't you? [*Pause*]

ROSE MARY: Ah, Abie darling, that's the trouble, I do love you.

ABIE: [*Embraces her—slight pause*] And you want our married life to be a happy one, don't you?

ROSE MARY: It's going to be, I can see that much from here.

ABIE: Then listen, dear, let him think your name is Murpheski. Make him like Miss Murpheski, then maybe Miss Murpheski can persuade him to open his heart a little bit to Miss Murphy. See what I mean?

ROSE MARY: You mean, I'm to let him think I'm Jewish until he likes me?

ABIE: Yes.

ROSE MARY: If he learns to like me, you think he might sanction our marriage?

ABIE: I'm sure of it. You know when you married me this morning you took me for better or for worse.

ROSE MARY: This is the worst I ever heard of.

ABIE: I'd do as much for you. You know your father isn't going to be easy either.

ROSE MARY: Don't remind me of my father at this minute. Your father is enough trouble for one day.

ABIE: That's what I say, dear, let's win my father over to our side, then when your father comes on from California, we'll have my father to help win your father.

ROSE MARY: You don't know my *father*—[*They kiss*]

SOLOMON: [*Enters*] Vell, dod's dod! [*Smiling again upon them, they stop kissing—look a bit uneasy and separate as they turn to him*] Go right ahead, don't let me interrupt!

ABIE: [*Rising*] Oh, Dad, come over here—I want you to know Miss Murpheski better. [*Brings him to davenport*]

SOLOMON: [*Sits on davenport*] Vell, dod's fair enough! I am glad of vone thing today! [*Both look at* SOLOMON *expectantly*] Dod you ain't an actress—!

ROSE MARY: Then I'm glad I'm not, too!

SOLOMON: What do you do for a living?

ROSE MARY: [*The question has been fired so quickly at her she is stunned*] Nothing.

SOLOMON: *Dod's* a great way to live. I don't believe in it.

ROSE MARY: My father never would let me work. I must study.

SOLOMON: [*Smiling again*] Your father he has money!

[*All this time,* ABIE *is fidgeting about, embarrassed*]

ABIE: He's in business on the Coast.

SOLOMON: Vat business, Abie? Cloiding?

ROSE MARY: No, contracting!

SOLOMON: [*Immediately freezing again*] Murpheski—contracting?

ABIE: Contracting for clothes.

SOLOMON: What!

ROSE MARY: [*Getting* ABIE'S *meaning quickly*] Yes, contracting for clothes.

SOLOMON: Contracting for— Oh, yes, yes, I know. I know. I must—look him up. [*Pleased at this—takes out notebook, writes*] Look him up. You know a lod aboud her father's business, Abie. [*Jokingly*]

ABIE: Why, I know what Miss Murpheski has told me.

SOLOMON: Vell, the cloiding is a good pizzness. [ABIE *and* ROSE MARY *exchange glances, both are nervous and trying to make a hit*] Abie!

ABIE: Yes, Dad?

SOLOMON: Vhy didn't you speak before of Miss Murpheski to me?

ABIE: Oh, I don't know.

SOLOMON: [*Nudges* ROSE MARY] I hate to tell you, Miss Murpheski, never before has Abie had such a nice little Jewish girl.

ROSE MARY: [*Trying to laugh*] Is that so?

SOLOMON: You tell 'em! But, Rose Mary—that's a fine name for a Jewish girl. Rose Mary!

ABIE: Why don't you tell Dad how you got the Mary part of it.

SOLOMON: [*Turning to* ROSE MARY] Vod does he mean got the Mary's?

ROSE MARY: [*Not knowing what* ABIE *is thinking of saying*] Why you see, Mr. Levy— You tell him, Abie.

ABIE: [*Short embarrassed pause*] Well, you see, Dad, her name is really Rosie!

SOLOMON: [*Smiling broadly*] Rosie! Vell, I thought so!

ABIE: Rosie Murpheski!

SOLOMON: Yeh, but the Mary's?

ROSE MARY: [*Coming to* ABIE'S *rescue, who is hardly able to come up for air*] Well, I thought Mary was such a pretty name, so I took it.

SOLOMON: Give it back! Rosie is a peautiful name. You don't need the rest of it.

ROSE MARY: All right, if you say so.

SOLOMON: [*This flatters him*] You hear dod, Abie? If I say so! Oh, Abele— [*Laughs*] I never knew you had such a good taste. [*Looking at* ROSE MARY *and pinching her cheek*] And Abie—has known you ever since the Var?

ROSE MARY: Yes—but you see I live in California. I went home as soon as I came back from France.

SOLOMON: Are you visiting somebody here now?

ROSE MARY: No, I'm staying at the Pennsylvania.

SOLOMON: In the depot?

ABIE: Dad! The Pennsylvania Hotel!!!!

SOLOMON: Oi, such an expense! Abie right away quick you should get Rosie's trunk away from dod place.

ROSE MARY: But Mr. Levy!

SOLOMON: Tut—tut—tut! *This* is your New York home. I like you, Rosie. I vouldn't have you staying in such a hotel.

ABIE: But Dad, maybe Miss Murpheski prefers to stay in a hotel.

SOLOMON: Nonsense! Rosie stays here, where she can get some nice Kosher food. [*Turns to* ROSIE] You like dod?

ROSE MARY: [*Isn't able to say anything to it*] I love it.

SOLOMON: [*To* ABIE] See, she loves it. I vouldn't think of letting her go avay from here. [*He turns to* ROSE MARY, *smiles—she smiles back—*ABIE *is frantic—but can say nothing*] Abie, run over to the Cohen's, and ask Mrs. Cohen if Mr. Cohen can come over. I want him to meet Rosie.

ABIE: Why not ask Mrs. Cohen, too. She's a peach, Miss Murpheski—you'd like her.

SOLOMON: [*Skeptically*] Yes. Esk *her*, too. She hasn't any appendix, but she's a nice woman.

ROSE MARY: Oh, I see—she's just been operated on?

SOLOMON: Yes. About three or four years ago. She'll tell you about it.

ABIE: You might as well hear it tonight and get it over with. She tells everybody.

ROSE MARY: I love to hear of operations.

SOLOMON: Then run along, Abie. And, Abie—

ABIE: Yes, Dad.

SOLOMON: Don't hurry back. Joke. Yes. [*He laughs at his own jokes all the time*]

ABIE: [*Laughs*] Dad, shall I ask the Cohens to stay for dinner?

SOLOMON: For vhat? We're not celebrating anything. A business for giving dinners for nothing. [ABIE *exits, going through hall, smiling.* SOLOMON *turns to* ROSE MARY. *Pause*] I don't know how Abie ever kept you a secred so long.

ROSE MARY: Well, we were afraid you wouldn't like me.

SOLOMON: Ain't dod foolishness?

ROSE MARY: Abie wanted to tell you about me.

SOLOMON: Abie, is it? [*Nudging her jokingly*]

ROSE MARY: Hearing you call him Abie—it came natural to me.

SOLOMON: That's right. Keep it up! I like to hear you call him Abie! He's a vonderful boy, my Abie!

ROSE MARY: Indeed he is!

SOLOMON: You like him?

ROSE MARY: Very much; he's a splendid man.

SOLOMON: You don't know the half of it. All by myself I raised him.

ROSE MARY: [*Softly*] Yes, I know. Abie told me his mother died when he was born. [SOLOMON *nods his head, "yes"*] My mother died when I was born, too.

SOLOMON: [*Turning to her*] Your father raised you, too? [ROSE MARY *nods her head.* SOLOMON *throws up his hands*] I can sympathize with him.

[*At this* ROSE MARY *is taken back*]

ROSE MARY: My father is a wonderful man!

SOLOMON: Of course he is, isn't his name Murpheski! What did Abie say his first name was?

ROSE MARY: [*Thinking quickly*] Why—Solomon.

SOLOMON: Solomon Murpheski! [ROSE MARY *quickly crosses herself*] I'd like to shake the hand of Solomon Murpheski.

ROSE MARY: [*With double meaning*] I wish you could.

[MRS. COHEN *enters. She is a tall good-looking woman, very well dressed*]

MRS. COHEN: Hello, Mr. Levy. Abie gave me the key and told me to walk right in.

SOLOMON: [*Rises, goes to her*] Mrs. Cohen—I vant you to know Rosie. Miss Rosie Murpheski.

MRS. COHEN: [*Crosses to her.* ROSE MARY *rises*] Miss Murpheski! I am glad to know anybody what iss a friend of Abie's

SOLOMON: Sid down, Mrs. Cohen. Make yourself homely. [MRS. COHEN *sits on davenport*] Oh, won't you lay off your furs for a minute?

MRS. COHEN: No, thanks, I have to be going in a few minutes.

SOLOMON: You von't feel the good of it. What's the use of havin' furs if you can't feel them when you go oud. [*Gets chair at back*]

MRS. COHEN: I always wear somthink around me in the house, ever since my operation— [SOLOMON *drops chair*] don't I, Solomon?

SOLOMON: [*Places chair, facing davenport. Paying no attention*] Yes. Yes— just think, Mrs. Cohen, Abie has known Rosie ever since the Var.

MRS. COHEN: Ve can blame a lod of things on the Var, can't ve?

ROSE MARY: I hope you won't blame the War for me.

MRS. COHEN Vat a nize pleasant blame. Did you go over?

SOLOMON: Dod's vhere she met Abie.

MRS. COHEN: Oh, you poor dear, what a lot of suffering you must have seen.

ROSE MARY: I did.

SOLOMON: Abie got shot in the Argonne. He laid in the hospital for weeks.

MRS. COHEN: I can sympathize with anybody in a hospital.

SOLOMON: [*Trying to stop her*] Yes ve know, your appendix was amputated.

MRS. COHEN: You know, Miss Murpheski, it started with a little pain, right here. [*Indicating her abdomen*] Or was it here—

SOLOMON: Make up your mind.

MRS. COHEN: Now come to think of it—

SOLOMON: Don't think of it, Mrs. Cohen. Forged it!

MRS. COHEN: I vish I could.

SOLOMON: So do I. [*She looks at him. He smiles, changing the meaning*] It would be so much better for you, Mrs. Cohen.

MRS. COHEN: That is just what Isaac says. [*She sighs*] But I can't.

SOLOMON: [*To* ROSE MARY] Isaac is Mrs. Cohen's husbands. He'll be here in a few minutes. You'll like him, von't she, Mrs. Cohen?

MRS. COHEN: Oh, yes, he's *just a husband—*

[ROSE MARY *is amused at their conversation. The doorbell rings*]

SOLOMON: Now I vonder who dod can be?

MRS. COHEN: Abie, maybe, he gave me his key. I forgod to leave the door open for him.

SOLOMON: [*Rises and puts chair back*] I'll have to answer it. Sarah is so deaf she can't even hear the *doorbell anymore.* [*Doorbell rings again*] Stop ringling. Can't you see I'm coming! [*He exits out into the hall*]

MRS. COHEN: Miss Murpheski have you ever had an operation?

ROSE MARY: No, not yet.

MRS. COHEN: Then you've never taken ether.

ROSE MARY: No.

MRS. COHEN: Dey had to give me twelve smells! I was in the hospital for three weeks. Oh, vat a time I had. Miss Murpheski, you should know vat I suffered after my appendix was oud.

ROSE MARY: I thought you suffered while it was in.

MRS. COHEN: And oud, too.

[SOLOMON *enters followed by* ABIE]

SOLOMON: Mrs. Cohen, Abie says Isaac will be right over.

ABIE: Will you give me the key to the front door, Mrs. Cohen, before we both forget it.

MRS. COHEN: Now vhere did I pud that key? [*Finds key on neck of dress*] Oh, here it is.

SOLOMON: [ABIE *and* SOLOMON *exchange glances*] Mrs. Cohen, vhy don'd you take off your fur?

MRS. COHEN: I'm a sight.

ABIE: We don't mind. Do we, Miss Murpheski?

ROSE MARY: I'm a sight myself. I haven't combed my hair since morning.

SOLOMON: Mrs. Cohen, vill you please take Rosie upstairs to the spare room.

ABIE: I'll show her where it is.

SOLOMON: You'll do nothing of the kind. Mrs. Cohen, you know the house as vell as ve do.

MRS. COHEN: [*Rising*] Of course I do. Come on, Miss Murpheski. You probably feel as dirty as I do.

ROSE MARY: [*To* SOLOMON] I would like to wash my hands and powder my nose a bit.

SOLOMON: Run along, Rosie. [MRS. COHEN *leads the way.* ROSE MARY *follows her up the stairs.* ROSE MARY *takes* ABIE's *hand in passing. Throws a kiss at him.* ABIE *looks after them.* SOLOMON *crosses to chair, sits, chuckling all the while—then says*] Abie—kim a hare—tzurn-taten. [*His father's voice calls his attention.* ABIE *comes and sits*] Well, my son, you're getting some senses at last.

ABIE: You like her, Dad?

SOLOMON: She's a nice girl, Jewish and everything.

ABIE: [*Not so sure*] Yeh!

SOLOMON: How much money has she got?

ABIE: Oh, I don't know exactly. Her father is comfortably fixed, that is all I know.

SOLOMON: And your father is comfortably fixed, too! [*Smiling knowingly*]

ABIE: What do you mean?

SOLOMON: You like her, don'd you?

ABIE: Do I! [*This speaks volumes*]

SOLOMON: Who could help it?

ABIE: Do you really like her, Dad?

SOLOMON: She's a nice girl. Didn't I told you to vait ven you brought all those girls around, those Christian girls? Didn't I say "Abie, vait—someday you'll meet a nize little Jewish girl." Didn't I say that?

ABIE: You did, Dad!

SOLOMON: Uh—Bahama, aren't you glad you vaited?

ABIE: I'm glad I waited for Rose Mary!

SOLOMON: [*Grabs his hand angrily, almost yelling at him*] Please don'd call her Rose Mary. [*Smiles*] She's Rosie!

ABIE: All right—Rosie! But I don't care what she is; it's the girl I like, not her religion.

SOLOMON: Sure—fine! You don'd care, but I care! We'll have no "Schickies" in this family. [*He hits table*]

ABIE: You mean to say if Rosie were a Christian you would't like her?

SOLOMON: Bud she isn't!

ABIE: Oh, piffle!

SOLOMON: [*Getting angry*] Don'd you peefle me!

ABIE: I didn't mean it for you—

SOLOMON: [*Hitting table. Paying no attention to* ABIE's *semi-apology*] I von'd be peefled!

ABIE: [*Meekly*] All right.

SOLOMON: No, sir!

> [ABIE *says nothing, sits with his hands deep in his pockets, hunched down in chair*]

SOLOMON: Positivil! Ein umglik mit dem ziem meinen zoog ich azoi zoogt er azoi shut up. [ABIE *still says nothing.* SOLOMON *talks long strings of Jewish, then awakes to the fact that he is arguing against the wind; he looks at* ABIE. ABIE *pays no attention—seems lost in his own thoughts*] Vy don'd you say something?

ABIE: There is nothing to say.

SOLOMON: Don'd argue with me. You get a nice little Jewish girl and you don'd hang on to her.

ABIE: [*With double meaning*] I'm hanging on to her all right!

SOLOMON: Yeh, all right vhy don'd you marry her qvick?

ABIE: Dad, have I your consent?

SOLOMON: Do you vant *me* to ask her for you?

ABIE: No. I can do that.

SOLOMON: Vell, do it, and—if she says yes, I'll start you in some kind of a business. What would you like?

ABIE: I hate business.

SOLOMON: You'll need a business ven you start raising a fambly! Esk Rosie! She's got a common sense!

ABIE: [*Apprehensively*] Say, Dad—don't mention anything about a family to Rose Mary.

SOLOMON: [*Grabs head angrily*] Oi—Ich platz. Didn't I just tell you not to call her dod Rose Mary. [*Smiles*] She's Rosie!

ABIE: All right, Rosie! But, say, please don't mention anything about a family to her, will you?

SOLOMON: Vat's the matter? She pelieves in a fambly, don't she.

ABIE: [*Nervously*] Why, I don't know. I've never asked her that.

SOLOMON: Vell, say, if she don'd, after you marry her make her change her mind.

ABIE: Well, it is just as well not to say anything to her about it anyhow.

SOLOMON: Sure! Ve know, don'd ve! [*Nudging* ABIE *in the side*]

ABIE: [*Uncomfortably*] Yes!

> [MR. COHEN *enters. He is an undersized little man, very much stoop shouldered, slightly bald, and absolutely dominated by* MRS. COHEN. *He is the direct antithesis of his wife. She is beautiful, big, and loud. He is undersized, quiet and—retiring*]

COHEN: Hello, Solomon!

SOLOMON: [*Rising and going to* COHEN—*very excited*] Isaac, my friend, congratulate me.

COHEN: What's the matter? Has somethink happened?

SOLOMON: [*Smiling blandly*] You should esk me! You should esk me!

COHEN: [*Smiling, too*] I am esking you. Abie, has somebody died and left him some money?

SOLOMON: Money—money—there are greater things in life than money.

COHEN: Vell, don't keep me in suspenses!

SOLOMON: Go on, boy—you tell him.

ABIE: [*Rising nervously*] Why, there is nothing to tell him yet—

SOLOMON: [*Angrily*] Vot? Nothink to tell! Ain'd you going to esk Rosie to marry you?

ABIE: [*Nervously*] Yes— [*Hesitating on the "yes" a bit*]

SOLOMON: [*Mimicking him*] Yes— Dod's no vay to feel.

COHEN: Rosie? Who iss it Rosie?

SOLOMON: [*Very expressively*] Oi! You should see Abie's Rosie! Such a hair! Such a teeth! Such a figure!

COHEN: [*Reprovingly*] Solomon!

SOLOMON: [*Turning again very angrily*] And dot schlimiel he's known her since de Var! They should have been married with the childrens py this time.

ABIE: [*Looking toward the stairs*] Ssh!

SOLOMON: [*Indignantly*] I von't be shushed.

COHEN: Vhere is Rosie?

ABIE: She's upstairs with Mrs. Cohen.

SOLOMON: [*Almost weeping, slapping* COHEN, *nearly knocking him over*] Isaac, I love dod girl! She's vine vife for Abie! Und dod loafer he won't esk her yet.

COHEN: Solomon, control yourself! Abie hasn't esked her yet, maybe she won't hab 'em.

SOLOMON: [*Immediately forgetting his sadness*] Vot! Nod marry my Abie! Look what's talking. Who could refuse my Abie. Ain'd he my son?

ABIE: Listen, Dad!

SOLOMON: [*Turning to* ABIE] Vell, I'm listening!

ABIE: Do you like Rosie?

SOLOMON: Isaac, listen to him after all I have—

ABIE: [*Interrupting him*] Now wait a minute!

SOLOMON: Oi! Such a talk!

ABIE: Do you want Rosie for a daughter-in-law?

SOLOMON: Do I vant a million dollars?

ABIE: All right, I'll ask her. But you are quite sure *you* like her?

SOLOMON: [*Smiling at* COHEN *blandly*] Ain'd dod a son to hev?

COHEN: Vell, Solomon, you hev been hard to blease! I'll say dod for you! Abie has prought you least a dozen girls I've seen my own eyes with.

SOLOMON: But dey vere not Jewish!

[*As though this statement was the Alpha and Omega. At this* ABIE *gets a bit nervous again*]

ABIE: [*A bit angrily*] Well, I want you both to know that I'm not marrying Rosie because she's Jewish—I wouldn't care if she were Turkish!

COHEN: [*At the word "Turkish"*] Vell, dod wouldn't be so bad!

SOLOMON: [*Looks sternly at* COHEN. *Pause. Turns to* ABIE. *Sternly*] But *I* vould care!

ABIE: Then you don't like Rosie for herself.

SOLOMON: Well, boy, I think I like her preddy vell, for vone day.

ABIE: [*The idea striking him*] Then the longer you know her the better you'll like her.

[MRS. COHEN *enters coming down the stairs followed by* ROSE MARY. MRS. COHEN *is talking*]

MRS. COHEN: And the doctor said he never saw a case like mine. My appendix was so small you could hardly see it! [ROSE MARY *smiles*. COHEN *rises*] Papa here. [*Motioning casually toward* COHEN] Thought he was going to lose his mama. Didn't you, Papa?

COHEN: Yès, Mama. Yeh, yeh—

SOLOMON: Rosie [ROSIE *does not recognize her name, continues to be deeply interested in* ABIE] Rosie [*Still does not turn. He calls louder*] Rosie! [*He is so loud this time they both turn at the noise. When they turn he smiles*] Rosie, don't you know your name?

ROSE MARY: Oh, I beg your pardon. [*She leaves* ABIE *and comes to* SOLOMON]

SOLOMON: I want you to meet a very dear friend of mine, Mr. Cohen, Mrs. Cohen's husband.

ROSE MARY: [*Holds out her hand which he takes*] How do you do, Mr. Cohen?

COHEN: So this is Rosie!

SOLOMON: [*Smiling delightedly*] Is she the same I told you?

COHEN: Also, and more. It's a pleasure— [MRS. COHEN *pulls his coat tail. He is looking at* ROSE MARY *full length. He looks at* MRS. COHEN *for a second. She pulls him onto the davenport*] I'm sure, to meet you. [*Ad lib, to* MRS. COHEN]

SOLOMON: You know, Rosie, ve vere talking aboud you while you vas gone.

ROSE MARY: [*Turning to* SOLOMON] How lovely! What were you saying?

SOLOMON: Ve vere saying vot a lucky man he would be, who god you.

ROSE MARY: Oh, thank you.

SOLOMON: If I was young enough—I vould try myself.

ROSE MARY: Oh, Mr. Levy, your blarney is wonderful.

    [ABIE *eases away*]

SOLOMON: [*Immediately changing. Grabs his head*] Please don'd say dod void to me. I never allow it to be used in my house.

ROSE MARY: Why! [*This is more an exclamation than a question. She is so surprised by the change*]

SOLOMON: I had once dealings with a fellow named Murphy and what he didn't do to me. Every time I hear dot void blarney it reminds me of dot Irisher.

ROSE MARY: [*Nervously*] Then you don't like the Irish?

SOLOMON: Could you like the Irish? I'm asking you?

ABIE: Dad!

SOLOMON: [*Turning to him*] Vot's the matter?

ABIE: You don't have to get so excited about it.

SOLOMON: I am not excited! [*Turning to* ROSE MARY] Could you marry an Irishman?

ROSE MARY: [*Looking at* ABIE *with double meaning*] No, I couldn't!

SOLOMON: There! Vot did I told you? You know, Rosie—[*Thinking he has won the argument*] Ven you marry, you get you a nize little Jewish boy what keep his Yom Kippur. [*He passes* ROSE MARY *over to* ABIE]

ROSE MARY: I intend to.

SOLOMON: You hear dod, Abie? [COHEN *and* MRS. COHEN *listening to all this and smiling benignly upon* ABIE *and* ROSE MARY, *too.* COHEN *nudges* MRS. COHEN *who nods as much as to say "It meets with my approval."*] She is going to marry a little Jewish boy, ain'd dod nize? [*He turns to* COHEN *for his approval.* COHEN *nods his head.* ROSE MARY *and* ABIE *are a bit embarrassed but cannot help themselves*]

MRS. COHEN: [*Rises*] Come on, Papa! Ve hev to hev supper.

SOLOMON: You are goink to hev supper here! I should let you go home! Never!

COHEN: Bud, Solomon—

MRS. COHEN: Shud up, Isaac, didn't you hear vot Solomon said, he invited us.

COHEN: [*Melting immediately, he knows he had better*] Oh, is dod so, tanks! [*Shaking* SOLOMON's *hand*]

SOLOMON: Mrs. Cohen, you run and tell Sarah you are staying and if she don'd like it, you fix it yourself.

MRS. COHEN: Sarah won'd mind, she likes me. Ever since my operation, she likes to hear about it.

SOLOMON: Tell her again! [MRS. COHEN *exits*] It looks like a party! Yes? [*Beaming on them*]

MRS. COHEN: [*Sticks her head through the door and yells for* COHEN] Isaac! Come here vonce, I vant you! [*She immediately exits, knowing her word is law*]

SOLOMON: Maybe she's got another appendicitus!

COHEN: I ain'd so lucky.

MRS. COHEN: [*Off*] Isaac, come here, I want you.

COHEN: Oh, Mama! Always you want something. I vantcha—*I vantcha*— [*He rushes to door and exits. The doorbell rings*]

SOLOMON: Now, who can dod be?

ABIE: Let Sarah answer the bell, Dad, you spoil her.

SOLOMON: She can't hear the pell!

ABIE: Then get somebody who can.

SOLOMON: And discharge Sarah?

ABIE: Certainly.

SOLOMON: I know, Abie, bud if I discharge Sarah she can't get another job. [*He exits*]

ROSE MARY: Oh, Abie, he's really a dear!

ABIE: Of course, he is, and so are you.

[*He looks around to see that no one is looking and takes* ROSE MARY *in his arms. He kisses her. As he does so,* SOLOMON *returns, followed by the* RABBI. SOLOMON *motions the* RABBI *to be quiet;* SOLOMON *beams. The* RABBI *looks at the lovers in their embrace. He cannot understand the situation; he looks at* SOLOMON *gesticulating like a mad man, he is so happy.* SOLOMON *comes further down into the room;* ABIE *and* ROSE MARY *still hold the kiss.* SOLOMON *cannot contain himself any longer, so he yells, almost scaring the lovers to death*]

SOLOMON: [*Looks at watch, counts five*] Time!

[ROSE MARY *and* ABIE *jump as though shot*]

ROSE MARY: Oh!

ABIE: Dad!

SOLOMON: [*Beaming*] Don't plush, Rosie! I kissed Abie's mama just the same vay vonce!

ROSE MARY: Oh, Mr. Levy! [*She goes to* SOLOMON's *arms—embarrassed to tears*]

SOLOMON: Call me Papa! [*He takes her in his arms. Her head is on his shoulder*]

COHEN: [*Enters. To* RABBI] Hello, Doctor.

SOLOMON: Isaac, my friend, Abie did it [*Shakes* COHEN's *hand, turning to* RABBI *as he does so*] Didn't he did it, Doctor Samuels? Didn't he did it?

RABBI: I don't know what you are talking about, Solomon.

SOLOMON: Didn't you see what I saw before we came into the room just now, vid Abie and Rosie?

RABBI: Oh, you mean the kiss?

SOLOMON: [*Turning to* COHEN *delightedly*] You hear vod he say! He saw the same thing. Oh, such a happiness!

COHEN: [*Opens door and yells at the top of his voice*] Mama! Quick! Abie did it! Abie did It!

ABIE: [*Embarrassed for* ROSE MARY; *also for himself*] Dad, please! [*He takes* ROSE MARY *in his arms*]

MRS. COHEN: [*Entering out of breath. She has on an apron as though cooking*] Isaac, what iss it?

COHEN: Abie did it.

MRS. COHEN: [*Sees the* RABBI] Doctor Samuels, what is it?

SOLOMON: Mrs. Cohen [*Beaming*] Abie asked her!

MRS. COHEN: [*Loudly*] Oh! You sveet child! Ven you going to be married by the good Rabbi here?

ROSE MARY: Rabbi!

SOLOMON: Next week!

ROSE MARY: Abie!

SOLOMON: [*Interrupting*] Oh, you can be ready by next week, Rosie! I'll get the trousseaus—the svellest in the city! I'll go to Greenbergs. He gives me a discount.

ABIE: But, Father—Rose Mary and I want to tell you—

SOLOMON: [*Incensed at the interruption*] Young man, whose vedding iss dis?

ABIE: [*Now thoroughly going*] It's mine!

SOLOMON: Den keep *quiet, I'll run it!*

> [SOLOMON *and* MRS. COHEN *go to the* RABBI *in consultation.* ROSE MARY, *in consternation, is gathered into* ABIE'S *arms trying to pacify her.* COHEN *is in the seventh heaven of delight as*]

CURTAIN

ACT TWO

> SCENE: *The same. With the exception that the entire room is decorated with oranges. There are orange trees of all different sizes. Oranges in bunches hanging on the walls which are festooned with orange ribbons. The place looks like a veritable orange bower.*
>
> TIME: *One week later.*
>
> AT RISE: ROSE MARY *in her wedding dress steals into the living room from upstairs making sure no one is there, she is very mysterious about her movements. Then she goes to the telephone, picks it up and calls.*

ROSE MARY: *Pennsylvania-6-5600.* [*Then she looks around cautiously again*] Yes, hurry please! [*There is a pause as she waits for the number*] Hello, hello! [*She seems very agitated*] Pennsylvania-6-5600. Information? Can you tell me if the 6:30 from Chicago is on time? [*She pauses*] One hour late, but you think it will make up some of the time? Thank you. Goodbye. [*She hangs up*]

ABIE: [*Enters, listening to* ROSE MARY, *placing his hat on table*] Rose Mary! [*She turns and sees* ABIE; *almost shrieks*] Why, what is it, dear?

ROSE MARY: You shouldn't see me in my wedding dress until we're married! It's bad luck [*She almost weeps—together with her agitation over the telephone*]

ABIE: [*Putting his arms around her soothingly*] Nonsense, it's good luck to see you at any time.

ROSE MARY: I know, but we should be very careful. It might be true.

ABIE: [*Laughing*] Well, I didn't see you in your wedding dress before we were married. You forget we've been married a week today. This is our anniversary. We're celebrating our wedding by being wedded again.

ROSE MARY: I forgot! Oh, Abie, it's been an awful week!

ABIE: I know it, dear! [*Holding her in his arms*] But it will soon be over.

ROSE MARY: Abie, Father's train is an hour late.

ABIE: Good!

ROSE MARY: But they said they would probably make up some of the time.

ABIE: We mustn't delay the wedding a minute.

ROSE MARY: If my father arrives before the Rabbi marries us, both your father and my father will prevent it.

ABIE: Mrs. Abraham Levy, you speak as if you weren't married to me at all.

ROSE MARY: I know, Abie. But your father wouldn't believe we've ever been married with only a minister officiating. [*Turns to him*] Neither would my father. My father won't even pay any attention to the Rabbi.

ABIE: But my father will. According to him, we'll be married good and tight this time. And it is all his fault, he has arranged every bit of it.

ROSE MARY: Then, please God, he doesn't find out I'm not a little Jewish girl until the good Rabbi ties the knot. [*Sits on davenport*]

ABIE: Amen! [*Sits beside her*]

ROSE MARY: The knot that we had tied a week ago, a little tighter. Abie, I'm getting awfully nervous!

ABIE: Now don't worry, dear. Everything is going to be all right.

ROSE MARY: What time is it?

ABIE: [*Looking at his watch*] Six-fifteen.

ROSE MARY: I hope Father's train doesn't make up any time!

ABIE: In fifteen minutes you will be married to me for the second time.

ROSE MARY: [*Fervently*] I hope so!

SOLOMON: [*Comes down the stairs. He is all dressed for the wedding. He has on a suit a trifle large. He walks down center, pirouettes.*] Abie—Rosie— give a look—a regular dandy!

[*They both rise*]

ABIE: Father, I told you to have that suit made smaller.

SOLOMON: [*Facing him*] Vot? I paid fifty-nine dollars and ninety-eight cents for this suit. Und den you vont dot I should have some of it out? No, sir. I vant all I paid for.

ABIE: But, it doesn't fit!

SOLOMON: I don't vant it to fit.

ROSE MARY: Abie, it's lovely.

SOLOMON: You hear. That boy has no idea of the money. I could hire a suit but he says no, und I buy this to please him und den he ain't pleased yet.

ABIE: Yes I am, Dad.

SOLOMON: Fifty-nine dollars and ninety-eight cents to wear a suit for von night. I could hire a suit for three dollars und save fifty-six dollars and ninety-eight cents.

ROSE MARY: Never mind; you look wonderful.

SOLOMON: [*Holding out his arms*] And how sweet you look! Oi! Such a bride! Abie, look at her. Look at her! Und den tank me!

ABIE: The Rabbi hasn't married us yet.

SOLOMON: He'll soon be here! Oi! I hope nothink happened to his texes keb!

ABIE: Father, please don't borrow trouble! I'm nervous enough.

SOLOMON: You're nervous! Vot do you tink I am? But I shall nod rest until I see you two lovers unided for life.

ABIE: Neither shall I.

SOLOMON: Unided you stand, divided you don'd.

ROSE MARY: Abie and I are never going to be divided, are we, Abie?

ABIE: [*She is in his arms*] I'll say we're not.

SOLOMON: Dod's de vay my childrens should speak up. Dod's de vay, Rosie! Vell, vod you tink of the decorations, you haven't said it yet. I did it all for you, Rosie.

ROSE MARY: They're beautiful.

SOLOMON: Does dod bring California back to you?

ROSE MARY: It certainly does. I love oranges.

SOLOMON: Now I'm glad now I couldn't get the blossams. You know this is more of an economical idea. Ven the wedding is over, we can *eat* the fruit.

ABIE: [*Reprovingly*] Dad!!

SOLOMON: [*Not getting the tone*] Vod do I care for expenses, ven it's all for my little Rosie. I told Cohen this vedding vos goink to be the svellest blow-up in the Bronx. [*He stops for a second*] I vonder if dos musicians have come yet? I ordered dem for a quarter past six.

ABIE: [*Looking at his watch*] It's only that now!

SOLOMON: Den they should be here.

ABIE: [*Nervous and a bit impatient with his father's chatter*] Oh, Dad, give them a chance!

SOLOMON: I'm givink them money; why should I give dem chances, a business with chances, dey should be here playing already!

ABIE: Not until after the ceremony, Dad. I'm too nervous for music just now!

SOLOMON: [*Teasing him*] Abie! For why are you nervous?

ROSE MARY: Abie, isn't it time to begin?

SOLOMON: But, Rosie, your father isn't here yet.

ABIE: [*Nervously*] His train is late.

SOLOMON: [*Sits in chair*] Den ve'll vait for him.

ROSE MARY: No—no! [SOLOMON *looks at her in surprise*] It's bad luck to wait, isn't it, Abie?

ABIE: Positively.

SOLOMON:[*Perplexed*] Yeh, but who vill give the bride avay?

ROSE MARY: I'll give myself away!

SOLOMON: Oi! I never did hear of such a talk!

ABIE: I know how to get around it!

SOLOMON: Giving the bride away?

ABIE: Yes.

SOLOMON: Ven the Rabbi esks, who gives the bride avay, you speaks oud of your turn and says, "Nobody, I take her myself!"

ABIE: Just tell the Rabbi to omit that part of the ceremony.

SOLOMON: Vat, leave oud somtink, ven it costs me so much money for the decoratings?

ROSE MARY: [*Pleadingly; hugs* SOLOMON] Please don't make us wait!

SOLOMON: [*Changing immediately*] Abie! You see she can't vait!

ABIE: I'm more impatient than Rosie!

SOLOMON: Never did I see such love. [*Doorbell rings.* ROSE MARY *and* ABIE *start nervously,* SOLOMON *smiles broadly. He rises*] Rosalie, maybe dod is your papa, our very good friend Solomon Murpheski! I vond to shake his hands!

   [*He exits, going to door. Slight pause.* ROSE MARY *almost in tears.* ABIE *reassuringly embraces her*]

ROSE MARY: Abie!

ABIE: Don't weaken! If it's your father— [*She starts*] We'll have to face it. That's all!

   [*Voices are heard out in hall*]

SOLOMON, MR. and MRS. COHEN: Maziltof! [*Leads the way in from the hall, followed by* COHEN *and* MRS. COHEN. ABIE *is standing with his arm protectingly about* ROSE MARY *waiting for the blow to fall*] Isaac, look!

COHEN: A regular tscotska.

SOLOMON: [*Very proudly*] Ain'd she a bride?

MRS. COHEN: [*Going to* ROSE MARY] My dear, your gown is beautiful!

COHEN: But, Mama, look vots in the gown.

MRS. COHEN: Isaac!!!! [MRS. COHEN *gives him a hard look*]

SOLOMON: Yess! [*Beaming—as doorbell rings again*] Rosie, mabe dod is de papa!

   [*He is delighted to think so.* ABIE *and* ROSE MARY *look almost frightened to death again*]

COHEN: Ain'd her papa here yet? [*Sits.* MRS. COHEN *sits next to him*]

SOLOMON: Answer the door, Abie, and leave it open so the peoples can valk right in.

> [ABIE *looks at* ROSE MARY. *She crosses herself surreptitiously.* ABIE *goes and exits*]

MRS. COHEN: Ain'd you afraid to leave the door open?

SOLOMON: Vid a vedding goink on? Nefer! Always leave the door open for veddings and funerals! It's stylish.

COHEN: Rosie, have you heard from the papa?

ROSE MARY: Yes, his train is an hour late.

MRS. COHEN: Musd ve vait an hour?

SOLOMON: Rosie von'd vait! [*Thinking this is a huge joke.* ROSE MARY *doesn't pay much attention to their chatter. She is back of the davenport looking apprehensively at the hall arch, thinking it might be her father*]

MRS. COHEN: Vell, I don't blame her. It's bad luck! Ve delayed our vedding fifteen minutes, und I always said, dod'd de reason I god my appendicitis!

> [ISAAC *puts hat under chair.* RABBI *enters followed by* ABIE. RABBI *goes to shake hands with* SOLOMON. ABIE *goes to* ROSE MARY]

SOLOMON: [*Disappointed*] Oh! I thought dod vos Rosie's papa! Hello, Doctor Samuels! Vell, I guess you is as much importance.

RABBI: Yes—I'm the one who does it.

SOLOMON: Vell, Doctor Samuels, do it vell!

RABBI: I will, Solomon, have no fear. [*Smiling*] Well, how are the Cohens tonight?

COHEN: [*Rises*] Perfect. Couldn't be perfecter.

MRS. COHEN: Isaac, speak for yourself! I have my own feeling, vod you don'd know aboud.

> [COHEN *is squelched and sits meekly*]

ABIE: Doctor Samuels, hadn't we better start things?

RABBI: I'm ready! Rosie, where are your bridesmaids?

SOLOMON: They're upstairs vaiting. Go on up, Rosie, you've god to come down vid them!

RABBI: Is her father here?

SOLOMON: No, his train is late.

RABBI: Then what is the hurry?

SOLOMON: Rose vonts to be married!

RABBI: Yes, of course. But who will give the bride away?

SOLOMON: That's just it!

MRS. COHEN: Isaac, you give the bride away.

COHEN: Sure, I don'd care.

SOLOMON: Sure, you don'd care. It don'd cost you noddings.

RABBI: Does that meet with your approval, Rosie?

ROSE MARY: [*Who is by now very nervous*] Oh, yes, yes!

SOLOMON: Vell run along den, Rosie!

ROSE MARY: [*Picking up her skirts preparing to go*] Goodbye, Abie. I'll meet you at the altar, if I'm lucky!

[*She rushes out and upstairs. They all look after her*]

SOLOMON: She's so afraid sometink is going to happen. I don'd know vod!

MRS. COHEN: She is nervous! All brides are! I remember I was dreadfully nervous. Vosn't I, Papa?

COHEN: Oh, yes, Mama! Bud you soon god over your nervousness, Mama!

MRS. COHEN: A vedding is almost as bad as an operation.

COHEN: Concentrate, Mama, concentrate!

[RABBI *is looking around room in perplexity.* SOLOMON *sees him, he swells all up again*]

SOLOMON: Vell! Vod you tink? Some decorations, yes?

RABBI: Splendid, Solomon, but why all the oranges?

SOLOMON: All for Rosie! She comes from California! Ve couldn't ged the flowers, so I ged's the fruit! Real California *Navy* oranges. *Ain'd* dod an idea?

COHEN: Peautiful! Significance!

MRS. COHEN: Are they sveet?

SOLOMON: Yes, bud don't eat them! If you ged hungry please vait!

COHEN: Solomon, I don'd know how you thought of it. You're a genius!

SOLOMON: Vell, my Abie vill only be married vonce.

[ABIE *glances at* SOLOMON *and exits*]

COHEN: Doctor Samuels, vod shall I do ven you ask for the bride?

RABBI: Well—

MRS. COHEN: Isaac, don'd led them know how already dumb you are yet!

COHEN: What you mean how dumb I am yet?

[*Ad lib argument*]

SOLOMON: Order—order—order—Mrs. Cohen, Isaac vonts to know!

MRS. COHEN: He's been married! He vent to his own vedding!

COHEN: I didn't vent. Dey took me. Doctor Samuels, what shall I do when you esk for the bride?

RABBI: Don't get nervous, Isaac, it is very easy. You'll know exactly what to do when the time comes.

MRS. COHEN: Pud me somevhere so I can nudge him.

COHEN: Mama, I don'd vont to be nudged!

[MRS. COHEN *gives him a look*]

SOLOMON: [*Looks disgustedly at* COHENS] Mrs. Cohen, I don'd tink anybody should be nudged at this vedding.

RABBI: [*Looking at his watch*] It is time to begin, Solomon.

SOLOMON: I'll tell them to start the moosic! They should be earning their money already before! [*He goes to door left*]

MRS. COHEN: Iss everybody here?

SOLOMON: You should see. I god it all fixed like a theater, everybody is seated holding the front seats to see the show good.

RABBI: Isaac you go upstairs and wait for the bride! You bring her down on your arm.

[COHEN *gets hat and immediately starts for the stairs*]

COHEN: The Bride! Sure! Fine!

MRS. COHEN: [*Follows him to arch*] Und Isaac, vait outside the door! [COHEN *exits upstairs, very quickly*] If I don't tell him, he goes right in by the bride. [*She exits left*]

[ABIE *enters*]

RABBI: [*Going over to* ABIE *and slapping him affectionately on the shoulder*] Good luck, son!

[*Music—"Oh, Promise Me"—starts softly*]

ABIE: [*Smiles at the* RABBI] Thanks!

[RABBI *goes to* SOLOMON, *pats him affectionately, and exits left.* SOLOMON *has been looking at* ABIE *affectionately, he goes up to him, puts his arm around him.* ABIE *gets hat from table and crosses to* SOLOMON]

SOLOMON: My little Abie! Sure it seems like only yesterday, I vos vaiting for your mama, just like you are vaiting for Rosie now. My son, I hope you can keep Rosie by your side until your hair is white like mine!!! My Rebecca didn't stay so long wid me. Only a little vhile—but no one couldn't take her place. I tink you lofe Rosie the same way.

ABIE: I do, Dad. I love Rosie better than my life.

SOLOMON: Dod's the vay, Abie! Und I lofe Rosie, too!

ABIE: I'm so glad of that, Dad! Will you always love her?

SOLOMON: Sure, why nod? Ain'd she Jewish and everything?

[*At this* ABIE *is squelched. The music stops.* RABBI *enters*]

RABBI: Solomon, everything is all ready and waiting. The best man is here!

SOLOMON: Iss it time for the moosic?

RABBI: Yes!

SOLOMON: [*Getting excited*] Vait till I gife the high sign! [*He goes to door left and waves his hand frantically to the orchestra which is offstage*] Go on—start to commence! Go on! Ve're waiting. [*Music begins, the wedding march*] There! Now vod do ve do?

[*The music softens*]

RABBI: Abie. [*Indicates* ABIE's *hat, he puts it on*] Now come. [*Exit* RABBI]

ABIE: Dad, I'm nervous as a cat!

SOLOMON: It vill soon be over. [*He slaps his back affectionately*] Don't be
nervous! [ABIE *exits left.* SOLOMON *is more nervous than* ABIE. *He goes to
table, gets his hat, puts it on, starts out left, then rushes to the foot of
stairs and putting his hand to his mouth, calls*] Isaac! Don't forget to
bring up the rear! Abie's goink in now! Come on! [*He runs about like a
madman. All of this time the "Wedding March" is being softly played off
left. The six* BRIDESMAIDS *are seen coming down the stairs. Then a* LITTLE
FLOWER GIRL *strewing flowers in front of the bride,* ROSE MARY, *who comes
down the steps on* COHEN's *arm, her eyes downcast.* THE BRIDESMAIDS *exit
left.* COHEN *and* ROSE MARY *with* LITTLE FLOWER GIRL *in front of them,
follow the* BRIDESMAIDS *off left.* SOLOMON *looks about, to see that they are
all in*] I guess dod's all! [*Puts on his hat and slowly crosses to door. As*
SOLOMON *gets to door, music strikes up loudly. Very pleased, he exits same
door, closing it behind him. The music is still heard playing through the
closed door. The room is empty. Only the music which finally stops.
There is another long pause. The doorbell rings one short ring. Then
there is another pause. Then the bell rings again, a longer ring. Another
pause. Then a long definite ring. Then voice is heard with a distinct
brogue in the hall*]

PATRICK: Come on in, Father. This must be the house. [*He enters, hangs hat
on tree.* PATRICK MURPHY, ROSIE's *father, enters the room, followed by*
FATHER WHALEN. PATRICK *is a big, burly Irishman, redfaced, brawny. The
kind who fights at the drop of a hat, but if appealed to in the right way,
would give his last dollar.* FATHER WHALEN, *the priest, is a good-looking
man of the scholarly type. Gentle, and kind. Irish, but of the esthetic
type*]

FATHER WHALEN: Patrick, we shouldn't enter a man's house without an
invitation.

PATRICK: This is the house all right. Didn't the children outside the door say
the wedding was to be here. [*As he starts away from* FATHER WHALEN, *he
spies the decoration of oranges; he looks about the place, blinking his
eyes to make sure he is not "seeing things"*] Father Whalen, do you see
what I see?

FATHER WHALEN: [*Looks about the room. He is surprised, too*] Yes!

PATRICK: What do you see?

FATHER WHALEN: [*Smiles*] I see oranges.

PATRICK: Dozens of them?

FATHER WHALEN: [*Surprised at this unusual feature*] Why, yes!

PATRICK: [*In sudden fear*] Glory be to God, Father, she's marrying a
Protestant!

FATHER WHALEN: Don't jump at conclusions!

PATRICK: I'm going to get to the bottom of this! [*He yells. Through door left*] Oh, Rose Mary! Rose Mary!!

FATHER WHALEN: Take it easy, son, take it easy!

PATRICK: Take it easy, with all them oranges staring me in the face! Rose Mary! Rose Mary!! [*Going to door right, opening it and calling*]

FATHER WHALEN: Patrick! You know love has never been a respecter of religion!

PATRICK: Who said anything about love? I'm talking about them oranges! [*To* FATHER WHALEN] I hate orange! 'Tis the color of the damned A.P.A.'s—Rose Mary! Rose Mary!

> [*The left door flies open and* SOLOMON *enters, closing the door behind him. Pantomimes* PATRICK *to hush.* PATRICK *walks down to him*]

SOLOMON: Shh! Sh! Shush, shush, please be quiet! You're interrupting the whole works!

PATRICK: [*To* FATHER WHALEN, *seeing* SOLOMON *and getting his dialect*] He's no A.P.A.

SOLOMON: [*Suddenly beaming*] Is your name Murpheski?

PATRICK: [*Not getting him yet*] What?

SOLOMON: Are you Solomon Murpheski?

PATRICK: [*Looking at* FATHER WHALEN *then back to* SOLOMON] Say, are you trying to kid me?

SOLOMON: No. I'm expecting Solomon Murpheski.

PATRICK: My name is Patrick Joseph Murphy.

SOLOMON: Gewald!

PATRICK: Not Gewald—Murphy! And I'm looking for my daughter. Is she here?

SOLOMON: [*Making a face at the name* MURPHY] Nobody by dod name is here. Voddo you vant?

PATRICK: I'm looking for the home of Michael Magee!

SOLOMON: [*Laughs*] Michael Magee! Listen to him! Efeter I've been telling you—

PATRICK: What is your name?

SOLOMON: [*Proudly*] Solomon Levy! Does dod sound like Michaels Magee?

PATRICK: Well, I'll tell the world it doesn't!

SOLOMON: Den please go vay!

FATHER WHALEN: Come, Patrick, I told you we were in the wrong house.

SOLOMON: [*Starts for the door left*] Absitivle! Close the door und lock id ven you go oud.

PATRICK: Wait a minute!

SOLOMON: [*Impatiently*] Oi, please be quick! It vill soon be over. Isaac is giving the bride avay. Und I vont to see it. It's the first thing in his life he ever gave avay, I'm telling you.

[*Laughs heartily.* PATRICK *walks slowly down to him*]

PATRICK: [*Laughs*] I'm very sorry. But I'm looking for my daughter. She is to be married tonight to a young fellow by the name of Michael Magee. I thought this was the address she gave me.

SOLOMON: No, sir! A girl by the name of Rosie Murpheski is marrying my son, Abraham Levy.

PATRICK: Ah, I see! Oh, but would you mind telling me, what you are doing with all the A.P.A. decorations?

SOLOMON: Oh, you liked id.

PATRICK: I'm not saying anything about that. But it seems very funny to have oranges for decorations.

SOLOMON: Vell, I tell you why! The girl's from California!

PATRICK: So's my daughter!

SOLOMON: Bud my son is marrying a Jewish girl!

PATRICK: My daughter is marrying an Irish boy!

SOLOMON: [*Almost shouting*] My son isn't Irish!

PATRICK: Well, my God! My daughter isn't Jewish!

FATHER WHALEN: Come, Patrick!

PATRICK: [*Turning to* FATHER WHALEN] But, Father, where can Rose Mary be?

SOLOMON: Wait a minute! [*In terror*] Did you say Rose Marys?

PATRICK: [*Coming close to him*] Shure I said it! That's my daughter's name!

SOLOMON: [*Suddenly grabbing his head*] Oi vey is mire! Do you suppose it could be true?

PATRICK: [*Looking at him in amazement*] What's the matter, are you having a fit?

SOLOMON: [*Pays no attention to* PATRICK, *but starts for door left, yelling at the top of his lungs*] Vait a minute! Stob it! Vait a minute! Stob it!

VOICE: [*Off*] Mas ameah, hoosen veim ha calo!

[*As* SOLOMON *gets to the door, the music starts up, which denotes the end of a Jewish ceremony.* GUESTS *cry "Maseltof," music plays*]

SOLOMON: [*Holding his head*] It's too late! It's too late! [*He staggers into a chair*]

PATRICK: What's that? Sounds like a riot!

[COHEN *enters. Does a wild sort of a dance*]

COHEN: Solomon, did you see me give the bride away?

SOLOMON: Vhere is Abie?

COHEN: He'll be here in a minute. Everybody is kissing the bride. Und, believe me, Solomon, she is some bride! I hated to give her away!

PATRICK: [*To* FATHER WHALEN] There is something wrong here?

COHEN: [*Seeing him; crossing to him*] Oh, is it a detective, vatching the vedding presents?

PATRICK: [*Turns to him*] I'm no detective! I'm a contractor!

SOLOMON: Oi! Oi! The contractor! [*Holds his head*]

COHEN: [*Advances*] Oh, you're the papa?

PATRICK: What do you mean, the papa?

COHEN: Don't you know bot iss it, a papa?

PATRICK: [*Raising his fist*] Don't you "papa" me!

FATHER WHALEN: [*Softly*] Control yourself, Patrick!

SOLOMON: Oi! Patrick!

COHEN: Abie heard the doorbell ring und he thought it vos the papa. He sent me on ahead to see for sure.

PATRICK: Abie! And who in the hell is Abie?

COHEN: He's your new son-in-law!

PATRICK: [*To* FATHER WHALEN] Did you hear that, Father? Abie! My new son-in-law! Well, that name better have an O or a Mac stuck in front of it!

COHEN: A Mac or an O in the front of a beautiful name like Levy?

PATRICK: [*To* FATHER WHALEN] My God! Did you hear that other name, Father? Abie Levy, my new son-in-law!

FATHER WHALEN: Sit down, Patrick, sit down!

[PATRICK *and* FATHER WHALEN *ad lib., both shaking heads and arguing, sit on davenport*]

COHEN: And a fine boy he is, too! He met Rose Marys when the Var vas here.

SOLOMON: Oi! Oi!

COHEN: Solomon, for why do you do dod? Oi! Oi!

[MRS. COHEN *enters. She is all aglow*]

MRS. COHEN: [*To* SOLOMON] Vod a vedding! Solomon, you have did yourself proud for vonce.

SOLOMON: Oi! Oi!

MRS. COHEN: Vod's the matter? Iss the expense worrying you already yet?

COHEN: [*Now thoroughly alarmed at* SOLOMON's *distress*] Mama, he's been doink dod since I came in, after the wedding.

MRS. COHEN: Solomon, heve you god a pain?

SOLOMON: I've god a sometink. I didn't vont, but now I've god it!

MRS. COHEN: That's the way I felt, too, about my appendix.

SOLOMON: It ain't my appendixes! I vish it vas!

MRS. COHEN: Solomon! If you vished it vas, you vish it vasn't! I know, I had the operation. Didn't I, Papa?

COHEN: Yes, Mama!

[*All this time* PATRICK *is looking on as though he would like to wring them all by the necks*]

FATHER WHALEN: Well, Patrick, if our Rose Mary has married this boy, we'll have to make the best of it!

COHEN: Sure! They are crazy aboud each other. Never did I see such love.

SOLOMON: They are both crazy!

COHEN: Solomon, Rosie is a wonderful girl. I vould take her in a minute.

MRS. COHEN: Isaac! [*She swings about her fan, just grazing* COHEN's *face*]

COHEN: [*Covering himself*] Vouldn't ve, Mama? [*Enter* RABBI]

MRS. COHEN: I vould take her in a minute, vouldn't ve, papa?

SOLOMON: I'd sell her for a nickel!

PATRICK: [*Rising*] You don't have to! I'm going to take her away for nothing.

SOLOMON: Oi! If you vould do me such a favor!

COHEN: But, Solomon, you had the Rabbi marry them yourself, for vhy have you changed?

SOLOMON: Esk him! [*Pointing to* PATRICK]

COHEN: [*To* PATRICK] Do you know?

PATRICK: I have a sneaking suspicion I do! [*Doubles up his fist*]

COHEN: [*To* MRS. COHEN] Mama, I don'd like dose sneaking suspiciousness!

[RABBI *goes to* PATRICK]

RABBI: Are you Rosie's father?

PATRICK: *Rosie's* father? [*Turning to* FATHER WHALEN]

SOLOMON: Oi! Oi!

RABBI: Why, Solomon, what is the matter, has something happened?

SOLOMON: [*Pointing to* PATRICK] Look at him! And ask me! I shall die from shame! His name's Murphy!

PATRICK: [*In a rage*] You'll die for shame at looking at me! Shure, you won't be able to see me, you won't be able to see anybody—you won't have room enough to open your eyes, your poor little abbreviated excuse for an apostrophe! [*Starts for* SOLOMON, FATHER WHALEN *stops him*]

SOLOMON: [*Rising, to* PATRICK] I didn't hear a word you said, but I'll get even for it!

RABBI: Solomon, don't do anything rash.

SOLOMON: Dod little Irisher! Marrying my son Abie against his vill. No vonder, she vouldn't vait. She vas afraid he'd back oud. The—the—the little—Irish A.P.A.

[*He exits left quickly.* PATRICK *starts right after him;* FATHER WHALEN *holding his arm*]

PATRICK: Let me loose, Father—let me loose.

FATHER WHALEN: Patrick, where are you going?

PATRICK: [*Breaking away*] I'm going after that little runt and make him eat those words along with every damned orange in this place! [*Exits left*]

COHEN: Come on, Mama! Ve god to help Solomon. [*Starting after* PATRICK]

MRS. COHEN: Isaac! Don'd bud in. If you come between them you'll get hit both vays! [*She exits*]

COHEN: [*Following her*] When I get through with that Irishman, I'll make him eat all the oranges in California!

[FATHER WHALEN *and* RABBI *look at each other for a second, then they smile*]

MRS. COHEN: [*Off*] Isaac! Isaac!

FATHER WHALEN: It looks like war between the Murphys and the Levys.

RABBI: Yes, I pity the young folks!

FATHER WHALEN: So do I. They are going to have their hands full. Poor Rose Mary!

RABBI: I feel sorry for Abie, too. He's a fine lad.

FATHER WHALEN: And Rose Mary's a wonderful girl. But what are we going to do about it?

RABBI: Seems to me, it's a little too late to do anything.

FATHER WHALEN: Yes, there is no use locking the barn door after the mare has gone. You married them, didn't you?

RABBI: Yes, and Solomon asked me to tie the knot good and tight.

[*He smiles at this.* FATHER WHALEN *laughs, too*]

FATHER WHALEN: [*Looking at* RABBI, *closely*] You know, your face is very familiar.

RABBI: I have been thinking the same of yours. You live here in New York?

FATHER WHALEN: No! California. I came on with Patrick for Rose Mary's wedding. [RABBI *indicates davenport.* FATHER WHALEN *sits and then the* RABBI *sits*] Have you ever been in California?

RABBI: No—never west of Pittsburgh!

FATHER WHALEN: And I have never been east, except during the War. I went over there!

RABBI: I went over there, too!

FATHER WHALEN: Maybe that's where we met.

RABBI: Most likely. That is where Abie and Rosie met—Abie did his bit. He was quite a hero.

FATHER WHALEN: Wounded?

RABBI: Very badly!

FATHER WHALEN: Shure, I have comforted a great many boys of your faith in their last hours when there wasn't a good rabbi around.

RABBI: And I did the same thing for a good many boys of your faith—when we couldn't find a good priest.

FATHER WHALEN: We didn't have much time to think of any one religion on the battle fields.

RABBI: I'll say not!

FATHER WHALEN: Shure, they all had the same God above them. And what with all the shells bursting, and the shrapnel flying, with no one knowing just what moment death would come, Catholics, Hebrews, and Protestants alike forgot their prejudice and came to realize that all faiths and creeds have about the same destination after all.

RABBI: [Shaking his head] True. Very true.

FATHER WHALEN: Shure, we're all trying to get to the same place when we pass on. We're just going by different routes. We can't all go on the same train.

RABBI: And just because your not riding on my train, why should I say your train won't get there?

FATHER WHALEN: Exactly!

RABBI: You know [Rises] I wish I could remember where I met you.

FATHER WHALEN: [Rises] I feel the same way. However, as long as we both feel that we have met before, we're old friends. My name's Whalen. John Whalen. [Holding out his hand cordially]

RABBI: And mine is Samuels! Jacob Samuels! [Taking FATHER WHALEN'S hand, clasping it warmly]

FATHER WHALEN: John Whalen and Jacob Samuels! [Laughs] Shure, 'tis almost as bad as Murphy and Levy!

RABBI: [Laughing, too] Yes, except that we're not married! [They both laugh heartily at this]

> [PATRICK and SOLOMON heard quarrelling off left. BRIDESMAIDS scream and rush on to RABBI; where he tries to pacify them. ROSE MARY dashes out of door. She stops on seeing FATHER WHALEN. Goes to him, throws herself into his arms]

ROSE MARY: Oh, Father Whalen!

FATHER WHALEN: There—there—child!

ROSE MARY: Can't you do something with Father? He's gone mad!

FATHER WHALEN: Such a pretty bride, too! [He looks around at the GIRLS] Faith, dear, you look frightened to death!

ROSE MARY: I have reason to be, Father! You ought to hear Abie's father and my father fight! Oh, such language!!

RABBI: Girls, wait in here, out of the way. It is just as well to keep out of sight of both fathers. Don't you think so, Father Whalen?

[*The* GIRLS *exeunt with bit of chatter*]

FATHER WHALEN: I do that! Shure, there's no use waving a red flag at a bull, unless you want more trouble.

[RABBI *closes doors after them*]

ROSE MARY: We couldn't have any more trouble!

RABBI: Oh, yes you can, my child—much more than this!

[ABIE *enters on the run; he stops on seeing* ROSE MARY; *takes a deep breath of relief*]

ABIE: Oh!—I thought you had gone! [*Goes to her*]

ROSE MARY: Isn't it awful?

ABIE: It's worse than I expected!

FATHER WHALEN: Is this Abie?

ROSE MARY: Oh, pardon me, Father—I thought you'd met him! Abie, this is Father Whalen.—Father brought him all the way from California to marry us!

FATHER WHALEN: [*Holds out his hand as* ABIE *hesitates, before he sees* FATHER WHALEN *is so cordial*] I'm glad to know you, Son!

ABIE: Father Whalen, I'm glad to know *you!*

RABBI: Where are the fond fathers?

[*Loud ad lib off left*]

SOLOMON: [*Off*] I tell you, don't push!

PATRICK: [*Off. A growl*]

FATHER WHALEN: Ah!

ABIE: There they are.

ROSE MARY: Oh, dear!

ABIE: It's all your father's fault, if he hadn't come, everything would have been all right!

ROSE MARY: It is not my father's fault! It's your father's! I never saw such a man!

[FATHER WHALEN *turns away, smiling*]

ABIE: My father is wonderful, he's just a little stirred up right now, that is all!

ROSE MARY: *All!* If he is only stirred up now, what is he like when he's really mad?

FATHER WHALEN: Here—here! Don't you two start to fight, too! [*Pats* ROSE MARY *on the shoulder*]

RABBI: That is just what the two fathers would like!

ABIE: There—there—Rose Mary, dear! Don't cry!

ROSE MARY: [*Crying*] But your father said he'd sell me for a nickel!

ABIE: [*Taking her in his arms*] But you don't belong to my father, you belong to me! And I wouldn't sell you for the whole world with a fence around it!

[FATHER WHALEN *and the* RABBI *exchange glances and smile*]

ROSE MARY: And my father said he was going to take me away from you and have the marriage annulled. He says that no rabbi cuts any ice with him!

ABIE: Well, the rabbi didn't marry him, he married us!

SOLOMON: [*Runs in; stops*] Abie, take your arm avay from her!

PATRICK: [*Entering after* SOLOMON; *stops, too*]

SOLOMON: No, ve just found out that you ain'd married at all!

RABBI: I beg your pardon. I have married a great many people—I know my business!

SOLOMON: No reflection, Doctor Samuels! It ain'd your fault this vone didn't took!

ABIE: What do you mean we are not married?

PATRICK: Her name isn't Murpheski! It's Murphy. Murpheski!! [*Making a face*] And another thing—that license you got isn't legal with that name on it!

SOLOMON: [*Smiling delightedly*] You see! Doctor Samuels, you merried Rose Murpheski—dhere ain'd no Rose Murpheski, so dhere ain'd no merriage! Oi! Vod a relief!

PATRICK: Rose Mary—take off that dress and veil! I am going to take you home!

SOLOMON: I'll send you a letter of tenks for it!

PATRICK: [*Looking down belligerently on him*] I don't want anything from you but silence, and plenty of that!

SOLOMON: All right! All right!

PATRICK: [*Turns back to* ROSE MARY] Rose Mary!

[*She hasn't moved from* ABIE'S *side*]

ABIE: She isn't going with you or anyone else.

SOLOMON: Abie, don'd be foolish. You ain'd married!

ABIE: Yes, we are!!

SOLOMON: Bud id didn't took! Esk anybody! They'll tell you the same thing! You married Rosie Murpheski. She ain'd!

RABBI: I'm afraid there might be some truth in what your father says, Abie!

ROSE MARY: We are married whether you like it or not! Aren't we, Abie?

ABIE: Yes, dear, and if this marriage didn't take—

SOLOMON: I von'd let you merry her again!

ABIE: You can't prevent it!

PATRICK: But I can!!

ABIE: Well, I married Rose Mary Murphy just one week ago today in Jersey City!

[ABIE *takes* ROSE MARY *in his arms.* SOLOMON *grabs his head*]

SOLOMON: Oi!! I nefer did like dod town!

PATRICK: Rose Mary, is this true?

ROSE MARY: Yes.

SOLOMON: Oi, such a headache!

PATRICK: Were you married by a priest?

[ROSE MARY *frightened—looks at* ABIE]

ABIE: No. By a Methodist minister!

SOLOMON: It's gettink worse!

PATRICK: Then you are not married!

ABIE: Well, try and take her away from me!

PATRICK: If you thought you were married so good and tight last week, why did you do it over again?

SOLOMON: To make it vorser!

[SOLOMON *and* PATRICK *look at one another as if to start another fight*]

ABIE: To satisfy my father.

SOLOMON: [*Getting furious*] To satisfy me! Say, do you tink I am satisfied? Look at me!

PATRICK: [*Shouting, staring toward* SOLOMON] You have nothing on me!

[SOLOMON, *frightened, goes to the* RABBI, *his hand on his heart*]

FATHER WHALEN: [*Crosses to* PATRICK] Patrick, as I told you before, you'd better make the best of it! The children have done all they could to satisfy both fathers.

PATRICK: Did they try to satisfy me? No! They get a Methodist minister first and a rabbi next—would I let a minister or rabbi marry me?

FATHER WHALEN: Well, marriages by ministers and rabbis are as legally binding as by priests or others!

PATRICK: They are not married!

SOLOMON: I'm going to phone my lawyer! [*He starts for the door left yelling*] Cohen! Oh, Isaac!

[PATRICK *follows him.* SOLOMON *exits*]

PATRICK: [*To* ROSE MARY] Get into your street clothes, young lady. Father Whalen, you see that she doesn't run away with him! I'm going after this poor fish and see what his lawyer has to say. They're not going to put anything over on me. [*Exits*]

[*This leaves* RABBI, FATHER WHALEN, ROSE MARY *and* ABIE]

ROSE MARY: [*Crying*] Abie!

ABIE: What is it, dear? [*Trying to soothe her*]

ROSE MARY: He doesn't believe we are married. He says it didn't take!

ABIE: But we are!

ROSE MARY: Oh, I told you we should have been married by a priest in Jersey City!

ABIE: Your father wouldn't be satisfied no matter who married us!

RABBI: Father Whalen, I wouldn't suggest it, but as long as the young folks have made a business of getting married, I don't think it would do any harm to marry them again in her faith, do you?

FATHER WHALEN: I don't think so!

ROSE MARY: Father Whalen, would you?

FATHER WHALEN: Where is the telephone?

ABIE: On the table!

FATHER WHALEN: I must get permission from my superior. [FATHER WHALEN *goes to telephone. Looks in address book for number. Then takes telephone*]

ABIE: But Doctor Samuels, why all this red tape?

RABBI: [ROSE MARY *goes to* FATHER WHALEN] Every great institution must have organization, my boy, and we must respect their rules and regulations.

FATHER WHALEN: Give me Vanderbilt zero, two, three, four. That's right. Vanderbilt, zero, two, three, four.

ROSE MARY: [*Nervously*] Suppose your superior says no?

ABIE: [*To* ROSE MARY] Suppose he isn't in?

FATHER WHALEN: Sssh— Hello—Vanderbilt zero, two, three, four? Is his Grace, the Archbiship in? Father Whalen from California, speaking. I'm sorry to trouble, but it's a very serious matter. Yes, yes, I must speak to him personally.

ROSE MARY: Tell him to hurry. Father will be here any minute!

RABBI: Father Whalen, there is a phone extension in the other room. You had better talk from it.

ABIE: But they are liable to want to use this one, and then they'll hear!

RABBI: I'll guard this phone, until the matter is settled one way or the other. [*To* ABIE] Show Father where it is!

ABIE: This way, Father Whalen.

[*He hurriedly starts for arch and exits*]

RABBI: Hurry, you haven't much time.

FATHER WHALEN: [*Starts*] Come, Rose Mary! [*Turns in doorway*] And if his Grace says yes, I'll tie the charmed knot so tight, it'll make you dizzy! [*Exits*]

ROSE MARY: Doctor Samuels! Say a prayer for us.

RABBI: What will I say?

ROSE MARY: Say please God, make the Archibishop say yes. [*She exits*]

RABBI: All right! [*He closes door with a satisfied smile on his face*]

MRS. COHEN: [*Enters; sees* RABBI] Nefer did I see such a night! [*Sits on davenport*] Nefer was I so tired! Oh, dear! If my appendix wasn't out, I know I'd have it again!

RABBI: You mustn't worry about it. Everything is going to be all right!

[PATRICK *enters. He looks around*]

PATRICK: Where is my daughter?

RABBI: I think you told her to change her dress.

PATRICK: Oh, she has gone to do it?

RABBI: You told her to, didn't you?

PATRICK: Where's the telephone in this house? I want to make reservations for California. I'm going to get out of this town on the first train and take me daughter with me!

RABBI: [*Goes to telephone*] I'll get your number for you, Mr. Murphy. What road do you want to go by? The Penn?

PATRICK: The fastest road out of New York, and the sooonest. [RABBI *takes receiver off and listens*] What's the matter, won't Central answer?

RABBI: The line's busy!

PATRICK: You never can get a number when you want it! [*Starts for telephone*] Here, give me that phone. I'll show you how to get it!

RABBI: No, no, Mr. Murphy—I insist on getting your number for you!

PATRICK: I know, but—

RABBI: There is someone speaking now, and we must not disturb them!

PATRICK: But if you'll allow—

RABBI: It would not be the right thing to do!

PATRICK: Yes, but if you'll—

rabbi: You wouldn't want to be disturbed, would you?

PATRICK: [*Disgusted*] Ah!

RABBI: Central—give me Penn—six, five, six hundred.

PATRICK: Whoever it is, by this time they should be through talking!

RABBI: All right, thank you! [*Hangs up*]

PATRICK: What's the matter now?

RABBI: The line's busy!

PATRICK: [*In rage*] Oh, I'll never get out of this damn town!

[SOLOMON *enters, followed by* COHEN]

SOLOMON: Oo—ah—

COHEN: Oo-ah—oo!

SOLOMON: [*To* RABBI] My lawyer says dod no matter vod I say, dhey are married so tight, it would make your head curl! [*Sits in chair*]

MRS. COHEN: Vod you tink! Didn't you tell Doctor Samuels to tie a good knot?

SOLOMON: [*Almost a scream*] I should be so foolish! Oi! Oi!

PATRICK: [*Bounds across room to* SOLOMON *and just misses tramping on* COHEN, *who is in the way*] If you don't stop saying Oi, Oi, you'll drive me to drink!

> [PATRICK *turns, looks at* COHEN, *who, frightened, crosses and sits left of* MRS. COHEN. *As* PATRICK *continues to look at him,* MRS. COHEN *passes* COHEN *to right of her and then looks defiantly at* PATRICK]

SOLOMON: Did you hear that I'll drive him to drink! I'd like to drive you to something for wishing an Irish wife on my Abie!

PATRICK: Wishing it on him! The devil take him and all his.

RABBI: Ssh! Ssh! You know what it says in the Scriptures about family quarrels?

PATRICK: Family quarrels! Do I look like a member of this family? [*He looks around at them*] No, and my daughter isn't going to be. Thank heaven, she wasn't married by a priest!

RABBI: And would that make any difference to you, Mr. Murphy?

SOLOMON: Dod's vhere he is lucky! He can do something widout fear or trembling. Bud vid me! [*Pointing to* RABBI] You tie the knot and I'm tied to it!

PATRICK: I'm going to untie that knot, don't you worry!

SOLOMON: Worry if you untie it? If you please, I'll be very much obliged.

PATRICK: [*Goes to telephone*] I don't want you to be anything but out of my life. Penn six, five, six hundred and don't you tell me the line's busy!

ABIE: [*Off*] With this ring I do thee wed.

> [RABBI *opens the door, disclosing wedding party*—FATHER WHALEN'S *voice is heard coming out clear and strong*]

FATHER WHALEN: I now pronounce you man and wife. "Those whom God hath joined together, let no man put asunder."

> [*As this is heard,* SOLOMON *comes to; he listens as though he cannot believe his ears.* PATRICK *is spellbound for the second, too*]

PATRICK: My God! They've done it again!

> [SOLOMON *turns, looks up at left corner door, where is the picture of* ABIE *and* ROSE MARY *with* FATHER WHALEN *between them, the* BRIDES-MAIDS *grouped around them. He collapses in chair as*]

CURTAIN

ACT THREE

SCENE: *In* ABIE'S *and* ROSE MARY'S *little modest apartment.*

It is small and not elegantly furnished, but everything shows that a woman's hand has tastefully arranged everything.

There is a door direct center at back, which leads into a foyer. Another door center at back of foyer leads to the hall outside. A door down right leads into the dining room. A window up right. Another door up left leads into the bedroom. There is a table left center with a chair on either side of it. A console with mirror above it is down left. A Christmas tree stands in the upper right corner. Other furniture to dress the room.

There is a small table with a chair between right door and window; a service table left of the center arch; a chair above the console.

TIME: *It is Christmas Eve. One year later.* ABIE *and* ROSE MARY *are discovered. She is sitting on chair near Christmas tree.* ABIE *is kneeling beside her. She is holding a baby. The moonlight is streaming through the window on them. All lights are out.* ROSE MARY *is singing an Irish Lullaby "Too-ra-loo-ra." Together, they rise, and walk slowly to bedroom door, she singing softly. She goes out.* ABIE *looks after her for a second, then turns on lights.*

ROSE MARY: [*Re-enters*] Oh, I hope that baby sleeps now.

ABIE: So do I. Hurry up, dear. [*Gets up on chair at tree*]

ROSE MARY: Well, what do you want next? [*Holding two ornaments up to him*]

ABIE: Where's the star that goes on the top?

ROSE MARY: [*Getting it from table*] Here it is. [*She takes it over to him, he puts it on the highest part of the tree*]

ABIE: The star of Bethlehem! Only we haven't any Wise Men to see it!

ROSE MARY: This is the babies' Christmas tree, star and all.

[ABIE *gets off chair*]

ABIE: Of course it is! So we should worry about the Wise Men, eh what? [*They embrace*]

ROSE MARY: [*Goes over to the table, picks up another ornament which she takes back to* ABIE] Say, Abie, did your father ever have a Christmas tree for you?

ABIE: My father, a Christmas tree? [*He laughs*]

ROSE MARY: Christmas wouldn't be Christmas to me without a tree.

ABIE: Well, my father doesn't believe there is such a day in the year.

ROSE MARY: [*Handing him another ornament*] Didn't you ever get things?

ABIE: [*Putting it on the tree*] You mean presents?

ROSE MARY: Yes.

ABIE: Not directly from Father. But I found out later that he used to give Sarah money to get things for me, so I would have toys and things. Like the other boys.

ROSE MARY: You know, Abie, I can't understand. Our fathers seemed to love us so much, yet they won't forgive us for marrying.

ABIE: [*Gets down from the chair and puts his arm around her*] Now, don't start to worry again about that. You are not strong enough yet. Aren't we happy?

ROSE MARY: Oh, Abie! [*Looking up into his face lovingly*] But you worry, too!

ABIE: Oh, I know it. But every time I do, I say to myself, "Well, old boy, you've got the dearest, [*Kiss*] sweetest, [*Kiss*] wife in the world, so why worry?"

ROSE MARY: That's right, we have each other.

ABIE: Don't forget our family, too!

ROSE MARY: Oh, Abie, I put the baby's bottle of milk on the electric stove to heat, and forgot all about it. I bet I've broken another bottle. I'm always breaking them. [*She tiptoes off*]

> [ABIE *sings* "Too-ra-loo-ra," *as she shuts the door. The doorbell rings. He goes to the door. As he opens the outside door in the foyer,* MR. *and* MRS. COHEN *are there. They enter.* MRS. COHEN *first,* COHEN *behind so close he cannot be seen until she steps aside.* COHEN *pulls cane out of coat and frightens* MRS. COHEN]

ABIE: Well, look who's here! Come in, Mrs. Cohen! How are you, Mr. Cohen?

MRS. COHEN: Hello, Abie! [*Bustling in with her regular spirit*] Ve vere just goink home from the theatre und I said to Isaac come on, let's go see Abie and Rosie a minute. Didn't I, Papa?

COHEN: You did, Mama.

ABIE: I'm glad you did. Won't you take off your things?

COHEN: Yes, Abie!

MRS. COHEN: Sure, why not? Isaac! Be a gentleman once in a while! [*She stoops and* COHEN *takes off her coat*] Where's our little Rose Mary? [*Sits*]

ABIE: She went to fix the baby's milk.

MRS. COHEN: Oh, how I love babies!

ABIE: Yes, I've been a proud father just a month today.

COHEN: [*Back from foyer, hanging up things*] Don' the time fly? And you can do so much in a little while!

MRS. COHEN: Have you heard from your father yet?

ABIE: No. Not a word.

COHEN: [*Sits*] Ve haven't mentioned it to him at all. Hev ve, Mama?

MRS. COHEN: Not a word! But he keeps talking about children all the time.

ABIE: [*Eagerly*] Does he really?

MRS. COHEN: Says he's goink to leave all his moneys to poor children.

COHEN: Yeh, and I esked him, if the money vos goink to be left just for Jewish children, und he said—

MRS. COHEN: Yes, Abie, he said it!

ABIE: Said what?

MRS. COHEN: Go on, Isaac, tell him what he said.

COHEN: How can I tell him when always you butts in? All the time!

MRS. COHEN: I butts in?

COHEN: Yes, always you butts in, Mama!

ABIE: Well, come, come, what did he say?

COHEN and MRS. COHEN: [*Together*] Well, he said—

COHEN: [*Excited*] Mama, we can't say it together individually!

MRS. COHEN: All right, go on tell him, I don't care.

COHEN: You said tell him in the first place.

MRS. COHEN: [*Angry*] Well, tell, I'm shut! Shtum shoin! [*Puts hand over mouth*]

COHEN: Well, he said, he said—now you made me forget it, see that?

MRS. COHEN: [*Laughing*] I made him forget it!

COHEN: Abie, vhere vas I?

ABIE: Why, you were saying that my father was going to leave his money to Jewish children.

MRS. COHEN: Dots it, Abie!

COHEN: Fangst shoin vider un! Don't you know the old saying silence is fourteen carats—he said "Certainly nod! His money vas goink to all kins of childrens."

MRS. COHEN: Yes, sir, Abie! He said, "Can children help it vhen dhere parents are voolish?"

COHEN: Und I said, "Vell, vhy nod leave id to Abie's children, they're poor?"

MRS. COHEN: He said, "I'm goink to leave my money to many childrens."

COHEN: Und I said, "Vell, give Rose and Abie a chance, dey might hev a lot, dey certain heven't wasted any time yet."

ABIE: Poor Dad! You know, I think he is just dying to see what a son of his son's looks like.

COHEN: *Shure!* Vhy nod? I'd like to see it, too!

MRS. COHEN: Isaac, you ain'd got a son. How can you see vhat his son looks like?

COHEN: I said if I had vone, I'd like to see it!

MRS. COHEN: But you haven't!

[ROSE MARY enters the room]

COHEN: Mama always you argue with me here.

MRS. COHEN: But how can you see your son—

COHEN: [Rises] Yeh, but vhy argue in other people's houses? Soon we'll be home. Home!

ROSE MARY: Hello, there!

MRS. COHEN: [Goes to her and kisses her] Didn't expect us so late, did you?

ROSE MARY: Awfully glad you stopped in. We're waiting up for Christmas.

COHEN: I'm sorry, ve can't stay a minute

MRS. COHEN: Isaac! [She gives him a look]

COHEN: [Quickly] Yes, ve can!

ROSE MARY: I have something awfully good to eat.

ABIE: And it's Kosher.

MRS. COHEN: Papa, we're goink to stay!

COHEN: Mama say we stay! We stay!

ROSE MARY: How do you like the tree?

[They all turn, look at it]

COHEN: [Not very enthusiastic] Fine!

ROSE MARY: Abie trimmed it all by himself. [She is bustling about like a good little housewife]

COHEN: You don't say so?

ROSE MARY: Excuse me, I must see about my ham, it's in the oven. [She exits]

COHEN: [Delighted] Abie, did she say ham?

MRS. COHEN: Isaac, do you ead ham?

COHEN: Vell, Mama, I tasted it vonce. You would like id!

MRS. COHEN: Abie, ham ain'd Kosher food!

ABIE: I know it isn't! The ham is for Rose Mary and her friends. The Kosher food is for me and my friends.

COHEN: I hope Rosie ain'd god too many friends.

MRS. COHEN: Isaac! Over there! Zits!

[COHEN jumps and goes to table]

ABIE: Don't worry though, it is a large ham. I bought it myself! [The doorbell rings] Excuse me.

MRS. COHEN: Sure. Vy not?

[ABIE answers bell. It is FATHER WHALEN. MR. and MRS. COHEN sit at the table]

FATHER WHALEN: Good evening, Abie!

ABIE: [*Delighted*] Father Whalen! Come right in! Give me your hat and coat. I was never so glad to see anyone in my life! How have you been?

FATHER WHALEN: Splendid— [*Taking off his coat*] And how is the good wife?

ABIE: Wonderful!!

FATHER WHALEN: And the family?

ABIE: Great! You know the Cohens, Father?

FATHER WHALEN: Why, of course. [*Taking off gloves*]

COHEN: Shure! I know de Father! Merry Christmas!

[*Both* MR. *and* MRS. COHEN *rise*]

FATHER WHALEN: How are you both?

MRS. COHEN: Ve heven't seen you since the vedding! Oi! Vod a battle!

FATHER WHALEN: Everything seems peaceful enough now.

MRS. COHEN: Yes, seems dod vay.

[FATHER WHALEN *nods for them to sit, which they do*]

ABIE: [*Calls*] Rose Mary! Look!

ROSE MARY: [*Entering*] Oh, Father Whalen, I can't believe my eyes! Is it really you?

FATHER WHALEN: Your eyes are not deceiving you, Rose Mary!

MRS. COHEN: [*Smiling benignly*] She's glad to see somebody from home!

ROSE MARY: How's Father! Have you seen him lately? Is he well? He won't even write to us.

FATHER WHALEN: To be sure he's well. Fit as a fiddle!

ROSE MARY: Did he send his love?

FATHER WHALEN: No, dear, not by me. [*She looks disappointed*] But I think he would have liked to. [ROSE MARY *turns away*] There—there—Rose Mary! [*He motions to* ABIE *to go to her*]

ABIE: [*Seeing that* ROSE MARY *is sad, taking her in his arms*] Don't you care, dear! We should worry about your old father!

ROSE MARY: But I do care! He's my father!

MRS. COHEN: Vell, dod ain'd your fault!

[COHEN *shows his disgust at this remark. Bangs hand on table.* MRS. COHEN *turns to him.* COHEN *points to* FATHER WHALEN *and bangs hand on table again.* MRS. COHEN *turns back to* COHEN *and bangs table.* COHEN *is squelched*]

ROSE MARY: Father Whalen, come with me, I want to show you something. [*She is very sweet about this, takes* FATHER WHALEN'S *hand and leads him to bedroom door*] You've never seen anything so cunning in your life!

COHEN: Oi! Such a sveetness! If I vos the papa of a sveetness like dod, I vouldn't speak to anybody!

FATHER WHALEN: Lead me to it! I'm crazy about babies!

[ROSE MARY *leads the way into the room,* FATHER WHALEN *following.* ABIE *fixes tree*]

ROSE MARY: Right in there, and don't make any noise. You know young babies sleep all the time!

FATHER WHALEN: [*Tiptoeing into room*] I won't.

ROSE MARY: [*Before she exits*] Mrs. Cohen, will you look at my ham and see that it doesn't burn? [ROSE MARY *exits after* FATHER WHALEN, *closing the door.* MRS. COHEN *looks in blank amazement at* ABIE *and* COHEN]

MRS. COHEN: Look at a ham! I never looked at a ham in my life!

COHEN: [*Amused*] Go on, Mama, look at it! It von't bite you.

ABIE: If I knew anything about it, I'd attend to it myself!

COHEN: So vould I! [*Rising*]

MRS. COHEN: Never mind! Zits! I'll do id— [*Crosses to door*] I'll do id, bud it's against my vill! [*With great effort she says that last and exits.* ABIE *smiles to himself*]

COHEN: I hope she don'd do anythink to spoil dod ham! I don'd trust Mama vid pork!

ABIE: [*Laughing*] She can't do anything to hurt it!

COHEN: Vell, I'd feel safer vatching her! I'm nod goink to take any chances. She's liable to make a fish out of it. [*Exits*]

ROSE MARY: [*Enters, followed by* FATHER WHALEN, *who closes the door*] Abie, did she go?

ABIE: Right in where the ham is. [*Exits*]

FATHER WHALEN: Where is everybody?

ROSE MARY: They're all in with the ham. Will you excuse me a second till I see if everything is all right? You know I'm chief cook and bottle washer now.

FATHER WHALEN: To be sure I will. Go right ahead! I understand! [ROSE MARY *starts to go*] And Rose Mary— [*Goes to her*] I have a little Christmas present for you.

ROSE MARY: Oh, what is it?

FATHER WHALEN: I'll tell you later. Go in the kitchen until I call you.

[*As soon as* ROSE MARY *exits* FATHER WHALEN *goes to center door. Opens same, beckons. A second later* PATRICK *enters. He has Christmas toys wrapped in paper. Everything for a girl*]

PATRICK: [*Puts package back of table*] I wondered where you had gotten to!

FATHER WHALEN: They have company.

PATRICK: They have?

FATHER WHALEN: [*Pause*] The Cohens! [PATRICK *who is taking off coat, makes motion as if to put it on again*] You remember them?

PATRICK: I'd like to forget them! [*Sees tree, hangs coat on tree in hall*]

FATHER WHALEN: So you've been shopping, eh?

PATRICK: Yes, I saw a little store down the street and thought I'd get a few things for my grandaughter.

FATHER WHALEN: Suppose it isn't that kind of baby?

PATRICK: What—they have a boy?

FATHER WHALEN: I said, suppose!

PATRICK: A boy would have to have the name of Levy tacked on to him forever. That would be terrible!

FATHER WHALEN: Well, Levy isn't a bad name.

PATRICK: Huh!

[ABIE *enters, stands very quietly. They do not see him*]

FATHER WHALEN: If it's good enough for Rose Mary; it ought to be good enough for her baby.

PATRICK: That's the trouble! It isn't good enough for Rose Mary! Why, she is a direct descendant of the Kings of Ireland!

FATHER WHALEN: Well, Abie might be a direct descendant of the Kings of Jerusalem!

ABIE: No! Just plain Jew. But I love Rose Mary, Mr. Murphy, more than you do!

PATRICK: Oh, you do, do you?

ABIE: Yes, for I wouldn't do anything in the world to cause her the tiniest bit of unhappiness. Can you say as much?

PATRICK: Listen to him!

FATHER WHALEN: The lad is right, Patrick. Abie, will you do something for me?

ABIE: Anything, Father!

FATHER WHALEN: Keep everybody in the kitchen as long as you can, will you?

ABIE: Don't you want Rose Mary?

FATHER WHALEN: Not yet, laddie! I'll call you! [*The doorbell rings*] I'll answer the door! You keep them in there!

ABIE: All right! I suppose you know what you are doing, Father!

FATHER WHALEN: I do, lad, trust me!

[As ABIE *exits,* FATHER WHALEN *turns to see* PATRICK *looking into a whiskey decanter on sideboard. He smiles and goes to center door, opening same. It is the* RABBI]

RABBI: Well, well, if it isn't my old friend, John Whalen!

FATHER WHALEN: Jacob Samuels, how are you?

[*The* RABBI *enters, takes off hat and coat.* PATRICK *is sore at the interruption*]

PATRICK: Huh! The Jew parson!

FATHER WHALEN: Come in!

RABBI: Where are the young folks?

FATHER WHALEN: [*In soft tone; pointing to kitchen*] In there.

> [RABBI *starts to go.* FATHER WHALEN *touches him on shoulder, and points to* PATRICK]

RABBI: [*Looks at* PATRICK] Is that Mr. Murphy?

PATRICK: [*Looking at him as though he would like to fight*] It is that!

RABBI: You came all the way from California to spend your Christmas with Rosie?

PATRICK: I did not. I didn't come to see Rose Mary! 'Tis the child I came to see and if it looks Irish, it gets all my money.[RABBI *and* FATHER WHALEN *smile at each other*] Father Whalen, I'll be right back. I couldn't carry everything up the stairs at once. [*He turns and exits*]

FATHER WHALEN: His bark is far worse than his bite. He's dying to see his daughter.

> [*Both sit at table*]

RABBI: Of course he is. So is Solomon just as anxious to see his son.

FATHER WHALEN: The young folks have stuck it out. They deserve to be forgiven.

RABBI: 'Tis the young folks who should do the forgiving. Their only crime is loving not wisely but well.

FATHER WHALEN: Abie's a fine boy!

RABBI: [*Not to be outdone*] And Rosie's a fine girl!

FATHER WHALEN: Indeed she is!

RABBI: Father, did you show Patrick the— [*Pointing to bedroom*]

FATHER WHALEN: No, not yet. I knew he was anxious so I thought a little punishment would be good for him. The stubborn old Mick! [*They laugh*] Patrick is sure it's a girl.

RABBI: And Solomon is just as sure it's a boy. I must take a peek myself! [*Goes to bedroom door, and looks in. Motions for* FATHER WHALEN *to come*] Father did you ever see anything so sweet in your life?

FATHER WHALEN: Never! [*Looking over* RABBI'S *shoulder*] And I've seen a great many babies, too!

> [*They exit, tiptoeing off; closing the door. The door center opens cautiously, and* SOLOMON *sticks his head in the door. He has overcoat, hat and earmuffs on; looks in; removes coat and hat, looks about then removes earmuffs, hangs them up; then enters with pillow sham containing Teddy Bear, horse, engine, drum and sticks; goes to back of table. Crosses to right, listens, then sits on chair near tree; takes out toys, places them on the floor: takes out horse, whose tail is off. He looks it over, finally finding where tail belongs and puts it on. As he*]

puts engine on floor PATRICK *enters with phonograph.* PATRICK *puts phonograph left of tree, then goes to package back of table, and begins to open it.* SOLOMON *puts drum down and* PATRICK *hears it. He looks toward door right, then they both spy each other.* SOLOMON *and* PATRICK *turn, face each other, both come center, then sniff—turn away two steps and look at each other; then* SOLOMON *gets Teddy Bear and places it under the tree—*PATRICK *pushes Teddy Bear over to make room for his doll—triumphant attitude.* PATRICK *gets doll placed under tree—same business as* SOLOMON. SOLOMON *gets horse and places Teddy Bear on it—*same business. PATRICK *unwraps go-cart, places doll in it, same business.* SOLOMON *gets engine, runs it on table several times.* PATRICK *gets phonograph, starts it—it has a record, an Irish Jig—places it under tree—dances a few steps.* SOLOMON *gets toy drum, beats it, trying to drown out jig.* PATRICK *gets toy horn, faces* SOLOMON, *blowing it.* RABBI *returns, followed by* FATHER WHALEN]

RABBI: Here, here!

FATHER WHALEN: Glory be to God!

RABBI: What is this? Your second childhood? [PATRICK *and* SOLOMON *both look foolish.* PATRICK *turns off phonograph*]

PATRICK: I wanted to see that everything worked right for my granddaughter.

SOLOMON: [*Rising, laughing sarcastically*] Listen to him, he thinks it's a girl!

PATRICK: [*Glowering at him*] Do you know what it is?

SOLOMON: No! But I know it isn't a girl!

FATHER WHALEN: Come on, Patrick, be reasonable!

SOLOMON: Oi! Oi! Such a name! Patrick! Patrick Murphy!

PATRICK: Patrick's a grand old name! It speaks for itself!

SOLOMON: Vell, ven you call Solomon, you don'd have to use your imagination.

   [*All this time* FATHER WHALEN *and* RABBI *are standing back; trying to get a chance to stop them*]

RABBI: Solomon! Solomon!

FATHER WHALEN: Patrick!

SOLOMON: Oi! Dod I should live to see my son married to a Murphy!

PATRICK: Well, you may not know it, but your time has almost come!

RABBI: Come, come, this will never do! If you are going to fight like this, it would have been better to have stayed away!

PATRICK: What? Me stay away from my granddaughter on Christmas?

SOLOMON: She would be better, if she didn't have a grandpapa!

PATRICK: And are you speaking for yourself?

SOLOMON: I heven't a granddaughter!

FATHER WHALEN: Well, if you had one, I don't think she'd own you!

PATRICK: And that's no lie! [*Turning away*]

FATHER WHALEN: Or you either, Patrick!

PATRICK: [*Surprised*] What's the idea?

FATHER WHALEN: She'd be ashamed of the fighting. You know, Patrick, the Irish are a great people!

PATRICK: Don't I know it!

SOLOMON: Huh! Say some more funny things!

FATHER WHALEN: And the Jews are a wonderful people!

PATRICK: That's the best joke tonight!

FATHER WHALEN: Now if the Jews and the Irish would only stop fighting, and get together, they'd own a corner of the world!

RABBI: You're right, Father, and I think they ought to start getting together right here!

PATRICK: [*Starting for* SOLOMON] That suits me, by golly, that suits me!

SOLOMON: Pas kudnack!

FATHER WHALEN: [*Stops him; crosses to* SOLOMON] I'm an Irishman, and I never saw a finer lad in my life than Abraham Levy!

RABBI: [*Crosses to* PATRICK] I'm a Jew, and I never saw a finer girl in the world than Rosie!!

PATRICK: Her name isn't Rosie! It's Rose Mary!

RABBI: Very well, Rose Mary, if that pleases you better!

SOLOMON: The Rose Mary's don'd please me better! It's Rosie!

PATRICK: Whose daughter is she?

SOLOMON: She ain'd your daughter any more. You disowned her, you said so. Ain'd you?

RABBI: Here, here, neither of you should say anything! Both of you ought to be ashamed. Instead of making the best of a bad situation, you make it worse!

FATHER WHALEN: 'Tis the truth he's speaking, Patrick!

RABBI: Now Abie and Rosie—

PATRICK: Rose Mary! ⎱
SOLOMON: Rosie! ⎰ [*Spoken together*]

RABBI: Very well, Abie and his wife have been very happy here. For one year—neither one of you have given a cent toward helping them. And some of the times have been pretty hard. Abie only makes a small salary and Rosie has had to do all the work, even do her own washing.

SOLOMON: Vell, dod's a good pizzness for the Irish!

[PATRICK *starts for* SOLOMON, *but* FATHER WHALEN *motions him back*]

PATRICK: Well, that's better than peddling shoestrings!

SOLOMON: They named vonce a song "The Irish Washerwoman."

PATRICK: I could say something insulting, but I won't, you funny wizened-up-old Shylock!

SOLOMON: Did you give them any money yourself this year? No! You stingy old A.P.A.

PATRICK: [*Starting after* SOLOMON] Don't call me. an A.P.A. I belong to the Ancient Order of Hibernians—and believe me, that ain't no A.P.A. hangout!

[FATHER WHALEN *stops him.* RABBI *goes to* SOLOMON]

RABBI: Solomon, why do you call him an A.P.A.?

SOLOMON: I don't know. It makes him mad. [*To* FATHER WHALEN] I never knew there vos any difference between them.

PATRICK: My God! Will you listen to the dumb thing. Any difference between them? And I live to hear such a thing!

SOLOMON: Vell, nod being Irish myself, I should know the difference. Bud— I'm glad I insulted you. I'll say it again.

PATRICK: [*Going toward him threateningly*] If you say it once more, it will be the last thing you say in this world! Now speak up, or forever hold your peace! [*By this time he is standing over* SOLOMON]

SOLOMON: [*Smiling up at him*] Vell, if I say id, I vill forever hold my peace!

PATRICK: You bet you will! [*He walks away*]

SOLOMON: I don'd have to say id!

PATRICK: [*Satisfied that he has won the battle*] You're wise!

SOLOMON: I'll tink it! [*Laughs*]

PATRICK: [*Spinning around immediately to him*] Oh, you'll tink it, will you? [*Raising his fist*]

SOLOMON: [*Blandly*] Vell, I'm not tinking it now!

PATRICK: [*Walking away again*] It's a good thing!

SOLOMON: Bud I have an active mind! [PATRICK *immediately turns to him again*] I can tink of the weather—[*Snapping his fingers*] Like dod!

PATRICK: In a few minutes, you're going to go where the weather is so hot a thermometer can't register it!

SOLOMON: Dod is good! I'll keep id dod vay for your arrival!

FATHER WHALEN: Now, aren't you two ashamed of yourselves?

RABBI: Grown men! Fathers!

FATHER WHALEN: Grandfathers!

PATRICK: If you will only let me see my granddaughter, I'll go!

SOLOMON: I vont to see Abie's first born!

RABBI: I'll bring the baby to you. [*Exits*]

PATRICK: My graddaughter!

SOLOMON: If it's a girl, you can hev it, I don'd vant it!

FATHER WHALEN: Oh, yes, you will, Mr. Levy!

PATRICK: If it's a girl she gets all my money!

SOLOMON: If she's a boy, she gets all mine!

RABBI: [*Enters*] Father Whalen! Will you take little Patrick Joseph.

PATRICK: Patrick Joseph! A boy named for me?

FATHER WHALEN: Yes. [*He exits, the* RABBI *follows*]

PATRICK: [*Gloating over the name*] Patrick Joseph Murphy—Levy. *Oh!!!* I won't say the rest! [Crosses to table] It ought to be the happiest day of your life to think you're lucky enough!

SOLOMON: Tut, tut—I thought you wouldn't hev a boy!

PATRICK: This is different. 'Tis named for me! [*Slams chair down in rage*]

SOLOMON: Dod's enough! Patrick Joseph! Ph! To tink I should live to have that name in my family! [PATRICK *sits—his back to* SOLOMON] To think my Abie's first born should be called Patrick Joseph!

PATRICK: I'm going to call my grandson Pat, for short!

SOLOMON: [*Looks daggers at* PATRICK. *Picks up chair, places it back to back to* PATRICK'S *with a bang, and sits*] I won't call him Patrick. I'll call him Mr. Levy!

PATRICK: That's the trouble with your race; you won't give in; acknowledge when they're beaten!

SOLOMON: Give in, is it! That's the trouble with the Irish! Dod's the reason it took you so long to get free!

PATRICK: Well, at least we've always had a country—that's more than you can say!

SOLOMON: Ve god a country, too! Jerusalem is free! Ve god it back!

PATRICK: Now that you got it, what are you going to do with it?

SOLOMON: Ve really don'd need it! Ve own all the other peoples!

PATRICK: Well, you don't own Ireland, thank God!!

SOLOMON: No, maybe dod's vot's the matter wid it!

> [PATRICK *rises and starts after him.* SOLOMON *holds chair up to defend himself*]

PATRICK: I won't stand it, I won't—I'll break every bone—

FATHER WHALEN: [*Enters with baby, he sees the two fighting*] Patrick! [PATRICK *turns and sees* FATHER WHALEN *with the baby which he brings to* PATRICK. PATRICK *takes the baby*] Look out for its head.

PATRICK: [*Takes baby and goes to chair with the greatest of care. While* SOLOMON *sorrowfully looks on*] Hello, Pat! [Sits]

SOLOMON: Oi, Pat! [*Cries, sits*]

RABBI: [*Enters with other baby. He goes to* SOLOMON *while* FATHER WHALEN *closes door*] Solomon!

SOLOMON: [*His head bowed, gradually raises his head, sighing*] Ah, what's the use? [*He sees baby, looks at* PATRICK, *sees other baby, then rises delighted*] Twinses?

RABBI: Yes.

PATRICK: Glory be to God!

SOLOMON: My Abie is a smart boy; you see—he wouldn't forget his old papa. Doctor Samuels, is this one named after my papa?

RABBI: No, Solomon, it couldn't be. It's a girl!

SOLOMON: [*His expression changes*] Take it back—I don't vant it!

RABBI: Oh, yes, you do—it's a wonderful baby. Come, Solomon, look at her!

SOLOMON: I wouldn't do it.

RABBI: Poor little Rebecca—

SOLOMON: [*His heart softens*] Rebecca—that's a fine name. Give me a look. [*He takes baby quickly from* RABBI]

RABBI: Look out, Solomon, look out for its head.

SOLOMON: Dot's all right, I was a baby vonce. [*He goes to chair, sits*]

PATRICK: Father Whalen. [*Motions for him.* FATHER WHALEN *goes to him*] Are you sure this is the boy?

FATHER WHALEN: Certainly, it has the pink ribbon.

PATRICK: I haven't much confidence in ribbon.

SOLOMON: [*Motions for* RABBI] Doctor Samuels, sometimes they get twinses mixed.

RABBI: They haven't been mixed, Solomon. You have little Rebecca!

SOLOMON: [*Playing with baby*] Yeh! Coochy coo! [*Takes rattle from pocket, and shakes it*]

PATRICK : [*Takes chicken balloon from his pocket and blowing it up, stands it on table. Holds baby to see*] Look, Pat!

[RABBI *and* FATHER WHALEN *laugh and exit*]

SOLOMON: Rebecca, look! [*After wind is out of chicken*] Look for nothing.

PATRICK: [*Who is beginning to get lost in the interest of the baby*] Shure, I have to give Abie credit—the boy here is the dead image of him!

SOLOMON: [*Delighted*] No, is it?

PATRICK: Look!

[*Both rise.* SOLOMON *goes a bit closer and looks at the baby*]

SOLOMON: He is, isn't he?

PATRICK: Didn't I tell you?

SOLOMON: Und the girl is just like Rosie! She's beautiful! Give a look!

[*Each is looking at the baby in the other man's arms*]

PATRICK: She looks just like my little Rose Mary! It takes me back to the time I first held her in my arms—her mother didn't live!

SOLOMON: [*Softly*] Abie's didn't, too!

PATRICK: I wonder if you'd mind if I held little Rebecca in me arms for awhile!

SOLOMON: Certainly nod! Give me little Patrick! [*They look for some place to put the babies to exchange. Finally* PATRICK *puts his on the table, and takes baby from* SOLOMON] Look out for the cup.

PATRICK: What???

SOLOMON: Excuse me, please, look out for its head!

PATRICK: Ah, talk United States! Ah shure, I feel more natural with a girl! Guess I'm more used to it!

SOLOMON: [*Puzzled at how to pick up the baby, picks it up*] Me, too! I feel more natural vid a boy! Patrickal!

[*They both sing lullabies,* SOLOMON *singing "Oyitzki Iz Gegangen, etc."* PATRICK *singing "Too-ra-loo-ra-loo-ra"*]

PATRICK: She ought to be called Rose Mary.

SOLOMON: Yes, maybe some day she could marry a good Irishman like yourself, and keep it all alike, yes?

PATRICK: You know, Sol.

SOLOMON: Yes, Pat?

PATRICK: That boy should be named for you. Solomon Levy.

SOLOMON: Solomon. It does sound better!

PATRICK: Let's change the names!

SOLOMON: Maybe Abie and Rosie vont let us!

[ROSE MARY *enters followed by* ABIE. *The men do not see them*]

PATRICK: To be sure, they'll let us!

SOLOMON: Maybe we could apologize and esk them to fergive us.

PATRICK: Well, if I can feel ashamed of myself, and I am—God knows you ought to be!

SOLOMON: [*Resents the insult, then smiles*] I feel like ten cents worth of liverwurst!

[ROSE MARY *and* ABIE *run to their fathers.* ROSE MARY *kisses* PATRICK *and* ABIE *puts his arms around* SOLOMON]

ROSE MARY: Daddy!

ABIE: Oh, Dad!

SOLOMON: It's all right!

[MRS. COHEN *enters followed by* COHEN *carrying four plates.* RABBI *and* FATHER WHALEN *also enter*]

MRS. COHEN: Merry Christmas! [*She is carrying the ham*]

SOLOMON: Mrs. Cohen, vod is dod you're carrying?

MRS. COHEN: It's a baked ham! [*She puts it on table, followed by* COHEN *with plates*]

[SOLOMON's *smile disappears. The Christmas bells start to ring out*]

SOLOMON: Vod iss it? A fire?

PATRICK: A fire! 'Tis Christmas! Merry Christmas, Sol!

SOLOMON: Goot Yonteff, Patrick!

CURTAIN

Harvey

MARY CHASE

MARY CHASE

One of the theatre's most affable comedies, *Harvey*, in its original engagement, ran for 1,775 performances, establishing it as the third longest-running play in Broadway history. A combination of fantasy and farce in which the central character—a six-foot-one-and-a-half-inch white rabbit—never appears on stage, it has become part of our theatrical folklore.

The enthusiastic reception given the Mary Chase comedy by its first night audience was duplicated in most of the following day's press. Howard Barnes lauded it in the *New York Herald Tribune* as "One of those blessed theatrical events which occur all too rarely on Broadway. It is stage sorcery at its whimsical best." John Chapman of the *Daily News* offered the pronouncement that *"Harvey* is the most delightful, droll, endearing, funny and touching piece of stage whimsy I ever saw." Others found it "a play of great charm and imagination," one that offers "a beguiling, rewarding, utterly irresistible evening in the theatre."

An immediate "hot ticket," *Harvey* went on to win the 1944–45 Pulitzer Prize, edging out Tennessee Williams's *The Glass Menagerie*, which was accoladed by the New York Drama Critics' Circle as the season's finest play. Coincidentally, both deal with characters who try to escape from reality by living in a world of fantasy. In the Williams drama, Laura Wingfield has her "glass menagerie" and in Mrs. Chase's comedy Elwood P. Dowd has his "pooka."

Since the Pulitzer Prize ostensibly is awarded for "the original American play performed in New York which shall best represent the educational value and power of the stage in raising the standard of good morals, good taste, and good manners," the award to *Harvey* was greeted with raised eyebrows in some quarters. After all, the misadventures of an amiable alcoholic and his furry companion hardly followed the doctrine of the award's intent. Nonetheless, the play was a popular choice, especially to audiences who came to the theater to be entertained rather than to be "educated." For decades thereafter, the gentle Elwood Dowd and his unseen friend won sympathetic understanding in nations around the world and in almost every language because of their plea for tolerance of human individuality, however eccentric. The miracle of *Harvey*, so termed by one critic, is in "the common sense that comes through it. For all its departures into the delights of pure nonsense, it reveals the fundamental wisdom to be

225

gained from those whose grip on reality is not as deathlike as the rest of us maintain it should be, teaching the lesson in sheer, unhackneyed fun."

While some critics referred to Harvey as an invisible rabbit; others as a rabbit seen only by Elwood; and still others, as an imaginary rabbit, Harvey originally did appear on stage during the Boston tryout. Since the stage directions specifically stated that Harvey crosses the stage and enters Dr. Chumley's office, an actor garbed in a rabbit's costume played the scene, somewhat to the detriment of the fantasy. Finally, producer Brock Pemberton convinced the author that the rabbit should not be visible to the audience, strengthening the theory that even literal-minded playgoers might accept the idea that Elwood could persuade others to believe in his pooka. In the New York production, the effect of Harvey's crossing the stage was attained by having a door open, followed by a pause of about eight seconds, then having the opposite door to Dr. Chumley's office open. It became one of the play's more memorable moments.

In 1949, *Harvey* was staged in London where it ran for 610 performances, and a film version was released in 1951. The play was revived in New York in 1970 with James Stewart (who appeared in the movie) and Helen Hayes.

Mary (Coyle) Chase was born on December 25, 1907, in Denver, Colorado. Her interest in pookas and banshees was derived from the Celtic origin of her parents, who came to this country from Ireland. She attended the University of Denver and the University of Colorado, and later became a reporter for the *Rocky Mountain News*. She was married to Robert L. Chase in 1928.

After her marriage, she left newspaper work but continued to write stories and plays. Her first produced play, *Me Third*, was written for the Federal Theatre Project in Denver. Under the title *Now You've Done It* it was presented in New York in 1937, but it was a failure. Other plays, until the emergence of *Harvey*, made little dent and from 1941 to 1944 she served as publicity director for the National Youth Administration in Denver.

With *Harvey* an established success, she turned back to the theatre and subsequently wrote *Mrs. McThing* (which starred Helen Hayes); *Bernadine*; and *Midgie Purvis* (with Tallulah Bankhead in the title role), among other comedies.

Mary Chase was given the William MacLeod Raine Award from the Colorado Authors League in 1944, and in 1947 the University of Denver honored her with the degree of doctor of letters.

HARVEY was first produced at the Forty-eighth Street Theatre, New York, on November 1, 1944, by Brock Pemberton. The cast was as follows:

MYRTLE MAE SIMMONS	*Jane Van Duser*
VETA LOUISE SIMMONS	*Josephine Hull*
ELWOOD P. DOWD	*Frank Fay*
MISS JOHNSON	*Eloise Sheldon*
MRS. ETHEL CHAUVENET	*Frederica Going*
RUTH KELLY, R.N.	*Janet Tyler*
MARVIN WILSON	*Jesse White*
LYMAN SANDERSON, M.D.	*Tom Seidel*
WILLIAM R. CHUMLEY, M.D.	*Fred Irving Lewis*
BETTY CHUMLEY	*Dora Clement*
JUDGE OMAR GAFFNEY	*John Kirk*
E. J. LOFGREN	*Robert Gist*

Directed by Antoinette Perry
Settings by John Root

The action of the play takes place in a city in the Far West in the library of the old Dowd family mansion and the reception room of Chumley's Rest.

Time: The Present.

ACT ONE

SCENE 1: *The library, late afternoon.*
SCENE 2: *Chumley's Rest, an hour later.*

ACT TWO

SCENE 1: *The library, an hour later.*
SCENE 2: *Chumley's Rest, four hours later.*

ACT THREE

Chumley's Rest, a few minutes later.

ACT ONE

The time is midafternoon of a spring day. The scene is the library of the old Dowd family mansion—a room lined with books and set with heavy, old-fashioned furniture of a faded grandeur. The most conspicuous item in the room is an oil painting over a black marble Victorian mantelpiece. This is the portrait of a lantern-jawed older woman. There are double doors at the right. These doors, now pulled apart, lead to the hallway and across to the parlor, which is not seen. Telephone is on small table at left. This afternoon there is a festive look to the room—silver bowls with spring flowers set about. From the parlor to the right comes the sound of a bad female voice singing, "I'm Called Little Buttercup."

AT RISE: MYRTLE MAE *is discovered coming through door from parlor, and as telephone rings, she goes to it.*

MYRTLE: Mrs. Simmons? Mrs. Simmons is my mother, but she has guests this afternoon. Who wants her? [*Respectful change in tone after she hears who it is*] Oh—wait just a minute. Hang on just a minute. [*Goes to doorway and calls*] Psst—Mother! [*Cranes her neck more*] Psst—Mother! [*Crooks her finger insistently several times. Singing continues*]

VETA: [*Enters, humming "Buttercup"*] Yes, dear?

MYRTLE: Telephone.

VETA: [*Turning to go out again*] Oh, no, dear. Not with all of them in there. Say I'm busy.

MYRTLE: Mother. It's the Society Editor of the *Evening News Bee—*

VETA: [*Turning*] Oh—the Society Editor. She's very important.[*She fixes her hair and goes to phone. Her voice is very sweet. She throws out chest and assumes dignified pose*] Good afternoon, Miss Ellerbe. This is Veta Simmons. Yes—a tea and reception for the members of the Wednesday Forum. You might say—program tea. My mother, you know—[*Waves hand toward portrait*] the late Marcella Pinney Dowd, pioneer cultural leader, she came here by ox team as a child and she founded the Wednesday Forum. [MYRTLE *is watching out door*] Myrtle—how many would you say?

MYRTLE: Seventy-five, at least. Say a hundred.

VETA: [*On phone*] Seventy-five. Miss Tewksbury is the soloist, accompanied by Wilda McCurdy, accompanist.

MYRTLE: Come on! Miss Tewksbury is almost finished with her number.

VETA: She'll do an encore.

MYRTLE: What if they don't give her a lot of applause?

VETA: I've known her for years. She'll do an encore. [MYRTLE *again starts to leave*] You might say that I am entertaining, assisted by my daughter, Miss Myrtle Mae Simmons. [*To* MYRTLE— *indicates her dress*] What color would you call that?

MYRTLE: Rancho Rose, they told me.

VETA: [*Into phone*] Miss Myrtle Mae Simmons looked charming in a modish Rancho Rose-toned crepe, picked up at the girdle with a touch of magenta on emerald. I wish you could see her, Miss Ellerbe.

MYRTLE: [*Looks through door*] Mother—please—she's almost finished and where's the cateress?

VETA: [*To* MYRTLE] Everything's ready. The minute she's finished singing we open the dining-room doors and we begin pouring. [*Into phone*] The parlors and halls are festooned with smilax. Yes, festooned. [*Makes motion in air with finger*] That's right. Yes, Miss Ellerbe, this is the first party we've had in years. There's a reason but I don't want it in the papers. We all have our troubles, Miss Ellerbe. The guest list? Oh, yes—

MYRTLE: Mother—come.

VETA: If you'll excuse me now, Miss Ellerbe. I'll call you later. [*Hangs up*]

MYRTLE: Mother—Mrs. Chauvenet just came in!

VETA: [*Arranging flowers on phone table*] Mrs. Eugene Chauvenet Senior! Her father was a scout with Buffalo Bill.

MYRTLE: So that's where she got that hat!

VETA: [*As she and* MYRTLE *start to exit*] Myrtle, you must be nice to Mrs. Chauvenet. She has a grandson about your age.

MYRTLE: But what difference will it make, with Uncle Elwood?

VETA: Myrtle—remember! We agreed not to talk about that this afternoon. The point of this whole party is to get you started. We work through those older women to the younger group.

MYRTLE: We can't have anyone here in the evenings, and that's when men come to see you—in the evenings. The only reason we can even have a party this afternoon is because Uncle Elwood is playing pinochle at the Fourth Avenue Firehouse. Thank God for the firehouse!

VETA: I know—but they'll just have to invite you out and it won't hurt them one bit. Oh, Myrtle—you've got so much to offer. I don't care what anyone says, there's something sweet about every young girl. And a man takes that sweetness, and look what he does with it. [*Crosses to mantel with flowers*] But you've got to meet somebody, Myrtle. That's all there is to it.

MYRTLE: If I do they say, That's Myrtle Mae Simmons! Her uncle is Elwood P. Dowd—the biggest screwball in town. Elwood P. Dowd and his pal—

VETA: [*Puts hand on her mouth*] You promised.

MYRTLE: [*Crossing above table, sighs*] All right—let's get them into the dining room.

VETA: Now when the members come in here and you make your little welcome speech on behalf of your grandmother—be sure to do this. [*Gestures toward portrait on mantel*]

MYRTLE: [*In fine disgust—business with flowers*] And then after that, I mention my Uncle Elwood and say a few words about his pal Harvey. Damn Harvey! [*In front of table, as she squats*]

VETA: [*The effect on her is electric. She runs over and closes doors*] Myrtle Mae—that's right! Let everybody in the Wednesday Forum hear you. You said that name. You promised you wouldn't say that name and you said it.

MYRTLE: [*Rising*] I'm sorry, Mother. But how do you know Uncle Elwood won't come in and introduce Harvey to everybody? [*Places flowers on mantel*]

VETA: This is unkind of you, Myrtle Mae. Elwood is the biggest heartache I have. Even if people do call him peculiar he's still my brother, and he won't be home this afternoon.

MYRTLE: Are you sure?

VETA: Of course I'm sure.

MYRTLE: But Mother, why can't we live like other people?

VETA: Must I remind you again? Elwood is not living with us—we are living with him.

MYRTLE: Living with him and Harvey! Did Grandmother know about Harvey?

VETA: I've wondered and wondered about that. She never wrote me if she did.

MYRTLE: Why did she have to leave all her property to Uncle Elwood?

VETA: Well, I suppose it was because she died in his arms. People are sentimental about things like that.

MYRTLE: You always say that and it doesn't make sense. She couldn't make out her will after she died, could she?

VETA: Don't be didactic, Myrtle Mae. It's not becoming in a young girl, and men loathe it. Now don't forget to wave your hand.

MYRTLE: I'll do my best. [*Opens door*]

VETA: Oh, dear—Miss Tewksbury's voice is certainly fading!

MYRTLE: But not fast enough. [*She exits*]

VETA: [*Exits through door, clapping hands, pulling down girdle*] Lovely, Miss Tewksbury—perfectly lovely. I loved it.

[*Through door at left enters* ELWOOD P. DOWD. *He is a man about forty-seven years old with a dignified bearing, and yet a dreamy expression in his eyes. His expression is benign, yet serious to the point of gravity. He wears an overcoat and a battered old hat. This hat, reminiscent of the Joe College era, sits on the top of his head. Over his arm he carries another hat and coat. As he enters, although he is alone, he seems to be ushering and bowing someone else in with him. He bows the invisible person over to a chair. His step is light, his movements quiet and his voice low-pitched]*

ELWOOD: [*To invisible person*] Excuse me a moment. I have to answer the phone. Make yourself comfortable, Harvey. [*Phone rings*] Hello. Oh, you've got the wrong number. But how are you, anyway? This is Elwood P. Dowd speaking. I'll do? Well, thank you. And what is your name, my dear? Miss Elsie Greenawalt? [*To chair*] Harvey, it's a Miss Elsie Greenawalt. How are you today, Miss Greenawalt? That's fine. Yes, my dear. I would be happy to join your club. I belong to several clubs now—the University Club, the Country Club and the Pinochle Club at the Fourth Avenue Firehouse. I spend a good deal of my time there, or at Charlie's Place, or over at Eddie's Bar. And what is your club, Miss Greenawalt? [*He listens—then turns to empty chair*] Harvey, I get the *Ladies Home Journal, Good Housekeeping,* and the *Open Road for Boys* for two years for six twenty-five. [*Back to phone*] It sounds fine to me. I'll join it. [*To chair*] How does it sound to you, Harvey? [*Back to phone*] Harvey says it sounds fine to him also, Miss Greenawalt. He says he will join, too. Yes— two subscriptions. Mail everything to this address. . . . I hope I will have the pleasure of meeting you some time, my dear. Harvey, she says she would like to meet me. When? When would you like to meet me, Miss Greenawalt? Why not right now? My sister seems to be having a few friends in and we would consider it an honor if you would come and join us. My sister will be delighted. 343 Temple Drive—I hope to see you in a very few minutes. Goodby, my dear. [*Hangs up*] She's coming right over. [*Moves to* HARVEY] Harvey, don't you think we'd better freshen up? Yes, so do I. [*He takes up hats and coats and exits*]

VETA: [*Enters, followed by* MAID] I can't seem to remember where I put that guest list. I must read it to Miss Ellerbe. . . . Have you seen it, Miss Johnson?

MAID: No, I haven't, Mrs. Simmons.

VETA: Look on my dresser.

[MAID *exits*]

MYRTLE: [*Enters*]. Mother—Mrs. Chauvenet—she's asking for you. [*Turning—speaking in oh-so-sweet tone to some one in hall*] Here's Mother, Mrs. Chauvenet. Here she is. [*Enter* MRS. CHAUVENET. *She is a woman of about sixty-five—heavy, dressed with the casual sumptuousness of a wealthy Western society woman—in silvery gold and plush, and mink scarf even though it is a spring day. She rushes over to* VETA]

MRS. CHAUVENET: Veta Louise Simmons! I thought you were dead. [*Gets to her and takes hold of her*]

VETA: [*Rushing to her, they kiss*] Aunt Ethel! [*Motioning to* MYRTLE *to come forward and meet the great lady*] Oh, no—I'm very much alive— thank you—

MRS. CHAUVENET: [*Turning to* MYRTLE] And this full-grown girl is your daughter—I've known you since you were a baby.

MYRTLE: I know.

MRS. CHAUVENET: What's your name, dear?

VETA: [*Proudly*] This is Myrtle—Aunt Ethel. Myrtle Mae—for the two sisters of her father. He's dead. That's what confused you.

MRS. CHAUVENET: Where's Elwood?

VETA: [*With a nervous glance at* MYRTLE MAE] He couldn't be here, Aunt Ethel—now let me get you some tea.

MRS. CHAUVENET: Elwood isn't here?

VETA: No—

MRS. CHAUVENET: Oh, shame on him. That was the main reason I came. [*Takes off scarf—puts it on chair*] I want to see Elwood.

VETA: Come—there are loads of people anxious to speak to you.

MRS. CHAUVENET: Do you realize, Veta, it's been years since I've seen Elwood?

VETA: No—where does the time go?

MRS. CHAUVENET: But I don't understand it. I was saying to Mr. Chauvenet only the other night—what on earth do you suppose has happened to Elwood Dowd? He never comes to the club dances any more. I haven't seen him at a horse show in years. Does Elwood see anybody these days?

VETA *and* MYRTLE: [*With a glance at each other*] Oh, yes—Aunt Ethel. Elwood sees somebody.

MYRTLE: Oh, yes.

MRS. CHAUVENET: [*To* MYRTLE] Your Uncle Elwood, child, is one of my favorite people. [VETA *rises*] Always has been.

VETA: Yes, I remember.

MRS. CHAUVENET: Is Elwood happy, Veta?

VETA: Elwood's very happy, Aunt Ethel. You don't need to worry about Elwood—[*Looks through doorway. She is anxious to get the subject on something else*] Why, there's Mrs. Frank Cummings—just came in. Don't you want to speak to her?

MRS. CHAUVENET: [*Peers out*] My—but she looks ghastly! Hasn't she failed though?

VETA: If you think she looks badly—you should see him!

MRS. CHAUVENET: Is that so? I must have them over. [*Looks again*] She looks frightful. I thought she was dead.

VETA: Oh, no.

MRS. CHAUVENET: Now—what about tea, Veta?

VETA: Certainly— [*Starts forward to lead the way*] If you will forgive me, I will precede—

[ELWOOD *enters,* MRS. CHAUVENET *turns back to pick up her scarf from chair, and sees him*]

MRS. CHAUVENET: [*Rushing forward*] Elwood! Elwood Dowd! Bless your heart.

ELWOOD: [*Coming forward and bowing as he takes her hand*] Aunt Ethel! What a pleasure to come in and find a beautiful woman waiting for me!

MRS. CHAUVENET: [*Looking at him fondly*] Elwood—you haven't changed.

VETA: [*Moves forward quickly, takes hold of her*] Come along, Aunt Ethel— you musn't miss the party.

MYRTLE: There's punch if you don't like tea.

MRS. CHAUVENET: But I do like tea. Stop pulling at me, you two. Elwood, what night next week can you come to dinner?

ELWOOD: Any night. Any night at all, Aunt Ethel—I would be delighted.

VETA: Elwood, there's some mail for you today. I took it up to your room.

ELWOOD: Did you, Veta? That was nice of you. Aunt Ethel—I want you to meet Harvey. As you can see he's a pooka. [*Turns toward air beside him*] Harvey, you've heard me speak of Mrs. Chauvenet? We always called her Aunt Ethel. She is one of my oldest and dearest friends. [*Inclines head toward space and goes "Hmm!" and then listens as though not hearing first time. Nods as though having heard someone next to him speak*] Yes—yes—that's right. She's the one. This is the one. [*To* MRS. CHAUVENET] He says he would have known you anywhere. [*Then as a confused, bewildered look comes over* MRS. CHAUVENET'S *face and as she looks to left and right of* ELWOOD *and cranes her neck to see behind him—*ELWOOD *not seeing her expression, crosses towards* VETA *and* MYRTLE MAE] You both look lovely. [*Turns to the air next to him*] Come on in with me, Harvey— We must say hello to all of our friends—[*Bows to* MRS. CHAUVENET] I beg your pardon, Aunt Ethel. If you'll excuse me for one moment— [*Puts his hand gently on her arm, trying to turn her*]

MRS. CHAUVENET: What?

ELWOOD: You are standing in his way—[*She gives a little—her eyes wide on him*] Come along, Harvey. [*He watches the invisible* HARVEY *cross to door, then stops him*] Uh-uh! [ELWOOD *goes over to door. He turns and pantomimes as he arranges the tie and brushes off the head of the invisible* HARVEY. *Then he does the same thing to his own tie. They are all watching him,* MRS. CHAUVENET *in horrified fascination, the heads of* VETA *and* MYRTLE *bowed in agony*] Go right on in, Harvey. I'll join you in a minute. [*He pantomimes as though slapping him on the back, and ushers him out. Then turns and comes back to* MRS. CHAUVENET] Aunt Ethel, I can see you are disturbed about Harvey. Please don't be. He stares like that at everybody. It's his way. But he liked you. I could tell. He liked you very much. [*Pats her arm reassuringly, smiles at her, then calmly and confidently goes on out. After his exit* MRS. CHAUVENET, MYRTLE, *and* VETA *are silent. Finally* VETA —*with a resigned tone—clears her throat*]

VETA: [*Looking at* MRS. CHAUVENET] Some tea—perhaps—?

MRS. CHAUVENET: Why, I—not right now—I—well—I think I'll be running along.

MYRTLE: But—

VETA: [*Putting a hand over hers to quiet her*] I'm so sorry—

MRS. CHAUVENET: I'll—I'll be talking to you soon. Goodby—goodby—

> [*She exits quickly.* VETA *stands stiffly—her anger paralyzing her.* MYRTLE *finally tiptoes over and closes one side of door—peeking over, but keeping herself out of sight*]

MYRTLE: Oh, God— [*Starts to run for doorway*] Oh, my God!

VETA: Myrtle—where are you going?

MYRTLE: Up to my room. He's introducing Harvey to everybody. I can't face those people now. I wish I were dead.

VETA: Come back here. Stay with me. We'll get him out of there and upstairs to his room.

MYRTLE: I won't do it. I can't. I can't.

VETA: Myrtle Mae! [MYRTLE *stops.* VETA *goes over to her and pulls her to where they are directly in line with doorway*] Now—pretend I'm fixing your corsage.

MYRTLE: [*Covering her face with her hands in shame*] Oh, Mother!

VETA: We've got to. Pretend we're having a gay little chat. Keep looking. When you catch his eye, tell me. He always comes when I call him. Now, then—do you see him yet?

MYRTLE: No—not yet. How do you do, Mrs. Cummings.

VETA: Smile, can't you? Have you no pride? I'm smiling— [*Waves and laughs*] and he's my own brother!

MYRTLE: Oh, Mother—people get run over by trucks every day. Why can't something like that happen to Uncle Elwood?

VETA: Myrtle Mae Simmons, I'm ashamed of you. This thing is not your uncle's fault. [*Phone rings*]

MYRTLE: Ouch! You're sticking me with that pin!

VETA: That's Miss Ellerbe. Keep looking. Keep smiling. [*She goes to phone*]

MYRTLE: Mrs. Cummings is leaving. Uncle Elwood must have told her what Harvey is. Oh, God!

VETA: [*On phone*] Hello—this is Mrs. Simmons. Should you come in the clothes you have on— What have you on? Who is this? But I don't know any Miss Greenawalt. Should you what?—May I ask who invited you? Mr. Dowd! Thank you just the same, but I believe there has been a mistake.— Well, I never!

MYRTLE: Never what?

VETA: One of your Uncle Elwood's friends. She asked me if she should bring a quart of gin to the Wednesday Forum!

MYRTLE: There he is—he's talking to Mrs. Halsey.

VETA: Is Harvey with him?

MYRTLE: What a thing to ask! How can I tell? How can anybody tell but Uncle Elwood?

VETA: [Calls] Oh, Elwood, could I see you a moment, dear? [To MYRTLE] I promise you your Uncle Elwood has disgraced us for the last time in this house. I'm going to do something I've never done before.

MYRTLE: What did you mean just now when you said this was not Uncle Elwood's fault? If it's not his fault, whose fault is it?

VETA: Never you mind. I know whose fault it is. Now lift up your head and smile and go back in as though nothing had happened.

MYRTLE: You're no match for Uncle Elwood.

VETA: You'll see. [ELWOOD is coming]

MYRTLE: [As they pass at door] Mother's waiting for you. [She exits]

VETA: Elwood! Could I see you for a moment, dear?

ELWOOD: Yes, sister. Excuse me, Harvey.

[VETA steps quickly over and pulls double doors together]

VETA: Elwood, would you mind sitting down in here and waiting for me until the party is over? I want to talk to you. It's very important.

ELWOOD: Of course, sister. I happen to have a little free time right now and you're welcome to all of it, Veta. Do you want Harvey to wait, too?

VETA: [Quite seriously—not in a pampering, humoring tone at all] Yes, Elwood. I certainly do. [She steals out—watching him as she crosses through door]

[After she has gone out we see doors being pulled together from the outside and hear the click of a lock. ELWOOD goes calmly over to bookcase, peruses it carefully, and then when he has found the book he wants, takes it out and from behind it pulls a half-filled pint bottle of liquor]

ELWOOD: [Looking at book he holds in one hand] Ah—Jane Austen. [He gets one chair, pulls it down, facing front. Gets chair and pulls it right alongside. Sits down, sets bottle on floor between chairs] Sit down, Harvey. Veta wants to talk to us. She said it was important. I think she wants to congratulate us on the impression we made at her party. [Reads.

Turns to HARVEY. *Inclines head and listens, then looks at back of book and answers as though* HARVEY *had asked what edition it is, who published it, and what are those names on the fly leaf; turning head toward empty chair each time and twice saying* "Hmm?"] Jane Austen—De Luxe Edition—Limited—Grosset and Dunlap—The usual acknowledgements. Chapter One—

AND THE CURTAIN FALLS

SCENE TWO

The office in the main building of Chumley's Rest—a sanitarium for mental patients. The wall at back is half plaster and half glass. There is a door up center, through which we can see the corridor of the sanitarium itself. In the right wall is a door which is lettered "Dr. Chumley." On right wall is a bookcase, a small filing-case on top of it. Across the room is another door lettered "Dr. Sanderson." Down left is the door leading from the outside. There is a big desk at right angles with footlights, with chair either side of desk. At right is a table with chairs on either side.

The time is an hour after the close of Scene One.

AT RISE: MISS RUTH KELLY, *head nurse at Chumley's Rest, is seated left of desk, taking notes as she talks to* VETA SIMMONS, *who stands.* MISS KELLY *is a very pretty young woman of about twenty-four. She is wearing a starched white uniform and cap. As she talks to* VETA *she writes on a slip of paper with a pencil.*

KELLY: [*Writing*] Mrs. O. R. Simmons, 343 Temple Drive, is that right?

VETA: [*Nodding, taking handkerchief from handbag*] We were born and raised there. It's old but we love it. It's our home. [*Crosses to table, puts down handbag*]

KELLY: And you wish to enter your brother here at the sanitarium for treatment. Your brother's name?

VETA: [*Coming back to desk—raising handkerchief to eyes and dabbing*] It's—oh—

KELLY: Mrs. Simmons, what is your brother's name?

VETA: I'm sorry. Life is not easy for any of us. I'll have to hold my head up and go on just the same. That's what I keep telling Myrtle and that's what Myrtle Mae keeps telling me. She's heartbroken about her Uncle Elwood—Elwood P. Dowd. That's it. [*Sits on chair beside desk*]

KELLY: [*Writing*] Elwood P. Dowd. His age?

VETA: Forty-seven the twenty-fourth of last April. He's Taurus—Taurus—the bull. I'm Leo, and Myrtle is on a cusp.

KELLY: Forty-seven. Is he married?

VETA: No, Elwood has never married. He stayed with mother. He was always a great home boy. He loved his home.

KELLY: You have him with you now?

VETA: He's in a taxicab down in the driveway. [KELLY *rings buzzer*] I gave the driver a dollar to watch him, but I didn't tell the man why. You can't tell these things to perfect strangers.

> [*Enter* WILSON. *He is the sanitarium strongarm. He is a big burly attendant, black-browed, about twenty-eight.* KELLY *crosses in front of desk toward bookcase*]

KELLY: Mr. Wilson, would you step down to a taxi in the driveway and ask a Mr. Dowd if he would be good enough to step up to Room number 24— South Wing G?

WILSON: [*Glaring*] *Ask* him?

KELLY: [*With a warning glance toward* VETA] This is his sister, Mrs. Simmons. [KELLY *crosses to cabinet for card*]

WILSON: [*With a feeble grin*] How do—why, certainly—be glad to *escort* him. [*Exits*]

VETA: Thank you.

KELLY: [*Handing* VETA *her printed slip*] The rates here, Mrs. Simmons— you'll find them printed on this card.

VETA: [*Waving it away*] That will all be taken care of by my mother's estate. The late Marcella Pinney Dowd. Judge Gaffney is our attorney.

KELLY: Now I'll see if Dr. Sanderson can see you.

VETA: Dr. Sanderson? I want to see Dr. Chumley himself.

KELLY: Oh, Mrs. Simmons, Dr. Sanderson is the one who sees everybody. Dr. Chumley sees no one.

VETA: He's still head of this institution, isn't he? He's still a psychiatrist, isn't he?

KELLY: [*Shocked at such heresy*] Still a psychiatrist! Dr. Chumley is more than that. He is a psychiatrist with a national reputation. Whenever people have mental breakdowns they at once think of Dr. Chumley.

VETA: [*Pointing*] That's his office, isn't it? Well, you march right in and tell him I want to see him. If he knows who's in here he'll come out here.

KELLY: I wouldn't dare disturb him, Mrs. Simmons. I would be discharged if I did.

VETA: Well, I don't like to be pushed off onto any second fiddle.

KELLY: Dr. Sanderson is nobody's second fiddle. [*Her eyes aglow*] He's young, of course, and he hasn't been out of medical school very long, but Dr. Chumley tried out twelve and kept Dr. Sanderson. He's really wonderful—[*Catches herself*] to the patients.

VETA: Very well. Tell him I'm here.

KELLY: [*Straightens her cap. As she exits into door, primps*] Right away.

VETA: [*Rises, takes off coat—puts it on back of chair, sighs*] Oh, dear—oh, dear.

> [WILSON *and* ELWOOD *appear in corridor.* ELWOOD *pulls over a little from* WILSON *and sees* VETA]

ELWOOD: Veta—isn't this wonderful—!

> [WILSON *takes him forcefully off upstairs.* VETA *is still jumpy and nervous from the surprise. Enter* DR. SANDERSON. LYMAN SANDERSON *is a good-looking young man of twenty-seven or twenty-eight. He is wearing a starched white coat over dark trousers. His eyes follow* MISS KELLY, *who has walked out before him and gone out, closing doors. Then he sees* VETA, *pulls down his jacket, and gets a professional bearing.* VETA *has not heard him come in. She is still busy with the compact*]

SANDERSON: [*Looking at slip in his hand*] Mrs. Simmons?

VETA: [*Startled—she jumps*] Oh—oh, dear—I didn't hear you come in. You startled me. You're Dr. Sanderson?

SANDERSON: [*He nods*] Yes. Will you be seated, please?

VETA: [*Sits*] Thank you. I hope you don't think I'm jumpy like that all the time, but I—

SANDERSON: Of course not. Miss Kelly tells me you are concerned about your brother. Dowd, is it? Elwood P. Dowd?

VETA: Yes, Doctor—he's—this isn't easy for me, Doctor.

SANDERSON: [*Kindly*] Naturally these things aren't easy for the families of patients. I understand.

VETA: [*Twisting her handkerchief nervously*] It's what Elwood's doing to himself, Doctor—that's the thing. Myrtle Mae has a right to nice friends. She's young and her whole life is before her. That's my daughter.

SANDERSON: Your daughter. How long has it been since you began to notice any peculiarity in your brother's actions?

VETA: I noticed it right away when Mother died, and Myrtle Mae and I came back home from Des Moines to live with Elwood. I could see that he—that he— [*Twists handkerchief—looks pleadingly at* SANDERSON]

SANDERSON: That he—what? Take your time, Mrs. Simmons. Don't strain. Let it come. I'll wait for it.

VETA: Doctor—everything I say to you is confidential? Isn't it?

SANDERSON: That's understood.

VETA: Because it's a slap in the face to everything we've stood for in this community the way Elwood is acting now.

SANDERSON: I am not a gossip, Mrs. Simmons. I am a psychiatrist.

VETA: Well—for one thing—he drinks.

SANDERSON: To excess?

VETA: To excess? Well—don't you call it excess when a man never lets a day go by without stepping into one of those cheap taverns, sitting around with riffraff and people you never heard of? Inviting them to the house— playing cards with them—giving them food and money. And here I am trying to get Myrtle Mae started with a nice group of young people. If that isn't excess I'm sure I don't know what excess is.

SANDERSON: I didn't doubt your statement, Mrs. Simmons. I merely asked if your brother drinks.

VETA: Well, yes, I say definitely Elwood drinks and I want him committed out here permanently, because I cannot stand another day of that Harvey. Myrtle and I have to set a place at the table for Harvey. We have to move over on the sofa and make room for Harvey. We have to answer the telephone when Elwood calls and asks to speak to Harvey. Then at the party this afternoon with Mrs. Chauvenet there— We didn't even know anything about Harvey until we came back here. Doctor, don't you think it would have been a little bit kinder of Mother to have written and told me about Harvey? Be honest, now—don't you?

SANDERSON: I really couldn't answer that question, because I—

VETA: I can. Yes—it certainly would have.

SANDERSON: This person you call Harvey—who is he?

VETA: He's a rabbit.

SANDERSON: Perhaps—but just who is he? Some companion—someone your brother has picked up in these bars, of whom you disapprove?

VETA: [*Patiently*] Doctor—I've been telling you. Harvey is a rabbit—a big white rabbit—six feet high—or is it six feet and a half? Heaven knows I ought to know. He's been around the house long enough.

SANDERSON: [*Regarding her narrowly*] Now, Mrs. Simmons, let me understand this—you say—

VETA: [*Impatient*] Doctor—do I have to keep repeating myself? My brother insists that his closest friend is this big white rabbit. This rabbit is named Harvey. Harvey lives at our house. Don't you understand? He and Elwood go every place together. Elwood buys railroad tickets, theater tickets, for both of them. As I told Myrtle Mae—if your uncle was so lonesome he had to bring something home—why couldn't he bring home something human? He has me, doesn't he? He has Myrtle Mae, doesn't he? [*She leans forward*] Doctor—[*She rises to him. He inclines toward her*] I'm going to tell you something I've never told anybody in the world before. [*Puts her hand on his shoulder*] Every once in a while I see that big white rabbit myself. Now isn't that terrible? I've never even told that to Myrtle Mae.

SANDERSON: [*Now convinced. Starts to rise*] Mrs. Simmons—

VETA: [*Straightening*] And what's more—he's every bit as big as Elwood says he is. Now don't ever tell that to anybody, Doctor. I'm ashamed of it.

SANDERSON: I can see that you have been under a great nervous strain recently.

VETA: Well—I certainly have.

SANDERSON: Grief over your mother's death depressed you considerably?

VETA: Nobody knows how much.

SANDERSON: Been losing sleep?

VETA: How could anybody sleep with that going on?

SANDERSON: Short-tempered over trifles?

VETA: You just try living with those two and see how your temper holds up.

SANDERSON: [*Presses buzzer*] Loss of appetite.

VETA: No one could eat at a table with my brother and a big white rabbit. Well, I'm finished with it. I'll sell the house—be appointed conservator of Elwood's estate, and Myrtle Mae and I will be able to entertain our friends in peace. It's too much, Doctor. I just can't stand it.

SANDERSON: [*Has been repeatedly pressing a buzzer on his desk. He looks with annoyance toward hall door. His answer now to* VETA *is gentle*] Of course, Mrs. Simmons. Of course it is. You're tired.

VETA: [*She nods*] Oh, yes, I am.

SANDERSON: You've been worrying a great deal.

VETA: [*Nods*] Yes, I have. I can't help it.

SANDERSON: And now I'm going to help you.

VETA: Oh, Doctor. . . .

SANDERSON: [*Goes cautiously to door—watching her*] Just sit there quietly, Mrs. Simmons. I'll be right back. [*He exits*]

VETA: [*Sighing with relief, rises and calls out as she takes coat*] I'll just go down to the cab and get Elwood's things.

[*She exits out.* SANDERSON, KELLY *and* WILSON *come in*]

SANDERSON: Why didn't someone answer the buzzer?

KELLY: I didn't hear you, Doctor—

SANDERSON: I rang and rang.[*Looks into his office. It is empty*] Mrs. Simmons— [*Looks out door, shuts it, comes back*] Sound the gong, Wilson. That poor woman must not leave the grounds.

WILSON: She's made with a getaway, huh, Doc? [WILSON *presses a button on the wall and we hear a loud gong sounding*]

SANDERSON: Her condition is serious. Go after her.

[WILSON *exits*]

KELLY: I can't believe it.

[SANDERSON *picks up phone*]

SANDERSON: Main gate. Henry, Dr. Sanderson. Allow no one out of the main gate. We're looking for a patient. [*Hangs up*] I shouldn't have left her alone, but no one answered the buzzer.

KELLY: Wilson was in South, Doctor.

SANDERSON: [*Making out papers*] What have we available, Miss Kelly?

KELLY: Number 13, upper West R., is ready, Doctor.

SANDERSON: Have her taken there immediately, and I will prescribe preliminary treatment. I must contact her brother. Dowd is the name, Elwood P. Dowd. Get him on the telephone for me, will you please, Miss Kelly?

KELLY: But, Doctor—I didn't know it was the woman who needed the treatment. She said it was for her brother.

SANDERSON: Of course she did. It's the oldest dodge in the world—always used by a cunning type of psychopath. She apparently knew her brother was about to commit her, so she came out to discredit him. Get him on the telephone, please.

KELLY: But, Doctor—I thought the woman was all right, so I had Wilson take the brother up to No. 24 South Wing G. He's there now.

SANDERSON: [*Staring at her with horror*] You had Wilson take the brother in? No gags, please, Kelly. You're not serious, are you?

KELLY: Oh, I did, Doctor. I did. Oh, Doctor, I'm terribly sorry.

SANDERSON: Oh, well then, if you're sorry, that fixes everything. [*He starts to pick up house phone and finishes the curse under his breath*] Oh—no! [*Buries his head in his hands*]

KELLY: I'll do it, Doctor. I'll do it. [*She takes phone*] Miss Dumphy—will you please unlock the door to Number 24—and give Mr. Dowd his clothes and—? [*Looks at* SANDERSON *for direction*]

SANDERSON: Ask him to step down to the office right away.

KELLY: [*Into phone*] Ask him to step down to the office right away. There's been a terrible mistake and Dr. Sanderson wants to explain—

SANDERSON: Explain? Apologize!

KELLY: Thank heaven they hadn't put him in a hydro tub yet. She'll let him out.

SANDERSON: [*Staring at her*] Beautiful—and dumb, too. It's almost too good to be true.

KELLY: Doctor—I feel terrible. I didn't know. Judge Gaffney called and said Mrs. Simmons and her brother would be out here, and when she came in here—you don't have to be sarcastic.

SANDERSON: Oh, don't I? Stop worrying. We'll squirm out of it some way.

[*Thinking—starts toward right door*]

KELLY: Where are you going?

SANDERSON: I've got to tell the chief about it, Kelly. He may want to handle this himself.

KELLY: He'll be furious. I know he will. He'll die. And then he'll terminate me.

SANDERSON: [*Catches her shoulders*] The responsibility is all mine, Kelly.

KELLY: Oh, no—tell him it was all my fault, Doctor.

SANDERSON: I never mention your name. Except in my sleep.

KELLY: But this man Dowd—

SANDERSON: Don't let him get away. I'll be right back.

KELLY: But what shall I say to him? What shall I do? He'll be furious.

SANDERSON: Look, Kelly—he'll probably be fit to be tied—but he's a man, isn't he?

KELLY: I guess so—his name is Mister.

SANDERSON: Go into your old routine—you know—the eyes—the swish—the works. I'm immune—but I've seen it work with some people—some of the patients out here. Keep him here, Kelly—if you have to do a strip tease. [*He exits*]

KELLY: [*Very angry. Speaks to closed door*] Well, of all the—oh—you're wonderful, Dr. Sanderson! You're just about the most wonderful person I ever met in my life. [*Kicks chair*]

WILSON: [*Has entered in time to hear last sentence*] Yeah—but how about giving me a lift here just the same?

KELLY: What?

WILSON: That Simmons dame.

KELLY: Did you catch her?

WILSON: Slick as a whistle. She was comin' along the path hummin' a little tune. I jumped out at her from behind a tree. I says "Sister—there's a man wants to see you." Shoulda heard her yell! She's whacky, all right.

KELLY: Take her to No. 13 upper West R.

WILSON: She's there now. Brought her in through the diet kitchen. She's screamin' and kickin' like hell. I'll hold her if you'll come and undress her.

KELLY: Just a second, Wilson. Dr. Sanderson told me to stay here till her brother comes down.

WILSON: Make it snappy— [*Goes out*]

[ELWOOD *enters.* KELLY *rises*]

KELLY: You're Mr. Dowd?

ELWOOD: [*Carrying other hat and coat over his arm. He bows*] Elwood P.

KELLY: I'm Miss Kelly.

ELWOOD: Let me give you one of my cards. [*Fishes in vest pocket—pulls out card*] If you should want to call me—call me at this number. Don't call me at that one. That's the old one.

KELLY: Thank you.

ELWOOD: Perfectly all right, and if you lose it—don't worry, my dear. I have plenty more.

KELLY: Won't you have a chair, please, Mr. Dowd?

ELWOOD: Thank you. I'll have two. Allow me. [*He brings another chair. Puts extra hat and coat on table. Motions* HARVEY *to sit in chair. He stands waiting*]

KELLY: Dr. Sanderson is very anxious to talk to you. He'll be here in a minute. Please be seated.

ELWOOD: [*Waving her toward chair right of desk*] After you, my dear.

KELLY: Oh, I really can't, thank you. I'm in and out all the time. But you mustn't mind me. Please sit down.

ELWOOD: [*Bowing*] After you.

KELLY: [*Sits.* ELWOOD *sits on chair he has just put in place*] Could I get you a magazine to look at?

ELWOOD: I would much rather look at you, Miss Kelly, if you don't mind. You really are very lovely.

KELLY: Oh—well. Thank you. Some people don't seem to think so.

ELWOOD: Some people are blind. That is often brought to my attention. And now, Miss Kelly—I would like to have you meet—

[*Enter* SANDERSON. MISS KELLY *rises and backs up to below desk.* ELWOOD *rises when she does, and he makes a motion to the invisible* HARVEY *to rise, too*]

SANDERSON: [*Going to him, extending hand*] Mr. Dowd?

ELWOOD: Elwood P. Let me give you one of my cards. If you should want—

SANDERSON: Mr. Dowd—I am Dr. Lyman Sanderson, Dr. Chumley's assistant out here.

ELWOOD: Well, good for you! I'm happy to know you. How are you, Doctor?

SANDERSON: That's going to depend on you, I'm afraid. Please sit down. You've met Miss Kelly, Mr. Dowd?

ELWOOD: I have had that pleasure, and I want both of you to meet a very dear friend of mine—

SANDERSON: Later on—be glad to. Won't you be seated, because first I want to say—

ELWOOD: After Miss Kelly—

SANDERSON: Sit down, Kelly—[*She sits, as does* ELWOOD—*who indicates to* HARVEY *to sit also*] Is that chair quite comfortable, Mr. Dowd?

ELWOOD: Yes, thank you. Would you care to try it? [*He takes out a cigarette*]

SANDERSON: No, thank you. How about an ash tray there? Could we give Mr. Dowd an ash tray? [KELLY *gets it.* ELWOOD *and* HARVEY *rise also.* ELWOOD *beams as he turns and watches her.* KELLY *puts ash tray by* DOWD, *who moves it to share with* HARVEY] Is it too warm in here for you, Mr. Dowd? Would you like me to open a window? [ELWOOD *hasn't heard. He is watching* MISS KELLY]

KELLY: [*Turning, smiling at him*] Mr. Dowd—Dr. Sanderson wants to know if he should open a window?

ELWOOD: That's entirely up to him. I wouldn't presume to live his life for him.

[*During this dialogue* SANDERSON *is near window.* KELLY *has her eyes on his face.* ELWOOD *smiles at* HARVEY *fondly*]

SANDERSON: Now then, Mr. Dowd, I can see that you're not the type of person to be taken in by any high-flown phrases or beating about the bush.

ELWOOD: [*Politely*] Is that so, Doctor?

SANDERSON: You have us at a disadvantage here. You know it. We know it. Let's lay the cards on the table.

ELWOOD: That certainly appeals to me, Doctor.

SANDERSON: Best way in the long run. People are people, no matter where you go.

ELWOOD: That is very often the case.

SANDERSON: And being human are therefore liable to mistakes. Miss Kelly and I have made a mistake here this afternoon, Mr. Dowd, and we'd like to explain it to you.

KELLY: It wasn't Doctor Sanderson's fault, Mr. Dowd. It was mine.

SANDERSON: A human failing—as I said.

ELWOOD: I find it very interesting, nevertheless. You and Miss Kelly here? [*They nod*] This afternoon—you say? [*They nod.* ELWOOD *gives* HARVEY *a knowing look*]

KELLY: We do hope you'll understand, Mr. Dowd.

ELWOOD: Oh, yes. Yes. These things are often the basis of a long and warm friendship.

SANDERSON: And the responsibility is, of course, not hers—but mine.

ELWOOD: Your attitude may be old-fashioned, Doctor—but I like it.

SANDERSON: Now, if I had seen your sister first—that would have been an entirely different story.

ELWOOD: Now there you surprise me. I think the world and all of Veta—but I had supposed she had seen her day.

SANDERSON: You must not attach any blame to her. She is a very sick woman. Came in here insisting you were in need of treatment. That's perfectly ridiculous.

ELWOOD: Veta shouldn't be upset about me. I get along fine.

SANDERSON: Exactly—but your sister had already talked to Miss Kelly, and there had been a call from your family lawyer, Judge Gaffney—

ELWOOD: Oh, yes. I know him. Know his wife, too. Nice people. [*He turns to* HARVEY—*cigarette business: he needs a match*]

SANDERSON: Is there something I can get for you, Mr. Dowd?

ELWOOD: What did you have in mind?

SANDERSON: A light—here—let me give you a light. [*Crosses to* DOWD, *lights his cigarette.* ELWOOD *brushes smoke away from the rabbit*] Your sister was extremely nervous and plunged right away into a heated tirade on your drinking.

ELWOOD: That was Veta.

SANDERSON: She became hysterical.

ELWOOD: I tell Veta not to worry about that. I'll take care of that.

SANDERSON: Exactly. Oh, I suppose you take a drink now and then—the same as the rest of us?

ELWOOD: Yes, I do. As a matter of fact, I would like one right now.

SANDERSON: Matter of fact, so would I, but your sister's reaction to the whole matter of drinking was entirely too intense. Does your sister drink, Mr. Dowd?

ELWOOD: Oh, no, Doctor. No. I don't believe Veta has ever taken a drink.

SANDERSON: Well, I'm going to surprise you. I think she has and does—constantly.

ELWOOD: I am certainly surprised.

SANDERSON: But it's not her alcoholism that's going to be the basis for my diagnosis of her case. It's much more serious than that. It was when she began talking so emotionally about this big white rabbit—Harvey—yes, I believe she called him Harvey—

ELWOOD: [*Nodding*] Harvey is his name.

SANDERSON: She claimed you were persecuting her with this Harvey.

ELWOOD: I haven't been persecuting her with Harvey. Veta shouldn't feel that way. And now, Doctor, before we go any further I must insist you let me introduce—[*He starts to rise*]

SANDERSON: Let me make my point first, Mr. Dowd. This trouble of your sister's didn't spring up overnight. Her condition stems from trauma.

ELWOOD: [*Sits down again*] From what?

SANDERSON: From trauma—Spelled T-R-A-U-M-A. It means shock. Nothing unusual about it. There is the birth trauma. The shock to the act of being born.

ELWOOD: [*Nodding*] That's the one we never get over—

SANDERSON: You have a nice sense of humor, Dowd—hasn't he, Miss Kelly?

KELLY: Oh, yes, Doctor.

ELWOOD: May I say the same about both of you?

SANDERSON: To sum it all up—your sister's condition is serious, but I can help her. She must however remain out here temporarily.

ELWOOD: I've always wanted Veta to have everything she needs.

SANDERSON: Exactly.

ELWOOD: But I wouldn't want Veta to stay out here unless she liked it out here and wanted to stay here.

SANDERSON: Of course. [*To* KELLY] Did Wilson get what he went after? [KELLY *nods*]

KELLY: Yes, Doctor. [*She rises*]

SANDERSON: What was Mrs. Simmons' attitude, Miss Kelly?

KELLY: Not unusual, Doctor.

SANDERSON: [*Rising*] Mr. Dowd, if this were an ordinary delusion—something reflected on the memory picture—in other words, if she were seeing something she had seen once—that would be one thing. But this is more serious. It stands to reason nobody has ever seen a white rabbit six feet high.

ELWOOD: [*Smiles at* HARVEY] Not very often, Doctor.

SANDERSON: I like you, Dowd.

ELWOOD: I like you, too, Doctor. And Miss Kelly here. [*Looks for* MISS KELLY, *who is just crossing in front of window seat.* ELWOOD *springs to his feet.* KELLY *sits quickly.* ELWOOD *motions* HARVEY *down and sits, himself*] I like her, too.

SANDERSON: So she must be committed here temporarily. Under these circumstances I would commit my own grandmother. [*Goes to desk*]

ELWOOD: Does your grandmother drink, too?

SANDERSON: It's just an expression. Now will you sign these temporary commitment papers as next-of-kin—just a formality?

ELWOOD: You'd better have Veta do that, Doctor. She always does all the signing and managing for the family. She's good at it.

SANDERSON: We can't disturb her now.

ELWOOD: Perhaps I'd better talk it over with Judge Gaffney?

SANDERSON: You can explain it all to him later. Tell him I advised it. And it isn't as if you couldn't drop in here any time and make inquiries. Glad to have you. I'll make out a full visitor's pass for you. When would you like to come back? Wednesday, say? Friday, say?

ELWOOD: You and Miss Kelly have been so pleasant I can come back right after dinner. About an hour.

SANDERSON: [*Taken aback*] Well—we're pretty busy around here, but I guess that's all right.

ELWOOD: I don't really have to go now. I'm not very hungry.

SANDERSON: Delighted to have you stay—but Miss Kelly and I have to get on upstairs now. Plenty of work to do. But I tell you what you might like to do.

ELWOOD: What might I like to do?

SANDERSON: We don't usually do this—but just to make sure in your mind that your sister is in good hands—why don't you look around here? If you go through that door—[*Rises—points beyond stairway*] and turn right just beyond the stairway you'll find the occupational therapy room down the hall, and beyond that the conservatory, the library, and the diet kitchen.

ELWOOD: For Veta's sake I believe I'd better do that, Doctor.

SANDERSON: Very well, then. [*He is now anxious to terminate the interview. Rises, shakes hands*] It's been a great pleasure to have this little talk with you, Mr. Dowd. [*Gives him pass*]

ELWOOD: [*Walking toward him*] I've enjoyed it too, Doctor—meeting you and Miss Kelly.

SANDERSON: And I will say that for a layman you show an unusually acute perception into psychiatric problems.

ELWOOD: Is that a fact? I never thought I knew anything about it. Nobody does, do you think?

SANDERSON: Well—the good psychiatrist is not found under every bush.

ELWOOD: You have to pick the right bush. Since we all seem to have enjoyed this so much, let us keep right on. I would like to invite you to come with me now down to Charlie's Place and have a drink. When I enjoy people I like to stay right with them.

SANDERSON: Sorry—we're on duty now. Give us a rain check. Some other time be glad to

ELWOOD: When?

SANDERSON: Oh—can't say right now. Miss Kelly and I don't go off duty till ten o'clock at night.

ELWOOD: Let us go to Charlie's at ten o'clock tonight.

SANDERSON: Well—

ELWOOD: And you, Miss Kelly?

KELLY: I—[*Looks at* SANDERSON]

SANDERSON: Dr. Chumley doesn't approve of members of the staff fraternizing, but since you've been so understanding perhaps we could manage it.

ELWOOD: I'll pick you up out here in a cab at ten o'clock tonight and the four of us will spend a happy evening. I want you both to become friends with a very dear friend of mine. You said later on so later on it will be. Goodbye, now. [*Motions goodbye to* HARVEY. *Tips hat, exits*]

KELLY: Whew—now I can breathe again!

SANDERSON: Boy, that was a close shave all right, but he seemed to be a pretty reasonable sort of fellow. That man is proud—what he has to be proud of I don't know. I played up to that pride. You can get to almost anybody if you want to. Now I must look in on that Simmons woman.

KELLY: Dr. Sanderson—! [SANDERSON *turns*] You say you can get to anybody if you want to. How can you do that?

SANDERSON: Takes study, Kelly. Years of specialized training. There's only one thing I don't like about this Dowd business.

KELLY: What's that?

SANDERSON: Having to make that date with him. Of course the man has left here as a good friend and booster of this sanitarium—so I guess I'll have to go with him tonight—but you don't have to go.

KELLY: Oh!

SANDERSON: No point in it. I'll have a drink with him, pat him on the back and leave. I've got a date tonight, anyway.

KELLY: [*Freezing*] Oh, yes—by all means. I didn't intend to go, anyway. The idea bored me stiff. I wouldn't go if I never went anywhere again. I wouldn't go if my life depended on it.

SANDERSON: [*Stepping back to her*] What's the matter with you, Kelly? What are you getting so emotional about?

KELLY: He may be a peculiar man with funny clothes, but he knows how to act. His manners were perfect.

SANDERSON: I saw you giving him the doll-puss stare. I didn't miss that.

KELLY: He wouldn't sit down till I sat down. He told me I was lovely and he called me dear. I'd go to have a drink with him if you weren't going.

SANDERSON: Sure you would. And look at him! All he does is hang around bars. He doesn't work. All that corny bowing and getting up out of his chair every time a woman makes a move. Why, he's as outdated as a cast-iron deer. But you'd sit with him in a bar and let him flatter you—You're a wonderful girl, Kelly

KELLY: Now let me tell you something—you—

[*Enter the great* DR. WILLIAM CHUMLEY. DR. CHUMLEY *is a large, handsome man of about fifty-seven. He has gray hair and wears rimless glasses which he removes now and then to tap on his hand for emphasis. He is smartly dressed. His manner is confident, pompous, and lordly. He is good and he knows it*]

CHUMLEY: Dr. Sanderson! Miss Kelly! [*They break apart and jump to attention like two buck privates before a* C.O.]

KELLY *and* SANDERSON: Yes, Doctor?

CHUMLEY: Tell the gardener to prune more carefully around my prize dahlias along the fence by the main road. They'll be ready for cutting next week. The difficulty of the woman who has the big white rabbit—has it been smoothed over?

SANDERSON: Yes, Doctor. I spoke to her brother and he was quite reasonable.

CHUMLEY: While I have had many patients out here who saw animals, I have never before had a patient with an animal that large. [*Puts book in bookcase*]

SANDERSON: Yes, Doctor. She called him Harvey.

CHUMLEY: Harvey. Unusual name for an animal of any kind. Harvey is a man's name. I have known several men in my day named Harvey, but I have never heard of any type of animal whatsoever with that name. The case has an interesting phase, Doctor [*Finishes straightening books*]

SANDERSON: Yes, Doctor.

CHUMLEY: I will now go upstairs with you and look in on this woman. It may be that we can use my formula 977 on her. I will give you my advice in prescribing the treatment, Doctor.

SANDERSON: Thank you, Doctor.

CHUMLEY: [*Starts to move across stage and stops, draws himself up sternly*] And now—may I ask—what is that hat and coat doing on that table? Whose is it?

SANDERSON: I don't know. Do you know, Miss Kelly? Was it Dowd's?

KELLY: [*Above table, picking up hat and coat*] He had his hat on, Doctor. Perhaps it belongs to a relative of one of the patients.

CHUMLEY: *Hand me the hat.* [KELLY *hands it. Looking inside*] There may be some kind of identification— Here—what's this—what's this? [*Pushes two fingers up through the holes*] Two holes cut in the crown of his hat. See!

KELLY: That's strange!

CHUMLEY: Some new fad—put them away. Hang them up—get them out of here.

[KELLY *takes them into office and comes out again.* WILSON *comes in*]

WILSON: [*Very impressed with* DR. CHUMLEY *and very fond of him*] Hello, Dr. Chumley.

CHUMLEY: Oh, there you are.

WILSON: How is every little old thing?

[DR. CHUMLEY *picks up pad of notes from desk*]

CHUMLEY: Fair, thank you, Wilson, fair.

WILSON: Look—somebody's gonna have to give me a hand with this Simmons dame—order a restraining jacket or something. She's terrible. [*To* KELLY] *Forgot me*, didn't you? Well, I got her corset off all by myself.

CHUMLEY: We're going up to see this patient right now, Wilson.

WILSON: She's in a hydro-tub now—my God—I left the water *running on her!* [*Runs off upstairs, followed by* KELLY. BETTY CHUMLEY, *the Doctor's wife, enters. She is a good-natured, gay, bustling woman of about fifty-five*]

BETTY: Willie—remember your promise—. Hello, Dr. Sanderson. Willie, you haven't forgotten Dr. McClure's cocktail party? We promised them faithfully.

CHUMLEY: That's right. I have to go upstairs now and look in on a patient. Be down shortly— [*Exits upstairs*]

BETTY: [*Calling after him*] Give a little quick diagnosis, Willie—we don't want to be late to the party. I'm dying to see the inside of that house.

[*Enter* ELWOOD. *He doesn't see* BETTY *at first. He looks around the room carefully*] Good evening.

ELWOOD: [*Removing his hat and bowing*] Good evening. [*Puts hat on desk. Walks over to her*]

BETTY: I am Mrs. Chumley. Doctor Chumley's wife.

ELWOOD: I'm happy to know that. Dowd is my name. Elwood P. Let me give you one of my cards. [*Gives her one*] If you should want to call me—call me at this one. Don't call me at that one, because that's—[*Points at card*] the old one.[*Starts one step. Looking*]

BETTY: Thank you. Is there something I can do for you?

ELWOOD: [*Turns to her*] What did you have in mind?

BETTY: You seem to be looking for someone.

ELWOOD: [*Walking*] Yes, I am. I'm looking for Harvey. I went off without him.

BETTY: Harvey? Is he a patient here?

ELWOOD: [*Turns*] Oh, no. Nothing like that.

BETTY: Does he work here?

ELWOOD: [*Looking out door*] Oh, no. He is what you might call my best friend. He is also a pooka. He came out here with me and Veta this afternoon.

BETTY: Where was he when you last saw him?

ELWOOD: In that chair there—with his hat and coat on the table.

BETTY: There doesn't seem to be any hat and coat around here now. Perhaps he left?

ELWOOD: Apparently. I don't see him anywhere. [*Looks in* SANDERSON'S *office*]

BETTY: What was that word you just said—pooka?

ELWOOD: [*Looking in hallway*] Yes—that's it.

BETTY: Is that something new? [*Looks in hallway*]

ELWOOD: Oh, no. As I understand it. That's something very old.

BETTY: Oh, really? I had never happened to hear it before.

ELWOOD: I'm not too surprised at that. I hadn't myself, until I met him. I do hope you get an opportunity to meet him. I'm sure he would be quite taken with you.

BETTY: Oh, really? Well, that's very nice of you to say so, I'm sure.

ELWOOD: Not at all. If Harvey happens to take a liking to people he expresses himself quite definitely. If he's not particularly interested, he sits there like an empty chair or an empty space on the floor. Harvey takes his time making his mind up about people. Choosey, you see.

BETTY: That's not such a bad way to be in this day and age.

ELWOOD: Harvey is fond of my sister, Veta. That's because he is fond of me, and Veta and I come from the same family. Now you'd think that feeling would be mutual, wouldn't you? But Veta doesn't seem to care for Harvey. Don't you think that's rather too bad, Mrs. Chumley?

BETTY: Oh, I don't know, Mr. Dowd. I gave up a long time ago expecting my family to like my friends. It's useless.

ELWOOD: But we must keep on trying [Sits]

BETTY: Well, there's no harm in trying, I suppose.

ELWOOD: Because if Harvey has said to me once he has said a million times— "Mr. Dowd, I would do anything for you." Mrs. Chumley—

BETTY: Yes—

ELWOOD: Did you know that Mrs. McElhinney's Aunt Rose is going to drop in on her unexpectedly tonight from Cleveland?

BETTY: Why, no I didn't—

ELWOOD: Neither does she. That puts you both in the same boat, doesn't it?

BETTY: Well, I don't know anybody named—Mrs.—

ELWOOD: Mrs. McElhinney? Lives next door to us. She is a wonderful woman. Harvey told me about her Aunt Rose. That's an interesting little news item, and you are perfectly free to pass it around.

BETTY: Well, I—

ELWOOD: Would you care to come downtown with me now, my dear? I would be glad to buy you a drink.

BETTY: Thank you very much, but I am waiting for Dr. Chumley and if he came down and found me gone he would be liable to raise—he would be irritated!

ELWOOD: We wouldn't want that, would we? Some other time, maybe? [He rises]

BETTY: I'll tell you what I'll do, however.

ELWOOD: What will you do, however? I'm interested.

BETTY: If your friend comes in while I'm here I'd be glad to give him a message for you.

ELWOOD: [Gratefully] Would you do that? I'd certainly appreciate that. [Goes to desk for his hat]

BETTY: No trouble at all. I'll write it down on the back of this. [Holds up card. Takes pencil from purse] What would you like me to tell him if he comes in while I'm still here?

ELWOOD: Ask him to meet me downtown—if he has no other plans.

BETTY: [Writing] Meet Mr. Dowd downtown. Any particular place downtown?

ELWOOD: He knows where. Harvey knows this town like a book.

BETTY: [Writing] Harvey—you know where. Harvey what?

ELWOOD: Just Harvey.

BETTY: I'll tell you what.

ELWOOD: What?

BETTY: Doctor and I are going right downtown—to Twelfth and Montview. Dr. McClure is having a cocktail party.

ELWOOD: [*He writes that down on pad on desk*]. A cocktail party at Twelfth and Montview.

BETTY: We're driving there in a few minutes. We could give your friend a lift into town.

ELWOOD: I hate to impose on you—but I would certainly appreciate that.

BETTY: No trouble at all. Dr. McClure is having this party for his sister from Wichita.

ELWOOD: I didn't know Dr. McClure had a sister in Wichita.

BETTY: Oh—you *know* Dr. McClure?

ELWOOD: No.

BETTY: [*Puts Elwood's card down on desk*] But—[*Sits*]

ELWOOD: You're quite sure you haven't time to come into town with me and have a drink?

BETTY: I really couldn't—but thank you just the same.

ELWOOD: Some other time, perhaps?

BETTY: Thank you.

ELWOOD: It's been very pleasant to meet you, and I hope to see you again.

BETTY: Yes, so do I.

ELWOOD: Goodnight, my dear. [*Tips hat—bows—goes to door, turns*] You can't miss Harvey. He's very tall—[*Shows with hands*] Like that—[*Exits*]

> [CHUMLEY *enters, followed by* SANDERSON *and* KELLY. CHUMLEY *goes to desk.* KELLY *crosses to office for* CHUMLEY'S *hat and coat*]

CHUMLEY: [*Working with pen on deskpad*] That Simmons woman is uncooperative, Doctor. She refused to admit to me that she has this big rabbit. Insists it's her brother. Give her two of these at nine—another at ten—if she continues to be so restless. Another trip to the hydro room at eight, and one in the morning at seven. Then we'll see if she won't cooperate tomorrow, won't we, Doctor?

SANDERSON: Yes, Doctor.

CHUMLEY: You know where to call me if you need me. Ready, pet?

BETTY: Yes, Willie—and oh, Willie—

CHUMLEY: Yes—

BETTY: There was a man in here—a man named—let me see—[*Picks up card from desk*] Oh, here is his card—Dowd—Elwood P. Dowd.

> [KELLY *enters. She has* DR. CHUMLEY'S *hat*]

SANDERSON: That's Mrs. Simmons' brother, Doctor. I told him he could look around, and I gave him full visiting privileges.

CHUMLEY: She mustn't see anyone tonight. Not anyone at all. Tell him that.

SANDERSON: Yes, Doctor.

BETTY: He didn't ask to see her. He was looking for someone—some friend of his.

CHUMLEY: Who could that be, Dr. Sanderson?

SANDERSON: I don't know, Doctor.

BETTY: He said it was someone he came out here with this afternoon.

SANDERSON: Was there anyone with Dowd when you saw him, Miss Kelly?

KELLY: No, Doctor—not when I saw him.

BETTY: Well, he said there was. He said he last saw his friend sitting right in that chair there with his hat and coat. He seemed quite disappointed.

KELLY: [*A funny look is crossing her face*] Dr. Sanderson—

BETTY: I told him if we located his friend we'd give him a lift into town. He could ride in the back seat. Was that all right, Willie?

CHUMLEY: Of course—of course—

BETTY: Oh, here it is. I wrote it down on the back of this card. His friend's name was Harvey.

KELLY: Harvey!

BETTY: He didn't give me his last name. He mentioned something else about him—pooka—but I didn't quite get what that was.

SANDERSON *and* CHUMLEY: Harvey!

BETTY: [*Rises*] He said his friend was very tall—. Well, why are you looking like that, Willie? This man was a very nice, polite man, and he merely asked that we give his friend a lift into town, and if we can't do a favor for someone, why are we living?

SANDERSON: [*Gasping*] Where—where did he go, Mrs. Chumley? How long ago was he in here?

CHUMLEY: [*Thundering*] Get me that hat! By George, we'll find out about this! [KELLY *goes out to get it*]

BETTY: I don't know where he went. Just a second ago.

[SANDERSON, *his face drawn, sits at desk and picks up house phone.* CHUMLEY, *with a terrible look on his face, has started to thumb through phone book*]

SANDERSON: [*On house phone*] Main gate—Henry—Dr. Sanderson—

CHUMLEY: [*Thumbing through book*] Gaffney—Judge Gaffney—

SANDERSON: Henry—did a man in a brown suit go out through the gate a minute ago? He did? He's gone? [*Hangs up and looks stricken.* KELLY *enters with hat*]

CHUMLEY: [*Has been dialing*] Judge Gaffney—this is Dr. William Chumley—the psychiatrist. I'm making a routine checkup on the spelling of a name before entering it into our records. Judge—you telephoned out here this afternoon about having a client of yours committed? How is that name spelled? With a W, not a U—Mr. Elwood P. Dowd. Thank you, Judge— [*Hangs up—rises—pushes chair in to desk—takes hat from* KELLY. *Stands silently for a moment, contemplating* SANDERSON] Dr. Sanderson—I believe your name is Sanderson?

SANDERSON: Yes, Doctor.

CHUMLEY: You know that much, do you? You went to medical school—you specialized in the study of psychiatry? You graduated—you went forth. [*Holds up hat and runs two fingers up through holes in it*] Perhaps they neglected to tell you that a rabbit has large pointed ears! That a hat for a rabbit would have to be perforated to make room for those ears?

SANDERSON: Dowd seemed reasonable enough this afternoon, Doctor.

CHUMLEY: Doctor—the function of a psychiatrist is to tell the difference between those who are reasonable, and those who merely talk and act reasonably. [*Presses buzzer, flings hat on desk*] Do you realize what you have done to me? You don't answer. I'll tell you. You have permitted a psychopathic case to walk off these grounds and roam around with an overgrown white rabbit. You have subjected me—a psychiatrist—to the humiliation of having to call—of all things—a lawyer to find out who came out here to be committed—and who came out here to commit!

[WILSON *enters*]

SANDERSON: Dr. Chumley—I—

CHUMLEY: Just a minute, Wilson—I want you. [*Back to* SANDERSON] I will now have to do something I haven't done in fifteen years. I will have to go out after this patient, Elwood P. Dowd, and I will have to bring him back, and when I do bring him back your connection with this institution is ended—as of that moment! [*Turns to* WILSON—*others are standing frightened*] Wilson, get the car. [*To* BETTY] Pet, call the McClures and say we can't make it. Miss Kelly—come upstairs with me and we'll get that woman out of the tub—[*Starts upstairs on the run*]

KELLY: [*Follows him upstairs*] Yes—Doctor—

[SANDERSON *turns on his heel, goes into his office.* WILSON *is getting into a coat in hall*]

BETTY: I'll have to tell the cook we'll be home for dinner. She'll be furious. [*She turns*] Wilson—

WILSON: Yes, ma'am.

BETTY: What is a pooka?

WILSON: A what?

BETTY: A pooka.

WILSON: You can search me, Mrs. Chumley.

BETTY: I wonder if it would be in the Encyclopedia here? [*Goes to bookcase and takes out book*] They have everything here. I wonder if it is a lodge, or what it is![*Starts to look in it, then puts it on table open*] Oh, I don't dare to stop to do this now. Dr. Chumley won't want to find me still here when he comes down.[*Starts to door very fast*] He'll raise—I mean—oh, dear! [*She exits*]

WILSON: [*Picks up book, looks in it. Runs forefinger under words*] P-o-o-k-a. "Pooka. From old Celtic mythology. A fairy spirit in animal form. Always very large. The pooka appears here and there, now and then, to this one and that one at his own caprice. A wise but mischievous creature. Very fond of rum-pots, crack-pots," and how are you, Mr. Wilson? [*Looks at book startled—looks at doorway fearfully—then back to book*] How are you, Mr. Wilson? [*Shakes book, looks at in surprise*] Who in the encyclopedia wants to know? [*Looks at book again, drops it on table*] Oh—to hell with it! [*He exits quickly*]

CURTAIN

ACT TWO

SCENE ONE

The Dowd library again, about an hour later.
    AT RISE: *Doorbell is ringing and* MYRTLE *enters. She calls behind her.*
MYRTLE: That's right. The stairs at the end of the hall. It goes to the third floor. Go right up. I'll be with you in a minute.

    [JUDGE OMAR GAFFNEY *enters, an elderly white-haired man. He looks displeased*]
JUDGE: [*Looking around*] Well, where is she?
MYRTLE: Where is who? Whom do you mean, Judge Gaffney? Sit down, won't you?
JUDGE: I mean your mother. Where's Veta Louise?
MYRTLE: Why, Judge Gaffney! You know where she is. She took Uncle Elwood out to the sanitarium.
JUDGE: I know that. But why was I called at the club with a lot of hysteria? Couldn't even get what she was talking about. Carrying on something fierce.
MYRTLE: Mother carrying on! What about?
JUDGE: I don't know. She was hysterical.
MYRTLE: That's strange! She took Uncle Elwood out to the sanitarium. All she had to do was put him in. [*Goes back, opens door, and looks through,*

calling] Did you find it? I'll be right up. [*Waits. Turns to him*] They found it.

JUDGE: Who? Found what? What are you talking about?

MYRTLE: When Mother left the house with Uncle Elwood I went over to the real estate office to put the house on the market. And what do you think I found there? [*She sits*]

JUDGE: I'm not a quiz kid.

MYRTLE: Well, I found a man there who was looking for an old house just like this to cut up into buffet apartments. He's going through it now.

JUDGE: Now see here, Myrtle Mae. This house doesn't belong to you. It belongs to your Uncle Elwood.

MYRTLE: But now that Elwood is locked up, Mother controls the property, doesn't she?

JUDGE: Where is your mother? Where is Veta Louise?

MYRTLE: Judge, she went out to Chumley's Rest to tell them about Harvey and put Uncle Elwood in.

JUDGE: Why did she call me at the club when I was in the middle of a game, and scream at me to meet her here about something important?

MYRTLE: I don't know. I simply don't know. Have you got the deed to this house?

JUDGE: Certainly, it's in my safe. Myrtle, I feel pretty bad about this thing of locking Elwood up.

MYRTLE: Mother and I will be able to take a long trip now—out to Pasadena.

JUDGE: I always liked that boy. He could have done anything—been anything—made a place for himself in this community.

MYRTLE: And all he did was get a big rabbit.

JUDGE: He had everything. Brains, personality, friends. Men liked him. Women liked him. I liked him.

MYRTLE: Are you telling me that once Uncle Elwood was like other men— that women actually liked him—I mean in that way?

JUDGE: Oh, not since he started running around with this big rabbit. But they did once. Once that mailbox of your grandmother's was full of those little blue-scented envelopes for Elwood.

MYRTLE: I can't believe it.

JUDGE: Of course there was always something different about Elwood.

MYRTLE: I don't doubt that.

JUDGE: Yes—he was always so calm about any sudden change in plans. I used to admire it. I should have been suspicious. Take our average man looking up and seeing a big white rabbit. He'd do something about it. But not Elwood. He took that calmly, too. And look where it got him!

MYRTLE: You don't dream how far overboard he's gone on this rabbit.

JUDGE: Oh, yes I do. He's had that rabbit in my office many's the time. I'm old but I don't miss much. [*Noise from upstairs*] What's that noise?

MYRTLE: The prospective buyer on the third floor. [*Looks up.* VETA *is standing in doorway, looking like something the cat dragged in. Shakes her head sadly; looks into the room and sighs; her hat is crooked.* MYRTLE *jumps up*] Mother! Look, Judge—

JUDGE: [*Rising*] Veta Louise—what's wrong, girl?

VETA: [*Shaking her head*] I never thought I'd see either of you again. [MYRTLE *and* JUDGE *take* VETA *to chair*]

MYRTLE: Take hold of her, Judge. She looks like she's going to faint. [JUDGE *gets hold of her on one side and* MYRTLE *on the other. They start to bring her into the room*] Now, Mother—you're all right. You're going to be perfectly all right.

JUDGE: Steady—steady, girl, steady.

VETA: Please—not so fast.

JUDGE: Don't rush her, Myrtle— Ease her in.

VETA: Let me sit down. Only get me some place where I can sit down.

JUDGE: [*Guiding her to a big chair*] Here you are, girl. Easy, Myrtle—easy.

> [VETA *is about to lower herself into chair. She sighs. But before she can complete the lowering,* MYRTLE MAE *lets out a yelp and* VETA *straightens up quickly*]

MYRTLE: Oh—[*She picks up envelope off chair. Holds it up*] The gas bill.

VETA: [*Hand at head*] Oh—oh, my— [*Sits*]

JUDGE: Get her some tea, Myrtle. Do you want some tea, Veta?

MYRTLE: I'll get you some tea, Mother. Get her coat off, Judge.

JUDGE: Let Myrtle get your coat off, Veta. Get her coat off, Myrtle.

VETA: Leave me alone. Let me sit here. Let me get my breath.

MYRTLE: Let her get her breath, Judge.

VETA: Let me sit here a minute and then let me get upstairs to my own bed where I can let go.

MYRTLE: What happened to you, Mother?

VETA: Omar, I want you to sue them. They put me in and let Elwood out.

JUDGE: What's this?

MYRTLE: Mother!

VETA: [*Taking off hat*] Just look at my hair.

MYRTLE: But why? What did you say? What did you do? [*Kneels at* VETA's *feet*] You must have done something.

VETA: I didn't do one thing. I simply told them about Elwood and Harvey.

JUDGE: Then how could it happen to you? I don't understand it.

VETA: I told them about Elwood, and then I went down to the cab to get his things. As I was walking along the path—this awful man stepped out. He was a white slaver. I know he was. He had on one of those white suits. That's how they advertise.

MYRTLE: A man—what did he do, Mother?

VETA: What did he do? He took hold of me and took me in there and then he—[*Bows her head.* MYRTLE *and* JUDGE *exchange a look*]

JUDGE: [*Softly*] Go on, Veta Louise. Go on, girl.

MYRTLE: [*Goes over, takes her hand*] Poor Mother— Was he a young man?

JUDGE: Myrtle Mae—perhaps you'd better leave the room.

MYRTLE: Now? I should say not! Go on, Mother.

JUDGE: [*Edging closer*] What did he do, Veta?

VETA: He took me upstairs and tore my clothes off.

MYRTLE: [*Shrieking*] Oh—did you hear that, Judge! Go on, Mother. [*She is all ears*]

JUDGE: By God—I'll sue them for this!

VETA: And then he set me down in a tub of water.

MYRTLE: [*Disappointed*] Oh! For heaven's sake! [*Rises*]

VETA: I always thought that what you were showed on your face. Don't you believe it, Judge! Don't you believe it, Myrtle. This man took hold of me like I was a woman of the streets—but I fought. I always said if a man jumped at me—I'd fight. Haven't I always said that, Myrtle?

MYRTLE: She's always said that, Judge. That's what Mother always told me to do.

VETA: And then he hustled me into that sanitarium and set me down in that tub of water and began treating me like I was a—

MYRTLE: A what—?

VETA: A crazy woman—but he did that just for spite.

JUDGE: Well, I'll be damned!

VETA: And those doctors came upstairs and asked me a lot of questions—all about sex-urges—and all that filthy stuff. That place ought to be cleaned up, Omar. You better get the authorities to clean it up. Myrtle, don't you ever go out there. You hear me?

JUDGE: This stinks to high heaven, Veta. By God, it stinks!

VETA: You've got to do something about it, Judge. You've got to sue them.

JUDGE: I will, girl. By God, I will! If Chumley thinks he can run an unsavory place like this on the outskirts of town he'll be publicly chastised. By God, I'll run him out of the State!

VETA: Tell me, Judge. Is that all those doctors do at places like that—think about sex?

JUDGE: I don't know.

VETA: Because if it is they ought to be ashamed—of themselves. It's all in their head anyway. Why don't they get out and go for long walks in the fresh air? [*To* MYRTLE] Judge Gaffney walked everywhere for years—didn't you, Judge?

JUDGE: Now let me take some notes on this. You said—these doctors came up to talk to you—Dr. Chumley and— What was the other doctor's name?

VETA: Sanderson— [*Sits up straight—glances covertly at them and becomes very alert*] But, Judge, don't you pay any attention to anything he tells you. He's a liar. Close-set eyes. They're always liars. Besides—I told him something in strictest confidence and he blabbed it.

MYRTLE: What did you tell him, Mother?

VETA: Oh, what difference does it make? Let's forget it. I don't even want to talk about it. You can't trust anybody.

JUDGE: Anything you told this Dr. Sanderson you can tell us, Veta Louise. This is your daughter and I am your lawyer.

VETA: I know which is which. I don't want to talk about it. I want to sue them and I want to get in my own bed. [JUDGE *rises*]

MYRTLE: But, Mother—this is the important thing, anyway. Where is Uncle Elwood?

VETA: [*To herself*] I should have known better than to try to do anything about him. Something protects him—that awful pooka—

MYRTLE: Where is Uncle Elwood? Answer me.

VETA: [*Trying to be casual*] How should I know? They let him go. They're not interested in men at places like that. Don't act so naïve, Myrtle Mae. [*Noise from upstairs*] What's that noise?

MYRTLE: I've found a buyer for the house.

VETA: What?

MYRTLE: Listen, Mother, we've got to find Uncle Elwood—no matter who jumped at you we've still got to lock up Uncle Elwood.

VETA: I don't know where he is. The next time *you* take him, Judge. Wait until Elwood hears what they did to me. He won't stand for it. Don't forget to sue them, Judge— Myrtle Mae, all I hope is that never, never as long as you live a man pulls the clothes off you and dumps you down into a tub of water. [*She exits*]

MYRTLE: [*Turning to* JUDGE] Now, see—Mother muffed everything. No matter what happened out there—Uncle Elwood's still wandering around with Harvey.

JUDGE: [*Pondering*] The thing for me to do is take some more notes.

MYRTLE: It's all Uncle Elwood's fault. He found out what she was up to— and he had her put in. Then he ran.

JUDGE: Oh, no—don't talk like that. Your uncle thinks the world and all of your mother. Ever since he was a little boy he always wanted to share everything he had with her.

MYRTLE: I'm not giving up. We'll get detectives. We'll find him. And, besides—you'd better save some of that sympathy for me and Mother— you don't realize what we have to put up with. Wait till I show you something he brought home about six months ago, and we hid it out in the garage. You just wait—

JUDGE: I'm going up to talk to Veta. There's more in this than she's telling. I sense that.

MYRTLE: [*As she exits*] Wait till I show you, Judge.

JUDGE: All right. I'll wait.

> [WILSON *enters*]

WILSON: Okay—is he here?

JUDGE: What? What's this?

WILSON: [*Stepping into hallway, calling*] Not here, Doctor—okay— [*To* JUDGE] Doctor Chumley's comin' in, anyway. What's your name?

JUDGE: Chumley—well, well, well—I've got something to say to him! [*Sits*]

WILSON: What's your name? Let's have it.

JUDGE: I am Judge Gaffney—where is Chumley?

WILSON: The reason I asked your name is the doctor always likes to know who he's talkin' to. [*Enter* CHUMLEY] This guy says his name is Judge Gaffney, Doctor.

JUDGE: Well, well, Chumley—

CHUMLEY: Good evening, Judge. Let's not waste time. Has he been here?

JUDGE: Who? Elwood—no—but see here, Doctor—

WILSON: Sure he ain't been here? He's wise now. He's hidin'. It'll be an awful job to smoke him out.

CHUMLEY: It will be more difficult, but I'll do it. They're sly. They're cunning. But I get them. I always get them. Have you got the list of the places we've been, Wilson?

WILSON: [*Pulling paper out of his pocket*] Right here, Doctor.

CHUMLEY: [*Sits*] Read it.

WILSON: We've been to seventeen bars, Eddie's Place, Charlie's Place, Bessie's Barn-dance, the Fourth Avenue Firehouse, the Tenth and Twelfth and Ninth Avenue firehouses, just to make sure. The Union Station, the grain elevator—say, why does this guy go down to a grain elevator?

JUDGE: The foreman is a friend of his. He has many friends—many places.

CHUMLEY: I have stopped by here to ask Mrs. Simmons if she has any other suggestions as to where we might look for him.

JUDGE: Doctor Chumley, I have to inform you that Mrs. Simmons has retained me to file suit against you—

CHUMLEY: What?

JUDGE: For what happened to her at the sanitarium this afternoon . . .

CHUMLEY: A suit!

JUDGE: And while we're on that subject—

WILSON: That's pretty, aint' it, Doctor? After draggin' your tail all over town trying to find that guy.

CHUMLEY: What happened this afternoon was an unfortunate mistake. I've discharged my assistant who made it. And I am prepared to take charge of this man's case personally. It interests me. And my interest in a case is something no amount of money can buy. You can ask any of them.

JUDGE: But this business this afternoon, Doctor—

CHUMLEY: Water under the dam. This is how I see this thing. I see it in this way—[MYRTLE *has come into the room. She is carrying a big flat parcel, wrapped in brown paper. Stands it up against wall and listens*] The important item now is to get this man and take him out to the sanitarium where he belongs.

MYRTLE: [*Coming forward*] That's right, Judge—that's just what I think—

JUDGE: Let me introduce Miss Myrtle Mae Simmons, Mr. Dowd's niece, Mrs. Simmons's daughter.

[CHUMLEY *rises*]

MYRTLE: How do you do, Dr. Chumley.

CHUMLEY: [*Giving her the careful scrutiny he gives all women*] How do you do, Miss Simmons.

WILSON: Hello, Myrtle—

MYRTLE: [*Now seeing him and looking at him with a mixture of horror and intense curiosity*] What? Oh—

CHUMLEY: Now, then—let me talk to Mrs. Simmons.

MYRTLE: Mother won't come down, Doctor. I know she won't. [*To* JUDGE] You try to get Mother to talk to him, Judge.

JUDGE: But, see here; your mother was manhandled. She was—God knows what she was—the man's approach to her was not professional, it was personal. [*Looks at* WILSON]

CHUMLEY: Wilson—this is a serious charge.

WILSON: Dr. Chumley, I've been with you for ten years. Are you gonna believe—what's your name again?

JUDGE: Gaffney. Judge Omar Gaffney.

WILSON: Thanks. You take the word of this old blister Gaffney—

CHUMLEY: Wilson!

WILSON: Me! Me and a dame who sees a rabbit!

JUDGE: It's not Mrs. Simmons who sees a rabbit. It's her brother.

MYRTLE: Yes, it's Uncle Elwood.

JUDGE: If you'll come with me, Doctor—

CHUMLEY: Very well, Judge. Wilson, I have a situation here. Wait for me. [*He and* JUDGE *exit*]

WILSON: O.K., Doctor.

> [MYRTLE MAE *is fascinated by* WILSON. *She lingers and looks at him. He comes over to her, grinning*]

WILSON: So your name's Myrtle Mae?

MYRTLE: What? Oh—yes— [*She backs up. He follows*]

WILSON: If we grab your uncle you're liable to be comin' out to the sanitarium on visiting days?

MYRTLE: Oh, I don't really know—I—

WILSON: Well, if you do, I'll be there.

MYRTLE: You will? Oh—

WILSON: And if you don't see me right away—don't give up. Stick around. I'll show up.

MYRTLE: You will—? Oh—

WILSON: Sure. [*He is still following her*] You heard Dr. Chumley tell me to wait?

MYRTLE: Yeah—

WILSON: Tell you what—while I'm waiting I sure could use a sandwich and a cup of coffee.

MYRTLE: Certainly. If you'll forgive me I'll precede you into the kitchen. [*She tries to go. He traps her*]

WILSON: Yessir—you're all right, Myrtle.

MYRTLE: What?

WILSON: Doctor Chumley noticed it right away. He don't miss a trick. [*Crowds closer; raises finger and pokes her arm for emphasis*] Tell you somethin' else, Myrtle—

MYRTLE: What?

WILSON: You not only got a nice build—but, kid, you got something else, too.

MYRTLE: What?

WILSON: You got the screwiest uncle that ever stuck his puss inside our nuthouse.

> [MYRTLE *starts to exit in a huff, and* WILSON *raises hand to give her a spank, but she turns and so he puts up raised hand to his hair. They exit. The stage is empty for a half second and then* ELWOOD *comes in, goes to phone, dials a number*]

ELWOOD: Hello, Chumley's Rest? Is Doctor Chumley there? Oh—it's Mrs. Chumley! This is Elwood P. Dowd speaking. How are you tonight? Tell me, Mrs. Chumley, were you able to locate Harvey?—Don't worry about it. I'll find him. I'm sorry I missed you at the McClure cocktail party. The people were all charming and I was able to leave quite a few of my cards. I waited until you phoned and said you couldn't come because a patient had escaped. Where am I? I'm here. But I'm leaving right away. I must find Harvey. Well, goodbye, Mrs. Chumley. My regards to you and anybody else you happen to run into. Goodbye. [*Hangs up, then he sees the big flat parcel against wall. He gets an "Ah, there it is!" expression on his face, goes over and takes off paper. We see revealed a very strange thing. It is an oil painting of* ELWOOD *seated on a chair while behind him stands a large white rabbit, in a blue polka-dot collar and red necktie.* ELWOOD *holds it away from him and surveys it proudly, then looks around for a place to put it. Takes it over and sets it on mantel. It obscures the picture of Marcella Pinney Dowd completely. He gathers up wrapping-paper, admires the rabbit again, tips his hat to it and exits. Phone rings and* VETA *enters, followed by* DR. CHUMLEY]

VETA: Doctor, you might as well go home and wait. I'm suing you for fifty thousand dollars and that's final. [*Crosses to phone—her back is to mantel; she hasn't looked up*]

CHUMLEY: [*Follows her*] Mrs. Simmons—

VETA: [*Into phone*] Yes— Well, all right.

CHUMLEY: This picture over your mantel.

VETA: That portrait happens to be the pride of this house.

CHUMLEY: [*Looking at her*] Who painted it?

VETA: Oh, some man. I forget his name. He was around here for the sittings, and then we paid him and he went away. Hello—yes— No. This is Dexter 1567. [*Hangs up*]

CHUMLEY: I suppose if you have the money to pay people, you can persuade them to do anything.

VETA: Well, Dr. Chumley— [*Walks over and faces him*] When you helped me out of that tub at your place, what did I say to you?

CHUMLEY: You expressed yourself. I don't remember the words.

VETA: I said, "Dr. Chumley, this is a belated civility." Isn't that what I said?

CHUMLEY: You said something of the sort—

VETA: You brought this up; you may as well learn something quick. I took a course in art this last winter. The difference between a fine oil painting and a mechanical thing like a photograph is simply this: a photograph shows only the reality; a painting shows not only the reality but the dream behind it—. It's our dreams that keep us going. That separate us from the beasts. I wouldn't even want to live if I thought it was all just eating and sleeping and taking off my clothes. Well—putting them on again— [*Turns—sees picture—screams—totters—falls back*] Oh—Doctor—oh—hold me—oh—

CHUMLEY: [*Taking hold of her*] Steady now—steady—don't get excited. Everything's all right. [*Seats her in chair*] Now—what's the matter?

VETA: [*Pointing*] Doctor—that is *not* my mother!

CHUMLEY: I'm glad to hear that.

VETA: Oh, Doctor. Elwood's been here. He's been here.

CHUMLEY: Better be quiet. [*Phone rings*] I'll take it. [*He answers it*] Hello. Yes, yes—who's calling? [*Drops his hand over mouthpiece quickly*] Here he is. Mrs. Simmons, it's your brother!

VETA: [*Getting up. Weak no longer*] Oh—let me talk to him!

CHUMLEY: Don't tell him I'm here. Be casual.

VETA: Hello, Elwood—[*Laughs*] Where are you? What? Oh—just a minute. [*Covers phone*] He won't say where he is. He wants to know if Harvey is here.

CHUMLEY: Tell him Harvey *is* here.

VETA: But he isn't.

CHUMLEY: Tell him. That will bring him here, perhaps. Humor him. We have to humor them.

VETA: Yes—Elwood. Yes, dear. Harvey is here. Why don't you come home? Oh, oh, oh—well—all right. [*Looks around uncomfortably. Covers phone again*] It won't work. He says for me to call Harvey to the telephone.

CHUMLEY: Say Harvey is here, but can't come to the telephone. Say—he—say—he's in the bathtub.

VETA: Bathtub?

CHUMLEY: Say he's in the bathtub, and you'll send him over there. That way we'll find out where he is.

VETA: Oh, Doctor!

CHUMLEY: Now, you've got to do it, Mrs. Simmons.

VETA: Hello, Elwood. Yes, dear. Harvey is here but he can't come to the telephone, he's in the bathtub. I'll send him over as soon as he's dry. Where are you? Where, Elwood? [*Bangs phone*]

CHUMLEY: Did he hang up?

VETA: Harvey just walked in the door! He told me to look in the bathtub—it must be a stranger. But I know where he is. He's at Charlie's Place. That's a bar over at Twelfth and Main.

CHUMLEY: [*Picking up his hat from table*] Twelfth and Main. That's two blocks down and one over, isn't it?

VETA: Doctor—where are you going?

CHUMLEY: I'm going over there to get your brother and take him out to the sanitarium, where he belongs.

VETA: Oh, Dr. Chumley—don't do that. Send one of your attendants. I'm warning you.

CHUMLEY: But, Mrs. Simmons, if I am to help your brother—

VETA: He can't be helped. [*Looks at picture*] There is no help for him. He must be picked up and locked up and left.

CHUMLEY: You consider your brother a dangerous man?

VETA: Dangerous!

CHUMLEY: Why?

VETA: I won't tell you why, but if I didn't, why would I be asking for a permanent commitment for him?

CHUMLEY: Then I must observe this man. I must watch the expression on his face as he talks to this rabbit. He does talk to the rabbit, you say?

VETA: They tell each other everything.

CHUMLEY: What's that?

VETA: I said, of course he talks to him. But don't go after him, Doctor. You'll regret it if you do.

CHUMLEY: Nonsense. You underestimate me, Mrs. Simmons.

VETA: Oh, no, Doctor. You underestimate my brother.

CHUMLEY: Not at all. Don't worry now. I can handle him! [He exits]

VETA: [After he has gone] You can handle him? That's what you think! [Calls] Myrtle Mae! See who's in the bathtub. OH!

CURTAIN

SCENE TWO

The main office at Chumley's Rest again, four hours later.
   AT RISE: KELLY *is on the phone.* WILSON *is helping* SANDERSON *carry boxes of books out of his office and onto table.*

KELLY: Thank you. I may call later. [Hangs up]

WILSON: How about the stuff in your room, Doctor—upstairs?

SANDERSON: All packed—thanks—Wilson.

WILSON: Tough your gettin' bounced. I had you pegged for the one who'd make the grade.

SANDERSON: Those are the breaks.

WILSON: When you takin' off?

SANDERSON: As soon as Dr. Chumley gets back.

WILSON: [To KELLY] Did you get a report back yet from the desk sergeant in the police accident bureau?

KELLY: Not yet. I just talked to the downtown dispensary. They haven't seen him.

WILSON: It's beginning to smell awful funny to me. Four hours he's been gone and not a word from him. [Goes to SANDERSON—extends hand] I may not see you again, Doctor, so I want to say I wish you a lot of luck and I'm mighty sorry you got a kick in the atpray.

SANDERSON: Thanks, Wilson—good luck to you, too—

WILSON: [*Starts to exit, but stops at door, turns toward* KELLY] Look, Kelly, let me know when you hear from the desk sergeant again. If there's no sign of the doctor, I'm goin' into town and look for him. He should know better'n to go after a psycho without me.

SANDERSON: I'd like to help look for the doctor, too, Wilson.

WILSON: That's swell of you, Doctor, right after he give you the brush.

SANDERSON: I've no resentment against Dr. Chumley. He was right. I was wrong. [*He rises*] Chumley is the biggest man in his field. It's my loss not to be able to work with him.

WILSON: You're not so small yourself, Doctor—

SANDERSON: Thanks, Wilson.

WILSON: Don't mention it. [*Exits*]

KELLY: [*Taking deep breath*] Dr. Sanderson—

SANDERSON: [*Without looking up*] Yes—

KELLY: [*Plunging in*] Well, Doctor—[*Takes another deep breath*] I'd like to say that I wish you a lot of luck, too, and I'm sorry to see you leave.

SANDERSON: [*Going on with his work*] Are you sure you can spare these good wishes, Miss Kelly?

KELLY: [*She flushes*] On second thought—I guess I can't. Forget it.

SANDERSON: [*Now looking up*] Miss Kelly—This is for nothing—just a little advice. I'd be a little careful if I were you about the kind of company I kept.

KELLY: I beg your pardon, Doctor?

SANDERSON: You don't have to. I told you it was free. I saw you Saturday night—dancing with the drip in the Rose Room down at the Frontier Hotel.

KELLY: [*Putting books on desk*] Oh, did you? I didn't notice you.

SANDERSON: I'd be a little careful of him, Kelly. He looked to me like a schizophrenic all the way across the floor.

KELLY: You really shouldn't have given him a thought, Doctor. He was my date—not yours. [*Hands book to* SANDERSON]

SANDERSON: That was his mentality. The rest of him—well—

KELLY: But she was beautiful, though—

SANDERSON: Who?

KELLY: That girl you were with—

SANDERSON: I thought you didn't notice?

KELLY: You bumped into us twice. How could I help it?

SANDERSON: Not that it makes any difference to you, but that girl is a charming little lady. *She* has a sweet kind disposition and *she* knows how to conduct herself.

KELLY: Funny she couldn't rate a better date on a Saturday night!

SANDERSON: And she has an excellent mind.

KELLY: Why doesn't she use it?

SANDERSON: Oh, I don't suppose you're to be censured for the flippant hard shell you have. You're probably compensating for something.

KELLY: I am not, and don't you use any of your psychiatry on me.

SANDERSON: Oh—if I could try something else on you—just once! Just to see if you'd melt under any circumstances. I doubt it.

KELLY: You'll never know, Doctor.

SANDERSON: Because you interest me as a case history—that's all. I'd like to know where you get that inflated ego—

KELLY: [Now close to tears] If you aren't the meanest person—inflated ego— case history! [Turns and starts out]

SANDERSON: Don't run away. Let's finish it.

    [Phone rings]

KELLY: Oh, leave me alone. [Goes to answer it]

SANDERSON: Gladly. [Exits]

KELLY: [In angry, loud voice] Chumley's Rest. Yes—Sergeant. No accident report on him either in town or the suburbs. Look, Sergeant—maybe we better— [Looks up as door opens and ELWOOD enters. He is carrying a bouquet of dahlias] Oh, never mind, Sergeant. They're here now. [Hangs up. Goes toward ELWOOD] Mr. Dowd—!

ELWOOD: [Handing her flowers] Good evening, my dear. These are for you.

KELLY: For me—oh, thank you!

ELWOOD: They're quite fresh, too. I just picked them outside.

KELLY: I hope Dr. Chumley didn't see you. They're his prize dahlias. Did he go upstairs?

ELWOOD: Not knowing, I cannot state. Those colors are lovely against your hair.

KELLY: I've never worn burnt orange. It's such a trying color.

ELWOOD: You would improve any color, my dear.

KELLY: Thank you. Did Dr. Chumley go over to his house?

ELWOOD: I don't know. Where is Dr. Sanderson?

KELLY: In his office there—I think.

ELWOOD: [Going over to door and knocking] Thank you.

SANDERSON: [Enters] Dowd! There you are!

ELWOOD: I have a cab outside, if it's possible for you and Miss Kelly to get away now.

SANDERSON: Where is Dr. Chumley?

ELWOOD: Is he coming with us? That's nice.

KELLY: [*Answering question on* SANDERSON'S *face*] I don't know, Doctor.

ELWOOD: I must apologize for being a few seconds late. I thought Miss Kelly should have some flowers. After what happened out here this afternoon the flowers really should be from you, Doctor. As you grow older and pretty women pass you by, you will think with deep gratitude of these generous girls of your youth. Shall we go now?

[KELLY *exits*]

SANDERSON: [*Pressing buzzer*] Just a moment, Dowd— The situation has changed since we met this afternoon. But I urge you to have no resentments. Dr. Chumley is your friend. He only wants to help you.

ELWOOD: That's very nice of him. I would like to help him, too.

SANDERSON: If you'll begin by taking a cooperative attitude—that's half the battle. We all have to face reality, Dowd—sooner or later.

ELWOOD: Doctor, I wrestled with reality for forty years, and I am happy to state that I finally won out over it. [KELLY *enters*] Won't you and Miss Kelly join me—down at Charlie's?

[*Enter* WILSON]

WILSON: Here you are! [*Goes over to* ELWOOD] Upstairs, buddy—we're going upstairs. Is the doctor O.K.? [*He asks* SANDERSON *this*]

ELWOOD: There must be some mistake. Miss Kelly and Dr. Sanderson and I are going downtown for a drink. I'd be glad to have you come with us, Mr.—

WILSON: Wilson.

ELWOOD: —Wilson. They have a wonderful floor show.

WILSON: Yeah? Well—wait'll you see the floor show we've got— Upstairs, buddy!

SANDERSON: Just a minute, Wilson. Where did you say Dr. Chumley went, Dowd?

ELWOOD: As I said, he did not confide his plans in me.

WILSON: You mean the doctor ain't showed up yet?

KELLY: Not yet.

WILSON: Where is he?

SANDERSON: That's what we're trying to find out.

KELLY: Mr. Dowd walked in here by himself.

WILSON: Oh, he did, eh? Listen, you—talk fast or I'm workin' you over!

ELWOOD: I'd rather you didn't do that, and I'd rather you didn't even mention such a thing in the presence of a lovely young lady like Miss Kelly—

SANDERSON: Mr. Dowd, Dr. Chumley went into town to pick you up. That was four hours ago.

ELWOOD: Where has the evening gone to?

WILSON: Listen to that! Smart, eh?

SANDERSON: Just a minute, Wilson. Did you see Dr. Chumley tonight, Dowd?

ELWOOD: Yes, I did. He came into Charlie's Place at dinner time. It is a cozy spot. Let's all go there and talk it over with a tall one.

WILSON: We're going no place— Now I'm askin' you a question, and if you don't button up your lip and give me some straight answers I'm gonna beat it out of you!

ELWOOD: What you suggest is impossible.

WILSON: What's that?

ELWOOD: You suggest that I button up my lip and give you some straight answers. It can't be done.

SANDERSON: Let me handle this, Wilson.

WILSON: Well, handle it, then. But find out where the doctor is.

SANDERSON: Dr. Chumley *did* come into Charlie's Place, you say?

ELWOOD: He did, and I was very glad to see him.

WILSON: Go on—

ELWOOD: He had asked for me, and naturally the proprietor brought him over and left him. We exchanged the conventional greetings. I said, "How do you do, Dr. Chumley," and he said, "How do you do, Mr. Dowd." I believe we said that at least once.

WILSON: Okay—okay—

ELWOOD: I am trying to be factual. I then introduced him to Harvey.

WILSON: To who?

KELLY: A white rabbit. Six feet tall.

WILSON: Six feet!

ELWOOD: Six feet one and a half!

WILSON: Okay—fool around with him, and the doctor is probably some place bleedin' to death in a ditch.

ELWOOD: If those were his plans for the evening he did not tell me.

SANDERSON: Go on, Dowd.

ELWOOD: Dr. Chumley sat down in the booth with us. I was sitting on the outside like this. [*Shows*] Harvey was on the inside near the wall, and Dr. Chumley was seated directly across from Harvey where he could look at him.

WILSON: That's right. Spend all night on the seatin' arrangements!

ELWOOD: Harvey then suggested that I buy him a drink. Knowing that he does not like to drink alone, I suggested to Dr. Chumley that we join him.

WILSON: And so?

ELWOOD: We joined him.

WILSON: Go on—go on.

ELWOOD: We joined him again.

WILSON: Then what?

ELWOOD: We kept right on joining him.

WILSON: Oh, skip all the joining!

ELWOOD: You are asking me to skip a large portion of the evening—

WILSON: Tell us what happened—come on—please—

ELWOOD: Dr. Chumley and Harvey got into a conversation—quietly at first. Later it became rather heated and Dr. Chumley raised his voice.

WILSON: Yeah—why?

ELWOOD: Harvey seemed to feel that Dr. Chumley should assume part of the financial responsibility of the joining, but Dr. Chumley didn't seem to want to do that.

KELLY: [*It breaks out from her*] I can believe *that* part of it!

WILSON: Let him talk. See how far he'll go. This guy's got guts.

ELWOOD: I agreed to take the whole thing because I did not want any trouble. We go down to Charlie's quite often—Harvey and I—and the proprietor is a fine man with an interesting approach to life. Then the other matter came up.

WILSON: Cut the damned double talk and get on with it!

ELWOOD: Mr. Wilson, you are a sincere type of person, but I must ask you not to use that language in the presence of Miss Kelly. [*He makes a short bow to her*]

SANDERSON: You're right, Dowd, and we're sorry. You say—the other matter came up?

ELWOOD: There was a beautiful blonde woman—a Mrs. Smethills—and her escort seated in the booth across from us. Dr. Chumley went over to sit next to her, explaining to her that they had once met. In Chicago. Her escort escorted Dr. Chumley back to me and Harvey and tried to point out that it would be better for Dr. Chumley to mind his own affairs. Does he have any?

WILSON: Does he have any what?

ELWOOD: Does he have any affairs?

WILSON: How would I know?

KELLY: Please hurry, Mr. Dowd—we're all so worried.

ELWOOD: Dr. Chumley then urged Harvey to go with him over to Blondie's Chicken Inn. Harvey wanted to go to Eddie's instead. While they were arguing about it I went to the bar to order another drink, and when I came back they were gone.

WILSON: Where did they go? I mean where did the doctor go?

ELWOOD: I don't know—I had a date out here with Dr. Sanderson and Miss

Kelly, and I came out to pick them up—hoping that later on we might run into Harvey and the doctor and make a party of it.

WILSON: So—you satisfied? You got his story—[*Goes over to* ELWOOD, *fists clenched*] O.K. You're lyin' and we know it!

ELWOOD: I never lie, Mr. Wilson.

WILSON: You've done somethin' with the doctor and I'm findin' out what it is—

SANDERSON: [*Moving after him*] Don't touch him, Wilson—

KELLY: Maybe he isn't lying, Wilson—

WILSON: [*Turning on them. Furiously*] That's all this guy is, a bunch of lies! You two don't believe this story he tells about the doctor sittin' there talkin' to a big white rabbit, do you?

KELLY: Maybe Dr. Chumley *did* go to Charlie's Place.

WILSON: And saw a big rabbit, I suppose.

ELWOOD: And why not? Harvey was there. At first the doctor seemed a little frightened of Harvey but that gave way to admiration as the evening wore on—. The evening wore on! That's a nice expression. With your permission I'll say it again. The evening wore on.

WILSON: [*Lunging at him*] With your permission I'm gonna knock your teeth down your throat!

ELWOOD: [*Not moving an inch*] Mr. Wilson—haven't you some old friends you can go play with?

[SANDERSON *has grabbed* WILSON *and is struggling with him*]

WILSON: [*He is being held. Glares fiercely at* ELWOOD. KELLY *dials phone*] The nerve of this guy! He couldn't come out here with an ordinary case of d.t.'s. No. He has to come out with a six-foot rabbit!

ELWOOD: Stimulating as all this is, I really must be getting downtown.

KELLY: [*On phone*] Charlie's Place? Is Dr. Chumley anywhere around there? He was there with Mr. Dowd earlier in the evening. What? Well, don't bite my head off! [*Hangs up*] My, that man was mad. He said Mr. Dowd was welcome any time, but his friend was not.

ELWOOD: That's Mr. McNulty the bartender. He thinks a lot of me. Now let's all go down and have a drink.

WILSON: Wait a minute—

KELLY: Mr. Dowd— [*Goes over to him*]

ELWOOD: Yes, my dear—may I hold your hand?

KELLY: Yes—if you want to. [ELWOOD *does*] Poor Mrs. Chumley is so worried. Something must have happened to the doctor. Won't you please try and remember something—something else that might help her? Please—

ELWOOD: For you I would do anything. I would almost be willing to live my life over again. Almost. But I've told it all.

KELLY: You're sure?

ELWOOD: Quite sure—but ask me again, anyway, won't you? I liked that warm tone you had in your voice just then.

SANDERSON: [*Without realizing he is saying it*] So did I. [*Looks at* KELLY]

WILSON: Oh, nuts!

ELWOOD: What?

WILSON: Nuts!

ELWOOD: Oh! I must be going. I have things to do.

KELLY: Mr. Dowd, what is it you do?

ELWOOD: [*Sits, as* KELLY *sits at desk*] Harvey and I sit in the bars and we have a drink or two and play the juke box. Soon the faces of the other people turn toward mine and smile. They are saying "We don't know your name, Mister, but you're a lovely fellow." Harvey and I warm ourselves in all these golden moments. We have entered as strangers—soon we have friends. They come over. They sit with us. They drink with us. They talk to us. They tell about the big terrible things they have done. The big wonderful things they *will* do. Their hopes, their regrets, their loves, their hates. All very large because nobody ever brings anything small into a bar. Then I introduce them to Harvey. And he is bigger and grander than anything they offer me. When they leave, they leave impressed. The same people seldom come back—but that's envy, my dear. There's a little bit of envy in the best of us—too bad, isn't it?

SANDERSON: [*Leaning forward*] How did you happen to call him Harvey?

ELWOOD: Harvey is his name.

SANDERSON: How do you know that?

ELWOOD: That was rather an interesting coincidence, Doctor. One night several years ago I was walking early in the evening along Fairfax Street— between Eighteenth and Nineteenth. You know that block?

SANDERSON: Yes, yes.

ELWOOD: I had just helped Ed Hickey into a taxi. Ed had been mixing his rye with his gin, and I felt he needed conveying. I started to walk down the street when I heard a voice saying: "Good evening, Mr. Dowd." I turned and there was this great white rabbit leaning against a lamppost. Well, I thought nothing of that, because when you have lived in a town as long as I have lived in this one, you get used to the fact that everybody knows your name. Naturally, I went over to chat with him. He said to me: "Ed Hickey is a little spiffed this evening, or could I be mistaken?" Well, of course he was not mistaken. I think the world and all of Ed but he was spiffed. Well, anyway, we stood there and talked, and finally I said—"You have the advantage of me. You know my name and I don't know yours." Right back at me he said: "What name do you like?" Well, I didn't even have to think a minute: Harvey has always been my favorite name. So I said, "Harvey," and this is the interesting part of the whole thing. He said—"What a coincidence! My name happens to be Harvey."

SANDERSON: What was your father's name, Dowd?

ELWOOD: John. John Frederick.

SANDERSON: Dowd, when you were a child you had a playmate, didn't you? Someone you were very fond of—with whom you spent many happy, carefree hours?

ELWOOD: Oh, yes, Doctor. Didn't you?

SANDERSON: What was his name?

ELWOOD: Verne. Verne McElhinney. Did you ever know the McElhinneys, Doctor?

SANDERSON: No.

ELWOOD: Too bad. There were a lot of them, and they circulated. Wonderful people.

SANDERSON: Think carefully, Dowd. Wasn't there someone, somewhere, sometime, whom you knew—by the name of Harvey? Didn't you ever know anybody by that name?

ELWOOD: No, Doctor. No one. Maybe that's why I always had such hopes for it.

SANDERSON: Come on, Wilson, We'll take Mr. Dowd upstairs now.

WILSON: I'm taking him nowhere. You've made this your show—now run it. Lettin' him set here—forgettin' all about Dr. Chumley! O.K. It's your show—you run it.

SANDERSON: Come on, Dowd— [*Pause. Putting out his hand*] Come on, Elwood—

ELWOOD: [*Rises*] Very well, Lyman. [SANDERSON *and* KELLY *take him to door*] But I'm afraid I won't be able to visit with you for long. I have promised Harvey I will take him to the floor show.

[*They exit.* WILSON *is alone. Sits at desk, looks at his watch*]

WILSON: Oh, boy! [*Puts head in arms on desk.* DR. CHUMLEY *enters.* WILSON *does not see him until he gets almost to the center of the room*]

WILSON: [*Jumping up, going to him*] Dr. Chumley—Are you all right?

CHUMLEY: All right? Of course I'm all right. I'm being followed. Lock that door.

WILSON: [*Goes to door, locks it*] Who's following you?

CHUMLEY: None of your business!

[*Exits into office and locks door behind him.* WILSON *stands a moment perplexed, then shrugs shoulders, turns off lights and exits. The stage is dimly lit. Then from door left comes the rattle of the doorknob. Door opens and shuts, and we hear locks opening and closing, and see light from the hall. The invisible* HARVEY *has come in. There is a* count of eight while he crosses the stage, then door of CHUMLEY'S office opens and closes, with sound of locks clicking. Harvey has gone in—and then—]

CURTAIN

ACT THREE

The sanitarium office at Chumley's Rest, a few minutes later.

AT RISE: Lights are still dim as at preceding curtain. There is a loud knocking and the sound of CHUMLEY's voice calling, "Wilson! Wilson!"

WILSON: [Enters, opens outside door. CHUMLEY enters, white-faced] How didja get out here, Doctor? I just saw you go in there.

CHUMLEY: I went out through my window. Wilson—don't leave me!

WILSON: No, Doctor.

CHUMLEY: Get that man Dowd out of here.

WILSON: Yes, Doctor. [Starts to exit]

CHUMLEY: No—don't leave me!

WILSON: [Turning back—confused] But you said—

CHUMLEY: Dumphy—on the telephone.

WILSON: Yes, Doctor. [Crosses to phone] Dumphy—give that guy Dowd his clothes and get him down here right away.

[A knock on the door]

CHUMLEY: Don't leave me!

WILSON: Just a minute, Doctor. [Turns on lights. Opens door] Judge Gaffney.

JUDGE: I want to see Dr. Chumley. [Enter JUDGE and MYRTLE MAE]

WILSON: Hiya, Myrtle.

MYRTLE: Hello.

JUDGE: Chumley, we've got to talk to you. This thing is serious.

MYRTLE: It certainly is.

JUDGE: More serious than you suspect. Where can we go to talk? [Moves toward CHUMLEY's office]

CHUMLEY: [Blocking door] Not in there.

WILSON: The Doctor doesn't want you in his office.

CHUMLEY: No, sir.

JUDGE: Then sit down, Dr. Chumley. Sit down, Myrtle Mae.

CHUMLEY: [*Dazed*] Sit down, Dr. Chumley. Sit down, Myrtle Mae. Don't go, Wilson. Don't leave me.

JUDGE: Now, Chumley, here are my notes—the facts. Can anybody hear me?

WILSON: Yeah, we can all hear you. Is that good?

JUDGE: [*Gives* WILSON *a look of reproof*] Now, Chumley, has it ever occurred to you that possibly there might *be* something like this rabbit Harvey?

MYRTLE: Of course there isn't. And anybody who thinks so is crazy. [CHUMLEY *stares at her*] Well, don't look at me like that. There's nothing funny about me. I'm like my father's family—they're all dead.

JUDGE: Now, then, my client, the plaintiff, Mrs. Veta Louise Simmons, under oath, swears that on the morning of November second while standing in the kitchen of her home, hearing her name called, she turned and saw this great white rabbit, Harvey. He was staring at her. Resenting the intrusion, the plaintiff made certain remarks and drove the creature from the room. He went.

CHUMLEY: What did she say to him?

JUDGE: She was emphatic. The remarks are not important.

CHUMLEY: I want to know how she got this creature out of her sanitarium—I mean—her home.

MYRTLE: I hate to have you tell him, Judge. It isn't a bit like Mother.

WILSON: Quit stalling. Let's have it.

JUDGE: She looked him right in the eye and exclaimed in the heat of anger— "To hell with you!"

CHUMLEY: [*Looking at door*] "To hell with you!" He left?

JUDGE: Yes, he left. But that's beside the point. The point is—is it perjury or is it something we can cope with? I ask for your opinion.

[KELLY *enters from stairs;* SANDERSON *comes from diet kitchen*]

SANDERSON: Ruthie! I've been looking all over for you.

CHUMLEY: Dr. Sanderson, disregard what I said this afternoon. I want you on my staff. You are a very astute young man.

KELLY: Oh, Lyman! Did you hear?

SANDERSON: Oh, baby!

KELLY: See you later. [*Exits, blowing him a kiss.* SANDERSON *exits into his office*]

MYRTLE: You've just got to keep Uncle Elwood out here, Doctor.

CHUMLEY: No. I want this sanitarium the way it was before that man came out here this afternoon.

MYRTLE: I know what you mean.

CHUMLEY: You do?

MYRTLE: Well, it certainly gets on anyone's nerves the way Uncle Elwood knows what's going to happen before it happens. This morning, for instance, he told us that Harvey told him Mrs. McElhinney's Aunt Rose would drop in on her unexpectedly tonight from Cleveland.

CHUMLEY: And did she?

MYRTLE: Did she what?

CHUMLEY: Aunt Rose—did she come just as Harvey said she would?

MYRTLE: Oh, yes. Those things always turn out the way Uncle Elwood says they will—but what of it? What do we care about the McElhinneys?

CHUMLEY: You say this sort of thing happens often?

MYRTLE: Yes, and isn't it silly? Uncle Elwood says Harvey tells him everything. Harvey knows everything. How could he when there is no such thing as Harvey?

CHUMLEY: [Goes over, tries lock at door] Fly-specks. I've been spending my life among fly-specks while miracles have been leaning on lampposts on Eighteenth and Fairfax.

VETA: [Enters. Looks around cautiously. Sighs with relief] Good. Nobody here but people.

MYRTLE: Oh, Mother! You promised you wouldn't come out here.

VETA: Well, good evening. Now Myrtle Mae, I brought Elwood's bathrobe. Well, why are you all just sitting here? I thought you'd be committing him.

JUDGE: Sit down there, girl. [Motioning to chair near WILSON]

VETA: I will not sit down there.

WILSON: How about you and me stepping out Saturday night, Myrtle Mae?

VETA: Certainly not. Myrtle Mae, come here.

MYRTLE: I'm sorry.

VETA: Is everything settled?

CHUMLEY: It will be

[SANDERSON enters from his office.]

SANDERSON: Doctor, may I give an opinion?

CHUMLEY: Yes, do. By all means.

VETA: [Sniffing] His opinion! Omar—he's the doctor I told you about. The eyes!

SANDERSON: It's my opinion that Elwood P. Dowd is suffering from a third-degree hallucination and the— [Pointing at VETA's back] other party concerned is the victim of auto-suggestion. I recommend shock formula number 977 for him and bed rest at home for— [Points again]

CHUMLEY: You do?

SANDERSON: That's my diagnosis, Doctor. [*To* VETA] Mr. Dowd will not see this rabbit any more after this injection. We've used it in hundreds of psychopathic cases.

VETA: Don't you call my brother a psychopathic case! There's never been anything like that in our family.

MYRTLE: If you didn't think Uncle Elwood was psychopathic, why did you bring him out here?

VETA: Where else could I take him, I couldn't take him to jail, could I? Besides, this is not your uncle's fault. Why did Harvey have to speak to him in the first place? With the town full of people, why did he have to bother Elwood?

JUDGE: Stop putting your oar in. Keep your oar out. If this shock formula brings people back to reality, give it to him. That's where we want Elwood.

CHUMLEY: I'm not sure that it would work in a case of this kind, Doctor.

SANDERSON: It always has.

VETA: Harvey always follows Elwood home.

CHUMLEY: He does?

VETA: Yes. But if you give him the formula and Elwood doesn't see Harvey, he won't let him in. Then when he comes to the door, I'll deal with him.

MYRTLE: Mother, won't you stop talking about Harvey as if there was such a thing?

VETA: Myrtle Mae, you've got a lot to learn and I hope you never learn it. [*She starts up toward* WILSON. ELWOOD *is heard offstage humming*]

JUDGE: Sh! Here he is.

[ELWOOD *enters*]

ELWOOD: Good evening, everybody.

VETA: Good evening, Elwood. I've brought you your bathrobe.

ELWOOD: Thank you, Veta.

JUDGE: Well, Chumley, what do we do? We've got to do something.

VETA: Oh, yes, we must.

MYRTLE: I should say so.

CHUMLEY: [*Looking at door*] Yes, it's imperative.

ELWOOD: Well, while you're making up your minds, why don't we all go down to Charlie's and have a drink?

VETA: You're not going anywhere, Elwood. You're staying here.

MYRTLE: Yes, Uncle Elwood.

JUDGE: Stay here, son.

ELWOOD: I plan to leave. You want me to stay. An element of conflict in any discussion is a good thing. It means everybody is taking part and nobody is left out. I like that. Oh—how did you get along with Harvey, Doctor?

CHUMLEY: Sh-h!

JUDGE: We're waiting for your answer, Doctor.

CHUMLEY: What?

JUDGE: What is your decision?

CHUMLEY: I must be alone with this man. Will you all step into the other room? [MYRTLE *exits*] I'll have my diagnosis in a moment.

VETA: Do hurry, Doctor.

CHUMLEY: I will.

VETA: You stay here, Elwood. [*She and* JUDGE GAFFNEY *exit*]

CHUMLEY: Here, Mr. Dowd. Let me give you this chair. [*Indicates chair*] Let me give you a cigar. [*Does so*] Is there anything else I can get you?

ELWOOD: [*Seated in chair*] What did you have in mind?

CHUMLEY: Mr. Dowd—[*Lowers voice, looks toward office*] What kind of a man are you? Where do you come from?

ELWOOD: [*Getting out card*] Didn't I give you one of my cards?

CHUMLEY: And where on the face of this tired old earth did you find a thing like him?

ELWOOD: Harvey the pooka?

CHUMLEY: [*Sits*] Is it true that he has a function—that he—?

ELWOOD: Gets advance notice? I'm happy to say it is. Harvey is versatile. Harvey can stop clocks.

CHUMLEY: What?

ELWOOD: You've heard that expression, "His face would stop a clock"?

CHUMLEY: Yes. But why? To what purpose?

ELWOOD: Harvey says that he can look at your clock and stop it and you can go away as long as you like with whomever you like and go as far as you like. And when you come back not one minute will have ticked by.

CHUMLEY: You mean that he actually—? [*Looks toward office*]

ELWOOD: Einstein has overcome time and space. Harvey has overcome not only time and space—but any objections.

CHUMLEY: And does he do this for you?

ELWOOD: He is willing to at any time, but so far I've never been able to think of any place I'd rather be. I always have a wonderful time just where I am, whomever I'm with. I'm having a fine time right now with you, Doctor. [*Holds up cigar*] Corona-Corona.

CHUMLEY: I know where I'd go.

ELWOOD: Where?

CHUMLEY: I'd go to Akron.

ELWOOD: Akron?

CHUMLEY: There's a cottage camp outside Akron in a grove of maple trees, cool, green, beautiful.

ELWOOD: My favorite tree.

CHUMLEY: I would go there with a pretty young woman, a strange woman, a quiet woman.

ELWOOD: Under a tree?

CHUMLEY: I wouldn't even want to know her name. I would be—just Mr. Brown.

ELWOOD: Why wouldn't you want to know her name? You might be acquainted with the same people.

CHUMLEY: I would send out for cold beer. I would talk to her. I would tell her things I have never told anyone—things that are locked in here. [*Beats his breast.* ELWOOD *looks over at his chest with interest*] And then I would send out for more cold beer.

ELWOOD: No whisky?

CHUMLEY: Beer is better.

ELWOOD: Maybe under a tree. But she might like a highball.

CHUMLEY: I wouldn't let her talk to me, but as I talked I would want her to reach out a soft white hand and stroke my head and say, "Poor thing! Oh, you poor, poor thing!"

ELWOOD: How long would you like that to go on?

CHUMLEY: Two weeks.

ELWOOD: Wouldn't that get monotonous? Just Akron, beer, and "poor, poor thing" for two weeks?

CHUMLEY: No. No, it would not. It would be wonderful.

ELWOOD: I can't help but feel you're making a mistake in not allowing that woman to talk. If she gets around at all she may have picked up some very interesting little news items. And I'm sure you're making a mistake with all that beer and no whisky. But it's your two weeks.

CHUMLEY: [*Dreamily*] Cold beer at Akron and one last fling! God, man!

ELWOOD: Do you think you'd like to lie down for awhile?

CHUMLEY: No. No. Tell me, Mr. Dowd, could he—would he do this for me?

ELWOOD: He could and he might. I have never heard Harvey say a word against Akron. By the way, Doctor, where is Harvey?

CHUMLEY: [*Rising. Very cautiously*] Why, don't you know?

ELWOOD: The last time I saw him he was with you.

CHUMLEY: Ah!

ELWOOD: Oh! He's probably waiting for me down at Charlie's.

CHUMLEY: [*With a look of cunning toward his office*] That's it! He's down at Charlie's.

ELWOOD: Excuse me, Doctor. [*Rises*]

CHUMLEY: No, no, Mr. Dowd. Not in there.

ELWOOD: I couldn't leave without saying good-night to my friend, Dr. Sanderson.

CHUMLEY: Mr. Dowd, Dr. Sanderson is not your friend. None of those people are your friends. *I* am your friend.

ELWOOD: Thank you, Doctor. And I'm yours.

CHUMLEY: And this sister of yours—she is at the bottom of this conspiracy against you. She's trying to persuade me to lock you up. Today she had commitment papers drawn up. She's got your power of attorney and the key to your safety box. She brought you out here—

ELWOOD: My sister did all that in one afternoon? Veta is certainly a whirlwind.

CHUMLEY: God, man, haven't you any righteous indignation?

ELWOOD: Dr. Chumley, my mother used to say to me, "In this world, Elwood"—she always called me Elwood—she'd say, "In this world, Elwood, you must be oh, so smart or oh, so pleasant." For years I was smart. I recommend pleasant. You may quote me.

CHUMLEY: Just the same, I will protect you if I have to commit her. Would you like me to do that?

ELWOOD: No, Doctor, not unless Veta wanted it that way. Oh, not that you don't have a nice place out here, but I think Veta would be happier at home with me and Harvey and Myrtle Mae. [KELLY *enters with flower in hair, goes to put magazines on table.* ELWOOD *turns to her*] Miss Kelly! "Diviner grace has never brightened this enchanting face!" [*To* CHUMLEY] Ovid's Fifth Elegy. [*To* MISS KELLY] My dear, you will never look lovelier!

KELLY: I'll never feel happier, Mr. Dowd. I know it. [*Kisses him*]

CHUMLEY: Well!

KELLY: Yes, Doctor. [*Exits.* WILSON *enters hall in time to see the kiss*]

ELWOOD: I wonder if I would be able to remember any more of that poem?

WILSON: Say, maybe this rabbit gag is a good one. Kelly never kissed me.

ELWOOD: [*Looking at* WILSON] Ovid has always been my favorite poet.

WILSON: O.K., pal— You're discharged. This way out— [*Takes him by arm downstage*]

CHUMLEY: Wilson! Take your hands off that man!

WILSON: What?

CHUMLEY: Apologize to Mr. Dowd.

WILSON: Apologize to him—this guy with the rabbit?

CHUMLEY: [*Looking toward his office*] Apologize! Apologize—

WILSON: I apologize. This is the door.

ELWOOD: If I leave, I'll remember. [WILSON *exits*]

CHUMLEY: Wait a minute, Dowd. Do women often come up to you and kiss you like Miss Kelly did just now?

ELWOOD: Every once in a while.

CHUMLEY: Yes?

ELWOOD: I encourage it, too.

CHUMLEY: [*To himself*] To hell with decency! I've got to have that rabbit! Go ahead and knock.

　　　[ELWOOD *starts for* SANDERSON's *door just as* SANDERSON *comes out*]

ELWOOD: Dr. Sanderson, I couldn't leave without—

SANDERSON: Just a minute, Dowd—[*To* CHUMLEY] Doctor, do you agree with my diagnosis?

CHUMLEY: Yes, yes! Call them all in.

SANDERSON: Thank you, Doctor. Mrs. Simmons—Judge Gaffney—will you step in here for a minute, please?

　　　[VETA *enters*]

VETA: Is it settled?

　　　[MYRTLE *and* JUDGE *enter*]

CHUMLEY: I find I concur with Dr. Sanderson!

SANDERSON: Thank you, Doctor.

MYRTLE: Oh, that's wonderful! What a relief!

JUDGE: Good boy!

ELWOOD: Well, let's celebrate—[*Takes little book out of his pocket*] I've got some new bars listed in the back of this book.

CHUMLEY: [*Speaking to others in low tone*] This injection carries a violent reaction. We can't give it to him without his consent. Will he give it?

VETA: Of course he will, if I ask him.

CHUMLEY: To give up this rabbit—I doubt it.

MYRTLE: Don't ask him. Just give it to him.

ELWOOD: "Bessie's Barn Dance. Blondie's Chicken Inn. Better Late Than Never—Bennie's Drive In"—

VETA: Elwood!

ELWOOD: We'll go to Bennie's Drive In. We should telephone for a table. How many of us will there be, Veta?

VETA: [*Starting to count, then catching herself*] Oh—Elwood!

CHUMLEY: Mr. Dowd, I have a formula—977—that will be good for you. Will you take it?

JUDGE: Elwood, you won't see this rabbit any more.

SANDERSON: But you will see your responsibilities, your duties—

ELWOOD: I'm sure if you thought of it, Doctor, it must be a very fine thing. And if I happen to run into anyone who needs it, I'll be glad to recommend it. For myself, I wouldn't care for it.

VETA: Hear that, Judge! Hear that, Doctor! That's what we have to put up with.

ELWOOD: [*Turning to look at her*] Veta, do you want me to take this?

VETA: Elwood, I'm only thinking of you. You're my brother and I've known you for years. I'd do anything for you. That Harvey wouldn't do anything for you. He's making a fool out of you, Elwood. Don't be a fool.

ELWOOD: Oh, I won't.

VETA: Why, you could amount to something. You could be sitting on the Western Slope Water Board right now if you'd only go over and ask them.

ELWOOD: All right, Veta. If that's what you want, Harvey and I will go over and ask them tomorrow.

VETA: Tomorrow! I never want to see another tomorrow. Not if Myrtle Mae and I have to live in the house with that rabbit. Our friends never come to see us—we have no social life; we have no life at all. We're both miserable. I wish I were dead—but maybe you don't care!

ELWOOD: [*Slowly*] I've always felt that Veta should have everything she wants. Veta, are you sure? [VETA *nods*] I'll take it. Where do I go, Doctor?

CHUMLEY: In Dr. Sanderson's office, Dowd.

ELWOOD: Say goodbye to the old fellow for me, won't you? [*Exits.* CHUMLEY *exits*]

JUDGE: How long will this take, Doctor?

SANDERSON: Only a few minutes. Why don't you wait? [*Exits*]

JUDGE: We'll wait. [*Sits*]

VETA: [*Sighs*] Dr. Sanderson said it wouldn't take long.

MYRTLE: Now, Mother, don't fidget.

VETA: Oh, how can I help it?

MYRTLE: [*Picks up edge of draperies*] How stunning! Mother, could you see me in a housecoat of this material?

VETA: [*To* MYRTLE—*first looking at draperies. Sighs again*] Yes, dear, but let me get a good night's sleep first.

[*Loud knocking at door*]

JUDGE: Come in. [*Enter* CAB DRIVER] What do you want?

CAB DRIVER: I'm lookin' for a little, short— [*Seeing* VETA] Oh, there you are! Lady, you jumped outta the cab without payin' me.

VETA: Oh, yes. I forgot. How much is it?

CAB DRIVER: All the way out here from town? $2.75.

VETA: [*Looking in purse*] Two seventy-five! I could have sworn I brought my coin purse—where is it? [*Gets up, goes to table, turns pocketbook upside down. Nothing comes out of it but a compact and a handkerchief*]

Myrtle, do you have any money?

MYRTLE: I spent that money Uncle Elwood gave me for my new hairdo for the party.

VETA: Judge, do you have $2.75 I could give this man?

JUDGE: Sorry. Nothing but a check.

CAB DRIVER: We don't take checks.

JUDGE: I know.

VETA: Dr. Chumley, do you happen to have $2.75 I could borrow to pay this cab driver?

CHUMLEY: [*He has just entered, now wearing white starched jacket*] Haven't got my wallet. No time to get it now. Have to get on with this injection. Sorry. [*Exits*]

VETA: Well, I'll get it for you from my brother, but I can't get it right now. He's in there to get an injection. It won't be long. You'll have to wait.

CAB DRIVER: You're gonna get my money from your brother and he's in there to get some of that stuff they shoot out here?

VETA: Yes, it won't be but a few minutes.

CAB DRIVER: Lady, I want my money now.

VETA: But I told you it would only be a few minutes. I want you to drive us back to town, anyway.

CAB DRIVER: And I told you I want my money now or I'm nosin' the cab back to town, and you can wait for the bus—at six in the morning.

VETA: Well, of all the pig-headed, stubborn things—!

MYRTLE: I should say so.

JUDGE: What's the matter with you?

CAB DRIVER: Nothin' that $2.75 won't fix. You heard me. Take it or leave it.

VETA: [*Getting up*] I never heard of anything so unreasonable in my life. [*Knocks*] Dr. Chumley, will you let Elwood step out here a minute. This cab driver won't wait.

CHUMLEY: [*Off*] Don't be too long.

[*Enter ELWOOD. CHUMLEY follows*]

VETA: Elwood, I came off without my coin purse. Will you give this man $2.75? But don't give him any more. He's been very rude.

ELWOOD: [*Extending his hand*] How do you do? Dowd is my name. Elwood P.

CAB DRIVER: Lofgren's mine. E. J.

ELWOOD: I'm glad to meet you, Mr. Lofgren. This is my sister, Mrs. Simmons. My charming little niece, Myrtle Mae Simmons. Judge Gaffney and Dr. Chumley. [*All bow coldly*]

CAB DRIVER: Hi—

ELWOOD: Have you lived around here long, Mr. Lofgren?

CAB DRIVER: Yeah, I've lived around here all my life.

ELWOOD: Do you enjoy your work?

CAB DRIVER: It's O.K. I been with the Apex Cabs fifteen years and my brother Joe's been drivin' for Brown Cabs pretty near twelve.

ELWOOD: You drive for Apex and your brother Joe for Brown's? That's interesting, isn't it, Veta? [VETA *reacts with a sniff*] Mr. Lofgren—let me give you one of my cards. [*Gives him one*]

CHUMLEY: Better get on with this, Mr. Dowd.

ELWOOD: Certainly. One minute. My sister and my charming little niece live here with me at this address. Won't you and your brother come and have dinner with us some time?

CAB DRIVER: Sure—be glad to.

ELWOOD: When—when would you be glad to?

CAB DRIVER: I couldn't come any night but Tuesday. I'm on duty all the rest of the week.

ELWOOD: You must come on Tuesday, then. We'll expect you and be delighted to see you, won't we, Veta?

VETA: Oh, Elwood, I'm sure this man has friends of his own.

ELWOOD: Veta, one can't have too many friends.

VETA: Elwood, don't keep Dr. Chumley waiting—that's rude.

ELWOOD: Of course. [*Gives him bill*] Here you are—keep the change. I'm glad to have met you and I'll expect you Tuesday with your brother. Will you excuse me now?

CAB DRIVER: Sure. [ELWOOD *exits.* CHUMLEY *follows*] A sweet guy.

VETA: Certainly. You could just as well have waited.

CAB DRIVER: Oh, no. Listen, lady. I've been drivin' this route fifteen years. I've brought 'em out here to get that stuff and drove 'em back after they had it. It changes 'em.

VETA: Well, I certainly hope so.

CAB DRIVER: And you ain't kiddin'. On the way out here they sit back and enjoy the ride. They talk to me. Sometimes we stop and watch the sunsets and look at the birds flyin'. Sometimes we stop and watch the birds when there ain't no birds and look at the sunsets when it's rainin'. We have a swell time and I always get a big tip. But afterward—oh—oh— [*Starts to exit again*]

VETA: Afterwards—oh—oh! What do you mean afterwards—oh—oh?

CAB DRIVER: They crab, crab, crab. They yell at me to watch the lights, watch the brakes, watch the intersections. They scream at me to hurry. They got no faith—in me or my buggy—yet it's the same cab—the same driver— and we're goin' back over the very same road. It's no fun—and no tips—[*Turns to door*]

VETA: But my brother would have tipped you, anyway. He's very generous. Always has been.

CAB DRIVER: Not after this he won't be. Lady, after this, he'll be a perfectly normal human being and you know what bastards they are! Glad I met you. I'll wait. [*Exits*]

VETA: [*Starts to run for door*] Oh, Judge Gaffney—Myrtle Mae! Stop it—stop it—don't give it to him! Elwood, come out of there.

JUDGE: You can't do that. Dr. Chumley is giving the injection.

MYRTLE: Mother—stop this—

VETA: [*Pounding on door*] I don't want Elwood to have it! I don't want Elwood that way. I don't like people like that.

MYRTLE: Do something with her, Judge—Mother, stop it—

VETA: [*Turning to her*] You shut up! I've lived longer than you have. I remember my father. I remember your father. I remember—

CHUMLEY: [*Opens door*] What's this? What's all this commotion?

WILSON: [*Enters*] What's the trouble, Doctor? She soundin' off again?

JUDGE: She wants to stop the injection.

VETA: You haven't—you haven't already given it to him, have you?

CHUMLEY: No, but we're ready. Take Mrs. Simmons away, Wilson.

VETA: Leave me alone. Take your hands off me, you white slaver!

JUDGE: You don't know what you want. You didn't want that rabbit, either.

VETA: And what's wrong with Harvey? If Elwood and Myrtle Mae and I want to live with Harvey it's nothing to you! You don't even have to come around. It's our business. Elwood—Elwood!

[ELWOOD *enters. She throws herself weepingly into his arms. He pats her shoulder*]

ELWOOD: There, there, Veta. [*To others*] Veta is all tired out. She's done a lot today.

JUDGE: Have it your own way. I'm not giving up my game at the club again, no matter how big the animal is. [*He exits*]

VETA: Come on, Elwood—let's get out of here. I hate this place. I wish I'd never seen it!

CHUMLEY: But—see—here—

ELWOOD: It's whatever Veta says, Doctor.

VETA: Why, look at this! That's funny. [*It's her coin purse*] It must have been there all the time. I could have paid that cab driver myself. Harvey! Come on, Myrtle Mae. Come on, Elwood. Hurry up. [*She exits.* MYRTLE *follows*]

ELWOOD: Good night, Doctor Chumley. Good night, Mr. Wilson.

VETA: [*Offstage*] Come along, Elwood.

ELWOOD: Doctor, for years I've known what my family thinks of Harvey. But I've often wondered what Harvey's family thinks of me. [*He looks beyond* CHUMLEY *to the door of his office*] Oh—there you are! Doctor—do you mind? [*Gestures for him to step back*] You're standing in his way. [*There is the sound of a lock clicking open and the door of* CHUMLEY'S *office opens wide. The invisible* HARVEY *crosses to him and as they exit together*] Where've you been? I've been looking all over for you—

CURTAIN

LIFE WITH FATHER: Vinnie Day, the mother (Dorothy Stickney), brings on one of the first storms when Father (Howard Lindsay) finds her accounts carelessly kept. *Photo: Theatre Collection, New York Public Library*

LIFE WITH FATHER: Family breakfast in the Day home. (Howard Lindsay, John Drew Devereaux, Richard Simon, Dorothy Stickney, Larry Robinson, and Raymond Roe). *Photo: Theatre Collection, New York Public Library*

ABIE'S IRISH ROSE: Abie and Rosemary are married—for a third time. *Photo: Theatre Collection, New York Public Library*

Above: HARVEY: Eloise Sheldon, John Kirk, Jane Van Duser, Jesse White, Josephine Hull, Fred Irving Lewis, and Frank Fay. *Photo: Theatre Collection, New York Public Library*

Right: HARVEY: Harvey is being welcomed by Elwood P. Dowd (Frank Fay). *Photo: Theatre Collection, New York Public Library*

MARY, MARY: Bob (Barry Nelson, center) has his "say" as the others look on (John Cromwell, Barbara Bel Geddes, Michael Rennie, and Betsy von Furstenberg). *Photo: The Joseph Abeles Collection*

MARY, MARY: Mary (Barbara Bel Geddes) is interrupted in the middle of a conversation by Dirk Winston (Michael Rennie). *Photo: The Joseph Abeles Collection*

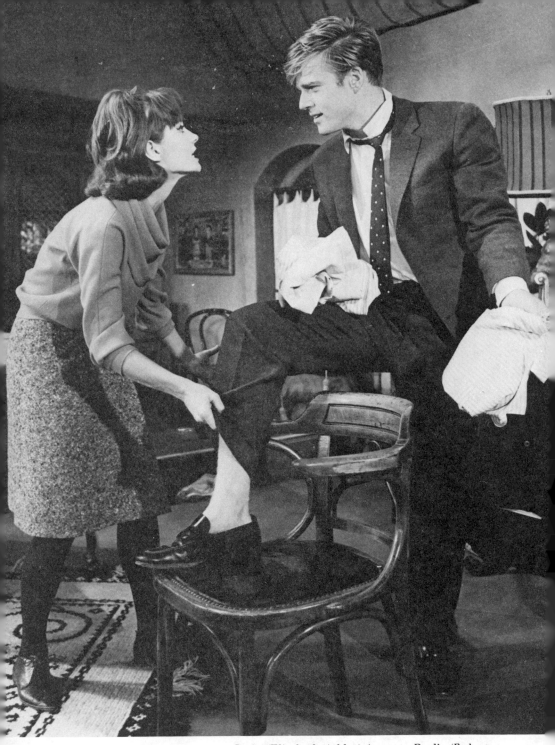

BAREFOOT IN THE PARK: Corie (Elizabeth Ashley) inspects Paul's (Robert Redford) stockingless foot after his "barefoot" walk in the park. *Photo: The Joseph Abeles Collection*

BAREFOOT IN THE PARK: Victor Velasco (Kurt Kasznar) offers his prize hors d'oeuvre, "knichi," to Corie (Elizabeth Ashley) as Mother (Mildred Natwick) and Paul (Robert Redford) look slightly disenchanted. *Photo: The Joseph Abeles Collection*

ARSENIC AND OLD LACE: Mortimer (Allyn Joslyn) frantically stops Mr. Gibbs (Henry Herbert) from drinking the elderberry wine proffered by the Brewster sisters (Josephine Hull and Jean Adair). *Photo: Theatre Collection, New York Public Library*

ARSENIC AND OLD LACE: Jonathan Brewster (Boris Karloff) menacingly confronts his aunts Abby (Josephine Hull) and Martha (Jean Adair). *Photo: Theatre Collection, New York Public Library*

TOBACCO ROAD: Jeeter Lester (Henry Hull, center) surrounded by family and friends. *Photo: Theatre Collection, New York Public Library*

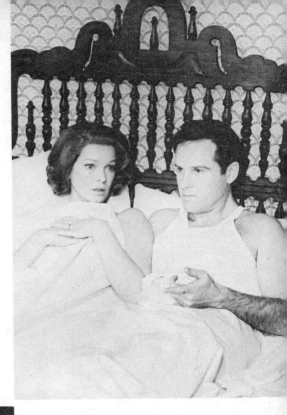

SAME TIME, NEXT YEAR: Doris (Ellen Burstyn) and George (Charles Grodin) in the opening scene of the play. *Photo: Martha Swope*

SAME TIME, NEXT YEAR: Some years later. Doris (Ellen Burstyn) enjoys a repast as George (Charles Grodin) sizes her up. *Photo: Martha Swope*

ANGEL STREET: the *frisson* of the rising and falling light grips the attention of Mrs. Manningham (Judith Evelyn) and Inspector Rough (Leo G. Carroll). *Photo: Theatre Collection, New York Public Library*

ANCEL STREET: A tense moment in the Manningham household. (Leo G. Carroll, Judith Evelyn, and Vincent Price). *Photo: Theatre Collection, New York Public Library*

CACTUS FLOWER: The morning after; a beaming Stephanie (Lauren Bacall) and a disapproving Julian (Barry Nelson). *Photo: Henry Grossman*

Mary, Mary

JEAN KERR

JEAN KERR

The longest running play of the 1960s, Jean Kerr's *Mary, Mary* tallied 1,572 performances, making it sixth in Broadway's record of dramatic longevity. At one point during its marathon engagement, four companies were presenting the comedy to the American public. Its appeal to playgoers in New York and in other cities was unmistakable.

In lesser hands than Mrs. Kerr's the comedy about a garrulous young woman endowed with utter frankness, and her broken marriage which we are convinced from the outset will be repaired during the course of the evening, could easily have been trapped into the idiom of soap opera. But the author eschewed the sentiment that the situation might normally be imbued with and peppered it with enough buoyant humor and comic inventiveness to keep it floating on an amusing keel.

Aided by an expert cast (including Barbara Bel Geddes, Barry Nelson and Michael Rennie) under the direction of Joseph Anthony, the comedy immediately took hold with audiences and, to a slightly lesser degree, with the critics. Howard Taubman of *The New York Times* communicated to his readers: "Mrs. Kerr, who has won national celebrity as a humorous writer, does not let her public down in the new comedy that opened last night at the Helen Hayes Theatre. Her mind is agile, her observation of the small frailties of people is sharp and her skill at coining a lively phrase is sure." Brooks Atkinson of the same newspaper, described it as "a clever entertainment" that contains "an explosion of witty remarks."

According to John Gassner, "So far as subject and plot are concerned, Jean Kerr wasn't particularly original in *Mary, Mary,* but she was able to give almost everything in it the high polish without which there can be no high comedy. *Mary, Mary* is an exceptionally well written and well organized example of this vanishing commodity.... Mrs. Kerr is a natural-born writer and a master of feminine wit, in which a tolerant understanding of human foibles is a large part."

A film version of *Mary, Mary* was released in 1963, with Debbie Reynolds as the voluble heroine. But while the stage may have a tolerance for talk (Shakespeare, Shaw, etc.) films do not and the movie was rejected by most as a "talkfest."

Jean Kerr, wife of author-drama critic Walter Kerr, and the mother of five sons and a daughter, was born in Scranton, Pennsylvania. An alumnus of Catholic University, Washington, D.C., her first play, *Jenny Kissed Me*, was produced in New York in 1948. This was followed by the revue *Touch and Go* (written with her husband); two sketches for *John Murray Anderson's Almanac; King of Hearts* (in collaboration with Eleanor Brooke); the musical *Goldilocks* (with her husband as coauthor); *Mary, Mary; Poor Richard;* and *Finishing Touches*.

A leading American humorist, Mrs. Kerr also has written four best-selling books: *Please Don't Eat the Daisies; The Snake Has All the Lines; Penny Candy;* and, most recently, *How I Got To Be Perfect*.

MARY, MARY was first produced at the Helen Hayes Theatre, New York, on March 8, 1961, by Roger L. Stevens. The cast was as follows:

BOB MCKELLAWAY	*Barry Nelson*
TIFFANY RICHARDS	*Betsy von Furstenberg*
OSCAR NELSON	*John Cromwell*
DIRK WINSTEN	*Michael Rennie*
MARY MCKELLAWAY	*Barbara Bel Geddes*

Directed by Joseph Anthony
Designed by Oliver Smith
Costumes by Theoni V. Aldredge
Lighting by Peggy Clark
Associate Producer: Lyn Austin
Produced in association with Collin Productions, Inc.

ACT ONE
A Saturday morning in winter.

ACT TWO
Saturday night, late.

ACT THREE
Sunday morning.

CHARACTERS:

BOB MC KELLAWAY: *a young independent publisher in his thirties*

MARY MC KELLAWAY: *his former wife, divorced within the year and now working on her own*

TIFFANY RICHARDS: *Bob's present fiancée, in her twenties, independently wealthy*

OSCAR NELSON: *a fiftyish tax lawyer and a friend of both Bob and Mary*

DIRK WINSTEN: *recently from Hollywood, and a wartime friend of Bob*

SCENE: *The action takes place in Bob McKellaway's living room, which is also an office away from the office, in a New York apartment building. The place is well kept, and obviously belongs to a man of taste and intelligence, but it is neither chic nor overly expensive. When the lights are lowered, it has a cozy, domestic feel to it, as though it had already been shared with a woman, though Bob is a bachelor at the moment and has let his homework rather overrun the place. He is a publisher by profession, heading his own small company, and he has a cluttered desk at one side of the room. Otherwise the customary sofa, chairs, liquor cabinet, bookshelves, a fish tank, and so on. There are entrances to five other areas: a main door to the outside corridor, a door to the bedroom, one to the kitchen, one to a linen closet, and one to what is obviously a cubbyhole filled with business files.*

ACT ONE

AT RISE: BOB *is on the telephone. Several morning newspapers, open to the book page, are spread out in front of him. He dials a number.*

BOB: I want to speak to Mr. Howard Nieman. [*The doorbell rings once, perfunctorily*] Okay, I'll hold on.

TIFFANY: [*Letting herself in at the front door; she carries a jar of wheat germ*] Bob!

BOB: Hi, honey.

TIFFANY: [*Leaving the door ajar and coming into the room apprehensively*] I've read the reviews. How are you feeling?

BOB: I'm not exactly dancing with glee.

TIFFANY: Well, it's not fair!

BOB: [*Rising, phone in hand*] Shhhh! This is Nieman. I'm waiting for him to get off the other line.

TIFFANY: [*Coming to* BOB *at the desk*] But it isn't fair. You publish books of quality and distinction and you should get the credit.

BOB: You're one hundred percent correct and beautiful besides. [*They kiss*] [*Into the phone*] Hello, Howard! How are you? [*He sits, pulling newspaper toward him*] Yes, sure I read the notices. Well, Howard, we were both hoping for a better break, but on the other hand there are a lot of good quotes here. [*Running his finger down a page and having some difficulty finding a decent quote*] "A magician with words" and so forth.

　　[TIFFANY *hangs her coat on the railing, and quietly feeds wheat germ to the fish*]

And with a book like yours we can hope for something more in the weeklies. I'm confident we'll go into another printing. What did you think about the notices? Sure, we all wish Orville Prescott would write a novel. Look, Howard, please calm down. I hope you're not going around talking this way. Well, for one thing, people don't read reviews that carefully. All you do is spread the bad word. [*Rises, fidgeting*] Let me give you some advice from Jake Cooper, in publicity. In his coarse but memorable phrase, nobody knows you've got a boil on your behind if you don't tell them. [BOB *listens a second longer, then shrugs and hangs up*]

TIFFANY: What did he say?

BOB: He said the boil was not on his behind. [*Picks up a newspaper*] It was on page 34 of the New York *Times*.

TIFFANY: Why shouldn't he be mad? It's a wonderful book!

BOB: That's what I like. Loyalty. [*Suddenly remembering, picking up a box of candy*] I have a present for you and I forgot about it.

TIFFANY: A present?

BOB: It's Valentine's Day. [*Bringing her the box*] Did you forget? To the sweet. Will you be my valentine? [*Kiss*]

TIFFANY: Sure I'll be your valentine. [*She pulls* BOB *down onto the sofa. He is kissing her as* OSCAR *appears from the corridor with a brief case*]

OSCAR: [*Pushing the door wider*] The door is open. Shall I come in?

BOB: Oh, Oscar—by all means. Tiffany, I want you to meet Oscar Nelson. My old friend and my new tax lawyer.

TIFFANY: Hello.

BOB: And this is Tiffany Richards. We're getting married next month.

OSCAR: And she'll be deductible. [*Comes down to shake hands with* TIFFANY] Congratulations. [BOB *closes the door*]

TIFFANY: Well, I'm very happy he's got you as a tax lawyer. Don't you think it's just outrageous—the government investigating his back taxes just like he was Frank Sinatra?

OSCAR: Under the law we're all equals.

BOB: Oscar—think of that clunk from the FBI who came charging in here and accused me of fleecing the government of six thousand dollars!

OSCAR: Wait, wait, wait. In the first place, this clunk is not from the FBI. He's from the Internal Revenue Service, a small but real distinction. In the second place, he is not accusing you of anything. He is merely asking you to produce proof that this six thousand dollars was legitimate professional expenses.

BOB: All I can tell you is that I am not coughing up any six thousand dollars. I'll move to Alaska.

OSCAR: You're too late. It's come into the Union.

TIFFANY: Darling, there's nothing to be upset about. Mr. Nelson will handle this man. [*Rises*] Now *I'm* going to get you your midafternoon cocktail. [*To* OSCAR] Would you like one?

OSCAR: Not this early, thank you.

TIFFANY: It's not alcohol. It's raw milk, brewer's yeast, and wheat germ.

OSCAR: Not this early, thank you.

BOB: [*Aware of* OSCAR's *expression*] It does sound awful, but it's incredible the energy it gives you.

OSCAR: I'll have to try it sometime.

TIFFANY: You have no intention of trying it. And you know what? You should, because you're definitely undernourished. Look at your ears.

OSCAR: What about them? I know they stick out.

TIFFANY: They're whitish. Here, let me look at your fingernails. [*She picks up his hand*] See how pale they are? A really healthy person will have pink ears and pink fingernails. Another thing—a healthy person will have a tongue the color of beefsteak.

OSCAR: [*Backing away, hand to mouth*] No, no—I will spare you that.

TIFFANY: I'm going to bring you a cocktail, and you try it. [*She goes off to the kitchen and closes the door*]

BOB: You think that's a lot of damn nonsense.

OSCAR: How did you know?

BOB: Because that's what I thought, in the beginning. But I have seen the results and I am completely sold. And if you want to know—I *love* being clucked over.

OSCAR: I'm delighted to hear it. And your ears were never lovelier. Now, shall we get down to business? [*Goes to the desk with his brief case*]

BOB: Please, let's. I'm in a real mess, Oscar. Actually, it's been a muddle ever since I started to pay alimony. And now this tax thing. What am I going to do? You probably read those notices today. I won't make anything on the Nieman book. Somewhere, something's got to give. And it's got to be straightened out before Tiffany and I get married.

OSCAR: [*Spreading out various papers on the desk*] We'll see what we can do.

BOB: What I want is a bird's-eye view of my whole financial picture. What I'm spending. What I should be spending. Where I should be cutting corners.

OSCAR: All right. I've already come to a few conclusions, but I'll want to look at your files—[*Makes a gesture toward the inner office*]

BOB: Thanks, Oscar. And I appreciate your coming over here on a Saturday. In fact, I appreciate your taking on this whole dumb job. I didn't think you would.

OSCAR: Why not?

BOB: Well, [*Glancing toward the kitchen door*] you wouldn't handle the divorce.

OSCAR: Bob, how could I have handled the divorce? Mary was just as much my friend as you were. Besides, I never thought you'd go through with it. I thought of you as the golden couple—smiling over steaming bowls of Campbell's chicken soup—

BOB: Oh, brother.

OSCAR: What happened?

BOB: [*With a shrug*] What happens to any marriage. You're in love, and then you're not in love. I married Mary because she was so direct and straightforward and said just exactly what she meant.

OSCAR: And why did you divorce her?

BOB: Because she was so direct and straightforward and said just exactly what she meant.

OSCAR: When did you see her last?

BOB: Eight, nine months ago.

OSCAR: Well, you're going to see her this afternoon.

BOB: Like hell!

OSCAR: Bob, I called Mary in Philadelphia and asked her—as a special favor—to come up here this afternoon.

BOB: But why would you do that? Why in God's name would you—?

OSCAR: Why? Because you have five thousand dollars' worth of canceled checks that you can neither identify nor explain. Some of them Mary signed. I'm hoping that her memory will be a little better than yours.

BOB: [*Searching for an out*] But I've got an appointment here in ten minutes. Do you remember Dirk Winsten?

OSCAR: The movie actor? Sure.

BOB: We were in the Navy together. Now he's moved into this building.

OSCAR: Well, it's nice you two old sailors can get together. There ought to be many a salty story, many a hearty laugh.

BOB: You don't get the picture. He's written a book.

OSCAR: A book?

BOB: That's right. The story of his life in three hundred and eighteen ungrammatical pages. [*Hands him a manuscript from the low bookcase*]

OSCAR: [*Glancing at it*] *Life Among the Oranges*. Not a bad title.

BOB: It's all right, I suppose. [*Picks up a small bowl of dried apricots and begins to eat one, nervously*] I can't imagine it on our lists.

OSCAR: I gather you're not going to do it.

BOB: Of course I'm not going to do it. But I dread talking to him. There is no right way to tell an author you don't want to publish his book.

OSCAR: If it's not going to be sweet, make it short. I can take Mary into the office—

BOB: Oh—Mary. [*Suddenly turning on* OSCAR] Don't you leave me alone with her for one minute, do you hear?

OSCAR: She's only five feet three.

BOB: Never mind that. [*Going to the file cabinet, upset, and picking up a set of galleys*] And when will I get to these galleys? They have to be back to the printer on Monday.

OSCAR: What are you eating?

BOB: Dried apricots. [OSCAR *remains silent*] They're full of vitamin C.

OSCAR: The things I'm learning today! [*Indicating the galleys* BOB *is fretting over*] What's that one like?

BOB: It's absolutely fascinating. I want you to read it. [*Enthusing, partly to distract himself*] It's told in the first person, and when the story opens we're coming back from a funeral. But only gradually do we come to realize that the narrator of the story is the dead man.

OSCAR: It sounds sensitive, very sensitive.

BOB: [*An extravagant little flare-up*] Oscar, I can think of only one sure way to clean up in this business! A new series. I could take the great sex novels—*Lady Chatterley, Peyton Place*—and have them rewritten for the ten-to-twelve age group.

[TIFFANY *enters with drinks, bringing one to* BOB]

TIFFANY: It took me longer because the Waring Blendor was broken. . . .

BOB: Thank you, darling.

TIFFANY: And I had to use an egg beater. [*Handing a glass to* OSCAR, *who rises*] You've *got* to *taste* it, anyway. [*He doesn't*]

BOB: [*Taking over*] Honey, I want you to put on your new gray bonnet and get out of here.

TIFFANY: [*Surprised*] Bob! Aren't we driving up to Goshen? Dad's expecting us!

BOB: Certainly. I'll pick you up at five-thirty. No, make it six.

TIFFANY: [*Really puzzled*] But why do I have to go?

BOB: Because in my winning, boyish way, I'm asking you to.

TIFFANY: I know why! Because that sexy movie actor is coming. You think in ten minutes I'll be sitting on his lap giving little growls of rapture.

BOB: Nonsense. Why should you care about vulgar good looks when you have me? No—[*With a sigh and moving away from her*]—the truth is my ex-wife is descending upon me this afternoon.

OSCAR: It was my suggestion. I thought she might be able to shed some light on this tax matter.

TIFFANY: [*Abruptly*] I'm delighted. I want to meet her. I've always wanted to meet her.

BOB: Well, you're not *going* to meet her—

TIFFANY: [*Sitting down, firmly, in a chair*] Yes, I am.

[OSCAR, *sensing that he'd better, slips away into the inner office with his papers and closes the door*]

BOB: Darling, you are a sweet, reasonable girl, and I insist that you stay in character. Besides, I have those galleys to finish. [*As though to conclude the matter*] Kiss me, and stop all this nonsense.

TIFFANY: [*Deliberately refusing to move*] I won't. I am not going to turn into Joan Fontaine.

BOB: What the hell are you talking about?

TIFFANY: Don't you remember Joan Fontaine in *Rebecca*? She was always thinking about the first Mrs. de Winter. She used to imagine that she could see her ghost on the stair case with that straight black Indian hair floating out behind her. Don't you remember? And she'd shudder when she saw the monogram on the silver brushes.

BOB: [*With a snort*] Silver brushes! Mary used to use plastic combs with little tails, and she'd crack off the tails so they'd fit in her purse. And her hair was tied back in a bun. Tiffany—this is so silly!

TIFFANY: I'll tell you another reason why I ought to meet Mary. We'd probably have a lot in common. Daddy says that a man goes on making the same mistake indefinitely.

BOB: Is that supposed to be an epigram? Because I don't get it.

TIFFANY: Practically everybody Daddy knows is divorced. It's not that they're worse than other people, they're just richer. And you do begin to see the pattern. You know Howard Pepper. When he divorced his first wife, everybody said "Oh, what he endured with Maggie! It was hell on earth!" Then when he married the new girl, everybody said "She's so *good* for him." Except when you met her she looked like Maggie, she talked like Maggie, it was Maggie all over agin. And now his *third* wife—

BOB: Okay, okay. I get the whole ghastly picture. But I promise you on my sacred oath as a Yale man that you don't resemble my ex-wife in any way, shape, or form.

TIFFANY: Is that good?

BOB: [*Relaxing for a moment with* TIFFANY *on the sofa*] Good? It's a benediction from heaven. You—sweet, idiot child—soothe my feathers. Mary always always ruffled them. Life with Mary was like being in a phone booth with an open umbrella—no matter which way you turned, you got it in the eye.

TIFFANY: Well, at last—a plain statement! Now that you've opened up a little, tell me, where did you meet her? Who introduced you?

BOB: I don't think we *were* introduced.

TIFFANY: You picked her up.

BOB: In a way. Do you remember that novel we published—*Our Kingdom Come?* It was sort of an allegory—the pilot of the plane turned out to be God?

TIFFANY: I don't think so.

BOB: Well, they made a play out of it. So, of course, I had to go to the opening night. And it was awful. Really grisly. After the second act, we were all standing out on the sidewalk. We were too stunned to talk. In fact, there didn't seem to be anything to say. Finally this girl spoke. She was standing there by herself in a polo coat, smoking—and she said, "Well, it's *not* uneven." So I laughed, and we started to talk—

TIFFANY: And you said, "We don't have to go back in there, let's have a drink—"

BOB: See? I don't have to tell you. You know. [*Rises and gets her coat*]

TIFFANY: [*Rising, too, pursuing the subject*] Did you kiss her that night?

BOB: Come on. Put on your coat. You're just stalling for time.

TIFFANY: I'll bet you did.

BOB: What?

TIFFANY: Kiss her that night.

BOB: I didn't kiss her for weeks.

TIFFANY: I don't believe it. You kissed me on the second night—in the elevator—do you remember?

BOB: [*Thinking of* MARY] Oh, I made certain fumbling attempts—but she'd make some little joke, like "Let's not start something we can't finish in a cab on Forty-fourth Street"—

TIFFANY: Well, for goodness sake, where was she when you finally did kiss her? On an operating table, under ether?

BOB: No, as it happens she was in a cab on Forty-fourth Street. Somehow or other she got her fingers slammed in the door. She pretended it was nothing, and we were chatting along. Then suddenly—this was blocks later—she started to cry. I looked at her fingers. [*Taking* TIFFANY'S *hand*] Two of the nails were really smashed. And it started out I was just trying to comfort her, and—

TIFFANY: That is the most *un*romantic story I ever heard!

BOB: They certainly won't get a movie out of it. [*Urging her toward door*] I told you it wasn't worth discussing.

TIFFANY: [*Picks up her handbag*] I know, I kept fishing. Did she cry a lot in taxicabs?

BOB: She never cried again. Not anyplace—ever—not once.

[OSCAR *appears from inner office, frowning over a sheaf of papers*]

OSCAR: These figures for the year—can they represent the *total* profit?

BOB: I'm afraid so. [*Doorbell.* BOB *thinks quickly*] Oscar, will you get that?

TIFFANY: Just let me *meet* her. Two minutes and I promise I'll go!

BOB: [*Pulling her toward the kitchen*] We'll go out the back door and I'll get you a cab.

TIFFANY: I feel like I was caught in a raid!

[OSCAR *has been looking on as* BOB *gets* TIFFANY *into the kitchen*]

BOB: I'm *not* adult and Noël Coward would wash his hands of me. [*He slips into the kitchen, too, and closes the door as* OSCAR *crosses to the main door and opens it not to* MARY *but to* DIRK WINSTEN, *who has a large, partially wrapped piece of wood carving in his arms*]

OSCAR: Hello. Come in.

DIRK: I'm—

OSCAR: Yes, I know. You're Dirk Winsten. Bob will be right back. My name is Oscar Nelson. [*We hear* TIFFANY *giggling and protesting "Please, Bob— please!" off in the kitchen area.* OSCAR *and* DIRK *hear it, too*] Her name is Tiffany Richards. [*Squeals from* TIFFANY, *off*]

DIRK: It kind of makes me homesick for the back lot at Paramount. I thought I was late, but. . . .

[OSCAR, *puzzled, is looking at the package in* DIRK'S *arms*]

Suppose I take this thing downstairs and I'll be back in ten minutes.

OSCAR: I think recess should be over by that time.

DIRK: [*Feeling he should explain the package*] I saw this in an antique shop. [*Undoing the wrapping a bit*] It's supposed to be Geronimo, but it looks so much like Jack Warner I couldn't resist.

> [*He goes, closing the door.* OSCAR *notices the drink* TIFFANY *has left for him. He tastes it, then crosses to the liquor table and pours a generous slug into the drink. He takes a sip. It's better. He looks at his finger-nails, then goes to the mantel, puts down his drink, picks up a mirror, and examines his tongue. While he is doing so,* MARY *enters by the main door. She puts down her overnight bag and then sees* OSCAR]

MARY: Oscar!

OSCAR: Mary, darling.

MARY: Are you sick?

OSCAR: Of course not. I'm out of my mind. [*Going to her and embracing her*] Hey! I want you to concentrate and give me a better hug than that!

> [*We are aware that* MARY *is somewhat abstracted and apprehensive. Also that she is getting her feel of the room again, after all this time*]

MARY: Oscar—dear Oscar—it's lovely to see you. [*Hesitantly*] Where's—?

OSCAR: He'll be right back. He just—[*Interrupting himself, staring at her*] Wait a minute! What's happened to you? You look absolutely marvel-ous.

MARY: Did you say that right?

OSCAR: Apparently not, because I didn't get an answer.

MARY: [*Adopting a television commercial tone, mechanically*] Well, you see, I *had* been using an ordinary shampoo, which left a dull, unattractive film on my hair. . . .

OSCAR: Come on, I'm interested. The hair is different—the clothes—the make-up. Clearly loving hands have been at work.

MARY: [*Putting her coat and handbag aside and sitting down, tentatively*] Yes, but you're not supposed to notice. I mean you're supposed to have an appreciative gleam in your eye, but you don't have to remind me of the dreary hours at Elizabeth Arden's—

OSCAR: Appreciative gleam? I've been casting you lustful glances. You're just too pure to notice. What caused the transformation?

MARY: [*Still not located in space*] Well, being divorced is like being hit by a Mack truck. If you live through it, you start looking very carefully to the right and to the left. While I was looking I noticed that I was the only twenty-eight-year-old girl wearing a polo coat and no lipstick.

OSCAR: You were? I never noticed. [*Starting toward kitchen*] But let me see if I can locate our—

MARY: [*Quickly taking a cigarette from a box on the table*] No, no—please—wait. Let me have a cigarette first.

OSCAR: [*Lighting it for her*] You nervous?

MARY: Certainly not. But I haven't seen Bob in nine months. I guess I can last another five minutes. Besides, you and I have a lot to talk about. How's Jennifer?

OSCAR: [*Quiet and offhand tone*] Well, she had this illegitimate baby after she met that man from Gristede's, but it's all right now. . . .

MARY: [*Nodding, looking about the room*] Oh? Good! And how's everything at the office?

OSCAR: You haven't heard one word I said.

MARY: [*Caught*] You're right. I'm not listening. And I *am* nervous. I shouldn't have come.

OSCAR: [*Puts his hands on the arm of her chair. Sympathetically*] Mary, do you still—

MARY: [*Quickly*] I don't still—anything.

OSCAR: I'm sorry. I should have realized that—

MARY: Stop it. Don't give me that sad spaniel expression, as though you'd just looked at the X-rays. I'm all right, Doctor. Just fine.

> [BOB *appears from kitchen, stops short. His words are awkwardly spaced*]

BOB: Well. Hello. You did get here.

OSCAR: Of course, she knew the address. [OSCAR *starts toward the office*]

BOB: [*Not wanting to be left alone*] Oscar! [MARY *gets to her feet, ill at ease*]

OSCAR: Be right back. [OSCAR *goes into office, leaving the door open.* MARY *turns toward* BOB *and her nerves now vanish. But* BOB's *are quickly in bad shape*]

MARY: Hello.

BOB: [*A step to her*] You look very different. You've changed. I was going to ask you how you've been. But I can see. You've been fine.

MARY: How about you? Did you ever clear up that case of athlete's foot?

BOB: [*Almost under his breath*] No—you haven't changed.

MARY: [*This flusters her briefly. She crosses to the desk, dips a hand into the bowl of dried apricots*] Well, you know what they say—the more we change, the more we stay the same. Good Lord! These are dried apricots.

BOB: What did you think they were?

MARY: Ears.

BOB: [*Ignoring it*] I want to say that I appreciate your coming. I'm sure you didn't *want* to.

MARY: [*Circling below the desk toward a plant on a low bookcase*] Nonsense. It put my mind at ease. You can't think how often I've worried about the philodendron.

BOB: [*Picking up tax papers*] I'm sure. Now, Oscar has explained to you that my—our—1962 income tax returns are being—

MARY: I advise you to make a clean breast of it. Admit everything.

BOB: This does not happen to be a subject for comedy. I've got to get this straightened out. I'm getting married in two weeks.

MARY: [*Really stunned*] Oh?

BOB: I thought you knew. Surely Oscar must have—

MARY: Of course! And it went right out of my head. [*Sitting near the desk*] But how nice! Do I know her?

BOB: No, you don't.

MARY: Do you?

BOB: [*Chooses to ignore this*] Her name is Tiffany Richards.

MARY: Tiffany. I'll bet she uses brown ink. And when she writes she draws little circles over the *i*'s.

BOB: She is a beautiful, lovely girl with a head on her shoulders.

MARY: How useful!

BOB: [*Spluttering with irritation*] You really do have a talent for—you've been here five minutes, and already I'm—

MARY: [*With maddening calm*] Have a dried apricot.

BOB: [*Striding to office door*] Oscar, have you fallen asleep in there?

OSCAR: [*Off*] Coming!

BOB: [*Moving away from* MARY *as* OSCAR *appears from office*] Shall we get on with this? [*To* MARY] I know you have to get back to Philadelphia—

MARY: I'm staying in town tonight, so you may consider that my time is your time.

OSCAR: [*Sits at the desk, handing* MARY *a batch of canceled checks*] Okay, Mary, will you look through these checks? Most of them you've signed.

MARY: Oh, dear—I'm not going to remember *any* of these, Oscar—

OSCAR: It'll come. Just give yourself time. You understand that we're particularly looking for items that might be deductible. Business entertaining, professional gifts, and so forth.

MARY: [*Working her way through the checks*] L. Bernstein—seventy-eight dollars. That's impossible. The only L. Bernstein I know is Leonard Bernstein and I don't know Leonard Bernstein.

OSCAR: [*Pointing it out*] This is L. Bernstein, D.D.S. A dentist.

BOB: [*Shaking his head*] I told you—Sidney Bauer is my dentist.

MARY: Dentist, dentist, dentist. [*Snapping her fingers*] Listen—it's that man in Boston!

BOB: What man in Boston?

MARY: Don't you remember that crazy restaurant where you go down all the stairs? And you thought you got a stone in the curry—but it was your inlay?

BOB: Oh.

MARY: And we drove all the way out to Framingham because he was the only dentist who'd take you on Sunday?

BOB: Yeah, yeah, yeah.

MARY: By the way, how is that inlay?

BOB: Just grand. How are your crowns? [*They turn from each other*]

OSCAR: [*Stopping this*] *And* we have Mrs. Robert Connors—three hundred dollars.

BOB: Mrs. Connors?

MARY: I thought so long as you walked this earth you'd remember Mrs. Connors. Bootsie Connors and her fish?

BOB: Oh, God. That ghastly weekend in Greenwich.

OSCAR: Okay, tell Daddy.

BOB: Do you remember that young English critic, Irving Mannix?

OSCAR: The angry young man?

BOB: This was two years ago, when he was just a cross young man. At that time he was writing long scholarly articles proving that Shakespeare was a homosexual.

MARY: Sort of the intellectual's answer to *photoplay*.

BOB: Anyway, he was staying here. And we'd been invited to a party at the Connors'.

MARY: So we brought along dear old Irving.

BOB: Do you know the Connors' place in Greenwich?

OSCAR: No.

BOB: Well the living room is about the size of the ballroom at the St. Regis. You feel it would be just the place to sign a treaty. [*As they become interested in the details of the story* BOB *and* MARY *gradually forget their present situation and relax*] Anyway, it was all too rich for Irving and he started to lap up martinis. In fifteen minutes he was asking our hostess if it was true that the Venetian paneling had been brought over piece by piece from Third Avenue.

OSCAR: Why didn't you take this charmer home?

BOB: Because he passed out. In the library.

MARY: [*It comes back*] On that damn velvet sofa.

BOB: But he came to just long enough to light a cigarette. Presently the sofa was on fire—really on fire. Our hero jumped up and, with stunning presence of mind, put out the blaze with a tank of tropical fish.

MARY: And these were no run-of-the-bowl goldfish. They came from Haiti and were friends of the family. I mean, they had *names*.

OSCAR: Well, he was a writer. I think we can call that professional entertainment. Okay—we have twenty-five dollars to the Beach Haven Inn.

MARY: That must be yours.

BOB: Nonsense! I was never in ... [*And then he remembers*] The Booksellers—

MARY and BOB: [*Together*] Convention.

BOB: That awful hotel with the iron deer in front.

MARY: [*Nodding, her eyes lighting up*] With the night clerk who looked like Norman Vincent Peale and was so suspicious.

BOB: No wonder he was suspicious! [*To* OSCAR, *indicating* MARY] He turns around to get the key and this one says just loud enough for him to hear, "Darling, are we doing the right thing? Maybe we ought to *wait*."

MARY: He was *delighted* to come face to face with sin.

BOB: That's probably why he charged us four bucks to bring up three bottles of beer.

MARY: [*To* OSCAR] He forgot the bottle opener, and we had to pry them open on the handle of the radiator.

BOB: And one of them was warm or something, so it shot up to the ceiling and all over one of the beds. Se we both had to sleep in the other twin bed.... [*His voice has slowed down on this last thought. The remembering is suddenly a bit painful. There is a short, awkward silence before* MARY *gets to her feet, deliberately breaking the mood*]

MARY: Oscar, we're being inefficient. We don't need total recall—just the facts. I'll take these checks into the office and make notes on the ones I can remember. [*Almost before they realize it, she has left them.* OSCAR *and* BOB *look at one another, then* BOB *looks away*]

OSCAR: Mary looks wonderful, don't you think?

BOB: Great.

OSCAR: Like a million bucks.

BOB: [*Nettled*] I'm afraid the figure that comes into my mind is five thousand bucks in alimony.

OSCAR: [*Notices* DIRK, *who has just stuck his head in at the main door*] Your friend from California.

BOB: [*Relieved at the interruption; his exuberance is a bit excessive after the strain with* MARY] Dirk! It's good to see you! How long has it been?

DIRK: I don't know. We were still in sailor suits.

BOB: [*Indicating* OSCAR] By the way, do you know—

OSCAR: We've met.

BOB: You know, Dirk is the expert we *should* consult! [*To* DIRK] You've been married four or five times. How the hell did you manage it?

DIRK: [*Relaxing into a chair*] I feel like a failure to admit that I was only married three times. Actually, I married my first wife twice—so while there were three marriages, there were just two wives involved.

BOB: Now what? Do you pay both of them alimony?

DIRK: No, my second wife just married a very nice plastic surgeon. He fell in love with her while removing a wart from her shoulder blade. I always thought there was a popular song in that.

BOB: What about your first wife?

DIRK: She died.

BOB: See? Them that has, gets!

OSCAR: [*Rises, picks up manuscript from desk, and gives it to* BOB] I know you two have business to talk about—[BOB *glances at* DIRK's *manuscript, and his face shows his dismay at having to deal with it*]—so I'll get back to my arithmetic. [*He joins* MARY *in the small office, closing the door*]

DIRK: Yes! Down to business.

BOB: [*Avoiding the subject and trying to hold onto his own momentary better spirits*] Dirk, you look great. Younger than ever. How do you do it?

DIRK: I'll tell you this—it gets harder and harder. If I don't get ten full hours' sleep, they can't do a close-up. If I eat a ham sandwich after four o'clock, it shows on the scale. Ham sandwich, hell. I can gain weight from two Bayer aspirins.

BOB: You sound like the curator of your own museum. Come on, now. It's been worth it, hasn't it?

DIRK: Sure. Except that you develop such nutty habits. Do you know what all middle-aged actors do when they're alone in taxicabs?

BOB: What do they do?

[DIRK *now demonstrates the business of biting, open-mouthed, from left to right, to strengthen the jaw muscles*]

What's that for?

DIRK: It firms up the jawline, old boy. I'll tell you what I dream of doing. My dearest ambition in life is to let my damn jawline go. In fact, that's why I wrote this book.

BOB: [*Brought back to the subject, embarrassed*] I see. But—uh—

DIRK: Have you read it?

BOB: Certainly I've read it. Now—the question is, shall I be perfectly frank? [DIRK *immediately rises and picks up the manuscript as if to go*] You bruise easily. Have you shown this to anybody else?

DIRK: My agent, who thought it was brave, haunting, and hilarious. I brought it to you first because I knew you.

BOB: I'm sorry, Dirk—but the truth is it's not a book at all. For the moment we'll rule out the quality of the writing.

DIRK: Let's not rule out anything. What about the quality of the writing?

BOB: Well, it's—it's—

DIRK: Is "lousy" the word you're groping for?

BOB: Well, let's say it's not prose. Actually, it's not even punctuated. I get the feeling that you waited until you were out of breath and then threw in a semicolon.

DIRK: Hm.

BOB: However, that could be fixed. What can't be fixed is the content. It's nothing but anecdotes, really. It's as though you were just taking up where Louella left off.

DIRK: I gather you do not wish to publish this book. Do you think someone else would take it?

BOB: There are a couple of fringe outfits that I imagine would—

DIRK: I don't want a fringe outfit. Tell me this. How much does it cost to publish a book? Any book?

BOB: It depends on the size of the first printing, the length of the book, the kind of promotion—

DIRK: Let's get down to cases. How much would it cost to bring out my book with a first printing of, say, twelve thousand copies?

BOB: Oh—eight, nine thousand dollars.

DIRK: Let's say I made a check out to you for eighteen thousand dollars. Would you do the book?

BOB: If you proposition women with this same kind of finesse you must get your face slapped a lot.

DIRK: I thought it was worth a try, but don't get mad.

BOB: I'm not mad. I'm surprised. Why does that book mean so much to you? Obviously it isn't the money.

DIRK: It may sound naïve to say it—but being a star has never killed my urge to become an actor. Ten years ago I started to campaign for real parts. But the formula was still making money. So I went right on—passionate kisses and then I'd build the Suez Canal—passionate kisses and then I'd open the golden West—

BOB: What do you figure—you're all through in Hollywood?

DIRK: Technically, no. I have two more pictures to go on my present contract. But when I left, they knew and I knew that I was the sinking ship leaving the rats.

BOB: By why this jump into literature?

DIRK: Well, my press agent thought ... what the hell, why blame him? *I* thought it might stir up a little interest in me as a man instead of a windup toy. In my fantasies I imagined it would be serialized in *The Saturday Evening Post* with pictures of me looking very seedy. And all of a sudden producers would be saying, "Don't laugh, but do you know who'd be perfect for the degenerate father—Dirk Winsten!"

[MARY *enters from the office, leaving the door open*]

MARY: Bob, I've done my half. Oscar would like to see you. [*Seeing* DIRK] Oh, excuse me.

DIRK: [*Rising, pleasantly*] Hello, there.

BOB: This is my—former wife, Mary McKellaway.

MARY: You're Dirk Winsten. And your real name is Winsten Krid. Dirk is Krid spelled backwards.

DIRK: Good Lord, how did you remember that?

MARY: Oh, I have a head full of the most useless information. I still remember the names of each of the Dionne quintuplets, and the width of the Amazon River.

DIRK: Oh?

MARY: You have no idea how few people care about the width of the Amazon River. I understand you've written a book.

DIRK: That's what I understood, until I talked to Bob here.

MARY: Bob's a special case. He was frightened at an early age by a best seller. [*She is picking up her coat and handbag*]

DIRK: He was?

BOB: I was not. Why do you say that? It's simply not true. I happen to believe that there's great wisdom in Emerson's remark that you should never read any book until it's a year old. And I'd like to think I'm publishing the kind of books that will be around next year. I'm fed up with novels about tangled lives in Scarsdale—or Old Salem for that matter: [*Quoting, in a mock literary rhythm*] "All he knew was that he was a man and she was a woman or had he made some dreadful mistake."

OSCAR: [*Off*] Bob! Are you coming?

BOB: [*On his way to office*] Be right back, Dirk.

DIRK: Don't think about me. We're all through. I wouldn't want you to be any clearer.

MARY: Bob, I suppose I might as well go, too.

BOB: [*Turns back to* MARY, *something new on his mind*] Right now?

MARY: Well, don't you have a date?

BOB: I am meeting Tiffany—but couldn't you spare just five minutes? There's something I'd like to ask you. [*Assuming her consent,* BOB *goes into the office.* MARY *stares after him a moment, absently reaching for a cigarette. Then she becomes aware of* DIRK *again, who has started for the main door but is now hesitating, watching her*]

MARY: I used to love your movies. Of course, I didn't see all of them, either. My mother wouldn't let me.

DIRK: That's all right. I didn't see all of them, either. My agent wouldn't let me. Are you a writer?

MARY: No, I work for the *Ladies' Home Journal.* I edit the letters to the editor.

DIRK: You mean they have to be edited?

MARY: [*Nodding*] It does seem a little like incest, doesn't it?

DIRK: Bob did say you were his *former* wife, didn't he?

MARY: That's right.

DIRK: I'm so glad.

MARY: Why?

DIRK: Because I can ask you to dinner. Will you have dinner with me?

MARY: Tonight?

DIRK: You have a date?

MARY: No—no.

DIRK: Then what's wrong with tonight?

MARY: I guess I think we should have known each other longer—like, say, another five minutes.

DIRK: You think you're letting yourself in for an orgy. You think I will ply you with liquor, lure you to my sinful bachelor lodgings, and chase you around the king-size bed.

MARY: [*With a look toward the office*] Well, I've never been plied with liquor. Maybe I'd like it, but—

DIRK: Come on, we'll have dinner. And *Duck Soup* is playing at the Museum of Modern Art. I promise you I'll be so respectable you'll find me quite tiresome.

MARY: [*On an impulse*] I have a new dress that would look pretty silly all by itself in Schrafft's. Why not? I'd love to. Do you want to pick me up here? What time?

DIRK: Half an hour? [*It occurs to him he'd better check*] By the way, you don't—live here, do you?

MARY: Oh, no. We're not as civilized as all that. This is business.

DIRK: Fine. [*Passing office door*] See you, Bob. I've got a call in to the Coast. [*On his way to the main door, turning back to* MARY] Half an hour?

> [MARY *nods, smiling.* DIRK *goes, closing the door.* MARY *turns, a little unsure of herself, sees the galleys on the sofa table, abstractedly picks them up, and puts her cigarette on an ash tray on the table. At almost the same time,* BOB *appears from the office, as though in response to* DIRK's *farewell, then realizes he is alone with* MARY]

BOB: Oh. Mary—thanks for waiting—I—

MARY: [*She has been aware of his return, but has not looked at him. Now she deliberately reads from the galleys, in a somewhat questioning voice*] "He was alone in the middle of the field. He was grateful once again to be in possession of his own body. The Queen Anne's lace waved in the breeze like a thousand tiny handkerchiefs..." [*Looks up*] This sounds suspiciously like our friend O'Brynner. [*Glancing at the first page of the galleys*] And no wonder! I thought you weren't going to do this one.

BOB: Why?

MARY: Because this man writes like a sick elf.

BOB: [*Wanting to brush the matter aside before he is irritated again*] Let's skip that. [*In a hesitant, slightly strained voice*] Mary—

MARY: [*Adopting his tone*] Bob—

BOB: I've been thinking. [*Starts to sit on the ottoman*]

MARY: I thought you had an odd expression.

BOB: [*Jumping up again, a sudden, desperate explosion*] Could you—would it be absolutely impossible for you to listen to me for three minutes without making one single wisecrack?

MARY: [*Stung—but concealing it*] I could try.

BOB: [*Earnestly*] I wish you would. I really wish you would. There is something I want to ask you and I can't do it through a barrage of flippantries.

MARY: You'd be surprised. I don't feel flippant at all. What is it you want to ask me?

BOB: [*Sitting*] You—know I'm getting married again.

MARY: Yes, I know that.

BOB: Well, I find myself stewing over a very curious thing Tiffany said today.

MARY: Oh?

BOB: Her idea was that people go right on making the same mistakes. I had an eerie feeling that there was something true about that. [*Realizing that he is groping*] What I'm trying to say is that I have by God got to make a better job of it this time. [MARY *turns her head away.* BOB *leans toward her*] Yes?

MARY: I didn't say anything.

BOB: But you were thinking—

MARY: [*Turns back to him sharply*] Look, you say your lines, I'll say my lines. You're hoping for better luck this time. *I* hope you'll have better luck this time. Beyond that, I don't see—

BOB: You could tell me what *I* did wrong. When we broke up, I spent many drunken hours thinking how it was all your fault. [MARY *starts to speak*] Yes, I know I'm painting a charming portrait of myself—Bob McKellaway as a slob and sorehead. But that's how I felt.

MARY: And that's how you still feel.

BOB: No, by the time I calmed down and cleared the last of your bobby pins out of the bathroom, I realized that half the trouble had to be me.

MARY: You think it can be divided into two equal parts—like a sandwich?

BOB: I think success has no rules, but you can learn a great deal from failure.

MARY: I see. And what you're really looking for is the formula for instant marriage.

BOB: No, I'm not as sappy as that. I'm prepared to make a number of different mistakes this time. I would like not to make the same ones. And I would like some advice.

MARY: Had you thought of writing to Dear Abby? [*He rises and moves away. She is immediately penitent*] Bob, I'm sorry for that. That's the kind of thing I promised not to say. [BOB *returns to her hopefully*] But what you're asking is impossible. I can't give you a report card. Is he punctual? Does he complete the task assigned? But you know what? This is so like you. This determination to be sensible in a situation where it isn't sensible to be sensible. You want to analyze, analyze. Like those people who take an overdose of sleeping pills, and sit there making notes while they're dying. "Four A.M. Vision beginning to blur." You'd do that. You would.

BOB: Maybe.

MARY: What shall I say? That you used to leave your ties on the coffee table? And you always grabbed *The New Yorker* first and took it to the bathroom? And you never talked to me in cars?

BOB: Of course I talked in cars.

MARY: Yes, to the traffic signals. "Come on, dammit, turn green."

BOB: I concentrate when I drive.

MARY: And you were always asking solemn, editorial-type questions beginning Don't You Ever. Don't You Ever order lunch meat? Don't You Ever put the lid back on the mayonnaise? Don't You Ever put your cigarettes out?

BOB: [*Brandishing* MARY's *still-smoking cigarette and putting it out with great vigor*] Because you never in your life put a cigarette out!

MARY: And you always, always put the ice-cube trays back without filling them.

BOB: [*Gesturing toward the kitchen*] Ice-cube trays? Is that all you remember?

MARY: Aren't you forgetting one small detail? You're the one who walked out.

BOB: Technically, I suppose that's true.

MARY: Technically? There was nothing technical about it. You got up in the middle of the night and slammed out of here. And you know what? I never knew why.

BOB: Like hell you didn't.

MARY: All I knew was, one moment you were in bed, and the next minute you were banging drawers and dumping shirts into a suitcase.

BOB: And that's *all* you remember? [*Coming nearer*] Let me reconstruct the scene for you. You were in bed reading *McCall's*. I was in the bathroom brushing my teeth. Then I put the lights out, came to bed, put my arms around you, and you said, "Okay, let's get those colored lights going."

MARY: I said that?

BOB: I wouldn't be capable of inventing it.

MARY: And was that so terrible?

BOB: Maybe not. But let us say that it had the effect of a cold shower when I wasn't in the mood for a cold shower.

MARY: I see.

BOB: I grant you it was a very small straw to be the last straw. Another time it would have bounced off me. But it had been such a stinker of a day. We got bad notices on the Caine book. The deal for the serial rights fell through. Oh, the usual. Except that I felt a peculiar need for some warmth. I guess I felt I needed a wife.

MARY: [*Hotly*] I think I was wifely—a lot.

BOB: Sure. On and off. Between jokes.

[MARY *grabs a sofa pillow as though she were going to hit him with it, but is deflected by* OSCAR's *return from the office. He sees what she is doing*]

OSCAR: Please don't be embarrassed on my account. I'm delighted. I hate a friendly divorce. A lawyer is never entirely comfortable with a friendly divorce, any more than a good mortician wants to finish his job and then have the patient sit up on the table. [MARY, *without saying a word, picks up her coat, her suitcase, gloves, and handbag and leaves by the main door.* OSCAR *looks at* BOB] Did you read Walter Lippmann today? I thought it was an awfully good piece.

BOB: Oscar, don't be urbane all the time. I can't stand it. [*Fuming*] You see why I didn't want to see her again? When you said she was coming, I should have walked out that front door! I don't understand it. I thought she had lost the power to enrage me. Maybe I took the bandages off too soon. Maybe I—[*Stops as he sees* MARY *returning with her suitcase*] Did you forget something?

MARY: No, dammit, I *remembered* something. Having made my dramatic exit, I realized that this is where I'm being picked up. I *have* to stay here for another ten minutes.

BOB: I see.

MARY: And furthermore, I will have to use your room to change in. [*To* OSCAR] Oscar, if the phone rings, it may be for me. Will *you* take it? The Algonquin is supposed to call and confirm my room for tonight.

BOB: There's a new telephone in the . . . [MARY *goes off to the bedroom, not exactly slamming the door but letting it close pretty arrogantly behind her.* BOB *starts to follow but is stopped by* OSCAR]

OSCAR: Never mind her. We have something more important to talk about.

[*Sitting at the desk*] I have been over all the figures and am now ready to give my State of the Union address.

BOB: [*Trying to tear his mind away from* MARY, *but still edgy and upset*] First, tell me about that tax thing.

OSCAR: Oh, my guess is that we'll get it down somewhere in the neighborhood of eighteen hundred, two thousand dollars.

BOB: That would be more like it.

OSCAR: You said you wanted my advice on the overall picture. Let me ask you a couple of questions. Tiffany comes from a wealthy family, doesn't she?

BOB: What has that got to do with anything?

OSCAR: A lot. She has to be supported. You can't support her. I have now been through what we shall laughingly call your books, and you're not supporting yourself.

BOB: You're joking.

OSCAR: Then why aren't you laughing?

BOB: Look. If you're trying in some left-handed way to tell me I can't get married, you're wasting your breath. I'm thirty-six years old, and this is a—

OSCAR: Free country? Don't you believe it. People pick up the most erroneous ideas from popular songs. Let me tell you something. If all you've got is the sun in the morning and the moon at night, you're in trouble.

BOB: What are you talking about? I take eighteen thousand a year out of the company—plus bonuses.

OSCAR: That's right.

BOB: That may be cigarette money to the Rockefellers, but it still feels like a lot to me. Hell, my father never made more than five thousand a year in his life and he put four boys through college.

OSCAR: Let's not dwell on the glories of the past. *I* have the figures for *this* year. Do you want to hear them?

BOB: No. [*Starts for bedroom and stops*] Oh, yes, I suppose so.

OSCAR: [*Referring to a work sheet*] We start with your base salary—eighteen thousand—plus one thousand dollars sales bonus. By the way, that was down from preceding years.

BOB: Sales were down.

OSCAR: So that's nineteen thousand dollars. Against that, we have: thirty-two hundred, rent; two thousand, eighty, maid service; four thousand, nine hundred, food and liquor; five thousand, alimony to Mary—

BOB: And that's ridiculous. [*Shouting at the bedroom door*] She's working.

OSCAR: That was the decision of the court. You can't do anything about it. [*Picking up where he left off*] Five thousand to Mary. Six hundred and eighty, club dues and entertainment. Six hundred, clothes. Nine hundred, books, furnishings, dry cleaning. Eleven hundred, insurance and medical. Twenty-seven hundred, taxes. We now have a total of twenty-one thousand, one hundred and sixty dollars. You do have three thousand in available savings, but most of that will go for that old tax bill.

BOB: Here, let me see that thing. [*Takes work sheet from* OSCAR]

OSCAR: You can juggle those figures any way you want to. But you're not going to change the fact that you are already spending twenty-one thousand on an income of nineteen. It's not just that you can't support another wife. You'd be ill-advised to buy a canary.

BOB: It can't be as complicated as you're pretending—

OSCAR: Actually, it's even more complicated. You must keep in mind that if you ever wanted to divorce Tiffany, you'd be in a hopeless position, financially.

BOB: [*Outburst*] I'm not going to divorce Tiffany! Why would I divorce Tiffany?

OSCAR: Your attitude does you credit.

BOB: Here. Some of these expenses I can cut.

OSCAR: Yes, you could move to a cheaper apartment. You don't have to belong to the New York Athletic Club. You might save seven or eight hundred dollars. However, I have met Tiffany. I doubt that you could keep her in cashmere sweaters for that. She doesn't work, does she?

BOB: Oh, she does volunteer things.

OSCAR: Maybe her father would give her an allowance.

BOB: Maybe we could take in boarders. Any more bright ideas? What the hell am I supposed to do? Stay single for the rest of my life and sleep around? Or do I remain celibate and take cold showers and get plenty of exercise?

OSCAR: Fortunately, you belong to the Athletic Club. [*Telephone rings.* OSCAR *answers it*] Hello. That's right. Can I take the message? [MARY, *in dressing gown, pokes her head out of the bedroom door*] I see. Will you wait one minute? [*To* MARY] They haven't got a single but they can give you a suite!

MARY: Tell them never mind. I'm not paying twenty-four dollars for one night. I'll go to the Biltmore.

BOB: [*Not graciously, just realistically*] If you want to, you can stay here. I'm going to be in Goshen for the weekend.

MARY: Stay here?

BOB: I won't be here. You'll be perfectly safe.

MARY: I'm not worried. I was perfectly safe when you *were* here. [MARY *disappears, shutting the door again*]

BOB: I shouldn't have divorced her. I should have shot her.

OSCAR: [*Into phone*] Thank you, she'll make other arrangements. [*Doorbell, as* OSCAR *hangs up*]

BOB: [*Going to the front door*] With my luck, this'll be a telegram saying that my rich old uncle died and left his money to a kindly waitress. [BOB *opens the door to* DIRK, *and is surprised to see him*] Oh. Hello again.

DIRK: Hello. Is she ready?

BOB: Who?

DIRK: Do I get a choice? I'm calling for Mary.

BOB: For Mary? For what?

DIRK: For dinner. Isn't that all right? Should my mother have called your mother?

BOB: Don't be ridiculous. I just didn't know, that's all.

OSCAR: You see, Bob thinks when he brings a book back to the library, it'll never go out again.

BOB: Bob doesn't think anything. I had always supposed that Mr. Winsten only went out with women whose names ended in *a*. Like Lana. Or Ava. And I'm a little puzzled as to why he wants to take my ex-wife to dinner.

DIRK: Because she looked hungry. You damn fool! Because she strikes me as an exceptionally attractive girl.

BOB: And you would know.

DIRK: That's right. I don't want to pull rank or anything—but I think it might be fair to assume I know at least as much about women as you do about books. Perhaps more.

BOB: Look, you misunderstand me. I am delighted that you find my former wife attractive. I'm charmed that you are taking her out. If you decide to marry her, I'll send up rockets. In fact, you can count on me as your best man.

OSCAR: Marry her and you count on him as your publisher.

BOB: [*Overheated*] Absolutely! Now, there's a brilliant idea! Why didn't I think of it? Oscar's got a head on both his shoulders. I could solve your problems, you could solve my problems.

DIRK: You've got to be joking.

BOB: [*Lying back on the sofa and kicking off his loafers*] Why? This is the age of the deal! You scratch me and I'll scratch you! Don't you read the papers? Why should I be out of touch?

OSCAR: Bob—

DIRK: No, let's listen to him. I couldn't be more impressed. It stirs memories of the past—I keep thinking, "Louis B. Mayer, thou shouldst be living at this hour!"

BOB: [*To* OSCAR] See? You're shocked. But he's been around!

DIRK: And back. It couldn't be more reasonable. He has an unmarketable wife and I have an unmarketable book. He thinks we should pool our lack of resources. I haven't had such a fascinating offer in years.

[*The bedroom door opens and* MARY *appears, beautiful in a low-cut dress*]

MARY: Hello! I think I'm all collected. [*All rise. She senses the tension in the air*] What are you all staring at? Is something showing?

DIRK: Yes, and it looks delicious. Are we ready? [*He gets* MARY's *coat as* MARY *goes to* OSCAR *and kisses him*]

MARY: [*To* BOB] I suppose it's all right if I pick up that bag later tonight?

BOB: Certainly. But how will you get in?

MARY: [*Waving a bunch of keys from out of her handbag*] I still have my keys. Have you been missing things?

DIRK: Shall we run along? I double-parked down there.

MARY: [*Breezing through doorway, calling back to* OSCAR *and* BOB] Good night!

BOB and OSCAR: [*She's already gone*] Good night.

DIRK: [*Ready to go, turning back to* BOB *from the doorway, grinning*] I think you've got yourself a deal. [DIRK *goes, closing door behind him.* BOB *heaves a great sigh of exasperation and snatches up the galleys*]

OSCAR: [*After watching* BOB *for a moment*] I've known you for twenty years and i never realized you had this flair for comedy. [*No answer from* BOB, *trying to concentrate on galleys*] You *were* joking?

BOB: [*Crossly*] Of course I was joking. [*Looking up as the thought crosses his mind*] But wouldn't I like to see him try! It'd be an education for him. [OSCAR *pokes the work sheet under his nose*] Don't, don't, don't. I don't want to hear another word about my untidy affairs. [*Turns his attention to galleys again*]

OSCAR: [*Following* BOB *to the desk*] What's the matter with you?

BOB: [*Sharply, not lyrically, and without looking up*] Say I'm weary, say I'm sad, say that health and wealth have missed me, and you've said it. [BOB *is now rapidly crossing out great sections of the galleys*]

OSCAR: Why are you *slashing* at those galleys?

BOB: Because this man writes like a sick elf! [*And* BOB *is going at it with renewed vigor as the curtain falls*]

CURTAIN

ACT TWO

The moment the curtain is up, DIRK *and* MARY *enter by the main door, stomping their feet and brushing snow from their clothes. It is shortly after midnight and the room is dark except for the glow from the window.* MARY *turns on the hall light just inside the front door.*

DIRK: Did you get wet?

MARY: No, except for my hair.

DIRK: It doesn't look wet.

MARY: No, but you watch. In five minutes it'll be so fuzzy I'll be able to cut a piece off and clean my suede shoes.

DIRK: Would you feel safer if I left the door open?

MARY: Oh dear! I felt perfectly safe until you asked that question.

DIRK: The question is withdrawn.

MARY: Isn't this the silliest snowstorm? [*Going to the window, looking out*]

DIRK: [*Closing the door and following her*] I come from California. I think it's a lovely snowstorm.

MARY: But those great big flakes swirling around! It looks so phoney. Like— do you remember those big glass paperweights and you turned them upside down and it snowed? That's how it looks. [*Turns and is surprised to find him right behind her. Unsettled, she points to her bag near the bedroom door*] Here's that damn bag. Remember—you're not coming back out with me. I'll get a cab.

DIRK: In *this?* You'd never. And here I am—ready—willing—cheaper.

MARY: If I had a brain in my head, I'd have taken it with me and we could have dropped it off at the Biltmore. [MARY *is holding the suitcase in her hand. As* DIRK *goes to take it from her, his hand rests on hers a moment*]

DIRK: Does everybody tell you how pretty you are?

MARY: [*Takes her hand away—flustered*] Oh, you *are* a good actor! You could play anything. [*Changing the subject*] You know what? It's really idiotic, our going back out in that blizzard. We're not delivering the serum. [*She comes into the room and turns on a lamp*] Why don't I just stay here? [DIRK *puts the bag down and looks toward the bedroom. In answer to his unspoken question*] Oh, he's safely in Goshen with a beautiful, lovely girl with a head on her shoulders. [*She has remembered* BOB's *description word for word.* DIRK *stares at her a second, then heads for the bar table*]

DIRK: Do you suppose we can have a drink, or did Bob get the custody of the liquor?

MARY: [*She is already a couple of cocktails in, and is beginning to like it*] Sure, let's have a drink. But make mine light. I'm beginning to feel that champagne. [*She turns on another lamp*] Do you realize we were three hours in that restaurant? That's the nice thing about having dinner with somebody you're not married to. [*She starts to sit on the sofa, then after a glance at* DIRK, *who is making the drinks, discreetly chooses a chair*] You have so much more to talk about.

DIRK: All I found out about you is that you're allergic to penicillin and you love *The Catcher in the Rye.*

MARY: That's all? That's a lot. I want to hear about you. Are you going to get your book published?

DIRK: I am going to make every possible effort. [*Hands her a drink*] That's mostly water. [*He moves a chair close to her and sits*] You and Bob must have spent a lot of time with authors. What do *they* talk about?

MARY: You don't think they talk about *books?* They talk about first serial rights, second serial rights, movie rights, and how they're going to form a corporation to publish their next one so they can call it a capital gain and move to Jamaica.

DIRK: They sound just like actors.

MARY: It's terrible when you feel a writer is trying out his material on you. You never know exactly what reaction they expect, but you have to keep looking so *interested* your eyebrows get tired. [*She has made a concentrated face to show what she means.* DIRK *grins*]

DIRK: I know a guy who used to work with Disney. He'd actually tell you the whole plot of an animated cartoon—frame by frame. But he was a classic case. He could bore the birds back onto the trees. He never stopped talking—never. If he took a drink, he'd hold his hand up—[*He demonstrates this*]—so you couldn't put a word in until he was back with you. [MARY *laughs at the demonstration, then calms down into a small silence, which* DIRK *fills*] Your eyes are so blue—and so liquid. I feel they might spill right down your cheeks.

MARY: [*Quick with the answer, moving away to get a cigarette, leaving her drink behind*] That's because I need glasses and won't wear them.

DIRK: [*Curious and interested*] Why do you do that?

MARY: Do what?

DIRK: You jump when you get a compliment.

MARY: [*Too quickly*] No, I don't.

DIRK: You're actually embarrassed.

MARY: [*A shade defensively, lighting her cigarette*] Why should I be embarrassed?

DIRK: I don't know. But you are. You come bustling in to change the subject, like a nervous hostess who's discovered that two of the guests are quarreling. [*Imitating the hostess*] "Now, come along, Harry—there's somebody very nice that I want you to meet."

MARY: [*Sits at one end of sofa*] All right. Pay me pretty compliments and I won't change the subject.

DIRK: And you won't make jokes? [MARY *is stunned by the echo of* BOB's *remark*]

MARY: What? What?

DIRK: Shouldn't I have said that?

MARY: No, that's all right. It's been said before. Just recently, in fact. I suppose I should take a course and find out what a girl should answer when a gentleman says "Tell me, pretty maiden, are there any more at home like you?" Though it would hardly pay. It doesn't come up that often.

DIRK: I thought little girls learned things like that when they were three years old. [*He moves nearer to her, bringing her drink*]

MARY: Oh, but I'm a very retarded case. It's only just this year I learned how to put my hair up in rollers.

DIRK: What did you do before that?

MARY: I wore it pinned back in a bun. And when it had to be cut, *I* cut it, or I went somewhere and *they* cut it. Lately I've been going to Elizabeth Arden, and I want you to know that it's a whole new way of life.

DIRK: So I'm told.

MARY: At Arden's they don't just cut your hair—never. They *shape* it. And they honestly think a good shaping is as important as a cure for cancer. The hairdresser really blanched when he saw my bun. I could hear him thinking, "Thank God she came to me—another month and it might have been too late."

DIRK: Well, I think your hair looks lovely. Now say thank you.

MARY: Thank you.

DIRK: See how easy it is?

MARY: [*Jumping up, self-conscious*] I—Oh—Tell me about your book. [*Picks up the manuscript*]

DIRK: [*Taking the manuscript from* MARY] What can I tell you? It weighs three quarters of a pound. It takes eight-four cents in stamps to mail it. [*Tosses it on sofa table and goes to the bar for another drink*]

MARY: Don't talk like that. You mustn't lose faith in it just because Bob didn't like it. Bob's a good publisher but he makes mistakes. Did you have any help with this book?

DIRK: You mean, did I *tell* it to somebody? No.

MARY: I'm glad. All these "as told to" books have such a spooky flavor about them. First the personality is all drained off. Then, to compensate, something else is pumped in—sex or religion or Scott Fitzgerald. I fully expect that any day now we're going to have The Confessions of Saint Augustine—as told to Gerold Frank.

DIRK: [*Returning to her*] Mary—

MARY: What?

DIRK: You just said Bob makes mistakes. But how did he ever let you slip through his fingers?

MARY: Just lucky, I guess.

DIRK: I think I am beginning to see the clue to this little puzzle.

MARY: What puzzle?

DIRK: You.

MARY: I'd love to think I was a puzzle. A woman of mystery. Smiling and enigmatic on the surface—but underneath, a tigress. [*Change of mood, straightforward*] I hate to admit it, but what you see is all there is. Underneath this plain girlish exterior, there's a very plain girl.

DIRK: Ah, but what happened to make you *decide* it was such a plain exterior? It was the divorce, wasn't it? It was Bob.

MARY: Bob? I decided *that* when I was thirteen years old. We can't blame Bob for everything.

DIRK: At thirteen, all by yourself, you decided that?

MARY: [*Sitting on the ottoman*] Oh, there were people around, but I can't say they gave me any argument. Do you ever look at little girls?

DIRK: How little?

MARY: [*Rather intensely, as she remembers and thinks about it. The intensity is perhaps increased by the amount she's had to drink*] You take two little girls. One of them is pink and round, with curly hair and yards of eyelashes. The other one is pale and bony, with thin, wispy hair and two little ears poking through—like the handles on a sugar bowl. Okay, which one of these little girls is going to have to wear braces on her teeth?

DIRK: The wispy one.

MARY: [*As though awarding him a prize*] You've got it. [*Seeing herself again, taking a sip of her drink*] That was me. Braces on my teeth, Band-Aids on my knees, freckles on my nose. All elbows and shoulder blades. For two years running I got picked to play the consumptive orphan in *Michael O'Halloran*.

DIRK: That was talent.

MARY: That was typecasting.

DIRK: All adolescents go through something. I had the worst case of acne in the history of the world. For three years I was a Technicolor marvel. You wouldn't remember when Fleischmann's Yeast was the big thing. I used to eat Fleischmann's Yeast and drink water until I couldn't move without gurgling. I imagine I was actually fermenting.

MARY: I never ate yeast, but once I sent away secretly for Stillman's freckle cream. I guess I used too much, because I just peeled and peeled. I had to pretend it was a sunburn.

DIRK: I used to pretend I hated everybody. Especially girls, because I was too self-conscious to talk to them.

MARY: You made a spectacular recovery.

DIRK: I may even have overdone it. But why didn't you—

MARY: Make a recovery? Well, it was sort of different with me. When I was a kid, I mean really a kid, I never worried about the way I looked, because I thought—I *knew*—I'd grow up to be beautiful just like my sister Clara.

DIRK: Was she so beautiful?

MARY: Clara? She had bright red hair and brown eyes and she always had a faintly startled look, as if she'd just come out of a dark theater into the sunlight. People who met her would be so busy staring they'd forget to finish their sentences.

DIRK: I can see that would have been something of a cross for you.

MARY: No, I thought it was insurance. Clara was six years older than I was, and I thought "I'll grow up to look just like that." One day I was measuring myself—I was about fourteen—and I realized I hadn't grown at all, not an inch, in a whole year. And then it came to me. I wasn't going to grow any more. I was *up*. And I didn't look anything at all like Clara.

DIRK: And you weren't satisfied to look like Mary?

MARY: I certainly was not. I went rushing to my father, and I asked him when I was going to look like Clara. Poor man. He didn't know what to say.

DIRK: What did he say?

MARY: He said "Darling, we wouldn't want two Claras. You're the bright one." That did it. I could have faced being plain, but to be plain *and* bright! In the high school I went to, that was a beatable combination.

DIRK: So you decided to get on the debating team.

MARY: How did you know?

DIRK: Girls who feel they are not going to be invited to dances always get on the debating team.

MARY: And I worked on the school newspaper. And I imagined all the time that I was really Catherine Earnshaw.

DIRK: Catherine who?

MARY: The girl in *Wuthering Heights*. Cathy.

DIRK: Oh, Merle Oberon.

MARY: That's right. I used to dream that somewhere there was a strange, dark man whose heart was quietly breaking for me. On rainy nights I'd open the window and imagine I could hear him calling—"Oh, my wild, sweet Cathy!" The colds I got! And of course the only dark man I ever saw was the middle-aged dentist who used to adjust the braces on my teeth.

DIRK: And you're still cross about it.

MARY: Is that how I sound? I don't feel that way. I feel wistful. I think of that sappy little girl and I wonder what happened to her.

DIRK: Nothing happened. She hasn't changed at all.

MARY: You mean I haven't changed at all? That's a hell of a thing to say.

DIRK: Oh, I'm certain you've changed in appearance. That's clear enough. But you yourself haven't changed. Somewhere inside you, you're *still* wearing braces on your teeth.

MARY: Oh, come, come. I came to the big city. I learned to tip waiters. I read *The New Yorker.* I got married.

DIRK: And nothing took. Do you know what's strange?

MARY: What?

DIRK: Here you are—so lovely. And nobody falls in love with you.

MARY: Oh, is that so? And where did you get that idea?

DIRK: From you.

MARY: You're crazy. I never said—listen, lots of people—well, Bob certainly was in love with me—

DIRK: You really thought so?

MARY: Of course! Why else would he marry me? There was no dowry, or anything.

DIRK: I don't know. Why did he?

MARY: [*Seriously unsettled beneath her insistent assurance*] Because he felt that—because we both—listen, what is this? [*Rises*] I haven't answered so many idotic questions since I tried to open a charge account at Saks! [*Moves away to the fireplace*] There must be a genteel, ladylike way of telling you that it's none of your damn business!

DIRK: I knew I'd get a rise out of you when I said that about Bob.

MARY: Then why did you say it?

DIRK: Of course Bob was in love with you. But you don't believe it. You never believed it.

MARY: [*Turns to him, alert*] What did he tell you?

DIRK: Nothing. You're the evidence. Women who believe they're attractive have a certain air about them. You don't. Your reflexes are off.

MARY: [*Now furious*] I will match my reflexes with your manners any old day! And now, unless you have some other little speech all rehearsed, I suggest you go upstairs or downstairs or wherever it is you call home!

DIRK: Now you're mad.

MARY: Oh, you *are* the quick one! Nothing is wasted on you. Of course I'm mad! What did you expect I'd be?

DIRK: I didn't know. I never met anybody quite like you before.

MARY: We're even. I never met anybody like you, either. [*Sitting at one end of the sofa*] Which doesn't explain why I let myself be taken in by that richer, milder, long-lasting M-G-M charm.

DIRK: Oh, *were* you—taken in?

MARY: I must have been. Why else would I sit here—babbling like an idiot, pouring out my little girlish secrets! That's not part of my regular act. I don't learn. [DIRK *sits near* MARY *on sofa*] I guess I never will learn.

DIRK: [*Putting his hands on her shoulders and speaking earnestly and directly*] Mary, do you know what I feel? I feel—

MARY: [*Coolly, sarcastically*] You feel as though you were seeing me—for the first time.

DIRK: I'll tell you something you ought to learn. You really ought to learn when to shut up. [*With real dispatch, he takes her into his arms and kisses her firmly.* MARY *is too startled at first to protest, and later she is maybe too interested. When they break off,* DIRK *puts one finger gently to her lips*] Shh! Now once more—quickly, before you lose your nerve. [*He kisses her again*]

MARY: [*Finally*] I feel dizzy.

DIRK: That's suitable.

MARY: It's just that I haven't kissed anybody, lately. But it's like riding a bicycle. It does come back to you.

DIRK: And you don't even have to worry about the calories.

MARY: You know—you're very nice. And about ninety-five per cent correct.

DIRK: About what?

MARY: About a lot of things. But why are you bothering with me?

DIRK: I'm being bribed.

MARY: [*Taking it as a joke, of course*] I *knew* that. But there must be other reasons. I like *you* because you hurt my feelings and made me lose my temper.

DIRK: And that's a reason?

MARY: To me it is. I've gone so long not reacting to anything, it seems somehow reassuring. It's like—well—if you were absolutely convinced that you had no feeling in your hand, you'd be relieved to burn your fingers.

DIRK: [*Picking up her hand and kissing it*] What can we do for those fingers? I like you because I think that, with any encouragement, I might fall in love with you. [*She is silent*] If you're going to say anything, say what you're thinking. Don't invent something.

MARY: [*Facing up to this*] I'm thinking I'd really like to believe that. So I will.

DIRK: That's my girl

[*And he is kissing her again as* BOB *enters.* BOB, *too, is snowy as he comes in the main door. He stops dead at what he sees*]

BOB: Mary. What are you doing here?

DIRK: Don't ask rhetorical questions. Surely you can see what she's doing.

BOB: [*Embarrassed, bothered by some instinctive reaction he doesn't understand, and trying to be cordial. After all, it's what he hoped for. His reactions are actually disturbingly mixed*] All I meant, really, was to indicate my surprise that Mary was *here.* I thought we left it that she was going to the Biltmore. I mean—what is the situation now? [*To* MARY, *and still floundering*] I mean, are you just coming or going?

MARY: [*Sweetly. She's a little bit high*] I'm staying. What about you?

DIRK: We thought you were on your way to Goshen.

BOB: [*Taking off his coat*] I *was* on my way to Goshen, but there's a blizzard out there. We couldn't even get on the thruway.

MARY: And I wasn't privy to your change of plans. [*Turns to* DIRK] Do you know I never in my whole life used the word privy before?

DIRK: Not even for—?

MARY: [*Shaking her head rapidly*] Nope, never. Don't you hate places where they have cute names for the men's room?

DIRK: I hate places where they have cute names for the places. Did you ever hear of a nightclub called the Chez When?

[BOB *moves toward the desk aimlessly. They are continuing their conversation as though he hadn't come in*]

MARY: [*Eyes widening*] No.

DIRK: What do you call it when the words are accidentally twisted? Where the minister says the Lord is a shoving leopard—?

MARY: I think that's a spoonerism. I'm always getting words twisted like that. I was buying a hammock for the porch at home. And in a crowded elevator I said, "Miss, where do you have perch forniture?"

DIRK: Perch forniture?

MARY: Don't you know the unsuitable things that would go on in perch forniture?

[*As they laugh, they become more aware of* BOB, *who is feeling very much like a fifth wheel and not liking it*]

DIRK: Bob, why don't you get yourself a drink?

BOB: Thank you. You're the soul of hospitality. [*He does go to get himself a drink*]

DIRK: Well. . . .

MARY: Pay no attention to Bob. It's just that he's systematic. He has his day all planned out. He makes a list. And the snow wasn't on his list and you weren't on his list.

DIRK: [*A sly look at* BOB] But we had such an interesting chat at six o'clock. I thought I was definitely in his plans—on his list.

BOB: I'm sorry if I sounded rude. But it happens to be one-thirty, and any hour now I'd like to know where I'm going to lay my head. [*To* MARY] Did I understand you to say you were staying here?

MARY: [*Giddily*] Yes. I'm sleepy. I do not wish to go out into the night that covers me black as the pit from pole to pole. Remember, women and children first. That's the law of the sea. And I'm sure it goes for snowstorms.

BOB: Naturally, I don't expect you to go out in this. [*Unable to restrain a note of irony*] Would it be all right if I slept here on the couch?

MARY: Certainly. Be your guest.

DIRK: [*To* MARY] Our host is beginning to look glassy-eyed. And since we seem to be sitting on his final resting place, I'd better leave. [*Rising*] But it was a lovely evening. [*Takes* MARY's *hand*]

MARY: [*Rising with* DIRK] I thought so. I really thought so. [*They go hand in hand toward the door.* DIRK *gets his coat*]

DIRK: I'll call you first thing in the morning. Is ten o'clock too early?

MARY: Ten o'clock is fine. [DIRK *kisses her lightly but definitely*]

DIRK: [*To* MARY] Good night—[*To* BOB, *cheerily*] Good night!

BOB: Night. [DIRK *goes, closing the main door behind him. There is a slight moment of awakwardness, then* BOB *goes toward the closet*] Well, I'll get myself a blanket and some sheets. I imagine that extra blanket is still in the storage closet.

MARY: [*Hasn't stirred*] I imagine.

BOB: [*Having got out a sheet and blanket*] Too bad we can't open the window. This place is full of smoke. [*Waving his arms about to dispel imaginary smoke*]

MARY: Uh-hm.

BOB: [*Picks up a large ash tray from the coffee table and dumps the contents of the sofa table ash tray and the mantel ash tray into it. Then empties the large one into the fireplace. Finally, he speaks his mind*] I must say that I'm rather surprised at you.

MARY: [*Bright, cheery*] Yes. I'm a little surprised at me, too.

BOB: You've been drinking.

MARY: [*Airily*] Yep, that's exactly what I've been doing. It's taught me a valuable lesson. You know what's the matter with this country? Too much sobriety. Too many sober persons.

BOB: May I suggest that you get yourself to bed before you pass right out?

MARY: No, you may not suggest one thing. I do not require your solasitude.

BOB: Solasitude? Solicitude!

MARY: [*Pleasantly stretching out on the sofa*] All right, that's what I do not require. I feel fine, splendid, top of the morning.

BOB: [*Cleaning desk ash tray*] I don't get it. I thought you were the conservative, slow-to-warm-up type. Miss Birds Eye Frozen.

MARY: There *was* a rumor like that going round. Isn't it nice to know there's nothing in it.

> [BOB *empties the contents of the bookcase and desk ash trays into a wastebasket*]

BOB: Mary, look. What you do is none of my business. I know that.

MARY: I'm glad you know that.

BOB: [*Edging toward her, worried*] I never wanted to see you retire to a convent. You ought to go out with men. You should get married again. To some man who's in love with you.

MARY: [*Listening*] What other kind of man would marry me?

BOB: There are men and men. And—well, you don't know what you're getting into here. The idea of you sitting around necking with that bum! What the hell do you know about him?

MARY: Well, let's see. He had a very bad case of acne when he was fourteen years old.

BOB: That clarifies everything. I'm telling you this league is too fast for you, dearie. These glamour boys collect women like stamps—if you want to be added to thc collection.

MARY: [*Sits up on sofa, finally speaking up for herself*] All right. I'll tell you something. He thinks he's falling in love with me.

BOB: [*Alarmed; feeling responsible*] He said that? Oh, that bastard! But you *couldn't* have believed him?

MARY: Why not?

BOB: Now, honestly. Does it seem very likely that that big, caramel-covered movie idol would come along and just one, two, three, bang, fall in love with a girl like you?

MARY: [*Sharply hurt, and now fighting tears*] I guess I thought it was possible—even with a girl like me. Isn't that the height of something or other?

BOB: [*Distressed at what he has said*] Wait, I didn't mean a girl like you—I meant any ordinary—

MARY: I *know* what you meant. How could you be clearer? I'm the drab, colorless type and I should know better than to believe it when somebody tells me I'm—pretty. . . . [*She can't help the catch in her voice, try as she may*]

BOB: [*Completely unsettled*] Are you going to cry about it?

MARY: Maybe. Maybe. Why not?

BOB: Because you never cry.

MARY: How do you know I never? How do you know? I'll cry if I please! And I please! [*And she lets herself go, having a real, satisfactory cry*]

BOB: Mary—

MARY: [*Flinging herself face down on sofa*] Don't you Mary me!

BOB: [*Out of his depth and railing against it*] It must have something to do with the position of the moon—I don't get it. Some joker tells you you're beautiful and you go all to pieces. I used to tell you you were beautiful and your detachment was marvelous to behold! [*Leans over her*]

MARY: [*Sits up—flaring*] You never, never, never told me I was beautiful!

BOB: Of course I did!

MARY: No, you didn't. You said you liked the way I looked.

BOB: That's the same thing.

MARY: It most certainly is not the same thing! The world is full of people that you like the way they look, but you wouldn't say they were beautiful!

BOB: Like who, for instance?

MARY: Like Mrs. Roosevelt!

BOB: [*Incredulous, entirely serious, and wonderfully maddening*] You didn't think Mrs. Roosevelt was beautiful? My God—the character in that face. . . !

MARY: See? Now I'm a Communist. I'm picking on Mrs. Roosevelt! I *loved* Mrs. Roosevelt. And I'm not talking about character. If there is one thing I'm not interested in having any more of—if there's one thing I'm lousy with—it's character! Oh, why did you come back here tonight? I felt so good. Now I'm cold sober and everything is spoiled!

BOB: [*Backtracking*] I see that you're upset. I'm sorry if I—

MARY: You're not sorry. You're merely embarrassed.

BOB: What I *am* is surprised. I never thought I'd find you sobbing on the sofa. For all the world like any other woman. Actually, it's quite becoming. [*Sits near* MARY *and offers his handkerchief*]

MARY: [*Taking it and wiping her eyes*] Thank you. I'm so relieved to know that.

BOB: Funny you never cried in the whole five years we were married.

MARY: I figured you were sensitive enough for both of us. You decided right at the beginning that I was the airy type—impervious to wind and weather and small disappointments.

BOB: You make it sound as though I invented your character. For that matter, what's wrong with being the airy type?

MARY: [*Getting up*] It got to be a bit of a strain. I felt like I was on some damn panel show, twenty-four hours a day. Smiling, affable, humming little snatches of song. Laughing when I didn't know the answers. But affable, affable, affable! You don't know how I longed to get up some morning and feel free for once to be depressed, to be constipated, to be boring. [*Pause*] All right. I was boring.

BOB: No, you were not boring. It's strange we talked so much without communicating. [*The fact has hit him, and he's considering it*]

MARY: It was hard to communicate with you. You were always communicating with yourself. The line was busy.

BOB: [*Surprised*] Is that the way it seemed to you?

MARY: It seemed to me that you were taking your emotional temperature six times a day. I could almost hear you asking yourself: "Am I nervous? Am I tense? Did that upset me?" How are you feeling right now? [BOB *almost doesn't hear this last thrust. He is seriously and soberly thinking back.* MARY *picks up the sheet and blanket*]

BOB: You're right, of course. I do have a bad habit of asking myself questions—silly questions. But—am I nervous, am I tense? That's more or less reasonable. [*Looking at her*] It was really more foolish than that. I used to ask myself—why doesn't she love me?

MARY: [*Shocked, unbelieving*] You asked yourself—that?

BOB: All the time.

MARY: [*Throws bedclothes on sofa, exploding*] That's why I hate intellectuals! They're all so dumb!

BOB: What kind of a statement is that?

MARY: An idiotic statement. I should save my breath and remember that I'm talking to the most sensible man in the western hemisphere.

BOB: Why do you harp on that? I'm not all that sensible.

MARY: But you are! You lead a sensible life. You eat a sensible breakfast. You limit yourself to one pack of cigarettes a day—no more than two cocktails before dinner. You're even sensible about sex.

BOB: Would you like to explain that crack?

MARY: Any man that would tap his wife on the shoulder at eleven o'clock and say "Are you in the mood tonight—because if you're not, I'm going to take a sleeping pill" is just about as sensible as you can get!

BOB: [*Blanching*] Of course, I don't have Mr. Dirk Winsten's technique in these matters.

MARY: No, you don't, more's the pity.

BOB: Look, I didn't mean to bring out your heavy artillery. I merely wanted to save you—

MARY: From what? From Dirk? But I don't want to be saved.

BOB: Just a minute. Surely you—

MARY: If he's just toying with my affections, okay. Maybe I'm in the mood to have my affections toyed with.

BOB: Mary, I promise you—you don't have the whole picture—

MARY: But I've seen the previews. And there's not one thing in this whole world you can do about it. [*Going toward the bedroom*]

BOB: [*Starts to follow her, but stops to steel himself*] Mary, I'm ashamed to tell you this, but I think I just *have* to—

MARY: [*Fiercely*] No, you don't have to, and you're not going to! I won't listen. I had a lovely time—a lovely time, do you hear? And you're not going to spoil it for me! Good night! [*She stomps off into the bedroom, letting the door bang behind her firmly*]

    [BOB *sees* DIRK'S *manuscript on sofa table, seizes it, and starts to throw it into the fireplace, then thinks better of it. He goes to his desk and picks up the telephone*]

BOB: Mr. Winsten's apartment, please. [*He fidgets, but the wait is not long*] Dirk? You asleep? No, I didn't call to ask if you were asleep. I'm coming down there. I've got to talk to you. [*Pause to listen*] Who's there with you—your agent? Is she pretty? Oh, all right, all right. I believe you. Then you've got to come up here. . . . You make it sound like I was asking you to drive to New Rochelle. It's only one flight up. No, it won't keep until Monday. Listen, it'll only take five minutes—okay, okay. [*Hangs up*]

    [MARY *appears from the bedroom with an alarm clock.* BOB *crosses quickly away from the phone*]

MARY: [*Coolly*] Do you want the alarm or shall I keep it?

BOB: You can keep it. I'm hardly likely to *oversleep* on that damn sofa. I'm lucky if I get to sleep. [*Turning off one of the lights*]

MARY: All right. I'll take the sofa. It doesn't bother me.

BOB: [*Quickly, alarmed that she'll still be on hand when* DIRK *arrives*] No, no, absolutely not. That's out of the question. Now if you're going to bed, would you go to bed? [*He starts pacing to the window and back to the bar table*]

MARY: [*Crossing casually to the alcove bookcase*] What's the matter with you? What are you pacing up and down like that for?

BOB: [*Stops pacing*] I'm waiting for you to go, instead of which—what are you doing?

MARY: Looking for something to read.

BOB: The place is full of books. What do you want?

MARY: I want something guaranteed not to improve my mind. [*Glancing at books*] The Gathering Storm . . . The Riddle of Rilke. . . . [*Spies* DIRK'S *manuscript on the desk*] Oh. Dirk's book. The very thing. [*She starts for the bedroom, slowing down as her interest is caught by something in the manuscript*]

BOB: Okay, now. Will you go to bed?

MARY: [*Slightly puzzled by his urgency*] I'm going. I'm going.

[*Taking her suitcase with her, she goes into the bedroom and closes the door.* BOB *breathes a sigh of relief, goes to the main door, opens it slightly so that* DIRK *will not have to ring, then returns to finish making himself a drink. At just this moment* DIRK *can be seen arriving in the corridor. As he is about to put his finger to the bell,* BOB *notices and dives for the door*]

BOB: *Don't* push that damn buzzer!

DIRK: What's the problem?

BOB: I simply don't want Mary to hear that bell.

DIRK: Shall I come in?

BOB: Yes, of course. [*Drawing him into the room, slightly away from bedroom door. Suddenly he is awkward and nervous in this new situation*] Listen, can I make you a drink?

DIRK: No, I don't want a drink. I merely want to know why you hauled me up here in the middle of the night.

BOB: Actually, it's only two o'clock. The thing is, I thought that we should— really, what I mean is that I should—[*Doesn't know how to begin*] You're sure you don't want a drink?

DIRK: Positive.

BOB: [*After staring at him helplessly for a second*] Well, I want a drink. [*Goes and gets the one he was making*]

DIRK: All right. Let's have it.

BOB: [*Gulping a shot, and taking the plunge*] Look here, Winsten . . . you know damn well that all this talk about you and Mary—and my publishing your book—was supposed to be a joke.

DIRK: I thought it was funny.

BOB: Okay, you knew I wasn't serious. Then why—why—?

DIRK: Ah, but you *were* serious! You had the wild-eyed look of a man who knows he has just spoken a true word in jest.

BOB: Look, I shot off my face. A bad habit I must nip in the full bloom. However, I wish to make it absolutely clear that I never intended at any time to make a deal with you involving Mary.

DIRK: And I thought it was an admirable plan! You wouldn't have been losing a wife, you'd have been gaining an author.

BOB: But you've got the whole thing straight now?

DIRK: Certainly.

BOB: [*Relieved*] I never dreamt that you were *this* anxious to get into print. And I certainly never thought that Mary—of all people—would sink into girlish incoherence at her first exposure to an actor.

DIRK: Why do you say "of all people—Mary"?

BOB: Because she's got some sense. That she could swallow that corny line!

DIRK: Do you describe everything you don't understand as corny?

BOB: What do you mean?

DIRK: Nothing. I suppose it's all right for me to go now—or did you have some other little confidence to tell me?

BOB: No, that's all. And thank you for coming. You can see I had to clear this up. I'll make your excuses to Mary in the morning.

DIRK: You will what?

BOB: I'll tell her you had to go back to Hollywood—for retakes, or whatever people go back to Hollywood for.

DIRK: And why will you tell her that?

BOB: Well, you don't think you'd be doing her a kindness to continue this little farce?

DIRK: I'm not interested in doing her a kindness. And I *am* going to see her.

BOB: [*Not understanding at all*] But why? I thought we understood each other. I thought we talked things out!

DIRK: Yes, and you listened very carefully to every word you had to say.

BOB: What do you mean by that?

DIRK: I mean you should take that paper bag off your head. You notice everything but the obvious. What kind of a jerk are you? How dare you suppose that Mary is some kind of a charity case? Where do you get off to suggest that any man who's interested in her has to have three ulterior motives?

BOB: [*At a real loss now*] I don't think *that*. I never thought—

DIRK: Well, you gave a very good imitation of somebody who thought that. What I told Mary may well have sounded corny. It seems that I lack literary qualities everywhere. [*Levelly*] But it wasn't a line. [BOB *sinks into the chair at his desk, confused*] You know, talking to you, I begin to see why Mary is so shy.

BOB: [*Aghast*] Mary? *Shy?*

DIRK: That's right. Shy *and* insecure. You probably don't believe that, either, even though you're at least two-thirds responsible.

BOB: [*He can't be hearing anything right*] How could I be responsible?

DIRK: I don't know. My guess is that you treated her as though she were intelligent.

BOB: She *is* intelligent.

DIRK: [*Waving it aside*] Shhh! She'll hear you! [*Going toward door, pausing to size him up*] Where did you get the habit of making assumptions based only on assumptions? Was your father a lawyer?

BOB: [*Staring at him*] I'll put it all in a letter.

DIRK: All right. Before I go, I want to say only one thing. Leave her alone.

Just leave her alone. Okay? [BOB *isn't grasping*] I mean—tonight. [*With a gesture to the sofa*]

BOB: [*Rising as this penetrates, dumfounded*] Are you nuts? I'm getting married in two weeks!

DIRK: Dandy. I'll send you a pair of book ends.

[*He leaves.* BOB *follows him to the door and angrily shoots the bolt. He turns out the hall light, takes off his jacket, picks up the sheet, then throws it down and starts for the bedroom door. He starts to knock on it, but doesn't. Biting his lip, he looks around the room, sees the telephone. With an inspiration, he hurries to it*]

BOB: Operator? Would you ring this number for me? *My* number. Thank you. [*He hangs up until the phone rings. Then he waits until it stops ringing after three rings. Picks it up*] Mary? This is Bob. I'm in the living room. [*Pause, while he listens for her to speak. Then the bedroom door whips open and* MARY *appears in the doorway, in pajamas, with the bedroom receiver in her hand*]

MARY: My God, you *are* in the living room! [*Stares at receiver in her hand, then at him*] What do you want? [*Holds up one finger, getting into the spirit of the thing, and is repeating her question into receiver as she returns to the bedroom*] What do you want?

BOB: [*Exasperated now, into phone*] Oh, stop it! Hang up! You're just trying to make me feel foolish!

MARY: [*Appearing in bedroom doorway again, with receiver*] I'm trying to make *you* look foolish! Who called who from the living room?

BOB: Well, I wasn't going to go barging into your bedroom! [*He hangs up his phone*] I had something to say to you and there seemed to be no reason why I couldn't say it on the telephone.

MARY: [*Turning to go*] I'll go back in. You call me again.

BOB: Stay right there! [MARY *merely reaches into the bedroom to hang up her receiver*] This won't take one minute. I just feel—in all fairness—that I have an obligation to tell you—[*It's a struggle for him, but he's game*]— that I was wrong, apparently, about Mr. Winsten.

MARY: And by what curious process did you arrive at this conclusion?

BOB: I talked to him. He was just up here.

MARY: [*Her eyes popping*] He *wasn't*—you *didn't*—!

BOB: It was all right. Don't worry. [*Facing her*] He merely told me that I was an insensitive clunk who never appreciated you.

MARY: And what did you say?

BOB: Oh, a number of stupid things. It was not my finest hour. Of course, when he says I didn't appreciate you, that's hogwash. I appreciated you, all right. [*Sits on the sofa*] I just wasn't able to handle you.

MARY: [*Softened by* BOB's *direct attitude and drifting into the room*] Don't reproach yourself. I didn't win any prizes for the way I handled you. It takes at least one to make a marriage.

BOB: Do you know how helpless you feel if you have a full cup of coffee in your hand and you start to sneeze? There's nothing to do but just let it splash. That's how I feel in all my relationships any more. Helpless— unable to coordinate—splashing everybody.

MARY: You're just tired.

> [*Without thinking about it, they seem to have drifted into a perfectly familiar domestic situation*]

BOB: Listen, you should have heard my various exchanges with Winsten today! And thank God you didn't! Talk about a comedy of errors! I try to grasp all sides of the picture. Nobody believes that—but I try.

MARY: Bob, honey—I mean, Bob—I believe it. I certainly believe it. I honestly think you're so busy grasping all sides of the picture that you never stand back and see it.

BOB: [*Willing to consider this*] Okay. Give me an example.

MARY: All right. I've been reading Dirk's book. I haven't got very far, but I think it's good.

BOB: Come on now—

MARY: No, you're going to let me finish. It may not win a Pulitzer prize, but it's readable. It's so nice and gossipy. I think it would sell.

BOB: I never said it wouldn't sell. I said I didn't want to do it.

MARY: But why not?

BOB: Oh, we've had this out a hundred times.

MARY: Bob, you won't believe this, but I'm glad you have standards. I wouldn't want you to settle for trash. But it's no crime to stay in business. You've got to keep the shop open or you won't be there when a masterpiece comes along. [*Quickly*] Let me get it. [*She dodges briefly into the bedroom for the manuscript, talking as she does, while* BOB *sits and stares at her*] I'm willing to make you a small bet that you can open it at any page at all and find something that's—nice, interesting. [*Coming back and sitting at one end of the sofa. The atmosphere is casual and they are, for all intents and purposes, man and wife at home alone*] Maybe it goes to pieces at the end, but I wouldn't know about that. Okay, we'll just open it anywhere. [*Reading from manuscript*] "... Starlets have a reputation for being dumb only because they have such blank expressions. And the smarter they are, the blanker they look, because they've learned that it's impossible to register any emotion without using some muscle which, in time, will produce a wrinkle. Even to look a tiny bit puzzled causes twin lines over the bridge of the nose. [*Glancing at* BOB *to do the expression for him; it strikes her as amusing.* BOB *is simply looking at her. She goes on*] By the time she is thirty, a starlet has been carefully taught to smile like a dead halibut. The eyes widen, the mouth drops open, but the eye muscles are never involved." [*Turning to* BOB *to explain*] They don't smile like this—[*She smiles as most people do*] See? You get all these wrinkles. [*Touching her forehead with her fingers to show him*] They go like this. [*She lets her mouth drop open in a mechanized, slack smile that doesn't involve the eyes.* BOB *is not really hearing her as he looks at her. She becomes aware he isn't responding*] You don't think that's funny.

BOB: [*Forced to say something, unable to identify what he's really feeling, the wrong thing pops out*] Haven't you got a robe? [*He rises and crosses away*]

MARY: [*Blank*] What do you mean, haven't I got a robe?

BOB: [*Awkward*] Well—do *you* think it's right for you to be sitting here in your night clothes?

MARY: [*Blowing*] My night clothes! Good Lord, you'd think it was a black lace bikini! Eight million times you've seen me in pajamas!

BOB: We were married then.

MARY: [*Staring after him*] Well, look at it this way. The divorce won't be final for two weeks.

BOB: [*Turns on a lamp*] That may be precisely the point.

MARY: Oh, my, we are so proper! Do you feel yourself in danger of being compromised? Don't worry so much. If I should suddenly throw myself upon you, you could always scream.

BOB: Oh, shut up.

MARY: [*Continuing blithely*] However, as it happens, I don't have a robe but there must be something around here. [*Sees his overcoat on the window seat*] Yes, here we are. [*Puts it on; it is, of course, too big for her*] I trust this will show my good faith and restore your sense of fitness.

BOB: And how do you think you look in that?

MARY: [*Sweetly*] I don't know. Kind of cute, maybe?

BOB: Boy! All of a sudden you're cocky as hell, aren't you?

MARY: All of a sudden? It took months. It was work, work, work every minute!

BOB: But it's been worth it. Think of having Dirk Winsten making passes at you! It must be like getting the Good Housekeeping Seal of Approval.

MARY: Um—sort of.

BOB: When you kissed him, I just hope you didn't damage his porcelain crowns.

MARY: [*Giggling*] Well, we can't worry about everything. But never mind his crowns, let's talk about his book. [*Reaching for the manuscript on the sofa, secretly pleased at* BOB's *attitude*]

BOB: I refuse to talk about anything with you in that damn coat. You look like Jackie Coogan in *The Kid*. Here—take it off! [*Reaches for the coat*]

MARY: [*Pretending to be shocked, as though fighting for her virtue*] Oh, no—no—please!

BOB: [*Starting to unbutton it*] Take it off. You only put it on to make me feel like an idiot.

MARY: [*Struggling*] You're going to break the buttons.

BOB: To hell with the buttons. [*He finally gets the coat off—and they stand facing each other in a moment of nervous intimacy. Instinctively,* MARY *puts her hand to the top of her pajamas.* BOB *backs away slightly*] No, that's as far as I mean to go. [*Angrily*] Now would you do me a favor, please? Will you please go to bed?

MARY: [*Below sofa, unsettled herself, now*] Certainly. But what are you so intense about?

BOB: I'm the intense type. Surely you've remarked on that before. I'm asking myself how I feel. And I feel wretched.

MARY: What's the matter?

BOB: You know damn well what's the matter! I feel all involved again. And I won't have it! I will not have it! I was getting over you so nicely. I was cured. My God, I feel like somebody who was getting out of the hospital after nine long months and fell down in the lobby and broke a leg. [*Because he is furious with himself*] And you did it deliberately!

MARY: Did it—did what?

BOB: If you want to pretend that your only purpose in the last half hour was to change my opinion of that book—all right!

MARY: [*Turns away, more quietly*] But I gather I'm not fooling you—great student of character that you are.

BOB: Okay, what *did* you have in mind—curling up on the sofa, cute as all get-out in your little blue pajamas? No, I'll tell you. You were conducting a little experiment.

MARY: I was?

BOB: You wanted to see—just for the record—if Old Bob wouldn't leap to the bait like our friend Mr. Winsten. You just wanted to check and see if I had any little twinges left. [*She says nothing*] Well?

MARY: [*Very quietly*] I'm just wondering if that could possibly be true.

BOB: There's no reason for you to be kept in suspense. Yes, if you want to know, I do still feel twinges. God help me. Every now and then a sharp one. Now what do you say?

MARY: [*Thoughtful for a split second, then, in her perplexity, reverting to type*] Well, I don't know—it *sounds* like a gall bladder attack. [BOB *stares a second, then turns on his heel and grabs his jacket.* MARY *impulsively, and now all regret*] Bob, where are you going?

BOB: [*Putting on his jacket wildly*] Where am I going? Out! What am I going to do? Nothing! [*He struggles to get quickly into his overcoat, making a mess of the procedure*]

MARY: Bob, don't be silly! It's still snowing! You'll get pneumonia.

BOB: [*Hurls his overcoat to the floor and storms out*] Don't you worry your little head. [*Leaving the door open*]

MARY: [*Shouting after him*] But where can you possibly go at this hour in the morning? They'll think you're crazy—! [MARY *stands there a moment, her back to us. Then she slowly turns and picks up* BOB's *coat. She comes down to a chair, the coat clutched in her arms. After a second or so, she begins to recite mechanically, like a child writing "lines" as a punishment*] I must keep my big mouth shut. . . . I must keep my big mouth shut. . . . I must keep my big mouth shut. . . .

CURTAIN

ACT THREE

Next morning, rather early.

   The stage is empty but the doorbell is ringing. The sofa is made up with sheet and blanket, but these are obviously unrumpled. In a moment MARY *comes from the bedroom, still half-asleep. She is in her pajamas.*

MARY: Bob . . . [*Staring at the sofa*] Oh. He didn't come back at all. [*She stumbles to the phone*] Hello. [*Doorbell*] Hello. For heaven's sakes, hello. [*Doorbell again.* MARY *now realizes it isn't the phone*] Oh. Excuse me. [*Hangs up*] I'm coming. [*Before she can get to the door, it opens. It is* TIFFANY] Oh, hello. Good morning. Oh—you're—I mean, you must be—

TIFFANY: [*After a moment of staring at* MARY, *without showing her surprise, she closes the door and speaks cheerily*] I'm Tiffany Richards. And you're Mary, aren't you? Well, I'm delighted to meet you. May I come in?

MARY: Certainly. By all means. I don't know *where* Bob is . . .

TIFFANY: [*Taking off her coat*] He's probably taking a walk. Lately I've been getting him to take a walk before breakfast. It's the very best thing for a sluggish colon.

MARY: [*Vaguely, still sleepy and not knowing where to settle or what to do next*] Yes, I can imagine it would be.

TIFFANY: [*Opening the curtains*] I never dreamt I'd find you here. But I'm so pleased it worked out this way. I've been dying to meet you. And it's a good thing Bob isn't here.

MARY: Why?

TIFFANY: Oh, he'd be bustling me right out the front door. For some reason, he was determined I wasn't going to meet you. You know, you're much shorter than I expected.

MARY: [*Not bitchy*] Of course I don't have any shoes on.

TIFFANY: It's just that Bob always makes you sound so overpowering. I expected somebody with a husky voice who said "darling" a lot. Harlequin glasses, big jangling bracelets, black velvet toreador pants.

MARY: But I do have a bracelet that jangles. I just don't wear it to bed.

TIFFANY: No, I can tell what you're like just by looking at you. I think you're nice.

MARY: Oh, dear.

TIFFANY: What's the matter?

MARY: It's so early. And you want to be frank and disarming.

TIFFANY: But what's wrong with that?

MARY: [*Going toward the bedroom, quickly and apologetically*] Oh, nothing, nothing at all. It's just my low metabolism. I don't grasp things this early in the day. I mean, I hear voices, all right, but I can't pick out the verbs. [*Goes into the bedroom*]

TIFFANY: [*Taking a dried apricot from the bowl*] You probably don't eat right. My grandmother is like that.

MARY: [*Returning, rummaging through her purse*] Oh, no. It's not possible! The way I feel and I don't even have a cigarette.

TIFFANY: Look, I wouldn't bother you, but Bob will be back and then I'll *never* get a chance to ask you.

MARY: [*Looks in the cigarette box on the sofa table*] Ask me? Ask me what? [*From now on* MARY *is making an abstracted effort to listen to* TIFFANY *but what she is really doing is making a methodical and increasingly desperate effort to find a cigarette somewhere around the apartment*]

TIFFANY: I guess I should warn you that I'm a very practical kind of person. People tease me about it all the time. Last Christmas, when I went to Palm Beach, everybody thought I was crazy because I took along my sun lamp, except it rained every day and I was the only one who came back with a tan.

MARY: Yes, but what did you want to ask me?

TIFFANY: I'm getting to that. Daddy always said that before you move into a house, you should consult the former tenant.

MARY: Oh. [*Checking the bookshelves and* BOB's *desk for a cigarette*]

TIFFANY: The person who's been living there will know where the storm windows are and whether there's a leak in the basement. Why should you spend six months finding out for yourself?

MARY: [*At the desk, too foggy to understand*] They don't have storm windows in this building.

TIFFANY: I'm not talking about the apartment. I'm talking about Bob.

MARY: You want to know if Bob has a leak in the basement? [*Her last resort*] Excuse me—you don't have a cigarette on you, do you?

TIFFANY: I'm sorry. I don't smoke. It's not that I worry about lung cancer, but it does stain your teeth.

MARY: Well, I worry terribly about lung cancer. I also worry about shortness of breath and heart disease. But what really worries me right this minute is that I'm not going to find a cigarette. [*Begins looking through the desk drawers*]

TIFFANY: Oh, I guess you never do find out. My cousin Harriet knew this boy for seven years. I mean she *thought* she knew him. But on the day they were married they took an overnight train to Chicago. And when they shut the door of their roomette, do you know the first thing he did?

MARY: No, and don't tell me.

TIFFANY: Well, he picked up a book of matches, opened the cover, and started picking his teeth. Like this.' [*Demonstrates "picking his teeth" with a lid of book matches. The key turns in the front door and* BOB *enters, the Sunday papers under his arm. He stops, startled and then embarrassed to find the two girls together*] Hi.

BOB: [*Pulling himself together with an effort*] Well. This is cozy. [*Then rattled again, quick to overexplain*] Tiffany, I should have explained to you last night that you'd find Mary here. [*Stopping to listen to himself*] Of course, I didn't *know* last night. [*Now really confused, looking at* MARY] I suppose you've introduced yourselves.

TIFFANY: [*Rising and kissing* BOB *on the cheek*] Oh yes, of course! [*She goes into the kitchen*]

BOB: Good morning, Mary.

MARY: Good morning, Bob. Did you have to go without your overcoat?

BOB: At the time I thought so.

MARY: I made up your bed because I expected—[BOB *takes off his jacket*] What did you do?

BOB: Walked, mostly. [*Looking for a cigarette on the low bookcase*]

MARY: Don't tell me you're out of cigarettes, too?

BOB: [*Patting his pockets. But they're empty*] Yes, but you'll find some in the desk drawer.

MARY: No, I looked.

BOB: Well, did you try behind the—

MARY: Yes, and I tried the liquor cabinet and the stamp drawer. [TIFFANY *returns with wheat germ for the fish*] And the last refuge of all—the Chinese vase—

BOB: [*Starting his own search*] Don't tell me I'm going to have to go trudging back out in the snow!

TIFFANY: Just for a cigarette? Would you like some breakfast? There's some orange-flavored yogurt.

BOB: Oh, no, no. Lord, no! Tiffany, be a lamb and fold up these sheets. There may be some under the—

MARY: See! If you hadn't dumped every single ash tray last night I could have found some medium-sized butts.

[TIFFANY *folds up the blanket, watching* MARY *and* BOB *feverishly search every conceivable nook*]

BOB: We must remain calm. It is statistically impossible that in this whole big apartment there isn't one single—just ask yourself: Where would you go if you were a cigarette? [*From beneath the cushion of a chair he brings up a battered half package*] Look! Success! [MARY *runs to him*]

MARY: [*As though cooing over a new baby*] There! Did you ever see anything so pretty in your life? [BOB *is digging for matches to light* MARY's *cigarette*]

TIFFANY: But they're all squashed!

[MARY *and* BOB *simply turn to stare at* TIFFANY, *simultaneously and incredulously. Then they turn their attention to the serious business of getting the cigarettes lighted, after which they exhale. Forgetting themselves, they speak in unison*]

MARY and BOB: Mmmm—that's *real* coffee! [*Becoming aware of what they have just done, they are a little embarrassed and pause awkwardly*]

TIFFANY: [*Looking up as she puts blanket away*] Coffee? What's that about coffee?

BOB: [*Firmer*] Nothing. Absolutely nothing.

TIFFANY: It must be something.

BOB: [TIFFANY *is obviously waiting for an explanation.* BOB *launches into it lamely*] We once heard this announcer on television. It was late at night and I suppose the poor joker was confused from having to talk about so many products all day. Anyway, he started to do a cigarette commercial. He sucked in and smiled and said "Mmmm—that's *real* coffee." [TIFFANY *does not react*] You see, it *wasn't* worth going into. [*Determined to be brisk and cheerful*] All of which reminds me that I haven't had any coffee. I think I'd better start some up. [BOB *goes into the kitchen almost too quickly, closing the door. There is a slight pause as* TIFFANY *looks at* MARY]

TIFFANY: How long does it take to have little private jokes?

MARY: What?

TIFFANY: Never mind. [*She begins to fold the sheet on the sofa*] I must stop asking questions for which there are no answers. [*Stops folding and looks reflectively at the sheet*] This sheet isn't even mussed. [*Looks at sofa*] Nobody slept on this sofa last night.

MARY: No. Bob was going to, but—

TIFFANY: He changed his mind.

MARY: [*Not wanting to go into what really happened*] That couch is a little short for him. Anyway, he decided that—

TIFFANY: —he'd rather sleep with you.

> [*She finishes folding the sheet, matter-of-factly.* MARY's *mouth drops open, but not for long*]

MARY: You mean—for old times' sake? No, indeed. Bob went—well, as a matter of fact, I don't *know* where he went. But he certainly wasn't there. As you will discover when you ask him.

TIFFANY: I won't ask him.

MARY: [*Looking at her*] Because you don't believe me.

TIFFANY: No, I don't.

MARY: Tiffany, when you get a little older, you'll learn not to *invent* problems. All you have to do is wait, and real ones turn up.

TIFFANY: In a way—I think I'm just as glad it happened.

MARY: You are.

TIFFANY: Bob's attitude toward you has always been a little mysterious. I'm hoping this may clear the air.

MARY: Your theory is that he's a little bit homesick and a trip back to the old place may cure him?

TIFFANY: All right, yes. That's what I think. [BOB *returns briskly from the kitchen, carrying a tray with coffee cups and an electric coffee maker on it*]

MARY: Bob. I'm afraid our little secret is out.

BOB: [*Casually, unraveling electric cord*] What little secret?

MARY: No, Bob, please. Tiffany *knows*. And she's being very understanding.

BOB: [*Glancing at* MARY *but kneeling to put the cord into the light socket*] Would you care to be plainer? I'm simply not up to riddles this morning.

MARY: Certainly. I'm trying to tell you that Tiffany is glad we slept together last night. She thinks it will clear the air.

BOB: [*Hearing it, and instantly up*] What did you say? What?

MARY: [*Blithely*] I really must get dressed. [MARY *goes off to the bedroom, closing the door behind her*]

BOB: [*Turning to* TIFFANY] Did I hear her correctly?

TIFFANY: [*Offering him the bowl of apricots*] Bob, whatever you do—please don't apologize.

BOB: [*Waving the bowl away and circling her*] You're damn right I won't apologize!

TIFFANY: All right, but are you going to snap at *me*?

BOB: Wait a minute. You accept this as a *fact*—and you're not even disturbed?

TIFFANY: Should I be?

BOB: Well, I can think of six reasons why you ought to be. And you can't even think of one?

TIFFANY: It isn't like it was somebody new. It isn't even like you planned it. You're put back into an old situation, and you fall into an old pattern.

BOB: I see.

TIFFANY: Anybody will tell you that the force of habit is stronger than—than love, even.

BOB: And in spite of the fact that I shack up with my ex-wife, you're willing to marry me?

TIFFANY: Certainly.

BOB: My God, haven't you got any principles, any ethics?

TIFFANY: [*Aroused, finally*] How did my principles ever get into this? What have *I* done?

BOB: [*Turning away and rubbing his forehead violently. Then he collapses into the chair behind the desk and begins rummaging through the desk drawers*] I've got to take some aspirin. I've got to clear my head.

TIFFANY: What's the matter?

BOB: You've heard of a lost weekend. Well, this has been a found weekend and it's worse.

TIFFANY: I'll get some water.

> [*She goes into the kitchen, leaving the door ajar.* BOB *now brings out, one by one, about a dozen bottles of pills of varying sizes, including aspirin*]

BOB: I feel in my bones that this is going to be one little peach of a day. I've got to take something to clear my head or I'm going to goof. I'm going to make some crucial mistake. [TIFFANY *returns with a glass of water*] And where the hell is Oscar?

TIFFANY: On Sunday, what do you want with Oscar?

BOB: [*Taking the glass and two aspirins*] There!

TIFFANY: Also take two of those large vitamins. [*With a glance at the bedroom door;* MARY *is on her mind*]

BOB: Why? [*He opens a bottle and takes out three capsules*]

TIFFANY: Alcohol works directly on the blood stream. [*He swallows one*] If you drink too much it lowers the white count, which is one reason why—

BOB: [*With another one in his mouth*] No, no—don't give me the details. [*Down a third*] Now I've taken three. There. I can feel my white blood count going up already.

TIFFANY: [*Suddenly noticing the bottle and picking it up*] Bob. You didn't take these?

BOB: You told me to.

TIFFANY: You idiot! These aren't vitamins.

BOB: What are they?

TIFFANY: Sleeping pills. [BOB *snatches the bottle from her and looks at it*]

BOB: [*To heaven in despair*] Oh, great. Great!

TIFFANY: Do you feel peculiar?

BOB: Not yet.

TIFFANY: Well, you will. We'd better get something.

BOB: It's not going to kill me. You have to take a whole bottle—a hundred and twenty, or something. [*Doorbell.* TIFFANY *starts to answer it*] That'll be Oscar.

TIFFANY: [*On her way to door*] Don't sit down. [BOB *jumps up*] I think you're supposed to keep walking around.

BOB: You're thinking of concussion.[*He drops into a chair again*]

TIFFANY: [*Opening the door.* DIRK *appears*] Oh—come in! You're Dirk Winsten, aren't you?

DIRK: Yes. And you're—?

TIFFANY: I'm Tiffany Richards. [*Pulling* DIRK *into the room*] And we've got a problem. Bob has taken some sleeping pills.

DIRK: Bob has!

BOB: Tiffany, please! Don't turn this into a melodrama. [*To* DIRK] I just—

TIFFANY: [*To* DIRK, *pointing to the coffee maker*] Do you think you could get him some coffee? I'll go to the drugstore and see if I can get some benzedrine or Dexamil—

BOB: They won't give you that without a prescription.

TIFFANY: [*Slipping on her coat*] They'll give me something, don't you worry. I'd call a doctor, but they want to ask you a lot of crazy questions, like are you depressed. [*To* DIRK] You'll watch out for him, won't you?

DIRK: Like a mother. Now, don't worry.[TIFFANY *rushes out the front door.* DIRK *wanders casually down to* BOB] Why did you do it?

BOB: Because my life has suddenly become ashes. I didn't know which way to turn.

DIRK: Come off it. How many did you take?

BOB: Three. Look, I got the bottles mixed up. I thought I was taking vitamins. Any more questions?

DIRK: Yeah. Where's Mary?

BOB: [*Crossly*] Well, the last time I saw her, she was in pajamas, so I think we may safely suppose she's dressing.

DIRK: What the hell are you so irritable about?

BOB: Because I had a rotten night! I drank too much, slept too little—

DIRK: You're not fooling anybody. You're mad as a hornet because I'm here to get Mary.

BOB: Why should I be mad? I'm delighted!

DIRK: You *sound* delighted.

BOB: Never mind my inflections. I just haven't had your training.

DIRK: You know, there's something very mysterious about your feeling for Mary. It's like gas. You can't get it up and you can't get it down.

BOB: [*The thought registers with* BOB *but he doesn't blanch*] There's a touch of the poet in you. [MARY *enters from the bedroom, dressed, and looking just splendid*]

MARY: [*Very cheery, seeing* DIRK] Good morning!

DIRK: Good morning. You just getting up?

MARY: Oh, I've been up for an hour. In fact, I've already had a heart-to-heart talk with Miss Richards.

BOB: [*Going to the bar table*] I've got to have some coffee.

MARY: [*Sweetly*] And would you bring me some, please? And a Danish that's—

BOB: [*Mechanically, swerving from the coffee maker toward the kitchen*]— cut down the middle, and no butter. I'll get it. [*Goes into the kitchen, closing the door*]

DIRK: I woke up this morning thinking: What nice thing just happened to me? And it was you.

MARY: You're very sweet. And not like a movie actor at all.

DIRK: [*Pouring her a cup of coffee*] Sure I am. Movie actors are just ordinary, mixed-up people—with agents.

MARY: I should think it would be fun to be Dirk Winsten.

DIRK: It is. There are all kinds of advantages. I can go into any restaurant at all and the headwaiter will automatically bring me a large pepper mill. Doctors don't get pepper mills—or lawyers. Not only that, but the head- waiter stands right there until I use it. I don't want him to feel a failure, so I grind away. With the result that I've had too much pepper on everything for twenty years. I love the way you smile.

MARY: [*Nervous, but meaning every word of it*] Dirk, I want you to know that I will never forget last evening. You couldn't possibly know what you did for me.

DIRK: Yes, but what have I done for you lately?

MARY: I'm not joking. I'm terribly pleased—and gratified.

DIRK: [*Urgently*] Gratified, hell! I don't want you to be gratified. I want you to be interested. I want you to say it would cause you a real pang if you thought you weren't going to see me again.

MARY: Oh, Dirk, it would—it does.

DIRK: I got a call from the studio at eight o'clock. They insist that I fly to New Orleans this morning for some personal appearance stuff. That picture of mine is opening there Thursday.

MARY: In New Orleans?

DIRK: [*Nodding*] The picture is called *King of the Mardi Gras*. That's how the great minds in publicity operate—the mayor meets me at the airport and hands me a praline or some damn thing. There's nothing I can do about it. It's in my contract. Anyway, here's the point. Why don't you come along?

MARY: But Dirk! I'm a working girl.

DIRK: Surely they could carry on without you for one week. Never underestimate the power of the *Ladies' Home Journal*.

MARY: But you just don't *do* that. . . !

DIRK: Sure you do. You call up and say that you've just had a recurrence of an old football injury. We could have a lot of fun. We could get to know each other.

MARY: But Dirk, I don't go off on trips with movie stars—I read about people like that in the *Journal-American* and I'm scandalized!

DIRK: Come on. Be rash. Fly now, pay later. [BOB *returns with an empty paper carton*]

BOB: Dirk, we seem to be all out of everything. Could I ask you to go down to the bakery and get a half-dozen Danish? It's for Mary.

MARY: Oh, let's have toast—anything.

BOB: No, there's nothing out there. I'd go myself, but I'm feeling so groggy.

DIRK: [*Rising and looking at his watch*] I don't *have* all that time . . . [*And looking at* MARY]

BOB: It's right in the building. Go left after you get out of the elevator.

DIRK: Well, I started life as a messenger boy.

MARY: Oh, don't bother.

DIRK: That's all right. I have to see if they've got my luggage in the lobby anyway. [*With a curious glance at* BOB, *then at* MARY] Mary—think about it. . . [*He goes*]

MARY: I don't know who ate them, but there was a whole bagful last night.

BOB: I stuffed them in the wastebasket.

MARY: You what?

BOB: I wanted to get him out of here so I could talk to you.

MARY: [*Starting for door as though to stop* DIRK] If that isn't the dumbest thing! Why should he have to—?

BOB: [*Grabbing her and spinning her around*] It won't hurt him a bit. You know—I'd like to shake you until your teeth rattled.

MARY: Oh, come on! In your whole life you never even shook a bottle of magnesia.

BOB: Why, why, *why* would you tell Tiffany that we slept together last night?

MARY: [*Honestly*] Look, Bob, whether you believe it or not, I said nothing to give Tiffany that impression.

BOB: [*This rocks him a little*] Then why did she—?

MARY: I don't know. Some people have such a talent for making the best of a bad situation that they go around creating bad situations so they can make the best of them.

BOB: [*Trying to think*] She didn't seem upset at all.

MARY: Upset? I got the impression she was delighted.

BOB: I know. I don't understand it. I don't understand anything. [*He sinks into a chair*] Mary, I'm so miserable.

MARY: Why?

BOB: You should know why. Look. In all the months we've been separated, have you been happier?

MARY: [*Reflectively*] No.

BOB: Have you—ever thought we might get back together again?

MARY: [*Trying to hide the emotion she feels*] It crossed my mind. [*She sits near him, tentatively*]

BOB: [*After a breath*] *Would* you consider it?

MARY: [*Struggling to control the relief and joy that want to come into her voice*] Bob, do you know what you're saying? Do you *mean* it?

BOB: [*Surprisingly making no move toward her*] I do mean it. [*Thinking, and even turning away*] I've been behaving like a damn adolescent—refusing to face the simple facts.

MARY: [*A little taken aback*] What simple facts?

BOB: Look at the whole thing in sequence. [*Counting the items on his fingers, logically*] A—I wanted a divorce from you because—well, it boils down to something as simple as I didn't think you understood me. Okay. [*Next finger*] B—the minute we got divorced, I discovered what I should have known in the first place—that I'm the kind of man who has to be married.

MARY: [*Hurt now, but keeping a level tone*] Is that what you discovered?

BOB: [*Going on with his explanation as though he were addressing a committee, completely unaware of the effect on* MARY] Absolutely. This business of going from flower to flower never did appeal to me. I hate to live alone. I hate to sleep alone. I keep finding myself, at four o'clock in the morning, sitting in the bathroom reading old magazines. So—I decided to get married again. That's C. In the circumstances, it seemed the logical thing to do.

MARY: [*Taking his tone*] I'd say so—yes.

BOB: But wait a minute. Now I discover that Tiffany really believes that I would actually sleep with one woman on the very eve of marrying another. By this time she should know me better than that. It isn't in my character. I'm really too square. But the point remains. *She* doesn't understand me, either.

MARY: [BOB *doesn't notice the acid that begins to creep into her voice*] Okay, we've had A, B, and C. What about D?

BOB: [*Innocent, and eager to go on explaining*] Well, I ask myself—am I walking with my eyes wide open into another case of incompatibility? In five years will there be another divorce? I don't think I could face it. [*He sinks onto the sofa, yawning*]

MARY: [*Casually, still playing along, though we can hear what's going on inside her*] No, and there would be more alimony, too.

BOB: Oh! More alimony, more scenes, more confusion! The thing is, you and I may be incompatible, but we know all about it now. I think we should get married again. It would be the sensible, reasonable thing to do. Don't you? [*He doesn't have to wait too long for his answer.* MARY *rises*]

MARY: You clunk. You block of wood. You're dumb—you're obtuse— you're—do you know something? I was so much in love with you that when you left I thought I'd die. That's right—big, healthy, well-adjusted Mary—I thought I might just possibly die! I used to sleep with the light on because in the beginning I'd wake up in the dark and forget where I was—and I'd reach out for you. Do you know if I saw a man ahead of me in the subway who walked like you or had shoulders like you, I used to feel faint, really faint. And you have the gall to stand there and talk to me about the sensible reasons why I should come back to you. You and your damn, stinking ABC's! [*She starts for the bedroom*]

BOB: [*With his head blown off*] Wait a minute—just because I try to be rational doesn't mean I don't *feel* anything—

MARY: Well, we won't really know until after the autopsy. Let me give you a little piece of advice. I think you should go right ahead and marry Tiffany. It would be more than a marriage. It would be a merger. You should be as happy as two IBM machines clicking away together!

BOB: [*Trying to salvage his dignity*] So you're not coming back.

MARY: That's right. A—I don't want to, B—I don't want to, C—I don't want to!

   [*She starts into the bedroom.* OSCAR *has let himself in,* DIRK *having left the door part-way open*]

OSCAR: What don't you want to do?

MARY: Oh, hello, Oscar— [*She stops in the bedroom doorway, all passion spent*]

OSCAR: [*Closing the door—to* BOB] I got your message. I'm shocked to see you looking so well.

BOB: What do you mean?

OSCAR: [*Getting out of his coat*] The answering service said it was absolutely urgent that I get over here this morning. *Urgent* was underlined three times.

BOB: Oh. [*An embarrassed glance in* MARY's *direction*]

OSCAR: I presumed that you were at death's door—waiting for me to draw up your will.

BOB: Of course not. It was really nothing that important. Actually it was really something minor. I mean, it could have—

MARY: [*Whirling on* BOB, *exasperated*] Oh, stop it! Why don't you tell him why you called him up this morning and asked him to come over? [*To* OSCAR] He thought he'd come back and find nobody here but *me*—and he'd be left alone with me. But think of it—you're too late! The damage has been done.

BOB: [*Outraged, blowing*] That's right! Listen to *her!* She knows my mind so much better than I do.

MARY: Oscar, when you go back over his accounts, you may deduct the amount he pays me in alimony. I don't want it. I never wanted it. I'm working now, and I don't need it.

BOB: [*Angrily*] Oh, don't be noble, there's no necessity!

MARY: Oh, but there is! [*To* OSCAR] Do you realize that if this poor soul had to go on paying alimony to me, he could never divorce Tiffany? Oscar, I sat at home and waited nine long months for him to call. Well, I'm not sitting home any longer. [*Heading for the bedroom*] Now I'm going to pack. [MARY *goes, slamming door behind her*]

OSCAR: Congratulations. You seem to have solved everything.

BOB: Oh, Oscar, you don't know what you're talking about! Even my problems have problems! [*Uncontrollably, he yawns right in* OSCAR's *face, then plunges on without pausing, in the same overwrought way*] What am I going to do? I can't marry Tiffany. She pushes in the bottoms of chocolates!

OSCAR: I never thought you would marry Tiffany.

BOB: Stop sounding like an owl and tell me what to do!

OSCAR: Get Mary back.

BOB: That's the conclusion I came to. But how?

OSCAR: Ask her.

BOB: Ask her? Last night I pleaded with her. Today I tried to be reasonable!

OSCAR: [*Quietly*] So that's what she's so mad about?

BOB: Yeah! And can you explain to me why *that* should make a woman mad?

OSCAR: Not in the time we have at our disposal. But I can tell you you'd be better off giving her one idiotic reason.

BOB: What do you mean?

OSCAR: Tell her you want her back so you can bite her shoulders.

BOB: You try and tell her something! Do you know that she's actually convinced I never noticed she was pretty? What does she think—I just arrived in from Mars? [*Yawn*] I've got two eyes. Hell, she always was pretty. When I first saw her with that pale hair and that pale face I thought she looked like a lovely piece of white porcelain.

OSCAR: Did you tell her?

BOB: Are you crazy? She would have said "White porcelain—you mean like the kitchen sink?"

OSCAR: Come on, now, you exaggerate.

BOB: Exaggerate? You don't know the half of it. She thinks I'm made of cast iron. She thinks I've never felt even a pang. Like I was some sort of vegetable. Do you know why I put that stinking phone in the bedroom? Because after we broke up I thought she might call me in the middle of the night some night and I wanted to be sure that I'd hear it. And before she gets out of here this afternoon I'm going to tell her about that phone. She's going to hear a few plain truths. She's not going to call me a block of wood. [*He starts toward the bedroom*] She's not going to—[*He is stopped by the return of* TIFFANY, *who hurries in by the main door with a small package*]

TIFFANY: Darling, how do you feel now? Are you all right? Hello, Mr. Nelson. I don't know what this is but he said it would help. [*Gives him a small box wrapped in blue paper*]

BOB: Thank you, darling. It was sweet of you to dash out and get things. [*But he is plainly befuddled by his own mixed emotions*]

TIFFANY: [*Sensing the problem*] Bob—you have something to tell me. You've had something to tell me ever since you came in this morning.

BOB: [*Evasive*] What? No, I didn't—I don't.

[OSCAR *is trying to make himself invisible by examining the fish tank*]

TIFFANY: You think you're inscrutable. You're the most scrutable man I ever met. Now, *tell* me—sleepy or no. You know, if you repress things, eventually you become devious—tell me!

BOB: Tiffany! Oscar is going to think *you've* taken an overdose of something.

TIFFANY: Don't worry about Oscar. He hasn't been surprised by anything since Truman was elected president. Tell me!

BOB: [*Trying to avoid a showdown, scarcely knowing his own mind and not up to a decision anyway*] Tiffany—honey—please—

TIFFANY: [*Crisply*] All right, I'll tell you. You've discovered that you're still in love with Mary.

[OSCAR *perks up an ear*]

BOB: [*Shocked*] Did I say anything whatsoever to lead you to think that?

TIFFANY: Of course not. And you never would. You'd be much too embarrassed. You'd think it was adolescent and in rather bad taste. Instead, you were going to tell me all the reasons why it would be a mistake for me to marry you. [BOB *is trying to shake his head "no," but she goes confidently on. To* OSCAR] I figured it all out while I was going to the drugstore.

BOB: [*Groaning and blinking his eyes*] No, no—not today!

OSCAR: What *are* the reasons? I'm interested even if Bob isn't.

TIFFANY: [*Systematically and incontrovertibly*] Well, one, he's thirteen years older than I am. That may not seem important now, but in ten years the gap will seem even wider. Then, two—[*She is just as thorough and efficient in her reasoning as* BOB *was with* MARY]—he's a divorced man, which makes him a bad risk to start with. A girl of my age really deserves better than that. Finally, he's not a rich man, never will be a rich man, and he could never provide the Dior originals and the sable stoles that a girl of my upbringing would naturally expect. [*She has given a good imitation of* BOB, *without sounding unlike herself*]

BOB: Nonsense! I never would have brought up that part about the money. It never occurred to me.

TIFFANY: [*Slowly, pointedly, only a shade regretfully*] But all the rest of it— did occur to you?

BOB: [*Terribly embarrassed, and really fighting off sleep now*] Oh, Lord, I don't mind that I'm a bastard. What hurts is that I seem to be such an *inept* bastard. [*Yawning in spite of himself*] Tiffany, what can I say that—
      [*At this moment* DIRK *returns by the main door, a bag of buns in his hand*]

DIRK: I've got the buns.

OSCAR: Congratulations!

DIRK: [*Noticing that although* BOB *is standing up, supporting himself with the back of a chair, his eyes are closed*] I thought only horses could sleep standing up.

OSCAR: Bob is exceptional. We shall not see his like again. [MARY *enters from the bedroom with her suitcase and coat*]

OSCAR: [*To* BOB] What is the matter with you? [BOB *shakes his head to wake himself*]

BOB: I should have cards printed; I took three sleeping pills by accident. [*He lets himself into a chair, puts his feet on another, and instantly drowses off*]

TIFFANY: Freud says there are no accidents. I think he wanted to pass out.

MARY: He was anticipating the popular demand. Dirk, I'll bet if I said I was coming to New Orleans with you—you'd go right into shock.

DIRK: What do you want to bet? Mary, are you . . . coming?

MARY: [*Struggling toward a decision*] I have half a mind to. I used to be superior to this kind of thing. But any minute now I'll be too old.

DIRK: That's right, you'll be seventy and you'll have nothing to repent.

OSCAR: May I come, too? She might need a lawyer.

TIFFANY: But you wouldn't go and leave Bob like that!

MARY: We could cover him with a sheet. [*She starts to eat a bun, reflectively*]

TIFFANY: How can you be so unfeeling?

MARY: My dear he has you. And when he wakes up he has all those dried apricots.

TIFFANY: But he doesn't have me. Not any more. We had an intelligent talk and I'm leaving.

MARY: That's my boy.

OSCAR: I wish he could hear this. I suggest you toss a coin. The loser takes Bob. [*He gives* BOB *an urgent, if surreptitious, poke in the ribs*]

BOB: What, what? [*Jumping up, grabbing more coffee*] There's something important going on. I've got to stay awake.

DIRK: [*Quickly, to* MARY] Honey, you know this plane is being met by a gaggle of city officials. That means you have to decide right now. We have to leave in ten minutes.

MARY: Yes, I realize that. . . !

OSCAR: [*Crossing to* MARY] You understand that once you get on that plane you can't change your mind and get off at 125th Street. Now I think we should thrash this out.

TIFFANY: [*Composing herself formally on the ottoman*] Yes, that's what I think.

MARY: Sure, why don't we call in David Susskind and have a panel discussion. [BOB *falls asleep again*] Oh, Oscar, I don't mean to be short with you but if I want to go with Dirk why shouldn't I?

TIFFANY: Well, for one thing, when a conservative person like you decides to embark on an indiscretion, you should practice up on little things before you fly off with a movie actor. You don't start at the top.

OSCAR: You see what she means. There's a hierarchy of skills.

DIRK: Just a minute. What makes you all so certain that I'm just a movie star on the make and that Mary is another pickup?

TIFFANY: Well, you use a cigarette holder . . . and her very own husband wants her back.

MARY: He is no longer my very own husband.

TIFFANY: But he was and . . .

OSCAR: May I take this one? Remember you and Bob chose each other. Now you'd tell me that you chose Bob in spite of his faults. I'd tell you that you chose him because of his faults. What is missing in him is probably necessary for what is missing in you. Let us not to the marriage of true impediments admit minds.

DIRK: Am I hearing right? Are you suggesting that these two people stay together for mutual therapy? I haven't heard anything so dumb since my press agent told me he was getting married because it made it easier to register at the Plaza.

TIFFANY: Under what circumstances are you in favor of marriage?

DIRK: What do you mean, in favor? Marriage isn't something that has to be supported like low-cost housing or the bill of rights. It's something that happens like a sneeze ... like lightning. Mary, I'll ask you once more. Will you take a chance? Will you come?

OSCAR: Why should she take a chance? [To MARY, forcibly] You still yearn after *Bob.* I know you do.

[OSCAR's *stress on the word "Bob"* has penetrated the fog, like an alarm bell. BOB *comes to slightly and looks around*]

MARY: Are we going to be naïve about this? Asking me whether I yearn after Bob is about as sensible as asking a reformed alcoholic whether he ever thinks about bourbon! What difference does it make? I'm on the wagon for good and sufficient reasons. And I feel a lot better. Dirk, I *am* going with you.

BOB: Where are you going? [To OSCAR] Where is she going?

DIRK: She is going to New Orleans with me.

BOB: [*Coming between* MARY *and* DIRK] Nonsense. I wouldn't let her go as far as the mailbox with you.

DIRK: Look, van Winkle, you have nothing whatever to say about it.

BOB: That's what you think. [*Fighting hard for consciousness*] I have something very important to say—and—I've been trying to say it since six o'clock this morning. [*He teeters a bit, tries to get a grip on himself*] Now *everybody* listen—[*With them all attentive, his mind starts to go blank again. He leans against the frame of the closet door and slowly slides to the floor. He is asleep again*]

MARY: [*Worried now*] Maybe we should call a doctor. I don't like his color.

DIRK: I don't like his color. I didn't like it yesterday. Come on Mary, let's leave Wynken, Blynken and Nod. [*He picks up* MARY's *suitcase and his coat*]

MARY: But what if he's really—?

BOB: [*With a supreme effort he rises*] Wait a minute, now. It's coming to me. [*Crossing blindly to* TIFFANY] Mary ... [*Sees his mistake and turns blinking to find* MARY]

MARY: [*Going to* BOB *and extending her hand*] I don't know whether you can hear me, but—good-by, Bob.

BOB: [*Focusing on* DIRK] You are one of the chief causes of why I am so confused. [*Puts his arm around* MARY] Don't you ever kiss my wife again.

MARY: Bob—you're making a fool of yourself—

BOB: [*Turning on* MARY *and pushing her toward the window seat*] You shut up! [*Back to* DIRK] You leave her alone. She can't cope with a lounge lizard like you. She's got more goodness in her whole body than you've got in your little finger! [*He looks dazedly at* OSCAR. OSCAR *shakes his head, as if to say* "No, you didn't get that right."]

MARY: [*Moving toward the door*] All right, Dirk—the poor soul doesn't know what he's talking about—

[DIRK *exits with her suitcase and* MARY *is following him when* BOB *summons a last burst of energy and lunges after her*]

BOB: Oh, don't I? I'm talking about you—you dumb little idiot—and you're not going anywhere with anybody! [*He grabs* MARY *around the waist and propels her into the storage closet. The others exclaim almost simultaneously*]

MARY: Bob!

DIRK: [*Reentering. He has dropped the suitcase in the hall*] Are you out of your. . . ?

[*But* BOB *has quickly shut the door, and locked it with a key. He turns to the others fiercely*]

BOB: I haven't slept in nine months and I'm sick of it!

DIRK: Hand me that key. If you were in *good* condition, I could take it from you.

BOB: That is an absolutely true statement. [*He walks to the window and calmly tosses the key through it*]

DIRK: What did you do that for?

BOB: I was going to swallow it, but it was too big. [*He collapses on the window seat, leans out for some air, and almost overbalances.* OSCAR *grabs his feet to keep* BOB *from falling out.* TIFFANY *screams*]

MARY: [*Off*] Let me out of here this minute!

DIRK: [*Going to the closet door, calling through*] Mary, can you hear? That lunatic has thrown the key out into the snow! [*A big groan from* MARY, *off*] What are we going to do?

OSCAR: Oh, the snow will melt in a day or two.

TIFFANY: In the movies, they just break the door down.

DIRK: In the movies the door is pieced together by the prop men so all you have to do is blow on it!

MARY: [*Off*] Dirk! Dirk! Are you still there?

DIRK: [*Exasperated*] Sure, I'm still here!

MARY: [*Off*] Well, you shouldn't be! Go this minute!

DIRK: No!

MARY: [*Off*] Please, Dirk! Those people will be waiting. The studio will be furious!

DIRK: Let them be furious! [*Starting for the desk*] I'll call them up. [*Remembers*] Oh, Lord, I can't even *get* them now! And if I don't show up all the columns will say I was drunk or being held somewhere on a morals charge. [*Turning on* BOB *as if he'd like to wring his neck*]

MARY: [*Off, urgently*] Dirk!

DIRK: [*Going to the closet door*] I *am* going, honey. I don't see what else to do. I'll call you tonight and we'll set up something. [*To* OSCAR] I depend on you as the only sane member of the group to get her out of there.

BOB: Well, it's been grand seeing you. Do come again.

DIRK: [*To* TIFFANY *and* OSCAR, *ignoring* BOB] Good-by. Where's my damn book? [*He sees it and starts for it*]

BOB: [*Snatching up the manuscript*] What are you talking about? You offered this book to me. You can't take it back.

DIRK: You said it stank.

BOB: I did not. I said it wasn't punctuated. I'll punctuate it. [*Weaving toward the window seat*]

OSCAR: [*To* DIRK] You'd better let him keep it or he'll throw it out in the snow.

DIRK: And I left Hollywood and came to New York because I wanted to be among intelligent people! [*Getting into his coat with a sigh*] You know I made three pictures for Cecil B. De Mille and he once said to me: "If you want to get hold of a woman, don't talk to her, get hold of her—pick her up and carry her away." I thought to myself: "This man is a jerk." [*With a glance toward heaven*] Cecil, forgive me. [DIRK *exits.* OSCAR *picks up a telephone book*]

BOB: [*Forcing himself to snap to, and going to the closet door*] Mary! Mary! [*Knocks*]

TIFFANY: You don't suppose *she's* fallen asleep?

BOB: No, I suppose she's too mad to talk.

OSCAR: [*At the desk, opening the classified section of the phone book*] Why don't you try calling a locksmith? Just start with the A's. . . . [TIFFANY *is picking up her coat*]

TIFFANY: I'd stay if there was anything I could do.

BOB: [*Blinking*] Oh—Tiffany.

TIFFANY: [*Holds out her hand*] Good-by.

BOB: Goodby. [*They shake hands. He helps her on with her coat*] Tiffany, you really are a very sweet girl.

TIFFANY: Yes, I am. [*Turning to* OSCAR] Good-by, Mr. Nelson.

OSCAR: Good-by, my dear. If you're ever looking for a job, I have a large law office and could always use a girl like you.

TIFFANY: Thank you. [BOB *is now dialing a number from the phone book*]

OSCAR: [*Following* TIFFANY *toward the door*] You're not too upset, are you?

TIFFANY: Oh, I'll be upset tomorrow, when the novocain wears off. But even tomorrow I think I'm going to feel it's just as well.

OSCAR: Why?

TIFFANY: I was attracted to Bob in the first place because he wasn't attracted to me. That intrigued me. I don't want to sound conceited but when you're twenty-one and you're sort of pretty and very rich, you get used to men falling in love with you. But now I ask myself—is it enough that a man is *not* attracted to you? Good-by. [*She goes*]

BOB: [*On the telephone*] Is this.the locksmith? I've got a woman locked in here. Certainly I know the woman. Could you come right over? I know it's Sunday. Okay, so it's extra. Ninety-one East Seventy-first Street. [*To* OSCAR, *who is getting into his coat*] He'll be right over.

OSCAR: Good. Then I may safely take my departure.

BOB: [*Rising, in terror*] Oscar—you wouldn't leave me alone with her?

OSCAR: You'll have the locksmith.

BOB: What will I say?

OSCAR: As little as possible. [*He starts out*]

BOB: [*Clutching* OSCAR *by the arms*] Please stay.

OSCAR: No, my dear boy. This dismal scene you needs must act alone.

BOB: Do you think she'll take the next plane after him?

OSCAR: Well, there are other rooms, other keys.

BOB: [*Reeling a little, but steadying himself*] You're a big help.

OSCAR: All my clients tell me that. I'll call you tomorrow. [OSCAR *goes*]

[BOB, *left alone, goes nervously to the closet door*]

BOB: Mary? Mary, please answer me. [*He kneels down and calls through the keyhole*] The locksmith is coming—[*The closet door opens unexpectedly and* MARY *appears. She walks past him into the room. He blinks*] How did you get the door open?

MARY: My keys. [*Shows them*]

BOB: [*Rising*] You mean you could have. . . ?

MARY: Yes. I could have.

BOB: [*Shaking himself, then nodding vaguely*] I know I behaved like a slob . . . doing this.

MARY: Like a slob.

BOB: I made a spectacle of myself.

MARY: You certainly did. It was the silliest thing I ever saw. And do you know what? I was so proud.

BOB: [*It's all getting through to him*] Mary! My sweet, beautiful darling. I always thought you were beautiful. I thought you were as beautiful as—a piece of white porcelain.

MARY: White porcelain? You mean like—[*She catches herself*] Oh, that's very sweet. [*He goes to her and takes her in his arms, her head on his shoulder*] I missed your shoulder more than anything.

BOB: A hundred times I would have crawled on my hands and knees to Philadelphia, but I was afraid—Mary, come home.

MARY: I'm home. [*They kiss. As they do,* BOB *begins to go slack again, sinking slowly onto the sofa*]

BOB: Oh, Mary, what am I going to do?

MARY: [*Sitting next to him as he stretches out helplessly*] Why, what's the matter, darling?

BOB: I'm falling asleep again.

MARY: [*She lifts his legs onto her lap*] That's all right.

BOB: Yeah. But how will we get those colored lights going?

MARY: We'll manage. [*She starts to take off his shoes and, smiling,* BOB *falls asleep as the* CURTAIN FALLS]

Barefoot in the Park

NEIL SIMON

NEIL SIMON

Neil Simon's second Broadway play, *Barefoot in the Park,* remains, at this writing, his longest running comedy. Opening at the Biltmore Theatre in New York on October 23, 1963, it ran for 1,530 performances. Hailed by reviewers as "a bubbling, rib-tickling comedy," *Barefoot in the Park* proved durable indeed and for almost four years entertained hundreds of thousands of theatregoers both on Broadway and on tour.

Ever since 1961, Neil Simon has reigned supreme as our foremost writer of contemporary comedies. His gilt-edged chain of successes began with his initial Broadway play, *Come Blow Your Horn,* which ran for 677 performances. This was followed by the book for the musical *Little Me* (1962); *Barefoot in the Park* (1963); *The Odd Couple* (1965); the musical *Sweet Charity* (1966); *The Star-Spangled Girl* (1966); and *Plaza Suite* (1968).

In December of that same year, Mr. Simon unveiled another success, the musical *Promises, Promises* (with music by Burt Bacharach and lyrics by Hal David). In 1969 his Broadway entry was *Last of the Red Hot Lovers;* followed in almost annual succession by *The Gingerbread Lady* (1970); *The Prisoner of Second Avenue* (1971); *The Sunshine Boys* (1972); *The Good Doctor,* adapted from short stories of Chekhov (1973); *God's Favorite* (1974); *California Suite* (1976); *Chapter Two* (1977); and the 1979 musical *They're Playing Our Song* (with music by Marvin Hamlisch and lyrics by Carole Bayer Sager).

The author was born in the Bronx, New York, on July 4, 1927. He attended New York University and the University of Denver. His initial theatrical affiliation came as a sketch writer (in collaboration with his brother Danny) for resort revues at Camp Tamiment, Pennsylvania. From there he moved on to television, supplying comedy material for such personalities as Phil Silvers, Jackie Gleason, Red Buttons, Tallulah Bankhead and, notably, for Sid Caesar and Imogene Coca in *Your Show of Shows.* An accomplished hand at comedy, he later contributed sketches to two Broadway revues, *Catch a Star* (1955) and *New Faces of 1956.*

In 1965 the dramatist won an Antoinette Perry (Tony) Award as the year's best author for *The Odd Couple,* and in 1968 he was the recipient of the Sam S. Shubert Award in recognition of his outstanding contribution to the American theatre. A similar honor was bestowed upon him in 1975 by the presentation of a Special Tony Award for his overall work in the theatre.

An acknowledged master of comedy technique, when asked for his "prescription" for successful comedy writing, Mr. Simon replied: "The idea of a prescription for comedy is obviously ridiculous. What works for one playwright rarely works for another, and even the fact that a certain approach succeeded for a writer before does not mean that it will surely produce an amusing play for that same scribe a second time."

Mr. Simon, however, would be the first to agree that comedy, as with all forms of drama, must originate with the characters, for valid and appreciable humor only can emerge from their involvements in, and reactions to, a situation. "In the first of 112 versions of *Come Blow Your Horn*, the opening five minutes of the play were crammed with good jokes . . . in fact, some of the best I had ever written . . . and the scene was terrible. The audience, knowing nothing of the characters or situation, could not have cared less. Now I know enough to *start* with the *characters*."

While Neil Simon's plays may be regarded by some as merely lighthearted entertainments, there is, if one digs deeply enough beyond the surface of laughter, an underlying element of human truths, particularly in his later works. As London's respected drama critic Herbert Kretzmer wrote in *The Daily Express:* "Mr. Simon's genius has been not only to write some of the funniest one-line gags now being spoken on the English-speaking stage, but to suggest also something of the pain, aspiration and panic behind all those flip phrases."

His wit and comedic expertise also have brightened many films. Besides preparing the movie versions of his own plays, he has enlivened the screen with his scenarios for, among others, *The Out-of-Towners; The Heartbreak Kid; Murder by Death; The Cheap Detective;* and *The Goodbye Girl.*

A film version of *Barefoot in the Park* (with Jane Fonda and Robert Redford) was released in 1967.

BAREFOOT IN THE PARK was first produced at the Biltmore Theatre, New York, on October 23, 1963, by Saint Subber. The cast was as follows:

CORIE BRATTER	*Elizabeth Ashley*
TELEPHONE MAN	*Herbert Edelman*
DELIVERY MAN	*Joseph Keating*
PAUL BRATTER	*Robert Redford*
MRS. BANKS	*Mildred Natwick*
VICTOR VELASCO	*Kurt Kasznar*

Directed by Mike Nichols
Setting by Oliver Smith
Costumes by Donald Brooks
Lighting by Jean Rosenthal

The entire action of the play takes place in the top-floor apartment in a brownstone on East Forty-eighth Street, New York City.

ACT ONE

About 5:30 on a cold February afternoon.

ACT TWO

SCENE 1: *Four days later, about 7:00 P.M.*
SCENE 2: *Later that night, about 2:00 A.M.*

ACT THREE

The following day, about 5:00 P.M.

ACT ONE

A large one-room apartment on the top floor of an old brownstone on East Forty-eighth Street off Third Avenue. The room is barren. A ladder, a canvas drop cloth, and a couple of empty paint cans stand forlornly in the center of the room. There is a huge skylight which pours the bright February sunshine glaringly into the room. Through the skylight we can see the roofs and windows of brownstones across the street and the framework of a large building under construction. Crests of clinging snow can be seen in the two windows under the skylight. At stage right, there is the entrance door, a step below the apartment itself. At stage left, four steps lead to a raised area from which two doors open, the upstage one leading to a bathroom, the other to the bedroom. We will soon learn that the latter is not really a bedroom, but a small dressing room. The bathroom has only a shower and a sink and what-have-you. On another raised section up right is the kitchen. It's not really a kitchen, but just an old stove, an older refrigerator, and a chipped sink standing nakedly between them. Upstage left of this area is another platform on which stand a steamer trunk and a few suitcases. The room has just been freshly painted— not carefully, maybe not professionally, but painted. There is a small Franklin stove downstage left below the platform, and an open closet downstage right. Completing the furnishings of the room are a railing that runs downstage of the entrance wall, and a radiator that sits high on the upstage left wall. For all the room's drabness and coldness, there is great promise here. Someone with taste, imagination, and personality can make this that perfect love nest we all dream about. That person is now putting the key in the door.

It opens and CORIE BRATTER *enters. She is lovely, young, and full of hope for the future. She enters the apartment, looks around, and sighs as though the world were just beginning. For her, it is. She is wearing Levis and a yellow top under a large, shaggy white fur coat; she carries a bouquet of flowers. After rapturously examining the room, she takes the small paint can, fills it with water, and puts in the flowers, throwing the wrapping on the floor. The first bit of color in the room. As she crosses to put the "vase" on top of the Franklin stove, the doorbell buzzes. She puts the flowers down, crosses to the door, buzzes back, and then opens the door and shouts down:*

CORIE: Hello?

[*From the depths, possibly from the bottom of the earth we hear a voice shout up*]

VOICE: Bratter?

CORIE: [*Yelling back*] Yes. Up here! . . . Top floor!

[*She crosses to the suitcases, opens the medium-sized one and takes out a large bottle of champagne which she puts into the refrigerator*]

VOICE: [*From below, this time a little closer*] Hello?

CORIE: [*Rushes to the door again and shouts down*] Up here! You have another floor to go.

[*Crossing back to the open suitcase she takes out three small logs and carries them to the Franklin stove. As she drops them in front of the stove, the owner of the voice appears at the door: a tall, heavy-set man in his mid-thirties, in a plaid wool jacket and baseball cap. He is breathing very, very hard*]

TELEPHONE MAN: Tel—[*He tries to catch his breath*]—Telephone Company.

CORIE: Oh, the phone. Good. Come on in.

[*He steps in, carrying a black leather repair kit*]

TELEPHONE MAN: That's quite a—[*Gasp, gasp*]—quite a climb.

CORIE: Yes, it's five flights. If you don't count the front stoop.

TELEPHONE MAN: I *counted* the front stoop. [*Gasp, gasp . . . he looks at his notebook*] Paul Bratter, right?

CORIE: *Mrs.* Paul Bratter.

TELEPHONE MAN: [*Still checking the book*] Princess phone?

CORIE: The little one? That lights up? In beige?

TELEPHONE MAN: The little . . . [*Gasp, gasp*] That lights up . . . [*Gasp, gasp*] In beige . . . [*Gasp, gasp. He swallows hard*]

CORIE: Would you like a glass of water?

TELEPHONE MAN: [*Sucking for air, nods*] Please!

CORIE: [*Crosses to the sink*] I'd offer you soda or a beer but we don't have anything yet.

TELEPHONE MAN: A glass of water's fine.

CORIE: [*Suddenly embarrassed*] Except I don't have a glass either.

TELEPHONE MAN: Oh!

CORIE: Nothing's arrived yet . . . You could put your head under and just schlurp.

TELEPHONE MAN: No, I'm okay. Just a little out of shape. [*As he climbs stiffly up the step out of the well, he groans with pain. After looking about*] Where do you want the phone?

CORIE: [*Looks around*] The phone . . . Let me see . . . Gee, I don't know. Do you have any ideas?

TELEPHONE MAN: Well, it depends what you're gonna do with the room. You gonna have furniture in here?

CORIE: Yes, it's on its way up.

TELEPHONE MAN: [*He looks back at the stairs*] Heavy furniture?

CORIE: I'll tell you what. [*She points to the telephone junction box on the wall left of the stairs*] Just put it over there and give me a long extension cord. If I can't find a place, I'll just hang it out the window.

TELEPHONE MAN: Fair enough. [*He crosses to the junction box, coughing and in pain*] Whoo!

CORIE: Say, I'm awfully sorry about the stairs. [*Taking the large suitcase, she starts to drag it into the bedroom*]

TELEPHONE MAN: [*On his knees; he opens his tool box*] You're really gonna live up here, heh? . . . I mean, every day?

CORIE: Every day.

TELEPHONE MAN: You don't mind it?

CORIE: [*Stopping on the stairs*] Mind it? . . . I love this apartment . . . besides [*She continues into the bedroom*] it *does* discourage people.

TELEPHONE MAN: What people?

CORIE: [*Comes out of the bedroom and starts for the other suitcases*] Mothers, friends, relatives, mothers. I mean no one just pops in on you when they have to climb five flights.

TELEPHONE MAN: You're a newlywed, right?

CORIE: Six days. What gave me away?

TELEPHONE MAN: I watch "What's My Line" a lot.

   [*The doorbell buzzes*]

CORIE: Oh! I hope that's the furniture.

TELEPHONE MAN: I don't want to see this.

CORIE: [*Presses the buzzer and yells down the stairs*] Helloooo! Bloomingdale's?

   [*From below, a voice*]

VOICE: Lord and Taylor.

CORIE: Lord and Taylor? [*Shrugs and takes the now empty suitcase and puts in into the closet*] Probably another wedding gift . . . From my mother. She sends me wedding gifts twice a day . . .

TELEPHONE MAN: I hope it's an electric heater. [*He blows on his hands*]

CORIE: [*Worried, she feels the steam pipe next to the closet*] Really? Is it cold in here?

TELEPHONE MAN: I can't grip the screwdriver. Maybe the steam is off.

CORIE: Maybe that's it. [*She gets up on the stairs and tests the radiator*]

TELEPHONE MAN: Just turn it on. It'll come right up.

CORIE: It *is* on. It's just not coming up.

TELEPHONE MAN: Oh! . . . Well, that's these old brownstones for you. [*He zips up his jacket*]

CORIE: I prefer it this way. It's a medical fact, you know, that steam heat is very bad for you.

TELEPHONE MAN: Yeah? In February?

[*Suddenly the* DELIVERY MAN *appears in the door, carrying three packages. He is in his early sixties and from the way he is breathing, it seems the end is very near. He gasps for air*]

CORIE: [*Crossing to him*] Oh, hi . . . Just put it down . . . anywhere.

[*The* DELIVERY MAN *puts the packages down, panting. He wants to talk but can't. He extends his hand to the* TELEPHONE MAN *for a bit of compassion*]

TELEPHONE MAN: I know. I know.

CORIE: I'm awfully sorry about the stairs. [*The* DELIVERY MAN *takes out a pad and pencil and holds them out limply toward* CORIE] What's this?

TELEPHONE MAN: I think he wants you to sign it.

CORIE: Oh, yes. [*She signs it quickly*] Wait, just a minute. [*She picks up her bag from where she had left it in the kitchen area and takes out some change*] Here you go . . . [*She puts it in his hand. He nods weakly and turns to go*] Will you be all right? . . . [*And for the first time he gets out some words. They are: "Argh, argh." He exits*]

CORIE: [*Closes the door behind him*] It's a shame, isn't it? Giving such hard work to an old man. [*She takes two of the packages and puts them with the remaining suitcases*]

TELEPHONE MAN: He's probably only twenty-five. They age fast on this route. [*He dials the phone and then talks into it*] Hello, Ed? Yeah . . . On . . . er . . . Eldorado five, eight, one, nine, one . . . Give me a straight check.

CORIE: [*Moving to* TELEPHONE MAN] Is that my number? Eldorado five, eight, one, nine, one [*The* TELEPHONE MAN *nods*] It has a nice sound, hasn't it?

TELEPHONE MAN: [*Why fool with a romantic*] Yeah, it's a beautiful number. [*The phone rings. He answers it, disguising his voice*] Hello? . . . [*He chuckles over his joke*] Good work, Mr. Bell, you've done it again. [*He hangs up, and turns to* CORIE] Well, you've got your phone. As my mother would say, may your first call be from the Sweepstakes.

CORIE: [*Takes the phone*] My very own phone. . . . Gives you a sense of power, doesn't it? Can I make a call yet?

TELEPHONE MAN: [*Putting the cover back on the junction box*] Your bill started two minutes ago.

CORIE: Who can I call? . . . I know. [*She starts to dial*]

TELEPHONE MAN: Oh, by the way. My name is Harry Pepper. And if you ever have any trouble with this phone, please, do me a favor, don't ask for Harry Pepper. [CORIE *hangs up, a look of disappointment on her face*] What's the matter, bad news?

CORIE: [*Like a telephone operator*] It is going to be cloudy tonight with a light snow.

TELEPHONE MAN: [*He looks up at the skylight*] And just think, you'll be the first one in the city to see it fall.

[*The doorbell buzzes.* CORIE *puts down the phone, and rushes to the door*]

CORIE: Oh, please, let that be the furniture and not Paul so Paul can see the apartment with furniture. [*She buzzes, opens the door, and yells downstairs*] Yes?

VOICE FROM BELOW: It's me!

CORIE: [*Unhappily*] Oh, hi, Paul. [*She turns into the room*] Well, I guess he sees the apartment without the furniture. [*She takes the remaining package and places it with the others on the landing under the windows*]

TELEPHONE MAN: [*Gathering up his tools*] How long d'ja say you were married?

CORIE: Six days.

TELEPHONE MAN: He won't notice the place is empty until June. [*He crosses to the door*] Well, Eldorado five, eight, one, nine, one. . . . Have a nice marriage. . . . [*He turns back into the room*] And may you soon have many extensions. [*He turns and looks at the climb down he has to make and moans*] Ooohh!

[*He is gone.* CORIE *quickly starts to prepare the room for* PAUL'S *entrance. She gathers up the canvas drop cloth and throws it into the closet*]

PAUL'S VOICE: Corie? . . . Where are you?

CORIE: [*Rushes back to the door and yells down*] Up here, hon . . . Top floor. . . . [*The phone rings*] Oh, my goodness. The phone. [*She rushes to it and answers it*] Hello? . . . Yes? . . . Oh, yes, he is . . . I mean he's on his way up. . . . Can you hold on for two more floors? [*She puts down the receiver and yells*] Paul. Hurry up, darling!

PAUL'S VOICE: Okay. Okay.

CORRIE: [*Into the phone*] Hello. He'll be with you in one more flight. Thank you. [*She puts the phone on the floor and continues to get the apartment ready. Rushing up the stairs, she closes the bedroom and bathroom doors. Surveying the room, she sees the wrapping from the flowers on the floor of the kitchen and the wadded-up newspapers on top of the stove. Quickly gathering them up, she stuffs them into the nearest hiding place—the refrigerator. Then dashing into the hall and closing the door behind her, she re-enters to make one more survey of her apartment. Satisfied with what she sees, she turns back to the open door, and yells down*] Now honey, don't expect too much. The furniture didn't get here yet and the paint didn't come out exactly right, but I think it's going to be beautiful. . . . Paul? . . . Paul, are you all right?

PAUL'S VOICE: I'm coming. I'm coming.

CORIE: [*Runs back to the phone and speaks into it*] He's coming. He's coming. [*She puts down the phone and looks at the door.* PAUL *falls in through the doorway and hangs on the rail at the entrance to the apartment.* PAUL *is twenty-six but breathes and dresses like fifty-six. He carries a heavy suitcase and an attaché case and all the dignity he can bear. He drops the attaché case at the railing*] Hi, sweetheart. [*She smothers him with kisses but all he can do is fight for air*] . . . Oh, Paul, darling. [PAUL *sucks for oxygen*] . . . Well? [*She steps back*] Say something.

PAUL: [*Breathing with great difficulty, he looks back down the stairs*] It's six flights . . . Did you know it's six flights?

CORIE: It isn't. It's five.

PAUL: [*Staggers up the step into the bathroom, and collapses onto the suitcase*] What about that big thing hanging outside the building?

CORIE: That's not a flight. It's a stoop.

PAUL: It may *look* like a stoop but it climbs like a flight. [*Gasp, gasp*]

CORIE: Is that *all* you have to say?

PAUL: [*Gasping*] I didn't think I'd get that much out. [*He breathes heavily*] It didn't seem like six flights when I first saw the apartment. [*Gasp*] Why is that?

CORIE: You didn't see the apartment. Don't you remember the woman wasn't home. You saw the third-floor apartment.

PAUL: Then that's why.

CORIE: [*Crossing above* PAUL] You don't like it. You really don't like it.

PAUL: I *do* like it. [*He squints around*] I'm just waiting for my eyes to clear first.

CORIE: I expected you to walk in here and say, "Wow." [*She takes his hand*]

PAUL: I will. [*He takes a deep breath*] Okay. [*He looks around, then says without enthusiasm*] "Wow."

CORIE: Oh, Paul. [*She throws herself onto* PAUL'S *knee*] It'll be beautiful, I promise you. You just came home too soon. [*She nuzzles him*]

PAUL: You know I missed you.

CORIE: Did you really?

PAUL: Right in the middle of the Monday morning conference I began to feel sexy.

CORIE: That's marvelous. [*They kiss*] Oh, boy. Let's take a cab back to the Plaza. We still have an hour before check-out time.

PAUL: We can't. We took a towel and two ash trays. We're hot. [*He kisses her*]

CORIE: My gosh, you still love me.

PAUL: After six days at the Plaza? What's the trick?

CORIE: [*Gets up and moves away*] But that was a honeymoon. Now we're on a regular schedule. I thought you'd come home tonight, and we'd shake hands and start the marriage. [*She extends her hand to him*]

PAUL: [*Rises*] "How do you do? . . ." [*They shake hands. Then* CORIE *throws herself into his arms and kisses him*]

CORIE: My turn to say "Wow" . . . For a lawyer you're some good kisser.

PAUL: [*With hidden import*] For a kisser I'm some good lawyer.

CORIE: What does that mean? . . . Something's happened? . . . Something wonderful? . . . Well, for Pete's sakes, what?

PAUL: It's not positive yet. The office is supposed to call and let me know in five minutes.

CORIE: [*Then she remembers*] Oh! They called!

PAUL: What . . . ?

CORIE: I mean they're calling.

PAUL: When. . . ?

CORIE: Now. . . . They're on the phone now.

PAUL: [*Looking around*] Where . . . ?

CORIE: [*Points to the phone*] There. . . .

PAUL: [*Rushes to the phone*] Why didn't you tell me?

CORIE: I forgot. You kissed me and got me all crazy.

PAUL: [*Into the phone*] Frank? . . . Yeah! . . . Listen what did—oh, very funny. [*Looks to* CORIE] "For a lawyer, I'm some good kisser." . . . Come on, come, tell me? . . . Well? . . . [*A big grin.* CORIE *feeling left out, sneaks over and tries to tickle him*] You're kidding? The whole thing? Oh, Frank, baby. I love you. . . . What do you mean, nervous? . . . I passed the bar, didn't I? . . . Yes, I'll go over everything tonight. [CORIE *reacts to "tonight" and slowly moves to the ladder*] I'll meet you in Schrafft's at eight o'clock in the morning. We'll go over the briefs. . . . Hey, what kind of a tie do I wear? I don't know. I thought maybe something flowing like Oliver Wendell Holmes. . . . Right. [*He stands up. He is bubbling with joy.* CORIE *has now climbed up the ladder*] Did you hear? . . . Did you hear? [*He moves up the ladder to* CORIE]

CORIE: What about tonight?

PAUL: I've got to be in court tomorrow morning . . . *I've got my first case!*

CORIE: What about tonight?

PAUL: I'll have to go over the briefs. Marshall has to be in Washington tomorrow and he wants me to take over . . . with Frank . . . but it's really my case. [*He hugs* CORIE] Oh, Corie, baby, I'm going to be a lawyer.

CORIE: That's wonderful. . . . I just thought we were going to spend tonight together.

PAUL: We'll spend tomorrow night together. [*He crosses to railing and gets his attaché case*] I hope I brought those affidavits.

CORIE: I brought a black lace nightgown. [*She crosses to the small suitcase*]

PAUL: [*Looks through affidavits from the case; his mind has now turned completely legal*] Marshall had everthing laid out when I was at the office. . . . It looks simple enough. A furrier is suing a woman for nonpayment of bills.

CORIE: [*Taking the nightgown out of the suitcase*] I was going to cook you spaghetti with the white clam sauce . . . in a bikini.

PAUL: We're representing the furrier. He made four specially tailored coats for this woman on Park Avenue. Now she doesn't want the coats.

CORIE: [*Takes off her sweatshirt, and slipping her arms through the nightgown straps, she drapes it over her*] Then I found this great thing on Eighth Street. It's a crossword puzzle with dirty words.

PAUL: But the furrier can't get rid of the coats. She's only four-foot-eight. He'd have to sell them to a rich little girl.

CORIE: . . . then I was going to put on a record and do an authentic Cambodian fertility dance.

PAUL: The only trouble is, he didn't have a signed contract. . . . [CORIE *begins her "fertility dance" and ends up collapsing on the bottom step of the ladder*] What are you doing?

CORIE: I'm trying to get you all hot and bothered and you're summing up for the jury. The whole marriage is over.

PAUL: [*Moves to* CORIE] Oh, Corie, honey, I'm sorry. [*He puts his arms around her*] I guess I'm pretty excited. You want me to be rich and famous, don't you?

CORIE: During the day. At night I want you to be here and sexy.

PAUL: I will. Just as soon as Birnbaum versus Gump is over. . . . I'll tell you what. Tomorrow night is your night. We'll do whatever you want.

CORIE: Something wild, insane, and crazy?

PAUL: I promise.

CORIE: Oh, Paul, how wonderful. . . . Can't we do it tonight?

PAUL: No, we can't do it tonight, because tonight I've got to work. [*He rises, and looks around*] Except where do I sit?

CORIE: The furniture will be here by five. They promised.

PAUL: [*Drops the affidavits into the attaché case, and looks at his watch*] Five? . . . It's five-thirty. [*He crosses to the bedroom stairs*] What do we do, sleep in Bloomingdale's tonight?

CORIE: They'll be here, Paul. They're probably stuck in traffic.

PAUL: [*Crossing up to the bedroom*] And what about tonight? I've got a case in court tomorrow. Maybe we should check into a hotel? [*He looks into the bedroom*]

CORIE: [*Rises and moves toward* PAUL] We just checked *out* of a hotel. I don't care if the furniture *doesn't* come. I'm sleeping in my apartment *tonight*.

PAUL: Where? Where? [*He looks into the bathroom, closes the door and starts to come back down the steps*] There's only room for *one* in the bathtub. [*He suddenly turns, goes back up the steps and opens the door to the bathroom*] Where's the bathtub?

CORIE: [*Hesitantly*] There is no bathtub.

PAUL: No bathtub?

CORIE: There's a shower. . . .

PAUL: How am I going to take a bath?

CORIE: You won't take a bath. You'll take a shower.

PAUL: I don't like showers. I like baths. Corie, how am I going to take a bath?

CORIE: You'll lie down in the shower and hang your feet over the sink. . . . I'm sorry there's no bathtub, Paul.

PAUL: [*Closes the door, and crosses down into the room*] Hmmmm. . . . Boy, of all the nights. . . . [*He suddenly shivers*] It's freezing in here. [*He rubs his hands*] Isn't there any heat?

CORIE: Of course there's heat. We have a radiator.

PAUL: [*Gets up on the steps and feels the radiator*] The *radiator's* the coldest thing in the room.

CORIE: It's probably the boiler. It's probably off in the whole building.

PAUL: [*Putting on his gloves*] No, it was warm coming up the stairs. [*He goes out the door into the hall*] See. . . . It's nice and warm out here.

CORIE: Maybe it's because the apartment is empty.

PAUL: The *hall* is empty too, but it's warm out here.

CORIE: [*Moves to the stove*] It'll be all right once I get a fire going.

PAUL: [*Goes to the phone*] A fire? You'd have to keep the flame going night and day . . . I'll call the landlord.

CORIE: [*Putting a log into the stove*] He's not home.

PAUL: Where is he?

CORIE: In Florida! . . . There's a handyman that comes Monday, Wednesday, and Fridays.

PAUL: You mean we freeze on Tuesdays, Thursdays, and Saturdays?

CORIE: He'll be here in the morning.

PAUL: [*Moving to the windows*] And what'll we do tonight? I've got a case in court in the morning.

CORIE: [*Moves to* PAUL] Will you stop saying it like you always have a case in court in the morning. This is your first one.

PAUL: Well, what'll we do?

CORIE: The furniture will be here. In the meantime I can light the stove and you can sit over the fire with your law books and a shawl like Abraham Lincoln. [*She crosses to the Franklin stove and gets matches from the top of it*]

PAUL: Is that supposed to be funny? [*He begins to investigate the small windows*]

CORIE: No. It was supposed to be nasty. It just came out funny. [*She strikes a match and attempts to light the log in the stove.* PAUL *tries the windows*] What are you doing? [*She gives up attempting to light the log*]

PAUL: I'm checking to see if the windows are closed.

CORIE: They're closed. I looked.

PAUL: Then why is it windy in here?

CORIE: [*Moves toward* PAUL] I don't feel a draft.

PAUL: [*Moves away from the windows*] I didn't say draft. I said wind . . . There's a brisk northeasterly wind blowing in this room.

CORIE: You don't have to get sarcastic.

PAUL: [*Moving up into the kitchen area*] I'm not getting sarcastic, I'm getting chapped lips. [*Looking up, he glimpses the hole in the skylight*]

CORIE: How could there be wind in a closed room?

PAUL: How's this for an answer? There's a hole in the skylight. [*He points up*]

CORIE: [*Looks up, sees it, and is obviously embarrassed by it*] Gee, I didn't see that before. Did you?

PAUL: [*Moves to the ladder*] I didn't see the *apartment* before.

CORIE: [*Defensively. She crosses to the railing and gets her coat*] All right, Paul, don't get upset. I'm sure it'll be fixed. We could plug it up with something for tonight.

PAUL: [*Gets up on the ladder*] How? How? That's twenty feet high. You'd have to fly over in a plane and *drop* something in.

CORIE: [*Putting on her coat*] It's only for one night. And it's not that cold.

PAUL: In February? Do you know what it's like at three o'clock in the morning? In February? Ice-cold freezing.

CORIE: It's not going to be freezing. I called the Weather Bureau. It's going to be cloudy with a light s— [*She catches herself and looks up*]

PAUL: What? [CORIE *turns away*] What? . . . A light what?

CORIE: Snow!

PAUL: [*Coming down the ladder*] Snow?? . . . It's going to snow tonight? . . . In here?

CORIE: They're wrong as often as they're right.

PAUL: I'm going to be shoveling snow in my own living room.

CORIE: It's a little hole.

PAUL: With that wind it could blow six-foot drifts in the bathroom. Honestly, Corie, I don't see how you can be so calm about all this.

CORIE: Well, what is it you want me to do?

PAUL: Go to pieces, like me. It's only natural.

CORIE: [*Goes to him and puts her arms around him*] I've got a better idea. I'll keep you warm . . . And there's no charge for electricity. . . . [*She kisses him*]

PAUL: I can see I haven't got much of a law career ahead of me.

CORIE: Good. I hope we starve. And they find us up here dead in each other's arms.

PAUL: "Frozen skinny lovers found on Forty-eighth Street." [*They kiss*]

CORIE: Are we in love again?

PAUL: We're in love again. [*They kiss again, a long passionate embrace. The doorbell buzzes*]

CORIE: [*Breaking away*] The bed. I hope it's the bed. [*She buzzes back, and then opens the door and yells down*] Helllooooo! Bloomingdale's? [*From below, a female voice: Surprise!* CORIE *turns to* PAUL] Oh, God.

PAUL: What's wrong.

CORIE: Please, let it be a woman delivering the furniture.

PAUL: A woman?

VOICE: Corie?

CORIE: But it's my mother.

PAUL: Your mother? Now?

CORIE: [*Taking off the nightgown and slipping into her top*] She couldn't wait. Just one more day.

PAUL: Corie, you've got to get rid of her. I've got a case in court tomorrow.

CORIE: It's ugly in here without furniture, isn't it. She's just going to hate it, won't she?

VOICE: Corie? Where are you?

CORIE: [*Crosses to the door and yells down the stairs*] Up here, Mom. Top floor.

PAUL: [*Hides the attaché case in a corner to the left of the windows*] How am I going to work tonight?

CORIE: She'll think this is the way we're going to live. Like gypsies in an empty store. [*Attempting to button her top*]

PAUL: [*Throwing the nightgown and lingerie into a suitcase*] Maybe I ought to sleep in the office.

CORIE: She'll freeze to death. She'll sit there in her fur coat and freeze to death.

PAUL: [*Helps her button her top*] I don't get you, Corie. Five minutes ago this was the Garden of Eden. Now it's suddenly Cannery Row.

CORIE: She doesn't understand, Paul. She has a different set of values. She's practical. She's not young like us.

PAUL: [*Gathers up the suitcase with lingerie and takes it into the bedroom*] Well, I'm twenty-six and cold as hell.

VOICE: [*Getting nearer*] Corie?

CORIE: [*Yells down at the door*] One more flight, Mother . . . Paul, promise me one thing. Don't tell her about the rent. If she asks, tell her you're not quite sure yet.

PAUL: [*Crossing to the door with his coat collar up around his face*] Not sure what my rent is? I *have* to know what my rent is. I'm a college graduate.

CORIE: [*Stopping* PAUL] Can't you lie a little? For me? You don't have to tell her it's a hundred and twenty-five.

PAUL: All right. How much is it?

CORIE Sixty?

PAUL: What?

CORIE: Sixty-five?

PAUL: Corie—

CORIE: Seventy-five, all right? Seventy-five dollars and sixty-three cents a month. Including gas and electricity. She'll believe that, won't she?

PAUL: *Anyone* would believe that. It's the hundred and twenty-five that's hard to swallow. [*He combs his hair*]

CORIE: She's taking a long time. I hope she's all right.

PAUL: I can't lie about the stairs. She's going to figure out it's six floors all by herself.

CORIE: Shh. Shh, she's here. [*She starts to open the door*]

PAUL: [*Grabs her*] Just promise *me* one thing. Don't let her stay too long because I've got a . . .

CORIE: [*With him*] . . . case in court in the morning . . . I know, I know . . . [*She opens the door and goes into the hall*] . . . Mother!

[MOTHER *shoots by her into the room and grabs the rail to keep from falling. She is in her late forties, pretty, but has not bothered to look after herself these past few years. She could use a permanent and a whole new wardrobe*]

PAUL: [*Rushes to support her*] Hello, Mom.

[MOTHER *struggles for air*]

MOTHER: Oh! . . . Oh! . . . I can't breathe.

CORIE: Take it easy, Mom. [*Holding her other arm*]

MOTHER: I can't catch my breath.

PAUL: You should have rested.

MOTHER: I did . . . But there were always more stairs.

CORIE: Paul, help her.

PAUL: Come on, Mom. Watch the step. [*He starts to lead her up the step into the room*]

MOTHER: More stairs? [*She steps up and* CORIE *and* PAUL *lead her toward* PAUL's *suitcase, still standing near the wall*]

CORIE: You want some water?

MOTHER: Later. I can't swallow yet.

PAUL: Here, sit down.

[*She sits on the suitcase*]

MOTHER: Oh, my.

CORIE: It's not *that* high, Mother.

MOTHER: I know, dear. It's not bad really ... What is it, nine flights?

PAUL: Five. We don't count the stoop.

MOTHER: I didn't think I'd make it ... If I'd known the people on the third floor I'd have gone to visit them ...

[PAUL *sits on the bottom step of the ladder*]

CORIE: This is a pleasant surprise, Mother.

MOTHER: Well, I really had no intention of coming up, but I had a luncheon in Westchester and I thought, since it's on my way home, I might as well drop in for a few minutes. . . .

CORIE: On your way home to New Jersey?

MOTHER: Yes. I just came over the Whitestone Bridge and down the Major-Deegan highway and now I'll cut across town and onto the Henry Hudson Parkway and up to the George Washington Bridge. It's no extra trouble.

PAUL: Sounds easy enough.

MOTHER: Yes. . . .

CORIE: We were going to ask you over on Friday.

MOTHER: Friday. Good. I'll be here Friday. . . . I'm not going to stay now, I know you both must be busy.

PAUL: Well, as a matter of fact. . . .

CORIE: [*Stopping him*] No, we're not, are we, Paul?

[*He kills her with a glance*]

MOTHER: Besides, Aunt Harriet is ringing the bell for me in ten minutes ... Just one good look around, that's all. I'm not sure I'm coming back.

CORIE: I wish you could have come an hour later. After the furniture arrived.

MOTHER: [*Gets up, looks, and stops cold*] Don't worry. I've got a marvelous imagination.

CORIE: WELL ... ?

MOTHER: [*Stunned*] Oh, Corie ... it's ... beautiful.

CORIE: You hate it. . . .

MOTHER: [*Moves toward windows*] No, no . . . It's a charming apartment. [*She trips over the platform*] I love it.

CORIE: [*Rushes to her*] You can't really tell like this.

MOTHER: I'm crazy about it.

CORIE: It's not your kind of apartment. I knew you wouldn't like it.

MOTHER: [*Moves down to* PAUL] I love it. . . . Paul, didn't I say I loved it? [*She takes his hand*]

PAUL: She said she loved it.

MOTHER: I knew I said it.

CORIE: [*To* MOTHER] Do you really, Mother? I mean are you absolutely crazy in love with it?

MOTHER: Oh, yes. It's very cute. . . . And there's so much you can do with it.

CORIE: I told you she hated it.

MOTHER: [*Moves toward the bedroom landing*] Corie, you don't give a person a chance. At least let me see the whole apartment.

PAUL: This is the whole apartment.

MOTHER: [*Cheerfully*] It's a nice, large room.

CORIE: There's a bedroom.

MOTHER: Where?

PAUL: One flight up.

CORIE: It's four little steps [*She goes up the steps to the bedroom door*] See. One-two-three-four.

MOTHER: [*To* PAUL] Oh. Split-level. [*She climbs the steps*] And where's the bedroom? Through there?

CORIE: No, *In* there. That's the bedroom . . . It's really just a dressing room but I'm going to use it as a bedroom.

MOTHER: [*At the bedroom door*] That's a wonderful idea. And you can just put a bed in here.

CORIE: That's right.

MOTHER: How?

[PAUL *moves to the steps*]

CORIE: It'll fit. I measured the room.

MOTHER: A double bed?

CORIE: No, an oversized single.

MOTHER: Oh, they're nice. And where will Paul sleep?

CORIE: With me.

PAUL: [*Moves up on the landing*] In an oversized single?

MOTHER: I'm sure you'll be comfortable.

CORIE: I'm positive.

[PAUL *moves back down the stairs and glumly surveys the room*]

MOTHER: It's a wonderful idea. Very clever. . . .

CORIE: Thank you.

MOTHER: Except you can't get to the closet.

CORIE: Yes, you can.

MOTHER: Without climbing over the bed?

CORIE: No, you *have* to climb over the bed.

MOTHER That's a good idea.

CORIE: [*Leaves the bedroom, crosses to the ladder, and climbs up*] Everything's just temporary. As they say in *McCall's*, it won't really take shape until the bride's own personality becomes more clearly defined.

MOTHER: I think it's *you* right now. [*She turns to the other door*] What's in here? . . . [*She opens the door and looks in*] The bathroom. . . . [*She closes the door*] No bathtub. . . . You really have quite a lot here, for one room. [*She moves down the steps*] And where's the kitchen? [*She sees the stove and refrigerator, stops in horror, and then crosses toward the kitchen*] Whoo, there it is. . . . Very cozy. I suppose you'll eat out a lot the first year.

CORIE: We're never eating out. It's big enough to make spaghetti and things.

MOTHER: What "things"?

CORIE: It's a dish I make called "Things." Honestly, Mother, we won't starve.

MOTHER: I know, dear. [*Under the skylight*] It's chilly in here. Do you feel a draft?

PAUL: [*Looks up*] Uh, stand over here, Mom. [*He moves her away from the hole to near the steam pipe next to the railing*]

CORIE: What you need is a drink. Paul, why don't you run down and get some Scotch?

PAUL: Now?

MOTHER: [*Crossing toward the Franklin stove*] Oh, not for me. I'm leaving in a few minutes.

PAUL: Oh. She's leaving in a few minutes.

CORIE: She can stay for one drink.

[PAUL *quietly argues with* CORIE *at the ladder*]

MOTHER: There's so much you can do in here. Lots of wall space. What color are you going to paint it?

CORIE: It's painted.

MOTHER: Very attractive.

PAUL: [*Looks at his watch*] Wow. Nearly six.

MOTHER: I've got to go.

CORIE: Not until you have a drink . . . [*To* PAUL] Will you get the Scotch?

[*He continues to argue with her*]

MOTHER: All right. I'll stay for just one drink.

PAUL: Good. I'll get the Scotch.

> [*He starts for the door*]

MOTHER: Button up, dear. It's cold.

PAUL: I've noticed that.

CORIE: And get some cheese.

> [PAUL *is gone*]

MOTHER: Paul! [PAUL *reappears at the door, and* MOTHER *extends her arms*] I just want to give my fella a kiss. And wish him luck. [PAUL *comes back in and crosses all the way over to* MOTHER. *She kisses him*] Your new home is absolutely beautiful. It's a perfect little apartment.

PAUL: Oh . . . thanks, Mom.

MOTHER: Then you *do* like it?

PAUL: Like it? [*He looks at* CORIE *and starts to exit*] Where else can you find anything like this . . . for seventy-five sixty-three a month? [*He exits, leaving* CORIE *and* MOTHER *alone.* CORIE *climbs down the ladder, and looks for some sign of approval from* MOTHER]

CORIE: Well?

MOTHER: Oh, Corie, I'm so excited for you. [*They embrace*]

CORIE: It's not exactly what you pictured, is it, Mother?

MOTHER: Well, it is *unusual*—like you. [*She crosses right*] I remember when you were a little girl you said you wanted to live on the moon. [*She turns back to* CORIE] I thought you were joking. . . . What about Paul? Is he happy with all this?

CORIE: He's happpy with me. I think it's the same thing. Why?

MOTHER: I worry about you two. You're so impulsive. You jump into life. Paul is like me. He looks first. [*She sits down on the suitcase*]

CORIE: He doesn't look. He stares. That's the trouble with both of you. . . . [*She places a paint can next to* MOTHER *and sits on it*] Oh, Mother, you don't know how I dreaded your coming up here. I was sure you'd think I was completely out of my mind.

MOTHER: Why should you think that, dear?

CORIE: Well, it's the first thing I've ever done on my own. Without your help. . . .

MOTHER: If you wanted it, I'm sure you would have asked for it . . . but you didn't. And I understand.

CORIE: I hope you do, Mother. It's something I just had to do all by myself.

MOTHER: Corie, you mustn't think I'm hurt. I'm not hurt.

CORIE: I'm so glad.

MOTHER: You mustn't think I'm hurt. I don't get hurt over things like that.

CORIE: I didn't think you would.

MOTHER: *Other* things hurt me, but not that. . . .

CORIE: Good. . . . Hey, let's open my presents and see what I've got. And you try to act surprised. [*She gets the presents and brings them to the paint can*]

MOTHER: You won't let me buy you anything. . . . Oh, they're just a few little things.

CORIE: [*Sitting down and shaking the smallest box vigorously*] What's in here? It sounds expensive.

MOTHER: Well, *now* I think it's a broken clock.

CORIE: [*Opens the box, and throws wrappings and tissue paper on the floor*] I'll bet you cleaned out Saks' gift department. I think I'm a regular stop on the delivery route now. [*She looks at the clock, replaces it in the box and puts it aside, and begins to open the largest box*]

MOTHER: Aunt Harriet was with me when I picked it out. [*She laughs*] She thinks I'm over here every day now.

CORIE: You know you're welcome, Mother.

MOTHER: I said, "Why, Harriet? Just because I'm alone now," I said. "I'm not afraid to live alone. In some ways it's better to live alone," I said. [CORIE *examines the blanket she finds in the package; then she closes the box, puts it aside, and begins to open the final package.* MOTHER *picks up a piece of tissue paper and smoothes it out on her lap*] But, you can't tell her that. She thinks a woman living alone, way out in New Jersey, is the worst thing in the world. . . . "It's not," I told her. "It's not the *worst* thing." . . .

CORIE: [*She has opened the package and now takes out the dismantled parts of a coffee pot*] Hey, does this come with directions?

MOTHER: If I knew about this kitchen, it would have come with hot coffee. [*She laughs*]

CORIE: [*Picks up the box with the clock and takes it with the parts of the coffee pot up into the kitchen*] Mother, you're an absolute angel. But you've got to stop buying things for me. It's getting embarrassing. [*She puts the clock on the refrigerator and the coffee pot on the sink*] If you keep it up I'm going to open a discount house. . . . [*She takes the blanket and places it with the suitcase near the windows*]

MOTHER: It's my pleasure, Corie. [*She begins to gather up wrappings and tissue paper and place them in the box which contained the coffee pot*] It's a mother's greatest joy to be able to buy gifts for her daughter when she gets married. You'll see someday. I just hope your child doesn't deprive *you* of that pleasure.

CORIE: I'm not depriving you, Mother.

MOTHER: I didn't say you were.

CORIE: [*Moves down to* MOTHER] Yes, you did.

MOTHER: Then why are you?

CORIE: Because I think you should spend the money on yourself, that's why.

MOTHER: Myself? What does a woman like me need? Living all alone . . . Way out in New Jersey. [*She picks up the box with wrappings in it and places it outside the front door*]

CORIE: [*Follows* MOTHER] It's only been six days. And you're five minutes from the city.

MOTHER: Who can get through that traffic in five minutes?

CORIE: Then why don't you move into New York?

MOTHER: Where . . . ? Where would I live?

CORIE: Mother, I don't care where you live. The point is, you've got to start living for yourself now. . . . [MOTHER *moves back into the room*] Mother, the whole world has just opened up to you. Why don't you travel? You've got the time, the luggage. All you need are the shots.

MOTHER: [*Sits on the suitcase*] Travel! . . . You think it's so easy for a woman of my age to travel alone?

CORIE: You'll meet people.

MOTHER: I read a story in the *Times*. A middle-aged woman traveling alone fell off the deck of a ship. They never discovered it until they got to France.

CORIE: [*Moves left and turns back to* MOTHER] I promise you, Mother, if *you* fell off a ship, *someone* would know about it.

MOTHER: I thought I might get myself a job.

CORIE: [*Straws in the wind*] Hey, that's a great idea. [*She sits on the paint can*]

MOTHER: [*Shrugs, defeated*] What would I do?

CORIE: I don't know what you would do. What would you *like* to do?

MOTHER: [*Considers*] I'd like to be a grandmother. I think that would be nice.

CORIE: A grandmother??? . . . What's your rush? You know, underneath that Army uniform, you're still a young, vital woman. . . . Do you know what I think you *really* need?

MOTHER: Yes, and I don't want to hear it. [*She gets up and moves away*]

CORIE: [*Goes to her*] Because you're afraid to hear the truth.

MOTHER: It's not the truth I'm afraid to hear. It's the *word* you're going to use.

CORIE: You're darn right I'm going to use that word. . . . It's love!

MOTHER: Oh. . . . Thank you.

CORIE: A week ago I didn't know what it meant. And then I checked into the Plaza Hotel. For six wonderful days. . . . And do you know what happened to me there?

MOTHER: I promised myself I wouldn't ask.

CORIE: I found *love* . . . spiritual, emotional, and physical love. And I don't think anyone on earth should be without it.

MOTHER: I'm not. I have you.

CORIE: I don't mean *that* kind of love. [*She moves to the ladder and leans against it*] I'm talking about late at night in. . . .

MOTHER: [*Quickly*] I *know* what you're talking about.

CORIE: Don't you even want to discuss it?

MOTHER: Not with *you* in the room.

CORIE: Well, what are you going to do about it?

MOTHER: I'm going back to New Jersey and give myself a Toni Home Permanent. Corie, sweetheart, I appreciate your concern, but I'm very happy the way I am.

CORIE: I'll be the judge of who's happy.

> [*They embrace. The door flies open and* PAUL *staggers in with the bottle of Scotch. He closes the door behind him and wearily leans his head against it, utterly exhausted*]

MOTHER: Oh, Paul, you shouldn't have run . . . Just for me. [*The doorbell buzzes,* AUNT HARRIET'S *special buzz*] . . . Ooh, and there's Harriet. I've got to go. [*She picks up her purse from next to the suitcase*]

CORIE: Some visit.

MOTHER: Just a sneak preview. I'll see you on Friday for the World Première . . . [*To* PAUL] Good-bye, Paul . . . I'm so sorry . . . [*To* CORIE] Good-bye, love . . . I'll see you on Friday . . . [PAUL *opens the door for her*] Thank you . . . [*She glances out at the stairs*] Geronimo . . . !

> [*She exits.* PAUL *shuts the door and, breathing hard, puts the bottle down at the foot of the ladder. He moves left, turns, and glares at* CORIE]

CORIE: What is it? . . . The stairs? [PAUL *shakes his head* "No"] The hole? [PAUL *shakes his head* "No"] The bathtub? [PAUL *shakes his head* "No"] Something new? [PAUL *nods his head* "Yes"] Well, what? . . .

PAUL: [*Leaning against the left wall*] Guess!

CORIE: Paul, I can't guess. Tell me.

PAUL: Oh, come on, Corie. Take a wild stab at it. Try something like, "All the neighbors are crazy."

CORIE: *Are* all the neighbors crazy?

PAUL: [*A pitchman's revelation*] I just had an interesting talk with the man down in the liquor store. . . . Do you know we have some of the greatest weirdos in the country living right here, in this house?

CORIE: Really? Like who? [*She puts the bottle on the kitchen platform*]

PAUL: [*Gathering his strength, he paces to the right*] Well, like to start with, in apartment One-C are the Boscos. . . . Mr. and Mrs. J. Bosco.

CORIE: [*Moving to the ladder*] Who are they?

PAUL: [*Paces to the left*] Mr. and Mrs. J. Bosco are a lovely young couple who just happen to be of the same sex and no one knows which one that is. . . . [*He moves up to left of the windows*] In apartment Three-C live Mr. and Mrs. Gonzales.

CORIE: So?

PAUL: [*Moves right above the ladder*] I'm not through. Mr. and Mrs. Gonzales, Mr. and Mrs. Armandariz, and Mr. Calhoun . . . [*He turns back to* CORIE] who must be the umpire. [*He moves left to left of the ladder, very secretively*] No one knows who lives in apartment Four-D. No one has come in or gone out in three years except every morning there are nine empty cans of tuna fish outside the door. . . .

CORIE: No kidding? Who do you think lives there?

PAUL: Well, it sounds like a big cat with a can opener. . . . [*He gets his attaché case from the corner, and turns to* CORIE] Now there *are* one or two normal couples in the building, but at this rent *we're* not one of them.

CORIE: Well, you've got to pay for all this color and charm.

PAUL: Well, if you figure it that way, we're getting a bargain. . . . [*He starts to go up the stairs, then turns back*] Oh, yes. I forgot. Mr. Velasco. Victor Velasco. He lives in apartment Six-A.

CORIE: Where's Six-A? [PAUL *points straight up*] On the roof?

PAUL: Attic. . . . It's an attic. [*He crosses up onto the bedroom landing*] He also skis and climbs mountains. He's fifty-eight years old and he's known as "The Bluebeard of Forty-eighth Street."

CORIE: [*Moves to the stairs*] What does that mean?

PAUL: [*Turns back to* CORIE] Well, it either means that he's a practicing girl-attacker or else he's an old man with a blue beard. [*He moves to the bedroom*] I'll say this, Corie. It's not going to be a dull two years.

CORIE: Where are you going?

PAUL: [*Turns back at the bedroom door*] I'm going to stand in the bedroom and work. I've got to pay for all this color and charm. If anything comes up, like the furniture or the heat, let me know. Just let me know. [*Bows off into the bedroom and slams the door*]

CORIE: [*After a moment of thought, she begins to fold up the ladder and put it against the left wall*] Can't I come in and watch you? . . . Hey, Paul, I'm lonesome . . . [*There is a knock at the door*] . . . and scared!

[*As* CORIE *puts the ladder against the wall,* VICTOR VELASCO, *fifty-eight and not breathing very hard, opens the door and enters. It's not that he is in such good shape. He just doesn't think about getting tired. There are too many other things to do in the world. He wears no topcoat. Just a sport jacket, an ascot, and a Tyrolean hat.* CORIE *turns and is startled to find him in the room*]

VELASCO: I beg your pardon. [*He sweeps off his hat*] I hope I'm not disturbing you. I don't usually do this sort of thing but I find myself in a rather embarrassing position and I could use your help. [*He discreetly catches his breath*] My name is Velasco. . . . Victor Velasco.

CORIE: [*Nervously*] Oh, Yes. . . . You live in the attic.

VELASCO: Yes. That's right. . . . Have me met?

CORIE: [*Very nervously*] No, not yet.

VELASCO: Oh. Well, you see, I want to use your bedroom.

CORIE: My bedroom?

VELASCO: Yes, You see, I can't get into my apartment and I wanted to use your window. I'll just crawl out along the ledge.

CORIE: Oh, did you lose your key?

VELASCO: No, I have my key. I lost my money. I'm four months behind in the rent.

CORIE: Oh! . . . Gee, that's too bad. I mean it's right in the middle of winter. . . .

VELASCO: You'll learn, as time goes by in this middle-income prison camp, that we have a rat fink for a landlord. . . . [*He looks about the room*] You don't have any hot coffee, do you? I'd be glad to pay you for it.

CORIE: No. We just moved in.

VELASCO: Really? [*He looks about the barren room*] What are you, a folk-singer?

CORIE: No. A wife. . . . They didn't deliver our furniture yet.

VELASCO: [*Moves toward* CORIE] You know, of course, that you're unbearably pretty. What's your name?

CORIE: Corie. . . . *Mrs.* Corie Bratter.

VELASCO: [*Takes it in stride*] You're still unbearably pretty. I may fall in love with you by seven o'clock. [*Catching sight of the hole in the skylight*] I see the rat fink left the hole in the skylight.

CORIE: Yes, I just noticed that. [*She crosses right, and looks up at the hole*] But he'll fix it, won't he?

VELASCO: I wouldn't count on it. My bathtub's been running since 1949. . . . [*He moves toward* CORIE] Does your husband work during the day?

CORIE: Yes. . . . Why? . . .

VELASCO: It's just that I'm home during the day, and I like to find out what my odds are. . . . [*He scrutinizes* CORIE] Am I making you nervous?

CORIE: [*Moving away*] Very nervous.

VELASCO: [*Highly pleased*] Good. Once a month, I try to make pretty young girls nervous just to keep my ego from going out. But, I'll save you a lot of anguish. . . . I'm fifty-six years old and a thoroughly nice fellow.

CORIE: Except I heard you were fifty-eight years old. And if you're knocking off two years, I'm nervous all over again.

VELASCO: Not only pretty but bright. [*He sits down on the paint can*] I wish I were ten years older.

CORIE: Older?

VELASCO: Yes. Dirty old men seem to get away with a lot more. I'm still at the awkward stage. . . . How long are you married?

CORIE: Six days. . . .

VELASCO: In love? . . .

CORIE: Very much. . . .

VELASCO: Damn. . . .

CORIE: What's wrong?

VELASCO: Under my present state of financial duress, I was hoping to be invited down soon for a free meal. But, with newlyweds I could starve to death.

CORIE: Oh. Well, we'd love to have you for dinner, as soon as we get set up.

VELASCO: [*Gets up, and stepping over the suitcase, moves to* CORIE] I hate generalizations. When?

CORIE: When? . . . Well, Friday? Is that all right?

VELASCO: Perfect. I'll be famished. I hadn't planned on eating Thursday.

CORIE: Oh, no . . . wait! On Friday night my mo— [*She thinks it over*] Yeah. Friday night will be fine.

VELASCO: It's a date. I'll bring the wine. You can pay me for it when I get here. . . . [*He moves to the stairs*] Which reminds me. You're invited to my cocktail party tonight. Ten o'clock. . . . You do drink, don't you?

CORIE: Yes, of course.

VELASCO: Good. Bring liquor. [*He crosses to* CORIE *and takes her hand*] I'll see you tonight at ten.

CORIE: [*Shivering*] If I don't freeze to death first.

VELASCO: Oh, you don't know about the plumbing, do you? Everything in this museum works backward. [*Crosses to the radiator on the wall*] For instance, there's a little knob up there that says, "Important—Turn right." . . . So you turn left. [*He tries to reach it but can't*]

CORIE: Oh, can you give me a little boost? . . .

VELASCO: With the greatest of physical pleasure. One, two, three . . . up. . . . [*He puts his arms around her, and lifts her to the radiator*] Okay? . . .

CORIE: [*Attempting to turn the knob*] I can't quite reach. . . .

PAUL: [*Comes out of the bedroom with an affidavit in his hand and his coat up over his head. He crosses to the head of the stairs*] Hey, Corie, when are they going to get here with— [*He stops as he sees* CORIE *in* VELASCO'S *arms.* VELASCO *looks at him, stunned, while* CORIE *remains motionless in the air*]

VELASCO: [*Puts* CORIE *down*] I thought you said he works during the day.

CORIE: Oh, Paul! This is Mr. Velasco. He was just showing me how to work the radiator.

VELASCO: [*Extending his hand*] Victor Velasco! I'm your upstairs neighbor. I'm fifty-eight years old and a thoroughly nice fellow.

PAUL: [*Lowers his coat, and shakes hands weakly*] Hello. . . .

CORIE: Mr. Velasco was just telling me that all the plumbing works backwards.

VELASCO: That's right. An important thing to remember is, you have to flush "up." [*He demonstrates*] With that choice bit of information, I'll make my departure. [*He crosses up onto the bedroom landing*] Don't forget. Tonight at ten.

PAUL: [*Looks at* CORIE] What's tonight at ten?

CORIE: [*Moves to the bottom of the stairs*] Oh, thanks, but I don't think so. We're expecting our furniture any minute. . . . Maybe some other time.

PAUL: What's tonight at ten?

VELASCO: I'll arrange it all for you in the morning. I'm also a brilliant decorator. [*He pats* PAUL *on the shoulder*] I insist you come.

CORIE: Well, it's really very nice of you.

VELASCO: [*Crossing to the bedroom door*] I told you. I'm a very nice person. A ce soir. . . . [*He exits into the bedroom*]

PAUL: [*To* CORIE] What's tonight at ten? . . . [*He suddenly realizes*] Where's he going? . . . [*He crosses to the bedroom*]

CORIE: [*Yelling after* VELASCO] Don't forget Friday. . . .

PAUL: [*To* CORIE] What's he doing in the bedroom? . . . What about Friday? [*He goes into the bedroom*]

CORIE: [*Rushes to the phone and dials*] He's coming to dinner. [*Into the phone*] Hello, Operator?

PAUL: [*Comes out of the bedroom*] That nut went out the window. [*He looks back into the bedroom*]

CORIE: I'm calling West Orange, New Jersey.

PAUL: [*Crosses down the stairs to* CORIE] Corie, did you hear what I said? There's an old nut out on our ledge.

CORIE:[*Into the phone*] Two, oh, one, seven, six, five, three, four, two, two.

PAUL: Who are you calling?

CORIE: My mother. On Friday night, she's going to have dinner with that old nut. [VELASCO *appears on the skylight, and carefully makes his way across.* CORIE *speaks into the phone*] Hello, Jessie . . . Will you please tell my mother to call me just as soon as she gets in!

[PAUL *turns and sees* VELASCO. VELASCO *cheerfully waves and continues on his way*]

CURTAIN

ACT TWO

SCENE ONE

Four days later. Seven o'clock, Friday evening.

*The apartment is no longer an empty room. It is now a home. It is
almost completely furnished, and the room, although a potpourri of
various periods, styles, and prices, is extremely tasteful and comfortable. No ultramodern, clinical interior for* CORIE. *Each piece was
selected with loving care. Since* CORIE'S *greatest aim in life is to spend
as much time as possible alone with* PAUL, *she has designed the room
to suit this purpose. A wrought-iron sofa stands in the middle of the
room, upholstered in a bright striped fabric. It is flanked by two old-
fashioned, unmatched armchairs, one with a romantically carved
wooden back; the other, a bentwood chair with a black leather seat. A
low, dark, wooden coffee table with carved legs is in front of the sofa,
and to the right is a small, round bentwood end table, covered with
green felt. Under the windows, a light-wood, Spanish-looking table
serves as a desk, and in front of it is a bamboo, straight-backed chair.
A large wicker basket functions as the wastebasket. A dark side table
with lyre-shaped legs fills the wall under the radiator, and below the
bedroom landing an open cane side table serves as a bar and telephone stand. To the right of the windows stands a breakfront with
shelves above and drawers below. The kitchen area is now partially
hidden by a four-fold bamboo screen that has been backed by fabric,
and potted plants have been placed in front of the screen. Straight-
backed bentwood chairs stand downstage right and left. The closet
has been covered by a drapery, the small windows by café curtains,
and the skylight by a large, striped Austrian curtain. Books now fill
the bookcase left of the kitchen, pictures and decorations have been
tastefully arranged on the walls, and lamps placed about the room.
The bedroom landing is graced with a bentwood washstand complete
with pitcher and basin which is filled with a plant. In the bathroom a
shower curtain and towels have been hung, and the bedroom boasts a
bed.*

*There is no one on stage. The apartment is dark except for a crack
of light under the bedroom door, and faint moonlight from the
skylight. Suddenly the front door opens and* CORIE *rushes in, carrying a
pastry box and a bag containing two bottles. After switching on the
lights at the door, she puts her packages on the coffee table, and
hangs her coat in the closet.* CORIE *wears a cocktail dress for the
festivities planned for tonight, and she sings as she hurries to get*

everything ready. She is breathing heavily but she is getting accustomed to the stairs. As she takes a bottle of vermouth and a bottle of gin out of the bag, the doorbell buzzes. She buzzes back, opens the door, and yells down the stairs.

CORIE: [*Yells*] Paul? [*We hear some strange, incoherent sound from below*] Hi, love ... [*She crosses back to the coffee table, and dumps hors d'oeuvres from the pastry box onto a tray*] Hey, they sent the wrong lamps ... but they go with the room so I'm keeping them. [*She crosses to the bar, gets a martini pitcher and brings it back to the coffee table*] ... Oh, do you have an Aunt Fern? ... Because she sent us a check ... Anyway, you have a cheap Aunt Fern ... How you doing? [*We hear a mumble from below.* CORIE *opens both bottles and pours them simultaneously into the shaker so that she has martinis made with equal parts of gin and vermouth*] ... Oh, and your mother called from Philly ... She and Dad will be up a week from Sunday ... And your sister has a new boy friend. From Rutgers ... He's got acne and they all hate him ... including your sister. [*She takes the shaker and while mixing the cocktails she crosses to the door*] ... Hey, lover, start puckering your lips 'cause you're gonna get kissed for five solid minutes and then ... [*She stops*] Oh, hello, Mr. Munshin. I thought it was my husband. Sorry. [*A door slams. She shrugs sheepishly and walks back into the room, closing the door behind her. As she goes up into the kitchen, the door opens and* PAUL *enters, gasping. He drops his attaché case at the railing, and collapses on the couch.* CORIE *comes out of the kitchen with the shaker and ice bucket*] It was you. I thought I heard your voice. [*She puts the ice bucket on the bookcase and the shaker on the end table*]

PAUL: [*Gasp, gasp*] Mr. Munshin and I came in together. [CORIE *jumps on him and flings her arms around his neck; he winces in pain*] Do you have to carry on—a whole personal conversation with me—on the stairs?

CORIE: Well, there's so much I wanted to tell you ... and I haven't seen you all day ... and it takes you so long to get up.

PAUL: Everyone knows the intimate details of our life. ... I ring the bell and suddenly we're on the air.

CORIE: Tomorrow I'll yell, "Come on up, Harry, my husband isn't home." [*She takes the empty box and bag, and throws them in the garbage pail in the kitchen*] Hey, wouldn't that be a gas if everyone in the building thought I was having an affair with someone?

PAUL: Mr. Munshin thinks it's *him* right now.

CORIE: [*Crossing back to the couch*] Well?

PAUL: Well what?

CORIE: What happened in court today? Gump or Birnbaum?

PAUL: Birnbaum!

CORIE: [*Jumps on his lap again. He winces again*] Oh, Paul, you won. You won, darling. Oh, sweetheart, I'm so proud of you. [*She stops and looks at him*] Well, aren't you happy?

PAUL: [*Glumly*] Birnbaum won the protection of his good name but no damages. We were awarded six cents.

CORIE: Six cents?

PAUL: That's the law. You have to be awarded something, so the court made it six cents.

CORIE: How much of that do you get?

PAUL: Nothing. Birnbaum gets the whole six cents. . . . And I get a going-over in the office. From now on I get all the cases that come in for a dime or under.

CORIE: [*Opening his collar and rubbing his neck*] Oh, darling, you won. That's all that counts. You're a good lawyer.

PAUL: Some lawyer. . . . So tomorrow I go back to sharpening pencils.

CORIE: And tonight you're here with me. [*She kisses his neck*] Did you miss me today?

PAUL: No.

CORIE: [*Gets off his lap and sits on the couch*] Why not?

PAUL: Because you called me eight times. . . . I don't speak to you that much when I'm home.

CORIE: [*Rearranging the canapés*] Oh, you're grouchy. I want a divorce.

PAUL: I'm not grouchy. . . . I'm tired. . . . I had a rotten day today. . . . I'm a little irritable . . and cold . . . and grouchy.

CORIE: Okay, grouch. I'll fix you a drink. [*She crosses to the bar and brings back three glasses*]

PAUL: [*Crosses to the closet, takes off his overcoat and jacket, and hangs them up*] I just couldn't think today. Couldn't think. . . . Moving furniture until three o'clock in the morning.

CORIE: Mr. Velasco moved. You complained. [*She pours a drink*]

PAUL: Mr. Velasco *pointed! I* moved! . . . He came in here, drank my liquor, made three telephone calls, and ordered me around like I was one of the Santini Brothers. [*He takes the drink from* CORIE, *and crosses to the dictionary on the table under the radiator. He takes a gulp of his drink and reacts with horror. He looks at* CORIE, *who shrugs in reply*]

CORIE: Temper, temper. We're supposed to be charming tonight.

PAUL: [*Taking off his tie*] Yeah, well, I've got news for you. This thing tonight has "fiasco" written all over it.

CORIE: [*Moves to the mirror on the washstand on the bedroom landing*] Why should it be a fiasco? It's just conceivable they may have something in common.

PAUL: [*Folding his tie*] Your mother? That quiet, dainty little woman . . . and the Count of Monte Cristo? You must be kidding. [*He puts the tie between the pages of the dictionary, and slams it shut*]

CORIE: Why? [*She puts on a necklace and earrings*]

PAUL: [*Crosses to the closet and gets another tie*] You saw his apartment. He wears Japanese kimonos and sleeps on rugs. Your mother wears a hairnet and sleeps on a board.

CORIE: What's that got to do with it?

PAUL: [*Crossing back to the mirror under the radiator and fixing his tie*] Everything. He skis, climbs mountains, and the only way into his apartment is up a ladder or across a ledge. I don't really think he's looking for a good cook with a bad back.

CORIE: The possibility of anything permanent never even occurred to me.

PAUL: Permanent? We're lucky if we get past seven o'clock . . .

[*The doorbell buzzes and Paul crosses to the door*]

CORIE: That's her. Now you've got me worried . . . Paul, did I do something horrible?

PAUL: [*Buzzing downstairs*] Probably.

CORIE: Well, do something. Don't answer the door. Maybe she'll go home.

PAUL: Too late. I buzzed. I could put a few Nembutals in his drink. It won't stop him but it could slow him down. [*He opens the door and yells downstairs*] Mom?

MOTHER'S VOICE: [*From far below*] Yes, dear. . . .

PAUL: [*Yelling through his hands*] Take your time. [*He turns back into the room*] She's at Camp Three. She'll try the final assault in a few minutes.

CORIE: Paul, maybe we could help her. [*She comes down the stairs*]

PAUL: [*Getting his blazer out of the closet*] What do you mean?

CORIE: [*Behind the couch*] A woman puts on rouge and powder to make her face more attractive. Maybe we can put some make-up on her personality.

PAUL: [*Puts his attaché case on the bookcase*] I don't think I want to hear the rest of this.

CORIE: All I'm saying is, we don't have to come right out and introduce her as "my dull fifty-year-old housewife mother."

PAUL: [*Crosses to the bar and pours a drink of Scotch*] Well, that wasn't the wording I had planned. What did you have in mind?

CORIE: [*Moves around the couch and sits on the right side of the couch*] Something a little more glamorous. . . . A former actress.

PAUL: Corie—

CORIE: Well, she *was* in *The Man Who Came to Dinner.*

PAUL: Your mother? In *The Man Who Came to Dinner?* . . . Where, in the West Orange P.T.A. show? [*He moves to the couch*]

CORIE: No! ... On Broadway.... And she was in the original company of *Strange Interlude* and she had a small singing part in *Knickerbocker Holiday*.

PAUL: Are you serious?

CORIE: Honestly. Cross my heart.

PAUL: Your mother? An actress? [*He sits next to* CORIE]

CORIE: Yes.

PAUL: Why didn't you ever tell me?

CORIE: I didn't think you'd be interested.

PAUL: That's fascinating. I can't get over it.

CORIE: You see. *Now* you're interested in her.

PAUL: It's a lie?

CORIE: The whole thing.

PAUL: I'm going to control myself. [*He gets up and crosses back of the couch*]

CORIE: [*Gets up and crosses to him at right of the couch*] What do you say? Is she an actress?

PAUL: No. [*He moves toward the door*]

CORIE: A fashion designer. The brains behind Ann Fogarty.

PAUL: [*Points to the door*] She's on her way up.

CORIE: A mystery writer ... under an assumed name.

PAUL: Let's lend her my trench coat and say she's a private eye.

CORIE: You're no help.

PAUL: I didn't book this act.

CORIE: [*Moves to* PAUL] Paul, who is she going to be?

PAUL: She's going to be your mother ... and the evening will eventually pass ... It just means ... that the Birdman of Forty-eighth Street is not going to be your father. [*He opens the door*] Hello, Mom.

    [MOTHER *collapses in and* PAUL *and* CORIE *rush to support her. They quickly lead her to the armchair at right of the couch*]

CORIE: Hello, sweetheart, how are you? [*She kisses* MOTHER, *who gasps for air*] Are you all right? [MOTHER *nods*] You want some water?

    [MOTHER *shakes her head "No" as* PAUL *and* CORIE *lower her into the chair. She drops her pocketbook on the floor*]

MOTHER: Paul ... in my pocketbook ... are some pink pills.

PAUL: [*Picks up her bag, closes the door, and begins to look for the pills*] Pink pills....

    [CORIE *helps* MOTHER *take off her coat*]

MOTHER: I'll be all right.... Just a little out of breath.... [CORIE *crosses to the coffee table and pours a drink*] I had to park the car six blocks away ... then it started to rain so I ran the last two blocks ... then my heel got caught in the subway grating . . . so I pulled my foot out and stepped in a puddle . . . then a cab went by and splashed my stockings . . . if the hardware store downstairs was open . . . I was going to buy a knife and kill myself.

[PAUL *gives her a pill, and* CORIE *gives her a drink*]

CORIE: Here, Mom. Drink this down.

PAUL: Here's the pill . . .

[MOTHER *takes the pill, drinks and coughs*]

MOTHER: A martini? To wash down a pill?

CORIE: It'll make you feel better.

MOTHER: I *had* a martini at home. It made me sick. . . . That's why I'm taking the pill. . . .

[CORIE *puts the drink down on the table*]

PAUL: [*Sitting on the end table*] You must be exhausted.

MOTHER: I'd just like to crawl into bed and cry myself to sleep.

CORIE: [*Offering her the tray of hors d'oeuvres*] Here, Mom, have an hors d'oeuvre.

MOTHER: No, thank you, dear.

CORIE: It's just blue cheese and sour cream.

MOTHER: [*Holds her stomach*] I wish you hadn't said that.

PAUL: She doesn't feel like it, Corie . . . [CORIE *puts the tray down and sits on the couch.* PAUL *turns to* MOTHER] Maybe you'd like to lie down?

CORIE: [*Panicky*] Now? She can't lie down now.

MOTHER: Corie's right. I can't lie down without my board . . . [*She puts her gloves into a pocket of her coat*] Right now all I want to do is see the apartment.

PAUL: [*Sitting on the couch*] That's right. You haven't seen it with its clothes on, have you?

MOTHER: [*Rises and moves to the left*] Oh, Corie. . . . Corie. . . .

CORIE: She doesn't like it.

MOTHER: [*Exhausted, she sinks into the armchair at left of the couch*] Like it? It's magnificent . . . and in less than a week. My goodness, how did you manage. Where did you get your ideas from?

PAUL: We have a decorator who comes in through the window once a week.

CORIE: [*Crossing to the bedroom*] Come take a look at the bedroom.

MOTHER: [*Crossing to the bedroom*] Yes, that's what I want to do . . . look at the bedroom. Were you able to get the bed in? [*She looks into the room*] Oh, it just fits, doesn't it?

PAUL: [*Moves to the stairs*] Just. We have to turn in unison.

MOTHER: It looks very snug . . . and did you find a way to get to the closet?

CORIE: Oh, we decided not to use the closet for a while.

MOTHER: Really? Don't you need the space?

PAUL: Not as much as we need the clothes. It flooded.

MOTHER: The closet flooded?

CORIE: It was an accident. Mr. Velasco left his bathtub running.

MOTHER: [*Moving down the stairs*] Mr. Velasco.... Oh, the man upstairs....

PAUL: [*Taking her arm*] Oh, then you know about Mr. Velasco?

MOTHER: Oh, yes. Corie had me on the phone for two hours.

PAUL: Did you know he's been married three times?

MOTHER: Yes.... [*She turns back to* CORIE] If I were you, dear, I'd sleep with a gun. [*She sits in the bentwood armchair*]

PAUL: Well, there's just one thing I want to say about this evening....

CORIE: [*Quickly, as she crosses to the coffee table*] Er ... not before you have a drink. [*She hands* MOTHER *the martini*] Come on, Mother. To toast our new home.

MOTHER: [*Holding the glass*] Well, I can't refuse that.

CORIE: [*Making a toast*] To the wonderful new life that's ahead of us all.

PAUL: [*Holds up his glass*] And to the best sport I've ever seen. Your mother.

MOTHER: [*Making a toast*] And to two very charming people ... that I'm so glad to be seeing again tonight ... your mother and father.

[CORIE *sinks down on the sofa*]

PAUL: [*About to drink, stops*] My what?

MOTHER: Your mother and father.

PAUL: What about my mother and father?

MOTHER: Well, we're having dinner with them tonight, aren't we? ... [*To* CORIE] Corie, isn't that what you said?

PAUL: [*Sits next to* CORIE *on the sofa*] Is that right, Corie? Is that what you said?

CORIE: [*Looks helpless, then plunges in*] Well, if I told you it was a blind date with Mr. Velasco upstairs, I couldn't have blasted you out of the house.

MOTHER: A blind date.... [*She doesn't quite get it yet*] With Mr. Velasco.... [*Then the dawn*] The one that...? [*She points up, then panics*] Good God! [*She takes a big gulp of her martini*]

PAUL: [*To* CORIE] You didn't even tell your mother?

CORIE: I was going to tell her the truth.

PAUL: [*Looks at his watch*] It's one minute to seven. That's cutting it pretty thin, isn't it?

MOTHER: Corie, how could you do this to me? Of all the people in the world....

CORIE: [*Gets up and moves to* MOTHER] I don't see what you're making such a fuss about. He's just a man.

MOTHER: My *accountant's* just a man. You make him sound like Douglas Fairbanks, Junior.

CORIE: He looks *nothing* like Douglas Fairbanks, Junior, . . . does he, Paul?

PAUL: No. . . . He just jumps like him.

MOTHER: I'm not even dressed.

CORIE: [*Brushing her* MOTHER'S *clothes*] You look fine, Mother.

MOTHER: For Paul's parents I just wanted to look clean. . . . *He'll* think I'm a nurse.

CORIE: Look, Mother, I promise you you'll have a good time tonight. He's a sweet, charming, and intelligent man. If you'll just relax I *know* you'll have a perfectly nice evening. [*There is a knock on the door*] Besides, it's too late. He's here.

MOTHER: Oh, no. . . .

CORIE: All right, now don't get excited.

MOTHER: [*Gets up and puts her drink on the coffee table*] You could say I'm the cleaning woman . . . I'll dust the table. Give me five dollars and I'll leave. [*She starts up the stairs to the bedroom*]

CORIE: [*Stops* MOTHER *on the stairs*] You just stay here. . . .

PAUL: [*Going to* MOTHER] It's going to be fine, Mom. [*He crosses to the door*]

CORIE: [*Leads* MOTHER *back to the sofa*] And smile. You're irresistible when you do. And finish your martini. [*She takes it from the table and hands it to* MOTHER]

MOTHER: Do you have a lot of these?

CORIE: As many as you need.

MOTHER: I'm going to need a lot of these. [*She downs a good belt*]

PAUL: Can I open the door?

CORIE: Paul, wait a minute. . . . Mother . . . your hair . . . in the back . . .

MOTHER: [*Stricken, she begins to fuss with her hair*] What? What's the matter with my hair?

CORIE: [*Fixing* MOTHER'S *hair*] It's all right now. I fixed it.

MOTHER: [*Moves toward* PAUL] Is something wrong with my hair?

PAUL: [*Impatient*] There's a man standing out there.

CORIE: Wait a minute, Paul. . . . [PAUL *moves back into the room and leans against the back of the armchair.* CORIE *turns* MOTHER *to her*] Now, Mother. . . . The only thing I'd like to suggest is . . . well . . . just try to go along with everything.

MOTHER: What do you mean? Where are we going?

CORIE: I don't know. But wherever it is . . . just relax . . . and be one of the fellows.

MOTHER: One of what fellows?

CORIE: I mean, don't worry about your stomach.

[*There is another knock on the door*]

MOTHER: Oh, my stomach. [*She sinks down on the couch*]

PAUL: Can I open the door now? . . .

CORIE: [*Moving to the right of the couch*] Okay, okay . . . open the door.

[PAUL *nods gratefully, then opens the door.* VELASCO *stands there, looking quite natty in a double-breasted, pin-striped blue suit. He carries a small covered frying pan in a gloved hand*]

PAUL: Oh, sorry to keep you waiting, Mr. Velasco. Come on in. . . .

VELASCO: [*Moving into the well, to* PAUL] Ah! Ho si mah ling. . . .

PAUL: No, no . . . It's Paul.

VELASCO: I know. I was just saying hello in Chinese. . . .

PAUL: Oh . . . hello.

VELASCO: [*To* CORIE] Corie, rava-shing. . . .

CORIE: [*Enthralled*] Oh. . . . What does that mean?

VELASCO: Ravishing. That's English.

CORIE: [*Taken aback*] Oh. . . . Ah, Paul. . . . Would you do the honors?

PAUL: Yes, of course. Mr. Velasco, I'd like you to meet Corie's mother, Mrs. Banks . . . [CORIE *steps back, unveiling* MOTHER *with a gesture*] Mother, this is our new neighbor, Mr. Velasco . . .

MOTHER: How do you do?

VELASCO: [*Sweeps to* MOTHER, *takes her hand, and bows ever so slightly*] Mrs. Banks . . . I've been looking forward so to meeting you. I invite your daughter to my cocktail party and she spends the entire evening talking of nothing but you.

[CORIE *moves up to left of the couch, taking it all in with great pleasure*]

MOTHER: Oh? . . . It must have been a dull party.

VELASCO: Not in the least.

MOTHER: I mean if she did nothing but talk about me. . . . *That* must have been dull. Not the party.

[PAUL *moves behind the couch to the coffee table and gets his drink*]

VELASCO: I understand.

MOTHER: Thank you. . . .

CORIE: [*To the rescue*] Oh, is that for us?

VELASCO: Yes. . . . I couldn't get the wine . . . my credit stopped . . . so instead . . . [*He puts the pan down on the end table and with a flourish lifts the cover*] . . . Knichi!

MOTHER: Knichi?

CORIE: It's an hors d'oeuvre. Mr. Velasco makes them himself. He's a famous gourmet.

MOTHER: A gourmet. . . . Imagine!

VELASCO: This won second prize last year at the Venice Food Festival.

MOTHER: Second prize. . . .

CORIE: Mr. Velasco once cooked for the King of Sweden, Mother.

MOTHER: Really? Did you work for him?

VELASCO: No. . . . We belong to the same club.

MOTHER: [*Embarrassed*] The same club. . . . Of course.

VELASCO: It's a Gourmet Society. There's a hundred and fifty of us.

MOTHER: All gourmets. . . .

VELASCO: That includes the King, Prince Phillip, and Darryl Zanuck.

MOTHER: Darryl Zanuck, too.

VELASCO: We meet once every five years for a dinner that we cook ourselves. In 1987 they're supposed to come to my house. [*He looks at his watch*] We have another thirty seconds. . . .

PAUL: Until what?

VELASCO: Until they're edible. [*He takes the cover off the pan, and puts it on the end table*] Now . . . the last fifteen seconds we just let them sit there and breathe. . . .

CORIE: [*Moves to the right*] Gee, they look marvelous.

VELASCO: When you eat this, you take a bite into history. Knichi is over two thousand years old. . . . Not this particular batch, of course. [*He laughs, but MOTHER laughs too loud and too long*]

CORIE: [*Again to the rescue*] Wow, what a great smell. . . . [*To VELASCO*] Mr. Velasco, would you be a traitor to the Society if you told us what's in it?

VELASCO: [*Secretively*] Well, if caught, it's punishable by a cold salad at the dinner . . . but since I'm among friends, it's bits of salted fish, grated olives, spices, and onion biscuits. . . . [*MOTHER reacts unhappily to the list of ingredients.* VELASCO *looks at his watch once more*] Ah, ready. . . . Five, four, three, two, one. . . . [*He holds the pan out to MOTHER*] Mrs. Banks?

MOTHER: [*Tentatively*] Oh . . . thank you. [*She takes one and raises it slowly to her mouth*]

CORIE: What kind of fish?

VELASCO: Eel!

PAUL: Eel?

MOTHER: [*Crumples with distaste*] Eel?? [*She doesn't eat it*]

VELASCO: That's why the time element is so essential. Eel spoils quickly. [MOTHER *crumples even more*] Mrs. Banks, you're not eating.

MOTHER: My throat's a little dry. Maybe if I finish my martini first. . . .

VELASCO: No, no. . . . That will never do. The temperature of the knichi is very important. It must be now. In five minutes we throw it away.

MOTHER: Oh! . . . Well, I wouldn't want you to do that. [*She looks at the knichi, then starts to take a nibble*]

VELASCO: Pop it!

MOTHER: I beg your pardon?

VELASCO: [*Puts down the pan and takes off his cooking glove*] If you nibble at knichi, it tastes bitter. You must pop it. [*He takes a knichi, tosses it from hand to hand three or four times and then pops it into his mouth*] You see.

MOTHER: Oh, yes. [*She tosses a knichi from hand to hand a few times and then tries to pop it into her mouth. But she misses and it flies over her shoulder.* VELASCO *quickly offers another. Although this time she succeeds in getting it into her mouth, she chokes on it*]

CORIE: [*Sitting next to her*] Mother, are you all right?

MOTHER: [*Coughing*] I think I popped it back too far.

CORIE: [*Takes* PAUL's *drink from him and hands it to* MOTHER] Here. . . . Drink this.

MOTHER: [*Drinks, gasps*] Ooh. . . . Was that my martini?

PAUL: [*Gets up and retrieves his drink*] No. My Scotch.

MOTHER: Oh, my stomach.

VELASCO: [*Moving left behind the couch*] The trick is to pop it right to the center of the tongue. . . . Then it gets the benefit of the entire palate. . . . Corie? [*He offers her the dish*]

CORIE: [*Takes one*] Well, here goes. [*She tosses it back and forth, then pops it perfectly*] How about that?

VELASCO: Perfect. You're the prettiest epicurean I've ever seen. . . . [*He offers the knichi to* PAUL] Paul?

PAUL: Er, no thank you. I have a bad arm.

CORIE: You can *try* it. You should try everything, right, Mr. Velasco?

VELASCO: As the French say, "At least once." . . . [PAUL *pulls up his sleeve, takes a knichi . . . then bites into it*] Agh. . . . Bitter, right?

CORIE: You know why, don't you?

PAUL: I didn't pop! I nibbled!

CORIE: Try another one and pop it.

PAUL: I don't want to pop another one. Besides, I think we're over the five-minute limit now, anyway.

VELASCO: [*Crossing to* MOTHER *behind the couch, he leans over to her very confidentially*] Taste is something that must be cultivated.

MOTHER: [*Almost jumps*] Er, yes, I've often said that. . . .

CORIE: Well, are we ready to go out to dinner?

MOTHER: [*Nervously*] You mean we're going out?

CORIE: We had a fire in our stove.

MOTHER: What happened?

PAUL: Nothing. We just turned it on.

CORIE: Mother, are you hungry?

MOTHER: Not terribly . . . no.

CORIE: Paul, you're the host. Suggest someplace.

PAUL: Well . . . er . . . how about Marty's on Forty-seventh Street?

CORIE: Marty's? That barn? You get a cow and a baked potato. What kind of a suggestion was that?

PAUL: I'm sorry. I didn't know it was a trick question.

CORIE: Tonight has to be something special. Mr. Velasco, you must know someplace different and unusual. . . .

VELASCO: [*Leaning against the end table*] Unusual? Yes, I know a very unusual place. It's the best food in New York. But I'm somewhat hesitant to suggest. . . .

CORIE: Oh, please. [*To* MOTHER] What do you say, Mother? Do you feel adventurous?

MOTHER: You know me, one of the fellows.

CORIE: [*To Velasco*] There you are. We place the evening in your hands.

VELASCO: A delightful proposition. . . . For dinner, we go to the Four Winds.

PAUL: Oh! The Chinese Restaurant? On Fifty-third Street?

VELASCO: No. . . . The Albanian restaurant on Staten Island.

MOTHER: [*Holds her stomach*] Staten Island?

CORIE: Doesn't it sound wild, Mother?

MOTHER: Yes . . . wild.

CORIE: I love it already. [*As she sweeps past* PAUL *on her way to the bedroom, she punches him on the shoulder*]

VELASCO: [*Sitting next to* MOTHER] Don't expect anything lavish in the way of decor. But Uzu will take care of the atmosphere.

MOTHER: Who's Uzu?

VELASCO: It's a Greek liqueur . . . Deceptively powerful. I'll only allow you one.

MOTHER: Oh . . . thank you.

CORIE: [*Coming out of the bedroom with her coat and purse*] It sounds perfect. . . . Let's go.

PAUL: It'll be murder getting a cab now.

VELASCO: I'll worry about the transportation. All you have to do is pick up the check.

CORIE: [*Back of the couch*] Mother has her car.

VELASCO: [*Rises, and turns to* PAUL] You see? My job is done. Mrs. Banks. . . . [*He holds up her coat.* PAUL *crosses to the closet and gets his overcoat*]

MOTHER: [*Putting on her coat*] Mr. Velasco, don't you wear a coat?

VELASCO: Only in the winter.

MOTHER: It's thirty-five.

VELASCO: [*Taking a beret out of his pocket*] For twenty-five I wear a coat . . . For thirty-five . . . [*He puts the beret on, and crosses to the door taking a scarf out of his pocket with a great flair.* PAUL *watches with great distaste and then crosses into the bedroom and opens the door*] Ready? . . . My group stay close to me. If anyone gets lost, we'll meet at the United States Embassy. [*He flings the scarf about his neck and exits.* MOTHER *desperately clutches* CORIE's *arm, but* CORIE *manages to push her out the door*]

CORIE: [*Turning back for* PAUL] What are you looking for?

PAUL: [*Comes out of the bedroom*] My gloves . . .

CORIE: [*With disdain*] You don't need gloves. It's only thirty-five. [*She sweeps out*]

PAUL: That's right. I forgot. [*Mimicking* VELASCO, *he flings his scarf around his neck as he crosses to the door*] We're having a heat wave. [*He turns off the lights and slams the door shut*]

CURTAIN

[*In the dark we hear the splash of waves and the melancholy toots of foghorns in the harbor sounding almost as sad as* PAUL *and* MOTHER *must be feeling at this moment*]

SCENE TWO

About 2:00 A.M.

    The apartment is still dark. We hear laughter on the stairs. The door opens and CORIE *rushes in. She is breathless, hysterical, and wearing* VELASCO's *beret and scarf.*

CORIE: Whoo. . . . I beat you. . . . I won. [*She turns on the lights, crosses to the couch, and collapses on it.* VELASCO *rushes in after her, breathless and laughing*]

VELASCO: [*Sinking to the floor in front of the couch*] It wasn't a fair race. You tickled me.

CORIE: Oh. . . . Ooh, I feel good. Except my tongue keeps rolling up. And when I talk it rolls back out like a noisemaker.

VELASCO: That's a good sign. It shows the food was seasoned properly.

CORIE: Hey, tell me how to say it again.

VELASCO: Say what?

CORIE: "Waiter, there's a fly in my soup."

VELASCO: Oh. "Poopla . . . sirca al mercoori."

CORIE: That's right. "Sirca . . . poopla al mercoori."

VELASCO: No, no. That's "Fly, I have a waiter in my soup."

CORIE: Well, I did. He put in his hand to take out the fly. [*She rises to her knees*] Boy, I like that singer. . . . [*She sways back and forth as she sings*] "Shama . . . shama . . . ela mal kemama" . . . [*She flings her coat onto the couch.* VELASCO *rises to a sitting position, crosses his legs, and plays an imaginary flute*] Hey, what am I singing, anyway?

VELASCO: [*Stretches prone on the floor*] It's an old Albanian folk song.

CORIE: [*Impressed with her own virtuosity*] "Shama shama . . ."? No kidding? What does it mean?

VELASCO: "Jimmy cracked corn and I don't care."

CORIE: Well, I don't. [*She feels her head*] Oh, boy. . . . How many Zuzus did I have? Three or four?

VELASCO: Uzus! . . . Nine or ten.

CORIE: Then it was ten 'cause I thought I had four. . . . How is my head going to feel in the morning?

VELASCO: Wonderful.

CORIE: No headaches?

VELASCO: No headache. . . . But you won't be able to make a fist for three days. [*He raises his hands and demonstrates by not being able to make a fist*]

CORIE: [*Holds out both hands and looks at them*] Yeah. Look at that. Stiff as a board. [*She climbs off the couch, and moves onto the floor next to* VELASCO] What do they put in Uzu anyway?

VELASCO: [*Holding up stiff hands*] I think it's starch.

CORIE: [*Looks at her two stiff hands*] . . . Hey, how about a game of ping-pong? We can play doubles. [CORIE *swings her two stiff hands at an imaginary ball*]

VELASCO: Not now. [*He sits up*] We're supposed to do something important. What was it?

CORIE: What was it? [*She ponders, then remembers*] Oh! . . . We're supposed to make coffee. [CORIE *places the shoes she has taken off under the sofa and moves toward the kitchen*]

VELASCO: [*Following her*] I'll make it. What kind do you have?

CORIE: Instant Maxwell House.

VELASCO: [*Crushed*] Instant coffee?

> [*He holds his brow with his stiff hands. He and* CORIE *disappear behind the screened kitchen continuing their babbling. Suddenly we hear scuffling in the hallway and* PAUL *struggles in through the door carrying* MOTHER *in his arms. From* PAUL'S *staggering we'd guess that* MOTHER *must now weigh about two thousand pounds. He makes it to the sofa, where he drops her, and then sinks in utter exhaustion to the floor below her. They both stare unseeing, and suck desperately for air.* CORIE *and* VELASCO, *who carries a coffee pot, emerge from the kitchen*]

CORIE: [*Crosses to* MOTHER] Forgot the stove doesn't work. Upstairs, everyone . . . for coffee. [CORIE *pulls* MOTHER's *coat but there is no reaction from* MOTHER *or* PAUL] Don't you want coffee?

> [PAUL *and* MOTHER *shake their heads "No"*]

VELASCO: [*Going to the door*] They'll drink it if we make it. . . .

CORIE: [*Following him*] Don't you two go away . . .

> [CORIE *and* VELASCO *exit, both singing "Shama, shama."* PAUL *and* MOTHER *stare silently ahead. They appear to be in shock, as if having gone through some terrible ordeal*]

MOTHER: [*Finally*] . . . I feel like we've died . . . and gone to heaven . . . only we had to climb up. . . .

PAUL: [*Gathering his strength*] . . . Struck down in the prime of life. . . .

MOTHER: . . . I don't really feel sick. . . . Just kind of numb . . . and I can't make a fist. . . . [*She holds up a stiff hand*]

PAUL: You want to hear something frightening? . . . My teeth feel soft. . . . It's funny . . . but the best thing we had all night was the knichi.

MOTHER: Anyway, Corie had a good time. . . . Don't you think Corie had a good time, Paul?

PAUL: [*Struggling up onto the couch*] Wonderful. . . . Poor kid. . . . It isn't often we get out to Staten Island in February.

MOTHER: She seems to get such a terrific kick out of living. You've got to admire that, don't you, Paul?

PAUL: I admire anyone who has three portions of poofla-poo pie.

MOTHER: [*Starts*] What's poofla-poo pie?

PAUL: Don't you remember? That gook that came in a turban.

MOTHER: I thought that was the waiter. . . . I tried, Paul. But I just couldn't seem to work up an appetite the way they did.

PAUL: [*Reassuring her*] No, no, Mom. . . . You mustn't blame yourself. . . . We're just not used to that kind of food. . . . You just don't pick up your fork and dig into a *brown* salad. . . .You've got to play around with it for a while.

MOTHER: Maybe I *am* getting old. . . .I don't mind telling you it's very discouraging. . . . [*With great difficulty, she manages to rouse herself and get up from the couch*] Anyway, I don't think I could get through coffee. . . . I'm all out of pink pills. . . .

PAUL: Where are you going?

MOTHER: Home . . . I want to die in my own bed. [*Exhausted, she sinks into a chair*]

PAUL: Well, what'll I tell them?

MOTHER: Oh, make up some clever little lie. [*She rallies herself and gets up*] Tell Corie I'm not really her mother. She'll probably never want to see me again anyway . . . Good night, dear. [*Just as* MOTHER *gets to the door, it opens and* CORIE *and* VELASCO *return*] Oh, coffee ready? [*She turns back into the room.* VELASCO *crosses to the bar as* CORIE *moves to behind the couch*]

CORIE: I was whistling the Armenian National Anthem and I blew out the pilot light.

VELASCO: [*Puts four brandy snifters he has brought in down on the bar, and taking a decanter from the bar begins to pour brandy*] Instead we're going to have flaming brandy . . . Corie, give everyone a match.

[CORIE *moves to the side table*]

MOTHER: I'm afraid you'll have to excuse me, dear. It *is* a little late.

CORIE: [*Moves toward* MOTHER] Mother, you're not going home. It's the shank of the evening.

MOTHER: I know, but I've got a ten-o'clock dentist appointment . . . at nine o'clock . . . and it's been a very long evening. . . . What I mean is it's late, but I've had a wonderful time. . . . I don't know what I'm saying.

CORIE: But, Mother. . . .

MOTHER: Darling, I'll call you in the morning. Good night, Paul. . . . Good night, Mr. Velasco. . . .

VELASCO: [*Putting down the brandy, he crosses to* CORIE] Good night, Paul. . . . Good night, Corie. . . .

CORIE: Mr. Velasco, you're not going, too?

VELASCO: [*Taking his beret and scarf from* CORIE *and putting them on*] Of course. I'm driving Mrs. Banks home.

MOTHER: [*Moves away in shock*] Oh, no! . . . [*She recovers herself and turns back*] I mean, oh, no, it's too late.

VELASCO: [*To* MOTHER] Too late for what?

MOTHER: The buses. They stop running at two. How will you get home?

VELASCO: Why worry about it now? I'll meet that problem in New Jersey. [VELASCO *moves to the door and* CORIE *in great jubilation flings herself over the back of the couch*]

MOTHER: And it's such a long trip. . . . [*She crosses to* CORIE] Corie, isn't it a long trip?

CORIE: Not really. It's only about thirty minutes.

MOTHER: But it's such an inconvenience. Really, Mr. Velasco, it's very sweet of you but—

VELASCO: Victor!

MOTHER: What?

VELASCO: If we're going to spend the rest of the evening together, it must be Victor.

MOTHER: Oh!

VELASCO: And I insist the arrangement be reciprocal. What is it?

MOTHER: What is what?

CORIE: Your name, Mother. [*To* VELASCO] It's Ethel.

MOTHER: Oh, that's right. Ethel. My name is Ethel.

VELASCO: That's better. . . . Now . . . are we ready . . . Ethel?

MOTHER: Well . . . if you insist, Walter.

VELASCO: Victor! It's Victor.

MOTHER: Yes. Victor!

VELASCO: Good night, Paul. . . . Shama shama, Corie.

CORIE: Shama shama!

VELASCO: [*Moves to the door*] If you don't hear from us in a week, we'll be at the Nacionál Hotel in Mexico City. . . . Room seven-oh-three! . . . Let's go, Ethel! [*And he goes out the door.* MOTHER *turns to* CORIE *and looks for help*]

MOTHER: [*Frightened, she grabs* CORIE's *arm*] What does he mean by that?

CORIE: I don't know, but I'm dying to find out. Will you call me in the morning?

MOTHER: Yes . . . about six o'clock! [*And in a panic, she exits*]

CORIE: [*Takes a beat, closes the door, smiles, and turns to* PAUL] Well . . . how about *that*, Mr. "This is going to be a fiasco tonight"? . . . He's taking her all the way out to New Jersey . . . at two o'clock in the morning. . . . That's what I call "The Complete Gentleman." . . . [PAUL *looks at her with disdain, rises and staggers up the stairs into the bedroom*] He hasn't even given a thought about how he's going to get home. . . . Maybe he'll sleep over. . . .Hey, Paul, do you think. . . ? No, not my mother. . . . [*She jumps up onto the couch*] Then again anything can happen with Rupert of Henzau. . . . Boy, what a night. . . . Hey! I got a plan. Let's take the bottle of Scotch downstairs, ring all the bells and yell "Police." . . . Just to see who comes out of whose apartment. . . . [*There is no answer from the bedroom*] . . . Paul? . . . What's the matter, darling? . . . Don't you feel well?

PAUL: [*Comes out of the bedroom, down the stairs, and crosses to the closet. He is taking his coat off and is angry*] What a rotten thing to do. . . . To your own mother.

CORIE: What?

PAUL: Do you have any idea how she felt just now? Do you know what kind of a night this was for her?

CORIE: [*Impishly*] It's not over yet.

PAUL: You didn't see her sitting here two minutes ago. You were upstairs with that Hungarian Duncan Hines. . . . Well, she was miserable. Her face was longer than that trip we took tonight. [*He hangs up his coat in the closet*]

CORIE: She never said a thing to me.

PAUL: [*Takes out a hanger and puts his jacket on it*] She's too good a sport. She went the whole cockeyed way. . . . Boy, oh boy . . . dragging a woman like that all the way out to the middle of the harbor for a bowl of sheep dip. [*He hangs his jacket up and crosses to the dictionary on the side table under the radiator. He takes his tie off and folds it neatly*]

CORIE: [*Follows him to the table*] It was Greek bean soup. And at least *she* tasted it. She didn't jab at it with her knife, throwing cute little epigrams like, "Ho, ho, ho . . . I think there's someone in there."

PAUL: [*Puts the tie between pages of the dictionary*] That's right. That's right. At least I was honest about it. You ate two bowls because you were showing off for Al Capone at the next table. [PAUL *searches for his wallet unsuccessfully*]

CORIE: What are you so angry about, Paul?

PAUL: [*Crossing to the closet*] I just told you. I felt terrible for your mother. [*He gets the wallet out of his jacket pocket*]

CORIE: [*Following after him to the front of the couch*] Why? Where is she at this very minute? Alone with probably the most attractive man she's ever met. Don't tell me *that* doesn't beat hell out of hair curlers and the "Late Late Show."

PAUL: [*Crossing onto bedroom landing*] Oh, I can just hear it now. What sparkling conversation. He's probably telling her about a chicken cacciatore he once cooked for the High Lama of Tibet and she's sitting there shoving pink pills in her mouth.

CORIE: [*Taking her coat from the couch and putting it on the armchair at right*] You never can tell what people talk about when they're alone.

PAUL: I don't understand how you can be so unconcerned about this. [*He goes into the bedroom*]

CORIE: [*Moving to the stairs*] Unconcerned. . . . I'm plenty concerned. Do you think I'm going to get one wink of sleep until that phone rings tomorrow? I'm scared to death for my mother. But I'm grateful there's finally the opportunity for something to be scared about. . . . [*She moves right, then turns back*] What I'm really concerned about is *you!*

PAUL: [*Bursts out of the bedroom, nearly slamming through the door*] Me? Me?

CORIE: I'm beginning to wonder if you're capable of *having* a good time.

PAUL: Why? Because I like to wear my gloves in the winter?

CORIE: No. Because there isn't the least bit of adventure in you. Do you know what you are? You're a Watcher. There are Watchers in this world and there are Do-ers. And the Watchers sit around watching the Do-ers do. Well, tonight you watched and I did.

PAUL: [*Moves down the stairs to* CORIE] Yeah. . . . Well, it was harder to watch what you did than it was for you to *do* what I was watching. [*He goes back up the stairs to the landing*]

CORIE: You won't even let your hair down for a minute? You couldn't even relax for one night. Boy, Paul, sometimes you act like a . . . a. . . . [*She gets her shoes from under the couch*]

PAUL: [*Stopping on the landing*] What . . . ? A stuffed shirt?

CORIE: [*Drops the shoes on the couch*] I didn't say that.

PAUL: That's what you're implying.

CORIE: [*Moves to the right armchair and begins to take off her jewelry*] That's what you're anticipating. I didn't say you're a stuffed shirt. But you are extremely proper and dignified.

PAUL: I'm proper and dignified? [*He moves to* CORIE] When . . . ? When was I proper and dignified?

CORIE: [*Turns to* PAUL] All right. The other night. At Delfino's. . . . You were drunk, right?

PAUL: Right. I was stoned.

CORIE: There you are. I didn't know it until you told me in the morning. [*She unzips her dress and takes it off*] You're a funny kind of drunk. You just sat there looking unhappy and watching your coat.

PAUL: I was watching my coat because I saw someone else watching my coat. . . . Look, if you want, I'll get drunk for you sometime. I'll show you a slob, make your hair stand on end. [*He unbuttons his shirt*]

CORIE: [*Puts her dress on the chair*] It isn't necessary.

PAUL: [*Starts to go, turns back*] Do you know . . . Do you know, in P. J. Clarke's last New Year's Eve, I punched an old woman. . . . Don't tell me about drunks. [*He starts to go*]

CORIE: [*Taking down her hair*] All right, Paul.

PAUL: [*Turns back and moves to behind the couch*] When else? When else was I proper and dignified?

CORIE: Always. You're always dressed right, you always look right, you always say the right things. You're very close to being perfect.

PAUL: [*Hurt to the quick*] That's . . . that's a *rotten* thing to say.

CORIE: [*Moves to* PAUL] I have never seen you without a jacket. I always feel like such a slob compared to you. Before we were married I was sure you slept with a tie.

PAUL: No, no. Just for very *formal* sleeps.

CORIE: You can't even walk into a candy store and ask the lady for a Tootsie Roll. [*Playing the scene out, she moves down to right side of the couch*] You've got to walk up to the counter and point at it and say, "I'll have that thing in the brown and white wrapper."

PAUL: [*Moving to the bedroom door*] That's ridiculous.

CORIE: And you're not. That's just the trouble. [*She crosses to the foot of the stairs*] Like Thursday night. You wouldn't walk barefoot with me in Washington Square Park. Why not?

PAUL: [*Moving to the head of the stairs*] Very simple answer. It was seventeen degrees.

CORIE: [*Moves back to the chair and continues taking down her hair*] Exactly. That's very sensible and logical. Except it isn't any fun.

PAUL: [*Moves down the stairs to the couch*] You know maybe I *am* too proper and dignified for you. Maybe you would have been happier with someone a little more colorful and flamboyant . . . like the Geek! [*He starts back to the bedroom*]

CORIE: Well, he'd be a lot more laughs than a stuffed shirt.

PAUL: [*Turns back on the landing*] Oh, oh . . . I thought you said I wasn't.

CORIE: Well, you are now.

PAUL: [*Reflectively*] I'm not going to listen to this. . . . I'm not going to listen. . . . [*He starts for the bedroom*] I've got a case in court in the morning.

CORIE: [*Moves left*] Where are you going?

PAUL: To sleep.

CORIE: Now? How can you sleep now?

PAUL: [*Steps up on the bed and turns back, leaning on the door jamb*] I'm going to close my eyes and count knichis. Good night!

CORIE: You can't go to sleep now. We're having a fight.

PAUL: *You* have the fight. When you're through, turn off the lights. [*He turns back into the bedroom*]

CORIE: Ooh, that gets me insane. You can even control your emotions.

PAUL: [*Storms out to the head of the stairs*] Look, I'm just as upset as you are. . . . [*He controls himself*] But when I get hungry, I eat. And when I get tired, I sleep. You eat and sleep, too. Don't deny it, I've seen you. . . .

CORIE: [*Moves right with a grand gesture*] Not in the middle of a crisis.

PAUL: What crisis? We're just yelling a little.

CORIE: You don't consider this a crisis? Our whole marriage hangs in the balance.

PAUL: [*Sits on the steps*] It does? When did that happen?

CORIE: Just now. It's suddenly very clear that you and I have absolutely *nothing* in common.

PAUL: Why? Because I won't walk barefoot in the park in winter? You haven't got a case, Corie. Adultery, yes. Cold feet, no.

CORIE: [*Seething*] Don't oversimplify this. I'm angry. Can't you see that?

PAUL: [*Brings his hands to his eyes, peers at her through imaginary binoculars, and then looks at his watch*] Corie, it's two-fifteen. If I can fall asleep in about half an hour, I can get about five hours' sleep. I'll call you from court tomorrow and we can fight over the phone. [*He gets up and moves to the bedroom*]

CORIE: You will *not* go to sleep. You will stay here and fight to save our marriage.

PAUL: [*In the doorway*] If our marriage hinges on breathing fish balls and poofla-poo pie, it's not worth saving. . . . I am now going to crawl into our tiny, little, single bed. If you care to join me, we will be sleeping from left to right tonight. [*He goes into the bedroom and slams the door*]

CORIE: You won't discuss it. . . . You're *afraid* to discuss it. . . . I married a coward!!. . . . [*She takes a shoe from the couch and throws it at the bedroom door*]

PAUL: [*Opens the door*] Corie, would you bring in a pail? The closet's dripping.

CORIE: Ohh, I hate you! I hate you! I really, really hate you!

PAUL: [*Storms to the head of the stairs*] Corie, there is one thing I learned in court. Be careful when you're tired and angry. You might say something you will soon regret. I-am-now-tired-and-angry.

CORIE: And a coward.

PAUL: [*Comes down the stairs to her at right of the couch*] And I will now say something I will soon regret. . . . Okay, Corie, maybe you're right. Maybe we have nothing in common. Maybe we rushed into this marriage a little too fast. Maybe Love isn't enough. Maybe two people should have to take more than a blood test. Maybe they should be checked for common sense, understanding, and emotional maturity.

CORIE: [*That hurt*] All right. . . . Why don't you get it passed in the

Supreme Court? Only those couples bearing a letter from their psychia-
trists proving they're well-adjusted will be permitted to be married.

PAUL: You're impossible.

CORIE: You're unbearable.

PAUL: You belong in a nursery school.

CORIE: It's a lot more fun than the Home for the Fuddy Duddies.

PAUL: [*Reaches out his hand to her*] All right, Corie, let's not get. . . .

CORIE: Don't you touch me. . . . Don't you touch me. . . .

> [PAUL *very deliberately reaches out and touches her.* CORIE *screams
> hysterically and runs across the room, away from him. Hysterically*] I
> don't want you near me. Ever again.

PAUL: [*Moves toward her*] Now wait a minute, Corie—

CORIE: No. [*She turns away from him*] I can't look at you. I can't even be in
the same room with you now.

PAUL: Why?

CORIE: I just can't, that's all. Not when you feel this way.

PAUL: When I feel what way?

CORIE: The way you feel about me.

PAUL: Corie, you're hysterical.

CORIE: [*Even more hysterically*] I am not hysterical. I know exactly what I'm
saying. It's no good between us, Paul. It never will be again.

PAUL: [*Throwing up his hands and sinking to the couch*] Holy cow.

CORIE: I'm sorry, I— [*She fights back tears*] I don't want to cry.

PAUL: Oh, for pete's sakes, cry. Go ahead and cry.

CORIE: [*At the height of fury*] Don't you tell me when to cry. I'll cry when I
want to cry. And I'm not going to have my cry until you're out of this
apartment.

PAUL: What do you mean, "out of this apartment"?

CORIE: Well, you certainly don't think we're going to live here together, do
you? After tonight?

PAUL: Are you serious?

CORIE: Of course I'm serious. *I want a divorce!*

PAUL: [*Shocked, he jumps up*] A *divorce?* What?

CORIE: [*Pulls herself together, and with great calm, begins to go up the
stairs*] I'm sorry, Paul, I can't discuss it any more. Good night.

PAUL: Where are you going?

CORIE: To bed. [*She turns back to* PAUL]

PAUL: You can't. Not now.

CORIE: You did before.

PAUL: That was in the middle of a fight. This is in the middle of a divorce.

CORIE: I can't talk to you when you're hysterical. Good night. [*She goes into the bedroom*]

PAUL: Will you come here? . . . [CORIE *comes out on the landing*] I want to know why you want a divorce.

CORIE: I told you why. Because you and I have absolutely nothing in common.

PAUL: What about those six days at the Plaza?

CORIE: [*Sagely*] Six days does not a week make.

PAUL: [*Taken aback*] What does *that* mean?

CORIE: I don't know what it means. I just want a divorce.

PAUL: You know, I think you really mean it.

CORIE: I *do!*

PAUL: You mean, every time we have a little fight, you're going to want a divorce?

CORIE: [*Reassuring*] There isn't going to be any more little fights. This is it, Paul! This is the end. Good night. [*She goes into the bedroom and closes the door behind her*]

PAUL: Corie, do you mean to say— [*He yells*] Will you come down here?!

CORIE: [*Yells from the bedroom*] Why?

PAUL: [*Screams back*] Because I don't want to yell. [*The door opens and* CORIE *comes out. She stands at the top of the stairs. He points to his feet*] All the way.

CORIE: [*Seething, comes all the way down and stands where he pointed*] Afraid the crazy neighbors will hear us?

PAUL: You're serious.

CORIE: Dead serious.

PAUL: You mean the whole thing? With signing papers and going to court, shaking hands, good-bye, finished, forever, divorced?

CORIE: [*Nodding in agreement*] That's what I mean . . .

PAUL: I see . . . Well . . . I guess there's nothing left to be said.

CORIE: I guess not.

PAUL: Right . . . Well, er . . . Good night, Corie. [*And he goes up the stairs*]

CORIE: Where are you going?

PAUL: [*Turns back on the landing*] To bed.

CORIE: Don't you want to talk about it?

PAUL: At two-thirty in the morning?

CORIE: I can't sleep until this thing is settled. [*She moves to the couch*]

PAUL: Well, it may take three months. Why don't you at least take a *nap?*

CORIE: You don't have to get snippy.

PAUL: Well, dammit, I'm sorry, but when I plan vacations I'm happy and when I plan divorces I'm snippy. [*He crosses to the bookcase and grabs his attaché case*] All right, you want to plan this thing, let's plan it. [*He storms to the coffee table and sweeps everything there onto the floor with his hand*] You want a quick divorce or a slow painful one?

CORIE: [*Horrified*] I'm going to bed. [*She goes up the stairs*]

PAUL: [*Shouts*] You stay here or you get no divorce from me.

CORIE: [*Stops on the landing*] You can try acting civilized.

PAUL: [*Putting down the attaché case*] Okay, I'll be civilized. But charm you're not going to get. [*He pushes a chair toward her*] Now sit down! . . . Because there's a lot of legal and technical details to go through. [*He opens the attaché case*]

CORIE: Can't you do all that? I don't know anything about legal things.

PAUL: [*Wheels on her and in a great gesture points an accusing finger at her*] Ah, haa. . . . Now *I'm* the Do-er and *you're* the Watcher! [*Relentlessly*] Right, Corie? Heh? Right? Right? Isn't that right, Corie?

CORIE: [*With utmost disdain*] . . . So this is what you're *really* like!

PAUL: [*Grimacing like the monster he is*] Yes. . . . Yes. . . .

CORIE: [*Determined she's doing the right thing. She comes down the stairs, and sits, first carefully moving the chair away from PAUL*] All right, what do I have to do?

PAUL: First of all, what grounds? [*He sits on the couch*]

CORIE: [*Not looking at PAUL*] Grounds?

PAUL: [*Taking a legal pad and a pencil out of the case*] That's right. Grounds. What is your reason for divorcing me? And remember, my failure to appreciate knichis will only hold up in a Russian court.

CORIE: You're a scream, Paul. Why weren't you funny when we were happy?

PAUL: Okay. . . . How about incompatible?

CORIE: Fine. Are you through with me?

PAUL: Not yet. What about the financial settlement?

CORIE: I don't want a thing.

PAUL: Oh, but you're entitled to it. Alimony, property? Supposing I just pay your rent. Seventy-five sixty-three a month, isn't it?

CORIE: Ha-ha. . . .

PAUL: And you can have the furniture and the wedding gifts. I'd just like to keep my clothes.

CORIE: [*Shocked, she turns to PAUL*] I hardly expected bitterness from you.

PAUL: I'm not bitter. That's a statement of fact. You're always wearing my pajamas and slippers.

CORIE: Only after you go to work.

PAUL: Why?

CORIE: Because I like the way they—never mind. It's stupid. [*She begins to sob, gets up and goes up the steps to the bedroom*] I'll sign over your pajamas and slippers.

PAUL: If you'd like, you can visit them once a month.

CORIE: [*Turns back on the landing*] That's bitter!

PAUL: You're damned right it is.

CORIE: [*Beginning to cry in earnest*] You have no right to be bitter.

PAUL: Don't tell me when to be bitter.

CORIE: Things just didn't work out.

PAUL: They sure as hell didn't.

CORIE: You can't say we didn't try.

PAUL: Almost two whole weeks.

CORIE: It's better than finding out in two *years*.

PAUL: Or twenty.

CORIE: Or fifty.

PAUL: Lucky, aren't we?

CORIE: We're the luckiest people in the whole world.

PAUL: I thought you weren't going to cry.

CORIE: Well, I am! I'm going to have the biggest cry I ever had in my life. And I'm going to enjoy it. [PAUL *drops the pencil and pad into the attaché case, and buries his head in a pillow from the couch*] Because I'm going to cry so loud, I'm going to keep you awake all night long. Good night, Paul! . . . I mean, *good-bye!*

[*She goes into the bedroom and slams the door, and we hear her crying.* PAUL *angrily slams his attaché case shut, gets up, and moves toward the stairs. At this moment, the bedroom door opens and* CORIE *throws out a blanket, sheet, and pillow which land at* PAUL's *feet. Then she slams the door shut again. Again we hear crying from the bedroom.* PAUL *picks them up and glares at the door*]

PAUL: [*Mimicking* CORIE] . . . all night long . . . work like a dog for a lousy six cents. . . . [*Seething,* PAUL *throws the bedding on the end table, and begins to try to make up the sofa with the sheet and blanket, all the while mumbling through the whole argument they have just had. As he puts the blanket over the sofa, he suddenly bursts out*] . . . Six days does not a week make.

[*The phone rings. For a moment,* PAUL *attempts to ignore it, but it keeps on ringing and he finally storms over to it and rips the cord from the wall. Then, still mumbling to himself, he crosses to the light switch near the door and shuts off the lights. Moonlight from the skylight falls onto the sofa.* PAUL *gets into his makeshift bed and finally settles down. And then . . . it begins to snow. Through the hole in the skylight it falls, down onto* PAUL'S *exposed head. He feels it and, after a quick moment, rises up on his knees and looks up at the hole. Soundlessly, he crumples into a heap*]

CURTAIN

ACT THREE

The following day. About 5:00 P.M.

   CORIE *is at the couch picking up the towels she has put down on the floor and the arm of the couch to soak up the water left by the previous night's snow. She picks up the towels with great distaste and uses one to rub off the arm. She looks up at the hole in the skylight, rolls the couch downstage so that it will not be under the skylight, and takes the towels up into the bathroom. As she disappears into the bathroom, the front door opens and* PAUL *comes in, collapsing over the railing. He looks haggard and drawn, not just from the stairs, but from a lack of sleep and peace of mind. Also, he has a cold, and as he leans there, he wearily blows his nose. He carries his attaché case and a newspaper. The doorbell buzzes, and as he presses the buzzer,* CORIE *comes out of the bathroom. They look silently at one another and then they both move, crossing each other wordlessly;* PAUL *goes up the steps to the bedroom and* CORIE *crosses up to the kitchen. Just before he gets to the bedroom door,* PAUL *sneezes.*

CORIE: [*About to go behind the screen, coldly, without looking at him*] God bless him!

   [PAUL *goes into the bedroom and slams the door.* CORIE *goes into the kitchen. She comes out with two plates, two knives and forks, and a napkin. Crossing to the table under the radiator, she puts down a plate with a knife and fork. Then putting the other setting down on the end table, she moves in all the way to the other side of the room. She goes back into the kitchen and emerges with two glasses. One she places on the side table and as she crosses toward the other table, our old friend Harry Pepper the* TELEPHONE MAN, *appears at the door. He is breathing as hard as ever. She sees him*]

CORIE: Oh, hi!

TELEPHONE MAN: [*Not too thrilled*] Hello again.

CORIE: How have you been?

TELEPHONE MAN: Fine. Fine, thanks.

CORIE: Good. . . . The telephone's out of order.

TELEPHONE MAN: I know. I wouldn't be here for a social call.

CORIE: Come on in. . . . [*He steps up into the apartment.* CORIE *closes the door behind him, and goes up into the kitchen to fill her glass with water*]

TELEPHONE MAN: [*Looking around*] Hey! . . . Not bad. . . . Not bad at all . . . you did a very nice job.

CORIE: [*Speaking from the kitchen*] Thanks. You know anyone who might want to rent it?

TELEPHONE MAN: You movin' *already?*

CORIE: [*Picking up the salt and pepper shakers*] I'm looking for a smaller place.

TELEPHONE MAN: [*Looks around with disbelief*] Smaller than this? . . . They're not easy to find.

CORIE: [*Coming out of the kitchen*] I'll find one. [*She places the glass of water and the shakers on the end table*]

TELEPHONE MAN: [*Moves to the phone*] Well, let's see what the trouble is. [*The* TELEPHONE MAN *picks up the receiver, jiggles the buttons, and listens, while* CORIE *moves the straight-backed bentwood chair to back of the end table. He puts down the receiver*] It's dead.

CORIE: I know. My husband killed it. [*She crosses to the side table under the radiator, and takes a candlestick and candle, and a small vase with a yellow rose*]

TELEPHONE MAN: [*Puzzled*] Oh! [*He looks down and notices that the wire has been pulled from the wall. He kneels down, opens his tool box, and cheerfully begins to replace the wire*] So how do you like married life?

CORIE: [*Puts the candlestick and vase down on her table; blandly*] Very interesting. [*She goes up into the kitchen*]

TELEPHONE MAN: Well, after a couple of weeks, what's not interesting? Yeah, it's always nice to see two young kids getting started. With all the trouble today, you see a couple of newlyweds, you figure there's still hope for the world. [*As* CORIE *comes out of the kitchen with a pot of food, a ladle, and a pot holder,* PAUL, *still in his overcoat and with his attaché case and newspaper, comes out of the bedroom and slams the door behind him. Both* CORIE *and the* TELEPHONE MAN *stop.* PAUL *goes into the bathroom and slams that door hard.* CORIE *grimaces and the* TELEPHONE MAN *is shocked. Puzzled*] Who's that?

CORIE: [*Rising above it*] Him!

TELEPHONE MAN: Your husband?

CORIE: [*Going to the bathroom door*] I suppose so. I wasn't looking. [*She pounds on the door with the ladle, and yells*] Dinnah—is served!

[*She crosses to the side table and begins to ladle food onto the plate. The bathroom door opens, and* PAUL *comes out*]

PAUL: [*Nods at the* TELEPHONE MAN *and then moves down the stairs to the couch*] I have my own dinner, thank you. [*He sits on the couch, puts his attaché case on the table, and opens it*]

CORIE: [*Ignoring* PAUL, *crosses to the* TELEPHONE MAN *and offers him the plate*] . . . Would you like some goulash?

TELEPHONE MAN: [*Embarrassed, he looks at* PAUL] Er, no, thanks. We're not allowed to accept tips.

[*He laughs at his small joke.* CORIE *takes the plate to the kitchen and drops the goulash, plate and all, into the garbage can. She then moves to her table and ladles goulash onto her plate.* PAUL, *meantime, has taken a small bag out of his attaché case. It contains a small bunch of grapes which he carefully places on top of his case.* CORIE *places the pot on the floor, and taking a book of matches from her apron pocket, she lights the candle. While she does this she sings to herself . . . "Shama, shama" . . .* PAUL *buries himself in his paper and begins to eat his grapes*]

TELEPHONE MAN: [*Taking all this in*] I'll be out of here as fast as I can. [*He dives back to his work*]

CORIE: [*Sitting down to eat*] Take your time. No one's rushing you.

[*The* TELEPHONE MAN *begins a nervous, tuneless hum as he works.* PAUL *continues to eat and read wordlessly. There is a long pause*]

PAUL: [*Without looking up*] Is there any beer in the house? [CORIE *does not answer. The* TELEPHONE MAN *stops humming and looks at her, hoping she will. . . . There is a pause. . . .* PAUL *is still looking at his newspaper*] I said, is there any beer in the house?

[*There is no answer*]

TELEPHONE MAN: [*He can't stand it any longer*] Would you like me to look?

CORIE: There is *no* beer in the house.

[PAUL *throws down his paper and storms toward the* TELEPHONE MAN, *who draws back in fright.* PAUL *stops at the bar and pours himself a drink*]

TELEPHONE MAN: [*With great relief, and trying to make conversation because no one else will*] That's *my* trouble . . . beer . . . I can drink ten cans in a night . . . of beer.

[PAUL *goes back to the couch and his newspaper. Not having eased the tension any, the* TELEPHONE MAN *goes back to his work and again begins his nervous humming*]

PAUL: [*After another pause, still looking at his newspaper*] Did my laundry come back today?

CORIE: [*With food in her mouth, she takes her own sweet time in answering*] Humph.

PAUL: [*Looks at her*] What does that mean?

CORIE: It meant your laundry came back today . . . They stuffed your shirts beautifully.

> [*Having watched this exchange, the* TELEPHONE MAN *desperately begins to whistle a pointless and innocuous tune*]

PAUL: [*Stung, takes a drink, then becoming aware of the* TELEPHONE MAN] Would you like a drink? [*There is no answer. The* TELEPHONE MAN *continues to work*] I said, would you like a drink?

TELEPHONE MAN: [*Startled, he looks up from his work*] Who?

PAUL: You!

TELEPHONE MAN: Me?

PAUL: Yes!

TELEPHONE MAN: OH! . . . NO!

PAUL: Right. [*He goes back to his newspaper*]

TELEPHONE MAN: [*Dives back to his work*] One more little screw should do it . . . There! [*Turns the screw, then says loud and elatedly*] I'm finished! I'm finished! [*He throws the tools quickly back into his kit*] That wasn't too long, was it?

CORIE: No. Thank you very much.

TELEPHONE MAN: [*Getting up and crossing to the door*] It's A.T.&T.'s pleasure. [*He nearly drops the kit, and in a panic rushes to the door. He is anxious to leave this scene*]

CORIE: [*Picks up the pot from the floor and moves to him at the door*] I'm sorry to keep bothering you like this.

TELEPHONE MAN: Oh, listen. Anytime.

CORIE: [*Very confidingly*] I don't think we'll be needing you again.

TELEPHONE MAN: Well, I wouldn't be too sure. . . . Phones keep breaking down now and then but er . . . [*He looks at* CORIE *as if trying to get some secret and personal message across to cheer her up*] . . . somehow, they have a way of getting fixed. You know what I mean. . . . [*He winks at her to indicate "Chin up." As he's winking,* PAUL *lowers his paper, turns around, and sees him. The* TELEPHONE MAN *is terribly embarrassed. So he winks at* PAUL. *Then, pulling himself together*] Well . . . 'bye.

> [*And he rushes out of the door.* CORIE *closes the door behind him and goes up into the kitchen with the pot and ladle. As soon as she is safely behind the screen,* PAUL *puts down his paper and runs to her table, where he swipes a mouthful of goulash. Dashing back to the couch, he is once more hidden behind his newspaper when* CORIE *comes out of the kitchen. She is now carrying a plate on which rests a*

small iced cake. She sits down, and pushing her plate aside, begins to eat her cake]

CORIE: Are you going to stay here again tonight?

PAUL: I haven't found a room yet.

CORIE: You've had all day to look.

PAUL: [*Using the nasal spray he had taken out of the attaché case with the bag of grapes*] I've been very busy. I work during the day, you know.

CORIE: You could look during your lunch hour.

PAUL: I *eat* during my lunch hour. I'll look during my looking hour. [*He puts down the spray and takes another drink*]

CORIE: You could look tonight.

PAUL: I intended to. [*He goes back to reading his paper*] But I'm coming down with a cold. I thought I'd just take a couple of aspirins and get right into the sofa.

CORIE: I'm sure you can find *some* place. . . . Why don't you sleep at your club?

PAUL: It's not *that* kind of a club. It's a locker room and a handball court . . . and to sleep there I'd have to keep winning the serve. [*He looks at* CORIE] Look, does it bother you if I stay here another couple of days?

CORIE: It's your apartment, too. Get out whenever you want to get out. [*The phone rings. When* PAUL *makes no move to answer it,* CORIE, *with great resignation, crosses to the phone and picks it up*] Hello? . . . Who? . . . Yes, it is. [CORIE *suddenly acts very feminine, in a somewhat lower, more provocative and confidential voice, even laughing at times as though she were sharing some private little joke. She seems to be doing this all for* PAUL's *benefit. Into the phone*] . . . Oh, isn't that nice. . . . Yes, I'm very interested. . . . [*Takes the phone and moves away from* PAUL] Thursday night? . . . Well, I don't see why not. . . .

PAUL: [*Doesn't like the sound of this*] Who is that?

CORIE: [*Ignores him and laughs into the phone*] . . . What's that? . . . Eight o'clock? . . . It sounds perfect.

PAUL: Who are you talking to?

CORIE: [*Still ignoring him*] . . . I see . . . But how did you get my number? . . . Oh, isn't that clever. . . .

PAUL: [*Crosses angrily and grabs the receiver*] Give me that phone.

CORIE: [*Struggling with him for it*] I will not. Get away from here, Paul. It's for me.

PAUL: I said give me that phone. [*Takes the receiver and its cradle from her.* CORIE *storms across to her table with great indignation, blows the candle out, and begins to take her setting into the kitchen.* PAUL, *into the phone*] Hello? . . . Who is this? . . . Who? . . . [*He looks at* CORIE *incredulously*]

No, madam, we're *not* interested in Bossa Nova lessons. [PAUL *hangs up and stares at* CORIE *as she comes out of the kitchen.* CORIE *does not look at him as she finishes clearing the table and takes the plates into the kitchen.* PAUL *moves back to the couch and sits*] I'm glad we didn't have children . . . because you're a crazy lady.

CORIE: [*Moves the chair back to the right, and carries the table back to the right of the couch*] I'll go where I want and do what I want. And I'm not going to stay in this house at nights as long as you're here.

PAUL: [*Putting down the paper*] I see. . . . Okay, Corie, when do you want me out?

CORIE: I want you out now. Tonight.

PAUL: [*Crossing to the closet*] Okay! Fine! [*He gets his suitcase and puts it on top of the end table*] I'll be out of here in five minutes. Is that soon enough for you?

CORIE: Not if you can make it in two.

PAUL: [*Opening the suitcase*] You can't wait, can you? You just can't wait till I'm gone and out of your life.

CORIE: Right. When do I get it?

PAUL: Get what?

CORIE: My divorce. When do I get my divorce?

PAUL: How should I know? They didn't even send us our marriage license yet.

CORIE: I'll get your Jockey shorts. [*She goes up into the bedroom*]

PAUL: [*Moves to the coffee table and takes his drink*] You can leave the suits. I'll pick them up in the spring when they're dry.

CORIE: [*In the bedroom*] You'd better ring the bell. 'Cause I'm buying a big dog tomorrow.

PAUL: [*Finishing his drink*] A dog. . . . Fine, fine. . . . Now you'll have someone to walk barefoot in the park with. [*The phone rings.* CORIE *comes out of the bedroom with a pile of Jockey shorts which she throws on the couch. She crosses to answer the phone*] If that's Arthur Murray, say hello. [*He gathers up the Jockey shorts and puts them in the suitcase*]

CORIE: [*Picks up the phone*] Hello. . . . Yes, Aunt Harriet. . . . What? . . . No, mother's not with me. . . . I'm positive. . . . She left about two in the morning. . . . What's wrong? . . . *What?*

PAUL: [*Crossing to the closet and getting a pair of pants*] What is it?

CORIE: [*Terribly frightened*] Mother??? . . . *My* Mother??? . . . Are you *sure?*

PAUL: [*Putting the pants in the suitcase*] What is it?

CORIE: [*Into the phone, now very nervous*] No, my phone's been out of order all day. . . . [*She gives* PAUL *a dirty look*] No, I don't know *what* could have happened.

PAUL: [*Blowing his nose*] What's the matter?

CORIE: All right, Aunt Harriet, don't get excited. . . . Yes. . . . Yes, I'll call as soon as I hear. [*She hangs up*]

PAUL: [*Moves to* CORIE] What happened to your mother?

CORIE: She didn't come home last night. Her bed wasn't slept in. Maybe I should call the police. [*She starts to pick up the phone*]

PAUL: All right, take it easy, Corie. . . .

CORIE: [*Turns back to* PAUL] Don't you understand? Jessie looked. She was not in her bedroom this morning. [*She picks up the phone*]

PAUL: [*Groping*] Well . . . well, maybe her back was bothering her and she went to sleep on the ironing board.

CORIE: You stupid idiot, didn't you hear what I said? My mother's been missing all night! . . . *My* mother!

PAUL: [*The Chief of Police*] All right, let's not crack up.

CORIE: [*Seething*] Will you go 'way. Get out of my life and go away! [*She slams the receiver down and crosses to the door*] I don't want to see you here when I get back.

PAUL: Where are you going?

CORIE: Upstairs to find out what happened to my mother. [*She opens the door*] And don't be here when I get back! [*She goes out and slams the door.* PAUL *goes to the door*]

PAUL: Oh, yeah . . . Well, I've got a big surprise for you. . . . [*He opens the door and yells after her*] I'm not going to be here when you get back. . . . [*Crossing to the dictionary on the side table*] Let's see how you like living alone. . . . [*He pulls ties out of the dictionary and throws them in the suitcase*] A dog . . . Ha! That's a laugh. . . . Wait till she tries to take him out for a walk. . . . He'll get one look at those stairs and he'll go right for her throat. [*Crossing into the bedroom*] You might as well get a parakeet, too. . . . So you can talk to him all night. [*Mimicking* CORIE] "How much can I spend for bird seeds, Polly? Is a nickel too much?" [*He comes out of the bedroom with shirts and pajamas*] Well, fortunately, I don't need anyone to protect me. [*Putting the clothes in the suitcase*] Because I am a man, sweetheart. . . . An independent, mature, self-sufficient man. [*He sneezes as he closes the suitcase*] God bless me! [*Feeling sorry for himself, he feels his head*] I probably got the flu. [*Crossing to the bar, he takes a bottle and glass*] Yeah, I'm hot, cold, sweating, freezing. It's probably a twenty-four-hour virus. I'll be all right. . . . [*He looks at his watch*] . . . tomorrow at a quarter to five. [*He pours another drink, puts down the bottle, and drinks. As he drinks, he notices the hole in the skylight. Stepping up onto the black leather armchair*] Oh! . . . Oh, thanks a lot, pal. [*He holds the glass up in toast fashion*] "And thus it was written, some shall die by pestilence, some by the plague . . . and one poor schnook is gonna get it from a hole in the ceiling." [*Getting down, he puts the drink on the side table*] Well, I guess that's it. [*He gets the bottle of Scotch from the bar, and glances at the bedroom*] Good-by, leaky closet.... [*To the bathroom*] Good-by, no bathtub.... [*Taking the attaché case from the coffee table, he looks up at the hole*] Good-by, hole ... [*Getting his suitcase*] Good-by, six flights.... [*As* PAUL *moves to the door,* CORIE *comes in. She holds her apron to her mouth, and is very disturbed*] Good-by, Corie.... [PAUL *stops in the doorway as* CORIE *wordlessly goes right by him and starts to go up the stairs to the bedroom*] Don't I get a good-by?... According to law, I'm entitled to a good-by!

CORIE: [*Stops on the stairs and slowly turns back to* PAUL, *in a heart-rending wail*] Good-by.... [*She goes into the bedroom and collapses on the bed*]

PAUL: Corie.... Now what is it? [*Alarmed, he drops the suitcase and attaché case, and puts the bottle on the end table*] Is it your mother?... Was it an accident?... [*He crosses to the bedroom*] Corie, for pete's sakes, *what happened to your mother?*

> [*Suddenly* MOTHER *rushes in through the open door. She is now dressed in a man's bathrobe many sizes too big for her. Over-sized man's slippers flap on her bare feet. But she is holding her pocketbook. Desperately clutching the bathrobe, she crosses to the bedroom*]

MOTHER: Corie, please, listen!... It's not the way it looks at all!

PAUL: [*Looks at her in amazement*] *Mother???*

MOTHER: [*Stops momentarily*] Oh, good morning, Paul. [*She goes up the stairs*] Corie, you've got to talk to me. [CORIE *slams the door to the bedroom shut*] There's a perfectly good explanation. [*Hysterical, in front of the closed door*] Corie, please.... You're not being fair.... [*She turns to* PAUL] Paul, make her believe me.

PAUL: [*Goes up the stairs and pounds on the bedroom door*] Now, you see.... Now are you satisfied?... [*He turns to* MOTHER, *being very forgiving*] It's all right, Mother, I understand. [*He starts for his suitcase*]

MOTHER: [*Shocked*] No!... *You don't understand!!!* [*She goes to* PAUL] You don't understand at all!!...

PAUL: [*Picking up the suitcase, attaché case, and bottle*] As long as you're all right, Mother. [*He looks at her, sadly shakes his head and exits*]

MOTHER: [*Trying to stop him*] No, Paul....You've got to believe me.... [*But* PAUL *is gone*] Oh, this is awful.... Somebody believe me. [*The bedroom door opens and* CORIE *comes out*]

CORIE: Paul! Where's Paul?...

MOTHER: [*Putting her bag down on the end table*] Corie, I'm going to explain everything. The bathrobe, the slippers.... It's all just a big mistake.

CORIE: [*Rushing to the front door*] Did he go? Did Paul leave?

MOTHER: [*Going to* CORIE] It happened last night. . . . when I left with Mr. Velasco. . . .

CORIE: [*Closing the door*] He was right. . . . Paul was right. [*She moves to the couch and sits*]

MOTHER: [*Following her*] It must have been the drinks. I had a great deal to drink last night. . . . [*She sits next to* CORIE] I had Scotch, martinis, coffee, black bean soup, and Uzus. . . .

CORIE: You don't have to explain a thing to me, Mother.

MOTHER: [*Horrified*] But I want to explain. . . . When I got outside I suddenly felt dizzy . . . and I fainted. . . . Well, I passed out. In the slush.

CORIE: I should have listened to him. . . . It's all my fault.

MOTHER: [*Desperately trying to make her see*] Then Victor picked me up and carried me inside. I couldn't walk because my shoes fell down the sewer.

CORIE: [*Deep in her own misery*] You hear about these things every day.

MOTHER: He started to carry me up here but his beret fell over his eyes, and he fell down the stairs. . . . He fell into apartment Three-C. I fell on his foot. . . . They had to carry us up.

CORIE: I thought we'd have a nice sociable evening, that's all.

MOTHER: . . . Mr. Gonzales, Mr. Armandariz, and Mr. Calhoun. . . . [*She sags in defeat*] They carried us up. . . .

CORIE: Just some drinks, dinner, and coffee. . . . That's all. . . .

MOTHER: And then they put us down. On the rugs. . . . Oh, he doesn't have beds . . . just thick rugs, and then I fell asleep. . . .

CORIE: Paul was right. He was right about so many things. . . .

MOTHER: And then when I woke up, Victor was gone. But I was there . . . in his bathrobe. [*She pounds the couch with her fist*] I swear that's the truth, Corie.

CORIE: [*Turns to* MOTHER] You don't have to swear, Mother.

MOTHER: But I want you to believe me. I've told you everything.

CORIE: Then where are your clothes?

MOTHER: *That* I can't tell you.

CORIE: Why not?

MOTHER: Because you won't believe me.

CORIE: I'll believe you.

MOTHER: You won't.

CORIE: I will. Where are your clothes?

MOTHER: I don't know.

CORIE: I don't believe you. [*She gets up and moves toward* MOTHER]

MOTHER: Didn't I say you wouldn't believe me? I just don't know where they are.... [*She gets up and moves to the right*] Oh, Corie, I've never been so humiliated in all my life....

CORIE: Don't blame yourself.... It's all my fault. *I* did it. I did this to you. [*She leans on the bar, holding her head*]

MOTHER: And I had horrible nightmares. I dreamt my fingers were falling off because I couldn't make a fist. [*She paces and catches sight of herself in the mirror*] Oh, God! I look like someone they woke up in the middle of the night on the *Andrea Doria!* [*She breaks into hysterical laughter, and then there is a pounding on the door*]

VELASCO'S VOICE: Hello. Anyone home? . . .

MOTHER: [*Terror-stricken*] It's him . . . [*She rushes to* CORIE] Corie, don't let him in. I can't face him now . . . not in his bathrobe. [*There is another pounding at the door*]

VELASCO'S VOICE: Somebody, please!

CORIE: [*Moving past* MOTHER] All right, Mother. I'll handle this. Go in the bedroom. . . .

MOTHER: [*Moving to the stairs*] Tell him I'm not here. Tell him anything.
[*The door opens and* VELASCO *steps in. He is now supporting himself with a cane and his foot is covered by a thick white stocking. As* VELASCO *enters*, CORIE *sinks into the armchair at right of the couch*]

VELASCO: [*Hobbling up the step and moving to the couch*] I'm sorry but I need some aspirins desperately. [*He catches sight of* MOTHER *who is furtively trying to escape up the stairs to the bedroom*] Hello, Ethel.

MOTHER: [*Caught, she stops and tries to cover her embarrassment*] Oh, hello, Victor.... Mr. Victor.... Mr. Velasco.

VELASCO: [*To* CORIE] Did you hear what happened to us last night? [*To* MOTHER] Did you tell her what happened to us last night?

MOTHER: [*Horrified*] Why ...? What happened to us last night? [*She composes herself*] Oh, you mean what happened to us last night. [*With great nonchalance, moving down the stairs*] Yes.... Yes.... I told her.

VELASCO: [*At the couch*] Did you know my big toe is broken?

MOTHER: [*Smiles*] Yes.... [*She catches herself*] I mean no.... Isn't that terrible?

VELASCO: I'll have to wear a slipper for the next month.... Only I can't find my slippers.... [*He sees them on* MOTHER's *feet*] Oh, there they are....

MOTHER: [*Looks down at her feet, as if surprised*] Oh, yes.... There's your slippers.

VELASCO: [*Sitting on the sofa and putting his foot up on the coffee table*] It took me forty minutes to walk up the stairs.... I'll have to hire someone to pull me up the ladder. [*To* CORIE] Corie, could I please have about three hundred aspirins?

[CORIE *crosses to the stairs*]

MOTHER: [*Appealing to* CORIE] A broken toe . . . Isn't that awful!

[CORIE *ignores her and goes into the bathroom*]

VELASCO: That's not the worst of it. I just had a complete examination. Guess what else I have?

MOTHER: What?

VELASCO: An ulcer! From all the rich food. . . . I have to take little pink pills like you.

MOTHER: Oh, dear. . . .

VELASCO: You know something, Ethel. . . . I don't think I'm as young as I think I am.

MOTHER: Why do you say that?

VELASCO: Isn't it obvious? Last night I couldn't carry you up the stairs. I can't eat rich foods any more . . . [*Very confidentially*] . . . and I dye my hair.

MOTHER: [*Moves to the couch*] Oh. . . . Well, it looks very nice.

VELASCO: Thank you. . . . So are you. . . .

MOTHER: [*Sitting next to* VELASCO] Oh. . . . Thank you.

VELASCO: I mean it, Ethel. You're a very unusual woman.

MOTHER: Unusual? . . . In what way?

VELASCO: [*Reflectively*] It's funny, but I can hardly feel my big toe at all now.

MOTHER: [*Insistent*] Unusual in what way?

VELASCO: Well, I took a look at you last night. . . . I took a long, close look at you. . . .Do you know what you are, Ethel?

MOTHER: [*Ready for the compliment*] What?

VELASCO: A good sport.

MOTHER: Oh. . . . A good sport.

VELASCO: To have gone through all you did last night. The trip to Staten Island, the strange food, the drinks, being carried up to my apartment like that. And you didn't say one word about it.

MOTHER: Well, I didn't have much chance to. . . . I did a lot of fainting.

VELASCO: Yes. . . . As a matter of fact, we both did. . . . If you remember. . . . [*Remembering, he begins to laugh*]

MOTHER: Yes. . . . [*She joins in. It is a warm, hearty laugh shared by two friends. After the laugh gradually dies out, there is a moment of awkward silence and then with an attempt at renewed gaiety,* MOTHER *says*] Mr. Velasco. . . . Where are my clothes?

VELASCO: Your clothes . . . ? Oh, yes. . . . [*He takes a piece of paper out of his pocket*] Here. [*He gives it to her*]

MOTHER: I'm sure I wore more than that.

VELASCO: It's a cleaning ticket. They're sending them up at six o'clock.

MOTHER: [*Taking the ticket*] Oh, they're at the cleaner's.... [*After a moment's hesitation*] When did I take them off?

VELASCO: You didn't.... You were drenched and out cold. Gonzales took them off.

MOTHER: [*Shocked*] Mr. Gonzales??

VELASCO: Not Mister! ... *Doctor* Gonzales!

MOTHER: [*Relieved*] Doctor.... Oh, *Doctor* Gonzales.... Well, I suppose that's all right. How convenient to have an M.D. in the building.

VELASCO: [*Laughing*] He's not an M.D. He's a Doctor of Philosophy.

MOTHER: [*Joins in the laughter with great abandon*] Oh, no....

> [CORIE *comes out of the bathroom with aspirin and a glass of water, and watches them laughing with bewilderment*]

CORIE: [*Goes behind the couch*] Here's the aspirins.

VELASCO: Thank you, but I'm feeling better now.

MOTHER: *I'll* take them. [*Takes an aspirin and a sip of water*]

VELASCO: [*Gets up and hobbles to the door*] I have to go. I'm supposed to soak my foot every hour . . .

MOTHER: Oh, dear.... Is there anything I can do?

VELASCO: [*Turns back*] Yes.... Yes, there is.... Would you like to have dinner with me tonight?

MOTHER: [*Surprised*] Me?

VELASCO: [*Nods*] If you don't mind eating plain food.

MOTHER: I love *plain* food.

VELASCO: Good.... I'll call the New York Hospital for a reservation.... [*He opens the door*] Pick me up in a few minutes.... We'll have a glass of buttermilk before we go. [*He exits*]

MOTHER: [*After a moment, she turns to* CORIE *on the stairs and giggles. Takes the grapes from the coffee table*] You know what? ... I'll bet I'm the first woman ever asked to dinner wearing a size forty-eight bathrobe.

CORIE: [*Lost in her own problem*] Mother, can I talk to you for a minute?

MOTHER: [*Puts down the bunch of grapes, gets up, and moves right*] I just realized. I slept without a board.... For the first time in years I slept without a board.

CORIE: Mother, will you listen....

MOTHER: [*Turns to* CORIE] You don't suppose Uzu is a Greek miracle drug, do you? [*She flips a grape back and forth and pops it into her mouth like a knichi*]

CORIE: Mother, before you go, there's something we've got to talk about.

MOTHER: [*Moving to* CORIE] Oh, Corie, how sweet.... You're worried about me.

CORIE: I am *not* worried about you.

MOTHER: [*Looks in the mirror*] Oh, dear. My hair. What am I going to do with my hair?

CORIE: I don't *care* what you do with your hair.

MOTHER: If *he* can dye it, why can't I? Do you think black would make me look too Mexican?

CORIE: Mother, why won't you talk to me?

MOTHER: [*Moving back of the couch*] Now? . . . But Victor's waiting. . . . [*She turns back to* CORIE] Why don't you and Paul come with us?

CORIE: That's what I've been trying to tell you. . . . Paul isn't coming back.

MOTHER: What do you mean? Where'd he go?

CORIE: I don't know. Reno. Texas. Wherever it is that men go to get divorced.

MOTHER: *Divorced???*

CORIE: That's right. Divorced. Paul and I have split up. For good.

MOTHER: I don't believe it.

CORIE: Why don't you believe it?

MOTHER: You? And Paul?

CORIE: Well, you just saw him leave here with his suitcase. What did you think he had in there?

MOTHER: I don't know. I know how neat he is. I thought maybe the garbage.

CORIE: Mother, I believe *you*. Why won't you believe me?

MOTHER: [*Moves left to the bentwood chair and sits facing* CORIE] Because in my entire life I've never seen two people more in love than you and Paul.

CORIE: [*Tearfully*] Well, it's not true. It may have been yesterday but it sure isn't today. It's all over, Mother. He's gone.

MOTHER: You mean he just walked out? For no reason at all? . . .

CORIE: He had a perfectly *good* reason. I *told* him to get out. *I* did it. Me and my big stupid mouth.

MOTHER: It couldn't have been all your fault.

CORIE: No? . . . No?? Because of me you're running around without your clothes and Paul is out there on the streets with a cold looking for a place to sleep. Who's fault is that?

MOTHER: Yours! . . . But do you want to know something that may shock you? . . . I still love you.

CORIE: You do? . . .

MOTHER: Yes, and Paul loves you, too.

CORIE: And I love him. . . . Only I don't know what he wants. I don't know how to make him happy. . . . Oh, Mom, what am I going to do?

MOTHER: That's the first time you've asked my advice since you were ten. [*She gets up and moves to* CORIE] It's very simple. You've just got to give up a little of you for him. Don't make everything a game. Just late at night in that little room upstairs. But take care of him. And make him feel important. And if you can do that, you'll have a happy and wonderful marriage. . . . Like two out of every ten couples. . . . But you'll be one of the two, baby. . . . [*She gently strokes* CORIE's *hair*] Now get your coat and go on out after him. . . . I've got a date. [*She crosses to the coffee table and picks up her handbag*] Aunt Harriet isn't going to believe a word of this. . . . [*Flourishing her bathrobe, she moves to the door and opens it*] I wish I had my Polaroid camera. . . .

> [*She pauses, blows* CORIE *a kiss, and exits.* CORIE *thinks a moment, wipes her eyes, and then rushes to the closet for her coat. Without stopping to put it on, she rushes to the door and opens it. As the door opens,* PAUL *is revealed at the doorway. He greets* CORIE *with a loud sneeze. His clothes are disheveled, his overcoat is gone, and he is obviously drunk, but he still is carrying his suitcase*]

CORIE: Paul! . . . Paul, are you all right? . . .

PAUL: [*Very carefully crossing to the coffee table*] Fine. . . . Fine, thank you. . . . [*He giggles*]

CORIE: [*Moves to him*] I was just going out to look for you.

PAUL: [*Puts the suitcase on the floor and starts to take out his clothes*] Oh . . . ? Where were you going to look? . . .

CORIE: I don't know. I was just going to look.

PAUL: [*Confidentially*] Oh . . . ! Well, you'll never find me. [*He throws a handful of clothes into the closet. He is apparently amused by some secret joke*]

CORIE: Paul, I've got so much to say to you, darling.

PAUL: [*Taking more clothes out of the suitcase*] So, have I, Corie. . . . I got all the way downstairs and suddenly it hit me. I saw everything clearly for the first time. [*He moves up left to behind the couch*] I said to myself, this is crazy. . . . Crazy! . . . It's all wrong for me to run like this. . . . [*He turns to* CORIE] And there's only one right thing to do, Corie.

CORIE: [*Moving to him*] Really, Paul? . . . What? . . .

PAUL: [*Jubilantly*] You get out! [*He breaks into hysterical laughter*]

CORIE: What? . . .

PAUL: Why should I get out? I'm paying a hundred twenty-five a month. . . . [*He looks about the apartment*] . . . for this. . . . You get out. [*He stuffs clothes into the dictionary*]

CORIE: But I don't want to get out!

PAUL: [*Crossing back to the suitcase and getting another handful of clothes*] I'm afraid you'll have to. . . . The lease is in my name. . . . [*He moves to the stairs*] I'll give you ten minutes to pack your goulash.

CORIE: [*Moves to him*] Paul, your coat! . . . Where is your coat?

PAUL: [*Draws himself up in indignation*] Coat? . . . I don't need a coat . . . It's only two degrees. . . . [*He starts to go up the stairs, slips and falls*]

CORIE: [*Rushing to him*] Paul, are you all right? . . .

PAUL: [*Struggling up*] You're dawdling, Corie. . . . I want you out of here in exactly ten minutes. . . .

CORIE: [*Holding him*] Paul, you're ice cold. . . . You're freezing! . . . What have you been doing?

PAUL: [*Pulls away from her and moves to a chair*] What do you think I've been doing? [*He puts his foot up on the seat*] I've been walking barefoot in the goddamn park.

CORIE: [*Pulls up his pants leg, revealing his stockingless foot*] Where's your socks? . . . Are you crazy?

PAUL: No. . . . No. . . . But guess what I am.

CORIE: [*Looks at him*] You're drunk!

PAUL: [*In great triumph, he moves right*] Ah . . . ! You finally noticed!!

CORIE: Lousy, stinkin' drunk!

PAUL: Ah, gee. . . . Thanks. . . .

CORIE: [*Moves to him and feels his forehead*] You're burning up with fever.

PAUL: How about that?

CORIE: You'll get pneumonia!

PAUL: If that's what you want, that is what I'll get.

CORIE: [*Leads him to the couch*] I want you to get those shoes off. . . . They're soaking wet. . . . [*She pushes him down onto the couch*]

PAUL: I can't. . . . My feet have swellened. . . .

CORIE: [*Pulling his shoes off*] I never should have let you out of here. I knew you had a cold. [*She puts the shoes on the side table*]

PAUL: [*Getting up and moving to the doorway*] Hey! Hey, Corie. . . . Let's do that thing you said before. . . . Let's wake up the police and see if all the rooms come out of the crazy neighbors. . . . [*He opens the door and shouts into the hall*] All right, everybody up. . . .

CORIE: [*Runs to him and pulls him back into the room*] Will you shut up and get into bed. . . . [*As she struggles with him, she tickles him, and* PAUL *falls to the floor behind the couch.* CORIE *closes the door behind her*] Get into bed. . . .

PAUL: You get in first.

CORIE: You're sick.

PAUL: Not *that* sick. . . . [*He lunges for her and she backs away against the door*]

CORIE: Stop it, Paul. . . .

PAUL: Come on, Corie. Let's break my fever. . . . [*He grabs her*]

CORIE: I said stop it! [*Struggling to get away*] I mean it, damn you. . . . Stop it! [*She gives him an elbow in the stomach and dodges away through the kitchen*]

PAUL: Gee, you're pretty when you're mean and rotten.

CORIE: Keep away from me, Paul. . . . [PAUL *moves toward her*] I'm warning you. . . . I'll scream. [CORIE *keeps the couch between her and* PAUL]

PAUL: [*Stops*] Shh. . . ! There's snow on the roof. We'll have an avalanche! . . .

CORIE: [*Dodging behind the chair*] You shouldn't be walking around like this. You've got a fever. . . .

PAUL: [*Moving to the chair*] Stand still! The both of you!

CORIE: [*Running up the stairs to the bathroom*] No, Paul . . . ! I don't like you when you're like this. [*She barricades herself in the bathroom*]

PAUL: [*Chasing her and pounding on the door*] Open this door!

CORIE: [*From the bathroom*] I can't . . . I'm scared.

PAUL: Of me?

CORIE: Yes.

PAUL: Why?

CORIE: Because it's not you anymore. . . . I want the old Paul back.

PAUL: That fuddy duddy?

CORIE: He's not a fuddy duddy. He's dependable and he's strong and he takes care of me and tells me how much I can spend and protects me from people like you. . . . [PAUL *suddenly has a brain storm and with great glee sneaks off into the bedroom*] And I just want him to know how much I love him. . . . And that I'm going to make everything here exactly the way he wants it. . . . I'm going to fix the hole in the skylight . . . and the leak in the closet. . . . And I'm going to put in a bathtub. . . . Because I want him to know how much I love him. . . . [*Slowly and cautiously opening the door*] Can you hear me, darling? . . . Paul? . . . [PAUL *appears on the skylight. He is crawling drunkenly along the ledge.* CORIE, *having gotten no answer, comes out of the bathroom and goes into the bedroom searching for* PAUL] Paul, are you all right?

> [*She comes out of the bedroom and crosses toward the front door. When she is beneath him,* PAUL *taps on the skylight and stands up.* CORIE, *looking up, sees him and screams*]

CORIE: [*Screams*] Paul. . . . You idiot. . . . Come down. . . . You'll kill yourself.

PAUL: [*Teetering on the ledge, yelling through the skylight*] I want to be a nut like everyone else in this building.

CORIE: [*Up on her knees on the couch, yelling back*] No! No, Paul! . . . I don't want you to be a nut. I want you to come down.

PAUL: I'll come down when you've said it again. . . . Loud and clear.

CORIE: What? . . . Anything, Paul. . . . Anything!

PAUL: My husband . . .

CORIE: "My husband . . ."

PAUL: Paul Bratter . . .

CORIE: "Paul Bratter . . ."

PAUL: . . . rising young attorney . . . [*He nearly falls off the ledge*]

CORIE: [*Screaming in fright*] ". . . rising young attorney . . ."

PAUL: . . . is a lousy stinkin' drunk. . . .

CORIE: ". . . is a lousy stinkin' drunk." . . . And I love him.

PAUL: And I love you, Corie. Even when I didn't like you, I loved you.

CORIE: [*Crossing to* PAUL] Then please, darling. . . . Please, come down.

PAUL: I. . . . I can't. . . . Not now.

CORIE: Why not?

PAUL: I'm going to be sick. . . . [*He looks around as if to find a place to be sick*]

CORIE: Oh, no!

PAUL: Oh, yes!

CORIE: [*Paces back and forth*] Paul. . . . Paul. . . . Don't move! I'll come out and get you.

PAUL: [*Holding on desperately*] Would you do that, Corie? Because I'm getting panicky!

CORIE: Yes. . . . Yes, darling, I'm coming. . . . [*She runs off into the bedroom*]

PAUL: Corie. . . . Corie. . . .

CORIE: [*Dashing out of the bedroom and down the stairs*] What, Paul? . . . What???

PAUL: Don't leave me. . . .

CORIE: You'll be all right, darling. Just hold on tight. And try to be calm. . . .

PAUL: How? What should I do?

CORIE: [*Ponders*] What should he do? [*To* PAUL] Sing, Paul!

PAUL: Sing??

CORIE: Sing. . . . Keep singing as loud as you can until I come out there. Promise me you'll keep singing, Paul. . . .

PAUL: Yes, yes. . . . I promise. . . . I'll keep singing. . . .

CORIE: [*Moving to the stairs*] But don't stop until I come out. . . . I love you, darling. . . . Keep singing, Paul. . . . Keep singing! [*She runs off into the bedroom*]

PAUL: [*Calling after her in desperation*] Corie, Corie, what song should I sing?? . . . Oh, God. . . . [*He pulls himself together*] "Shama, shama. . . ."

CURTAIN

Arsenic and Old Lace

JOSEPH KESSELRING

JOSEPH KESSELRING

The theatre, which is several thousand years old, has never produced anything quite like *Arsenic and Old Lace*. Nor have there ever been two more disarmingly homicidal characters on stage than the Brewster sisters of Joseph Kesselring's murder charade. Beaming with benevolence and as devout as any of the late Norman Rockwell's parishioners, they go about their charitable duties of proffering lethal elderberry wine to lonely old men with all the grace and innocent pleasure of hostessing a church tea. And not only has their erratic behavior brought permanent solace to the hapless victims, it also has established *Arsenic and Old Lace* as a modern classic and one of the theatre's all-time highest-grossing plays.

The macabre comedy made its debut at the Fulton Theatre, New York, on January 10, 1941, and ran for 1,444 performances. During that period, the original Broadway production and four touring companies grossed more than four million dollars. (Prevailing ticket prices were considerably lower than they are today.) In London, where it opened on December 23, 1942, the Kesselring murder romp established a new mark for an American importation—1,337 performances. During the harrowing period of the London blitz, when other West End offerings were forced to seek shelter in the provinces, *Arsenic and Old Lace* nonchalantly stayed right on at the Strand Theatre until 1946. The Brewster sisters, as usual, persevered.

Nor did these uncommonly genteel poison-cup artists confine their feral activities to the English-language stage: Through numerous foreign translations, they roamed the globe, providing chills and laughter in equal and profitable doses. And to add to the account: a motion picture version was made by Frank Capra in 1944, with Cary Grant abetted by Josephine Hull and Jean Adair in a recreation of their famed stage roles.

Arsenic and Old Lace nimbly combines the humor of farce with the mystery and suspense of melodrama. As Brooks Atkinson reported in *The New York Times:* "Mr. Kesselring has written a murder play as legitimate as farce-comedy. It is full of chuckles even when the scene is gruesome by nature. Swift, dry, satirical and exciting, it kept the first-night audience roaring with laughter."

Joseph Kesselring (1902–67) was born in New York City. At the age of twenty he joined the faculty of Bethel College, Kansas, as a professor of music and remained on campus until 1924. During the next eight years, he wrote, produced, and acted in vaudeville sketches and also turned out a number of published short stories and poems.

Aggie Appleby, Maker of Men (1933) was Kesselring's first play to reach Broadway. It was not a success, nor were his two succeeding attempts: *There's Wisdom in Women* (1935), and *Cross-Town* (1937).

Indeed, there was little in Kesselring's professional dossier to prepare Broadway and theatregoers for the riotous comedy and fresh invention of *Arsenic and Old Lace*. Consequently, rumors were rife that Howard Lindsay and Russel Crouse—the original producers of the play and who are represented in this collection by their dramatization of *Life With Father*—had transformed the show from straight melodrama to farce by adding humorous embellishments. Though they consistently denied this during their lifetimes, it was logical that the suspicion persisted, for Lindsay and Crouse had an almost unbeatable track record in the comedy department and were old and experienced hands at doctoring as well as at creating.

Subsequent to 1941, when the Brewster ménage took firm hold, Joseph Kesselring produced at least a half dozen other plays, but all are more or less forgotten. What matters most, however, is that he gave us *Arsenic and Old Lace*, a wildly satiric thriller, "one so funny that none of us will ever forget it."

ARSENIC AND OLD LACE was first produced at the Fulton Theatre, New York, on January 10, 1941, by Howard Lindsay and Russel Crouse. The cast was as follows:

ABBY BREWSTER	*Josephine Hull*
THE REV. DR. HARPER	*Wyrley Birch*
TEDDY BREWSTER	*John Alexander*
OFFICER BROPHY	*John Quigg*
OFFICER KLEIN	*Bruce Gordon*
MARTHA BREWSTER	*Jean Adair*
ELAINE HARPER	*Helen Brooks*
MORTIMER BREWSTER	*Allyn Joslyn*
MR. GIBBS	*Henry Herbert*
JONATHAN BREWSTER	*Boris Karloff*
DR. EINSTEIN	*Edgar Stehli*
OFFICER O'HARA	*Anthony Ross*
LIEUTENANT ROONEY	*Victor Sutherland*
MR. WITHERSPOON	*William Parke*

Directed by Bretaigne Windust
Setting and Costumes by Raymond Sovey

SCENE: *The living room of the Brewster home in Brooklyn.*
TIME: *1941*

ACT ONE

An afternoon in September.

ACT TWO

That same night.

ACT THREE

SCENE 1: *Later that night.*
SCENE 2: *Early the next morning.*

ACT ONE

The living room of the old Brewster home in Brooklyn. It is just as Victorian as the two sisters, ABBY *and* MARTHA BREWSTER, *who occupy the house with their nephew,* TEDDY.

Downstage, right, is the front door of the house, a large door with frosted glass panels in the upper half, beyond which, when it is open, can be seen the front porch and the lawn and shrubbery of the front garden of the Brewster house. On either side of the door are narrow windows of small panes of glass, curtained. Over the door is a small arch of colored glass. The remainder of the right wall is taken up by the first flight of stairs leading to the upper floors. In the upstage corner is a landing where the stairs turn to continue along the back wall of the room. In the right wall of the landing is an old-fashioned window, also looking out on to the porch. At the top of the stairs, along the back wall, is another landing, from which a door leads into the second-floor bedrooms, and an arch at the left end of this landing suggests the stairs leading to the third floor.

On stage level under this landing is a door which leads to the cellar. To the left of this door is a recess which contains a sideboard, on the top of which at either end are two small cabinets, where the sisters keep, among other things, bottles of elderberry wine. On the sideboard, among the usual impedimenta, are colored wine glasses. To the left of the recess is the door leading to the kitchen.

In the left wall of the room, there is a large window looking out over the cemetery of the neighboring Episcopal Church. This window has the usual lace curtains and thick drapes, which open and close by the use of a heavy curtain cord. Below the window is a large window seat, the lid of which has a thin pad of the same material as the drapes. When this lid is raised, the hinges creak audibly.

At the left of the foot of the stairs is a small desk, on which stands a dial telephone, and by this desk is a stool. Along the back wall, to the right of the cellar door, is an old-fashioned sofa. Left center in the room is a round table. There is a small chair right of this table and behind it, to the left of the table, a larger, comfortable armchair. On the walls are the usual pictures, including several portraits of the rather eccentric Brewster ancestors.

The time is 1941. Late afternoon in September. As the curtain rises, ABBY BREWSTER, *a plump little darling in her late sixties, is presiding at tea. She is sitting behind the table in front of a high silver tea service. At her left, in the comfortable armchair, is the* REV. DR. HARPER, *the elderly rector of the nearby church. Standing, at her right, thoughtfully sipping a cup of tea, is her nephew,* TEDDY, *in a frock coat, and wearing pince-nez attached to a black ribbon.* TEDDY *is in his forties and has a large mustache.*

ABBY: My sister Martha and I have been talking all week about your sermon last Sunday. It's really wonderful, Dr. Harper—in only two short years you've taken on the spirit of Brooklyn.

DR. HARPER: That's very gratifying, Miss Brewster.

ABBY: You see, living here next to the church all our lives, we've seen so many ministers come and go. The spirit of Brooklyn, we always say, is friendliness—and your sermons are not so much sermons as friendly talks.

TEDDY: Personally, I've always enjoyed my talks with Cardinal Gibbons—or have I met him yet?

ABBY: No, dear, not yet. [*Changing the subject*] Are the biscuits good?

TEDDY: Bully! [TEDDY *retires to the sofa, with his teacup and his thoughts*]

ABBY: Won't you have another biscuit, Dr. Harper?

DR. HARPER: Oh, no, I'm afraid I'll have no appetite for dinner now. I always eat too many of your biscuits just to taste that lovely jam.

ABBY: But you haven't tried the quince. We always put a little apple in with it to take the tartness out.

DR. HARPER: No, thank you.

ABBY: We'll send you over a jar.

DR. HARPER: No, no! You keep it here so I can be sure of having your biscuits with it.

ABBY: I do hope they don't make us use that imitation flour again. I mean with this war trouble threatening us. It may not be charitable of me, but I've almost come to the conclusion that this Mr. Hitler isn't a Christian.

DR. HARPER: [*With a sigh*] If only Europe were on another planet!

TEDDY: [*Sharply*] Europe, sir?

DR. HARPER: Yes, Teddy.

TEDDY: Point your gun the other way!

DR. HARPER: Gun?

ABBY: [*Trying to calm him*] Teddy!

TEDDY: To the West! There's your danger! There's your enemy! Japan!

DR. HARPER: Why, yes—yes, of course.

ABBY: Teddy!

TEDDY: No, Aunt Abby! Not so much talk about Europe and more about the Canal!

ABBY: Let's not talk about war. Have another cup of tea, dear?

TEDDY: No, thank you, Aunt Abby.

ABBY: Dr. Harper?

DR. HARPER: No, thank you. I must admit, Miss Abby, that war and violence seem far removed from these surroundings.

ABBY: It is peaceful here, isn't it?

DR. HARPER: Yes—peaceful. The virtues of another day—they're all here in this house. The gentle virtues that went out with candlelight and good manners and low taxes.

ABBY: [*Glancing about her contentedly*] It's one of the oldest houses in Brooklyn. It's just as it was when Grandfather Brewster built and furnished it—except for the electricity. We use it as little as possible—it was Mortimer who persuaded us to put it in.

DR. HARPER: [*Dryly*] Yes, I can understand that. Your nephew Mortimer seems to live only by electric light.

ABBY: The poor boy has to work so late. I understand he's taking Elaine to the theater again tonight. Teddy, your brother Mortimer will be here a little later.

TEDDY: [*Bearing his teeth in a broad grin*] Dee-lighted!

ABBY: We're so happy it's Elaine Mortimer takes to the theater with him.

DR. HARPER: Well, it's a new experience for me to wait up until three o'clock in the morning for my daughter to be brought home.

ABBY: Oh, Dr. Harper, I hope you don't disapprove of Mortimer.

DR. HARPER: Well . . .

ABBY: We'd feel so guilty if you did—sister Martha and I. I mean since it was here in our home that your daughter met Mortimer.

DR. HARPER: Of course, Miss Abby. And so I'll say immediately that I believe Mortimer himself to be quite a worthy gentleman. But I must also admit that I have watched the growing intimacy between him and my daughter with some trepidation. For one reason, Miss Abby.

ABBY: You mean his stomach, Dr. Harper?

DR. HARPER: Stomach?

ABBY: His dyspepsia—he's bothered with it so, poor boy.

DR. HARPER: No, Miss Abby, I'll be frank with you. I'm speaking of your nephew's unfortunate connection with the theater.

ABBY: The theater! Oh, no, Dr. Harper! Mortimer writes for a New York newspaper.

DR. HARPER: I know, Miss Abby, I know. But a dramatic critic is constantly exposed to the theater, and I don't doubt but that some of them do develop an interest in it.

ABBY: Well, not Mortimer! You need have no fear at all. Why, Mortimer hates the theater.

DR. HARPER: Really?

ABBY: Oh, yes! He writes awful things about the theater. But you can't blame him, poor boy. He was so happy writing about real estate, which he really knew something about, and then they just made him take this terrible night position.

DR. HARPER: My! My!

ABBY: But as he says, the theater can't last much longer and in the meantime, it's a living. [*Complacently*] I think if we give the theater another year or two. . . . [*There is a knock at the door. They all rise.* TEDDY *starts toward door*] Now who do you suppose that is? [*To* TEDDY] Never mind, Teddy, I'll go [*She goes to door and opens it*] Come right in, Mr. Brophy. [*Two uniformed policemen enter. They are* BROPHY *and* KLEIN]

BROPHY: Hello, Miss Brewster.

ABBY: How are you, Mr. Klein?

KLEIN: Very well, Miss Brewster.

TEDDY: [*To the policemen*] Gentlemen, what news have you brought me?

BROPHY: [*As he and* KLEIN *salute him*] Colonel, we have nothing to report.

TEDDY: [*Returning the salute*] Splendid! Thank you, gentlemen! At ease!

ABBY: [*To the policemen*] You know Dr. Harper.

KLEIN: Sure! Hello, Dr. Harper.

BROPHY: [*To* ABBY] We've come for the toys for the Christmas Fund.

ABBY: Oh, yes!

DR. HARPER: That's a splendid work you men do—fixing up discarded toys to give poor children a happier Christmas.

KLEIN: It gives us something to do when we have to sit around the station. You get tired playing cards and then you start cleaning your gun and the first thing you know you've shot yourself in the foot.

ABBY: Teddy, go upstairs and get that box in your Aunt Martha's room [TEDDY *starts for the stairs*] How is Mrs. Brophy today? Mrs. Brophy has been quite ill, Dr. Harper.

BROPHY: [*To* DR. HARPER] Pneumonia.

DR. HARPER: I'm sorry to hear that.

> [TEDDY *has reached the landing, where he stops and draws an imaginary sword*]

TEDDY: [*Shouting*] CHARGE! [*He charges up the stairs and exits through the door to the bedrooms. The others pay no attention to this*]

BROPHY: Oh, she's better now. A little weak still. . . .

ABBY: I'm going to get you some beef broth to take to her.

BROPHY: Don't bother, Miss Abby! You've done so much for her already.

ABBY: We made it this morning. Sister Martha is taking some to poor Mr. Benitzky right now. I won't be a minute. Sit down and be comfortable, all of you [*She goes into the kitchen.* DR. HARPER *sits again*]

BROPHY: She shouldn't go to all that trouble.

KLEIN: Listen, try to stop her or her sister from doing something nice—and for nothing! They don't even care how you vote. [*He sits on the window seat*]

DR. HARPER: When I received my call to Brooklyn and moved next door, my wife wasn't well. When she died—and for months before—well, if I know what pure kindness and absolute generosity are, it's because I've known the Brewster sisters.

[*At this moment* TEDDY *steps out on the balcony with a large brass bugle and blows a bugle call*]

BROPHY: [*To* TEDDY] Colonel, you promised not to do that!

TEDDY: But I have to call a Cabinet meeting to get the release of those supplies. [*He wheels and exits*]

BROPHY: He used to do that in the middle of the night. The neighbors raised Cain with us. They're a little afraid of him, anyway.

DR. HARPER: Oh, he's quite harmless.

KLEIN: Suppose he does think he's Teddy Roosevelt. There's a lot worse people he could think he was.

BROPHY: Damn shame—a nice family like this hatching a cuckoo.

KLEIN: Well, his father—the old girls' brother—was some sort of a genius, wasn't he? And their father—Teddy's grandfather—seems to me I've heard he was a little crazy, too.

BROPHY: Yeah—he was crazy like a fox. He made a million dollars.

DR. HARPER: Really? Here in Brooklyn?

BROPHY: Yeah—patent medicine. He was kind of a quack of some sort. Old Sergeant Edwards remembers him. He used the house here as sort of a clinic—tried 'em out on people.

KLEIN: Yeah, I hear he used to make mistakes occasionally, too.

BROPHY: The department never bothered him much because he was pretty useful on autopsies sometimes, especially poison cases.

KLEIN: Well, whatever he did, he left his daughters fixed for life. Thank God for that.

BROPHY: Not that they ever spend any of it on themselves.

DR. HARPER: Yes, I'm well acquainted with their charities.

KLEIN: You don't know a tenth of it. When I was with the Missing Persons Bureau I was trying to trace an old man that we never did find. . . . [*Rising*] Do you know there's a renting agency that's got this house down on its list for furnished rooms? They don't rent rooms, but you can bet that anybody who comes here looking for a room goes away with a good meal and probably a few dollars in their kick.

BROPHY: It's just their way of digging up people to do some good to.

[*The doorknob rattles, the door opens and* MARTHA BREWSTER *enters.*]

MARTHA *is also a plump, sweet, elderly woman with Victorian charm. She is dressed in the old-fashioned manner of* ABBY, *but with a high lace collar that covers her neck*]

MARTHA: [*Closing the door*] Well, isn't this nice?

BROPHY: Good afternoon, Miss Brewster.

MARTHA: How do you do, Mr. Brophy?

DR. HARPER: Good afternoon, Miss Brewster.

MARTHA: How do you do, Dr. Harper, Mr. Klein?

KLEIN: How do you do, Miss Brewster? We dropped in to get the Christmas toys.

MARTHA: Oh, yes! Teddy's Army and Navy. They wear out. They're all packed.

BROPHY: The Colonel's upstairs after them—it seems the Cabinet has to O.K. it.

MARTHA: Yes, of course. I hope Mrs. Brophy's better?

BROPHY: She's doing fine, ma'am. Your sister's getting some soup for me to take to her.

MARTHA: Oh, yes, we made it this morning. I just took some to a poor man who broke ever so many bones.

[ABBY *enters from the kitchen, carrying a small covered pail*]

ABBY: Oh, you're back, Martha. How was Mr. Benitzky?

MARTHA: It's pretty serious, I'm afraid. The doctor was there. He's going to amputate in the morning.

ABBY: [*Hopefully*] Can we be present?

MARTHA: No. I asked him, but he says it's against the rules of the hospital.

DR. HARPER: You couldn't be of any service—and you must spare yourselves something.

[TEDDY *enters on balcony with a box of toys and comes downstairs and puts the box down on the stool by the desk*]

ABBY: Here's the broth, Mr. Brophy. [*She hands the pail to* BROPHY]

BROPHY: Thank you, Miss Brewster.

ABBY: Be sure it's good and hot.

KLEIN: [*Looking into the box of toys*] This is fine—it'll make a lot of kids happy. [*Holding up a toy soldier*] That O'Malley boy is nuts about soldiers.

TEDDY: That's General Miles. I've retired him [KLEIN *holds up a toy ship*] What's this! The *Oregon!* [*He takes the ship from* KLEIN]

MARTHA: Put it back, dear.

TEDDY: But the *Oregon* goes to Australia.

ABBY: Now, Teddy. . . .

TEDDY: No, I've given my word to Fighting Bob Evans.

MARTHA: But, Teddy . . .

KLEIN: What's the difference what kid gets it—Bobby Evans, Izzy Cohen? We'll run along, ma'am, and thank you very much.

[*He picks up the box and he and* BROPHY *salute* TEDDY *and exit*]

ABBY: [*Closing door*] Not at all. Good-by.

MARTHA: Good-by.

DR. HARPER: I must be getting home.

ABBY: Before you go, Doctor—

[TEDDY *has reached the stair landing*]

TEDDY: CHARGE! [*He dashes up the stairs. At top, he stops and with a sweeping gesture over the balcony rail*] Charge the blockhouse! [*He dashes through the door*]

DR. HARPER: The blockhouse?

MARTHA: The stairs are always San Juan Hill.

DR. HARPER: Have you ever tried to persuade him that he wasn't Teddy Roosevelt?

ABBY: Oh, no!

MARTHA: He's so happy being Teddy Roosevelt.

ABBY: Once, a long time ago, we thought if he would be George Washington it would be a change and we suggested it to him.

MARTHA: But he stayed under his bed for days and wouldn't be anybody.

ABBY: And we'd so much rather he'd be Mr. Roosevelt than nobody.

DR. HARPER: Well, if he's happy—and what's more important, *you're* happy. You will see that he signs these. [*He takes some legal documents from his pocket and hands them to* ABBY]

MARTHA: What are they?

ABBY: Dr. Harper has made all the arrangements for Teddy to go to Happy Dale Sanitarium after we pass on.

MARTHA: But why should Teddy sign any papers now?

DR. HARPER: It's better to have it all settled. If the Lord should take you away suddenly, perhaps we couldn't persuade Teddy to commit himself and that would mean an unpleasant legal procedure. Mr. Witherspoon understands they're to be filed away until the time comes to use them.

MARTHA: Mr. Witherspoon? Who's he?

DR. HARPER: He's the Superintendent of Happy Dale.

ABBY: [*To* MARTHA] Dr. Harper has arranged for him to drop in tomorrow or the next day to meet Teddy.

DR. HARPER: I'd better be running along or Elaine will be over here looking for me. [*He leaves*]

ABBY: [*At door; calling after him*] Give Elaine our love. . . . And please don't think harshly of Mortimer because he's a dramatic critic. *Somebody* has to do those things.

MARTHA: [*Noticing the tea things*] Did you just have tea?

ABBY: [*As one who has a secret*] Yes—and dinner's going to be late, too.

    [TEDDY *enters on the balcony*]

MARTHA: So? Why?

    [TEDDY *starts downstairs*]

ABBY: Teddy! [*He stops halfway downstairs*] Good news for you! You're going to Panama and dig another lock for the canal.

TEDDY: Dee-lighted! Bully! Bully, bully! I shall prepare at once for the journey. [*He turns to go back upstairs, stops as if puzzled, then hurries to the landing and cries*] CHARGE! [*He rushes up and disappears*]

MARTHA: [*Elated*] Abby! While I was out?

ABBY: Yes, dear! I just couldn't wait for you. I didn't know when you'd be back and Dr. Harper was coming.

MARTHA: But all by yourself?

ABBY: Oh, I got along fine!

MARTHA: I'll run right downstairs and see! [*She starts happily for the cellar door*]

ABBY: Oh, no, there wasn't time. I was all alone.

    [MARTHA *looks around the room and toward the kitchen*]

MARTHA: Well?

ABBY: Martha . . . [*Coyly*] You just look in the window seat. [MARTHA *almost skips to the window seat, but just as she gets there, a knock is heard on the door. She stops. They both look toward the door.* ABBY *hurries to the door and opens it.* ELAINE HARPER *enters.* ELAINE *is an attractive girl in her twenties; she looks surprisingly smart for a minister's daughter*] Oh, it's Elaine! Come in, dear.

ELAINE: Good afternoon, Miss Abby. Good afternoon, Miss Martha. I thought Father was here.

MARTHA: He just this minute left. Didn't you meet him?

ELAINE: [*Pointing to the window*] No, I took the short cut through the cemetery. Mortimer hasn't come yet?

ABBY: No, dear.

ELAINE: Oh? He asked me to meet him here. Do you mind if I wait?

MARTHA: [*Cordially*] Not at all.

ABBY: Why don't you sit down?

MARTHA: But we really must speak to Mortimer about doing this to you.

ELAINE: Doing what?

MARTHA: He was brought up to know better. When a gentleman is taking a young lady out he should call for her at her house.

ELAINE: Oh, there's something about calling for a girl at a parsonage that discourages any man who doesn't embroider.

ABBY: He's done this too often—we're going to speak to him!

ELAINE: Don't bother! After young men whose idea of night life was to take me to prayer meeting, it's wonderful to go to the theater almost every night of my life.

MARTHA: It's comforting for us too, because if Mortimer has to see some of those plays he has to see, at least he's sitting next to a minister's daughter.

ABBY: My goodness, Elaine, what must you think of us—not having tea cleared away by this time. [*She picks up the tea tray and starts toward the kitchen*]

MARTHA: [*To* ABBY] Now don't bother with anything in the kitchen until Mortimer comes. Then I'll help you [ABBY *exits into the kitchen. To* ELAINE] He should be here any minute now.

ELAINE: Yes. Father must have been surprised not to find me at home—I'd better run over and say good night to him.

MARTHA: It's a shame you missed him.

ELAINE: If Mortimer comes you tell him I'll be right back. [*She has opened the door, but sees* MORTIMER *just outside*] Hello, Mort!

[MORTIMER BREWSTER *walks in. He is a dramatic critic*]

MORTIMER: Hello, Elaine. [*As he passes her going toward* MARTHA, *thus placing himself between* ELAINE *and* MARTHA, *he reaches back and pats* ELAINE *on the fanny*] Hello, Aunt Martha. [*He kisses her*]

MARTHA: [*Calling off*] Abby, Mortimer's here!

MORTIMER: [*To* ELAINE] Were you going somewhere?

ELAINE: I was just going over to tell Father not to wait up for me.

MORTIMER: I didn't know that was still being done, even in Brooklyn.

[ELAINE *closes the door, staying inside, as* ABBY *comes in from the kitchen*]

ABBY: Hello, Mortimer.

MORTIMER: Hello, Aunt Abby. [*He kisses her*]

ABBY: How are you, dear?

MORTIMER: All right. And you look well. You haven't changed much since yesterday.

ABBY: It was yesterday, wasn't it? We're seeing a great deal of you lately. [*She laughs and looks at* ELAINE] Sit down! Sit down! [*It looks as though she's going to settle down, too*]

MARTHA: [*Knowingly*] Abby—haven't we something to do in the kitchen? You know—the tea things.

ABBY: [*Getting it*] Oh, yes! Yes! [*Backing toward kitchen, joining* MARTHA] Well—you two just make yourselves at home. Just. . . .

MARTHA: Just make yourselves at home!

> [ABBY *and* MARTHA *exit happily into the kitchen.* ELAINE *moves over to* MORTIMER *ready to be kissed*]

ELAINE: Well, can't you take a hint?

MORTIMER: No. That was pretty obvious. A lack of inventiveness, I should say.

ELAINE: Yes—that's exactly what you'd say! [*She walks away, ruffled*]

MORTIMER: [*Not noticing the ruffle*] Where do you want to go for dinner?

ELAINE: I don't care. I'm not very hungry.

MORTIMER: Well, I just had breakfast. Suppose we wait until after the show?

ELAINE: But that'll make it pretty late, won't it?

MORTIMER: Not with the little stinker we're seeing tonight. From what I've heard about it, we'll be at Bleeck's by ten o'clock.

ELAINE: You ought to be fair to these plays.

MORTIMER: Are these plays fair to me?

ELAINE: I've never seen you walk out on a musical.

MORTIMER: That musical isn't opening tonight.

ELAINE: [*Disappointed*] No?

MORTIMER: Darling, you'll have to learn the rules. With a musical there are always four changes of title and three postponements. They liked it in New Haven but it needs a lot of work.

ELAINE: Oh, I was hoping it was a musical.

MORTIMER: You have such a light mind.

ELAINE: Not a bit! Musicals somehow have a humanizing effect on you [*He gives her a look*] After a serious play we join the proletariat in the subway and I listen to a lecture on the drama. After a musical you bring me home in a taxi and you make a few passes.

MORTIMER: Now wait a minute, darling, that's a very inaccurate piece of reporting.

ELAINE: Oh, I will admit that after the Behrman play you told me I had authentic beauty—and that's a hell of a thing to say to any girl. It wasn't until after our first musical you told me I had nice legs. And I have, too. [MORTIMER *stares at her legs for a moment, then walks over and kisses her*]

MORTIMER: For a minister's daughter you know a lot about life. Where did you learn it?

ELAINE: [*Casually*] In the choir loft.

MORTIMER: I'll explain that to you sometime, darling—the close connection between eroticism and religion.

ELAINE: Religion never gets as high as the choir loft. Which reminds me, I'd better tell Father please not to wait up for me tonight.

MORTIMER: [*Almost to himself*] I've never been able to rationalize it.

ELAINE: What?

MORTIMER: My falling in love with a girl who lives in Brooklyn.

ELAINE: Falling in love? You're not stooping to the articulate, are you?

MORTIMER: [*Ignoring this*] The only way I can regain my self-respect is to keep you in New York.

ELAINE: Did you say *keep?*

MORTIMER: No, I've come to the conclusion you're holding out for the legalities.

ELAINE: I can afford to be a good girl for quite a few years yet.

MORTIMER: And I can't wait that long. Where could we be married in a hurry—say tonight?

ELAINE: I'm afraid Father will insist on officiating.

MORTIMER: Oh, God! I'll bet your father could make even the marriage service sound pedestrian.

ELAINE: Are you, by any chance, writing a review of it?

MORTIMER: Forgive me, darling. It's an occupational disease. [*She smiles at him lovingly and walks toward him. He meets her halfway and they forget themselves for a moment in a sentimental embrace and kiss. When they come out of it, he turns away from her quickly*] I may give that show tonight a good notice!

ELAINE: Now, darling, don't pretend you love me *that* much.

[MORTIMER *looks at her with polite lechery*]

MORTIMER: Be sure to tell your father not to wait up tonight.

ELAINE: [*Aware that she can't trust either of them*] I think tonight I'd better tell him to wait up.

MORTIMER: [*Reassuringly*] Darling, I'll telephone Winchell to publish the banns.

ELAINE: Nevertheless . . .

MORTIMER: All right, everything formal and legal. But not later than next month.

ELAINE: Darling. [*She kisses him*] I'll talk it over with Father and set the date.

MORTIMER: Oh, no! We'll have to consult the Zolotow list. There'll be a lot of other first nights in October.

[TEDDY *enters from above and comes down the stairs carrying his bugle and dressed in tropical clothes and a solar topee. He sees* MORTIMER]

TEDDY: Hello, Mortimer! [*He goes to* MORTIMER *and they shake hands*]

MORTIMER: [*Gravely*] How are you, Mr. President?

TEDDY: Bully, thank you. Just bully. What news have you brought me?

MORTIMER: Just this, Mr. President—the country is squarely behind you.

TEDDY: [*Beaming*] Yes, I know. Isn't it wonderful? [*He shakes* MORTIMER'S *hand again*] Well, good-by. [*He shakes hands with* ELAINE] Good-by.

ELAINE: Where are you off to, Teddy?

TEDDY: Panama. [*He exits through the cellar door.* ELAINE *looks at* MORTIMER *inquiringly*]

MORTIMER: Panama's the cellar. He digs locks for the Canal down there.

ELAINE: You're so sweet with him—and he's very fond of you.

MORTIMER: Well, Teddy was always my favorite brother.

ELAINE: Favorite? Were there more of you?

MORTIMER: There's another brother—Jonathan.

ELAINE: I never heard of him. Your aunts never mention him.

MORTIMER: No, we don't like to talk about Jonathan. He left Brooklyn very early—by request. Jonathan was the kind of boy who liked to cut worms in two—with his teeth.

ELAINE: [*Shuddering*] What became of him?

MORTIMER: I don't know. He wanted to be a surgeon like Grandfather, but he wouldn't go to medical school—and his practice got him into trouble.

[ABBY *enters from the kitchen*]

ABBY: Aren't you going to be late for the theater?

MORTIMER: We're skipping dinner. [*Consulting his wristwatch, then to* ELAINE] We won't have to start for half an hour.

ABBY: Then I'll leave you two alone again.

ELAINE: Don't bother, darling. I'm going to run over to speak to Father. [*To* MORTIMER] Before I go out with you, he likes to pray over me a little. I'll be right back—I'll cut through the cemetery.

MORTIMER: Well, if the prayer isn't too long, I'd have time to lead you beside distilled waters.

[ELAINE *laughs and exits*]

ABBY: [*Happily*] That's the first time I ever heard you quote the Bible! We knew Elaine would be a good influence on you.

MORTIMER: Oh, by the way—I'm going to marry her.

ABBY: Oh, Mortimer! [*She runs to him and embraces him. Then she dashes to the kitchen door, as* MORTIMER *crosses toward the window*] Martha, Martha! Come right in here! I've got wonderful news for you! [MARTHA *hurries in from the kitchen*] Mortimer and Elaine are going to be married!

MARTHA: Married! Oh, Mortimer. [*She runs over to* MORTIMER, *who is looking out the window, embraces and kisses him*]

ABBY: We hoped it would happen just like this!

MARTHA: Elaine must be the happiest girl in the world!

MORTIMER: [*Looking out the window*] Happy! Just look at her leaping over those gravestones! [*He and* ABBY *wave to* ELAINE, *outside. He starts to turn away from the window but his attention is drawn to something*] Say! What's that?

MARTHA: [*Looking out*] What's what, dear?

MORTIMER: See that statue there? That's a *horundinida carnina*.

MARTHA: Oh, no—that's Emma B. Stout ascending to heaven.

MORTIMER: No—standing on Mrs. Stout's left ear. That bird—that's a red-crested swallow. I've only seen one of those before in my life.

ABBY: I don't know how you can think of birds now—with Elaine and the engagement and everything.

MORTIMER: It's a vanishing species. Thoreau was very fond of them. By the way, I left a large envelope around here last week. It's one of the chapters of my book on Thoreau. Have you seen it?

MARTHA: Well, if you left it here, it must be here somewhere.

> [MORTIMER *starts searching the room, looking in drawers, cupboards, desk, etc.*]

ABBY: When are you going to be married? What are your plans? There must be something more you can tell us about Elaine.

MORTIMER: Elaine? Oh, yes, Elaine thought it was brilliant.

MARTHA: What, Mortimer?

MORTIMER: My chapter on Thoreau!

ABBY: Well, when Elaine comes back I think we ought to have a little celebration. We must drink to your happiness. Martha, isn't there some of that Lady Baltimore cake left?

MARTHA: Oh, yes!

ABBY: And we'll open a bottle of wine.

MARTHA: And to think that it happened in this room! [*She exits into the kitchen*]

MORTIMER: Now, where could I have put that . . . ?

ABBY: Well, with your fiancée sitting beside you tonight, I do hope the play will be something you can enjoy for once. It may be something romantic. What's the name of it?

> [MORTIMER *is still searching for the envelope with the chapter in it*]

MORTIMER: *Murder Will Out!*

ABBY: Oh, dear!

> [*She disappears into the kitchen.* MORTIMER *doesn't notice her absence and goes on talking. He is beside the window seat*]

MORTIMER: When the curtain goes up the first thing you see will be a dead body.... [*He lifts the window seat and sees one. Not believing it, he drops the window seat again and turns away. He looks back quickly toward the window seat, opens it again, stares in. He goes slightly mad for a moment. He drops the window seat again and sits on it, as if to hold it down.* ABBY *comes into the room, carrying the silencer and tablecloth, which she puts on a chair and turns to the table, clearing it of its impedimenta. When* MORTIMER *speaks to her it is in a somewhat strained voice*] Aunt Abby!

ABBY: Yes, dear?

MORTIMER: You were going to make plans for Teddy to go to that sanitarium—Happy Dale.

ABBY: Yes, dear, it's all arranged. Dr. Harper was here today and brought the things for Teddy to sign. Here they are.

[*She takes the papers from the sideboard and hands them to him*]

MORTIMER: He's got to sign them right away!

ABBY: That's what Dr. Harper thinks. ... [MARTHA *enters from the kitchen, carrying a tray with the table silver. Throughout the scene the two sisters go ahead setting the table—three places*] Then there won't be any legal difficulties after we pass on.

MORTIMER: [*Glancing through the papers*] He's got to sign them this minute! He's down in the cellar—get him up here right away.

MARTHA: There's no such hurry as that.

ABBY: When he starts working on the Canal you can't get his mind on anything else.

MORTIMER: Teddy's got to go to Happy Dale *now—tonight!*

MARTHA: Oh, no, Mortimer! That's not until after we're gone!

MORTIMER: Right away, I tell you!—right away!

ABBY: Mortimer, how can you say such a thing? Why, as long as we live we won't be separated from Teddy.

MORTIMER: [*Trying to be calm*] Listen, darlings, I'm frightfully sorry, but I've got some shocking news for you. [*The sisters stop work and look at him with some interest*] Now, we've all got to try to keep our heads. You know, we've sort of humored Teddy because we thought he was harmless.

MARTHA: Why, he *is* harmless!

MORTIMER: He *was* harmless. That's why he has to go to Happy Dale—why he has to be confined.

ABBY: Mortimer, why have you suddenly turned against Teddy?—your own brother!

MORTIMER: You've got to know sometime. It might as well be now. Teddy's killed a man!

MARTHA: Nonsense, dear.

[MORTIMER *rises and points to the window seat*]

MORTIMER: There's a body in the window seat!

ABBY: [*Not at all surprised*] Yes, dear, we know.

MORTIMER: You *know?*

MARTHA: Of course, dear, but it has nothing to do with Teddy.

[*Relieved, they resume setting the table*]

ABBY: Now, Mortimer, just forget about it—forget you ever saw the gentleman.

MORTIMER: *Forget?*

ABBY: We never dreamed you'd peek.

MORTIMER: But who is he?

ABBY: His name's Hoskins—Adam Hoskins. That's really all I know about him—except that he's a Methodist.

MORTIMER: That's all you know about him? Well, what's he doing here? What happened to him?

MARTHA: He died.

MORTIMER: Aunt Martha, men don't just get into window seats and die.

ABBY: No, he died first.

MORTIMER: But how?

ABBY: Mortimer, don't be so inquisitive! The gentleman died because he drank some wine with poison in it.

MORTIMER: How did the poison get in the wine?

MARTHA: We put it in wine because it's less noticeable. When it's in tea it has a distinct odor.

MORTIMER: *You* put it in the wine?

ABBY: Yes. And I put Mr. Hoskins in the window seat because Dr. Harper was coming.

MORTIMER: So you knew what you'd done! You didn't want Dr. Harper to see the body!

ABBY: Not at tea! That wouldn't have been very nice! Now you know the whole thing and you can forget all about it. I do think Martha and I have the right to our own little secrets.

MARTHA: And don't you tell Elaine! [MORTIMER *stands looking at his aunts, stunned.* MARTHA *turns to* ABBY] Oh, Abby, while I was out I dropped in on Mrs. Schultz. She's much better, but she would like to have us take Junior to the movies again.

ABBY: We must do that tomorrow or the next day. [*They start toward the kitchen*]

MARTHA: This time we'll go where *we* want to go, Junior's not going to drag me into another one of those scary pictures.

ABBY: They shouldn't be allowed to make pictures just to frighten people. [*They exit into the kitchen.* MORTIMER, *dazed, looks around the room, goes to the telephone and dials a number*]

MORTIMER: [*Into telephone*] City desk. . . . Hello, Al. Do you know who this is? [*Pause*] That's right. Say, Al, when I left the office, I told you where I was going, remember? [*Pause*] Well, where did I say? [*Pause*] Uh-huh. Well, it would take me about half an hour to get to Brooklyn. What time have you got? [*He looks at his watch*] That's right. I must be here. [*He hangs up, sits for a moment, then suddenly leaps out of the chair toward the kitchen*] Aunt Martha! Aunt Abby! Come in here! [*The two sisters bustle in.* MORTIMER *turns to them in great excitement*] What are we going to do? What are we going to do?

MARTHA: What are we going to do about what, dear?

MORTIMER: There's a body in there!

ABBY: Yes, Mr. Hoskins'.

MORTIMER: Good God, I can't turn you over to the police. But what am I going to do?

MARTHA: Well, for one thing, stop being so excited.

ABBY: And for pity's sake stop worrying. We told you to forget the whole thing.

MORTIMER: *Forget it?* My dear Aunt Abby, can't I make you realize that something has to be done!

ABBY: [*A little sharply*] Mortimer, you behave yourself! You're too old to be flying off the handle like this!

MORTIMER: But Mr. Hotchkiss . . .

ABBY: Hoskins, dear.

MORTIMER: Well, whatever his name is, you can't leave him there!

MARTHA: We don't intend to, dear.

ABBY: Teddy's down in the cellar now digging a lock.

MORTIMER: You mean you're going to bury Mr. Hotchkiss in the cellar?

MARTHA: Why, of course, dear. That's what we did with the others.

MORTIMER: Aunt Martha, you can't bury Mr. . . . *Others?*

ABBY: The other gentlemen.

MORTIMER: When you say others—do you mean—others? More than one others?

MARTHA: Oh, yes, dear. Let me see, this is eleven, isn't it, Abby?

ABBY: No, dear, this makes twelve.

[MORTIMER *backs up and sinks stunned on the stool beside the desk*]

MARTHA: Oh, I think you're wrong, Abby. This is only eleven.

ABBY: No. When Mr. Hoskins first came in, it occurred to me that he would make a round dozen.

MARTHA: Well, you really shouldn't count the first one.

ABBY: Oh, I was counting the first one. So that makes it twelve.

> [*The telephone rings.* MORTIMER, *in a daze, turns toward it and without picking up the receiver speaks*]

MORTIMER: Hello! [*It rings the second time and he realizes it's the telephone and picks up the receiver*] Hello. Oh, hello, Al. My, it's good to hear your voice!

ABBY: [*To* MARTHA] But he *is* in the cellar, dear.

MORTIMER: [*To aunts*] Ssh! [*Into telephone*] Oh, no, Al, I'm as sober as a lark. No, I just called you because I was feeling a little Pirandello. Pirandel. . . . You wouldn't know, Al. Look, I'm glad you called. Get hold of George right away. He's got to review the play tonight. I can't make it. No, you're wrong, Al. I'll tell you about it tomorrow. . . . No— Well, George has got to cover the play tonight! This is my department and I'm running it! You get hold of George! [*He hangs up and sits for a moment, trying to collect himself*] Now, let's see, where were we? [*He suddenly leaps from his chair*] Twelve!

MARTHA: Yes, Abby thinks we ought to count the first one and that makes twelve.

MORTIMER: Now, let me get this. . . . [*Grabs* MARTHA *and sits her in a chair*] Who was the first one?

ABBY: Mr. Midgely. He was a Baptist.

MARTHA: Of course, I still think we can't take full credit for him because he just died.

ABBY: Martha means without any help from us. You see, Mr. Midgely came here looking for a room.

MARTHA: It was right after you moved to New York.

ABBY: And it didn't seem right that your nice room should go to waste when there were so many people who needed it.

MARTHA: He was such a lonely old man.

ABBY: All his kith and kin were dead and it left him so forlorn and unhappy.

MARTHA: And then when his heart attack came, and he sat dead in that chair, so peaceful—remember, Martha?—well, we decided then and there that if we could help other lonely old men to find that peace, we would.

> [MORTIMER *is immersed in their story for a moment*]

MORTIMER: He dropped dead, right in that chair. How awful for you!

MARTHA: Not at all! It was rather like old times. Your grandfather always used to have a cadaver or two around the house. You see, Teddy had been digging in Panama and he thought Mr. Midgely was a yellow fever victim.

ABBY: That meant he had to be buried immediately.

MARTHA: So we all took him down to Panama and put him in the lock.

[*Rising*] You see, that's why we told you not to bother about it. We know exactly what's to be done.

MORTIMER: And that's how all this started? That man walking in here and dropping dead?

ABBY: Well, we realized we couldn't depend on that happening again.

MARTHA: Remember those jars of poison that have been up on the shelves in Grandfather's laboratory all these years?

ABBY: You know the knack your Aunt Martha has for mixing things. You've eaten enough of her piccalilli!

MARTHA: Well, Mortimer, for a gallon of elderberry wine I take a teaspoonful of arsenic, and add a half-teaspoonful of strychnine, and then just a pinch of cyanide.

MORTIMER: [*Appraisingly*] Should have quite a kick.

ABBY: As a matter of fact, one of our gentlemen found time to say, "How delicious!"

MARTHA: Well, I'll have to get things started in the kitchen. [*She starts out*]

ABBY: [*To* MORTIMER] I wish you could stay to dinner, dear.

MARTHA: I'm trying out a new recipe.

MORTIMER: I couldn't eat a thing.

> [MARTHA *exits into the kitchen*]

ABBY: [*Calling after* MARTHA] I'll come and help you. [*She turns to* MORTIMER, *relieved*] Well, I feel better now that you understand. You have to wait for Elaine, don't you? [*She smiles*] How happy you must be! I'll leave you alone with your thoughts.

> [ABBY *exits, smiling.* MORTIMER *stands dazed and then summons his courage and goes to the window seat, opens it and peeks in, then closes it and backs away. He backs around the table and is still looking at the window seat when there is a knock at the door, immediately followed by* ELAINE's *entrance. This, however, does not arouse him from his thought. She smiles at him softly*]

ELAINE: I'm sorry I took so long, dear. [*She starts slowly toward him. As she approaches he looks in her direction and as her presence dawns on him he speaks*]

MORTIMER: Oh, it's you!

ELAINE: Don't be cross, darling! Father saw I was excited—so I told him about us and that made it hard for me to get away. [*She goes to him and puts her arm around him*] But, listen, darling—he's not going to wait up for me tonight.

MORTIMER: Elaine—you run on back home and I'll call you up tomorrow.

ELAINE: Tomorrow!

MORTIMER: [*Irritated*] You know I always call you up every day or two.

ELAINE: But we're going to the theater tonight.

MORTIMER: No—no, we're not.

ELAINE: Well, why not?

MORTIMER: Elaine, something's come up.

ELAINE: What, darling? Mortimer—you've lost your job!

MORTIMER: No—no! I haven't lost my job! I'm just not covering the play tonight. Now, you run along home, Elaine.

ELAINE: But I've got to know what's happened. Certainly, you can tell me.

MORTIMER: No, I can't, dear.

ELAINE: But if we're going to be married. . . .

MORTIMER: Married?

ELAINE: Have you forgotten that not fifteen minutes ago you proposed to me?

MORTIMER: I did? Oh—yes! Well, as far as I know, that's still on. But you go home now. I've got to do something.

ELAINE: Listen, you can't propose to me one minute and throw me out of the house the next.

MORTIMER: I'm not throwing you out of the house, darling. Will you get out of here?

ELAINE: No, I won't get out of here. Not until I've had some kind of explanation!

> [*She stalks across the room and almost sits on the window seat. He intercepts her*]

MORTIMER: Elaine! [*The telephone rings. He goes to it and answers*] Hello! Oh, hello, Al. Hold on just a minute, will you, Al? I'll be right with you. All right, it's important! But it can wait a minute, can't it? Hold on! [*He puts the receiver down on the table and goes back to* ELAINE] Elaine, you're a sweet girl and I love you. But I have something on my mind now and I want you to go home and wait until I call you.

ELAINE: Don't try to be masterful!

MORTIMER: [*Annoyed to the point of being literate*] When we're married and I have problems to face I hope you're less tedious and uninspired!

ELAINE: And when we're married, *if* we're married, I hope I find you adequate! [*She exits*]

MORTIMER: Elaine! [*He runs out on the porch after her, calling*] Elaine! [*He rushes back in, slams the door, and runs across to call to her out of the window. When he kneels on the window seat, he suddenly remembers Mr. Hoskins, and leaps off it. He dashes toward the kitchen, then he remembers Al is waiting on the telephone. He hurries across the room and picks up the receiver*] Al . . . ? Al . . . ? [*He hangs up and starts to dial again, when the doorbell rings. He lifts the receiver and speaks into it*] Hello . . . Hello . . . ?

> [ABBY *enters from the kitchen, followed by* MARTHA]

ABBY: It's the doorbell ringing. [*She goes to door and opens it, as* MORTIMER *hangs up and starts to dial*] How do you do? Come in.

    [MR. GIBBS *enters. A very disgruntled old man*]

GIBBS: I understand you have a room to rent.

ABBY: Yes. Won't you step in?

GIBBS: Are you the lady of the house?

ABBY: Yes, I'm Miss Brewster. This is my sister, another Miss Brewster.

GIBBS: My name is Gibbs.

ABBY: Oh, won't you sit down? I'm sorry we're just setting the table for dinner.

MORTIMER: [*Into the telephone*] Hello ... Let me talk to Al again. City desk! *Al! City desk!* What ... I'm sorry ... wrong number. [*He hangs up and dials again*]

GIBBS: May I see the room?

MARTHA: Why don't you sit down and let's get acquainted?

GIBBS: That won't do much good if I don't like the room.

ABBY: Is Brooklyn your home?

GIBBS: Haven't got a home. Live in a hotel. Don't like it.

MORTIMER: [*Into the telephone*] Hello. City desk.

MARTHA: Are your family Brooklyn people?

GIBBS: Haven't got any family.

ABBY: All alone in the world? Why, Martha.... [MARTHA *crosses to the sideboard for the wine*] Well, you've come to just the right place. Do sit down. [*She eases* GIBBS *into a chair by the table*]

MORTIMER: [*Into the telephone*] Hello, Al? Mort. We got cut off. ... Al, I can't cover the play tonight. That's all there is to it. I can't!

MARTHA: What church do you go to? There's an Episcopal church practically next door.

GIBBS: I'm Presbyterian. Used to be.

MORTIMER: [*Into the telephone*] What's George doing in Bermuda? Certainly, I told him he could go to Bermuda. ... It's my department, isn't it? Well, Al, you've got to get somebody. Who else is there around the office?

GIBBS: [*Rising*] Is there always this much noise?

MARTHA: Oh, he doesn't live with us.

MORTIMER: [*Into the telephone*] There must be *somebody* around the place. How about the office boy? You know, the bright one. The one we don't like. Well, look around the office ... I'll hold on.

GIBBS: I'd really like to see the room.

ABBY: It's upstairs. Won't you try a glass of our wine before we start up?

GIBBS: Never touch it.

MARTHA: We make this ourselves. It's elderberry wine.

GIBBS: [*To* MARTHA] Elderberry. [*Looking at the wine*] Haven't tasted elderberry wine since I was a boy. Thank you.

> [*He sits.* ABBY *pours a glass of wine for* MR. GIBBS]

MORTIMER: [*Into the telephone*] Well, there must be some printers around. Look, Al, the fellow who sets my copy. He ought to know about what I'd write. His name is Joe. He's the third machine from the left. . . . But, Al, he might turn out to be another Burns Mantle!

GIBBS: Do you have your own elderberry bushes?

MARTHA: No, but the cemetery's full of them.

MORTIMER: [*Into the telephone*] No, I'm not drinking, but I'm going to start now! [*He hangs up and starts for the sideboard. When he sees the wine bottle on the table, he rushes and gets a glass from the sideboard and starts pouring himself a glass of wine*]

MARTHA: [*Seeing* MORTIMER *pouring the wine*] Mortimer, eh . . . eh . . . eh!

MORTIMER: [*Engrossed in pouring the wine*] Huh?

MARTHA: [*To* MORTIMER] Eh . . . eh . . . eh! . . .

ABBY: [*Seeing what* MORTIMER *is doing*] Mortimer! Not that!

> [*She drags his arm down as he is about to drink.* MORTIMER *puts his glass down, then realizes that it must be the poisoned wine. Suddenly, he sees* MR. GIBBS *is about to drink.* MORTIMER *utters a blood-curdling cry and points his finger at* MR. GIBBS, *who puts his glass down on the table and stares at* MORTIMER, *terrified*]

MORTIMER: Get out of here! Do you want to be killed? Do you want to be poisoned? Do you want to be murdered?

> [*In the middle of the above speech,* MR. GIBBS *starts to run and dashes out of the house, with* MORTIMER *chasing him.* MORTIMER *slams the door behind* MR. GIBBS *and leans against it weakly*]

ABBY: [*To* MORTIMER] Now, you've spoiled everything.

MORTIMER: You can't do things like that! I don't know how I can explain this to you. But it's not only against the law, it's wrong! It's not a nice thing to do! People wouldn't understand. *He* wouldn't understand.

MARTHA: Abby, we shouldn't have told Mortimer.

MORTIMER: What I mean is . . . Well—this has developed into a very bad habit.

ABBY: Now, Mortimer, we don't try to stop you from doing the things you like to do. I don't see why you should interfere with us.

> [*The telephone rings.* MORTIMER *answers it*]

MORTIMER: [*Into the telephone*] Hello? Yes, Al. . . . All right, Al, I'll see the first act and I'll pan the hell out of it. But, Al, you've got to do this for me. Get hold of O'Brien. Our lawyer . . . the head of our legal department! Have him meet me at the theater. Now, don't let me down. O.K.

I'm starting now. [*He hangs up, then speaks to his aunts*] I've got to go to the theater. I can't get out of it. But before I go will you promise me something?

MARTHA: We'd have to know what it was first.

MORTIMER: I love you very much and I know you love me. You know I'd do anything in the world for you and I want you to do this little thing for me.

ABBY: What do you want us to do?

MORTIMER: Don't *do* anything. I mean—don't do *anything!* Don't let anyone in this house—and leave Mr. Hoskins right where he is.

MARTHA: Why?

MORTIMER: I want time to think—and I've quite a little to think about. You know I wouldn't want anything to happen to you.

ABBY: Well, what on earth could happen to us?

MORTIMER: Anyway—you'll do that for me, won't you?

MARTHA: Well, we were planning to hold services before dinner.

MORTIMER: Services?

MARTHA: [*A little indignant*] You don't think we'd bury Mr. Hoskins without a full Methodist service? He *was* a Methodist.

MORTIMER: Can't that wait until I get back?

ABBY: Oh, then you could join us!

MORTIMER: Yes! Yes!

ABBY: You'll enjoy the services, Mortimer—especially the hymns. [*To* MARTHA] Remember how beautifully Mortimer sang in the choir before his voice changed?

MORTIMER: And you're not going to let anybody in this house until I get back? It's a promise.

MARTHA: Well. . . .

ABBY: Oh, Martha—we can do that now that Mortimer's cooperating with us. All right, Mortimer.

MORTIMER: Have you got any paper? [ABBY *goes to the desk and gets a sheet of stationery*] I'll be back as soon as I can. [MORTIMER *takes out the commitment papers, looks at them*] There's a man I've got to see.

ABBY: Here's some stationery. Will this do?

MORTIMER: [*Taking it*] That's fine. I can save some time if I write my review on the way to the theater. [*He hurries out.* MARTHA *closes the door behind him.* ABBY *returns to setting the table*]

MARTHA: Mortimer didn't seem quite himself today.

ABBY: [*Lighting the candelabra*] Well, that's only natural—I think I know why.

MARTHA: [*Going up to landing to close the drapes on the window of the landing*] Why?

ABBY: He's just become engaged to be married. I suppose that always makes a man nervous.

MARTHA: I'm so happy for Elaine. And their honeymoon ought to give Mortimer a real vacation. I don't think he got much rest this summer. [*She comes down into the room again, turns off the electric lights, straightens the telephone on the desk, lights the standing lamp beside the desk*]

ABBY: Well, at least he didn't go kiting off to China or Spain.

MARTHA: I could never understand why he wanted to go to those places.

ABBY: Well, I think to Mortimer the theater has always seemed pretty small potatoes. He needs something really big to criticize—something like the human race.

MARTHA: Abby, if Mortimer's coming back for the services for Mr. Hoskins, we'll need another hymnal. There's one in my room. [*She starts upstairs*]

ABBY: It's really my turn to read the services, but since you weren't here when Mr. Hoskins came I want you to do it.

[MARTHA *stops on the stairs*]

MARTHA: [*Pleased*] That's very nice of you, dear. Are you sure you want me to?

ABBY: It's only fair.

MARTHA: I think I'll wear my black bombazine—and Mother's old brooch. [*She starts up again and* ABBY *starts toward the kitchen. The doorbell rings*]

ABBY: I'll go, dear.

MARTHA: [*Hushed*] We promised Mortimer we wouldn't let anyone in.

ABBY: Who do you suppose it is?

MARTHA: Wait a minute—I'll look. [*She is at the landing and turns to the landing window and peeks out the curtains*] It's two men—and I've never seen them before.

ABBY: Are you sure?

MARTHA: [*Peeking out again*] There's a car at the curb—they must have come in that.

ABBY: Let me look!

[*She hurries up the stairs. There is a knock at the door.* ABBY *peeks out the window*]

MARTHA: Do you recognize them?

ABBY: They're strangers to me.

MARTHA: We'll just have to pretend we're not home.

[*There is another knock, then the door is slowly opened and a tall man walks into the center of the room. He walks in with assurance and ease as though the room were familiar to him. He stands and looks about him—in every direction but that of the stairs. There is something sinister about the man—something that brings a slight chill in his presence. It is in his walk, his bearing and his strange resemblance to Boris Karloff. From the stair landing,* ABBY *and* MARTHA *watch him, almost afraid to speak. Having completed his survey of the room, the man turns and addresses someone outside the front door*]

JONATHAN: Come in, Doctor. [DR. EINSTEIN *enters. He is somewhat ratty in his appearance. His face wears the benevolent smirk of a man who lives in a haze of alcohol. There is something about him that suggests the unfrocked priest. He stands just inside the door, timid but expectant*] This is the home of my youth. [DR. EINSTEIN *looks about him timidly*] As a boy, I couldn't wait to escape from this house. And now I'm glad to escape back into it.

EINSTEIN: Yah, Chonny, it's a good hideout.

JONATHAN: The family must still live here. There's something so unmistakably Brewster about the Brewsters. I hope there's a fatted calf awaiting the return of the prodigal.

EINSTEIN: Yah, I'm hungry. [*He sees the fatted calf in the form of the two glasses of wine*] Look, Chonny! Drinks!

JONATHAN: As if we were expected! A good omen.

[EINSTEIN *almost scampers to the table, passing* JONATHAN, *also on his way to the table. As they are about to reach for the glasses,* ABBY *speaks*]

ABBY: Who are you? What are you doing here?

[EINSTEIN *and* JONATHAN *turn and see the two sisters*]

JONATHAN: Aunt Abby! Aunt Martha! It's Jonathan.

MARTHA: You get out of here!

JONATHAN: I'm Jonathan! Your nephew, Jonathan!

ABBY: Oh, no, you're not! You're nothing like Jonathan, so don't pretend you are! You just get out of here! [*A little belligerent, she comes two or three steps down the stairs*]

JONATHAN: Yes, Aunt Abby. I *am* Jonathan. And this is Dr. Einstein.

ABBY: And he's not Dr. Einstein either.

JONATHAN: Not Dr. Albert Einstein—Dr. Herman Einstein.

ABBY: Who are you? You're not our nephew, Jonathan!

JONATHAN: I see you're still wearing the lovely garnet ring that Grandma Brewster bought in England. [ABBY *gasps, looks at the ring and then looks toward* MARTHA] And you, Aunt Martha, still the high collar—to hide the scar where Grandfather's acid burned you.

[MARTHA's *hand goes to her throat. The two sisters stare at each other, then back at* JONATHAN]

MARTHA: His voice is like Jonathan's.

ABBY: Have you been in an accident?

JONATHAN: No. . . . [*His hand goes up to his neck*] My face. . . . [*He clouds*] Dr. Einstein is responsible for that. [*The two sisters look at* EINSTEIN] He's a plastic surgeon. [*Flatly*] He changes people's faces.

MARTHA: But I've seen that face before. [*To* ABBY] Remember when we took the little Schultz boy to the movies—and I was so frightened. It was that face!

[JONATHAN *grows tense and looks toward* EINSTEIN]

EINSTEIN: Chonny—easy! [*He goes quickly between* JONATHAN *and his aunts*] Don't worry! The last five years I give Chonny three faces. I give him another one right away. The last face—I saw that picture, too—just before I operate. And I was intoxicated.

JONATHAN: [*With a growing and dangerous intensity*] You see, Doctor— what you've done to me. Even my own family. . . .

EINSTEIN: [*To calm him*] Chonny—you're home!—in this lovely house! [*To the aunts*] How many times he tells me about Brooklyn—about this house—about his aunts that he loves so much! [*To* JONATHAN] They know you, Chonny. [*To the aunts*] You know it's Jonathan. Speak to him! Tell him so!

[ABBY *starts slowly downstairs*]

ABBY: Well—Jonathan—it's been a long time—what have you been doing all these years?

[MARTHA *starts to follow her cautiously*]

MARTHA: Yes, Jonathan, where have you been?

JONATHAN: [*Recovering his composure*] England, South Africa, Australia— the last five years, Chicago. Dr. Einstein and I have been in business together there.

ABBY: Oh! We were in Chicago for the World's Fair.

MARTHA: [*For want of something to say*] We found Chicago awfully warm.

EINSTEIN: Yah—it got hot for us, too.

JONATHAN: [*Turning on the charm*] It's wonderful to be in Brooklyn again. And you—Abby—Martha—you don't look a day older. Just as I remembered you—sweet, charming, hospitable. [*They exchange a quick look*] And dear Teddy? [*He indicates with his hand a lad of eight or ten*] Did he go into politics? [*Turns to* EINSTEIN] My little brother, Doctor, was determined to become President.

ABBY: Oh, Teddy's fine! Just fine. Mortimer's well, too.

JONATHAN: [*Grimly*] I know about Mortimer. I've seen his picture at the head of his column. He's evidently fulfilled all the promise of his early nasty nature.

ABBY: [*Defensively*] We're very fond of Mortimer.

[*There is a pause*]

MARTHA: [*Uneasily*] Well, Jonathan, it's very nice to have seen you again.

JONATHAN: [*Expanding*] Bless you, Aunt Martha! It's good to be home again.

[*He sits down. The two women look at each other with dismay*]

ABBY: Martha, we mustn't let what's on the stove boil over. [*She tugs at* MARTHA]

MARTHA: Yes. If you'll excuse us for just a minute, Jonathan—unless you're in a hurry to go somewhere.

[JONATHAN *looks at her balefully.* ABBY *exits to the kitchen taking the glasses of wine with her.* MARTHA *takes the bottle of wine from the table, puts it in the compartment of the sideboard, then hurries out after* ABBY]

EINSTEIN: Well, Chonny, where do we go from here? We got to think fast. The *police!* They got pictures of that face. I got to operate on you right away. We got to find some place—and we got to find some place for Mr. Spenalzo, too.

JONATHAN: Don't waste any worry on that rat.

EINSTEIN: But, Chonny, we got a hot stiff on our hands.

JONATHAN: Forget Mr. Spenalzo!

EINSTEIN: But we can't leave a dead body in the rumble seat! You shouldn't have killed him, Chonny. He's a nice fellow—he gives us a lift—and what happens . . . ? [*He gestures strangulation*]

JONATHAN: He said I looked like Boris Karloff! That's your work, Doctor. You did that to me!

EINSTEIN: Now, Chonny—we find a place somewhere—I fix you up quick!

JONATHAN: *Tonight!*

EINSTEIN: Chonny, I got to eat first. I'm hungry. I'm weak.

[ABBY *enters and comes spunkily up to* JONATHAN. MARTHA *hovers in the doorway*]

ABBY: Jonathan, we're glad that you remembered us and took the trouble to come and say "Hello." But you were never happy in this house and we were never happy while you were here. So we've just come in to say goodby.

JONATHAN: [*Smoothly*] Aunt Abby, I can't say your feeling toward me comes as a surprise. I've spent a great many hours regretting the heartaches I must have given you as a boy.

ABBY: You were quite a trial to us, Jonathan.

JONATHAN: But my great disappointment is for Dr. Einstein. [*The aunts look at* EINSTEIN] I promised him that no matter how rushed we were in passing through Brooklyn, I would take the time to bring him here for one of Aunt Martha's homecooked dinners.

[MARTHA *rises to this a bit*]

MARTHA: Oh?

ABBY: I'm sorry. I'm afraid there wouldn't be enough.

MARTHA: Abby, it's a good-sized pot roast.

JONATHAN: Pot roast!

MARTHA: I think the least we can do is . . .

JONATHAN: Thank you, Aunt Martha! We'll stay to dinner!

ABBY: Well, we'll hurry it along.

MARTHA: Yes! [*She exits into the kitchen*]

ABBY: If you want to freshen up, Jonathan—why don't you use the washroom in Grandfather's laboratory?

JONATHAN: Is that still there?

ABBY: Oh, yes! Just as he left it. Well, I'll help Martha get things started— since we're all in a hurry. [*She exits into kitchen*]

EINSTEIN: Well, we get a meal, anyway.

JONATHAN: Grandfather's laboratory! [*He looks upstairs*] And just as it was! Doctor, a perfect operating room!

EINSTEIN: Too bad we can't use it.

JONATHAN: After you finished with me. . . . Doctor, we could make a fortune here! The laboratory—that large ward in the attic—ten beds, Doctor—and Brooklyn is crying for your talents.

EINSTEIN: Why work yourself up, Chonny? Anyway, for Brooklyn we're a year too late.

JONATHAN: You don't know this town, Doctor. Practically everybody in Brooklyn needs a new face.

EINSTEIN: But so many of the old faces are locked up.

JONATHAN: A very small percentage—and the boys in Brooklyn are famous for paying generously to stay out of jail.

EINSTEIN: Take it easy, Chonny. Your aunts—they don't want us here.

JONATHAN: We're here for dinner, aren't we?

EINSTEIN: Yah—but after dinner?

JONATHAN: Leave that to me, Doctor, I'll handle it. This house will be our headquarters for years.

EINSTEIN: Oh, that would be beautiful, Chonny! This nice quiet house! Those aunts of yours—what sweet ladies! I love them already. [*Starts to the door*] I get the bags, yah?

JONATHAN: [*Stopping him*] Doctor! We must wait until we're invited.

EINSTEIN: But you just said . . .

JONATHAN: We'll be invited.

EINSTEIN: And if they say no?

JONATHAN: [*Grimly*] Doctor—two helpless old women . . . ? [*He sits on the sofa*]

EINSTEIN: [*Taking out flask, and relaxing on the window seat*] It's like comes true a beautiful dream. Only I hope you're not dreaming [*Takes a swig from the flask*] It's so peaceful.

JONATHAN: [*Stretching out on the sofa*] Yes, Doctor, that's what makes this house so perfect for us. It's so peaceful.

> [TEDDY *enters from the cellar, blows a blast on his bugle, then marches to the stairs and on up to the landing as the two men look at his tropical garb with some astonishment*]

TEDDY: [*On the landing*] CHARGE! [*He rushes up the stairs and off through the balcony door.* JONATHAN *has risen, watching him.* EINSTEIN *stares and takes another hasty swig from his flask*]

CURTAIN

ACT TWO

> JONATHAN, *smoking an after-dinner cigar, is occupying the most comfortable chair, completely at his ease.* ABBY *and* MARTHA, *sitting together on the window seat, are giving him a nervous attention in the attitude of people who wish their guests would go home.* EINSTEIN *is relaxed and happy. The dinner dishes have been cleared and the room has been restored to order.*

JONATHAN: Yes, those five years in Chicago were the busiest and happiest of my life.

EINSTEIN: And from Chicago, we go to South Bend, Indiana.

> [*He shakes his head as though he wishes they hadn't.* JONATHAN *gives him a look*]

JONATHAN: They wouldn't be interested in our experience in Indiana.

ABBY: Well, Jonathan, you've led a very interesting life, I'm sure. But we shouldn't have allowed you to talk so late. [*She starts to rise*]

JONATHAN: My meeting Dr. Einstein in London, I might say, changed my whole life. Remember, I had been in South Africa in the diamond business—then Amsterdam, the diamond market. I wanted to go back to South Africa—and Dr. Einstein made it possible for me.

EINSTEIN: A good job, Chonny. [*To the aunts*] When we take off the bandages, he look so different the nurse had to introduce me.

JONATHAN: I loved that face. I still carry the picture with me. [*He produces a picture from his pocket, looks at it a moment and then hands it to* MARTHA, *who takes it.* ABBY *looks over her shoulder*]

ABBY: That looks more the way you used to look, but still I wouldn't know you.

[MARTHA *returns the picture to* JONATHAN]

JONATHAN: I think we'll go back to that face, Doctor.

EINSTEIN: Yah! It's safe now.

ABBY: [*Rising*] I know that you both want to get to—where you're going.

MARTHA: Yes. [*She rises, too, hintingly*]

JONATHAN: My dear aunts—I am so full of that delicious dinner that I just can't move a muscle. [*He takes a puff of his cigar*]

EINSTEIN: Yes, it's nice here. [*He relaxes a little more*]

MARTHA: After all, it's very late and . . .

[TEDDY *at the head of the stairs, wearing his solar topee, carrying an open book and another solar topee*]

TEDDY: I found it! I found it!

JONATHAN: What did you find, Teddy?

TEDDY: [*Descending*] The story of my life—my biography. [*He goes to* EINSTEIN] Here's the picture I was telling you about, General. Here we are, both of us. [*He shows the open book to* EINSTEIN] "President Roosevelt and General Goethals at Culebra Cut." That's me, General, and that's you.

[EINSTEIN *looks at the picture*]

EINSTEIN: My, how I've changed!

[TEDDY *looks at* EINSTEIN, *a little puzzled, but makes the adjustment*]

TEDDY: Well, you see that picture hasn't been taken yet. We haven't even started work on Culebra Cut. We're still digging locks. And now, General, we will go to Panama and inspect the new lock. [*He puts the book down and hands* EINSTEIN *the solar topee*]

ABBY: No, Teddy—not to Panama!

EINSTEIN: We go some other time. Panama's a long way off.

TEDDY: Nonsense, it's just down in the cellar.

JONATHAN: The cellar?

MARTHA: We let him dig the Panama Canal in the cellar.

TEDDY: General Goethals, as President of the United States, Commander-in-Chief of the Army and Navy, and the man who gave you this job, I demand that you accompany me on the inspection of the new lock.

JONATHAN: Teddy! I think it's time for you to go to bed.

[TEDDY *turns and looks at* JONATHAN]

TEDDY: I beg your pardon. Who are you?

JONATHAN: I'm Woodrow Wilson. Go to bed.

TEDDY: No—you're not Wilson. But your face is familiar. [JONATHAN *stiffens*] Let me see. You're not anyone I know now. Perhaps later—on my hunting trip to Africa—yes, you look like someone I might meet in the jungle.

[JONATHAN *begins to burn*]

ABBY: It's your brother, Jonathan, dear. . . .

MARTHA: He's had his face changed.

TEDDY: So that's it—a nature faker!

ABBY: Perhaps you had better go to bed—he and his friend have to get back to their hotel.

[JONATHAN *looks at* ABBY *and then, rising, turns to* EINSTEIN]

JONATHAN: General Goethals—inspect the Canal.

EINSTEIN: All right, Mr. President. We go to Panama.

TEDDY: [*On his way to the cellar door*] Bully! Bully! [EINSTEIN *follows him.* TEDDY *opens the cellar door*] Follow, me, General. It's down south, you know.

[EINSTEIN *puts on the solar topee*]

EINSTEIN: Well—bon voyage.

[TEDDY *exits,* EINSTEIN *follows him off. When the cellar door closes* JONATHAN *turns to* ABBY]

JONATHAN: Aunt Abby, I must correct your misapprehension. You spoke of our hotel. We have no hotel. We came directly here. . . .

MARTHA: Well, there's a very nice little hotel just three blocks down the street. . . .

JONATHAN: Aunt Martha, this is my home!

ABBY: But, Jonathan, you can't stay here. [JONATHAN *gives her a look*] We need our rooms.

JONATHAN: You need them?

ABBY: Yes, for our lodgers.

JONATHAN: [*Alarmed for a moment*] Are there lodgers in this house?

MARTHA: Well, not just now, but we plan to have some.

JONATHAN: Then my old room is still free.

ABBY: But, Jonathan, there's no place for Dr. Einstein.

JONATHAN: He'll share the room with me.

ABBY: No, Jonathan, I'm afraid you can't stay here.

JONATHAN: [*Coldly*] Dr. Einstein and I need a place to sleep. This afternoon, you remembered that as a boy I could be disagreeable. It wouldn't be pleasant for any of us if . . .

MARTHA: [*To* ABBY, *frightened*] Perhaps we'd better let them stay here tonight.

ABBY: Well, just overnight, Jonathan.

JONATHAN: That's settled. Now, if you'll get my room ready . . .

MARTHA: [*Starting upstairs*] It only needs airing out. . . .

ABBY: [*Following*] We keep it ready to show to our lodgers. I think you and Dr. Einstein will find it comfortable.

JONATHAN: You have a most distinguished guest in Dr. Einstein. I'm afraid you don't appreciate his skill. But you shall. In a few weeks you'll see me looking like a very different Jonathan.

MARTHA: [*Stopping on the balcony*] But he can't operate here!

JONATHAN: When Dr. Einstein and I get organized . . . when we resume practice . . . I forgot to tell you—we're turning Grandfather's laboratory into an operating room. We expect to be very busy.

ABBY: [*On the balcony*] Jonathan, we're not going to let you turn this house into a hospital.

JONATHAN: A hospital! Heavens, no! It will be a beauty parlor!

[EINSTEIN *enters excitedly from the cellar*]

EINSTEIN: Hey, Chonny! Down in the cellar. . . . [*He sees the aunts and stops*]

JONATHAN: Dr. Einstein. My dear aunts have invited us to live with them.

EINSTEIN: Oh, you fixed it?

ABBY: Well, you're sleeping here tonight.

JONATHAN: Please get our room ready immediately.

MARTHA: Well. . . .

ABBY: For tonight.

[*They exit to the third floor*]

EINSTEIN: Chonny, when I was in the cellar, what do you think I find?

JONATHAN: What?

EINSTEIN: The Panama Canal.

JONATHAN: The Panama Canal!

EINSTEIN: Chonny, it just fits Mr. Spenalzo! A hole Teddy dug, four feet wide and six feet long.

JONATHAN: [*Pointing*] Down there?

EINSTEIN: You'd think they knew we were bringing Mr. Spenalzo along. Chonny, that's hospitality.

JONATHAN: Rather a good joke on my aunts, Doctor, their living in a house with a body buried in the cellar.

EINSTEIN: How do we get him in, Chonny?

JONATHAN: Yes, we can't just walk him through the door. [*Looks from door to window*] We'll drive the car up between the house and the cemetery and, after they've gone to bed, we'll bring Mr. Spenalzo in through the window.

EINSTEIN: Bed! Just think! We got a bed tonight. [*He takes out his bottle and starts to take a swig*]

JONATHAN: Easy, Doctor. Remember you're operating tomorrow. And this time you'd better be sober.

EINSTEIN: I fix you up beautiful.

JONATHAN: And if you don't . . .

[ABBY *and* MARTHA *enter on the balcony*]

ABBY: Your room's all ready, Jonathan.

JONATHAN: [*Crossing to the outside door*] Then you can go to bed. We're moving the car up behind the house.

MARTHA: It will be all right where it is—until morning.

[EINSTEIN *has opened the door*]

JONATHAN: I don't want to leave it in the street—that might be against the law. [*He and* EINSTEIN *exit*]

MARTHA: Abby, what are we going to do?

ABBY: [*Coming downstairs*] Well, we're not going to let them stay more than one night in this house, for one thing. What would the neighbors think? People coming into this place with one face and going out with another.

MARTHA: What are we going to do about Mr. Hoskins?

ABBY: Oh, yes, Mr. Hoskins. It can't be very comfortable for him in there. He's been so patient, the poor dear. I think Teddy ought to get Mr. Hoskins downstairs right away.

MARTHA: Abby, I will not invite Jonathan to the services.

ABBY: Oh, no, dear—we'll wait until they've gone to bed and then come down and hold the services.

[TEDDY *enters from the cellar*]

TEDDY: General Goethals was very pleased. He said the Canal was just the right size.

ABBY: Teddy, there's been another yellow fever victim.

TEDDY: Dear me—that will be a shock to the General.

MARTHA: Then we mustn't tell him about it.

TEDDY: But it's his department.

ABBY: No, we mustn't tell him about it. It would just spoil his visit, Teddy.

TEDDY: I'm sorry, Aunt Abby. It's out of my hands—he'll have to be told. Army regulations, you know.

ABBY: No, Teddy, we'll have to keep it a secret.

MARTHA: Yes!

TEDDY: A state secret?

ABBY: Yes, a state secret.

MARTHA: Promise?

TEDDY: You have the word of the President of the United States. Cross my heart and hope to die. [*Following the childish formula, he crosses his heart and spits*] Now let's see—how are we going to keep it a secret?

ABBY: Well, Teddy, you go back down in the cellar and when I turn out the lights—when it's dark—you come up and take the poor man down to the Canal. Go along, Teddy.

MARTHA: We'll come down later and hold services.

TEDDY: You may announce the President will say a few words. [*He starts to the cellar door, then stops*] Where is the poor devil?

MARTHA: In the window seat.

TEDDY: It seems to be spreading. We've never had yellow fever *there* before. [*He exits into the cellar*]

ABBY: When Jonathan and Dr. Einstein come back, let's see whether we can't get them to go to bed right away.

MARTHA: Yes, then they'd be asleep by the time we got dressed for the funeral. Abby, I haven't even seen Mr. Hoskins yet.

ABBY: Oh, my goodness, that's right—you were out. Well, you just come right over and see him now. [*They go to the window seat*] He's really very nice-looking—considering he's a Methodist.

   [MARTHA *is about to lift the window seat when* JONATHAN *thrusts his head through the window curtains. They jump back in fright*]

JONATHAN: We're bringing our luggage through here. [*He climbs into the room*]

ABBY: Your room's waiting for you. You can go right up.

   [*Two bags and a large instrument case are passed through the window.* JONATHAN *puts them down*]

JONATHAN: I'm afraid we don't keep Brooklyn hours. You two run along to bed.

ABBY: You must be very tired—both of you—and we don't go to bed this early.

JONATHAN: Well, you should. It's time I came home to take care of you.

MARTHA: Oh, we weren't planning to go until . . .

JONATHAN: [*Sternly*] Did you hear me say go to bed, Aunt Martha? [MARTHA *retreats upstairs.* EINSTEIN *comes through the window*] Take the bags upstairs. [*Putting the instrument case beside the window seat*] The instruments can go to the laboratory in the morning. [*He closes the window*] Now we're all going to bed.

[EINSTEIN *starts upstairs, reaching the upper landing, where he stops*]

ABBY: I'll wait till you're up, then turn out the lights. [*She retreats toward the light switch*]

JONATHAN: Another flight, Doctor. Run along, Aunt Martha. [MARTHA *goes to the upstairs door and opens it.* EINSTEIN *goes through the arch with the bags and* JONATHAN *stops on the landing, looks down at* ABBY] All right, Aunt Abby.

ABBY: [*Looking toward cellar door*] I'll be right up.

JONATHAN: Now, Aunt Abby! Turn out the lights.

[ABBY *snaps out the lights.* JONATHAN *waits until* ABBY *has come upstairs and she and* MARTHA *have gone through their door and closed it, then turns and goes up through the arch. The stage is entirely dark.* TEDDY *opens the cellar door, looks out and sees everything is safe, then switches the cellar light on and moves toward the window seat. In the darkness we hear the familiar creak of the window seat as it is opened. A few seconds later we see the faint shadow of* TEDDY *carrying a burden, passing through the cellar door, then this door is closed behind him shutting off the light. After a second or two* JONATHAN *and* EINSTEIN *come out on the upper landing.* JONATHAN *lights a match and in its light he comes down the stairs*]

EINSTEIN: [*On the balcony, listening at the aunts' door*] It's all right, Chonny. [*He comes downstairs*]

JONATHAN: I'll open the window. You go around and hand him through.

EINSTEIN: Chonny, he's too heavy for me. You go outside and push. I stay here and pull. Then together we get him down to Panama.

JONATHAN: All right. But be quick. I'll take a look around outside the house. When I tap on the glass you open the window. [JONATHAN *goes out front door, closing it behind him.* [EINSTEIN *moves toward the window, holding lighted match. He bumps into the table, burns his finger, and we hear him suck the burnt place. He continues to window in darkness. Then we hear a crash*]

EINSTEIN: Ach! Himmel! [*He lights a match and in its wavering light we see that he has fallen into the window seat*] Who left this open, the dummkopf? [*We hear tapping on the glass, as he closes the window seat and then we hear him open the window*] Chonny? O.K. Allez oop! Wait a minute, Chonny. You lost a leg somewhere. Ach! Now I got him [*There is a crash of a body and then the sound of a "Sh-h!" from outside*] That was me, Chonny. I schlipped.

JONATHAN'S VOICE: [*Off*] Quiet!

EINSTEIN: Well, his shoe came off. [*Pause*] All right, Chonny. I got him. Whew! [*In the silence there is a knock at the door*] Chonny! Somebody at the door! Go quick. No, I manage here. Go quick!

> [*There is a second knock at the door. There is a moment's silence and we hear the creak of the window seat, the noise of* EINSTEIN *struggling with Mr. Spenalzo's body, then another creak of the window seat. There is a third knock at the door, then it is opened and by the dim glow of a remote street light we see* ELAINE *peering into the room*]

ELAINE: [*Calling softly*] Miss Abby! Miss Martha! [*In the dim path of light she comes in and moves toward the center of the room, calling toward the staircase*] Miss Abby! Miss Martha! [JONATHAN *enters hurriedly and we hear the closing of the door.* ELAINE *whirls and gasps*] Who is it? Is that you, Teddy? [JONATHAN *advances on her*] Who *are you?*

JONATHAN: Who are *you?*

ELAINE: I'm Elaine Harper—I live next door!

JONATHAN: What are you doing here?

> [EINSTEIN *circles around* ELAINE *toward front door*]

ELAINE: I came over to see Miss Abby and Miss Martha.

JONATHAN: Turn on the lights, Doctor. [EINSTEIN *switches on the lights*] I'm afraid you've chosen an untimely moment for a social call. [*He moves past her toward the window expecting to see Mr. Spenalzo there. He doesn't, and this bewilders him*]

ELAINE: [*Trying to summon courage*] I think you'd better explain what you're doing here.

JONATHAN: We happen to live here. [JONATHAN *looks out the window in his search for the missing Mr. Spenalzo*]

ELAINE: You don't live here. I'm in this house every day and I've never seen you before. Where are Miss Abby and Miss Martha? What have you done to them?

JONATHAN: Perhaps we had better introduce ourselves. May I present Dr. Einstein. . . .

ELAINE: Dr. Einstein!

> [JONATHAN *moves toward the table and looks under the table cloth for Mr. Spenalzo*]

JONATHAN: A surgeon of great distinction—and—[*Not finding Mr. Spenalzo*] something of a magician.

ELAINE: And I suppose you're going to tell me you're Boris . . .

> [JONATHAN *stiffens and speaks sharply*]

JONATHAN: I'm Jonathan Brewster!

ELAINE: [*Almost with fright*] Oh—you're Jonathan!

JONATHAN: I see you've heard of me.

ELAINE: Yes—just this afternoon—for the first time. . . .

JONATHAN: And what did they say about me?

ELAINE: Only that there was another brother named Jonathan—that's all that was said. Well, that explains everything. Now that I know who you are I'll run along back home [*She runs to the door and finds it locked*]—if you'll kindly unlock the door.

> [JONATHAN *goes to the door and unlocks it.* ELAINE *starts toward the door, but* JONATHAN *turns and stops her with a gesture*]

JONATHAN: "That explains everything?" Just what did you mean by that? Why did you come here at this time of night?

ELAINE: I thought I saw someone prowling around the house. I suppose it was you.

> [JONATHAN *reaches back and locks the door again, leaving the key in the lock.* EINSTEIN *and* JONATHAN *both move slowly toward* ELAINE]

JONATHAN: You thought you saw someone prowling about the house?

ELAINE: Yes—weren't you outside? Is that your car?

JONATHAN: Oh, you saw someone at the car!

ELAINE: Yes.

JONATHAN: What else did you see?

ELAINE: Just that—that's all. That's why I came over here. I wanted to tell Miss Abby to call the police. But if it was you, and that's your car, I don't need to bother Miss Abby. I'll be running along. [*She takes a step toward the door.* JONATHAN *blocks her way*]

JONATHAN: What was the man doing at the car?

ELAINE: I don't know. You see I was on my way over here.

JONATHAN: I think you're lying.

EINSTEIN: Chonny, I think she tells the truth. We let her go now, huh?

JONATHAN: I think she's lying. Breaking into a house at this time of night. I think she's dangerous. She shouldn't be allowed around loose. [*He seizes* ELAINE's *arm. She pulls back*]

ELAINE: [*In a hoarse frightened tone*] Take your hands off me. . . .

JONATHAN: And now, young lady . . .

> [*The cellar door suddenly opens and* TEDDY *comes through and closes it with a bang. They all jump.* TEDDY *looks them over*]

TEDDY: [*Blandly*] It's going to be a private funeral. [*He starts for the steps*]

ELAINE: [*Struggling*] Teddy! Teddy! Tell these men who I am!

TEDDY: That's my daughter, Alice.

> [*She struggles to get away from* JONATHAN]

ELAINE: No! No! Teddy! Teddy!. [*Still struggling*]]

TEDDY: Now, Alice, don't be a tomboy. Don't play rough with the gentle-men. [*He has reached the landing on the stairs, draws his imaginary sword*] CHARGE! [*He charges up the stairs and off*]

ELAINE: Teddy! Teddy!

[JONATHAN *pulls her arm behind her back and claps a hand over her mouth*]

JONATHAN: Doctor, your handkerchief! [JONATHAN *takes* EINSTEIN's *hand-kerchief in his free hand and starts to stuff it in her mouth. As he releases his hand for this,* ELAINE *lets out a scream.* JONATHAN *claps his hand over her mouth again*] Doctor, the cellar!

[EINSTEIN *opens the cellar door, then dashes for the light switch and turns off the lights.* JONATHAN *forces* ELAINE *into the cellar and waits until* EINSTEIN *takes hold of her. In the dark, we hear*]

ABBY: What's the matter?

MARTHA: What's happening down there?

[JONATHAN *closes the cellar door on* EINSTEIN *and* ELAINE *as* ABBY *turns on the lights from the balcony switch and we see* ABBY *and* MARTHA *on the balcony. They are dressed for Mr. Hoskins' funeral. Mr. Hoskins is being paid the respect of deep and elaborate mourning*]

ABBY: What's the matter? What are you doing?

[JONATHAN *is holding the cellar door*]

JONATHAN: We caught a burglar—a sneak thief. Go back to your room.

ABBY: I'll call the police! [*She starts downstairs*]

JONATHAN: We've called the police. We'll handle this. You go back to your room. [*They hesitate*] Did you hear me? [ABBY *turns as if to start upstairs when the knob of the outside door is rattled followed by a knock. They all turn and look toward the door.* ABBY *starts down again*] Don't answer that!

[ELAINE *rushes out of the cellar.* EINSTEIN *follows, grabbing for her*]

ELAINE: Miss Abby! Miss Martha!

MARTHA: Why, it's Elaine!

[*There is a peremptory knock at the door.* ABBY *hurries over, unlocks it and opens it.* MORTIMER *enters carrying a suitcase. At the sight of him* ELAINE *rushes into his arms. He drops the suitcase and puts his arms around her.* EINSTEIN *and* JONATHAN *have withdrawn toward the kitchen door, ready to make a run for it*]

ELAINE: Oh, Mortimer, where have you been?

MORTIMER: To the Nora Bayes Theatre—and I should have known better. [*He sees* JONATHAN] My God, I'm still there!

ABBY: This is your brother Jonathan—and this is Dr. Einstein.

[MORTIMER *surveys the roomful*]

MORTIMER: I know this isn't a nightmare, but what is it?

JONATHAN: I've come back home, Mortimer.

MORTIMER: [*Looking at him and then at* ABBY] Who did you say that was?

ABBY: It's your brother Jonathan. He's had his face changed. Dr. Einstein performed the operation on him.

MORTIMER: Jonathan, you always were a horror, but do you have to look like one?

[JONATHAN *takes a step toward him.* EINSTEIN *pulls his sleeve*]

EINSTEIN: Easy, Chonny! Easy!

JONATHAN: Mortimer, have you forgotten the things I used to do to you? Remember the time you were tied to the bedpost—the needles—under your fingernails. I suggest you don't ask for trouble now.

MORTIMER: Yes, I remember. I remember you as the most detestable, vicious, venomous form of animal life I ever knew.

[JONATHAN *gets tense and takes a step toward* MORTIMER. ABBY *steps between them*]

ABBY: Now, don't you boys start quarreling again the minute you've seen each other.

MORTIMER: There won't be any fight, Aunt Abby. Jonathan, you're not wanted here, so get out!

JONATHAN: Dr. Einstein and I have been invited to stay.

MORTIMER: Oh, no—not in this house!

ABBY: Just for tonight.

MORTIMER: I don't want him anywhere near me.

ABBY: But we did invite them for tonight, Mortimer, and it wouldn't be very nice to go back on our word.

MORTIMER: [*Reluctantly giving in*] All right, tonight—but the first thing in the morning—out. Where are they sleeping?

ABBY: We put them in Jonathan's old room.

MORTIMER: [*Picking up his suitcase and starting up the stairs*] That's my old room. I'm moving into that room. I'm here to stay.

MARTHA: Oh, Mortimer, I'm so glad!

EINSTEIN: [*To* JONATHAN] Chonny, we sleep down here.

MORTIMER: You bet your life you'll sleep down here.

EINSTEIN: [*To* JONATHAN] You sleep on the sofa—I sleep on the window seat.

MORTIMER: [*Stopping suddenly, as he remembers Mr. Hoskins*] The window seat! Oh, well, let's not argue about it. That window seat's good enough for me tonight. [*Descending as he talks*] I'll sleep on the window seat.

EINSTEIN: Chonny—all this argument—it makes me think of Mr. Spenalzo.

JONATHAN: Spenalzo! Well, Mortimer, there's no real need to inconvenience you. We'll sleep down here.

MORTIMER: Jonathan, this sudden consideration for me is very unconvincing.

EINSTEIN: Come, Chonny, we get our things out of the room, yes?

MORTIMER: Don't bother, Doctor.

JONATHAN: You know, Doctor, I've completely lost track of Mr. Spenalzo.

MORTIMER: Who's this Mr. Spenalzo?

EINSTEIN: [*On the stairs*] Just a friend of ours Chonny's been looking for.

MORTIMER: Don't you bring anybody else in here!

EINSTEIN: [*Reassuringly*] It's all right, Chonny. While we pack I tell you about him.

[JONATHAN *starts upstairs*]

ABBY: Mortimer, you don't have to stay down here. I could sleep with Martha and you could have my room.

JONATHAN: [*On the balcony*] No trouble at all, Aunt Abby. We'll be packed in a few minutes, and then you can have the room, Mortimer.

MORTIMER: You're just wasting time. I told you I'm sleeping down here! [JONATHAN *exits through the arch.* MORTIMER *starts for stairs and almost bumps into* ELAINE] Oh, hello, Elaine!

ELAINE: Mortimer!

MORTIMER: [*Taking her in his arms*] What's the matter with you, dear?

ELAINE: I've almost been killed!

MORTIMER: You've almost been . . . Abby! Martha! [*He looks quickly at the aunts*]

MARTHA: It was Jonathan.

ABBY: He mistook her for a sneak thief.

ELAINE: No, it was more than that. He's some kind of a maniac. [*She draws close to* MORTIMER *again*] Mortimer, I'm afraid of him.

MORTIMER: Why, darling, you're trembling. [*Sitting* ELAINE *on sofa. To the aunts*] Have you got any smelling salts?

MARTHA: No, but do you think some hot tea or coffee . . . ?

MORTIMER: Coffee. Make some for me, too—and some sandwiches. I haven't had any dinner.

MARTHA: We'll get something for both of you.

[ABBY *takes off her hat and gloves and puts them on sideboard*]

ABBY: Martha, we can leave our hats downstairs here.

MORTIMER: You weren't going out anywhere, were you? Do you know what time it is? It's after twelve. Twelve! [*He glances hurriedly at the cellar door, remembering*] Elaine, you go along home.

ELAINE: What?

ABBY: Why, Mortimer, you wanted some sandwiches for you and Elaine. It won't take us a minute.

MARTHA: Remember, we wanted to celebrate your engagement. . . . That's what we'll do. We'll have a nice supper for you—and we'll open a bottle of wine.

MORTIMER: [*Reluctantly*] All right. [*The aunts exit to the kitchen. He calls after them*] No wine!

ELAINE: [*Rising*] Mortimer, what's going on in this house?

MORTIMER: What do you mean—What's going on in this house?

ELAINE: You were supposed to take me to dinner and the theater tonight. . . . You called it off. You asked me to marry you . . . I said I would . . . five minutes later you threw me out of the house. Tonight, just after your brother tries to strangle me, you want to chase me home. Now, listen, Mr. Brewster . . . before I go home, I want to know where I stand. Do you love me?

MORTIMER: [*Going to her*] I love you very much, Elaine. In fact, I love you so much I can't marry you.

ELAINE: [*Drawing away*] Have you suddenly gone crazy?

MORTIMER: I don't think so—but it's just a matter of time. [*He seats her on sofa*] You see, insanity runs in my family. [*He looks toward the kitchen*] It practically *gallops!* That's why I can't marry you, dear.

ELAINE: [*Unconvinced*] Now wait a minute. You've got to do better than that.

MORTIMER: No, dear—there's a strange taint in the Brewster blood. If you *really* knew my family—well—it's what you would expect if Strindberg had written *Hellzapoppin!*

ELAINE: Now, just because Teddy . . .

MORTIMER: No, it goes way back. The first Brewster—the one who came over on the *Mayflower*. You know, in those days the Indians used to scalp the settlers—he used to scalp the *Indians*.

ELAINE: Mortimer, that's ancient history.

MORTIMER: No, the whole family! Take my grandfather—he tried his patent medicines out on dead people to be sure he wouldn't kill them!

ELAINE: He wasn't so crazy. He made a million dollars.

MORTIMER: And then there's Jonathan. You just said he was a maniac. He tried to kill you.

ELAINE: But he's your brother, not you. I'm in love with you.

MORTIMER: And Teddy! You *know* Teddy. He thinks he's Roosevelt.

ELAINE: Even Roosevelt thinks he's Roosevelt.

MORTIMER: No, dear, no Brewster should marry. I realize now that if I'd met my father in time I would have stopped him.

ELAINE: Now, darling, all of this doesn't prove *you're* crazy. Just look at your aunts—they're Brewsters, aren't they?—and the sanest, sweetest people I've ever known.

MORTIMER: [*Glancing at the window seat and moving toward it*] Well, even they have their peculiarities!

[ELAINE *walks away from him*]

ELAINE: Yes, but what lovely peculiarities—kindness, generosity, human sympathy!

[MORTIMER *lifts the window seat to take a peek at Mr. Hoskins and sees Mr. Spenalzo*]

MORTIMER: [*To himself*] There's another one!

ELAINE: [*Turning to* MORTIMER] There are plenty of others! You can't tell me anything about your aunts.

MORTIMER: I'm not going to! [*Crossing to* ELAINE] Elaine, you've got to go home. Something very important has just come up.

ELAINE: Come up from where? We're here alone together.

MORTIMER: Elaine, I know I'm acting irrationally, but just put it down to the fact that I'm a mad Brewster.

ELAINE: If you think you're going to get out of this by pretending you're insane, you're crazy. Maybe you're not going to marry me, but I'm going to marry you. I love you, you dope!

MORTIMER: [*Pushing her toward the door*] Well, if you love me, will you get the hell out of here?

ELAINE: Well, at least take me home. I'm afraid!

MORTIMER: Afraid! A little walk through the cemetery?

ELAINE: [*Changing tactics*] Mortimer, will you kiss me good night?

[MORTIMER *goes over to her*]

MORTIMER: Of course. [*What* MORTIMER *plans to be a desultory peck,* ELAINE *turns into a production number.* MORTIMER *comes out of it with no loss of poise*] Good night, dear. I'll call you up in a day or two.

[*She walks to the door in a cold fury, opens it and starts out, then wheels on* MORTIMER]

ELAINE: You—you critic! [*She exits, slamming the door.* MORTIMER *turns and rushes determinedly to the kitchen door*]

MORTIMER: Aunt Abby, Aunt Martha! Come in here!

ABBY'S VOICE: We'll be in in just a minute, dear.

MORTIMER: Come in here now!

[ABBY *enters from the kitchen*]

ABBY: What do you want, Mortimer? Where's Elaine?

MORTIMER: I thought you promised me not to let anyone in this house while I was gone!

ABBY: Well, Jonathan just walked in.

MORTIMER: I don't mean Jonathan!

ABBY: And Dr. Einstein was with him.

MORTIMER: I don't mean Dr. Einstein! Who is that in the window seat?

ABBY: We told you—it's Mr. Hoskins.

MORTIMER: It is *not* Mr. Hoskins. [*He opens the window seat.* ABBY *goes over and looks down at Mr. Spenalzo*]

ABBY: [*Puzzled at the sight of a stranger*] Who can that be?

MORTIMER: Are you trying to tell me you've never seen this man before?

ABBY: I certainly am! Why, this is a fine how-do-you-do! It's getting so anyone thinks he can walk into our house.

MORTIMER: Now, Aunt Abby, don't try to get out of this. That's another one of your gentlemen!

ABBY: Mortimer, that man's an impostor! Well, if he came here to be buried in our cellar, he's mistaken.

MORTIMER: Aunt Abby, you admitted to me that you put Mr. Hoskins in the window seat.

ABBY: Yes, I did.

MORTIMER: Well, this man couldn't have just got the idea from Mr. Hoskins. By the way where *is* Mr. Hoskins?

ABBY: He must have gone to Panama.

MORTIMER: You buried him?

ABBY: Not yet, he's just down there waiting for the services, poor dear! We haven't had a minute what with Jonathan in the house.

MORTIMER: Jonathan. . . . [*At the mention of* JONATHAN's *name, he closes the window seat*]

ABBY: We've always wanted to hold a double funeral, but we're not going to read services over a perfect stranger.

MORTIMER: A stranger! Aunt Abby, how can I believe you? There are twelve men in the cellar and you admit you poisoned them.

ABBY: [*Drawing herself up*] I did. But you don't think I'd stoop to telling a fib? [*She bustles indignantly into the kitchen, calling*] Martha!

[MORTIMER *starts to pace.* JONATHAN, *having learned where Mr. Spenalzo is, enters from above and comes down the stairs hurriedly, making for the window seat. He sees* MORTIMER *and stops*]

JONATHAN: Mortimer, I'd like to have a word with you.

MORTIMER: A word's about all you'll have time for, Jonathan, because I've decided you and your doctor friend are going to have to get out of this house as quickly as possible.

JONATHAN: I'm glad you recognize the fact that you and I can't live under the same roof. But you have arrived at the wrong solution. Take your suitcase and get out! [*He starts toward the window seat*]

MORTIMER: Jonathan, you're beginning to bore me! [*He circles around the table, heading* JONATHAN *off*] You've played your one-night stand in Brooklyn. Move on!

JONATHAN: My dear Mortimer, just because you've graduated from the back fence to the typewriter, don't think you're grown up. [*He slips past* MORTIMER, *and sits on window seat*] I'm staying—you're leaving—and I mean now!

MORTIMER: If you think I can be frightened, Jonathan, if you think there's anything I fear. . . .

JONATHAN: [*Rising and facing* MORTIMER] I've led a strange life, Mortimer. But it's taught me one thing—to be afraid of nothing!

[*For a second they glare at each other with equal courage.* ABBY *marches in from kitchen, followed by* MARTHA]

ABBY: Martha, you just look and see what's in that window seat.

[*Both men throw themselves on the window seat and speak and gesture simultaneously*]

MORTIMER AND JONATHAN: Now, Aunt Abby. . . . [*Light dawns on* MORTIMER'S *face. He rises with smiling assurance*]

MORTIMER: Jonathan, let Aunt Martha see what's in the window seat. [JONATHAN *freezes dangerously*] Aunt Abby, I owe you an apology. I have very good news for you. Jonathan is leaving. He's taking Dr. Einstein and their cold companion with him. [*He walks to* JONATHAN] You're my brother, Jonathan. You're a Brewster. I'm giving you a chance to get away and take the evidence with you. You can't ask for more than that. [JONATHAN *doesn't move*] All right. In that case, I'll have to call the police. [MORTIMER *starts for the telephone*]

JONATHAN: Don't reach for that telephone [*He crosses quickly toward* MORTIMER] Are you still giving me orders after seeing what's happened to Mr. Spenalzo?

MARTHA: Spenalzo?

ABBY: I knew he was a foreigner.

JONATHAN: [*To* MORTIMER] Remember, what happened to Mr. Spenalzo can happen to you, too.

[*There is a knock at the door; it opens and* OFFICER O'HARA *sticks his head in*]

O'HARA: Oh, hello. . . .

ABBY: Hello, Officer O'Hara. Is there anything we can do for you?

O'HARA: Saw your lights on—thought there might be sickness in the house. Oh, you got company. Sorry I disturbed you.

[MORTIMER *hurries to* O'HARA *and pulls him through the door into the room*]

MORTIMER: No! Come in!

ABBY: Yes, come in!

MARTHA: Come right in, Officer O'Hara. This is our nephew, Mortimer.

O'HARA: Pleased to meet you.

ABBY: And this is another nephew, Jonathan.

O'HARA: Pleased to make your acquaintance. Well, it must be nice having your nephews visiting you. Are they going to stay with you for a bit?

MORTIMER: I'm staying. My brother Jonathan is just leaving.

[JONATHAN *starts for stairs.* O'HARA *stops him*]

O'HARA: I've met you here before, haven't I?

ABBY: I'm afraid not. Jonathan hasn't been home for years.

O'HARA: [*To* JONATHAN] Your face looks familiar to me. Perhaps I've seen a picture of you somewhere.

JONATHAN: I don't think so. [*He hurries up the stairs*]

MORTIMER: I'd hurry if I were you, Jonathan. You're all packed anyway, aren't you?

[JONATHAN *exits upstairs*]

O'HARA: Well, you'll be wanting to say your good-bys. I'll be running along. [*He starts for the door*]

MORTIMER: [*Stopping him*] What's the rush? I'd like to have you stick around until my brother goes.

O'HARA: I just dropped in to make sure everything was all right.

MORTIMER: We're going to have some coffee in a minute. Won't you join us?

ABBY: Oh, I forgot the coffee. [*She hurries out*]

MARTHA: I'd better make some more sandwiches. I ought to know your appetite by this time, Mr. O'Hara. [*She exits into the kitchen*]

O'HARA: [*Calling after her*] Don't bother. I'm due to ring in in a few minutes.

MORTIMER: You can have a cup of coffee with us. My brother will be going soon.

O'HARA: Haven't I seen a photograph of your brother around here some place?

MORTIMER: I don't think so.

O'HARA: He certainly reminds me of somebody.

MORTIMER: He looks like somebody you've probably seen in the movies.

O'HARA: I never go to the movies. I hate 'em. My mother says the movies is a bastard art.

MORTIMER: Yes. It's full of them. Your mother said that?

O'HARA: Yeah. My mother was an actress—a stage actress. Perhaps you've heard of her—Peaches Latour.

MORTIMER: Sounds like a name I've seen on a program. What did she play?

O'HARA: Her big hit was *Mutt and Jeff*. Played it for three years. I was born on tour—the third season.

MORTIMER: You were?

O'HARA: Yeah. Sioux City, Iowa. I was born in the dressing-room at the end of the second act and mother made the finale.

MORTIMER: What a trouper! There must be a good story in your mother. You know, I write about the theater.

O'HARA: You do? Say, you're not Mortimer Brewster, the dramatic critic? [MORTIMER *nods*] Say, I'm glad to meet you. We're in the same line of business.

MORTIMER: We are?

O'HARA: Yes, I'm a playwright. This being on the police force is just temporary.

MORTIMER: How long have you been on the force?

O'HARA: Twelve years. I'm collecting material for a play.

MORTIMER: I'll bet it's a honey.

O'HARA: Well, it ought to be. With all the drama I see being a cop. Mr. Brewster, you got no idea what goes on in Brooklyn.

MORTIMER: I think I have!

O'HARA: What time you got?

MORTIMER: Ten after one.

O'HARA: Gee, I got to ring in. [*He starts to go*]

MORTIMER: [*Stopping him*] Wait a minute! On that play of yours—you know, I might be able to help you.

O'HARA: You would? Say, it was fate my walking in here tonight. Look, I'll tell you the plot.

[JONATHAN *and* EINSTEIN *enter on the balcony carrying suitcases*]

MORTIMER: Oh, Jonathan, you're on your way, eh? Good! You haven't got much time, you know.

ABBY: [*Entering from kitchen*] Everything's about ready. [*She sees* JONATHAN *and* EINSTEIN] Oh, you leaving now, Jonathan? Well, good-by. Good-by Dr. Einstein. [*She notices the instrument case by the window*] Oh, doesn't this case belong to you?

MORTIMER: Yes, Jonathan. You can't go without *all* of your things! [*To* O'HARA] Well, O'Hara, it was nice meeting you. I'll see you again—we'll talk about your play.

O'HARA: Oh, I'm not leaving now, Mr. Brewster.

MORTIMER: Why not?

O'HARA: Well, you just offered to help me with my play, didn't you? You and me are going to write my play together.

MORTIMER: No, O'Hara, I can't do that. You see, I'm not a creative writer.

o'HARA: I'll do the creating. You just put the words to it.

MORTIMER: But, O'Hara . . .

o'HARA: No, sir, Mr. Brewster, I ain't going to leave this house till I tell you the plot. [o'HARA *sits on the window seat*]

JONATHAN: In that case, Mortimer, we'll be running along. [*He starts toward the outside door*]

MORTIMER: No, Jonathan! Don't try that! You can't go yet. You're taking *everything* with you. . . . [*To* o'HARA] Look, O'Hara, you run along now. My brother's just going and. . . .

o'HARA: I can wait. I've been waiting twelve years.

[MARTHA *enters with sandwiches and coffee on a tray*]

MARTHA: I'm sorry I was so long.

MORTIMER: Don't bring that in here! O'Hara, would you join us for a bite in the kitchen?

MARTHA: The kitchen?

ABBY: Jonathan's leaving.

MARTHA: Oh, that's nice! Come along, Mr. O'Hara. [*She takes the tray back into the kitchen*]

ABBY: Mr. O'Hara, you don't mind eating in the kitchen?

o'HARA: Where else would you eat? [*He exits to the kitchen*]

ABBY: Good-by, Jonathan, it's nice to have seen you again. [*She hurries into kitchen*]

MORTIMER: [*Closing the kitchen door after* ABBY] Jonathan, I'm glad you came back to Brooklyn because it gives me a chance to throw you out! [*He opens window seat*] And the first one out is your boy friend, Mr. Spenalzo.

o'HARA: [*Appearing in doorway*] Look, Mr. Brewster! [MORTIMER *hurriedly closes the window seat*] We can talk in here.

MORTIMER: No. I'll be right out, O'Hara. [*He pushes* o'HARA *back into the kitchen*]

JONATHAN: [*Scornfully*] I might have known you'd grow up to write a play with a policeman.

MORTIMER: Get going, now—all *three* of you! [*He exits; closing the door*]

JONATHAN: [*Putting the bags down*] Doctor, this affair between my brother and me has got to be settled.

EINSTEIN: Now, Chonny, we got trouble enough. Your brother gives us a chance to get away—what more could you ask?

JONATHAN: You don't understand, Doctor. [*Opening window seat*] This goes back many years.

EINSTEIN: Now, Chonny, let's get going.

JONATHAN: We're not going—we're going to sleep right here tonight.

EINSTEIN: With a cop in the kitchen and Mr. Spenalzo in the window seat?

JONATHAN: That's all he's got on us, Doctor. [*He closes the window seat*] We'll take Mr. Spenalzo down and dump him in the bay. That done, we're coming back here. And then if he tries to interfere . . .

EINSTEIN: Now, Chonny!

JONATHAN: Doctor, you know when I make up my mind . . .

EINSTEIN: Yeah—when you make up your mind, you lose your head! Brooklyn ain't a good place for you, Chonny.

JONATHAN: [*Peremptorily*] Doctor!

EINSTEIN: O.K. We got to stick together. Some day we get stuck together. [*He points to the bags*] If we're coming back do we got to take them with us?

JONATHAN: No. Leave them here. [*He looks toward upstairs, then toward the cellar door*] Hide them in the cellar. [EINSTEIN *moves toward the cellar with the instrument case*] Move fast! Spenalzo can go out the same way he came in.

> [EINSTEIN *exits into the cellar.* JONATHAN *goes to the foot of the staircase, takes the other bags to the cellar door, goes to the window and opens it.* EINSTEIN *comes up from the cellar, excited*]

EINSTEIN: Hey, Chonny! Come quick!

JONATHAN: What's the matter?

EINSTEIN: You know that hole in the cellar?

JONATHAN: Yes.

EINSTEIN: Well—we got an ace in the hole.

> [*They both disappear down the cellar steps.* MORTIMER *enters from kitchen, finishing a sandwich and looks around the room. He sees their two bags and notices the open window. He goes to the window seat, looks in and sees Mr. Spenalzo is still there, closes the window seat and, kneeling on it, leans out the window and calls softly*]

MORTIMER: Jonathan! Jonathan! [JONATHAN *and* EINSTEIN *come in through the cellar door unnoticed by* MORTIMER *and walk into the room*] Jonathan!

JONATHAN: Yes, Mortimer!

MORTIMER: [*Turning around and seeing* JONATHAN, *he speaks angrily*] Where have you two been? I thought I told you. . . .

JONATHAN: We're not going.

MORTIMER: Oh, you're not? You think I'm not serious about this, eh? Do you want the police to know what's in that window seat?

JONATHAN: [*Firmly*] We're staying here.

MORTIMER: All right! You asked for it! This gets me rid of you and O'Hara both at the same time. [*He goes to the kitchen door*] Officer O'Hara!

JONATHAN: If you tell O'Hara what's in the window seat, I'll tell him what's in the cellar.

MORTIMER: [*Closing the door swiftly*] The cellar?

JONATHAN: There's an elderly gentleman down there who seems to be very dead.

MORTIMER: What were you doing in the cellar?

EINSTEIN: What's *he* doing in the cellar?

[OFFICER O'HARA's *voice is heard offstage*]

O'HARA: [*Offstage*] No, thank you, ma'am. I've had plenty! They were fine!

JONATHAN: Now, what are you going to say to Officer O'Hara?

[O'HARA *walks in*]

O'HARA: Say, your aunts want to hear it, too. Shall I get them in here?

MORTIMER: [*Pulling him toward the outside door*] No, O'Hara! You can't do that now! You've got to ring in!

O'HARA: The hell with ringing in! I'll get your aunts in and tell you the plot.

MORTIMER: No, O'Hara, not in front of all these people! We'll get together alone someplace, later.

O'HARA: Say, how about the back room at Kelly's?

MORTIMER: [*Hurrying him toward door*] Fine! You go ring in and I'll meet you at Kelly's.

JONATHAN: Why don't you two go down in the cellar?

O'HARA: That's all right with me [*He starts for the cellar door*] Is this the cellar?

MORTIMER: [*Grabbing him*] No! We'll go to Kelly's. But you're going to ring in on the way, aren't you?

O'HARA: All right, that will only take a couple of minutes.

[MORTIMER *pushes him through the outside door, then turns to get his hat*]

MORTIMER: [*To* JONATHAN] I'll ditch this guy and be back in five minutes. I expect to find you gone. No! Wait for me. [*He exits, closing the door*]

JONATHAN: We'll wait for him, Doctor. I've waited a great many years for a chance like this.

EINSTEIN: We got him where we want him. Did he look guilty!

JONATHAN: Take the bags back to our room, Doctor.

[*He goes to the window and closes it.* ABBY, *who is wiping her hands on her apron, enters, followed by* MARTHA, *who has a saucer and dish towel in her hand*]

ABBY: Have they gone? [*She sees* JONATHAN *and* EINSTEIN] Oh—we thought we heard somebody leave.

JONATHAN: Just Mortimer—he'll be back in a few minutes. Is there any food left in the kitchen? I think Dr. Einstein and I would enjoy a bite.

MARTHA: You won't have time. . . .

ABBY: Yes, if you're still here when Mortimer gets back, he won't like it.

EINSTEIN: He'll like it! He's gotta like it!

JONATHAN: Get something for us to eat, while we bury Mr. Spenalzo in the cellar.

MARTHA: Oh, no!

ABBY: [*Spiritedly*] He can't stay in our cellar, Jonathan. You've got to take him with you.

JONATHAN: There's a friend of Mortimer's downstairs waiting for him.

ABBY: A friend of Mortimer's?

JONATHAN: He and Mr. Spenalzo will get along fine together. They're both dead.

MARTHA: They must mean Mr. Hoskins.

EINSTEIN: Mr. Hoskins?

JONATHAN: So you know about what's downstairs?

ABBY: Of course we do, and he's no friend of Mortimer's. He's one of our gentlemen.

EINSTEIN: Your gentlemen?

MARTHA: [*Firmly*] And we *won't* have any strangers buried in our cellar.

JONATHAN: But Mr. Hoskins. . . .

MARTHA: Mr. Hoskins isn't a stranger.

ABBY: Besides, there's no room for Mr. Spenalzo. The cellar's crowded already.

JONATHAN: Crowded? With what?

ABBY: There are twelve graves down there now.

JONATHAN: Twelve graves!

ABBY: That leaves very little room and we're going to need it.

JONATHAN: You mean you and Aunt Martha have murdered . . .

ABBY: Murdered! Certainly not! It's one of our charities.

MARTHA: What we've been doing is a mercy.

ABBY: [*With a gesture of dismissal*] So you take your Mr. Spenalzo out of here.

JONATHAN: [*Amazed and impressed*] You've done that—right in this house— and buried them down there?

EINSTEIN: Chonny, we been chased all over the world. . . . They stay right here in Brooklyn and do just as good as you do.

JONATHAN: What?

EINSTEIN: You got twelve, Chonny. They got twelve.

JONATHAN: [*His pride wounded*] I've got thirteen.

EINSTEIN: No, twelve, Chonny.

JONATHAN: Thirteen! There's Mr. Spenalzo! Then the first one in London. Two in Johannesburg—one in Sydney—one in Melbourne—two in San Francisco—one in Phoenix, Arizona. . . .

EINSTEIN: Phoenix?

JONATHAN: The filling station—the three in Chicago, and the one in South Bend. That makes thirteen!

EINSTEIN: But, Chonny, you can't count the one in South Bend. He died of pneumonia.

JONATHAN: [*His record at stake*] He wouldn't have got pneumonia if I hadn't shot him.

EINSTEIN: No, Chonny, he died of pneumonia. He don't count.

JONATHAN: He counts with me! I say *thirteen!*

EINSTEIN: No, Chonny. You got twelve. They got twelve. The old ladies are just as good as you are.

JONATHAN: [*Wheeling on them*] Oh, they are, are they? That's easily taken care of! All I need is one more!—that's all—just one more!

[MORTIMER *enters hastily, closing the door behind him and turns to them with a nervous smile*]

MORTIMER: Well—here I am!

[JONATHAN *looks at* MORTIMER *with the widening eyes of someone who has just solved a problem*]

CURTAIN

ACT THREE

SCENE ONE

The curtain rises on an empty stage. We hear voices, voices in disagreement, from the cellar, through the open cellar door.

MARTHA: [*Offstage*] You stop doing that!

ABBY: [*Offstage*] This is our house and this is our cellar and you can't do that!

EINSTEIN: [*Offstage*] Ladies! Please go back upstairs where you belong.

JONATHAN: [*Offstage*] Abby! Martha! Go upstairs!

MARTHA: [*Offstage*] There's no use of your doing what you're doing because it will just have to be undone!

ABBY: [*Offstage*] I tell you we won't have it!

[MARTHA *enters from the cellar*]

MARTHA: You'll find out! You'll find out whose house this is! [*She goes to the street door, opens it and looks out.* ABBY *enters from the cellar. Both women are wearing their hats*]

ABBY: I'm warning you! You'd better stop! [*To* MARTHA] Hasn't Mortimer come back yet?

MARTHA: [*She closes the door*] No.

ABBY: It's a terrible thing—burying a good Methodist with a foreigner!

MARTHA: I won't have our celler desecrated!

ABBY: And we promised Mr. Hoskins a full Christian funeral. . . . Where do you suppose Mortimer went?

MARTHA: I don't know. But he must be doing something. He said to Jonathan, "You just wait, I'll settle this!"

ABBY: Well, he can't settle it while he's out of the house. [*Turning to the cellar door*] That's all we want settled—what's going on down there. [MORTIMER *enters from the street carrying* TEDDY's *commitment papers in his hand*]

MORTIMER: [*Grimly*] All right. Now, where's Teddy?

ABBY: Mortimer, where have you been?

MORTIMER: I've been over to Dr. Gilchrist's. I've got his signature on Teddy's commitment papers.

MARTHA: Mortimer, what's the matter with you?

ABBY: Running around getting papers signed at a time like this!

MARTHA: Do you know what Jonathan is doing?

ABBY: He's putting Mr. Hoskins and Mr. Spenalzo in together.

MORTIMER: Oh, he is, is he? Well, let him. Is Teddy in his room?

MARTHA: Teddy won't be any help.

MORTIMER: When he signs these commitment papers, I can tackle Jonathan.

ABBY: What have they got to do with it?

MORTIMER: You had to tell Jonathan about those twelve graves! If I can make Teddy responsible for those, I can protect you, don't you see?

ABBY: No, I don't see. And we pay taxes to have the police protect us.

MORTIMER: [*Starting upstairs*] I'll be back down in a minute.

ABBY: Come, Martha. [*To* MORTIMER] We're going for the police.

[*The sisters get their gloves*]

MORTIMER: All right. [*He suddenly realizes what has been said*] The police! You can't go for the police! [*He rushes downstairs to the street door*]

MARTHA: Why can't we?

MORTIMER: Because, if you told them about Mr. Spenalzo, they'd find Mr.

Hoskins too; and that might make them curious, and they'd find out about the other gentlemen.

ABBY: Mortimer, we know the police better than you do. I don't think they'd pry into our private affairs if we asked them not to.

MORTIMER: But if they found your twelve gentlemen they'd have to report to headquarters.

MARTHA: [*Pulling on her gloves*] I'm not so sure they'd better. They'd have to make out a very long report. And if there's one thing a policeman hates to do, it's to write.

MORTIMER: You can't depend on that! It might leak out! And you couldn't expect a judge and jury to understand.

MARTHA: Judge Cullman would.

ABBY: [*Drawing on her gloves*] We know him very well.

MARTHA: He always comes to church to pray just before election.

ABBY: And he's coming here to tea some day. He promised.

MARTHA: We'll have to speak to him again about that, Abby. [*To* MOR-TIMER] His wife died a few years ago and it's left him very lonely.

ABBY: Come along, Martha.

[*She starts toward the door.* MORTIMER, *however, gets there first*]

MORTIMER: You can't do this! I won't let you. You can't leave this house and you can't have Judge Cullman to tea!

ABBY: Well, if you're not going to do something about Mr. Spenalzo, we are.

MORTIMER: But I am going to do something. We may have to call the police in later, but if we do, I want to be ready for them.

MARTHA: You've got to get Jonathan out of this house!

ABBY: And Mr. Spenalzo, too!

MORTIMER: Will you please let me do it my own way? I've got to see Teddy. [*He starts upstairs*]

ABBY: If they're not out of here by morning, Mortimer, we're going to call the police.

[MORTIMER *turns at the top of the stairs*]

MORTIMER: They'll be out. I promise you that! Go to bed, will you? And for God's sake get out of those clothes. You look like Judith Anderson. [*He exits upstairs*]

MARTHA: Well, that's a relief, Abby.

ABBY: If Mortimer is doing something at last then Jonathan's just going to a lot of unnecessary trouble. We'd better tell him. [JONATHAN *comes up the cellar steps and into the room*] Jonathan, you might as well stop what you're doing.

JONATHAN: It's all done. Did I hear Mortimer?

ABBY: Well, it will have to be undone. You're all going to be out of this house by morning.

JONATHAN: Oh, we are? In that case, you and Aunt Martha can go to bed and have a peaceful night's sleep.

MARTHA: [*Always a little frightened by* JONATHAN] Yes. Come, Abby.

[*They start up the stairs*]

JONATHAN: Good night, aunties.

[*The sisters turn at the top of the stairs*]

ABBY: Not good night, Jonathan. Good-by! By the time we get up you'll be out of this house. Mortimer's promised.

MARTHA: And he has a way of doing it, too!

JONATHAN: Then Mortimer is back?

ABBY: Yes, he's up here talking to Teddy.

MARTHA: Good-by, Jonathan.

ABBY: Good-by, Jonathan.

JONATHAN: [*Quietly*] Perhaps you'd better say good-by to Mortimer.

ABBY: Oh, you'll see Mortimer.

JONATHAN: [*Tense*] Yes, I'll see Mortimer.

[ABBY *and* MARTHA *exit.* JONATHAN *stands without moving. There is murder on his mind. After an appreciable pause* EINSTEIN *comes up from the cellar dusting himself off. He is wearing Mr. Spenalzo's shoes*]

EINSTEIN: Whew! That's all fixed up. Smooth like a lake. Nobody'd ever know they're there. [JONATHAN *still stands without moving*] That bed feels good already. Forty-eight hours we didn't sleep. Whew! Come on, Chonny, let's go up, yes?

[JONATHAN'S *eyes move to* EINSTEIN]

JONATHAN: You're forgetting, Doctor.

EINSTEIN: Vas?

JONATHAN: My brother Mortimer.

EINSTEIN: Chonny, tonight? I'm sleepy. We do that tomorrow—the next day.

JONATHAN: No, tonight. Now!

EINSTEIN: Chonny, please! I'm tired. . . . Tomorrow I got to operate. . . .

JONATHAN: You're going to operate tomorrow, Doctor. But tonight we take care of Mortimer.

EINSTEIN: Chonny, not tonight—we go to bed, eh?

JONATHAN: Doctor, look at me! [EINSTEIN *looks and straightens up*] You can see that it's going to be done, can't you?

EINSTEIN: Ach, Chonny! I can see! I know that look!

JONATHAN: It's a little late for us to dissolve our partnership.

EINSTEIN: O.K., Chonny. We do it. But the quick way? The quick twist, like in London. [*He gives that London neck another twist with his hands*]

JONATHAN: No, Doctor, I think this calls for something special. [JONATHAN *begins to anticipate a rare pleasure*] I think, perhaps, the Melbourne method.

EINSTEIN: Chonny—No!—Not that! Two hours! And when it was all over— what? The fellow in London was just as dead as the fellow in Melbourne.

JONATHAN: We had to work too fast in London. There was no aesthetic satisfaction in it. Now, Melbourne—ah, there was something to remember.

EINSTEIN: Remember! [*He shivers*] I wish I didn't. Chonny—not Melbourne—not me. . . .

JONATHAN: Yes, Doctor. Where are the instruments?

EINSTEIN: I won't do it, Chonny! I won't do it!

JONATHAN: Get your instruments!

EINSTEIN: No, Chonny!

JONATHAN: Where are they? Oh, yes. You hid them in the cellar. Where?

EINSTEIN: I won't tell you!

JONATHAN: I'll find them, Doctor.

> [*He exits to the cellar.* EINSTEIN *paces desperately for a moment.* TEDDY *steps out on the balcony with his bugle and lifts it as if to blow.* MORTIMER *dashes out after him and grabs his arm*]

MORTIMER: Don't do that, Mr. President!

TEDDY: I cannot sign any proclamation without consulting my cabinet.

MORTIMER: But this must be secret.

TEDDY: A secret proclamation? How unusual!

MORTIMER: Japan mustn't know until it's signed.

TEDDY: Japan? Those yellow devils! I'll sign it right away. You have my word for it. I can let the cabinet know later.

MORTIMER: Yes, let's go and sign it.

TEDDY: You wait here. If it's a secret proclamation it has to be signed in secret.

MORTIMER: At once, Mr. President.

TEDDY: I'll put on my signing clothes.

> [*He exits.* MORTIMER *comes downstairs.* EINSTEIN *takes* MORTIMER's *hat from the hall tree and meets him at the foot of the stairs*]

EINSTEIN: You go now, eh? [*He hands* MORTIMER *his hat*]

MORTIMER: No, Doctor, I'm waiting for something—something important. [MORTIMER *tosses his hat on the couch*]

EINSTEIN: [*Urging* MORTIMER *to the door*] Please, you go now!

MORTIMER: Dr. Einstein, I have nothing against you personally. You seem to be a nice fellow. If you'll take my advice, you'll get out of this house and get just as far away as possible. . . . There's going to be trouble.

EINSTEIN: Trouble, yah! You get out!

MORTIMER: All right, don't say I didn't warn you.

EINSTEIN: I'm warning *you*—get away quick!

MORTIMER: Things are going to start popping around here any minute.

EINSTEIN: [*Glancing nervously toward the cellar*] Chonny is in a bad mood. When he is like this—he is a madman! Things happen—terrible things!

MORTIMER: Jonathan doesn't worry me now.

EINSTEIN: Ach! Himmel! Don't those plays you see teach you anything?

MORTIMER: About what?

EINSTEIN: At least people in plays act like they got sense.

MORTIMER: Oh, you think so, do you? You think people in plays act intelligently. I wish you had to sit through some of the ones I have to sit through. This little opus tonight—for instance. In this play, there's a man . . . [JONATHAN *enters from the cellar, carrying the instrument case. He pauses in the doorway, unseen by* MORTIMER] . . . he's supposed to be bright. He knows he's in a house with murderers—he ought to know he's in danger. He's even been warned to get out of the house. Does he go? No, he stays there. I ask you—is that what an intelligent person would do?

EINSTEIN: You're asking me!

MORTIMER: He didn't even have sense enough to be scared—to be on guard. For instance, the murderer invites him to sit down.

EINSTEIN: You mean "Won't you sit down"?

MORTIMER: Believe it or not, that one was in there, too.

EINSTEIN: And what did he do?

MORTIMER: He sat down! Mind you—this fellow is supposed to be bright. [MORTIMER *sits down*] There he is—all ready to be trussed up. And what do they use to tie him with?

EINSTEIN: What?

MORTIMER: The curtain cord.

> [JONATHAN *finds an idea being thrust on him, draws his knife, and goes to the window*]

EINSTEIN: Well, why not? A good idea. Very convenient.

> [JONATHAN *cuts the curtain cord*]

MORTIMER: A little too convenient. When are playwrights going to use some imagination? [JONATHAN *has coiled the curtain cord and is moving behind* MORTIMER] The curtain cord!

EINSTEIN: He didn't see him get it?

MORTIMER: See him? He sat there with his back to him. That's the kind of stuff we have to suffer through night after night. And they say the critics are killing the theater. It's the playwrights that are killing the theater. So there he sat—the big dope—this guy that's supposed to be bright—waiting to be tied up and gagged!

[JONATHAN *drops the looped curtain cord over* MORTIMER'S *shoulders, pulls it taut and ties it behind the back of the chair. Simultaneously* EINSTEIN *leaps to* MORTIMER, *pulls* MORTIMER'S *handkerchief out of his pocket and gags him with it.* JONATHAN *steps to* MORTIMER'S *side*]

EINSTEIN: [*Tying* MORTIMER'S *legs*] You're right about that fellow—he *wasn't* very bright.

JONATHAN: Now if you don't mind, Mortimer—we'll finish the story. [MOR-TIMER *is making muted, unintelligible sounds.* JONATHAN *goes to the sideboard and brings the candelabra down to the table and lights the candles*] Mortimer, I've been away for twenty years, but never, my dear brother, were you out of my mind. . . . In Melbourne one night—I dreamt of you. . . . When I landed in San Francisco—I felt a strange satisfaction— Once again I was in the same country with you. [JONATHAN *turns out the lights, throwing the room into an eerie candlelight. He picks up the instrument case and sets it down on the table between the candelabra*] Now, Doctor—we go to work.

EINSTEIN: Please, Chonny—for me—the quick way—eh?

JONATHAN: Doctor, this must be an artistic achievement! After all, we're performing before a very distinguished critic.

EINSTEIN: Chonny. . . .

JONATHAN: [*Flaring*] Doctor. . . .

EINSTEIN: All right, Let's get it over! [JONATHAN *takes several instruments out of the case, handling them as potential accessories to torture. The last of these is a long probe, which he measures to* MORTIMER'S *face. Finally he begins to put on rubber gloves.* EINSTEIN *takes a bottle from his pocket, finds it empty*] Chonny, I gotta have a drink, I can't do this without a drink.

JONATHAN: Pull yourself together, Doctor!

EINSTEIN: I gotta have a drink! Chonny, when we walked in this afternoon— there was wine there. . . . [*He points to the table*] Remember? Where did she put it? [*He remembers*] Ah. . . . [*He goes to sideboard and opens it, finding the wine*] Look, Chonny! [*He takes the wine bottle to the table with two wine glasses*] We got a drink. [*He pours the wine into the two glasses, the second glass emptying the bottle.* MORTIMER, *who has been squirming, stops, eyeing the bottle, then* JONATHAN *and* EINSTEIN] That's all there is. I split it with you. We both need a drink! [EINSTEIN *hands one glass to* JONATHAN, *then raises the glass of poisoned wine and is about to drink*]

JONATHAN: One moment, Doctor! Please! Where are your manners? [*To* MORTIMER] Yes, Mortimer. I realize now that it was you who brought me back to Brooklyn. We drink to you! [*He raises his glass, sniffs the wine, hesitates, then proposes a grim toast*] Doctor—to my dear dead brother! [*They are raising their glasses to their lips, when* TEDDY, *fully and formally dressed, steps out of the upper door onto the balcony and blows a terrific blast on his bugle.* EINSTEIN *and* JONATHAN *drop their glasses, spilling the wine.* TEDDY *turns around and goes out again*]

EINSTEIN: Ach, Gott!

JONATHAN: Damn that idiot! He goes next! That's all. He goes next! [*He rushes to the staircase*]

EINSTEIN: No, Chonny, not Teddy! That's where I stop—not Teddy! [*He intercepts* JONATHAN *at the stairs*]

JONATHAN: We'll get to him later.

EINSTEIN: We don't get to him at all!

JONATHAN: Now we *have* to work fast!

EINSTEIN: Yah—the quick way—eh, Chonny?

JONATHAN: Yes—the quick way!

[*He darts behind* MORTIMER, *pulling a large silk handkerchief from his pocket and drops it around* MORTIMER's *neck. There is a knock at the door.* JONATHAN *and* EINSTEIN *are startled. The door opens and* OFFICER O'HARA *enters*]

O'HARA: Hey, the Colonel's gotta quit blowing that horn!

[JONATHAN *and* EINSTEIN *quickly stand between* MORTIMER *and* O'HARA]

JONATHAN: It's all right, officer. We're taking the bugle away from him.

O'HARA: There's going to be hell to pay in the morning. We promised the neighbors he wouldn't do that any more.

JONATHAN: It won't happen again, officer. Good night.

O'HARA: I better speak to him myself. Where are the lights? [O'HARA *turns on the lights.* EINSTEIN *and* JONATHAN *break for the kitchen door but stop when the lights go on.* O'HARA *closes the door and starts up the stairs.* MORTIMER *mumbles through the gag.* O'HARA *turns and sees him*] Hey, you stood me up! I waited an hour at Kelly's for you [*He comes downstairs.* MORTIMER *is trying to talk.* O'HARA *turns to* EINSTEIN] What happened to him?

EINSTEIN: He was explaining the play he saw tonight. That's what happened to a fellow in the play.

O'HARA: Did they have that in the play you saw tonight? [MORTIMER *nods his head*] Gee, they practically stole that from the second act of my play. In the second act just before . . . I'd better begin at the beginning. It opens in my mother's dressing room, where I was born—only I ain't born yet. [MORTIMER *mumbles and moves his head*] Huh? Oh, yes. [*He goes to*

MORTIMER *and starts to remove the gag, then hesitates*] No! You've got to hear the plot! [O'HARA *goes enthusiastically into his plot as the curtain is coming down*] Well, she's sitting there making up, see—when out of a clear sky the door opens—and a man with a black mustache walks in. . . .

CURTAIN

SCENE TWO

When the curtain rises again, daylight is streaming through the windows. MORTIMER *is still tied in his chair and seems to be in a semiconscious state.* JONATHAN *is asleep on the couch near the stairs.* EINSTEIN, *pleasantly intoxicated, is seated, listening. There is a bottle of whisky on the table and two glasses.* O'HARA, *with his coat off and his collar loosened, has progressed to the most exciting scene of his play.*

O'HARA: . . . there she is, lying unconscious across the table—in her longeray—the Chink is standing over her with a hatchet . . . [*He takes the pose*] . . . I'm tied up in a chair just like you are. . . . The place is an inferno of flames—it's on fire—great effect we got there—when all of a sudden—through the window—in comes Mayor La Guardia! [MORTIMER *is startled into consciousness, then collapses again.* O'HARA *is pacing with self-satisfaction.* EINSTEIN *pours himself a drink*] Hey, remember who paid for that—go easy on it.

EINSTEIN: Well, I'm listening, ain't I?

O'HARA: How do you like it, so far?

EINSTEIN: It put Chonny to sleep [EINSTEIN *goes over and shakes* JONATHAN] Hey, Chonny!—Chonny!—want a drink?

O'HARA: [*Pouring drink*] Let him alone—if he ain't got no more interest than that—he don't get a drink. [O'HARA *tosses a drink down and is ready to resume his story*] All right . . . It's three days later. . . . I been transferred and I'm under charges—that's because somebody stole my badge—all right, I'm walking my beat on Staten Island—forty-sixth precinct—when a guy I'm following, it turns out is really following *me*. . . . [*There is a knock at the door*] Don't let anybody in. [EINSTEIN *hurries to the landing window and looks out*] So I figure I'll outsmart him. There's a vacant house on the corner. I goes in.

EINSTEIN: [*Looking out*] It's cops!

O'HARA: I stands there in the dark and I sees the door handle turn.

EINSTEIN: [*Shaking* JONATHAN's *shoulder*] Chonny! It's cops! It's cops! [EINSTEIN *hurries up the stairs*] o'HARA: I pulls my gun, I braces myself against the wall and I say "Come in!" [OFFICERS BROPHY and KLEIN *walk in, see* o'HARA *with his gun pointed toward them, and start to raise their hands.* EINSTEIN *exits upstairs*] Hello, boys!

BROPHY: [*Recognizing* o'HARA] What the hell's going on here?

o'HARA: Hey, Pat, what do you know? This is Mortimer Brewster! He's going to write my play with me! I'm just telling him the story.

KLEIN: Did you have to tie him up to make him listen? [*He goes over and unties* MORTIMER]

BROPHY: Joe, you'd better report in at the station. The whole force is out looking for you.

o'HARA: Did they send you boys here for me?

KLEIN: We didn't know you was here.

BROPHY: We came to warn the old ladies that there's hell to pay. The Colonel blew that bugle again in the middle of the night.

KLEIN: From the way the neighbors have been calling in about it you'd think the Germans had dropped a bomb on Flatbush Avenue.

BROPHY: The Lieutenant's on the warpath. He says the Colonel's got to be put away some place.

[KLEIN *helps* MORTIMER *to his feet*]

MORTIMER: [*Weakly*] Yes! [*He staggers toward the stairs.* o'HARA *follows him*]

o'HARA: Listen, Mr. Brewster. I got to go, so I'll just run through the third act quick.

MORTIMER: Get away from me!

[BROPHY *goes to the telephone and dials*]

KLEIN: Say, do you know what time it is? It's after eight o'clock in the morning.

o'HARA: It is? Gee, Mr. Brewster, them first two acts run a little long. But I don't see anything we can leave out.

MORTIMER: You can leave it *all* out.

[BROPHY *sees* JONATHAN *on the couch*]

BROPHY: Who the hell is this guy?

MORTIMER: It's my brother.

BROPHY: Oh, the one that ran away? So he came back.

MORTIMER: Yes, he came back! [*He has reached the balcony*]

BROPHY: [*Into the telephone*] This is Brophy. Get me Mac. [*To* o'HARA] I'd better let them know I found you, Joe. [KLEIN *has wandered over to the other side of* JONATHAN *and looks down at him.* BROPHY *is looking at* o'HARA] Mac? Tell the Lieutenant he can call off the big man hunt. We got him. In the Brewster house. [JONATHAN *hears this and suddenly comes very awake, looking up to see a policeman on each side of him*] Do you want us to bring him in? Oh, all right—we'll hold him right here. [*He hangs up*] The Lieutenant's on his way over.

[JONATHAN *is now on his feet between the two policemen, under the impression that he is cornered*]

JONATHAN: So, I've been turned in, eh? [BROPHY *and* KLEIN *look at him with interest*] All right, you've got me! I suppose you and my stool-pigeon brother will split the reward?

KLEIN: Reward? [*Instinctively* KLEIN *and* BROPHY *both grab* JONATHAN *by an arm*]

JONATHAN: Now I'll do some turning in! You think my aunts are charming, sweet old ladies, don't you? Well, there are thirteen bodies buried in their cellar!

MORTIMER: [*Exits upstairs, calling:*] Teddy! Teddy!

KLEIN: What the hell are you talking about?

BROPHY: You'd better be careful what you say about your aunts—they happen to be friends of ours.

JONATHAN: I'll show you! I'll prove it to you! Come down in the cellar with me! [*He starts to drag them toward the cellar door*]

KLEIN: Wait a minute!

JONATHAN: Thirteen bodies—I'll show you where they're buried!

KLEIN: [*Refusing to be kidded*] Oh, yeah?

JONATHAN: Oh, you don't want to see what's down in the cellar!

[BROPHY *releases* JONATHAN'S *arm*]

BROPHY: Go on down in the cellar with him, Abe.

KLEIN: [*Stepping away from* JONATHAN] I'm not so sure I want to be down in the cellar with him. Look at that puss. He looks like Boris Karloff.

[JONATHAN, *at the mention of Boris Karloff, leaps at* KLEIN'S *throat*]

BROPHY: What d'you think you're doing?

KLEIN: Get him off me. Pat! Grab him! [BROPHY *swings on* JONATHAN *with his nightstick.* JONATHAN *falls, unconscious*] Well, what do you know about that?

[*There is a knock at the door*]

O'HARA: Come in!

[LIEUTENANT ROONEY *bursts in. He is a very tough, driving, dominating police officer*]

ROONEY: What the hell are you men doing here? I told you *I* was going to handle this.

KLEIN: Well, sir, we was just. . . . [KLEIN'S *eyes go to the prostrate* JONATHAN *and* ROONEY *sees him*]

ROONEY: What happened? Did he put up a fight?

BROPHY: This ain't the guy that blows the bugle. This is his brother. He tried to kill Klein.

KLEIN: [*Feeling his throat*] All I said was he looked like Boris Karloff.

[ROONEY *gives them a look*]

ROONEY: Turn him over!

BROPHY: We kinda think he's wanted somewhere.

[KLEIN *and* BROPHY *turn* JONATHAN *over and* ROONEY *takes a look at him*]

ROONEY: Oh, you kinda *think* he's wanted somewhere? If you guys don't look at the circulars we hang up in the station, at least you could read *True Detective*. Certainly he's wanted! In Indiana! Escaped from the Prison for the Criminal Insane—he's a lifer. For God's sake, that's how he was described—he looked like *Karloff!*

KLEIN: Was there a reward mentioned?

ROONEY: Yeah—and *I'm* claiming it.

BROPHY: He was trying to get us down in the cellar.

KLEIN: He said there was thirteen bodies buried down there.

ROONEY: Thirteen bodies buried in the cellar? And that didn't tip you off he came out of a nut house?

O'HARA: I thought all along he talked kinda crazy.

[ROONEY *sees* O'HARA *for the first time*]

ROONEY: Oh—it's Shakespeare! Where have you been all night—and you needn't bother to tell me!

O'HARA: I've been right here, sir, writing a play with Mortimer Brewster.

ROONEY: Yeah? Well, you're going to have plenty of time to write that play. You're suspended!

O'HARA: [*Getting his hat and coat*] Can I come over some time and use the station typewriter?

ROONEY: No! Get out! [O'HARA *gets out.* TEDDY *enters on the balcony and comes downstairs*] Take that guy somewhere else and bring him to. See what you can find out about his accomplice—the guy that helped him escape. He's wanted, too. [KLEIN *and* BROPHY *are bending over* JONATHAN] No wonder Brooklyn's in the shape it's in. With the police force full of flatheads like you. Falling for that kind of a story—thirteen bodies buried in the cellar!

[TEDDY *has reached* ROONEY'S *side*]

TEDDY: But there are thirteen bodies in the cellar.

ROONEY: [*Turning on him*] Who are you?

TEDDY: I'm President Roosevelt.

[ROONEY *goes slightly crazy*]

ROONEY: What the hell is this?

BROPHY: He's the fellow that blows the bugle.

KLEIN: Good morning, Colonel.

[BROPHY *and* KLEIN *salute* TEDDY. TEDDY *returns the salute.* ROONEY *almost salutes but stops halfway*]

ROONEY: Well, Colonel, you've blown your last bugle!

[TEDDY'S *attention has been attracted to the body on the floor*]

TEDDY: Dear me, another yellow fever victim!

ROONEY: What?

TEDDY: All the bodies in the cellar are yellow fever victims.

[ROONEY *takes a walk on this*]

BROPHY: No, Colonel, this is a spy we caught in the White House.

ROONEY: [*Pointing to* JONATHAN] Will you get that guy out of here? [BROPHY *and* KLEIN *pick up* JONATHAN] Bring him to and question him.

[MORTIMER *enters on the balcony carrying* TEDDY'S *commitment papers, and starts downstairs*]

TEDDY: If there's any questioning of spies—that's my department!

[BROPHY *and* KLEIN *drag* JONATHAN *into the kitchen.* TEDDY *starts to follow*]

ROONEY: Hey, you—keep out of that!

TEDDY: You're forgetting! As President, I'm also head of the Secret Service. [*He exits into the kitchen.* MORTIMER *has come down*]

MORTIMER: Captain—I'm Mortimer Brewster.

ROONEY: [*Dizzy by this time*] Are you sure?

MORTIMER: I'd like to talk to you about my brother Teddy—the one who blew the bugle.

ROONEY: Mr. Brewster, we ain't going to talk about that—he's got to be put away.

MORTIMER: I quite agree with you, Captain. In fact, it's all arranged for. I had these commitment papers signed by Dr. Gilchrist last night. Teddy has just signed them himself—you see. And I've signed them as next of kin.

[ROONEY *looks at the papers.* EINSTEIN *enters hurriedly through the arch, sees the policeman and sneaks back out of sight*]

ROONEY: Where's he going?

MORTIMER: Happy Dale. . . .

ROONEY: All right. I don't care where he goes as long as he goes!

MORTIMER: Oh, he's going all right. But I want you to understand that everything that's happened around here Teddy's responsible for. Now, those thirteen bodies in the cellar. . . .

ROONEY: Yeah—those thirteen bodies in the cellar! It ain't enough that the neighbors are afraid of him and his disturbing the peace with that bugle—

but can you imagine what would happen if that cockeyed story about thirteen bodies in the cellar got around? And now he's starting a yellow fever scare. Cute, ain't it?

MORTIMER: [*Greatly relieved and with an embarrassed laugh*] Thirteen bodies! Do you think anybody would believe that story?

ROONEY: You can't tell. Some people are just dumb enough. You don't know what to believe sometimes. A year ago, a crazy guy started a murder rumor over in Greenpoint and I had to dig up a half-acre lot, just to prove . . .

    [*There is a knock at the door*]

MORTIMER: Excuse me!

    [*He goes to the door and admits* ELAINE *and* MR. WITHERSPOON, *an elderly, tight-lipped disciplinarian. He is carrying a briefcase*]

ELAINE: [*Briskly*] Good morning, Mortimer!

MORTIMER: Good morning, dear.

ELAINE: This is Mr. Witherspoon. He's come to meet Teddy.

MORTIMER: To meet Teddy?

ELAINE: Mr. Witherspoon's the Superintendent of Happy Dale.

MORTIMER: [*Eagerly*] Oh, come right in! This is Captain . . .

ROONEY: Lieutenant Rooney. I'm glad you're here, Super, because you're taking him back with you today!

WITHERSPOON: Today! I had no idea . . .

ELAINE: Not today!

MORTIMER: Elaine, I've got a lot of business to attend to, so you run along home and I'll call you up.

ELAINE: Nuts! [*She walks over and plants herself on the window seat*]

WITHERSPOON: I didn't realize it was this immediate.

ROONEY: The papers are all signed. He goes today.

    [TEDDY *enters from the kitchen*]

TEDDY: [*Looking back*] It's insubordination! You'll find out I'm no molly-coddle. [*He advances into the room angrily*] When the President of the United States is treated that way, what's this country coming to?

ROONEY: There's your man, Super.

MORTIMER: Just a minute! [*He goes to* TEDDY *and speaks with great dignity*] Mr. President! I have very good news for you. Your term of office is over.

TEDDY: Is this March fourth?

MORTIMER: Practically.

TEDDY: Let's see! [*He thinks it over*] Oh—now I go on my hunting trip to Africa! Well, I must get started immediately. [*He starts across, sees* WITHERSPOON, *steps back to* MORTIMER, *and speaks sotto voce*] Is he trying to move into the White House before I've moved out?

MORTIMER: Who, Teddy?

TEDDY: [*Indicating* WITHERSPOON] Taft!

MORTIMER: This isn't Mr. Taft, Teddy. This is Mr. Witherspoon. He's going to be your guide in Africa.

TEDDY: Bully! Bully! [*He shakes* MR. WITHERSPOON's *hand*] Wait right here— I'll bring down my equipment. [MARTHA AND ABBY *enter on the balcony and come downstairs*] When the safari comes tell them to wait. [*To his aunts as he passes them on the stairs*] Good-by, Aunt Abby. Good-by, Aunt Martha. I'm on my way to Africa. Isn't it wonderful? [*He has reached the landing*] CHARGE! [*He charges up and out*]

MARTHA: Good morning, Mortimer.

MORTIMER: Good morning, darlings.

MARTHA: Good morning, Elaine. Well, we have visitors.

MORTIMER: This is Lieutenant Rooney.

ABBY: [*Going to him*] Well, Lieutenant, you don't look like the fuss-budget the policemen say you are.

MORTIMER: Why the Lieutenant is here—you know Teddy blew that bugle again last night.

MARTHA: Yes, we're going to speak to Teddy about that.

ROONEY: It's a little more serious than that, Miss Brewster.

MORTIMER: And you haven't met Mr. Witherspoon—he's the Superintendent of Happy Dale.

ABBY: How do you do?

MARTHA: Oh—you've come to meet Teddy.

ROONEY: He's come to *take* him.

MORTIMER: Aunties, the police want Teddy to go there *today*.

ABBY: Oh—no!

MARTHA: Not as long as we're alive!

ROONEY: I'm sorry, Miss Brewster, but it has to be done. The papers are all signed and he's going along with the Superintendent.

ABBY: We won't permit it! We'll promise to take the bugle away from him.

MARTHA: We won't be separated from Teddy!

ROONEY: I know how you feel, ladies, but the law's the law. He's committed himself and he's going.

ABBY: Well, if he goes, we're going too!

MARTHA: Yes, you'll have to take us with him!

MORTIMER: Well, why not?

WITHERSPOON: [*To* MORTIMER] It's sweet of them to want to, but it's impossible. You see, we can't take *sane* people at Happy Dale.

MARTHA: Mr. Witherspoon, if you'll let us live there with Teddy, we'll see that Happy Dale is in our will and for a very generous amount.

WITHERSPOON: The Lord knows we could use the money, but I'm afraid . . .

ROONEY: Now, let's be sensible about this, ladies. For instance, here I am wasting my morning when I've got serious work to do. You know there are still *murders* to be solved in Brooklyn.

MORTIMER: Yes! [*He remembers a few*] Oh, are there?

ROONEY: It ain't only his bugle-blowing and the neighbors all afraid of him, but things would just get worse. Sooner or later we'd be put to the trouble of digging up your cellar.

ABBY: Our cellar?

ROONEY: Yeah—your nephew is telling around that there are thirteen bodics buried in your cellar.

ABBY: But there are thirteen bodies in our cellar.

MARTHA: If that's why you think Teddy has to go away—you come down to the cellar with us and we'll prove it to you.

ABBY: There's one, Mr. Spenalzo—who doesn't belong there and is going to have to leave—and the other twelve are our gentlemen.

    [MORTIMER *crosses and stands in front of the cellar door to head them off*]

MORTIMER: I don't think the Lieutenant wants to go down in the cellar. He was just telling me that last year he had to dig up a half-acre lot—weren't you, Lieutenant?

ABBY: Oh, he doesn't have to dig here. The graves are all marked. We put flowers on them every Sunday.

ROONEY: Flowers? [*He thinks that one over and looks at* WITHERSPOON] Superintendent—don't you think you can find room for these ladies?

WITHERSPOON: Well, I . . .

ABBY: You come along with us—and see the graves.

ROONEY: I'll take your word for it, lady—I'm a busy man. How about it, Super?

WITHERSPOON: They'd have to be committed.

MORTIMER: Teddy committed himself. Can't they do that? Can't they sign the papers?

WITHERSPOON: Certainly.

MARTHA: Oh, if we can go with Teddy we'll sign the papers. Where are they?

ABBY: Yes, where are they?

    [*The sisters cross to the table and sit, ready to sign.* WITHERSPOON *produces the papers from his briefcase.* KLEIN *enters from kitchen*]

KLEIN: [To ROONEY] He's coming around, Lieutenant.

ABBY: Good morning, Mr. Klein.

MARTHA: Good morning, Mr. Klein. Are you here, too?

KLEIN: Yeah, me and Brophy have got your other nephew out in the kitchen.

ROONEY: Sign 'em up, Superintendent. I want to get this all cleaned up. Thirteen bodies!

[*He and* KLEIN *exit into the kitchen.* WITHERSPOON *and* MORTIMER *produce fountain pens*]

WITHERSPOON: [*To* MARTHA] If you'll sign right here.

[MARTHA *takes his pen*]

MORTIMER: [*Handing* ABBY *his pen*] And you here, Aunt Abby.

ABBY: I'm really looking forward to going. The neighborhood here has changed so.

MARTHA: Just think, a front lawn again!

[*They both sign.* EINSTEIN *enters on the balcony and comes downstairs stealthily*]

WITHERSPOON: Oh—we're overlooking something.

MARTHA: What?

WITHERSPOON: Well, we're going to need the signature of a physician.

[MORTIMER *straightens up, sees* EINSTEIN *slipping out the door*]

MORTIMER: Oh, Dr. Einstein! Will you come over here and sign some papers?

EINSTEIN: Please. . . .

MORTIMER: Come right along, Doctor. At one time last night, I thought the doctor was going to operate on me. [EINSTEIN *crosses nervously to the table*] Just sign right here.

[ROONEY *enters and goes to the telephone, unseen by* EINSTEIN, *and starts dialing.* KLEIN *has come in through the kitchen door*]

ABBY: Were you leaving, Doctor?

EINSTEIN: Yes, I think so.

MARTHA: Aren't you going to wait for Jonathan?

EINSTEIN: I don't think we're going to the same place.

[EINSTEIN *signs the papers hurriedly.* MORTIMER *suddenly rediscovers* ELAINE *patiently sitting on the window seat*]

MORTIMER: Oh, hello, darling! Glad to see you. Stick around.

ELAINE: Don't worry. I'm going to.

ROONEY: [*Into the telephone*] Hello, Mac? Rooney. We've picked up that guy that's wanted in Indiana. There's a description of his accomplice on the circular—it's right on the desk there. Read it to me. [EINSTEIN *starts for the kitchen but sees* KLEIN. *He retreats toward the front door but is stopped by* ROONEY's *voice.* ROONEY's *eyes are somewhat blankly on* EINSTEIN *through the following description*] Yeah—about fifty-four—five-foot-six—a hundred and forty pounds—blue eyes—talks with a German accent—poses as a doctor—Thanks, Mac. [*He hangs up*]

WITHERSPOON: [*To* ROONEY] It's all right, Lieutenant. The doctor here has just completed the signatures.

ROONEY: [*Going to* EINSTEIN *and shaking his hand*] Thanks, Doc. You're really doing Brooklyn a service.

[ROONEY *and* KLEIN *exit into kitchen*]

EINSTEIN: [*Bolts for the front door*] If you'll excuse me, I'd better hurry.

[*He exits, waving a good-by. The aunts wave gaily back*]

WITHERSPOON: [*To* MORTIMER] Mr. Brewster, you sign now as next of kin.

ABBY: [*A little upset by this*] Martha. . . .

[*The sisters go into a huddle*]

MORTIMER: Oh, yes, of course. Right here? [*He signs the papers*]

WITHERSPOON: Yes. . . . That's fine.

MORTIMER: That makes everything complete? Everything legal?

WITHERSPOON: Oh, yes.

MORTIMER: Well, Aunties, now you're safe!

WITHERSPOON: [*To the aunts*] When do you think you'll be ready to start?

ABBY: [*Nervously*] Well, Mr. Witherspoon, why don't you go up and tell Teddy what he can take along?

WITHERSPOON: Upstairs? [*He starts across the room*]

MORTIMER: I'll show you. [*He starts, but* ABBY *stops him*]

ABBY: No, Mortimer, you stay here. We want to talk to you. [*To* WITHERSPOON] Just up the stairs and turn left.

[WITHERSPOON *starts up, the sisters keeping an eye on him while talking to* MORTIMER]

MARTHA: Mortimer, now that we're moving—this house is really yours.

ABBY: Yes, Mortimer, we want you to live here.

MORTIMER: No, Aunt Abby, I couldn't do that. This house is too full of memories.

MARTHA: But you'll need a home when you and Elaine are married.

MORTIMER: Darlings, that's very indefinite.

ELAINE: [*Still in there fighting*] It's nothing of the kind. We're going to be married right away.

[*The sisters watch* WITHERSPOON *as he exits through the balcony door, then turn to* MORTIMER]

ABBY: Mortimer, we're really very worried about something.

MORTIMER: Now, Aunt Abby, you're going to love it at Happy Dale.

MARTHA: Oh, yes, we're very happy about the whole thing! That's just it! We don't want anything to go wrong.

ABBY: Will they investigate those signatures?

MORTIMER: Now, don't worry—they're not going to look up Dr. Einstein.

MARTHA: It's not his signature, dear, it's yours.

ABBY: You see, you signed as next of kin.

MORTIMER: Of course. Why not?

MARTHA: It's something we've never wanted to tell you, Mortimer. But now you're a man—and it's something Elaine should know, too. You see, you're not really a Brewster.

[MORTIMER *stares*]

ABBY: Your mother came to us as a cook—and you were born about three months afterward. But she was such a sweet woman—and such a good cook—and we didn't want to lose her—so brother married her.

MORTIMER: I'm—not—really—a—Brewster?

MARTHA: Now don't feel badly about it, Mortimer.

ABBY: And you won't let it make any difference, Elaine?

MORTIMER: Elaine! Did you hear—do you understand? I'm a bastard!

[ELAINE *leaps into his illegitimate arms*]

MARTHA: [*Relieved*] Well, I'll have to see about breakfast. [*She starts for the kitchen*]

ELAINE: Mortimer's coming to my house. Father's gone to Philadelphia and Mortimer and I are going to have breakfast together.

MORTIMER: Yes, I need some coffee. I've had quite a night.

ABBY: Well, Mortimer, in that case, I should think you'd want to get to bed.

MORTIMER: [*With a glance at* ELAINE] I do.

[*He leads her out.* ABBY *closes the door.* WITHERSPOON *enters from balcony door, carrying an armful of canteens.* TEDDY *enters with an enormous, two-bladed canoe paddle*]

TEDDY: Just a minute, Mr. Witherspoon. Take this with you!

[*He hands the paddle to* WITHERSPOON *and goes back through the balcony door.* WITHERSPOON, *encumbered, comes downstairs.* ROONEY *enters from the kitchen, followed by* JONATHAN, *handcuffed to* KLEIN *and* BROPHY]

ROONEY: We won't need the wagon. My car's out front.

MARTHA: [*Pleasantly*] Oh, you leaving now, Jonathan?

ROONEY: Yes. He's going to Indiana. Some people out there want to take care of him the rest of his life. [*To* JONATHAN] Come on.

[*The handcuffed three start*]

ABBY: Well, Jonathan, it's nice to know you have some place to go.

[JONATHAN *stops*]

JONATHAN: Good-by, Aunt Abby. Good-by, Aunt Martha.

MARTHA: We're leaving, too.

ABBY: We're going to Happy Dale.

JONATHAN: Then this house is seeing the last of the Brewsters.

MARTHA: Unless Mortimer would like to live here.

JONATHAN: I have a suggestion. Why don't you turn this property over to the church?

[*The aunts look at each other*]

ABBY: Well, we never thought of that.

JONATHAN: [*Dryly*] After all, it *should* be a part of the cemetery. [*He starts, then turns back*] Well, I won't be able to better my record now, but neither will you. At least, I have that satisfaction. The score stands even— *twelve to twelve.*

> [JONATHAN *and the policemen exit. The aunts bristle slightly, looking out after* JONATHAN]

MARTHA: Jonathan always was a mean boy. He never could stand to see anyone get ahead of him. [*She closes the door*]

ABBY: I wish we could show him he isn't so smart! [*She turns and her eyes fall on* WITHERSPOON, *standing looking out the window. She studies him.* MARTHA *turns from the door and sees* ABBY's *contemplation*] Mr. Witherspoon, does your family live with you at Happy Dale?

WITHERSPOON: I have no family.

ABBY: Oh. . . .

MARTHA: Well, I suppose you consider everyone at Happy Dale your family?

WITHERSPOON: I'm afraid you don't understand. As head of the institution, I have to keep quite aloof.

ABBY: That must make it very lonely for you.

WITHERSPOON: It does. But my duty is my duty.

ABBY: [*Benignly*] Well, Martha. . . . [MARTHA *immediately starts for the sideboard*] If Mr. Witherspoon won't have breakfast with us, I think at least we should offer him a glass of elderberry wine.

WITHERSPOON: Elderberry wine?

> [MARTHA *takes out a wine bottle but it is the one* EINSTEIN *has emptied. She reaches in for another*]

MARTHA: We make it oursleves. [*She uncorks the fresh bottle*]

WITHERSPOON: Why, yes! Of course, at Happy Dale our relationship will be more formal, but here . . . [*He sits, as* MARTHA *brings the wine with a single wine glass to the table*] You don't see much elderberry wine nowadays. I thought I'd had my last glass of it.

ABBY: Oh, no. . . .

MARTHA: [*Handing it to him*] Here it is!

> [WITHERSPOON *bows to the ladies and lifts the glass to his lips, but the* CURTAIN FALLS *before he does*]

Same Time, Next Year

BERNARD SLADE

BERNARD SLADE

Probably the most successful two-character comedy ever to grace the Broadway stage, Bernard Slade's *Same Time, Next Year* had a run of 1,444 performances and shares ninth place with *Arsenic and Old Lace* on the chart of longest-running plays.

Clive Barnes of *The New York Times* considered it "the funniest comedy about love and adultery to come Broadway's way in years. If that were not enough, it is also touching." Martin Gottfried of the *New York Post* concurred: "A very funny romantic play. It is also honest and true and heartfelt." Even *New York Magazine*'s generally caustic John Simon came under its spell: "I warmly recommend *Same Time, Next Year*. It is genuinely funny, often moving, and slyly perspicacious throughout."

Not only was the comedy cited but so were the performances by Ellen Burstyn (winner of an Antoinette Perry (Tony) Award for her portrayal of the errant housewife) and Charles Grodin (as her willing partner), and the wonderfully adroit direction by Gene Saks.

The play was nominated for a Tony, won a Drama Desk Award, and subsequently was presented in thirty-three foreign productions. The movie of *Same Time, Next Year* was released in 1978. Both Mr. Slade (who also wrote the screenplay) and Ellen Burstyn (costarred with Alan Alda in a recreation of her stage role) were nominated for Academy Awards for their work on the film.

Bernard Slade was born May 2, 1930, in St. Catherines, Ontario. He left Canada at the age of five for England where his father worked in the aircraft industry before and during the war. Educated in various parts of England ("My father was moved around a lot: North Wales, Brighton, Nottingham, the outskirts of London. I never lived in the same house two years in a row until I was married, and went to thirteen changes of schools; some I hit three times."), he returned to Canada at eighteen determined to be an actor. "In England there'd been repertory companies, one almost in every town. You'd go to them the way people go to movies. I was bitten by the acting bug, and now I started acting in summer stock."

He worked in stock and television for the next decade and with his wife, television actress Jill Foster, opened and maintained the Garden Center Theatre in Vineland, Canada, near Niagara Falls.

In 1957 he made the transition to writer and his first work was a television play, *The Long, Long Laugh,* the first of his many television scripts that were seen in Canada, England, and on all three American networks.

Mr. Slade next turned his hand to writing for the theatre and his initial effort, *Simon Says Get Married,* was presented at the Crest Theatre in Toronto. This was followed by *A Very Close Family* at the Manitoba Theatre.

In 1964 the Slades moved to Los Angeles where he was put under contract to Columbia Pictures, mainly for television work. He was the story editor and author of the first and sixteen other episodes of the *Bewitched* television series, and creator of the pilot programs for *The Flying Nun* and *The Partridge Family.*

On June 1, 1978, Mr. Slade returned to Broadway with his second success, *Tribute,* starring Jack Lemmon. What made the occasion particularly unique in theatrical circles was the fact that producer Morton Gottlieb paid off all his backers that same night from profits accrued from the out-of-town tryout engagements and the sale of motion picture rights.

Romantic Comedy, the third joint enterprise between playwright Bernard Slade and producer Morton Gottlieb, opened on Broadway in the autumn of 1979.

SAME TIME, NEXT YEAR was first produced at the Brooks Atkinson Theatre, New York, on March 13, 1975, by Morton Gottlieb, Dasha Epstein, Edward L. Schuman and Palladium Productions. The cast was as follows:

DORIS   *Ellen Burstyn*

GEORGE   *Charles Grodin*

Directed by Gene Saks
Scenery by William Ritman
Costumes by Jane Greenwood
Lighting by Tharon Musser
Associate Producers: Ben Rosenberg, Warren Crane

The entire action of the play takes place in a room in a traditional country-style inn, two hundred miles north of San Francisco.

ACT ONE

SCENE 1: *A day in February, 1951.*
SCENE 2: *A day in February, 1956.*
SCENE 3: *A day in February, 1961.*

ACT TWO

SCENE 1: *A day in February, 1965.*
SCENE 2: *A day in February, 1970.*
SCENE 3: *A day in February, 1975.*

ACT ONE

The Time: A day in February, 1951.

The Place: A bed-sitting room in the cottage of a country-style inn near Mendocino, north of San Francisco. The beamed ceilings, wood-burning fireplace, wallpaper, durable antique furniture, and burnished brass lamps and fittings give the setting a feeling of comfortable warmth and respectable tradition. The room is large enough to contain a sturdy double bed, chintz-covered sofa and armchairs, and a baby grand piano. There are two leaded pane glass windows, a closet door, a door leading to a bathroom and another door that opens to an outside patio. The room's aura of permanence is not an illusion. The decor has been the same for the past twenty-five years and will not change for the next twenty-five.

At Rise: GEORGE *and* DORIS *are asleep in bed. He is twenty-seven with a likable average face and an intense nervous energy that gives everything he does a slightly frenetic quality, but doesn't always cover his deep-seated insecurity. Something wakes him, and as he groggily turns over his eyes fall upon the sleeping form of* DORIS *beside him. He sits bolt upright in bed, instantly wide awake.*

GEORGE: [*Fervently*] Oh, Jesus! [*He slips out of bed and we see he is wearing only boxer shorts. He grabs his sports coat from the floor, puts it on and surveys the clothes strewn about the room. They include the rest of his clothes and her blouse, skirt, stockings, bra, girdle, and shoes*] Jesus H. Christ!

[*He looks back at* DORIS *and then quickly moves to the dresser where he grabs a bottle of Wildroot Cream Oil, massages it into his scalp and starts to comb his short, tousled hair.*

While he is doing this DORIS *wakes up, sits up in bed, watches him. At this point in time she is slightly overweight, with ordinary pretty looks and a friendly, unself-conscious, ingenuous manner that makes her immediately appealing despite the fact that at twenty-four she hasn't had the time or the education to find out who or what she is yet. When she speaks there is a forced gaiety to her voice*]

DORIS: Hey, that's a real sharp-looking outfit.

[*At the sound of her voice he turns around to look at her*]

GEORGE: Uh—hi.

[*They eye one another for a moment*]

DORIS: What time is it?

GEORGE: Uh—my watch is on the bedside table.

511

[*As she leans over to look at his watch, he makes a distracted attempt to clean up the room. This consists of picking up his trousers and his right shoe. He puts on his trousers during the following*]

DORIS: [*Puzzled*] It says ten to eleven.

GEORGE: No, it's twenty-five after seven. It's always three hours and twenty-five minutes fast.

DORIS: Why?

GEORGE: When I got it back from being fixed at the watchmaker's it was set three hours and twenty-five minutes fast. I decided to keep it that way.

DORIS: [*Bewildered*] Doesn't that mix you up?

GEORGE: No, I'm very quick with figures.

DORIS: But what about other people?

GEORGE: [*Agitated*] Look, it's *my* watch!

DORIS: What are you so sore about?

[*He takes a deep breath*]

GEORGE: [*Grimly*] Because we're in a lot of trouble.

DORIS: Yeah?

GEORGE: God, why do you have to look so—so luminous!

DORIS: Luminous?

GEORGE: I mean it would make everything so much easier if you woke up with puffy eyes and blotchy skin like most women.

DORIS: I guess God figured chubby thighs was enough.

GEORGE: Look, this thing is not just going to go away. We've got to talk about it.

DORIS: Okay. [*She gets out of bed, pulls the sheet out, puts it around her over her slip and heads across the room*]

GEORGE: What are you doing?

DORIS: I thought I'd clean my teeth first.

GEORGE: Dorothy, sit down. [*She opens her mouth to speak*] Please—sit. [*She moves to a chair, sits with the sheet wrapped around her.*

He paces for a moment, gathering his thoughts before he turns to face her. When he speaks it is with great sincerity] Dorothy, first of all, I want you to know last night was the most beautiful, fantastic, wonderful, crazy thing that's ever happened to me and I'll never forget it—or you.

DORIS: Doris.

GEORGE: What?

DORIS: My name's Doris.

GEORGE: [*Thrown*] Why didn't you say so earlier? All last night I called you Dorothy and you never said anything.

DORIS: I didn't expect us to end up this—you know—[*She trails off*] Then when I did try to tell you—you weren't listening.

GEORGE: When?

DORIS: [*Embarrassed*] It was—you know—in the middle of—things.

[*He fixes her with a look of smoldering intensity*]

GEORGE: It was incredible, wasn't it?

DORIS: It was—nice. [*Sensing he expects something more*] Especially the last time.

GEORGE: [*Anguished*] I know—I'm an animal! [*He throws the shoe he is holding into the sofa, moves away to look out of the window. She takes this opportunity to kneel down to gather up some of her clothes*] I don't know what got into me. I just—what was the matter with the other two times?

DORIS: What? Oh—well, the first time was so fast and the second—look, I feel funny talking about this.

GEORGE: [*Earnestly*] It was a very beautiful thing, Doris. There was nothing disgusting or dirty in what we did.

DORIS: Then how come you're looking so down in the dumps?

GEORGE: Because my wife is going to *kill* me!!

DORIS: Why should she find out?

GEORGE: She knows already.

DORIS: You said she was in New Jersey!

GEORGE: [*Gloomily*] It doesn't matter. She *knows.*

DORIS: How come?

GEORGE: Look, I don't want to talk about it! [*He stares at her*] Doris, was it as incredible for you as it was for me?

DORIS: [*Curiously*] Do all men like to talk about it a lot afterwards?

GEORGE: [*Defensively*] Why? You think I'm some sort of—eccentric or something?

DORIS: No, I just wondered. See, I was a virgin when I got married. At least technically.

GEORGE: Technically?

DORIS: Well, I was pregnant. I don't count that.

GEORGE: [*Doubtfully*] Doris, that counts.

DORIS: I mean it was by the man I married.

GEORGE: Oh, I'm sorry.

[*She sits, puts on stocking during following*]

DORIS: That's okay. Harry and me would've got married anyway. It just hurried things up a bit. [*Brightly*] Turns out I get pregnant if we drink from the same cup. [*He looks at her, pales a little, and gulps*] What's the matter?

GEORGE: [*Quickly*] It's okay. Trojans are very reliable.

DORIS: Who are?

GEORGE: Never mind.[*He stares at her*] We're in a lot of trouble, Doris.

DORIS: Why?

GEORGE: I think I love you.

DORIS: Better not start up something we can't finish, George.

GEORGE: Maybe it's too late for that. [*Suddenly*] It's crazy! It's really crazy! I mean I don't even know if you like *Catcher in the Rye!*

DORIS: What?

GEORGE: I have this test for people. If they don't like *Catcher in the Rye* or *Death of a Salesman* I won't even date them!

DORIS: I never even finished high school.

GEORGE: [*Wildly*] You see? I don't even *care!* And I'm really a *snob* about education! [*He moves and bleakly stares out of window.* DORIS *puts on her skirt and blouse during the following*] Of course I should've known this would happen. You see, there's something I didn't tell you about me, Doris.

DORIS: What?

GEORGE: When it comes to life I have a brown thumb. I mean nothing goes right. Ever.

DORIS: How do you mean?

GEORGE: Well, let me think of something that will give you the picture. [*He thinks*] Okay. I was eighteen when I first had sex. It was in the back seat of a parked 1938 Dodge sedan. Right in the middle of it—we were rear ended.

DORIS: Gee, that's terrible. Did you have insurance?

GEORGE: And take last night. You know what they were playing on the juke box when we met? [*She shakes her head*] "If I Knew You Were Coming I'd've Baked a Cake"!

DORIS: [*Puzzled*] So?

GEORGE: So that's going to be "our song"! [*He moves to angrily throw a log on the smoldering fire*] Other people would get "Be My Love" or "Hello, Young Lovers." Me—I get "If I knew You Were Coming I'd've Baked a Cake"!

DORIS: [*Sentimentally*] You're very romantic. I like that.

　　[*He looks at her*]

GEORGE: And what about you? I think I've fallen in love with you, Doris. Now you want to know the luck I have? I'm happily married!

DORIS: [*Curiously*] Are you Jewish?

GEORGE: [*Thrown*] No, I'm not Jewish. [*He takes off coat, puts on shirt*] As a matter of fact, I'm the result of a very strict Methodist upbringing.

DORIS: Is that why you feel so guilty?

GEORGE: Don't *you* feel guilty?

DORIS: Are you kidding? Half my high school graduating class became nuns.

GEORGE: Yeah, I guess Catholics have rules about this sort of thing.

DORIS: They have rules about everything. That's what's so great about being Catholic. You know where you stand and all.

[*He looks at her for a moment, shakes his head, starts to pace*]

GEORGE: I tell you, Doris, I feel like slitting my wrists.

DORIS: Are you Italian?

GEORGE: What's with you and nationalities?

DORIS: You're so emotional.

GEORGE: I happen to be a C.P.A. I mean I can be as logical as the next person.

DORIS: You don't strike me as an accountant type.

GEORGE: It's very simple. [*He shrugs*] My whole life has always been a mess. Figures always come out right. Black and white, nice and tidy. I like that. What are you?

DORIS: Italian.

GEORGE: [*Thrown*] Then why aren't you more emotional?

[*She moves to fire and warms her hands*]

DORIS: If you're brought up in a large Italian family it's enough to turn you off emotion for life, you know?

GEORGE: I wondered why you weren't crying or yelling or anything.

DORIS: I got up this morning and did all that in the john.

GEORGE: Crying?

DORIS: Yelling.

GEORGE: I didn't hear you.

DORIS: I put a towel in my mouth.

GEORGE: Oh, I'm sorry.

DORIS: That's okay. There's no use crying over spilt milk.

GEORGE: You're right.

DORIS: Then why are we feeling so lousy?

GEORGE: [*Soberly*] Because we're both decent, honest people and this thing is tearing us apart. I mean I know it wasn't our fault but I keep seeing the faces of my children and the look of betrayal in their eyes. I keep thinking of the trust my wife has placed in me. The times we've shared together. Our wedding vows. And you know the worst part of it all? Right at this moment, while I'm thinking all these things I have this fantastic hard on!

[*She looks at him for a moment, not moving*]

DORIS: [*Finally*] I wish you hadn't said that.

GEORGE: I'm sorry. I just feel we should be totally honest with each other.

DORIS: No, it's not that. I have to go to confession.

[*He looks at her for a second, breaks into rather a forced, incredulous laugh, moves away, turns to her, chuckles*]

GEORGE: This is really very funny, you know that?

DORIS: Tell me—I could use a good laugh.

GEORGE: We're both crazy! I mean this sort of thing happens to millions of people every day. We're just normal, healthy human beings who did a perfectly healthy, normal thing. You don't use actual names in confession, do you?

DORIS: No.

GEORGE: Good. You want to know what I think about marriage and sex?

DORIS: I don't want to miss confession, George.

GEORGE: After you've heard what I have to say maybe you won't need to even go. [*He moves and sits cross-legged before her*] Look, suppose you compare a husband or a wife to a good book. So you got this great book and you read it—it's terrific; you love it. So you read the book again. Still good. So you read it again and again and again and even after maybe a hundred times you still enjoy it. Well, you know the book by heart now, so for a little variety you read it standing up, then lying down, then upside down, backwards, sideways, every way you can think of. You still like it, but Jesus, how many ways are there to read a book? Just once in a while you want to hear a new story, right? It doesn't mean you *hate* the old book. You'll read it again—later. Who knows? Maybe you'll appreciate it more. [*A beat*] You understand what I'm saying?

DORIS: There's no use crying over split milk?

GEORGE: [*Getting to his feet*] Doris, you've missed the whole point!

DORIS: What is the point?

GEORGE: [*Intensely*] I've got to go to bed with you right now! [*He embraces her passionately and starts to smother her with kisses*]

DORIS: George, we can't!

GEORGE: Why not?

DORIS: You'll feel even worse afterward!

GEORGE: [*Still kissing her*] I won't, I won't! I'm over that now!

DORIS: How come?

GEORGE: I just remembered something!

DORIS: What?

GEORGE: The Russians have the bomb! We could all die tomorrow!

DORIS: [*Somewhat out of breath*] George—You're clutching at straws!

[*He grabs her by the shoulders, looks deep into her eyes*]

GEORGE: Don't you understand? We're both grown-up people who have absolutely nothing to be ashamed or afraid of!!!

[*There is a knock at the door. Both freeze, their eyes reflecting total panic. Then they go into frantic action as they both dive for the clothes on the floor. He gets her girdle but is not aware of what is in his hand. She, clutching the sheet and her shoes, bumps into him as she first tries to get under the bed and then heads for the bathroom door]*

GEORGE: [*Panic-stricken—in a desperate kiss*] Don't go into the bathroom!

[*She freezes*]

DORIS: Why not?

GEORGE: It's the first place thcy'll look! [*She heads for the window and climbs out onto the balcony as he frantically tries to make the room presentable. He looks around, sees she has disappeared but doesn't know where as he heads for the door*] I'm coming! [*He opens the door about six inches and squeezes outside, closing the door behind him. We hear a muffled exchange offstage before the door reopens and he reenters pushing a cart containing breakfast*] Doris? [*She doesn't appear and, puzzled, he looks under the bed, then in the closet, then moves to the window, pushes it open and leans outside*] Doris? [*While he is doing this she comes back into the room through the other window, moves to behind him, claps a firm hand on his shoulder, speaks in a deep voice*]

DORIS: You have a woman in here?

[*He leaps about a foot in the air with a yelp, turns to face her. She giggles and finally he gives a sheepish grin*]

GEORGE: It's okay, it was old Mr. Chalmers with my breakfast. I was very calm. He didn't suspect a thing.

DORIS: He didn't ask about the girdle?

GEORGE: What girdle? [*He looks in his hand, sees he is still clutching her girdle. Anguished*] Oh—great! Now he probably thinks I'm a—a homo!

DORIS: What do you care?

GEORGE: I stay here every year.

[*She moves to peek under platters on breakfast cart*]

DORIS: How come?

GEORGE: There's this guy I went to school with who went into the wine business near here. I fly out the same weekend every year to do his books.

DORIS: From New Jersey?

GEORGE: He was my first client. It's kind of a sentimental thing.

DORIS: Oh. [*She looks at him*] Uh—can I have my girdle back?

GEORGE: Oh, sorry—sure. [*He extends girdle, she reaches for it but he keeps hold of the other end, so they are both holding an end*] Doris, there's something I want to tell you.

DORIS: What?

GEORGE: You probably think I do this sort of thing all the time. I mean I know I must appear smooth and glib—sexually. Well, I want you to know that since I've been married this is the very first time I've done this. [*A beat*] Do you believe me?

DORIS: Sure, I could tell. Hey, you mind if I have some of your breakfast? I'm starved!

GEORGE: Oh, sure—help yourself, I'm not hungry. [*She takes her girdle, pulls a chair up to the cart and starts to eat as he starts to pace*] It's funny, even when I was single I was no good at quick, superficial affairs. I had to be able to really *like* the person before—[*Turning to her suddenly*] What do you mean, you could tell?

DORIS: What? Oh—I don't know—the way you tried to get your pants off over your shoes and then tripped and hit your head on the bed post. [*Her eyes twinkling*] Little things like that.

[*He smiles at her affectionately*]

GEORGE: It's great to be able to be totally honest with another person, isn't it?

DORIS: It sure is.

[*His expression changes*]

GEORGE: Doris, I haven't been totally honest with you.

DORIS: No?

GEORGE: No. [*He takes a deep breath*] Okay—here it comes—the big one. [*She waits expectantly*] I told you I was a married man with two children.

DORIS: You're not?

GEORGE: No. I'm a married man with *three* children.

DORIS: I don't get it.

GEORGE: I thought it would make me seem less married. [*Under her gaze he becomes agitated and starts to pace*] Look, I just didn't think it through. Anyway, it's been like a lead weight inside me all morning. I mean denying little Debbie like that. I'm sorry, I was under a certain stress or I wouldn't have done it. You understand?

DORIS: Sure, we all do nutty things sometimes. [*He smiles in relief*] So how come your wife doesn't travel with you?

GEORGE: Phyllis won't get on a plane.

DORIS: She's afraid of flying?

GEORGE: Crashing. [*He watches her eat for a moment. She looks up*]

DORIS: What's the matter?

GEORGE: Nothing. I just love the way you eat.

[*She grins at him, holds up coffee pot*]

DORIS: You wanta share a cup of coffee?

[*He nods, pulls up a chair opposite her, gazes at her as she pours coffee*]

GEORGE: Doris, I've been thinking. Sometimes if you *know* why something happened it makes it easier to understand.

DORIS: You mean like us?

GEORGE: Right. Doris, do you believe that two total strangers can look across a room and both have this sudden, overwhelming, totally irrational desire to possess one another in every possible way?

DORIS: [*She considers for a moment*] No.

GEORGE: [*Puzzled*] Neither do I—so I guess that can't be it. Then how did this whole thing start?

DORIS: It started when you sent me over that steak in the restaurant.

GEORGE: They didn't serve drinks. Steak was all they had.

DORIS: What made you do it?

GEORGE: Impulse. Usually I never do that sort of thing. I have this—this friend who says that life is saying "yes." [*He shrugs*] The most I can generally manage is "maybe."

DORIS: Your wife sounds like a nice person. [*He reacts*] So why'd you do it?

GEORGE: I guess I was lonely and you looked so—so vulnerable and—well, you had a run in your stocking and your lipstick was smeared.

DORIS: You thought I looked cheap?

GEORGE: [*Quickly*] No—beautiful. I'm attracted by flaws. I don't know—somehow they make people seem more human and—approachable. [*She gazes at him affectionately*] That's why I like Pete Reiser better than say—Joe DiMaggio.

DORIS: Pete Reiser's a baseball player?

GEORGE: He keeps running into walls. I like that.

DORIS: [*Gently*] You know something, George? You're a real nice guy. [*They smile tenderly at one another*] What made you think I was a medium rare?

GEORGE: I'm very intuitive.

DORIS: I'm well-done.

[*This jolts George out of his romantic mood*]

GEORGE: Well-done? How can anyone like meat well-done?

DORIS: Harry always has his that way.

GEORGE: Oh. What were you doing in the restaurant anyway?

DORIS: I was on my way to a retreat. I go this same weekend every year.

GEORGE: [*Thrown*] To—uh—meditate?

DORIS: Yeah, you might call it that. But not about God or anything. More about—well—myself. [*He waits, awkwardly*] See, I got pregnant when I was just eighteen and so I never had a chance to—well—live it up. Oh, I don't know what I'm trying to say. [*She shakes her head, gives a little laugh*] Sometimes I think I'm crazy.

GEORGE: Why?

DORIS: [*Awkwardly, thinking it out*] Well, look at my life. I got three little kids underfoot all the time, so I'm never alone. I live in a two-bedroom duplex in downtown Oakland, we got a 1948 Kaiser that's almost half paid for, a blond three-piece dinette set, a Motorola TV, and we go bowling at least once a week. [*A beat*] I mean, what else could anyone ask for? But sometimes things get me down, you know? It's dumb!

GEORGE: I don't think it's dumb.

DORIS: I don't know. Sometimes I—I don't know what I *think* about anything, you know? I mean I'm almost twenty-five and I still feel—well—half-formed. [*He doesn't say anything. A look of wonder comes to her face*] Will you listen to me? Honest, you make me say things out loud I haven't even *thought* to myself. [*She smiles at him*] I noticed that right after I met you last night.

GEORGE: [*Eagerly*] We had instant rapport! Did you notice that, too?

DORIS: No, but I know we really hit it off. [*A beat*] You want some more coffee?

> [*He shakes his head and watches her as she rises, moves to get sheet from where it was stuffed under the sofa, takes it to bed and starts to make bed*]

GEORGE: What happens to your kids when you go on your retreat?

DORIS: Oh, Harry takes them to see his mother in Bakersfield. It's her birthday.

GEORGE: She doesn't mind you not going?

DORIS: No, she hates me.

GEORGE: Why?

DORIS: Because I got pregnant.

> [*He moves to help her make up bed*]

GEORGE: But her son had something to do with that, too.

DORIS: She's blocked that out of her mind. Oh, I don't blame her. You see, Harry was in first year of dental college.

GEORGE: I don't get the connection.

DORIS: He had to drop out of school and take a job selling waterless cooking.

GEORGE: Oh. [*He moves away, watches her make up bed for a moment*] Look, Doris, naturally we're both curious about each other's husband and wife. But rather than dwelling on it and letting it spoil everything, why don't we do this? I'll tell you two stories—one showing the best side of my wife and the other showing the worst. Then you do the same about your husband. Okay?

DORIS: Okay.

GEORGE: I think I should go first.

DORIS: Why?

GEORGE: Because I already have my stories prepared. [*She nods, sits cross-legged on bed*] I'll start with the worst side of her.

DORIS: Go ahead.

GEORGE: [*Grimly*] Phyllis knows about us.

DORIS: You said that before. How could she possibly know?

GEORGE: Because she has this—thing in her head.

DORIS: You mean like a plate?

GEORGE: [*Thrown*] Plate?

DORIS: I got this uncle who was wounded in the war so they put this steel plate in his head and he says he can tell when it's going to rain.

[*He looks at her for a moment*]

GEORGE: Jesus, I'm in a lot of trouble.

DORIS: Why?

GEORGE: Because I find everything you say absolutely *fascinating!*

DORIS: Tell me about your wife's steel plate.

GEORGE: What? [*Brought back to earth, miserably*] No, it's not a plate—it's more like a bell. [*Becoming agitated*] I could be a million miles away but whenever I even *look* at another woman it goes off like a fire alarm! Last night at 1:22. I just know she sat bolt upright in bed with her head going, ding, ding, ding, ding! [*He nervously moves to breakfast cart and absently starts wiping off the lipstick marks on the coffee cup with his handkerchief*]

DORIS: How'd you know it was 1:22?

GEORGE: I have peripheral vision and I noticed my watch said 4:47.

DORIS: That's crazy.

GEORGE: Okay, I happen to have personal idiosyncrasies and I happen to like my watch to be—

DORIS: No, I didn't mean that. I mean about your wife's bell and all.

GEORGE: Look, I know it's just an imaginary bell but it's very real to me! [*He throws his lipstick-smeared handkerchief into the fire*]

DORIS: [*Incredulous*] You just threw your hankie into the fire.

GEORGE: We can't be too careful.

DORIS: Tell me something nice about her.

GEORGE: What? Oh—she made me believe in myself. [*He looks at her. Seriously*] It's probably hard for you to imagine, but I used to be very insecure.

DORIS: How did she do that? Make you believe in yourself?

GEORGE: She married me.

DORIS: Yes, that was very nice of her. [*He looks at her*] I mean bolstering you up and all.

[*He lies on the couch*]

GEORGE: Okay, your turn. Tell me the worst story first.

DORIS: Well—it's hard—

GEORGE: [*Eagerly*] To pick one?

DORIS: No, to think of one. Harry's the salt of the earth—everyone says so.

[*He sits upright*]

GEORGE: Look, you owe me one rotten story.

DORIS: Okay. This is not really rotten but—well— [*She gets off the bed, moves to fire, looks into it for a moment*] On our fourth anniversary we were having kind of a rough time. The kids were getting us down and—well, we'd gotten in over our heads financially but we decided to have some friends over anyway. [*She moves to look out of window*] Now Harry doesn't drink much, but that night he had a few beers and after the Gillette fights he and some of the guys started to talk and I overheard him say his time in the Army were the best years of his life.

GEORGE: [*Puzzled*] What's wrong with that? A lot of guys feel that way about the service.

[*She turns to face him*]

DORIS: Harry was in the Army four years. Three of those years were spent in a Japanese prison camp! [*A beat*] And he said this on our anniversary! Oh, I know he didn't mean to hurt me—Harry would never hurt anyone—but, well, it—hurt, you know? [*A beat*] You're the only person I've ever told.

GEORGE: You want some more coffee?

DORIS: I'll get lipstick on the cup.

GEORGE: I don't care. [*He moves to pour her coffee*]

DORIS: You wanta hear a story about the good side of him?

GEORGE: Not really.

DORIS: But you have to! I mean, I don't want you to get the wrong impression about Harry.

GEORGE: Okay, if you insist.

[*She moves to bed, plumps pillows*]

DORIS: Well, Harry's a real big, kind of heavyset sort of guy, you know?

GEORGE: I wish you hadn't told me that.

DORIS: Oh, you don't have to worry. He's gentle as—as a puppy. [*She sits on the downstage side of the bed, facing front and clasps a pillow to her chest*] Anyway, he tries to do different things with each of the kids, you know? [*He sits beside her on the bed, hands her coffee*] Thanks. So, he was having a hard time finding something special to do with Tony, our four-year-old. Then he gets the idea to take him out to the park and fly this big kite. Well, he tells Tony about it—really builds it up—and Tony gets real excited. So this one Saturday last winter they go out together, but there's no wind and Harry has trouble getting the kite to take off.

Well, it's kind of cold and Tony, who's pretty bored by now—he's only four years old—asks if he can sit in the car. Harry says, "Sure." [*She starts to smile*] About an hour later I happen to come by on my way home from the laundromat and I see Tony fast asleep in the car and Harry, all red in the face and out of breath, pounding up and down, all alone in the park, with this kite dragging along behind him on the ground. [*Her smile fades*] I don't know—somehow it really got to me.

> [*He looks at her, touched more by her reaction than by the story itself*]

GEORGE: Yeah, I know. Helen has some nice qualities, too.

DORIS: Who's Helen?

GEORGE: [*Puzzled*] My wife of course.

DORIS: You said her name was Phyllis.

> [*Caught—a split moment of panic*]

GEORGE: I know—I lied. [*She stares at him bewildered. Agitated*] Helen—Phyllis—what's the difference? I'm married! [*He gets up, paces*] Look, I was nervous and I didn't want to leave any *clues!* I mean I was scared you'd try to look me up or something!

DORIS: Is your real name George?

GEORGE: Of course it is! You don't think I'd lie about my own name, do you?

DORIS: [*Baffled*] You're crazy.

GEORGE: Well, I never claimed to be consistent!

DORIS: [*Gently*] Crazy. [*She holds out the coffee cup to him, their hands touch and they become aware of the contact. Their eyes meet. He sits beside her*]

GEORGE: [*Tenderly*] It's funny, isn't it? Here we are having breakfast in a hotel room, gazing into each other's eyes, and we're both married with six kids between us.

DORIS: You got pictures?

GEORGE: [*Thrown*] What?

DORIS: Pictures of your kids.

GEORGE: [*Uncomfortably*] *Well, sure,* but I don't think this is the time or place to—

> [*She moves for her purse*]

DORIS: I'll show you mine if you show me yours. [*Getting snapshots from purse*] I keep them in a special folder we got free from Kodak. [*She returns to bed, hands him snaps*] Where are yours?

GEORGE: [*Still off-balance*] Uh—You have to take the whole wallet. [*He extracts wallet from his back pocket, hands it to her. They are now seated side by side on the bed, looking at each other's snapshots*]

DORIS: Oh, they're cute! Is the one in the glasses and baggy tights the oldest?

GEORGE: [*Looking at snap*] Yes, that's Michael. Funny-looking kid, isn't he?

DORIS: He wants to be Superman?

GEORGE: Peter Pan. Sometimes it worries me. [*Looking at snaps in his hand*] Why is this one's face all screwed up?

DORIS: Oh, that's Paul—it was taken on a roller coaster. Isn't it natural? He threw up right after that.

GEORGE: Yeah, he's really—something. I guess he looks like Harry, huh?

DORIS: Both of us really. [*Looking at snap*] What's your little girl's name?

GEORGE: Debbie. That was taken on her second birthday. We were trying to get her to blow out the candles.

DORIS: She has her hand in the cake.

GEORGE: Yeah, neat is not her strong suit. [*They look at one another*]

DORIS: You have great-looking kids, George.

GEORGE: You, too.

DORIS: Thanks.

[*There is a slight pause*]

GEORGE: Doris?

DORIS: Yeah?

GEORGE: Let's dump the lot of them and run away together!

[*She looks at him astonished as the lights fade*]

SCENE TWO

The Time: *A day in February, 1956.*

The Place: *The same.*

At Rise: GEORGE, *wearing a charcoal suit and pink shirt of the period, has just hung a home-made sign reading "HAPPY FIFTH ANNIVERSARY, DARLING" on the front door. He has put on a few pounds, his hair has just started to thin, and at thirty-two he gives the impression of more substance. It is just an impression. Although his manner is more subdued than five years ago and his insecurities flash through less frequently, it is only because he has learned a degree of control of his mercurial moods. He takes a small birthday cake from a box and places it beside two plates and forks on the coffee table.*

DORIS: [*Offstage*] Damn!

GEORGE: What's the matter?

DORIS: [*Offstage*] It's my merry widow.

GEORGE: Your what?

DORIS: [*Offstage*] Merry widow. It mashes you in and pushes you out in all the right places. It also gives you this pale, wan look because it cuts off all circulation.

GEORGE: Be sure and let me know when you're coming out.

DORIS: [*Offstage*] Right now.

GEORGE: Wait a minute! [*He quickly moves to the piano, sits*] Okay—now

[*As she enters he sings and plays "If I Knew You Were Coming I'd've Baked a Cake."*

She is dressed in a strapless, black cocktail dress that was considered chic in the suburbs in the fifties; is slimmer than before and more carefully put together. The most striking physical change in her is her very blond hair, shaped in a Gina Lollobrigida cut. She has acquired some of the social graces of middle-class suburbia, is more articulate than before, and has developed a wry, deprecating wit that doesn't hide a certain terseness of manner.

He stops playing, moves to her and embraces her]

GEORGE: Happy anniversary, darling. [*He hands her a glass of champagne, they toast, drink, and he indicates the cake*] Cut the cake and make a wish. [*They move to sit on the sofa and he watches her as she cuts the cake*] What did you wish?

DORIS: I only have one wish.

GEORGE: What?

DORIS: That you keep showing up every year. [*They kiss*]

GEORGE: I'm always surprised that you do. I was really surprised the second year. [*He crosses to the piano and refills their glasses with champagne. He gives one to* DORIS] Of course I had less confidence in my personal magnetism then. You know that was one of the best ideas you ever had?

DORIS: Meeting here every year?

GEORGE: No, refusing to run off with me. Weren't you even tempted?

DORIS: Sure I was. I still am. But I had the feeling that if we had run off together we'd end up with—well—with pretty much the same sort of nice, comfortable marriage we both already had at home. [*They sit and drink*]

GEORGE: How are things at home?

DORIS: We moved to the suburbs. Right now everyone's very excited. Next week they're going to connect the sewers. Well, it's not exactly the life of Scott and Zelda, but we'll survive.

GEORGE: [*Surprised*] You started reading!

DORIS: Oh, you don't know the half of it. I joined the Book-of-the-Month Club.

GEORGE: Good for you.

DORIS: [*Kidding herself*] Listen, sometimes I even take the *alternate* selections.

GEORGE: [*Sincerely*] I'm really proud of you, honey.

DORIS: Well, it was either that or group mambo lessons. You still live in New Jersey?

GEORGE: No, we moved to Connecticut. We bought an old barn and converted it.

DORIS: What's it like?

GEORGE: Drafty. Helen's got the decorating bug. At my funeral just as they're closing the lid on my coffin I have this mental picture of Helen throwing in two fabric swatches and yelling, "Which one do you like?" That's the bad story about her.

DORIS: What else is new?

GEORGE: We had a baby girl.

DORIS: Oh, George, that's marvelous! You have pictures?

GEORGE: [*Grins*] I knew you'd ask that. [*He takes out pictures, hands them to her*]

DORIS: [*Looking at snaps*] Oh, she's adorable. It's funny. I still like to look at new babies but I don't want to *own* one anymore. You think that's a sign of maturity?

GEORGE: Could be. [*He takes out cigar*] Here, I even kept one of these for you to give to Harry. It's from Havana.

DORIS: Harry still thinks I go on retreat. What should I tell him? It came from a Cuban nun? [*She takes the cigar, moves to put it in her purse*] So how are the rest of the kids? How's Michael?

GEORGE: Oh, crazy as ever. He had this homework assignment, to write what he did on his summer vacation. Trouble is, he chose to write what he actually did.

DORIS: What was that?

GEORGE: Tried to get laid. He wrote in great comic detail about his unfortunate tendency to get an erection on all forms of public transportation. The school almost suspended him.

DORIS: You're crazy about him, aren't you?

GEORGE: He's a very weird kid, Doris.

DORIS: And he really gets to you. Come on—admit it.

GEORGE: Okay, I admit it. He's a nice kid.

DORIS: See? Was that so hard?

[*He looks at her for a moment, crosses to her, impulsively kisses her*]

DORIS: What was that for?

GEORGE: Everything. This. One beautiful weekend every year with no cares, no ties, and no responsibilities. Thank you, Doris. [*He kisses her again. The embrace grows more passionate. They break*]

DORIS: [*Breathlessly*] Gee, I just got all dressed up.

[*They sink onto the bed. He is lying half on top of her when the phone rings*]

DORIS: Someone has a rotten sense of timing.

GEORGE: Let it ring. It's probably only Pete wanting to know how much he owes the I.R.S.

DORIS: Chalmers probably told him we're in.

GEORGE: Damn! [*Without changing his position he reaches out and takes the phone*] Hello. [*His expression changes—slowly but drastically*] Is there anything wrong? Yes, this is Daddy—Funny? [*He slowly rolls off* DORIS *to a tense position on the edge of the bed*] Well, that's probably because Daddy was just—uh—I had a frog in my throat, sweetheart. It came out, huh? Which one was it? [*He sits with the phone in his hand, bent over, almost as if he has a stomachache*] Of course, the tooth-fairy will come, sweetheart—Why tonight, of course—It doesn't matter if you can't find it, darling, the tooth-fairy will know—Well, I wish I could be there to find it for you too, honey, but Daddy's working—Oh, in my room. [*At this point* DORIS *gets off the bed and unobtrusively starts to clean up the room*] Yes, it's a very nice room—Well, it has a fireplace and a sofa and a big comfortable b—[*He can't bring himself to say "bed"*)—bathroom. Well, I'd like you to come with me too, sweetheart. Maybe next year—I'm afraid not, sweetheart. You see Daddy has to finish up his—business—well, I'll try—Yes, I love you too, honey—Yes, very much. [*He hangs up and puts his head in his hands.*

DORIS *crosses to him and wordlessly puts a comforting hand on his shoulder*] Oh, God, I feel so *guilty!* [*He rises and moves away*]

DORIS: Debbie?

GEORGE: Her tooth came out. She can't find it and she's worried the tooth-fairy won't know! Oh, God, that thin, reedy little voice. Do you know what that *does* to me!

DORIS: Sure, that calm exterior doesn't fool me for a minute.

GEORGE: You think this is *funny?*

DORIS: Honey, I understand how you feel but I really don't think it's going to help going on and on about it.

GEORGE: Doris, my little girl said, "I love you, Daddy," and I answered her with a voice still *hoarse with passion!*

DORIS: I think I've got the picture, George.

GEORGE: Don't you ever feel guilty?

DORIS: Sometimes.

GEORGE: You've never said anything.

DORIS: I just deal with it in a different way.

GEORGE: How?

DORIS: Privately.

[*Agitated,* GEORGE *starts pacing around the room*]

GEORGE: I don't know, maybe men are more—sensitive than women.

DORIS: Have a drink, George.

GEORGE: Perhaps women are more pragmatic than men.

DORIS: What's that mean?

GEORGE: They adjust to rottenness quicker. I mean, they're more inclined to live for the moment. [*Offhandedly*] Anyway, you have the church.

DORIS: The church?

GEORGE: Well, you're Catholic, aren't you? You can get rid of all your guilt at one sitting. I have to *live* with mine.

DORIS: I think *I'll* have a drink. [*She moves to pour herself a drink*]

GEORGE: Boy, something like that really brings you up short! [*Holding out his trembling hands*] I mean *look* at me! I tell you, Doris—when she started talking about the tooth-fairy—well, it affected me in a very profound manner. [*A beat*] On top of that I have indigestion you can't *believe*. It hit me that hard, you know?

DORIS: George, I have three children, too.

GEORGE: Sure, sure—I know. I don't mean that you don't *understand*. It's just that we're different people and your guilt is less—acute.

DORIS: Honey, what do you want to do? Have a guilt contest? Is that going to solve anything?

GEORGE: What do you want me to do, Doris?

DORIS: I think it might be a terrific idea if you stopped talking about it. It's only making you feel worse.

GEORGE: I can't feel worse. That pure little voice saying—[*He stops, tries to shake it off with a jerk of his head*] No, you're right. Forget it. [*Shakes his head again*] Forget it! Talk about something else. Tell me about Harry. Tell me the good story about Harry. [*During the following,* GEORGE *tries to concentrate but is obviously distracted and nervous*]

DORIS: Okay. He went bankrupt.

[*This momentarily jolts him out of his problem*]

GEORGE: How can anyone go bankrupt selling TV sets?

DORIS: Harry has this one weakness as a salesman. It's a compulsion to talk people out of things they can't afford. He lacks the killer instinct. [*Reflectively*] It's one of the things I like best about him. Anyway, he went into real estate. [GEORGE *is staring out of the window*] Your turn.

GEORGE: What?

DORIS: Tell me your story about Helen.

GEORGE: I already did.

DORIS: You just told me the bad one. Why do you always tell that one first?

GEORGE: It's the one I look forward to telling the most.

DORIS: Tell me the nice story about her.

GEORGE: Oh. [*Moving about the room*] Well—Chris—that's our middle one—ran into a lawn sprinkler and gashed his knee really badly. Helen drove both of us to the hospital.

DORIS: Both of you?

GEORGE: I fainted.

DORIS: Oh.

GEORGE: The nice part was she never told anybody.

DORIS: You faint often?

GEORGE: Only in emergencies.

DORIS: Is it the sight of blood that—

GEORGE: Please, Doris! My stomach's squeamish enough already. Maybe I will have that drink. [*He moves to liquor, speaks overcasually*] Oh, listen, something just occurred to me. Instead of my leaving at the usual time tomorrow night would you mind if I left a little earlier?

DORIS: [*Puzzled*] When did you have in mind?

GEORGE: Well, there's a plane in half an hour.

[*She stares at him astounded*]

DORIS: You want to leave twenty-three hours early?

[*He moves to suitcase, starts to pack and continues through the following as she watches with unbelieving eyes*]

GEORGE: Look, I know how you feel—I really do—and I wouldn't even *suggest* it if you weren't a mother yourself and didn't understand the situation. I mean I wouldn't even *think* of it if this crisis hadn't come up. Oh, it's not just the tooth-fairy—she could have *swallowed* the tooth. I mean it could be lodged God knows where! Now I know this leaves you a bit—uh—at loose ends but there's no reason for you to leave, too. The room's all paid up. Anyway, I'm probably doing you a favor. If I did stay I wouldn't be very good company. Uh—have you seen my hairbrush? [*He looks around, sees it is beside her*] Doris, would you hand me my hairbrush? [*Without a word, she picks it up and throws it at him with much more force than necessary. It sails past his head and crashes against the wall. There is a pause*] I think I can explain that. You feel somewhat rejected and, believe me, I can understand that but I want you to know my leaving has nothing to do with *you and me!* [*She just stares at him*] Doris, this is an *emergency!* I have a *sick child* at home!

DORIS: [*Exploding*] Oh, will you *stop* it! It's got nothing to do with the goddam tooth-fairy! You're consumed with guilt and the only way you can deal with it is by getting as far away from me as possible!

GEORGE: Okay, I feel guilty. Is that so strange? [*Intensely*] Doris, don't you understand? We're *cheating!* Once a year we lie to our families and sneak off to a hotel in California and commit adultery! [*Holding up his hand*] Not that I want to stop doing it! But yes, I feel guilt. I admit it.

DORIS: [*Incredulous*] You *admit* it!? You take out ads! You probably stop strangers in the street! It's a wonder you haven't hired a *sky writer!* I'm amazed you haven't had your shorts monogrammed with a scarlet "A" as a conversation starter! You think that by *talking* about it, by wringing your hands and beating your breast it will somehow excuse what you're doing? So you wander around like—like an open nerve saying, "I'm cheating but look how *guilty* I feel so I must really be a nice guy!" And to top it all, you have the incredible arrogance to think you're the only one in the world with a conscience! Well, that doesn't make you a nice guy. You know what it makes you? A *horse's ass!* [*There is a pause*]

GEORGE: [*Finally*] You know something? I liked you better *before* you started reading.

DORIS: That's not why you're leaving, George.

GEORGE: Doris, it's not the end of the world. I'm not leaving you permanently. [*Turning to finish packing*] We'll see each other again next year. [*He shuts suitcase, snaps locks*]

DORIS: [*Quietly—with finality*] There's not going to be a next year, George.
    [*He turns to face her*]

GEORGE: You don't mean that. [*He suspects by her face that she does*] I can't believe that! Just because I have to leave early one year you're willing to throw away a lifetime of weekends? How can you be so—so *casual?*

DORIS: I don't see any point in going on.
    [*He starts to shake his head*]

GEORGE: Oh, no. Don't do that to me, Doris. [*He takes suitcase, moves to deposit it by the door during following*] Don't try to manipulate me. I get enough of that at home. [*Getting raincoat, putting it on*] That's not what our relationship is about.

DORIS: [*Soberly*] What is it about, George?

GEORGE: You don't *know?*

DORIS: Yes. But it seems to be completely different from how you think about us. That's why I think we should stop seeing each other.

GEORGE: [*Finally*] My God, you really *are* serious.

DORIS: George, what's the point of going on if we're going to come to each other burdened down with guilt and remorse? What joy is there in that?

GEORGE: [*Frustrated—indicating door*] Doris, I have a commitment there.

DORIS: [*Quietly*] And you don't have a commitment here?

GEORGE: [*Bewildered*] Here? I thought our only commitment was to show up every year.

DORIS: Nice and tidy, huh? Just two friendly sexual partners who meet once a year, touch and let go.

GEORGE: Okay—so maybe I was kidding myself. I'm human.

DORIS: Well, so am I.

GEORGE: [*Sincerely*] But you're different. Stronger. You always seem able to—cope.

> [*She moves away, looks into the fire. She speaks slowly, deliberately unemotional*]

DORIS: George, during the past year I picked up the phone and started to call you five times. I couldn't seem to stop thinking about you. You kept slopping over into my real life and it scared hell out of me. More to the point I felt *guilty*. So I decided to stop seeing you. [*He is shaken. She turns to face him*] At first I wasn't going to show up at all but then I thought I at least owed you an explanation. So I came. [*She turns away*] When you walked in the door I knew I couldn't do it. That despite the price it was all worth it. [*A pause*]

GEORGE: [*Finally—anguished*] Oh God, I feel so *guilty!!*

DORIS: [*Quietlyl—flatly*] I think you'd better leave, George. [*There is a pause*]

GEORGE: I love you, Doris. [*A beat*] I'm an idiot. I suspect I'm deeply neurotic, and I'm no bargain—but I do love you. [*He moves to her, gently turns her to face him*] Will you let me stay? [*They embrace, break, and gaze at one another*] Doris, what are we going to do?

> [*She reaches out and takes his hand*]

DORIS: Touch and hold on very tight. Until tomorrow.

> [*They embrace. The lights slowly fade and the curtain falls*]

SCENE THREE

The Time: *A day in February, 1961.*

> The Place: *The same.*

> At Rise: GEORGE, *still wearing his raincoat and hat, is talking on the phone. His unpacked suitcase is in the middle of the floor and it is apparent that he has just arrived. As he talks he takes off his raincoat and throws it on the bed.*

GEORGE: [*Irritably—into phone*] No, of course I haven't left Helen. I'm on a business trip. I come out here every year—I am not running away from the problem! [*Becoming more angry*] Of course I know it's serious. I still don't think it's any reason to phone me long distance and—look, frankly, I don't think this is any of your business and to be totally honest I resent—[*He gives an exasperated sigh*] Yes, I saw a doctor—He said it's no big deal, that every man has this problem at one time or another and—Look, if we *have* to discuss this you may as well learn to pronounce it correctly. It's impotence, not im*p*otence— [*Incredulous*] What do you mean, did I catch it in time? It's a slight reflex problem not a terminal illness! [*Frustrated*] It's not something you have to "nip in the bud." Look, how did you find out about this anyway?—Dropped a few hints? What *sort* of hints?—You asked her and she looked funny. Terrific [*Exasperated again*] Yes, of course I'm trying to do something about it—I don't have to tell you that—Look, will you let me deal with this in my own way? I'm going to be okay—Soon—I just *know*, that's all. [*Flaring*] I just *feel* it, okay?— I'm seeing someone out here who's an expert. [*His patience exhausted*] Look, I don't think we should be even *discussing* this!—I'm sorry, I'm going to hang up now. [*Firmly*] Goodby, Mother!

> [*He slams the receiver down, picks up his raincoat, looks at bed, throws raincoat over chair, turns blankets and sheets down, tosses hat into chair revealing that his hairline has receded noticeably. He then crosses to his suitcase, puts it on rack, opens it, extracts pajamas and robe and exits to bathroom. There is a slight pause before the front door opens and* DORIS *enters. She is obviously very, very pregnant. Her hair is back to her normal color and her face looks softer than before. Perspiring slightly, she puts her case down*]

DORIS: [*Calling*] George!

GEORGE: [*Offstage—from bathroom*] Be right out, darling! [DORIS, *holding her back, moves to look out of the window. When* GEORGE, *now dressed in robe and pajamas, enters from the bathroom her back is toward him. He stops, smiles at her tenderly*] How are you, lover?

> [*She turns to face him, revealing her eight months pregnant stomach. His smile fades and his expression becomes frozen. He just stares, unable to speak*]

DORIS: [*Finally*] I know. I've heard of middle-aged spread but this is ridiculous.

GEORGE: [*In a strangled voice*] My God, what have you done to yourself?

DORIS: Well, I can't take all the credit. It was a mutual effort. [*He continues to stare at her*] Honey, when you haven't seen an old friend for a year isn't it customary to kiss them hello?

GEORGE: [*Still stunned*] What? Oh, sure. [*He moves to her, gives her a rather perfunctory kiss*]

DORIS: Are you okay? You look funny.

GEORGE: [*Flaring—moving away*] Funny? I'm hysterical!

DORIS: What's that mean?

> [*He tries to regain control*]

GEORGE: Well—naturally, I'm—surprised, okay?

DORIS: *You're* surprised. I insisted on visiting the dead rabbit's grave! [*Puzzled*] Why are you wearing your pajamas and robe in the afternoon?

GEORGE: [*Irritably*] I'm rehearsing for a Noël Coward play! Why the hell do you think?

DORIS: Oh, I'm sorry, darling. I'm afraid all that dirty stuff is out. That is, unless you have a ladder handy.

GEORGE: Doris, do you mind? I'm in no mood for bad taste jokes!

DORIS: Oh, come on, honey—where's your sense of humor? Look at it this way—maybe it's nature's way of telling us to slow down. [*He watches her as she moves to a chair and awkwardly negotiates herself into the seat. She kicks off her shoes, massages her feet, looks up to find him staring at her with a baleful expression*] George, is there something on your mind?

[*He moves away to the window*]

GEORGE: Not anymore.

DORIS: Then why are you so jumpy?

[*He wheels to face her*]

GEORGE: You must be eight months pregnant!

DORIS: Why are you so shocked? I am married.

GEORGE: You think that excuses it?

DORIS: What exactly are you trying to say?

GEORGE: I just consider it damned—irresponsible!

DORIS: [*Amused*] Well, I have to admit, it wasn't planned!

GEORGE: [*Frustrated*] I mean coming here in—in that condition!

DORIS: Well, I'm sorry you're disappointed, darling, but we'll just have to find some other way to—communicate.

GEORGE: Great! You have any ideas?

DORIS: We could talk.

GEORGE: Talk? Talk I can get at home!

DORIS: [*Grinning*] Well, sex *I* can get at home. And as you can see, that's not just talk.

GEORGE: What the hell is that supposed to mean?

DORIS: [*Shrugs*] Well, I've never had any cause to complain about Harry in that department.

GEORGE: Oh, really? And what does that make me? Chopped liver?

[*She has been watching him with a curious expression*]

DORIS: George, what is the *matter* with you?

GEORGE: Matter? I'm the only man in America who just kept an illicit assignation with a woman who—who looks like a—frigate in full sail! And you ask what's the matter?

DORIS: [*Calmly*] No, there's something else. You're not yourself.

GEORGE: Let me be the judge of who I am, okay?

DORIS: Why are you so *angry?*

GEORGE: What was the crack about Harry? Is that supposed to reflect on me? You don't think I have normal desires and sex drives?

DORIS: Of course not. You're very normal. I just meant I look forward to seeing you for a lot of reasons *beside* sex. Do you think we would have lasted this long if that's all we had in common?

GEORGE: [*Grudgingly*] No, I guess not.

DORIS: We're friends as well as lovers, aren't we?

GEORGE: Yes. [*He sighs*] I'm sorry, Doris. I've—I've had a lot on my mind lately and—well, seeing you like that took the wind out of my sails. You want a drink?

DORIS: No, you go ahead. Alcohol makes me go a funny shade of pink. [*She watches him as he moves to extract a bottle from his suitcase*] You want to tell me about it?

GEORGE: No, it's not something I can really *talk* about. [*He moves to get glass, pours drink, shrugs*] It's just I was looking forward to an—intimate weekend.

DORIS: You think we can only be intimate through sex?

GEORGE: I think it sure helps.

DORIS: Oh, maybe at the beginning.

GEORGE: The beginning?

DORIS: Well, every year we meet it's a bit strange and awkward at first but we usually solve that in between the sheets with a lot of heavy breathing.

GEORGE: Doris, if we're not going to do it, would you mind not talking about it?

DORIS: I just meant maybe we need something else to—break the ice.

GEORGE: [*Pouring himself another drink*] I'm willing to try anything.

DORIS: How about this? Supposing I tell you something about myself I've never told anyone before in my life?

GEORGE: I think I've had enough surprises for one day.

DORIS: You'll like this one. [*She gets out of the chair with some difficulty and moves to look out of window. He watches and waits*] I've been having these sex dreams about you.

GEORGE: When?

DORIS: Just lately. Almost every night.

GEORGE: What sort of dreams?

  [*She turns to face him*]

DORIS: That's what's so strange. They're always the same. We're making love under water. In caves, grottos, swimming pools—but always under water.

Isn't that weird? [*She shrugs*] Probably something to do with me being pregnant.

GEORGE: Under water, huh?

    [*She nods*]

DORIS: Now you tell me some deep, dark secret about yourself.

GEORGE: I can't swim.

DORIS: [*Puzzled*] Literally?

GEORGE: [*Irritably*] Of course literally! When I tell you I can't swim I simply mean I can't swim!

DORIS: How come?

GEORGE: I just never learned when I was a kid. But I never told anybody— well, Helen found out when she pushed me off a dock and I almost drowned—but my kids don't even know. When we go to the beach I pretend I'm having trouble with my trick knee.

DORIS: You have a trick knee?

GEORGE: No. They don't know that either.

    [*She moves to him, puts her hand on his cheek*]

DORIS: You see, it worked. [*He looks puzzled*] We're talking just like people who have been to bed and everything. [*She moves to another chair, carefully lowers herself into it. The effort tires her*] Boy, I'll tell you—that Ethel Kennedy must really like kids.

GEORGE: Hey, I'm sorry about—earlier. I'm glad to see you anyway.

DORIS: You want to tell me what it was all about?

    [*He looks at her for a moment*]

GEORGE: Okay, I may as well get it out in the open. I mean it's nothing to be ashamed about. [*He takes a turn around the room*] It's very simple really. It's my—sex life. Lately, Helen hasn't been able to satisfy me.

DORIS: [*Surprised*] She's lost her interest in sex?

GEORGE: Oh, she tries—God knows. But I can tell she's just going through the motions.

DORIS: Do you have any idea why this is?

GEORGE: Well, Helen's always had a lot of hangups about sex. For one thing she's always thought of it as just a healthy, normal, pleasant function. Don't you think that's a bit twisted?

DORIS: Only if you're Catholic.

GEORGE: [*Earnestly*] You're joking but there's a lot to be said for guilt. I mean if you don't feel guilty or ashamed about it I think you're missing half the fun. To Helen—sex has always been good, clean—*entertainment*. No wonder she grew tired of it. [*He finds* DORIS' *gaze somewhat disconcerting*] Look, I don't know, for some reason my sex drive has increased while hers has decreased.

DORIS: That's odd. Usually, it's the other way around.

GEORGE: [*Defensively*] Are you accusing me of lying?

DORIS: Of course not. Why are you so edgy?

GEORGE: Because—well, I don't think it's fair to talk about this behind her back when she's not here to defend herself.

    [*She watches him as he moves to pour another drink*]

DORIS: Would you like to get to the more formal part of your presentation?

GEORGE: What? Oh—okay. I'll start with the nice story about her.

DORIS: You've never done that before. You must be mellowing.

GEORGE: Doris, do you mind? Where was I? Oh—yeah. We were checking into a hotel in London and there was a man in a morning coat and striped trousers standing at the front entrance. Helen handed him her suitcases and sailed on into the lobby. The man followed her in with her suitcases and very politely pointed out that not only didn't he work at the hotel but that he was the Danish Ambassador. Without batting an eye she said, "Well, that's marvelous. Maybe you can tell us the good places to eat in Copenhagen." And he did. The point is it doesn't bother her when she makes a total ass of herself. I really admire that.

DORIS: And what don't you admire?

GEORGE: It's that damned sense of humor of hers!

DORIS: Oh, those are the stories I like the best.

    [*He looks at her for a moment, then launches headlong into the story*]

GEORGE: We'd come home from a party and we'd had a few drinks and we went to bed and we started to make love. Well, nothing happened—for me—I couldn't—well, you get the picture. It was no big deal—and we laughed about it. Then about half an hour later, just as I was dropping off to sleep she said, "It's funny, when I married a C.P.A. I always thought it would be his eyes that would go first."

DORIS: [*Finally*] She was just trying to make you feel better, George.

GEORGE: Well, it didn't. Some things aren't funny. [DORIS *doesn't say anything*] I suppose what I'm trying to say is that the thing that bugs me most about Helen is that she broke my pecker!

DORIS: [*Gently*] You're impotent?

GEORGE: Slightly. [*He gives a shrug*] Okay, now five people know. Me, you, Helen and her mother.

DORIS: Who's the fifth?

GEORGE: Chet Huntley. I'm sure her mother has given him the bulletin for the six o'clock news.

DORIS: I thought that might be it.

GEORGE: You mean you can tell just by *looking* at me?

DORIS: [*Sympathetically*] When did it happen, honey?

GEORGE: Happen? Doris, we're not talking about a freeway accident! I mean you don't wake up one morning and say, "Oh shoot, the old family jewels have gone on the blink." It's a—a gradual thing.

DORIS: And you really blame Helen for this?

GEORGE: Of course not. I—I wanted to tell you but I just couldn't think of a graceful way of working it into the conversation. [*He gives a short, hard laugh*] To tell you the truth I was just waiting for you to say "What's new?" And I was going to say "Nothing, but I can tell you what's old."

DORIS: How's Helen reacting?

GEORGE: Oh, we haven't talked about it much but I get the feeling she regards it as a lapse in one's social responsibility. You know, rather like letting your partner down in tennis by not holding your serve. [*He gives a little laugh*] Look, it's not a great tragedy. As they say in Brooklyn, "Just wait 'til next year." [*She is not smiling*] Seriously, I'll be okay. Send no flowers. The patient's not dead yet—just resting. [*She extends her hand*] Doris, that statement hardly calls for congratulations.

DORIS: I need help to get out of this chair. [*He pulls her out of the chair. Takes his face between her hands. Simply*] I'm really sorry.

[*They look tenderly at one another for a moment before he suddenly jerks away*]

GEORGE: What the hell was that?

DORIS: The baby kicking.

GEORGE: [*Moving away*] Well, everyone else has taken a shot at me. Why not him?

DORIS: [*Puzzled*] It's strange. He hasn't been kicking lately. Maybe he resents the bumpy ride up here. [*She sees that* GEORGE *is not really listening*] Is there anything I can say that will help?

GEORGE: What? Honey, you can say anything you want except "It's all in your head." I mean I'm no doctor but I have a great sense of direction. [*As she starts to talk*] Look, to tell you the truth, I'm not too crazy about this whole discussion. Let's forget it, huh?

DORIS: Okay. What do you want to talk about?

GEORGE: Anything but sex. How'd you feel about being pregnant?

DORIS: Catatonic, incredulous, angry, pragmatic, and finally maternal. Pretty much in that order.

GEORGE: Your vocabulary's improving.

DORIS: Ah, you didn't know. You're talking to a high school graduate.

GEORGE: [*Puzzled*] How come?

DORIS: Well, I was confined to bed for the first three months of my pregnancy, so rather than it being a total loss I took a correspondence course.

GEORGE: [*Admiringly*] You're really something, you know that?

DORIS: There's kind of an ironic twist to all this.

GEORGE: Oh?

DORIS: Well, I didn't graduate the first time because I got pregnant. And now I did graduate because— [*She grins, taps her stomach*] Appeals to my sense of order.

GEORGE: [*Teasing*] I didn't know you had a sense of order.

DORIS: That's unfair. I'm much better at housework lately. Now I'm only two years behind in my ironing. Must be the nesting instinct. Anyway, the day my diploma came in the mail Harry bought me a corsage and took me out dancing. Well, we didn't really dance—we lumbered. Afterwards we went to a malt shop and had a fudge sundae. That's the nice story about him.

GEORGE: He still selling real estate?

DORIS: Insurance. He likes it. Gives him an excuse to look up all his old Army buddies.

> [*He regards her as she stands with her stomach thrust out and both hands pressed on either side of her back*]

GEORGE: Doris, are you comfortable in that position?

DORIS: Honey, when you're in my condition you're not comfortable in any position.

> [*He takes her arm, leads her to a chair*]

GEORGE: Come on, sit over here. [*He helps lower her into the chair. As he does a strange expression comes to his face*]

DORIS: Thanks. How are the kids?

GEORGE: [*Vaguely*] What? Oh, fine. Michael got a job with Associated Press.

DORIS: Oh, darling, that's marvelous. I'm so proud of him. [*She notices he is staring at her with an odd, fixed expression*] George, why are you looking at me like that?

GEORGE: [*Too quickly*] No reason. It—it's nothing.

DORIS: Does my stomach offend you?

GEORGE: No, it's not that. Tell me your other story about Harry.

DORIS: I had trouble telling him I was pregnant. When I finally did he looked at me for a moment and then said "Is there a revolver in the house?" George, you're doing it again! What *is* it?

GEORGE: [*Exploding*] It's obscene!

DORIS: [*Bewildered*] What is?

GEORGE: When I touched you I started to get excited!!!! [*He paces around*] What kind of pervert am I? [*He turns to look at her*] I'm staring at a two hundred pound woman and I'm getting hot! Just the *sight* of you is making me excited.

> [*She looks at him for a moment*]

DORIS: [*Finally*] Let me tell you something. That's the nicest thing anyone's said to me in months.

GEORGE: [*Very agitated*] It's not funny!

DORIS: Aren't you pleased?

GEORGE: Pleased? It reminds me of my seventh birthday!

DORIS: What?

GEORGE: My uncle gave me fifty cents. I ran two miles and when I got there the candy store was closed!

DORIS: [*Puzzled*] But doesn't this solve your—problem?

GEORGE: [*Frustrated*] The idea doesn't solve anything! It's the execution that counts!

DORIS: [*Pleased*] I really got to you, huh?

GEORGE: [*Tightly*] Excuse me. [*Without another word, he marches to the piano, sits and aggressively launches into a Rachmaninoff concerto. Surprisingly, he plays extremely well. Not quite concert hall material but close enough to fool a lot of people.* DORIS *watches, absolutely astounded. She finally recovers enough to get out of her chair and move to the piano where she watches him with an incredulous expression*]

DORIS: [*Finally*] That's incredible! Are you as good as I think you are?

[*He continues to play until indicated*]

GEORGE: How good do you think I am?

DORIS: Sensational.

GEORGE: I'm not as good as you think I am.

DORIS: You sound marvelous to me.

GEORGE: It's the story of my life, Doris. All the form and none of the ability.

DORIS: [*Puzzled*] But for ten years that piano has been sitting there and you haven't touched it. Why tonight?

GEORGE: It beats a cold shower.

DORIS: You play to release sexual tension?

GEORGE: Any kind of tension. Any frustration in my life and I head right for the piano. [*A wry shrug*] You don't even get this good without a lot of practice.

[DORIS *shakes her head in wonder*]

DORIS: George, you're full of surprises.

GEORGE: Yeah, I know—you live with a man for ten days but you never really know him.

DORIS: Why didn't you tell me you played before?

GEORGE: I had other ways of entertaining you.

DORIS: Well, I always knew you had wonderful hands.

[*He stops playing, looks at her*]

GEORGE: Look, lady, I only work here. I'm not allowed to date the customers.

[*She smiles, moves away. He starts playing again*]

DORIS: George? You still feel—frustrated?

GEORGE: I have the feeling it's going to take all six Brandenburg concertos.

DORIS: You'll be exhausted.

GEORGE: That's the idea.

DORIS: But—

GEORGE: [*Irritably*] Doris, I've been waiting three months for—for the balloon to go up! Well, it's up and it's not going to come down until something—

DORIS: Honey, come here. [*He stops playing, looks at her*] Come on.

[*He gets up from the piano and moves to her. She starts to untie his robe*]

GEORGE: Doris—

DORIS: It's okay. It'll be okay.

GEORGE: But you can't—

DORIS: I know that.

GEORGE: Then how—

DORIS: Don't worry, darling. We'll work something out. [*She kisses him very tenderly. Gradually he becomes more involved in the kiss until they are in a passionate embrace. Suddenly she backs away, clutching her stomach, her face a mixture of surprise and alarm. Then she grimaces with pain*]

GEORGE: [*Alarmed*] What is it? [*She is too busy fighting off the pain to answer*] Doris? [*The pain has knocked the breath out of her and she gasps to catch her breath*] Doris, for God's sake, what is it? [*She looks at him unbelievingly, not saying anything*] Doris, what *the hell is the matter?*

DORIS: [*Finally*] If—if memory serves me correctly—I just had a labor pain.

[*He stands stock still, trying to absorb this*]

GEORGE: You—you can't have! [*Clutching at straws*] Maybe it's indigestion.

DORIS: No, there's a difference.

GEORGE: How can you be *sure?*

DORIS: I've had both.

GEORGE: But you can't be in labor! When is the baby due?

DORIS: Not for another month.

[*He stares at her for a moment and then puts his hands to his head*]

GEORGE: My God, what have I *done?!*

DORIS: What have *you* done?

GEORGE: I brought it on. My—my selfishness.

DORIS: George, don't be ridiculous. You had nothing to do with it.

GEORGE: Don't treat me like a child, Doris!

DORIS: Will you stop getting so excited?

GEORGE: Excited? I thought I had troubles before. Can you imagine what *this* is going to do to my sex life?

DORIS: George, will you— [*She stops*] I think I'd better—sit down.

[*He quickly moves to her, leads her to a chair*]

GEORGE: [*Anguished*] Jesus, what kind of a man am I? What kind of man would do a thing like that?

DORIS: George, may I say something?

GEORGE: [*Very agitated—moving around*] Look, I appreciate what you're trying to do, honey, but nothing you can say will make me feel any better.

DORIS: I'm not trying to make you feel any better.

[*This stops him in his tracks*]

GEORGE: What are you trying to say?

DORIS: We're in a lot of trouble. I'm going to have a baby.

GEORGE: I know that.

DORIS: I mean now. I have a history of short labor and— [*She stops as another labor pain starts*]

GEORGE: Oh, Jesus! [*He quickly moves to her, kneels in front of her and she grabs his hand in a viselike grip as she fights off the pain*] Oh, Jesus! [*The pain starts to subside*] How—how do you feel?

DORIS: Like—like I'm going to have a baby.

GEORGE: Maybe it's a false alarm. It has to be a false alarm!

DORIS: Honey, try and get a hold of yourself. Get on the phone and find out where the nearest hospital is.

GEORGE: Hospital? You want to go to a hospital?

DORIS: George, like it or not, I'm going to have a baby.

GEORGE: But we're not married! [*She stares at him*] I mean it's going to look—odd!

[*She gets up*]

DORIS: Get on the phone, George. [*Moving toward the bathroom*] And make sure you get the directions.

GEORGE: Where are you going?

DORIS: The bathroom.

GEORGE: Why?

DORIS: I don't have time to answer questions! [*She exits to bathroom. He quickly moves to telephone, frantically jiggles receiver bar*]

GEORGE: [*Into phone*] Hello, Mr. Chalmers? George. Can you tell me where the nearest hospital is?—Well, it's my—my wife. Something—unexpected came up. She got pregnant and now she's going to have the baby—How far is that? [*With alarm*] Oh, my God!—Get—get them on the phone for me, will you? [*He covers receiver with hand, calls out*] Are you okay, Doris? [*There is no answer. Panicking*] Doris! Doris, answer me!

DORIS: [*Offstage from the bathroom—obviously in pain*] In—a minute. I'm busy.

GEORGE: Oh, Jesus! [*Into phone*] Hello—hello, I'm staying at the Sea Shadows Inn just outside Mendocino and—I—I heard this—this groaning from—the next room. Well, I knocked on the door and found this—this lady—who I'd never met before, in labor and—Do *you* have to know that?—I still don't see why—Okay, George Peterson!—Well, I didn't time it exactly but—About three or four minutes I think—Hold on. [*Calling out*] Doris, who's your doctor?

DORIS: [*Offstage—with an effort*] Doctor Joseph—Harrington. Oakland. 555-78-78.

GEORGE: [*Into phone*] Doctor Joseph Harrington in Oakland. His number is 555-78-78—Yes, I have a car and I'm certainly willing to help out if—I'll get her there—Right, right—Uh, could you answer one question?—Would—uh—erotic contact during pregnancy be the cause of premature—No reason, I just wondered and—Right, I'll do that! [*He hangs up, calls out*] They're phoning your doctor. He'll meet us there at the hospital. [DORIS *appears in the doorway of the bathroom, a strange look on her face. She doesn't say anything*] Doris, did you hear me?

DORIS: I don't think we're going to make it to the hospital. [*The blood drains from his face*]

GEORGE: What?

DORIS: My water just burst.

GEORGE: Oh, dear God!

DORIS: We're going to have to find a doctor in the area.

GEORGE: But supposing we *can't!*

DORIS: You look terrible. You're not going to faint, are you?

GEORGE: [*In total shock*] Doris, I'm not a cab driver! I don't know how to deliver babies!

DORIS: George, this is no time to start acting like Butterfly McQueen. [*She heads toward the bed*] Get the nearest doctor on the phone.

[*He races back to phone as she half sits and half lies on the bed*]

GEORGE: [*Into phone*] Who's the nearest doctor?—Get him on the phone! Fast! This is an emergency! [DORIS *has gone into another labor spasm.*
GEORGE, *phone in hand, moves to her, puts his arm around her, grabs her hand*] It's okay—hold on. Hold on. Doris. Hold on. There—there—hold on. You okay?

DORIS: [*Weakly*] This'll—teach you to fool around—with a married woman. [*Blurting*] George, I'm scared!

GEORGE: You're going to be okay. Everything— [*Into phone*] Yes? [*Standing up—yelling*] His answering service! You don't understand. She's in the last stages of labor!—Well, get in your car and drive down to the goddam course! Just *get* him! [*He hangs up*] It's okay—he's on the golf course but it's just down the road. Chalmers is getting him. [DORIS *is staring at him with a look of total panic*] Doris, what is it?

DORIS: I—I—can feel the baby!!

[*He stares at her, absorbs the situation, and we see a definite transformation take place. He rolls up the sleeves of his robe*]

GEORGE: [*Calmly*] All right, lean back and try to relax. I'll be right back. [*He exits quickly to the bathroom*]

DORIS: [*Screaming*] George, don't leave me!

GEORGE: [*Offstage*] Hold on, baby.

DORIS: George!

[*He reappears with a pile of towels*]

GEORGE: It's okay, I'm here. It'll be all right.

DORIS: What—are those—for?

GEORGE: Honey, we're going to have a baby.

DORIS: We?

GEORGE: Right. But I'm going to need your help. [*She goes into a spasm of labor and he sits on the bed beside her*] Okay—bear down—bear down. Come on, baby.

[*The lights start to fade*]

You're going to be fine. Just fine. You think I play the piano well? Wait until you get a load of how I deliver babies.

[*The lights have faded and the stage is dark*]

ACT TWO

SCENE ONE

The Time: *A day in February, 1965.*
    The Place: *The same.*
    At Rise: GEORGE *is unpacking his suitcase. Thinner than the last time we saw him, he is wearing an expensive conservative suit, his hair is gray and is worn unfashionably short. His manner is more subdued than before and he looks and acts older than his years. The door*

opens and DORIS *bursts into the room. She is wearing a brightly colored granny gown, beads, sandals, and her hair is long and flowing. She is carrying a decal decorated duffel bag.*

DORIS: Hey, baby! What do ya say? [*She throws her duffel bag into a chair and herself into the arms of a very surprised* GEORGE. *She kisses him passionately, backs off and looks at him*] So—you wanta fuck?

[*He takes an astonished moment to absorb this*]

GEORGE: [*Finally*] What?

DORIS: [*Grins*] You didn't understand the question?

GEORGE: Of course I did. I just think it's a damned odd way to start a conversation.

DORIS: Yeah? I've always found it to be a great little icebreaker. Besides, I thought you might be feeling horny after your flight.

[GEORGE *continues to eye* DORIS *with a mild consternation*]

GEORGE: I didn't fly, I drove.

DORIS: From Connecticut?

GEORGE: From Los Angeles. We moved to Beverly Hills about ten months ago. [*He manages to yank his eyes away from (to him)* DORIS's *bizarre appearance and resumes hanging up his clothes*]

DORIS: How come?

GEORGE: Oh, a number of reasons. [*Shrugs*] I got fed up standing knee-deep in snow trying to scrape the ice off my windshield with a credit card. Besides, there are a lot of people out here with a lot of money who don't know what to do with it.

DORIS: And you tell them?

GEORGE: I'm what they call a Business Manager.

DORIS: Things going okay?

GEORGE: I can't complain. Why?

DORIS: Because you look shitty. [*He turns to look at her*] Are you all right, honey?

GEORGE: I'm fine.

DORIS: You sure there's not something bothering you?

GEORGE: Yes—you. Do you always go around dressed like a bad finger painting?

DORIS: [*Grinning*] No. I have to admit that today I am a little—well—visually overstated.

GEORGE: Why?

DORIS: I guess I wanted to make sure you knew you were dealing with the "new me." Sort of "show and tell."

GEORGE: You look like a refugee from Sunset Strip.

DORIS: Berkeley. I went back to school.

GEORGE: [*Bewildered*] What for?

DORIS: [*Grins*] You mean what do I want to be when I grow up?

GEORGE: Well, you have to admit it's a bit strange becoming a schoolgirl at your age.

DORIS: Are you kidding? Listen, it's not easy being the only one in the class with clear skin. [*She moves to get her duffel bag, unpacks it through the following*]

GEORGE: [*Sitting*] What made you do it?

DORIS: It was a dinner party that finally pushed me into it. Harry's boss invited us for dinner and I panicked.

GEORGE: Why?

DORIS: I'd spent so much time with kids I didn't know if I was capable of carrying on an intelligent conversation with anyone over five who wasn't a supermarket check-out clerk. Anyway, I went and was seated next to *the* boss. Well, I surprised myself. He talked—then I talked—you know, just like a real conversation. I was feeling real cool until I noticed him looking at me in a weird way. I looked down and realized that all the time we'd been talking I'd been cutting up the meat on his plate. At that moment I *knew* I had to get out of the house.

GEORGE: But why school?

[*She stretches out on the bed*]

DORIS: It's hard to explain. I felt restless and—undirected and I thought an education might give me some answers.

GEORGE: What sort of answers?

DORIS: [*Shrugs*] To find out where it's really at.

GEORGE: [*Gets up*] Jesus!

DORIS: What's the matter?

GEORGE: That expression.

DORIS: Okay. To find out who the hell I was.

GEORGE: You don't get those sort of answers from a classroom.

DORIS: I'm not in the classroom all the time. The demonstrations are a learning experience in themselves.

GEORGE: Demonstrations against what?

DORIS: The war of course. Didn't you hear about it? It was in all the papers.

GEORGE: [*Curtly*] Demonstrations aren't going to stop the war.

DORIS: You have a better idea?

GEORGE: Look, I didn't come up here to discuss politics.

DORIS: Well, so far you've turned down sex and politics. You want to try religion?

GEORGE: I think I'll try a librium.

[*She watches him as he takes pill out and moves to take it with a glass of water from the drink tray*]

DORIS: George, why are you so uptight?

GEORGE: That's another expression I hate.

DORIS: Uptight?

GEORGE: There's no such word.

DORIS: You remind me of when I was nine years old and I asked my mother what "fuck" meant. Know what she said? "There's no such word."

GEORGE: And now you've found out there is you feel you have to use it in every other sentence?

DORIS: George, what's bugging you?

GEORGE: Bugging me? I'll tell you what's "bugging" me. The blacks are burning down the cities, there's a Harvard professor telling my children the only way to happiness is to become a doped up zombie, and I have a teen-age son with hair so long that from the back he looks exactly like Yvonne de Carlo.

DORIS: [*Grins*] That's right, baby—let it all hang out.

GEORGE: I wish people would *stop* letting it "all hang out." Especially my daughter. It's a wonder she hasn't been arrested for indecent exposure.

DORIS: That's a sign of age, honey.

GEORGE: What is?

DORIS: Being worried about the declining morality of the young. Besides, there's nothing you can do about it.

GEORGE: We could start by setting some examples.

DORIS: What are you going to do, George? Bring back public flogging?

GEORGE: It might not be a bad idea. We could start with the movie producers. My God, have you seen the films they're making today? Half the time the audience achieves a climax before the movie does!

DORIS: It's natural for people to be interested in sex. You can't kid the body, George.

GEORGE: Maybe not but you can damn well be *firm* with it.

[*She giggles, gets off the bed, moves toward him*]

DORIS: When you were younger I don't remember you as being exactly a monk about that sort of thing.

GEORGE: That was different! Our relationship was not based upon a casual one night stand!

[*She affectionately rumples his hair*]

DORIS: No, it's been *fifteen* one night stands.

GEORGE: It's not the same. We've *shared* things. My God, I helped deliver your child, remember?

DORIS: Remember? I think of it as our finest hour. [*She kisses him lightly, moves away to pour herself a drink*]

GEORGE: How is she?

DORIS: Very healthy, very noisy, and very spoiled.

GEORGE: You don't feel guilty about leaving her alone while you're at school?

DORIS: Harry's home a lot. The insurance business has been kind of slow lately.

GEORGE: How does he feel about all this?

DORIS: When I told him I wanted to go back to school because I want some identity he lost his temper and said, "You want identity? Go build a bridge! Invent penicillin but get off my back!"

GEORGE: I always said Harry had a good head on his shoulders.

DORIS: George, that was the *bad* story about him. How's Helen?

GEORGE: Helen's fine. Just fine.

DORIS: Tell me a story that shows how really lousy she can be.

GEORGE: [*Surprised*] That's not like you.

DORIS: We seem to need something to bring us closer together.

GEORGE: I don't understand.

DORIS: I thought a really bad story about Helen might make you appreciate me more.

[*This finally gets a small smile from* GEORGE]

GEORGE: Okay. [*She sits with her drink and listens*] As you know, she has this funny sense of humor.

DORIS: By funny I take it you mean peculiar?

GEORGE: Right. And it comes out at the most inappropriate times. I had signed this client—very proper, very old money. Helen and I were invited out to his house for cocktails to get acquainted with him and his wife. Well, it was all pretty awkward but we managed to get through the drinks all right. Then as we went to leave, instead of walking out the front door I walked into the hall closet. Now that wasn't so bad—I mean anybody can do that. The mistake I made was that I *stayed* in there.

DORIS: You stayed in the closet?

GEORGE: Yes. I don't know—I guess I figured they hadn't noticed and I'd stay there until they'd gone away—okay, I admit I didn't think things through. I was in there for a minute before I realized I'd—well—misjudged the situation. When I came out the three of them were just staring at me. All right, it was an embarrassing situation but I probably could have carried it off. Except for Helen. You know what she did?

DORIS: What?

GEORGE: She peed on the carpet.

DORIS: [*Incredulous*] She did *what?*

GEORGE: Oh, not right away. First of all, she started to laugh. Her face was all screwed up and the laughter was sort of—squeaky. Then she held her stomach and tears started to roll down her face. Then she peed on their Persian rug.

[DORIS *is having trouble keeping a straight face*]

DORIS: What did you say?

GEORGE: I said, "You'll have to excuse my wife. Ever since her last pregnancy she's had a problem." Then I offered to have the rug cleaned.

DORIS: Did that help?

GEORGE: They said it wasn't necessary. They had a maid. [DORIS *finally explodes into peals of laughter*] You think that's funny?

DORIS: I've been meaning to tell you this for years but I think I'd like Helen.

GEORGE: [*Irritated*] Would she come off any worse if I told you I lost the account?

DORIS: George, when did you get so *stuffy?*

GEORGE: Stuffy? Just because I don't like my wife urinating on my client's carpets does not mean I'm stuffy!

DORIS: Okay, maybe not just that but—well—look at you. [*She gets up, gestures at him*] I mean—Jesus—you scream Establishment.

GEORGE: I am not a faddist!

DORIS: What's that mean?

GEORGE: I have no desire to be like those middle-aged idiots with bell bottom trousers and Prince Valiant haircuts who go around saying "Ciao."

DORIS: I wasn't talking about *fashion.* I was talking about your attitudes.

GEORGE: My attitudes are the same as they always were. I haven't changed at all.

DORIS: Yes, you have. You used to be crazy and—and insecure and dumb and a terrible liar and—*human.* Now you seem so *sure* of yourself.

GEORGE: That's the last thing I am.

[*She is surprised by his admission*]

DORIS: Oh?

[*He looks at her for a moment, frowns, moves to look into the fire*]

GEORGE: I picked up one of Helen's magazines the other day and there was this article telling women what quality of *orgasms* they should have. It was called "The Big O." [*He turns to face her*] You know what really got to me? This was a magazine my mother used to buy for its *fruit cake* recipes.

DORIS: The times they are a changing, darling.

GEORGE: [*Troubled*] Too fast. I don't know, twenty, thirty years ago we were brought up with standards—all right, they *were* blacks and whites but they were standards. Today—it's so confusing.

DORIS: Well, that's at least a step in the right direction. [*She moves to him and kisses him*]

GEORGE: When did I suddenly become so appealing?

DORIS: When you went from pompous to confused. [*They kiss again*] So what's your pleasure? A walk by the ocean, dinner, or me?

GEORGE: You.

DORIS: Gee, I thought you'd never ask. [*She steps back a pace and whips her dress off over her head revealing that she is just wearing a pair of bikini panties*]

GEORGE: My God.

DORIS: What is it?

GEORGE: Doris—you're not wearing a *bra!*

    [*She giggles, embraces him*]

DORIS: Oh, George, you're so *forties*. [*She starts to nibble on his ear*]

GEORGE: [*Becoming passionate*] I happen to be an old-fashioned—man.

DORIS: The next thing you'll be telling me you voted for Goldwater.

GEORGE: I did.

    [*She takes a step back from him*]

DORIS: Are you putting me on?

GEORGE: Of course not. [*Without another word, she picks up her dress and puts it on*] What—what are you doing?

DORIS: [*Furious*] If you think I'm going to bed with any son of a bitch who voted for Goldwater you've got another think coming!

GEORGE: Doris, you can't do this to me! Not *now!*

DORIS: Oh, can't I? I'll tell you something—not only will I not go to bed with you—I want fifteen years of fucks back!

GEORGE: Doris, this is a very *delicate mechanism!!*

    [*She stares at him unbelievingly*]

DORIS: My God, how could you vote for a man like that?

GEORGE: [*Moving toward her*] Could we talk about this later?

DORIS: [*Pushing him away*] No, we'll talk about it *now!* Why?

GEORGE: [*Frustrated—yelling*] Because I have a son who wants to be a rock musician!!

DORIS: What kind of reason is *that?*

GEORGE: [*Sitting*] The best reason I can come up with right now in my condition!

DORIS: Well, you're going to have to do a lot better!

GEORGE: Okay, he was going to end the war!

DORIS: By bombing the hell out of innocent people!

GEORGE: What innocent people? They're *Reds!*

DORIS: They just wanted their country back!

GEORGE: Oh, I'm sick of hearing all that liberal crap! We've got the H-bomb. Why don't we use it?

DORIS: *Are you serious?*

GEORGE: Yes, I'm serious. Wipe the sons of bitches off the face of the earth!

    [*She stares at him for a moment*]

DORIS: [*Quietly, incredulous*] My God, I don't know anything about you. What sort of a man are you?

GEORGE: Right now—very frustrated.

DORIS: All this time I thought you were a liberal Democrat. You told me you worked for Stevenson.

GEORGE: [*In a tired voice*] That was years ago.

DORIS: What changed you? What happened to you?

GEORGE: [*Bitterly*] I grew up.

DORIS: Yeah, well in my opinion you didn't turn out too well.

GEORGE: Let's forget it, huh?

DORIS: Forget it? How can I forget it? I mean being stuffy and—and old-fashioned is one thing but being a Fascist is another!

GEORGE: [*Flaring*] I am not a Fascist!

DORIS: You're advocating mass murder!

GEORGE: Doris—drop it, okay! Just—drop it!

DORIS: How could you *do* this to me? Why, you stand for everything I'm against!

GEORGE: Then maybe you're against the wrong things!

DORIS: You used to think the same way I did.

GEORGE: I changed!

DORIS: *Why?*

GEORGE: Because Michael was killed! How the hell else did you expect me to feel!!

    [*There is a long pause as she stands transfixed, trying to absorb this*]

DORIS: [*Finally*] Oh—dear—God. How?

GEORGE: He was trying to get a wounded man onto a Red Cross helicopter and a sniper killed him.

    [*Without a word, she moves to him, starts to put her arms around him. He brushes her away, rises and moves to window and stares out*]

DORIS: [*Finally—almost in a whisper*] When?

    [*There is a pause*]

GEORGE: [*Dispassionately*] We heard in the middle of a big July 4th party.

Helen went completely to pieces—I'll never forget it. I didn't feel a thing. I thought I was in shock and it would hit me later. [*He turns to face her*] But you know something? It never did. The only emotion I can feel is blind anger. I didn't shed a tear. [*She doesn't say anything*] Isn't that the darnedest thing? I can't cry over my own son's death. I loved him but—for the life of me—I can't seem to cry over him. [*She doesn't move as he crosses to shakily pour himself a drink*] Doris, I'm sorry about—everything. Lately I've been a bit on edge and— [*The glass slips out of his hand, he tries to save it but it hits the dresser and smashes*] Oh, great! Will you look at that—I've gone and cut myself. If it isn't—one—damn thing—after—

[*He starts to sob.* DORIS *moves to him and puts her arms around him. He sinks into a chair, and buries his head into her chest as the curtain falls*]

SCENE TWO

The Time: *A day in February, 1970.*
    The Place: *The same.*
    At Rise: DORIS *and* GEORGE *are lying on top of the rumpled bed lazily enjoying the afterglow of lovemaking.* GEORGE *is wearing jeans with a butterfly on the seat and longish hair. His manner reflects a slightly self-conscious inner serenity.* DORIS *is wearing an attractive kimono but during the scene will don clothes and makeup that will project an image of chic, expensive, good taste.*

DORIS: It's amazing how good it can be after all these years, isn't it?
GEORGE: All these years? Honey, if you add up all the times we've actually made it together we're still on our honeymoon.
    [*A slight pause*]
DORIS: George, did you know I'm a grandmother?
GEORGE: No, but I think you picked a weird time to announce it.
DORIS: You think it's decadent having sex with a grandmother?
GEORGE: Only if it's done well. [*He pats her hand*] Anyway, you're the youngest looking grandmother I've ever had a peak experience with.
DORIS: [*Getting off bed*] My mother thanks you, my father thanks you, my hairdresser thanks you, and my plastic surgeon thanks you. [*He watches her as she lights a cigarette, sits at dresser, peers into mirror, starts to brush hair and apply makeup*] When Harry says, "You're not the girl I married," he doesn't know how right he is.
GEORGE: Didn't Harry like your old nose?
DORIS: He thinks this *is* my old nose.

GEORGE: He never noticed?

DORIS: [*Flippantly*] Pathetic, isn't it? A new dress I could understand—but a whole nose?

GEORGE: Well, to be totally honest I really can't see much of a difference either.

DORIS: Who cares? It looks different from *my* side. Makes me *act* more attractive.

GEORGE: Why do you feel you need a validation of your attractiveness?

DORIS: [*A slight shrug*] A woman starts feeling a little insecure when she gets to be forty-four.

GEORGE: Forty-five.

DORIS: See what I mean? Anyway, that's this year's rotten story about Harry. Got one about Helen?

> [*He grins, gets off bed, dons shirt, denim jacket, and sandals during the following*]

GEORGE: There was a loud party next door. Helen couldn't sleep and she didn't want to take a sleeping pill because she had to get up at six the next morning. So she stuffed two pills in her ears. During the night they melted. The next morning as the doctor was digging the stuff out of her ears he said, "You know these *can* be taken orally." Helen just laughed.

DORIS: If that's the worst story you can tell about her you must be a very happy man.

> [*He sits on the piano bench*]

GEORGE: Well, let's say I've discovered I have the *potential* for happiness.

> [*The phone rings.* DORIS *immediately moves to answer it*]

DORIS: [*Into phone*] Hello. [*Just a hint of disappointment*] Oh, hi, Liz. No, it's sixty—not sixteen guests—That's right—a brunch— We've catered a couple of parties for her before—No problem. She sets up tables around the pool and there's room for the buffet on the patio—Right. Anyone else call?—Okay, I'll be at this number. [*She hangs up, turns to* GEORGE, *who has been watching her*] Sorry, busy weekend. I had to leave the number.

GEORGE: Does Harry know you're here?

DORIS: No, he still thinks I go on the retreat. Don't worry. [*She moves and proceeds to get dressed during the following*]

GEORGE: I'm not worried.

DORIS: Then why are you frowning?

GEORGE: I'm getting some bad vibes again.

DORIS: Again?

GEORGE: When you first walked into the room I picked up on your high tension level. Then after we made love I sensed a certain anxiety reduction but now I'm getting a definite negative feedback.

DORIS: How long you been in analysis?

GEORGE: How did you know I was in analysis?

DORIS: [*Drily*] Just a wild guess. What made you go into therapy?

GEORGE: [*With a shrug*] My value system changed. [*He casually plays some soft, pleasant chords at the piano as he talks*] One day I took a look at my $150,000 house, the three cars in the garage, the swimming pool, and the gardeners and I thought—"*Why?*" I mean did I really want the whole status trip? So—I decided to try and find out what I did want and who I was.

DORIS: And you went from analysis to Esalen to Gestalt to Transactional to encounter groups to Nirvana.

[*He stops playing, swivels to face her, speaks in a calm, reasonable voice*]

GEORGE: Doris, just because many people are trying to expand their emotional horizons doesn't make the experience any less valid. I've learned a lot.

DORIS: I've noticed. For one thing you learned to talk as if you're reasoning with someone about to jump off a skyscraper ledge.

GEORGE: [*Grins*] Okay—okay. I know I tend to overcompensate for my emotionalism and sometimes there's a certain loss of spontaneity. I'm working on that.

DORIS: I'm glad to hear it. What else did you find out?

GEORGE: [*Simply*] That behind the walls I've built around myself I'm a warm, caring, loving, human being.

[*She looks at him for a moment*]

DORIS: I could have told you that twenty years ago. How does Helen feel about this "voyage of self discovery"?

GEORGE: At first she tended to overact.

DORIS: In what way?

GEORGE: She threw a grapefruit at me in the Thriftimart. It was natural that we'd have some interpersonal conflicts to work through but now it's cool. She's into pottery.

DORIS: But how do you make a living?

GEORGE: We live very simply, Doris—we don't need much. What bread we do need I can provide by simple, honest labor.

DORIS: Like what?

GEORGE: I play cocktail piano in a singles bar in the Valley.

[*The phone rings again.* DORIS *quickly moves to answer it*]

DORIS: [*Into phone*] Hello—Oh, hi, Liz—No way. Tell him that's our final offer—I don't care how good a location it is—That's bull, Liz, he needs us more than we need him. If he doesn't like it he can shove it but don't worry—he won't. Anything else?—Okay, you know the number. [*She hangs up*] I'm buying another store.

GEORGE: Why?

DORIS: Money. [*She continues to dress*]

GEORGE: Is that why you went into business? Just to make money.

DORIS: Of course not. I wanted money *and* power. And it finally penetrated my thick little head that attending C.R. groups with ten other frustrated housewives wasn't going to change anything.

GEORGE: C.R. groups?

DORIS: Consciousness raising. [*He nods*] I take it you *are* for Women's Liberation?

GEORGE: Listen, I'm for any kind of liberation.

DORIS: That's a cop out. Women have always been exploited by men and you know it.

GEORGE: We've *all* been shafted, Doris, and by the same things. [*He gets up*] Look, let me lay this on you. I go to a woman doctor. The first time she gave me a rectal examination she said, "Am I hurting you or are you tense?" I said, "I'm tense." Then she said, "Are you tense because I'm a woman?" and I said, "No, I get tense when *anybody* does that to me." [*A beat*] You see what I mean?

DORIS: I don't know but I *do* know that the only time a woman is taken seriously in this country is when she has the money to back up her mouth. The business has given me that.

GEORGE: [*Mildly*] Well, I guess it's nice to have a hobby.

DORIS: Hobby? We grossed over half a million dollars the first year.

GEORGE: Honey, if that's what you want I'm very happy for you. [*A slight shrug*] It's just that I'm not into the money thing anymore.

[*She looks at him for a moment*]

DORIS: [*Lightly*] George, you ever get the feeling we're drifting apart?

GEORGE: No. In many ways I've never felt closer to you.

DORIS: Really? I don't know, sometimes I think our lives are always—out of sync.

GEORGE: We all realize our potential in different ways at different times. All I ask is that you don't lay *your* trip on me, that's all.

[*She moves to purse, extracts check*]

DORIS: Then let me lay this on you. [*She hands him check*] Here—it's the money you loaned me to start the store.

GEORGE: [*Looking at check*] It's three times the amount I gave you.

DORIS: Return on your investment.

GEORGE: I can't accept this, Doris.

DORIS: [*Firmly*] You can and you will. I'm not going to have any lover of mine playing piano in a singles bar. Sounds tacky.

[*They smile at one another*]

GEORGE: You never used to order me around.

DORIS: I've come a long way, baby.

GEORGE: The important thing is, does it give you a sense of fulfillment?

DORIS: Fulfillment? Let me tell you about fulfillment. [*She moves to finish dressing*] I went into Gucci's the other day and I noticed a suede suit I liked and asked one of their snotty salesgirls the price. She said, "Seven hundred dollars," and started to walk away. I said, "I'll take five." She turned and said, "Five? Why on earth would you want five?" and I said, "I want them for my bowling team." *That's* fulfillment.

GEORGE: So you have everything you want?

DORIS: [*Lighting cigarette—flippantly*] With one minor exception. Somewhere along the way I seem to have lost my husband.

GEORGE: Lost him?

DORIS: Well, I don't know if I've lost him or simply misplaced him. He walked out of the house four days ago and I haven't heard from him since.

GEORGE: How do you feel about that?

DORIS: George, do me a favor—stop acting as if you're leading a human potential group. It really pisses me off.

GEORGE: That's cool.

DORIS: *What's* cool?

GEORGE: For you to transfer your hostility and feelings of aggression from Harry to me. As long as you *know* that's what you're doing.

DORIS: You mind if I tell you something, George? You're beginning to get on my nerves.

GEORGE: That's cool, too.

DORIS: Jesus!

GEORGE: I mean it. At least it's *honest*. That's the key to everything—total honesty.

DORIS: Oh, really? And are you totally honest with Helen?

GEORGE: I'm trying.

DORIS: Have you told her about us?

GEORGE: No—but I could. [*She grimaces*] Really, I think that today she's matured enough to handle it.

DORIS: George, you're full of shit.

GEORGE: I can buy that—if you're really being *honest*.

DORIS: Believe me, I'm being honest!

GEORGE: Well, at least it's a start. But what about that other garbage? [*She starts to speak*] Oh, come on, Doris! [*Imitating her*] "I don't know if I lost him or simply misplaced him." I mean what sort of crap is that?

[*She looks at him for a moment*]

DORIS: Okay, you have a point.

GEORGE: Is there someone else?

DORIS: I don't think so. I *know* there isn't with me. [*Getting agitated*] That's what really gets to me. Did you know I've been married for over twenty-five years and I've never cheated on him *once!* [*He doesn't say anything*] Well, you know what I mean.

GEORGE: What is it then? Boredom?

DORIS: No. Oh, Harry's not exactly Cary Grant anymore but then neither is Cary Grant.

GEORGE: So how do you feel about all this?

DORIS: You're doing it again, George. [*He doesn't say anything*] Okay, I think—

GEORGE: No, don't tell me what you think. Tell me what you *feel.*

DORIS: Like I've been kicked in the stomach.

GEORGE: That's good. [*She looks at him*] What else?

DORIS: Angry, hurt, betrayed, and—okay, a little guilty. But you know something? I *resent* the fact that he's made me feel guilty.

GEORGE: Why do you feel resentment?

DORIS: [*Angrily*] Look, I didn't marry Harry because he had a head for business! Okay, it so happens that I discovered I did. Or maybe I was just lucky—I don't know. The point is, I don't love Harry any less because he's a failure as a provider. Why should he love me any less because I'm a success? [*He doesn't say anything, she sighs*] I don't know—one of these days I'm going to know exactly how I *do* feel.

GEORGE: You don't know?

DORIS: It varies between Joan of Arc, Rosalind Russell, and Betty Crocker.

GEORGE: Well, I suppose most women are going through a transitional period.

DORIS: [*With a wry grimace*] Yeah, but what am I going to do tonight?

GEORGE: Have you told him you still love him?

DORIS: Love him? Why does he think I've been hanging around with him for twenty-seven years?

GEORGE: [*In his calm, reasonable voice*] I just mean that right now his masculinity is being threatened and he probably needs some validation of his worth as a man.

DORIS: And how the hell do I do all that? I mean that's *some* trick.

GEORGE: Total honesty, Doris. Is it so hard for you to tell him that you understand how he feels?

DORIS: Right now—it is, yes.

GEORGE: Oh?

DORIS: I mean why the hell should I apologize for doing something well? It's *his* ego that's screwed us up. I mean I really *resent* that!

GEORGE: You want him back?

DORIS: Right at this moment I'm not sure I do. Ask me tomorrow and I'll probably give you a different answer.

GEORGE: Why?

DORIS: [*Simply*] Tomorrow I won't have you.

GEORGE: I'm always with you in spirit.

DORIS: It's not easy to spiritually put your cold feet on someone's back.

GEORGE: Is that a proposal, Doris?

DORIS: You interested?

GEORGE: Are you?

DORIS: For two cents.

GEORGE: Leave Helen and Harry?

DORIS: Sure. Present a united back. [*He is looking at her, trying to determine whether she's serious*] Don't look so panicky, George. I'm only three quarters serious.

> [*There is a pause*]

GEORGE: Well, when you have your head together and are completely serious why don't you ask me again.

DORIS: I bet you say that to all the girls.

GEORGE: No.

> [*She cups his face in her hands and kisses him*]

DORIS: Thanks.

GEORGE: And stop feeling so insecure.

DORIS: About what?

GEORGE: You're as feminine as you always were.

> [*She looks at him for a moment*]

DORIS: I know Gloria Steinem would hate me but I'm glad you said that. [*She gives a little shrug*] I guess I'm not as emancipated as I thought I was.

GEORGE: None of us are.

> [*She grins at him*]

DORIS: You hungry?

GEORGE: Yes.

DORIS: Well, you're a lucky man because tonight our dinner is being catered by the chicest, most expensive French delicatessen in San Francisco.

GEORGE: How'd we swing that?

DORIS: The owner has a thing about you. [*As she moves toward the door*] It's all in the trunk of my car.

GEORGE: You need any help?

DORIS: Yes. Set the table, light the candles, and when I come back make me laugh.

GEORGE: I'll try.

DORIS: That's okay. If you can't make me laugh just hold my hand.

[*She exits. He moves to prepare the table for the food. The phone rings. He hesitates for a moment before picking up the receiver*]

GEORGE: [*Into the phone*] Hello—No, she's not here right now. Who is this? [*His face freezes*] Harry!—Uh, hold—hold on a moment. [*He places the phone on the floor, stares at it for a moment. Then he paces in a circle around it, his mind wrestling with the alternatives. He stops, stares at it, takes a deep breath, picks up the receiver*] Hello—Harry, we're two adult mature human beings and I've decided to be totally honest with you— No, Doris is not here right now but *I'd* like to talk to you—Because I know you and Doris have been having a rough time lately and—We're very close friends. I've known Doris for twenty years and through her I feel as if I know you—Well, we've been meeting the same weekend for twenty years—The Retreat? Well, we can get into that later but first I want you to know something. She loves you, Harry—she really loves you— I just know, Harry—Look, maybe if I told you a story she just told me this morning it would help you understand. A few months ago Doris was supposed to act as a den mother for your ten-year-old daughter Georgina and her Indian guide group. Well, she got hung up at the store and was two hours late getting home. When she walked into the house she looked into the living room and do you know what she saw? A rather overweight, balding, middle-aged man with a feather on his head sitting cross-legged on the floor very gravely and gently telling a circle of totally absorbed little girls what it was like to be in a World War II Japanese prison camp. She turned around, walked out of the house, sat in her car and thanked God for being married to a man like you—Are you still there, Harry?— Well, sometimes married people get into an emotional straitjacket and find it difficult to communicate how they truly feel about each other. Honesty is the key to everything—Yes, we've had a very close, very intimate relationship for twenty years and I'm not ashamed to admit that it's been one of the most satisfying experiences of my life—My name? My name is Father Michael O'Herlihy. [*The lights start to dim as he keeps talking*] No, she's out saying a novena right now—Yes, my son, I'll tell her to call you.

[*The curtain has fallen*]

SCENE THREE

The Time: *A day in February, 1975.*

The Place: *The same.*

At Rise: DORIS *is alone on the stage silently mouthing "twenty-one, twenty-two, twenty-three" as she finishes transferring some red roses from a box into a silver vase. She is well dressed but her clothes are softer, more feminine and less fashionable than the last time we saw her. She turns as* GEORGE *enters. His hair has been trimmed to a "conservatively long" length and his raincoat covers his comfortably rumpled sports coat, pants, and turtle neck sweater. They drink one another in for a moment before they embrace affectionately.*

GEORGE: You feel *good*.

DORIS: So do you. [*She looks at him*] But you *look* tircd.

GEORGE: [*Grins*] I've looked this way for years. You just haven't noticed. [*She doesn't say anything but we see the concern in her eyes. He turns away, takes off his raincoat and throws it over a chair during the following*] Anyway, I feel better now I'm here. This room's always had that effect on me.

DORIS: I know what you mean. I guess it proves that maybe you can't buy happiness but you can certainly *rent* it. [*She gazes around the room affectionately*] It never changes, does it?

GEORGE: About the only thing that doesn't.

DORIS: I find that comforting.

GEORGE: Even old Chalmers is the same. He must be seventy-five by now. [*He smiles at her*] Remember when we first met how even then we called him Old Chalmers? [*She nods*] He must have been about the same age we are now.

DORIS: *That* I don't find comforting.

GEORGE: We were very young. [*They gaze at one another for a moment*]

DORIS: Have we changed, George?

GEORGE: Of course. I grew up with you. Remember the dumb lies I used to tell?

DORIS: [*Nods*] I miss them.

GEORGE: I don't. It was no fun being that insecure.

DORIS: And what about me? Have I grown up, too?

GEORGE: Oh, I have the feeling you were already grown up when I met you. [*They smile at one another*] Tell me something.

DORIS: Anything.

GEORGE: Why is it that every time I look at you I want to put my hands all over you?

[*She moves to embrace him*]

DORIS: That's another thing that hasn't changed. You always were a sex maniac.

GEORGE: [*Nuzzling her*] Softest thing I've touched in months is Rusty, my cocker spaniel.

[*She looks at him in surprise*]

DORIS: Oh? [*He avoids the unspoken query by moving away to the fireplace*]

GEORGE: Let's see if I can get this fire going. [*She watches him as he throws another log on*] You know I figured out with the cost of firewood today it's cheaper to buy Akron furniture, break it up, and burn *it*.

DORIS: Things that tight?

GEORGE: No, I'm okay. I've been doing some teaching at U.C.L.A.

DORIS: Music?

GEORGE: Accounting. [*He shrugs, gestures at the window*] It seems with everything that's happening out there figures are still the only things that don't lie. [*She moves to pour two cups of coffee from a coffee pot that has been set up on a tray*] Doris, why'd you sell your business?

DORIS: [*Surprised*] How did you know that?

GEORGE: I'll tell you later. What made you do it?

DORIS: I was bought out by a chain. [*A slight shrug*] It was the right offer at the right time.

GEORGE: But I thought you loved working.

DORIS: Well, there was another factor. Harry had a heart attack. [*She hands him a cup of coffee*] It turned out to be a mild one but he needed me to look after him—so— [*She shrugs*]

GEORGE: You don't miss the action?

DORIS: Not yet. I guess I'm still enjoying being one of the idle rich.

[*He sits with his coffee as she moves to get a cup for herself*]

GEORGE: But what do you do with yourself?

DORIS: Oh—read, watch TV, play a little golf, visit our grandchildren—you know, all the jet set stuff.

GEORGE: Harry's okay now?

[*She sits opposite him*]

DORIS: Runs four miles a day and has a body like Mark Spitz. [*Grins*] Unfortunately, his face is still like Ernest Borgnine's. You want to hear a nice story about him?

GEORGE: [*Unenthusiastically*] Sure.

DORIS: Right after the heart attack when he came out of intensive care he looked up at the doctor and said, "Doc, give it to me straight. After I get out of the hospital will I be able to play the piano?" The doctor said, "Of course," and Harry said, "Funny, I couldn't play it *before*." [GEORGE *gives a polite smile, gets up, moves to look out of the window*] You don't understand—it wasn't that it was that funny. It's just that Harry *never* makes jokes but he saw how panicky I was and wanted to make me feel better.

GEORGE: Doris, how are you and Harry? You know—emotionally.

DORIS: Comfortable.

GEORGE: You're willing to settle for that?

[*She moves to pick up his raincoat*]

DORIS: Oh, it's not such a bad state. The word's been given a bad reputation by the young. [*She looks around for his luggage*] Where's your luggage? Still in the car?

GEORGE: I didn't bring any. [*She looks at him*] I—I can't stay, Doris.

DORIS: [*Puzzled*] Why?

GEORGE: Look, I have a lot to say and a short time to say it so I'd better start now. [*She waits. He takes a breath*] First of all, Helen's known about us for over ten years.

DORIS: [*Finally*] When did you find out?

GEORGE: Two months ago.

DORIS: She never confronted you with it before?

GEORGE: No.

[*She slowly sits*]

DORIS: I always wondered how we managed to pull it off. I guess we didn't. What made her finally tell you?

GEORGE: She didn't. She has this—this old friend—Connie—maybe I've mentioned her before. She told me. [*He shakes his head unbelievingly*] All those years and Helen never even hinted that she knew. [*A beat*] I guess that's the nicest story I've ever told about her.

DORIS: Your wife's an amazing woman, George.

GEORGE: She's dead. [*She just looks at him*] She died six months ago. Cancer. It was all—very fast. [*She slowly gets up, moves to look into the fire*] I'm sorry to blurt it out like that. I just couldn't think of a—a graceful way to tell you. [*She nods, her back still to him*] You okay, honey?

DORIS: It's so strange. I never met Helen. But—but I feel as if I've just lost my best friend. It's—crazy. [*He doesn't say anything. She turns to face him*] It must have been awful for you.

GEORGE: You cope. You don't think you can but—you cope.

[*She moves to him, touches his cheek with her hand*]

DORIS: The kids okay?

GEORGE: They'll survive. I don't think I could have gotten through the whole thing without them. [*He moves away*] Then of course there was—Connie.

DORIS: Connie?

GEORGE: She'd lost her husband a few years ago so there was a certain—empathy.

DORIS: Oh?

GEORGE: She's a friend, Doris. A very good friend. We've always felt very—comfortable—together. I suppose it's because she's a lot like Helen. [*She reacts with a slight frown*] Is there something the matter?

DORIS: I just wish you'd tried to reach me.

GEORGE: I did. That's when I found out you'd sold the stores. I called and they gave me your home number. I let the phone ring four times, then I hung up. But it made me feel better knowing you were there if I needed you.

DORIS: I wish you'd spoken to me.

GEORGE: I didn't want to intrude. I didn't feel I had the right.

DORIS: My God, that's terrible. We should have been together.

GEORGE: I've been thinking about us a lot lately. Everything we've been through together. The things we shared. The times we've helped each other. Did you know we've made love a hundred and thirteen times? I figured it out on my Bomar calculator. [*He is fixing fresh cups of coffee*] It's a wonderful thing to know someone that well. You know, there is nothing about you I don't know. It's two sugars, right?

DORIS: No, one.

GEORGE: Cream? [*She shakes her head*] So, I don't know everything about you. I don't know who your favorite movie stars are and I couldn't remember the name of your favorite perfume. I racked my brain but I couldn't remember.

DORIS: [*Smiles*] That's funny. It's My Sin.

GEORGE: But I do know that in twenty-four years I've never been out of love with you. I find that incredible. So what do you say, Doris, you want to get married?

DORIS: [*Lightly*] Married? We shouldn't even be doing this.

GEORGE: I'm serious.

DORIS: [*Looking at him*] You really are, aren't you?

GEORGE: What did you think I was—just another summer romance? A simple "yes" will do.

DORIS: There's no such thing, George.

GEORGE: What is it?

DORIS: I was just thinking of how many times I've dreamed of you asking me this. It's pulled me through a lot of bad times. I want to thank you for that.

GEORGE: What did you say to me all those times?

DORIS: I always said "yes."

GEORGE: Then why are you hesitating now? [*Pause*] Do you realize I'm giving you the opportunity to marry a man who has known you for twenty-four years and every time you walk by still wants to grab your ass?

DORIS: You always were a sweet talker.

GEORGE: That's because if I told you how I really felt about you it would probably sound like a medley of clichés from popular songs. Will you marry me?

DORIS: [*Pause*] I can't.

GEORGE: Why not?

DORIS: I'm already married.

GEORGE: You feel you have to stay because he needs you?

DORIS: No, it's more than that. George, try and understand. [*She moves away and turns to him*] When I look at Harry I don't only see the way he is now. I see all the other Harrys I've know. I'm sure he feels the same way about me. When we look at our children—our grandchildren—old movies on TV—anything—we share the same memories. [*A beat*] It's—comfortable. Maybe that's what marriage is all about in the end—I don't know. [*A slight pause*] Didn't you feel that way with Helen?

[*There is a short pause*]

GEORGE: [*Exploding*] Goddamit! [*He smashes his coffee cup into the fireplace*] I was the one who got you back together five years ago! Why did I *do* a stupid thing like that!? I mean why the hell was I so goddam generous!?

DORIS: Because you felt the same way about Helen then as I do about Harry now.

GEORGE: What's that got to do with anything?!

DORIS: If I hadn't gone back to Harry you might have been stuck with me permanently and you were terrified.

[*He looks at her, manages a sheepish grin*]

GEORGE: You could always see through me, couldn't you?

DORIS: That's okay. I always liked what I saw.

GEORGE: Well, I want you now.

DORIS: I'm still available once a year. [*He doesn't say anything*] Same time, same place? [*She catches a certain look in his eyes*] What is it?

[*He looks at her for a moment, paces, turns to face her*]

GEORGE: [*Awkwardly*] Doris—I—I need a wife. I'm just not the kind of man who can live alone. I want you to marry me but when I came here I—I knew there was an outside chance you'd say "no." What I'm trying to say is—if you don't marry me I'll probably end up marrying Connie. No—that's a lie—I will marry her. She knows why I came here today. She knows—all about you. The point is, she's not the sort of woman who would go along with our—relationship. [*A beat*] You understand? [DORIS *manages a nod*] I suppose what I'm saying is that if you don't marry me we won't ever see each other again. [DORIS *is frozen, he moves to take her hand*] You're trembling.

DORIS: The thought of never seeing you again terrifies me.

GEORGE: Doris, for God's sake—marry me!

DORIS: [*Finally—torn*] I'm sorry—I can't. [*He looks at her for a long moment*] Don't hate me, George.

GEORGE: I could never hate you. I was just trying to think of something that would break your heart, make you burst into tears and come with me.

DORIS: You know us Italians. We never cry.

[*He makes a gesture of helplessness, stands*]

GEORGE: What time is it? [*She holds out her wrist, he looks at her watch, reacts*] Five-fifty-five.

DORIS: No, it's only two-thirty. I always keep my watch three hours and twenty-five minutes fast.

GEORGE: [*Puzzled*] How long you been doing that?

DORIS: About twenty odd years.

GEORGE: Why would anyone want to do that?

DORIS: Personal idiosyncrasy.

[*There is an awkward pause*]

GEORGE: Well—I—I have a plane to catch. [*She nods, stands. They look at one another*] You know, I can't believe this is happening to us. [*She doesn't say anything*] Yeah. Well—

[*They embrace and kiss, clumsily and awkwardly, almost like two strangers. They break, he picks up his raincoat, moves to door, turns to look at her*]

GEORGE: Who were your favorite movie stars?

DORIS: Lon McAllister, Howard Keel, Cary Grant, Marlon Brando, and Laurence Olivier.

GEORGE: You've come a long way.

DORIS: We both have.

[*He opens door, looks at her*]

GEORGE: Always keep your watch three hours and twenty-five minutes fast, huh?

[*He exits quickly, shutting the door behind him.*

DORIS *stands for a moment trying to absorb the shock of his departure. Then, trancelike, she moves to the closet where she gets her suitcase, puts it on the sofa, and starts to pack but stops to look lovingly around the room, drinking in the memories before her eyes come to rest upon the vase of roses. She slowly moves to the roses, takes one out, closes her eyes and rests it gently against her cheek. She holds this pose for a long moment before her eyes jolt open as the door crashes open and* GEORGE, *perspiring and very agitated, bursts into the room, holding his suitcases. He drops his cases with a thump, fixes her with an angry, frustrated look*]

GEORGE: Okay, you win goddamit! You can't look a gift horse in the mouth!

DORIS: [*Astounded*] But—but what about Connie?

GEORGE: [*Yelling*] There is no Connie! I made her up! [*She just stares at him, dumbfounded*] No, that's a lie, too. There is a Connie but she's sixty-nine years old! [DORIS *is still speechless*] Doris, I wanted you to *marry* me and I figured if you thought there was someone else you'd—okay, maybe I didn't think it through. I was desperate, okay? [*Getting even more agitated*] Look, for once in my life I wanted a happy ending, can't you understand that?! Listen, I don't want to talk about it anymore! [*Still speechless she watches him march to the bed and start to furiously undress. He turns to look at her*] Okay! You're right about that, too! If you had married me we might have just ended up with a "comfortable" ending! [*She opens her mouth to speak*] Look, I'm in no mood to figure it out right now. All I know is I'm back and I'm going to keep coming back every year until our bones are too brittle to risk contact.[*She starts to laugh, her laughter builds and then almost imperceptibly changes to something else and we realize that she is crying. She moves blindly into his arms, still sobbing. He gently tips her face up so that he can look at her and speaks very softly*] After twenty-four years? Why now?

DORIS: [*Through her tears*] Because I love—happy—endings!

[*He picks her up, places her on the bed and as he lies beside her the lights slowly dim until there is just a pin spot on the vase of roses. Finally, this too fades, the stage is dark, and the play is over*]

CURTAIN

Angel Street

A VICTORIAN THRILLER

PATRICK HAMILTON

PATRICK HAMILTON

When Patrick Hamilton died in 1962, it was said editorially of him: "For more than thirty years Patrick Hamilton raised goose pimples on millions of theatregoers, and his plays are likely to continue to do so as long as thriller melodramas remain popular." There was more truth than poetry to this journalistic eulogy, for Hamilton's celebrated Victorian melodrama, *Angel Street*, remains to this day one of the most popular and frequently revived of all suspense dramas.

Its perennial allurement may be attributed to a combination of factors. It is a work that never permits the attention to wander even for the briefest moment; characters, situation, and dialogue all minister to the desired thrill. It is compact in construction, economical in style, and as the British historian J. C. Trewin wrote: "*Angel Street* has always kept a throat-constricting power, one bred of narrative and atmosphere and with an effect unfailing in performance, the *frisson* of the rising and falling light."

When the play was presented in England in 1938, it was known as *Gaslight* (as was the subsequent film version that costarred Ingrid Bergman and Charles Boyer). Following an engagement at the Richmond Theatre, it was brought to London where the Manninghams set up their rather demoniac housekeeping at the Apollo Theatre. Reports of its success gradually crossed the Atlantic and in due course contracts were arranged for an American presentation. Before its Broadway debut, however, the play encountered almost as many anxious moments as did the terrorized Mrs. Manningham. After a West Coast tryout that made little dent, Broadway regarded its chances for survival as practically nil. Production money was tight, and according to theatrical lore, when the play finally did manage to raise its curtain at the John Golden Theatre, tickets had been printed to cover only the opening night and the subsequent Saturday matinee and evening performances. In short, as the Broadway skeptics had prophesied, the Manninghams soon were destined to take up a more permanent residence at Cain's Warehouse. And as if that were not quite enough, the Victorian thriller opened on December 5, 1941, two days before Pearl Harbor.

Yet, the actualities of the theatre can be as astonishing as any piece of fiction, perhaps more so, and *Angel Street* reversed course and became an instant smash hit. It ran for over three years, achieving a record of 1,295 performances, making it one of the dozen longest-running nonmusical plays in Broadway history.

New York's professional aisle-sitters were generous in their praise for both play and production. Brooks Atkinson, from his lofty perch at *The New York Times*, sounded the clarion call that led directly to the box office of the John Golden Theatre: "As a creep show, Patrick Hamilton's Victorian melodrama remains close to the top of the class—literate and harrowing simultaneously." His colleagues were in accordance: "One of the most satisfying theatre adventures of the last decade . . . it really can keep you anchored to your seat bolt upright . . . a masterpiece of suspense."

The verdict was in . . .

Patrick Hamilton was born in Sussex, England, on March 17, 1904. Educated at Westminster, he began his association with the theatre as an actor and made his first appearance on stage in 1921. He established himself as a playwright with *Rope*, a 1929 drama of two Oxford undergraduates who commit murder for thrills. Although Hamilton always stoutly denied that it was suggested by the notorious Leopold–Loeb murder case in Chicago, the parallel proved beneficial to the play's long career. Among the author's other works for the stage are *John Brown's Body*, *The Duke in Darkness*, and *The Man Upstairs*. An accomplished novelist as well as dramatist, he published his first novel, *Monday Morning*, before he was twenty. Additional novels followed at brief intervals, but he is best known, perhaps, in the United States for *Hangover Square*.

In his foreword to *Rope*, Patrick Hamilton stated his credo as a dramatist. "I have gone all out to write a horror play and make your flesh creep. And there is no reason to believe that this reaction is medically or chemically any worse for you than making you laugh or cry. If I have succeeded, you will leave the theatre braced and recreated, which is what you go to the theatre for."

Angel Street was performed again in New York in 1948 with Uta Hagen and José Ferrer, and in 1975 with Dina Merrill and Michael Allinson.

Angel Street was first produced at the John Golden Theatre, New York, on December 5, 1941, by Shepard Traube (in association with Alexander H. Cohen). The cast was as follows:

MRS. MANNINGHAM	*Judith Evelyn*
MR. MANNINGHAM	*Vincent Price*
NANCY	*Elizabeth Eustis*
ELIZABETH	*Florence Edney*
ROUGH	*Leo G. Carroll*

Directed by Shepard Traube
Setting and Costumes by Lemuel Ayers
Lighting by Feder

The entire action of the play occurs in a house on Angel Street, located in the Pimlico district of London. The time is 1880.

ACT ONE

Late afternoon.

ACT TWO

Immediately afterward.

ACT THREE

Later the same night.

ACT ONE

The scene is a living room on the first floor of a four-storied house in a gloomy and unfashionable quarter of London, in the latter part of the last century. The room is furnished in all the heavily draped and dingy profusion of the period, and yet, amidst this abundance of parapher-nalia, an air is breathed of poverty, wretchedness, and age.

Fireplace down right. Door at right above fireplace leading to little room. Settee below fireplace with stool in front of it. Table center with chairs right and left of it. Window at left. Desk in front of window with chairs back and above it. Secretary against wall up right. Lamp on table. Sliding double doors at back left center leading to hall, to left the front door, to right the servants' quarters. A circular stair leading to the upper floors is at back up right center. Chairs down right and left.

The curtain rises upon the rather terrifying darkness of the late afternoon—the zero hour, as it were, before the feeble dawn of gas light and tea. In front of the fire, on the settee, MANNINGHAM *is stretched out and sleeping heavily. He is tall, good-looking, about forty-five. He is heavily moustached and bearded and perhaps a little too well dressed. His manner is suave and authoritative, with a touch of mystery and bitterness.* MRS. MANNINGHAM *is sitting sewing on the chair left of the table. She is about thirty-four. She has been good-looking, almost a beauty—but now she has a haggard, wan, frightened air, with rings under her eyes, which tell of sleepless nights and worse.*

Big Ben strikes five. Pause. From the street below, in the distance, can be heard the intermittent jingling of a muffin-man ringing his bell.

MRS. MANNINGHAM *listens to this sound for a few moments, furtively and indecisively, almost as though she is frightened even of this. Then she rustles quickly over to the window and looks down into the street. Then to the bell cord by the door, which she pulls. Then back to her sewing, which she gathers up and puts into a box, at the same time taking a purse therefrom. There is a knock at the door, and* ELIZABETH, *the cook and housekeeper, enters. She is a stout, amiable, subservient woman of about fifty. Signaling that her husband is asleep,* MRS. MANNINGHAM *goes over and whispers to her at the door, giving her some money from the purse.* ELIZABETH *goes out closing the doors.*

MR. MANNINGHAM: [*Whose eyes have opened, but whose position has not changed a fraction of an inch*] What are you doing, Bella?

MRS. MANNINGHAM: Nothing, dear. [*She crosses quietly and quickly to the secretary with her sewing and starts back to the doors]* Don't wake yourself.

[*There is a pause. She starts to window*]

MR. MANNINGHAM: [*Whose eyes are closed again*] What *are* you doing, Bella? Come here. . . .

MRS. MANNINGHAM: [*After hesitating, going to him*] Only for tea, my dear. Muffins—for tea— [*She takes his hand*]

MR. MANNINGHAM: Muffins—eh—?

MRS. MANNINGHAM: Yes, dear— He only comes so seldom—I thought I might surprise you.

MR. MANNINGHAM: Why are you so apprehensive, Bella? I was not about to reproach you.

MRS. MANNINGHAM: [*Nervously releasing her hand*] No, dear. I know you weren't.

MR. MANNINGHAM: That fire's in ashes. Ring the bell, will you, Bella dear, please?

MRS. MANNINGHAM: Yes. . . . [*She is going over to bell, but stops*] Is it merely to put coal on, my dear? I can do that.

MR. MANNINGHAM: Now then, Bella. We've had this out before. Be so good as to ring the bell.

MRS. MANNINGHAM: But, dear—Lizzie's out in the street. Let me do it. I can do it easily. [*She comes over to do it*]

MR. MANNINGHAM: [*Stopping her with outstretched hand*] No, no, no, no, no. . . . Where's the girl? Let the girl come up if Lizzie's out.

MRS. MANNINGHAM: But, my dear. . . .

MR. MANNINGHAM: Go and ring the bell, please, Bella—there's a good child. [MRS. MANNINGHAM *gives in, and goes back to ring the bell*] Now, come here. [*She does so*] What do you suppose the servants are for, Bella? [MRS. MANNINGHAM *does not answer. There is a pause; then gently*] Go on. Answer me. [*He rises*] What do you suppose servants are for?

MRS. MANNINGHAM: [*Shamefacedly, and scarcely audible, merely dutifully feeding him*] To serve us, I suppose, Jack—

MR. MANNINGHAM: Precisely. Then why—?

MRS. MANNINGHAM: But I think we should consider them a little, that's all.

MR. MANNINGHAM: Consider them? There's your extraordinary confusion of mind again. You speak as though they work for no consideration. I happen to consider Elizabeth to the tune of sixteen pounds per annum. And the girl ten. Twenty-six pounds a year all told. And if that is not consideration of the most acute and lively kind, I should like to know what is.

MRS. MANNINGHAM: Yes, Jack. I expect you are right.

MR. MANNINGHAM: I have no doubt of it, my dear. It's sheer weakmindedness to think otherwise. [*Pause*] What's the weather doing? Is it still as yellow?

MRS. MANNINGHAM: Yes, it seems to be denser than ever. Shall you be going out in this, Jack dear?

MR. MANNINGHAM: Oh—I expect so. Unless it gets very much worse after tea.

> [*There is a knock at the door.* MRS. MANNINGHAM *hesitates. There is another knock*]

Come in.

> [*Enter* NANCY, *the maid. She is a self-conscious, pretty, cheeky girl of nineteen*]

NANCY: [*Stands looking at both, as* MRS. MANNINGHAM *hesitates to tell her why she rang the bell*] Oh, I beg your pardon. I thought the bell rang—

MR. MANNINGHAM: Yes, we rang the bell, Nancy— [*Pause*] Go on, my dear, tell her why we rang the bell.

MRS. MANNINGHAM: Oh— Yes— We want some coal on the fire, Nancy, please.

> [NANCY *looks at her impudently, and then, with a little smile and toss of the head, goes over to put coal on the fire*]

MR. MANNINGHAM: [*After pause*] And you might as well light the gas, Nancy. This darkness in the afternoon is getting beyond endurance.

NANCY: Yes, sir. [*With another barely discernible little smile, she gets the matches, and goes to light the two incandescent mantles on each side of the fireplace. Manningham watches her as she lights the second mantle*]

MR. MANNINGHAM: You're looking very impudent and pretty this afternoon, Nancy. Do you know that?

NANCY: I don't know at all, sir, I'm sure.

MR. MANNINGHAM: What is it? Another broken heart added to your list?

NANCY: I wasn't aware of breaking any hearts, sir.

MR. MANNINGHAM: I'm sure that's not true. And that complexion of yours. That's not true, either. I wonder what mysterious lotions you've been employing to enhance your natural beauties.

NANCY: I'm quite natural, sir, I promise you. [*Crosses to light lamp on table*]

MR. MANNINGHAM: But you do it adroitly, I grant you that. What are your secrets? Won't you tell us the name of your chemist? Perhaps you could pass it on to Mrs. Manningham—and help banish her pallor. She would be most grateful, I have no doubt.

NANCY: I'd be most happy to, I'm sure, sir.

MR. MANNINGHAM: Or are women too jealous of their discoveries to pass them on to a rival?

NANCY: I don't know, sir— Will that be all you're wanting, sir?

MR. MANNINGHAM: Yes. That's all I want, Nancy— Except my tea.

NANCY: It'll be coming directly. sir. [NANCY *goes out*]

MRS. MANNINGHAM: [*After a pause, reproachfully rather than angrily*] Oh, Jack, how *can* you treat me like that?

MR. MANNINGHAM: But, my dear, you're the mistress of the house. It was your business to tell her to put the coal on.

MRS. MANNINGHAM: It *isn't* that! It's humiliating me like that. As though I'd do anything to my face, and ask for *her* assistance if I did.

MR. MANNINGHAM: But you seem to look on servants as our natural equals. So I treated her as one. [*Sits down on settee and picks up newspaper*] Besides, I was only trifling with her.

MRS. MANNINGHAM: It's strange that you can't see how you hurt me. That girl laughs at me enough already.

MR. MANNINGHAM: Laughs at you? What an idea. What makes you think she laughs at you?

MRS. MANNINGHAM: Oh—I know that she does in secret. In fact, she does so openly—more openly every day.

MR. MANNINGHAM: But, my dear—if she does that, doesn't the fault lie with you?

MRS. MANNINGHAM: [*Pause*] You mean that I'm a laughable person?

MR. MANNINGHAM: I don't mean anything. It's you who read meaning into everything, Bella dear. I wish you weren't such a perfect little silly. Come here and stop it. I've just thought of something rather nice.

MRS. MANNINGHAM: Something nice? What have you thought of, Jack?

MR. MANNINGHAM: I shan't tell you unless you come here.

MRS. MANNINGHAM: [*Going over and sitting on stool beside him*] What is it, Jack? What have you thought of?

MR. MANNINGHAM: I read here that Mr. MacNaughton—the celebrated ac-tor—is in London for another season.

MRS. MANNINGHAM: Yes. I read that. What of it, Jack?

MR. MANNINGHAM: What of it? What do you suppose?

MRS. MANNINGHAM: Oh, Jack dear. Do you mean it? Would you take me to see MacNaughton? You wouldn't take me to see MacNaughton, would you?

MR. MANNINGHAM: I not only would take you to see MacNaughton, my dear. I *am* going to take you to see MacNaughton. That is, if you want to go.

MRS. MANNINGHAM: Oh, Jack! What heaven—what heaven!

MR. MANNINGHAM: When would you like to go? You have only three weeks, according to his advertisement.

MRS. MANNINGHAM: Oh—what perfect heaven! Let me see. Do let me see!

MR. MANNINGHAM: There. You see? You can see him in comedy or tragedy—

according to your choice. Which would you prefer, Bella—the comedy or the tragedy?

MRS. MANNINGHAM: Oh—it's so hard to say! Either would be equally wonderful. Which would you choose, if you were me?

MR. MANNINGHAM: Well—it depends—doesn't it—upon whether you want to laugh, or whether you want to cry.

MRS. MANNINGHAM: Oh—I want to laugh. But then, I should like to cry, too. In fact, I should like to do both. Oh, Jack, what made you decide to take me?

MR. MANNINGHAM: Well, my dear, you've been very good lately, and I thought it would be well to take you out of yourself.

MRS. MANNINGHAM: Oh, Jack dear. You have been so much kinder lately. Is it possible you're beginning to see my point of view?

MR. MANNINGHAM: I don't know that I ever differed from it, did I, Bella?

MRS. MANNINGHAM: Oh, Jack dear. It's true. It's true. All I need is to be taken out of myself—some little change—to have some attention from you. Oh, Jack, I'd be *better*—I could really try to be better—you know in what way—if only I could get *out* of myself a little more.

MR. MANNINGHAM: How do you mean, my dear, exactly, *better*?

MRS. MANNINGHAM: You know. . . . You know in what way, dear. About all that's happened lately. We said we wouldn't speak about it.

MR. MANNINGHAM: Oh, no—don't speak about that.

MRS. MANNINGHAM: No, dear, I don't want to—but what I say is so important. I *have* been better—even in the last week. Haven't you noticed it? And why is it? Because you have stayed in, and been kind to me. The other night when you stayed and played cards with me, it was like old days, and I went to bed feeling a normal, happy, healthy, human being. And then, the day after, when you read your book to me, Jack, and we sat by the fire, I felt all my love for you coming back then, Jack. And I slept that night like a child. All those ghastly dreads and terrible, terrible fears seemed to have vanished. And all just because you had given me your time, and taken me from brooding on myself in this house all day and night.

MR. MANNINGHAM: I wonder if it is that—or whether it's merely that your medicine is beginning to benefit you?

MRS. MANNINGHAM: No, Jack dear, it's not my medicine. I've taken my medicine religiously—haven't I taken it religiously? Much as I detest it! It's more than medicine that I want. It's the medicine of a sweet, sane mind, of interest in something. Don't you see what I mean?

MR. MANNINGHAM: Well—we *are* talking about gloomy subjects, aren't we?

MRS. MANNINGHAM: Yes. I don't want to be gloomy, dear—that's the last thing I want to be. I only want you to understand. Say you understand.

MR. MANNINGHAM: Well, dear. Don't I seem to? Haven't I just said I'm taking you to the theatre?

MRS. MANNINGHAM: Yes, dear— Yes, you have. Oh, and you've made me so happy—so happy, dear.

MR. MANNINGHAM: Well, then, which is it to be—the comedy or the tragedy. You must make up your mind.

MRS. MANNINGHAM: [*With exulting solemnity*] Oh, Jack, which *shall* it be? [*Rising and showing her pleasure with delighted gestures*] What *shall* it be? It matters so little! It matters so wonderfully little! I'm going to the play! Do you understand that, my husband! I'm going to the play! [*She throws her arms around him and kisses him. There is a knock on the door*] Come in. [*Enter* NANCY, *carrying tray. Pause, as she starts to desk*] No, Nancy, I think we'll have it on the table today.

NANCY: [*Still with impudence*] Oh—just as you wish, madam.

> [*Pause, as she puts tray on table, arranges cups and puts books, etc., on one side*]

MRS. MANNINGHAM: [*At mantelpiece*] Tell me, Nancy—if you were being taken to the play, and had to choose between comedy and tragedy, which would *you* choose?

NANCY: Me, madam? Oh—I'd go for the comedy all the time.

MRS. MANNINGHAM: Would you? Why would you choose the comedy, Nancy?

NANCY: I like to laugh, madam, I suppose.

MRS. MANNINGHAM: Do you? Well—I daresay you're right. I must bear it in mind. Mr. Manningham's taking me next week, you see.

NANCY: Oh, yes? I hope you enjoy it. I'll bring the muffins directly.

> [*As* NANCY *goes out,* MRS. MANNINGHAM *puts out her tongue at her.* MANNINGHAM *sees this*]

MR. MANNINGHAM: My dear—what are you doing?

MRS. MANNINGHAM: The little beast! Let her put that in her pipe and smoke it.

MR. MANNINGHAM: But what has she done?

MRS. MANNINGHAM: Ah—you don't know her. She tries to torment and score off me all day long. You don't see these things. A man wouldn't. [MR. MANNINGAHM *rises*] She thinks me a poor thing. And now she can suffer the news that you're taking me to the theatre.

MR. MANNINGHAM: I think you imagine things, my dear.

MRS. MANNINGHAM: Oh, no, I don't. We've been too familiar with her. [*Arranging chairs, in an emotionally happy state*] Come along, my dear. You sit one side, and I the other—like two children in the nursery.

MR. MANNINGHAM: [*Stands with back to fire*] You seem wonderfully pleased with yourself, Bella. I must take you to the theatre more often, if this is the result.

MRS. MANNINGHAM: [*Sitting at the table*] Oh, Jack—I wish you could.

MR. MANNINGHAM: I don't really know why we shouldn't. I used to like nothing so much when I was a boy. In fact, you may hardly believe it, but I even had an ambition to be an actor myself at one time.

MRS. MANNINGHAM: I can well believe it, dear. Come along to your tea now.

MR. MANNINGHAM: You know, Bella, that must be a very superb sensation. To take a part and lose yourself entirely in the character of someone else. I flatter myself I could have made an actor.

MRS. MANNINGHAM: [*Pouring tea*] Why, of course, my dear. You were cut out for it. Anyone can see that.

MR. MANNINGHAM: [*Crosses slowly*] No—do you think so—seriously? I always felt a faint tinge of regret. Of course, one would have required training, but I believe I should have made out—and might have reached the top of the tree for all I know.

> "To be or not to be. That is the question.
> Whether 'tis nobler in the mind to suffer
> The slings and arrows of outrageous fortune,
> Or to take arms against a sea of troubles,
> And, by opposing, end them."

[NANCY *enters, sets the muffin dish down on table during the recitation and goes out*]

MRS. MANNINGHAM: You see how fine your voice is? Oh—you've made a great mistake.

MR. MANNINGHAM: [*Lightly*] I wonder.

MRS. MANNINGHAM: Then if you had been a famous actor, I should have had a free seat to come and watch you every night of my life. And then called for you at the stage door afterwards. Wouldn't that have been paradise?

MR. MANNINGHAM: [*As he sits at the table*] A paradise of which you would soon tire, my dear. I have no doubt that after a few nights you would be staying at home again, just as you do now.

MRS. MANNINGHAM: Oh, no, I wouldn't. I should have to keep my eye on you for all the hussies that would be after you.

MR. MANNINGHAM: There would be hussies after me, would there? That is an added inducement, then.

MRS. MANNINGHAM: Yes—I know it, you wretch. But you wouldn't escape me. [*Lifting cover of muffin dish*] They look delicious. Aren't you glad I thought of them? [*Passes the salt*] Here's some salt. You want heaps of it. Oh, Jack dear, you must forgive me chattering on like this, but I'm feeling so happy.

MR. MANNINGHAM: I can see that, my dear.

MRS. MANNINGHAM: I'm being taken to the play, you see. Here you are. I used to adore these as a child, didn't you? [*Offers muffin to* MR. MAN- NINGHAM] I wonder how long it is since we had them? We haven't had them since we've been married anyway. Or have we? Have we?

MR. MANNINGHAM: I don't know, I'm sure. [*Suddenly rising, looking at the wall upstage and speaking in a calm, yet menacing way*] I don't know— Bella—

MRS. MANNINGHAM: [*After pause, dropping her voice almost to a whisper*] What is it? What's the matter? What is it now?

MR. MANNINGHAM: [*Walking over to fireplace, and speaking with his back to her*] I have no desire to upset you, Bella, but I have just observed something very much amiss. Will you please rectify it at once, while I am not looking, and we will assume that it has not happened.

MRS. MANNINGHAM: Amiss? What's amiss? For God's sake don't turn your back on me: What has happened?

MR. MANNINGHAM: You know perfectly well what has happened, Bella, and if you will rectify it at once I will say no more about it.

MRS. MANNINGHAM: I don't know. I don't know. You have left your tea. Tell me what it is. Tell me.

MR. MANNINGHAM: Are you trying to make a fool of me, Bella? What I refer to is on the wall behind you. If you will put it back, I will say no more about it.

MRS. MANNINGHAM: The wall behind me? What? [*Turns*] Oh—yes—The picture has been taken down— Yes— The picture— Who has taken it down? Why has it been taken down?

MR. MANNINGHAM: Yes. Why has it been taken down? Why, indeed? You alone can answer that, Bella. Why was it taken down before? Will you please take it from wherever you have hidden it, and put it back on the wall again?

MRS. MANNINGHAM: But I haven't hidden it, Jack. [*Rises*] I didn't do it. Oh, for God's sake look at me. I didn't do it. I don't know where it is. Someone else must have done it.

MR. MANNINGHAM: Someone else? [*Turning to her*] Are you suggesting per- haps that I should play such a fantastic and wicked trick?

MRS. MANNINGHAM: No, dear, no! But someone else. [*Going to him*] Before God, I didn't do it! Someone else, dear, someone else.

MR. MANNINGHAM: [*Shaking her off*] Will you please leave go of me. [*Walk- ing over to bell*] We will see about "someone else."

MRS. MANNINGHAM: Oh, Jack—don't ring the bell. Don't ring it. Don't call the servants to witness my shame. It's not my shame for I haven't done it—but *don't* call the servants! Tell them not to come. [*He has rung the bell. She goes to him*] Let's talk of this between ourselves! Don't call that girl in. Please!

MR. MANNINGHAM: [*Shaking her off violently*] Will you please leave go of me and sit down there! [*She sits in chair above the desk. He goes to fireplace*] Someone else, eh? Well—we shall see. [MRS. MANNINGHAM *sobs*] You had better pull yourself together, hadn't you?—[*There is a knock at the door*] Come in. [*Enter* ELIZABETH] Ah, Elizabeth. Come in please, Elizabeth— Shut the door—well, come, come into the room. [*She does so*] Now, Elizabeth, do you notice anything amiss in this room?—Look carefully around the walls, and see if you notice anything amiss— [*Pause, as* ELIZABETH *looks around the room and when she sees the space of the missing picture she stands still*] Well, Elizabeth, what do you notice?

ELIZABETH: Nothing, sir—Except the picture's been taken down.

MR. MANNINGHAM: Exactly. The picture has been taken down. You noticed it at once. Now was that picture in its place when you dusted the room this morning?

ELIZABETH: Yes, sir. It was, sir. I don't understand, sir.

MR. MANNINGHAM: Neither do I, Elizabeth, neither do I. And now, before you go, just one question. Was it you who removed that picture, Elizabeth?

ELIZABETH: No, sir. Of course I ain't, sir.

MR. MANNINGHAM: You did not. And have you ever, at any time, removed that picture from its proper place?

ELIZABETH: No, sir. Never, sir. Why should I, sir?

MR. MANNINGHAM: Indeed, why should you?—And now please, Elizabeth, will you kiss that Bible, will you as a token of your truthfulness—fetch that Bible from my desk? [ELIZABETH *hesitates. Then she does so*] Very well, you may go. And please send Nancy in here at once.

ELIZABETH: Yes, sir. [ELIZABETH *goes out looking at both*]

MRS. MANNINGHAM: [*Going to him*] Jack—spare me that girl. Don't call her in. I'll say anything. I'll say that I did it. I did it, Jack, I did it. Don't have that girl in. Don't!

MR. MANNINGHAM: Will you have the goodness to contain yourself?

[*There is a knock at the door.* MRS. MANNINGHAM *sits again*]

Come in.

NANCY: Yes, sir. Did you want me?

MR. MANNINGHAM: Yes, I do want you, Nancy.—If you will look at the wall behind you, you will see that the picture has gone.

NANCY: [*Going upstage*] Why. My word. So it has. [*Turns*] What a rum go!

MR. MANNINGHAM: I did not ask for any comment on your part, Nancy. Kindly be less insolent and answer what I ask you. Did *you* take that picture down, or did you not?

NANCY: Me? Of course I didn't. [*Comes to him slyly*] What should I want to move it for, sir?

MR. MANNINGHAM: Very good. Now will you kiss that Bible lying there, please, as a solemn oath that you did not—and you may go.

NANCY: Willingly, sir. [*She does so, and places Bible on table again with a little smile*] If I'd done it I'd've—

MR. MANNINGHAM: That is all, Nancy. You may go. [NANCY *goes out. Going to Bible as if to replace it on the desk*] There! I think we may now be said to have demonstrated conclusively—

MRS. MANNINGHAM: [*Rises*] Give me that Bible! Give it to me! Let me kiss it, too! [*Snatches it from him*] There! [*Kisses it*] There! Do you see? [*Kisses it*] There! Do you see that I kiss it?

MR. MANNINGHAM: For God's sake be careful what you do. Do you desire to commit sacrilege above all else?

MRS. MANNINGHAM: It is no sacrilege, Jack. Someone else has committed sacrilege. Now see—I swear before God Almighty that I never touched that picture. [*Kisses it*] There! [*She comes close to him*]

MR. MANNINGHAM: [*He grabs Bible*] Then, by God, you are mad, and you don't know what you do. You unhappy wretch—you're stark gibbering mad—like your wretched mother before you.

MRS. MANNINGHAM: Jack—you promised you would never say that again.

MR. MANNINGHAM: [*Crosses right. Pause*] The time has come to face facts, Bella. If this progresses you will not be much longer under *my* protection.

MRS. MANNINGHAM: Jack—I'm going to make a last appeal to you. I'm going to make a last appeal. I'm desperate, Jack. Can't you see that I'm desperate? If you can't, you must have a heart of stone.

MR. MANNINGHAM: [*Turns to her*] Go on. What do you wish to say?

MRS. MANNINGHAM: Jack, I may be going mad, like my poor mother—but if I am mad, you have got to treat me gently. Jack—before God—I never lie to you knowingly. If I have taken down that picture from its place I have not known it. *I have not known it.* If I took it down on those other occasions I did not know it, either. Jack, if I steal your things—your rings—your keys—your pencils and your handkerchiefs, and you find them later at the bottom of my box, as indeed you do, then I do not know that I have done it— Jack, if I commit these fantastic, meaningless mischiefs—so meaningless—why should I take a picture down from its place? If I do all these things, then I am certainly going off my head, and must be treated kindly and gently so that I may get well. You must *bear* with me, Jack, *bear* with me—not storm and rage. God knows I'm trying, Jack, I'm trying! Oh, for God's sake believe me that I'm trying and be kind to me!

MR. MANNINGHAM: Bella, my dear—have you any idea where that picture is now?

MRS. MANNINGHAM: Yes, yes, I suppose it's behind the secretary.

MR. MANNINGHAM: Will you please go and see?

MRS. MANNINGHAM: [*Vaguely*] Yes—yes— [*She goes to upper end of secretary and produces it*] Yes, it's here.

MR. MANNINGHAM: [*Reproachfully; as he crosses to the desk, places the Bible on it*] Then you did know where it was, Bella. [*Turns to her*] You did know where it was.

MRS. MANNINGHAM: [*As she starts toward him*] No! No! I only *supposed* it was! I only supposed it was because it was found there before! It was found there twice before. Don't you see? I *didn't* know—I didn't!

MR. MANNINGHAM: There is no sense in walking about the room with a picture in your hand, Bella. Go and put it back in its proper place.

MRS. MANNINGHAM: [*Pause, as she hangs the picture on wall, then comes to the back of the chair right of table*] Oh, look at our tea. We were having our tea with muffins—

MR. MANNINGHAM: Now, Bella, I said a moment ago that we have got to face facts. And that is what we have got to do. I am not going to say anything at the moment, for my feelings are running too high. In fact, I am going out immediately, and I suggest that you go to your room and lie down for a little in the dark.

MRS. MANNINGHAM: No, no—not my room. For God's sake don't send me to my room!

MR. MANNINGHAM: There is no question of sending you to your room, Bella. You know perfectly well that you may do exactly as you please.

MRS. MANNINGHAM: I feel faint, Jack— [*He goes quickly to her and supports her*] I feel faint—

MR. MANNINGHAM: Very well— [*Leading her to settee*] Now, take things quietly and come and lie down, here. Where are your salts? [*Crosses to secretary, gets salts and returns to her*] Here they are—[*Pause*] Now, my dear, I am going to leave you in peace—

MRS. MANNINGHAM: [*Eyes closed, reclining*] Have you got to go? Must you go? Must you always leave me alone after these dreadful scenes?

MR. MANNINGHAM: Now, no argument, please. I had to go in any case after tea, and I'm merely leaving you a little earlier, that's all. [*Pause. Going into room up right and returning with undercoat on*] Now is there anything I can get for you?

MRS. MANNINGHAM: No, Jack dear, nothing. You go.

MR. MANNINGHAM: Very good— [*Goes toward his hat and overcoat which are on the chair above desk, and stops*] Oh, by the way, I shall be passing the grocer and I might as well pay that bill of his and get it done with. Where is it, my dear? I gave it to you, didn't I?

MRS. MANNINGHAM: Yes, dear. It's on the secretary. [*Half rising*] I'll—

MR. MANNINGHAM: No, dear—don't move—don't move. I can find it. [*At secretary and begins to rummage*] I shall be glad to get the thing off my chest. Where is it, dear? Is it in one of these drawers?

MRS. MANNINGHAM: No—it's on top. I put it there this afternoon.

MR. MANNINGHAM: All right. We'll find it— We'll find it— Are you sure it's here, dear? There's nothing here except some writing paper.

MRS. MANNINGHAM: [*Half rising and speaking suspiciously*] Jack, I'm quite sure it *is* there. Will you look carefully?

MR. MANNINGHAM: [*Soothingly*] All right, dear. Don't worry. I'll find it. Lie down. It's of no importance, I'll find it— No, it's not here— It must be in one of the drawers—

MRS. MANNINGHAM: [*She has rushed to the secretary*] It is not in one of the drawers! I put it out here on top! You're not going to tell me *this* has gone, are you?　　 } [*Together*]

MR. MANNINGHAM: My dear. Calm yourself. Calm yourself!

MRS. MANNINGHAM: [*Searching frantically*] I laid it out here myself! Where is it? [*Opening and shutting drawers*] Where is it? Now you're going to say I've hidden this!

MR. MANNINGHAM: [*Moving away*] My God!—What new trick is this you're playing upon me?

MRS. MANNINGHAM: It was there this afternoon! I put it there! This is a plot! This is a filthy plot! You're all against me! It's a plot! [*She screams hysterically*]

MR. MANNINGHAM: [*Coming to her and shaking her violently*] Will you control yourself! Will you control yourself!— Listen to me, madam, if you utter another sound I'll knock you down and take you to your room and lock you in darkness for a week. I have been too lenient with you, and I mean to alter my tactics.

MRS. MANNINGHAM: [*Sinks to her knees*] Oh, God help me! God help me!

MR. MANNINGHAM: May God help you, indeed. Now listen to me. I am going to leave you until ten o'clock. In that time you will recover that paper, and admit to me that you have lyingly and purposely concealed it—if not, you will take the consequences. You are going to see a doctor, madam, more than one doctor—[*Puts his hat on and throws his coat over his arm*] and they shall decide what this means. Now do you understand me?

MRS. MANNINGHAM: Oh, God—be patient with me. If I am mad, be patient with me.

MR. MANNINGHAM: I have been patient with you and controlled myself long enough. It is now for you to control yourself, or take the consequences. Think upon that, Bella. [*He starts to door*]

MRS. MANNINGHAM: Jack—Jack—don't go—Jack—you're still going to take me to the theatre, aren't you?

MR. MANNINGHAM: What a question to ask me at such a time. No, madam, emphatically, I am not. You play fair by me, and I'll play fair by you. But if we are going to be enemies, you and I, you will not prosper, believe me.

[MANNINGHAM *goes out.* Whimperingly, MRS. MANNINGHAM *rises, aiding herself by the mantel, and goes to the secretary searching through the drawers, then crosses to center, looks at the picture and shudders. Then turning to the table, she takes up the pitcher of water from the tea tray, crosses back to the secretary, opens the upper door, gets a glass, then opens a drawer and takes out a paper of medicine. She takes this medicine and follows it with a drink of water. This is obviously, incredibly nasty and almost chokes her. She staggers over to the table and replaces the pitcher of water and then turns down the table lamp. Then crossing to the settee, she sinks down on it with her head toward the fireplace and sobs. She mutters, "Peace—Peace—Peace." She breathes heavily as a clock in the house strikes six. Pause. There is a knock at the door. She does not hear it. There is another knock and* ELIZABETH *enters*]

ELIZABETH: Madam—madam—

MRS. MANNINGHAM: Yes!—Yes!—What is it, Elizabeth? Leave me alone.

ELIZABETH: [*Peering through the darkness*] Madam, there's somebody called.

MRS. MANNINGHAM: Who is it? I don't want to be disturbed.

ELIZABETH: It's a gentleman, madam—he wants to see you.

MRS. MANNINGHAM: Tell him to go, Elizabeth. He wants to see my husband. My husband's out.

ELIZABETH: No, madam—he wants to see you. You must see him, madam.

MRS. MANNINGHAM: Oh, leave me alone. Tell him to go away. I want to be left alone.

ELIZABETH: Madam, madam. I don't know what's going on between you and the Master, but you've got to hold up, madam. You've got to hold up.

MRS. MANNINGHAM: I am going out of my mind, Elizabeth. That's what's going on.

ELIZABETH: Don't talk like that, madam. You've got to be brave. You mustn't go on lying here in the dark, or your mind *will* go. You must see this gentleman. It's *you* he wants—not the Master. He's waiting to see you. Come, madam, it'll take you out of yourself.

MRS. MANNINGHAM: Oh, my God—what new torment is this? I'm not in a fit state, I tell you.

ELIZABETH: [*Crosses to table*] Come madam, I'll turn up the light. [*She does so. Then, she picks up box of matches, crosses to the desk lamp, lights it*] There. Now you'll be all right.

MRS. MANNINGHAM: Elizabeth! What have you done? I can't have anyone in. I'm not fit to be seen.

ELIZABETH: You look all right, madam. You mustn't take on so. Now—I'll call him in.

[ELIZABETH *goes to the door, and can be heard calling "Will you come in, please, sir?" The front door is heard to slam.* MRS. MANNINGHAM *rises, half paralyzed, then runs over to the mirror above the mantelpiece and adjusts her hair. She stands with her back to the fireplace, waiting.* ELIZABETH *returns, holding back the door.* DETECTIVE ROUGH *enters. He is middle-aged—graying, short, wiry, active, brusque, friendly, overbearing. He has a low warming chuckle and completely dominates the scene from the beginning*]

ROUGH: Thank you— Ah—good evening. [*As he crosses*] Mrs. Manningham, I believe—How are you, Mrs. Manningham?

MRS. MANNINGHAM: [*Shaking hands*] How do you do? I'm very much afraid—

ROUGH: You're very much afraid you don't know me from Adam? That's about the root of the matter, isn't it?

[ELIZABETH *goes out, closing the doors*]

MRS. MANNINGHAM: Oh, no—it's not that—but no doubt you have come to see my husband?

ROUGH: [*Who is still holding her hand, and looking at her appraisingly*] Oh, no! You couldn't be further out. [*Chuckling*] On the contrary, I have chosen this precise moment to call when I knew your husband was out. May I take off my things and sit down?

MRS. MANNINGHAM: Why, yes, I suppose you may.

ROUGH: You're a good deal younger and more attractive than I thought, you know. But you're looking very pale. Have you been crying?

MRS. MANNINGHAM: Really—I'm afraid I don't understand at all.

ROUGH: You will do so, madam, very shortly. [*Goes left, and begins to remove scarf*] You're the lady who's going off her head, aren't you? [*He puts his hat on the desk*]

MRS. MANNINGHAM: [*Terrified*] What made you say that? Who are you? What have you come to talk about?

ROUGH: Ah, you're running away with things, Mrs. Manningham, and asking me a good deal I can't answer at once. [*Taking off coat, and putting it on chair down left*] Instead of that, I am going to ask you a question or two— Now, please, will you come here, and give me your hands? [*Pause. She obeys*] Now, Mrs. Manningham, I want you to take a good look at me, and see if you are not looking at someone to whom you can give your trust. I am a perfect stranger to you, and you can read little in my face besides that. But I can read a great deal in yours.

MRS. MANNINGHAM: [*Pause*] What? What can you read in mine?

ROUGH: Why, madam, I can read the tokens of one who has traveled a very long way upon the path of sorrow and doubt—and will have, I fear, to travel a little further yet before she comes to the end. But I fancy she is coming toward the end, for all that. Come now, are you going to trust me, and listen to me?

MRS. MANNINGHAM: [*Pause*] Who are you? God knows I need help.

ROUGH: [*Still holding her hands*] I very much doubt whether God knows anything of the sort, Mrs. Manningham. If He did I believe He would have come to your aid before this. But I am here, and so you must give me your faith.

MRS. MANNINGHAM: [*Withdraws her hands*] Who are you? Are you a doctor?

ROUGH: Nothing so learned, ma'am. Just a plain police detective.

MRS. MANNINGHAM: Police detective?

ROUGH: Yes. Or was some years ago. At any rate, still detective enough to see that you've been interrupted in your tea. Couldn't you start again, and let me have a cup? [*He stands back of chair left of table and holds it for her*]

MRS. MANNINGHAM: Why, yes—yes. I will give you a cup. It only wants water. [*She begins to busy herself with hot water, cup, pot, etc., throughout the ensuing conversation*]

ROUGH: You never heard of the celebrated Sergeant Rough, madam? Sergeant Rough, who solved the Claudesley Diamond Case—Sergeant Rough, who hunted down the Camberwell dogs—Sergeant Rough, who brought Sandham himself to justice. [*He has his hand on back of chair, right of table, as he looks at her*] Or were all such sensations before your time?

MRS. MANNINGHAM: [*Looking up at* ROUGH] Sandham? Why, yes—I have heard of Sandham—the murderer—the Throttler.

ROUGH: Yes—madam—Sandham the Throttler. And you are now looking at the man who gave Sandham to the man who throttled *him*. And that was the common hangman. In fact, Mrs. Manningham—you have in front of you one who was quite a personage in his day—believe it or not.

MRS. MANNINGHAM: [*As she adds water to the tea*] I quite believe it. Won't you sit down? I'm afraid it won't be very hot.

ROUGH: Thank you— [*Sitting*] How long have you been married, Mrs. Manningham?

MRS. MANNINGHAM: [*Pouring tea*] Five years—and a little.

ROUGH: Where have you lived during all that time, Mrs. Manningham? Not here, have you?

MRS. MANNINGHAM: [*Putting milk in his cup and passing it to him*] No—first we went abroad—then we lived in Yorkshire, and then six months ago my husband bought this house.

ROUGH: You bought it?

MRS. MANNINGHAM: Yes. I had a bit of money. My husband thought this was an excellent investment.

ROUGH: You had a bit of money, eh? [*Taking cup*] That's very good. And does your husband always leave you alone like this in the evenings?

MRS. MANNINGHAM: Yes. He goes to his club, I believe, and does business.

ROUGH: Oh, yes— [*He is stirring his tea, thoughtfully*]

MRS. MANNINGHAM: Yes—

ROUGH: And does he give you a free run of the whole house while he's out?

MRS. MANNINGHAM: Yes— Well, no—not the top floor. Why do you ask?

ROUGH: Ah—not the top floor—

MRS. MANNINGHAM: No—no—will you have some sugar?

ROUGH: Thanks.

MRS. MANNINGHAM: [*Bending over eagerly to answer his questions*] What were you saying?

ROUGH: Before I go any further, Mrs. Manningham, I must tell you there's a leakage in this household. You have a maid called Nancy?

MRS. MANNINGHAM: Yes—yes—

ROUGH: And Nancy walks out of an evening with a young man named Booker in my employ. I only live a few streets away from you, you know.

MRS. MANNINGHAM: Oh, yes?

ROUGH: [*With a chuckle*] Well, there is hardly anything which goes on in this house, which is not described in detail to Booker, and from that quarter it reaches me.

MRS. MANNINGHAM: I knew it! I knew she talked. Now I know it, she shall be dismissed.

ROUGH: Oh, no—no such retribution is going to overtake her at the moment, Mrs. Manningham. In fact, I fancy you are going to be heavily in debt to your maid, Nancy. If it were not for her indiscretions I should not be here now, should I?

MRS. MANNINGHAM: What do you mean? What is this mystery? You must not keep me in the dark. What is it?

ROUGH: I'm afraid I shall have to keep you in the dark for a little, Mrs. Manningham, as I am still quite far down in the dark myself. Can I have another lump of sugar in this?

MRS. MANNINGHAM: Yes. [*Passes bowl to him*]

ROUGH: Thank you. [*Pause*] We were talking about the top floor. [*Helping himself to several lumps*] There is a bedroom above this, and above that again *is* the top floor? Is that right?

MRS. MANNINGHAM: Yes. But it's shut up. When we first took the house, my husband said we would not need the upstairs quarters—until there were children.

ROUGH: You've never been up to the top floor, Mrs. Manningham?

[*Pause*]

MRS. MANNINGHAM: No one goes up there.

ROUGH: Not even a servant to dust?

MRS. MANNINGHAM: No.

ROUGH: Rather funny?

MRS. MANNINGHAM: Funny? [*Pause*] I don't know— [*But she does think so*]

ROUGH: I think it is. Now, Mrs. Manningham, to ask a personal question. When did you first get the notion into your head that your reason was playing you tricks?

MRS. MANNINGHAM: [*About to drink her tea. Pause. Looks at* ROUGH *and then sets her cup down*] How did you know?

ROUGH: Never mind how I know. When did it begin?

MRS. MANNINGHAM: I always had that dread. My mother died insane, when she was quite young. When she was my age. But only in the last six months, in this house—things began to happen—

ROUGH: Which are driving you mad with fear?

MRS. MANNINGHAM: Yes. Which are driving me mad with fear.

ROUGH: Is it the house itself you fear, Mrs. Manningham?

MRS. MANNINGHAM: Yes. I suppose it is. I hate the house. I always did.

ROUGH: And has the top floor got anything to do with it?

MRS. MANNINGHAM: Yes, yes, it has. That's how all this dreadful horror began.

ROUGH: Ah—now you interest me beyond measure. Do tell me about the top floor.

MRS. MANNINGHAM: I don't know what to say. It all sounds so incredible— It's when I'm alone at night. I get the idea that—somebody's walking about up there— [*Looking up*] Up there— At night, when my husband's out— I hear noises, from my bedroom, but I'm too afraid to go up—

ROUGH: Have you told your husband about this?

MRS. MANNINGHAM: No. I'm afraid to. He gets angry. He says I imagine things which don't exist—

ROUGH: It never struck you, did it, that it might be your own husband walking about up there?

MRS. MANNINGHAM: Yes—that *is* what I thought—but I thought I must be mad. [*She turns to him*] Tell me how you knew.

ROUGH: Why not tell me first how *you* knew, Mrs. Manningham.

MRS. MANNINGHAM: [*Rises and goes toward fireplace*] It's true, then! It's true. I knew it. I knew it! When he leaves this house he comes back. He comes back and walks up there above—up and down—up and down. He comes back like a ghost. How does he get up there?

ROUGH: [*Rises, crosses to* MRS. MANNINGHAM] That's what we're going to find out, Mrs. Manningham. But there are such commonplace resources as roofs and fire escapes, you know. Now please don't look so frightened. Your husband is no ghost, believe me, and you are very far from mad. [*Pause*] Tell me now, what made you first think it was him?

MRS. MANNINGHAM: It was the light—the gas light— It went down and it went up— Oh, thank God I can tell this to someone at last. I don't know who you are, but I must tell you!

ROUGH: Now try to keep calm. You can tell me just as well sitting down, can't you? Won't you sit down?

MRS. MANNINGHAM: Yes—yes. [*She sits down on settee*]

ROUGH: [*Looks around*] The light, did you say? Did you see a light from a window?

MRS. MANNINGHAM: No. In this house, I can tell everything by the light of the gas. You see the mantle there. Now it's burning full. But if an extra light went on in the kitchen or someone lit it in the bedroom then this one would sink down. It's the same all over the house.

ROUGH: Yes—yes—that's just a question of insufficient pressure, and it's the same in mine. But go on, please.

MRS. MANNINGHAM: [*Pause*] Every night, after he goes out, I find myself waiting for something. Then all at once I look round the room and see that the light is slowly going down. Then I hear tapping sounds—persistent tapping sounds. At first I tried not to notice it, but after a time it began to get on my nerves. I would go all over the house to see if anyone had put on an extra light, but they never had. It's always at the same time—about ten minutes after he goes out. That's what gave me the idea that somehow *he* had come back and that it was *he* who was walking about up there. I go up to the bedroom but I daren't stay there because I hear noises overhead. I want to scream and run out of the house. I sit here for hours, terrified, waiting for him to come back, and I always know when he's coming, always. Suddenly the light goes up again and ten minutes afterwards I hear his key in the lock, and he's back again.

ROUGH: How very strange, indeed. You know, Mrs. Manningham, you should have been a policeman.

MRS. MANNINGHAM: Are you laughing at me? Do you think I imagine everything, too?

ROUGH: Oh, no! I was merely praising the keenness of your observation. I not only think you are right in your suppositions, I think you have made a very remarkable discovery, and one which may have very far-reaching consequences.

MRS. MANNINGHAM: Far-reaching? How?

ROUGH: Well, let's leave that for the moment. Tell me, that is not the only cause, is it, which has lately given you reason to doubt your sanity? Has anything else been happening? [*Pause*] Don't be afraid to tell me.

MRS. MANNINGHAM: Yes, there are other things. I hardly dare speak of them. It has been going on for so long. This business of the gas has only brought it to a head. It seems that my mind and memory are beginning to play me tricks.

ROUGH: Tricks? What sort of tricks? When?

MRS. MANNINGHAM: Incessantly—but more and more of late. He gives me
things to look after, and when he asks for them they are gone, and can
never be found. Then he misses his rings, or his studs, and I will hunt the
place for them, and he will find them lying hidden at the bottom of my
workbox. Twice the door of that room [*Looking at door up right*] was
found locked with the key vanished. That was also found at the bottom
of my box. Only today, before you came, that picture had been taken
from the wall and hidden. [ROUGH *looks around at picture*] Who could
have done it but myself? I try to remember. [*He turns to her*] I break my
heart trying to remember. But I can't. Oh, and then there was that
terrible business about the dog—

ROUGH: The dog?

MRS. MANNINGHAM: We have a little dog. A few weeks ago, it was found with
its paw hurt.—He believes ... Oh, God, how can I tell you what he
believes—that *I* had hurt the dog. He does not let the dog near me now.
He keeps it in the kitchen and I am not allowed to see it! I begin to
doubt, don't you see? I begin to believe I imagine everything. Perhaps I
do. Are *you* here? Is this a dream, too? Who are you? [*Rises*] I'm afraid
they are going to lock me up.

ROUGH: Do you know, Mrs. Manningham, it has occurred to me that you'd
be all the better for a little medicine.

MRS. MANNINGHAM: Medicine. Are you a doctor? You're not a doctor, are
you?

ROUGH: [*Chuckling*] No, I'm not a doctor, but that doesn't mean that a
little medicine would do you any harm.

MRS. MANNINGHAM: But I have medicine. He makes me take it. It does me
no good, and I hate it. How can medicine help a mind that's ill?

ROUGH:Oh—but mine's an exceptional medicine. I have some with me now.
You must try it.

MRS. MANNINGHAM: What medicine is it?

ROUGH: You shall sample it and see. [*He goes over to his coat*] You see, it
has been employed by humanity, for several ages, for the purpose of the
instantaneous removal of dark fears and doubts. That seems to fit you,
doesn't it?

MRS. MANNINGHAM: The removal of doubt. How could a medicine effect
that?

ROUGH: Ah—that we don't know. The fact remains that it does. Here we are.
[*Produces what is obviously a bottle of whiskey*] You see, it comes from
Scotland. Now, madam, have you such a thing handy as two glasses or a
couple of cups?

MRS. MANNINGHAM: Why—are you having some, too?

ROUGH: Oh, yes. I am having some above all things. We could use these cups, if you like.

MRS. MANNINGHAM: No. I will get two— [*She goes to secretary and brings out two glasses*]

ROUGH: Ah—thank you—the very thing. Now we shan't be long.

MRS. MANNINGHAM: What is it? I so dislike medicine. What does it taste like?

ROUGH: Delicious! Something between ambrosia and methylated spirits. Do you mean to say you've never tasted good Scotch whiskey, Mrs. Manningham?

MRS. MANNINGHAM: Whiskey? But I must not take whiskey. I can't do that!

ROUGH: [*Pouring it out*] You underestimate your powers, Mrs. Manningham. You see, I don't want you thinking you can't trust your reason. This will give you faith in your reason like nothing else—Now for some water— All right this will do. [*Takes water from pitcher and pours it into the glasses*] There! [*Hands glass to her*] Tell me— [*Is pouring water into his own*] Did you ever hear of the Cabman's Friend, Mrs. Manningham?

MRS. MANNINGHAM: The Cabman's Friend?

ROUGH: Yes. How nice to see you smile. Here's your very good health. [*Drinks*] Go on— [*She drinks*] There— Is it so nasty?

MRS. MANNINGHAM: No. I rather like it. My mother used to give us this as children when we had the fever.

ROUGH: Ah, then you're a hardened whiskey drinker. But you'll enjoy it better sitting down.

MRS. MANNINGHAM: Yes. [*Sitting down on chair below fireplace*] What were you saying? Who is the Cabman's Friend?

ROUGH: Ah. The Cabman's Friend. [*Crosses to her*] You should ask me who *was* the Cabman's Friend, Mrs. Manningham, for she was an old lady who died many years ago.

[*Pause, as he puts her whiskey on mantelpiece*]

MRS. MANNINGHAM: An old lady years ago? What has she to do with me?

ROUGH: A great deal, I fancy, if you will follow me patiently. Her name was Barlow—Alice Barlow, and she was an old lady of great wealth, and decided eccentricities. In fact, her principal mania in life was the protection of cabmen. You may think that an extraordinary hobby, but in her odd way she did a lot of good. She provided these men with shelters, clothing, pensions, and so forth, and that was her little contribution to the sum of the world's happiness; or rather her little stand against the sum of the world's pain. There is a great deal of pain in this world, Mrs. Manningham, you know. Well, it was not my privilege to know her, but it was my duty, on just one occasion, to see her. That was when her throat was cut open, and she lay dead on the floor of her own house.

MRS. MANNINGHAM: Oh, how horrible! Do you mean she was murdered?

ROUGH: Yes. She was murdered. I was only a comparatively young officer at the time. It made an extremely horrible, in fact I may say lasting, impression on me. You see, the murderer was never discovered but the motive was obvious enough. Her husband had left her the Barlow rubies and it was well known that she kept them, without any proper precautions, in her bedroom on an upper floor. She lived alone except for a deaf servant in the basement. Well, for that she paid the penalty of her life.

MRS. MANNINGHAM: But I don't see—

ROUGH: There were some sensational features about the case. The man seemed to have got in about ten at night, and stayed till dawn. Apart, presumably, from the famous rubies, there were only a few trinkets taken, but the whole house had been turned upside down, and in the upper room every single thing was flung about, or torn open. Even the cushions of the chairs were ripped up with his bloody knife, and the police decided that it must have been a revengeful maniac as well as a robber. I had other theories, but I was a nobody then, and not in charge of the case.

MRS. MANNINGHAM: What were your theories?

ROUGH: Well, it seemed to me, from all that I gathered here and there, that the old lady might have been an eccentric, but that she was by no means a fool. It seemed to me that she might have been one too clever for this man. We presume he killed her to silence her, but what then? What if she had *not* been so careless? What if she had got those jewels cunningly hidden away in some inconceivable place, in the walls, floored down, bricked in, maybe? What if the only person who could tell him where they were was lying dead on the floor? Would not that account, Mrs. Manningham, for all that strange confusion in which the place was found? Can't you picture him, Mrs. Manningham, searching through the night, ransacking the place, hour after hour, growing more and more desperate, until at last the dawn comes and he has to slink out into the pale street, the blood and wreckage of the night behind? And the deaf servant down in the basement sleeping like a log through it all.

MRS. MANNINGHAM: Oh, how horrible! How horrible indeed! And was the man ever found?

ROUGH: No, Mrs. Manningham, the man was never found. Nor have the Barlow rubies ever come to light.

MRS. MANNINGHAM: Then perhaps he found them after all, and may be alive today.

ROUGH: I think he is almost certainly alive today, but I don't believe he found what he wanted. That is, if my theory is right.

MRS. MANNINGHAM: Then the jewels may still be where the old lady hid them?

ROUGH: Indeed, Mrs. Manningham, if my theory is right the jewels *must* still

be where she hid them. The official conclusion was quite otherwise. The
police, naturally and quite excusably, presumed that the murderer had
got them, and there was no reopening of matters in those days. Soon
enough the public forgot about it. I almost forgot about it myself. But it
would be funny, wouldn't it, Mrs. Manningham, if after all these years I
should turn out to be right.

MRS. MANNINGHAM: Yes, yes, indeed. But what has this to do with me?

ROUGH: Ah, that is the whole question, Mrs. Manningham. What, indeed?
What has the obscure murder of an old lady fifteen years ago to do with
an attractive, though I am afraid at present, somewhat pale and wan
young woman, who believes she is going out of her mind? Well, I believe
there is a link, however remote, wild and strange it may be, and that is
why I am here.

MRS. MANNINGHAM: It's all so confusing. Won't you—

ROUGH: Do you conceive it possible, Mrs. Manningham, that that man
might never have given up hope of one day getting at the treasure which
lay there?

MRS. MANNINGHAM: Yes. Yes. Possibly. But how—

ROUGH: Can you conceive that he may have waited years—gone abroad, got
married even, until at last his chance came to resume the search begun on
that terrible night? [*Crossing down to her*] You don't follow where I am
leading at all, do you, Mrs. Manningham?

MRS. MANNINGHAM: Follow you? I think so.

ROUGH: You know, Mrs. Manningham, of the old theory that the criminal
always returns to the scene of his crime.

MRS. MANNINGHAM: Yes?

ROUGH: Ah, yes, but in this case there is something more than morbid
compulsion— There is real treasure there to be unearthed if only he can
search again, search methodically, without fear of interruption, without
causing suspicion. And how would he do that? [*All at once she rises*]
Don't you think . . . What's the matter, Mrs. Manningham?

MRS. MANNINGHAM: [*As she looks at brackets and backs away*] Quiet! Be
quiet! He has come back! Look at the light! It is going down! Wait!

   [*Pause, as light sinks*]

   There! He has come back, you see. He is upstairs now.

ROUGH: Dear me, now. How very odd that is. How very odd, indeed.

MRS. MANNINGHAM: [*Whispering*] He is in the house, I tell you. You must
go. He will know you are here. You must go.

ROUGH: How dark it is. You could hardly see to read.

MRS. MANNINGHAM: You must go. He is in the house. Please go.

ROUGH: [*Quickly coming to her*] Quiet, Mrs. Manningham, quiet! You have got to keep your head. Don't you see my meaning, yet? Don't you understand that this was the house?

MRS. MANNINGHAM: House? What house?

ROUGH: The old woman's house, Mrs. Manningham— This house, here, these rooms, these walls. Fifteen years ago Alice Barlow lay dead on the floor in this room. Fifteen years ago the man who murdered her ransacked this house—below and above—but could not find what he sought. What if he is still searching, Mrs. Manningham? What if he is up there—*still searching?* Now do you see why you must keep your head?

MRS. MANNINGHAM: But my husband, my husband is up there!

ROUGH: Precisely that, Mrs. Manningham. Your husband. [*Going and fetching her drink from mantelpiece*] You see, I am afraid you are married to a tolerably dangerous gentleman. Now drink this quickly, as we have a great deal to do.

[*He stands there, holding out glass to her. She remains motionless*]

CURTAIN

ACT TWO

No time has passed. MRS. MANNINGHAM *takes the whiskey from* ROUGH *in a mechanical way, and stares at him.*

MRS. MANNINGHAM: This house— How do you know this was the house?

ROUGH: Why, ma'am, because I was on the case, and came here myself, that's all.

MRS. MANNINGHAM: The idea is mad. I have been married five years. How can you imagine my husband is—what you imagine he may be?

ROUGH: Mrs. Manningham—

MRS. MANNINGHAM: Yes?—

[*Pause*]

ROUGH: When the police came into this place fifteen years ago, as you can understand there was a great deal of routine work to be done—interviewing of relatives and friends and so forth. Most of that was left to me.

MRS. MANNINGHAM: Well?—

ROUGH: Well, amongst all the acquaintances and relatives, nephews and nieces, etc., that I interviewed, there happened to be a young man of the name of Sydney Power. I suppose you have never heard that name at all, have you?

MRS. MANNINGHAM: Power?—

ROUGH: Yes, Sydney Power. It conveys nothing to you?

MRS. MANNINGHAM: Sydney Power. No—

ROUGH: [*During the following speech, he pours himself out another drink*] Well, he was a kind of distant cousin, apparently much attached to the old lady, and even assisting her in her good works. The only thing was that I remembered his face. Well, I saw that face again just a few weeks ago. It took me a whole day to recollect where I had seen it before, but at last I remembered.

MRS. MANNINGHAM: Well—what of it? What if you did remember him?

ROUGH: It was not so much my remembering Mr. Sydney Power, Mrs. Manningham. What startled me was the lady on his arm, and the locality in which I saw him.

MRS. MANNINGHAM: Oh—who was the lady on his arm?

ROUGH: *You* were the lady on his arm, Mrs. Manningham, and you were walking down this street.

MRS. MANNINGHAM: What are you saying? Do you mean you think my husband—my husband is this Mr. Power?

ROUGH: Well, not exactly, for if my theories are correct— [*He drinks*]

MRS. MANNINGHAM: What are you saying? [*Sits*] You stand there talking riddles. You are so cold. You are as heartless and cold as he is.

ROUGH: No, Mrs. Manningham, I am not cold, and I am not talking riddles. [*Puts his drink on table*] I am just trying to preserve a cold and calculating tone, because you are up against the most awful moment in your life, and your whole future depends on what you are going to do in the next hour. Nothing less. You have got to *strike* for your freedom, and *strike* now, for the moment may not come again.

MRS. MANNINGHAM: Strike—

ROUGH: You are not going out of your mind, Mrs. Manningham. You are slowly, methodically, systematically being *driven* out of your mind. And why? Because you are married to a criminal maniac who is afraid you are beginning to know too much—a criminal maniac who steals back to his own house at night, still searching for something he could not find fifteen years ago. Those are the facts, wild and incredible as they may seem. His name is no more Manningham than mine is. He is Sydney Power and he murdered Alice Barlow in this house. Afterward he changed his name, and he has waited all these years, until he found it safe to acquire this house in a legal way. He then acquired the empty house next door. Every night, for the last few weeks, he has entered that house from the back, climbed up onto its roof and come into this house by the skylight. I know that because I have seen him do it. You have watched the gas light, and, without knowing it, been aware of the same thing. He is up there now. Why he should employ this mad, secretive, circuitous way of getting at what he wants, God Himself only knows. For the same reason perhaps, that he employs this mad, secretive, circuitous way of getting rid of you: that is, by slowly driving you mad and into a lunatic asylum.

MRS. MANNINGHAM: Why?

ROUGH: The fact that you had some money, enough to buy this house is part of it, I expect. For now that he's got that out of you he doesn't need you any longer. Thank God you are not married to him, and that I have come here to save you from the workings of his wicked mind.

MRS. MANNINGHAM: Not married?—Not married?—He married me.

ROUGH: I have no doubt he did, Mrs. Manningham. Unfortunately, or rather fortunately, he contracted the same sort of union with another lady many years before he met you. Moreover the lady is still alive, and the English law has a highly exacting taste in monogamy. You see, I have been finding things out about Mr. Sydney Power.

MRS. MANNINGHAM: Are you speaking the truth? [*Rises*] My God—are you speaking the truth? Where is this wife now?

ROUGH: I'm afraid, she is the length of the world away—on the continent of Australia to be precise, where I know for a fact he spent two years. Did you know that?

MRS. MANNINGHAM: No. [*Pause. She crosses to front of settee and faces fireplace*] I—did—not—know—that.

ROUGH: Ah, yes. If only I could find her, things would be easier, and that's the whole root of the matter, Mrs. Manningham. So far I am only dealing in guesses and *half facts*. I have got to have evidence, and that is why I came to see you. *You have got to give me the evidence* or *help* me find it.

MRS. MANNINGHAM: [*Turning and facing* ROUGH] This is my husband. Don't you understand—this is my husband. He married me. Do you ask me to betray the man who married me?

ROUGH: By which you mean, of course, the man who has betrayed you into thinking that you are married to him—don't you?

MRS. MANNINGHAM: But I'm married to him. You must go. I must think this out. You must go. I must cling to the man I married. Mustn't I?

ROUGH: Indeed, cling to him by all means, but do not imagine you are the only piece of ivy on the garden wall. You can cling to him if you desire, as his fancy women in the low resorts of the town cling to him. That is the sort of wall you have to cling to, ma'am.

MRS. MANNINGHAM: [*Sits on settee*] Women? What are you suggesting?

ROUGH: I'm not suggesting anything. I am only telling you what I have seen. He comes to life at night, this gentleman upstairs, in more ways than one.

I have made it my business to follow him on some of his less serious excursions, and I can promise you he has a taste in *unemployed actresses* which he is at no pains to conceal.

MRS. MANNINGHAM: [*After pause*] God in heaven! . . . what *am* I to believe?

ROUGH: Mrs. Manningham, it is hard to take everything from you, but you are no more tied to this man, you are under no more obligation to him than those wretched women in those places. You must learn to be thankful for that.

MRS. MANNINGHAM: [*Pause*] What do you want me to do? What do you want?

ROUGH: I want his papers, Mrs. Manningham—his identity. There is some clue somewhere in this house, and we have got to get at it. Where does he keep his papers? [ROUGH *has now completely changed his tone, and is striding up and down in a businesslike way*]

MRS. MANNINGHAM: [*Rises*] Papers? I know of no papers. Unless his bureau—

ROUGH: Yes. His bureau? His bureau?

MRS. MANNINGHAM: Yes. There. [*Points to desk*] But he keeps it always locked. I have never seen it open.

ROUGH: Ah—he keeps it locked, does he?

MRS. MANNINGHAM: It is just his desk—his bureau—

ROUGH: [*Crosses to desk*] Very well. We will have a look inside.

MRS. MANNINGHAM: But it is locked. How can you, if it is locked?

ROUGH: Oh—it doesn't look so very formidable. [*Going to overcoat, to fetch ring of keys and implements*] You know, Mrs. Manningham, one of the greatest regrets of my life is that fate never made me one of two things— one was a gardener, the other a burglar—both quiet occupations, Mrs. Manningham. As for burgling I think, if I'd started young, and worked my way up, I should have been a genius. Now let's have a look at this.

MRS. MANNINGHAM: [*Crossing to him at desk*] But you must not touch this. He will know what you have done.

ROUGH: Come now, ma'am. You're working with me, aren't you—not against me? [*Looks at desk*] Yes— Yes— Now do you mind if I take off my coat? I'm a man who never feels at work until his coat's off. [*He is taking off his coat, and hanging it on chair down left, revealing a pink fancy shirt*] Quite a saucy shirt, don't you think? You didn't suspect I was such a dandy, did you? Now. [*Sits at desk and gets out keys*] Let's have a real look at this.

MRS. MANNINGHAM: [*After a pause*] But you must not tamper with that. He will know what you have done.

ROUGH: Not if we are clever enough. And this one here doesn't even ask for cleverness— You see, Mrs. Manningham, there are all manner of. . . .

MRS. MANNINGHAM: Stop—stop talking— Haven't you noticed? Haven't you noticed something?

ROUGH: Noticed? I've only . . .

MRS. MANNINGHAM: Stop! Yes—I was right. Look. Can't you see? The light!
It's going up. He's coming back.

ROUGH: The light?—

MRS. MANNINGHAM: Quiet! [*Pause, after which the light slowly goes up in a
tense silence. Whispering*] There. It's come back. You see. You must go.
Don't you see? He's coming back— He's coming back and you must go!

ROUGH: [*Rises*] God bless my soul. This looks as if the unexpected *has*
entered in.

MRS. MANNINGHAM: Yes. He *always* does the unexpected. I never know what
he'll do. You must go.

ROUGH: [*Without moving, looking up ruminatively*] I wonder. Yes. Well,
well— [*Puts the keys in his pocket and begins to put on his coat*] Now—
will you go and ring that bell for Elizabeth?

MRS. MANNINGHAM: Elizabeth. Why do you want her?

ROUGH: Do as I say, and ring the bell. At once. Please. Or you can go and
fetch her if you like. Now let me see.

MRS. MANNINGHAM: [*Ringing bell*] Go, please!—Go, please do! You must go
at once. [*Crossing to above desk*] Why do you want Elizabeth?

ROUGH: [*Picks up overcoat, puts it on, then his scarf and crosses below desk
to her*] All in good time. He's not going to jump through the window, you
know. In fact he can't be round at our front door in less than five
minutes—unless he's a magician. Now, can you see anything I've missed?

MRS. MANNINGHAM: No. No. [*Turns and sees whiskey bottle, quickly gets it
and gives it to* ROUGH] Yes, the whiskey here.

ROUGH: Oh, yes. I told you you'd make a good policeman. Don't forget the
glasses.

MRS. MANNINGHAM: Oh, do go, please, please go!

[ELIZABETH *enters.* MRS. MANNINGHAM *puts glasses away in secretary*]

ROUGH: Ah—Elizabeth—come here, will you?

ELIZABETH: [*Crosses to* ROUGH] Yes, sir?

ROUGH: Elizabeth, you and I have got to do a little quite calm, but rather
quick thinking. You've told me you're anxious to help your mistress,
Elizabeth?

ELIZABETH: Why, yes, sir, I told you I was, sir. But what's it all about?

ROUGH: Are you anxious to help your mistress, blindly, without asking any
questions?

ELIZABETH: Yes, sir. But you see—

ROUGH: Come now, Elizabeth. Are you or are you not?

ELIZABETH: [*After pause, looking at* MRS. MANNINGHAM, *in quiet voice*] Yes,
sir.

ROUGH: Good. Now, Elizabeth, Mrs. Manningham and I have reason to suppose that in about five minutes' time the master is returning to this house. He mustn't see me leaving. Would you be good enough to take me down to your kitchen and hide me away for a short space of time? You can put me in the oven if you like.

ELIZABETH: Yes, sir. But you see—

MRS. MANNINGHAM: [*As* ROUGH *crosses to window and looks out*] You must go! You must go! He won't see you if you go now.

ROUGH: What were you saying, Elizabeth?

ELIZABETH: Yes, sir. You could come to the kitchen. But—Nancy's down there, sir.

ROUGH: Nancy! What the devil's this now? I thought this was Nancy's afternoon off. Was it not arranged that I should come when Nancy was away?

ELIZABETH: [*Agitated*] Yes, sir. But for some reason she's stayed on. I think she's got a young man, and I couldn't make her go, could I, sir? If I'd done that, I'd've—

ROUGH: All right—all right. Then she was here when I came, and she knows I am here—is that it?

ELIZABETH: Oh, no— She was in the scullery when I answered the door, and I said it was a man who had come to the wrong house. She hasn't no idea, sir, and I'm—

ROUGH: All right. All right. That's better news. But it means you can't entertain me in the kitchen. Now where are you going to hide me, Elizabeth? Make up your mind quickly.

ELIZABETH: I don't know, sir. Unless you go to the bedroom. Mine and Nancy's, I mean.

ROUGH: That sounds altogether entrancing! Shall we go there now?

ELIZABETH: Yes, sir, but supposing Nancy went up there before she goes out?

ROUGH: You're a good soul and you think of everything, Elizabeth. [*Going to door up right*] Where does this lead to, and what's the matter with this?

ELIZABETH: [*Crossing to* ROUGH] It's where he dresses, where he keeps his clothes. Yes, sir. Go in there, sir. He won't see you there. There's a big wardrobe there, at the back.

ROUGH: Excuse me. [*He goes through door*]

MRS. MANNINGHAM: Oh, Elizabeth.

ELIZABETH: [*Crosses to* MRS. MANNINGHAM] It's all right, ma'am. Don't take on so. It'll be all right.

MRS. MANNINGHAM: I'm sure he ought to go.

ELIZABETH: No, ma'am. He knows best. He's bound to know best.

ROUGH: [*Coming back*] Perfect accommodation. [*As he trots across to win-*

dow for another peep. Has seen something] Yes, there he is. Now we really have got to hurry. Get off to bed, Mrs. Manningham, quick. And you, Elizabeth, go to your room. You can't get downstairs in time. Hurry, please. Elizabeth, turn down that lamp.

[ELIZABETH *does so. He goes to turn down gas*]

MRS. MANNINGHAM: To bed? Am I to go to bed?

ROUGH: [*Really excited for the first time*] Yes, quick. He's coming. Don't you understand? Go there and stay there. You have a bad headache—[*He crosses to fireplace and starts to turn down upstage gas bracket*]—a bad headache. [*Quite angry, turning from gas*] Will you go, in heaven's name!

[MRS. MANNINGHAM *goes upstairs and* ELIZABETH *exits, leaving the doors open, as* ROUGH *turns down the gas in the downstage bracket. There is a light from the hall through the open doors.* ROUGH *crosses to the left end of the settee, pauses a moment watching the hall, then, nimbly on tiptoes, crosses up to the open doors and listens. After a short pause, there is the sound of the front door closing. He stiffens and starts to quietly trot to the door up right and as he just about reaches it, feels his head, discovers his hat missing, and, turning quickly, trots to the desk, gets his hat, puts it on as he quickly crosses back to door up right and exits. There is a short pause and* MR. MANNINGHAM *appears in the doorway, peers into the room and enters, closes the doors and looks up the stairway, then crosses to upstage bracket, turns it up, then to the downstage bracket and turns it up. Then he goes back of the settee, puts his hat on the settee, crosses to the bell and rings it. Then leisurely, he starts to the fireplace. As he reaches the settee* ELIZABETH *opens the doors and enters*]

ELIZABETH: Did you ring, sir?

MR. MANNINGHAM: Yes, I did. [*Without yet saying why he has rung, he removes his coat and places it over settee, and then comes and stands with his back to the fireplace*] Where is Mrs. Manningham, Elizabeth?

ELIZABETH: I think she's gone to bed, sir. I think she had a bad headache and went to bed.

MR. MANNINGHAM: Oh, indeed. And how long has she been in bed, do you know?

ELIZABETH: She went just a little while ago, sir—I think, sir—

MR. MANNINGHAM: Oh. I see. Then we must be quiet, mustn't we? Walk about like cats.—Can you walk about like a cat, Elizabeth?

ELIZABETH: [*Trying to smile*] Yes, sir. I think so, sir.

MR. MANNINGHAM: Very well, Elizabeth. Walk about like a cat. All right. That's all.

ELIZABETH: Yes, sir. Thank you, sir.

[*Just as* ELIZABETH *is about to exit, he calls her back*]

MR. MANNINGHAM: Er—Elizabeth.

ELIZABETH: [*Coming back*] Yes, sir? [MANNINGHAM *is again silent*] Did you call, sir?

MR. MANNINGHAM: Yes. Why haven't you cleared away the tea things?

ELIZABETH: [*Crossing to table*] Oh—I'm sorry, sir. I was really just about to, sir.

MR. MANNINGHAM: Yes. I think you had better clear away the tea things, Elizabeth.

ELIZABETH: Yes, sir. [*After pause, putting a dish on the tray*] Excuse me, sir, but were you going to have some supper, sir?

MR. MANNINGHAM: [*Crossing to desk*] Oh, yes. I am going to have supper. The question is, am I going to have supper here?

ELIZABETH: Oh, yes, sir. Are you having it out, sir?

MR. MANNINGHAM: Yes, I am having it out. [MANNINGHAM *takes off his undercoat and puts it carefully over a chair left of table. He is beginning to undo his tie*] I have come back to change my linen. [*He is undoing his collar. There is a pause*]

ELIZABETH: [*Looks up and realizes his coat is off*] Do you want a fresh collar, sir? Shall I get you a fresh collar?

MR. MANNINGHAM: Why, do you know where my collars are kept?

ELIZABETH: Why, yes, sir. In your room, there, sir. Shall I get you one, sir?

MR. MANNINGHAM: What a lot you know, Elizabeth. And do you know the sort of collar I want tonight?

ELIZABETH: Why, yes, sir—I think I know the sort of collar, sir.

MR. MANNINGHAM: [*As he crosses toward door up right*] Then all I can say is you know a great deal more than I do— No— I think you must let me choose my own collar— [*Stops, turns to* ELIZABETH] That is, if I have your permission, Elizabeth.

ELIZABETH: [*Gazing at him*] Yes, sir—yes, sir—

> [MANNINGHAM *goes in.* ELIZABETH *puts on the table the plate she is holding and lowers her head, remaining motionless in suspense. Not a sound comes from the other room, and nearly a quarter of a minute goes by. At last,* MANNINGHAM *comes out in a perfectly leisurely way. He is putting his tie on and crosses down to mirror over fireplace, looking at himself in the mirror during the ensuing conversation*]

MR. MANNINGHAM: What did you think about Mrs. Manningham tonight, Elizabeth?

ELIZABETH: Mrs. Manningham, sir? In what way do you mean, sir?

MR. MANNINGHAM: Oh—just as regards her general health, Elizabeth.

ELIZABETH: I don't know, sir. She certainly seems very unwell.

MR. MANNINGHAM: Yes. I doubt if you can guess to what extent she is unwell.

[*Turns to* ELIZABETH] Or are you beginning to guess?

ELIZABETH: I don't know, sir.

MR. MANNINGHAM: I'm afraid I was compelled to drag you and Nancy into our troubles tonight. Perhaps I should not have done that.

ELIZABETH: It all seems very sad, sir.

MR. MANNINGHAM: [*Smiling and somewhat appealingly, as he takes a step toward* ELIZABETH] I'm at my wits' end, Elizabeth. You know that, don't you?

ELIZABETH: I expect you are, sir.

MR. MANNINGHAM: I have tried everything. Kindness, patience, cunning— even harshness, to bring her to her senses. But nothing will stop these wild, wild hallucinations, nothing will stop these wicked pranks and tricks.

ELIZABETH: It seems very terrible, sir.

MR. MANNINGHAM: You don't know a quarter of it, Elizabeth. You only see what is forced upon your attention—as it was tonight. You have no conception of what goes on all the time. [*He is looking at his tie*] No—not this one, I think—

ELIZABETH: Do you want another tie, sir?

MR. MANNINGHAM: Yes. [*He strolls again into the other room.* ELIZABETH *turns and watches the door intently. After a pause, he comes out with another tie. As he enters,* ELIZABETH *quickly turns to tea table. He crosses down to fireplace mirror. He is putting his tie on during the ensuing conversation*] I suppose you know about Mrs. Manningham's mother, Elizabeth?

ELIZABETH: No, sir. What of her, sir?

MR. MANNINGHAM: Not of the manner in which she died?

ELIZABETH: No, sir.

MR. MANNINGHAM: She died in the madhouse, Elizabeth, without any brain at all in the end.

ELIZABETH: Oh, sir!—How terrible, sir.

MR. MANNINGHAM: Yes, terrible indeed. The doctors could do nothing. [*Pause. Turns to* ELIZABETH] You know, don't you, that I shall have to bring a doctor to Mrs. Manningham before long, Elizabeth? [*As he crosses and gets his undercoat*] I have fought against it to the last, but it can't be kept a secret much longer.

ELIZABETH: No, sir— No, sir—

MR. MANNINGHAM: [*Putting on his undercoat*] I mean to say, you know what goes on. You can testify to what goes on, can't you?

ELIZABETH: Indeed, sir. Yes.

MR. MANNINGHAM: Indeed, you may *have* to testify in the end. Do you realize that? [*Pause. Sharp*] Eh?

ELIZABETH: [*Looking quickly up at him*] Yes, sir. I would only wish to help you both, sir.

MR. MANNINGHAM: [*Goes to settee, gets coat and puts it on, crosses to mirror and adjusts coat*] Yes, I believe you there, Elizabeth. You're a very good soul. I sometimes wonder how you put up with things in this household— this dark household. I wonder why you do not go. You're very loyal.

ELIZABETH: [*Looking at him in an extraordinary way. He cannot see her*] Always loyal to you, sir. Always loyal to you.

MR. MANNINGHAM: There now, how touching. I thank you, Elizabeth. You will be repaid later for what you have said, and repaid in more ways than one. You understand that, don't you?

ELIZABETH: Thank you, sir. I only want to serve, sir.

MR. MANNINGHAM: [*Crosses back of settee, gets hat*] Yes, I know that. Well, Elizabeth, I am going out. In fact, I'm even going to try to be a little gay. Can you understand that, or do you think it is wrong?

ELIZABETH: Oh, no, sir. No. You should get all the pleasure you can, sir, while you can.

MR. MANNINGHAM: I wonder—yes—I wonder—it's a curious existence, isn't it— Well—good night, Elizabeth. [MANNINGHAM *goes off*]

ELIZABETH: Good night, sir—good night.

[MANNINGHAM *has left the door open.* ELIZABETH *quickly crosses up to door and looks after him. After a pause,* ROUGH *comes forth and* ELIZABETH *turns to him. He and* ELIZABETH *stand there looking at each other. At last,* ROUGH *goes to the window and looks out. The front door is heard slamming*]

ROUGH: He was right when he said you would be repaid, Elizabeth. Though not in the way he thinks. [*Taking off hat, puts it on desk; then his overcoat and muffler and puts them on chair down left*] Will you go and get Mrs. Manningham?

ELIZABETH: Yes, sir. I'll get her, sir.

[*As she starts toward stairs,* MRS. MANNINGHAM *comes downstairs.* ROUGH *gets implements out of overcoat pocket*]

ROUGH: Ah—there you are.

MRS. MANNINGHAM: I saw him go.

[ELIZABETH *takes tray and exits*]

ROUGH: Now we must get back to work.

MRS. MANNINGHAM: What did he want? What did he come back for?

ROUGH: He only came to change his clothes. Turn up the lamp, will you? [MRS. MANNINGHAM *does so, and comes to him as he again reaches desk*] Now let's have another look at this.

MRS. MANNINGHAM: What if he comes back again? There is no light to warn us now.

ROUGH: Oh, you've realized that, have you? Well, Mrs. Manningham, we've just got to take that risk. [*Takes his keys from pocket*] This is going to be child's play, I fancy. Just a little patience—a little adroitness in the use. . . . [*The front door slams*] What's that?—Go and have a look, will you? [MRS. MANNINGHAM *rushes over to the window*] We seem to be rather bothered this evening, don't we?

MRS. MANNINGHAM: It's all right. It's only Nancy. I forgot. She usually goes out at this time.

ROUGH: She uses the front door—does she?

MRS. MANNINGHAM: Oh, yes. Indeed she does. She behaves like the mistress in this house.

ROUGH: A saucy girl. [*The top of the bureau opens*] Ah—here we are. Next to a key there's nothing a lock appreciates like kindness.

MRS. MANNINGHAM: Will you be able to close it again?

ROUGH: Yes. No damage done. There we are. [*He pulls the upstage drawer out and puts it on top of desk*] Now. Let's see. Doesn't seem much here— And when she got there the cupboard was bare—and so the poor detective—[*He picks up a brooch*]

MRS. MANNINGHAM: What is that in your hand? What is that in your hand?

ROUGH: [*Holding up brooch*] Why, do you recognize this?

MRS. MANNINGHAM: Yes! My brooch! Yes! Is there anything else there? What else is there?—Look, my watch! Oh, God, it's my watch!

ROUGH: This also is your property then?

MRS. MANNINGHAM: Yes. Both of them. This watch I lost a week ago—my brooch has been missing three months. And he said he would give me no more gifts because I lost them. He said that in my wickedness I hid them away! Inspector, is there anything else—? [*She crosses anxiously to upper end of the desk and looks over his shoulder*] Is there a bill there? [*He looks up at her*] Is there a grocery bill?

ROUGH: [*Searching drawer*] A grocery bill?—No— There doesn't seem to be— [*He has pulled out a letter which he drops on the desk*]

MRS. MANNINGHAM: [*Picking up letter*] One moment— One moment— This letter!—this letter! [*She goes on reading it*] It's from my cousin—my cousin—

ROUGH: Is your husband's correspondence with your relations very much to the point at the moment, Mrs. Manningham?

MRS. MANNINGHAM: You don't understand. [*Speaking rapidly*] When I was married I was cast off by all my relations. I have not seen any of them since I was married. They did not approve my choice. I have longed to see them again more than anything in the world. When we came to London—to this house, I wrote to them, I wrote to them twice. There never was any answer. Now I see why there never was any answer. [*Dazed*] This letter is to me. It's from my cousin.

ROUGH: [*Cynically*] Yet you never got it. Now you're beginning to understand, Mrs. Manningham?

MRS. MANNINGHAM: [*As she crosses to chair and sits*] Listen. Let me read to you what he says. Let me read it to you. [*Feverishly*] "Dear Cousin— All of us were overjoyed to hear from you again." [*Looks up at* ROUGH] Overjoyed, do you hear that? [*Returns to reading the letter*] He goes on to say that his family are in Devonshire, and that they have gone to the country. He says we must meet and recapture old times. [*She is showing signs of great emotion*] He says that they all want to see me—that I must go and stay with them—that they will give me—that they will give me their Devonshire cream to fatten my cheeks, and their fresh air to bring the sparkle back to my eyes . . . they will give me . . . they'll give me . . . [*Breaking down*] Dear God, they wanted me back! They wanted me back all the time!

ROUGH: [*Coming to her as she cries softly*] Poor child. You shall have your Devonshire cream and you shall have the fresh air to bring the sparkle back into your eyes. [*She looks up at him*] Why, I can see a sparkle in them already. If you will be brave now and trust me, you will not have to wait long. Are you going to trust me?

MRS. MANNINGHAM: Thank you, Inspector, for bringing me this letter. [ROUGH *crosses back to desk*] What do you wish me to do?

ROUGH: For the moment, nothing. Tell me. This drawer here. It seems to me to have a special lock. Has it ever been open to your knowledge?

MRS. MANNINGHAM: [*Hesitantly*] No.

ROUGH: No?—I suspected as much. Yes, this is a tougher proposition, I'm afraid. [*He goes to his overcoat and produces an iron instrument*]

MRS. MANNINGHAM: [*Rising and crossing to stop him*] What are you going to do? Are you going to force it?

ROUGH: [*Calmly*] If I possibly can. I don't know that . . .

MRS. MANNINGHAM: But you must not do that. You must not. What shall I say when my husband comes back?

ROUGH: [*Ironically. Getting his jimmy from coat*] I have no idea *what* you will say when he comes back, Mrs. Manningham. But then I have no idea what you will do, Mrs. Manningham, if I have no evidence to remove you from his loving care for good.

MRS. MANNINGHAM: [*Torn with doubts*] Oh, God. I am afraid. What can I do?

ROUGH: [*Sharply*] There is only one thing we *can* do—go ahead. If we go back now, we are lost. I am going to force it and gamble on finding something. Are you with me?

MRS. MANNINGHAM: [*Tormented as she studies him*] But, don't you see— All right. Force it! Force it! But be quick.

ROUGH: There's no hurry, madam. He's quite happy where he is—Now, I
don't like violent methods [*He is straining at lock*] of this sort—it makes
me feel like a dentist— There— [*There's a sound of splitting wood*] All
over now— Now, let's have a look.

MRS. MANNINGHAM: [*After pause, in which she watches him. As he pulls out
the drawer:*] Is there anything there? Is there anything there?

ROUGH: [*Looking at papers*] No, I don't see anything yet—I don't see
anything. Wait a minute— No— No— What's this? [*As he picks up a
bundle of papers*] Mr. Manningham—Mr. Manningham—Mr. Manningham—

MRS. MANNINGHAM: Is there nothing?

ROUGH: No— Not a thing. We have lost our gamble, ma'am. I'm afraid.

MRS. MANNINGHAM: [*Frightened*] Oh, dear me, what are we to do? What are
we to do?

ROUGH: Some rapid thinking at the moment. Don't have any fear, Mrs.
Manningham, I've been in many a tighter corner than this. Let's get those
things back to begin with, shall we? Give me the watch and the brooch.
[*Takes watch and brooch*] We must put them back where they were.

MRS. MANNINGHAM: Yes—here they are.

ROUGH: Here on the right, was it not?

MRS. MANNINGHAM: Yes. There— That's right. There.

ROUGH: [*Holding up brooch*] A nice piece of jewelry. When did he give you
this?

MRS. MANNINGHAM: Soon after we were married. But it was only secondhand.

ROUGH: Secondhand, eh? I'm afraid you got everything secondhand, from
this gentleman, Mrs. Manningham. Well—that's all right. [*He puts
brooch in drawer and drawer back in desk*] Now I must lock this up again,
[*Closes the second drawer*] if I can— [*About to lock first drawer*] Secondhand did you say?— How did you know that brooch was secondhand,
Mrs. Manningham?

MRS. MANNINGHAM: There's an affectionate inscription to someone else
inside.

ROUGH: [*Vaguely*] Oh— Is there?—[*Opens first drawer*] Why didn't you tell
me that—?

MRS. MANNINGHAM: Why—I only found it myself a little while ago.

ROUGH: [*As he takes out brooch*] Oh ... really. Do you know, I have a
feeling I have seen this somewhere before? Where is this inscription you
speak of?

MRS. MANNINGHAM: It is a sort of trick. I only discovered it by accident. You
pull the pin at the back. It goes to the right, and then to the left. It opens
out like a star.

ROUGH: [*As he opens it*] Oh, yes— Yes— Ah—here we are. Yes. [*He sits at table and takes out his jeweler's glass*] How very odd. What are these spaces here?

MRS. MANNINGHAM: There were some beads in it, but they were all loose and falling out—so I took them out.

ROUGH: Oh—there were some beads in it, but they were all loose and falling out—so you took them out. [*Pause*] Have you got them by any chance?

MRS. MANNINGHAM: Yes. I think so. I put them in a vase.

ROUGH: May I see them, please?

MRS. MANNINGHAM: Yes. [*Going to vase on mantelpiece*] They should still be here.

ROUGH: There should be nine altogether, I think.

MRS. MANNINGHAM: Yes, that's right, I think there were. Yes. Here they are. Here are some of them at any rate.

ROUGH: Let me see, will you?—Ah— Thank you. Try and find them all, will you? [*She goes back to mantel*] Did you happen to read this inscription at any time, ma'am?

MRS. MANNINGHAM: Yes, I read it. Why?

ROUGH: [*Reading*] "Beloved A.B. from C.B. Eighteen fifty-one." [*Looking up at her*] Does nothing strike you about that?

MRS. MANNINGHAM: No. What of it? What should strike me?

ROUGH: Really, I should have thought that as simple as A.B.C. Have you got the others? There should be four more.

MRS. MANNINGHAM: Yes. Here they are.

ROUGH: Thank you. That's the lot. [*He is putting them in brooch on the table*] Now tell me this—have you ever been embraced by an elderly detective in his shirt sleeves?

MRS. MANNINGHAM: What do you mean?

ROUGH: For that is your immediate fate at the moment. [*Puts down brooch, rises and comes to her*] My dear Mrs. Manningham. . . . [*Kisses her*] My dear, dear Mrs. Manningham! Don't you understand?

MRS. MANNINGHAM: No, what are you so excited about?

ROUGH: [*Picks up brooch*] There, there you are, Mrs. Manningham. The Barlow rubies—complete. Twelve thousand pounds' worth before your very eyes! [*Gives her brooch*] Take a good look at them before they go to the Queen.

MRS. MANNINGHAM: But it couldn't be—it couldn't. They were in the vase all the time.

ROUGH: Don't you see? Don't you see the whole thing? *This* is where the old lady hid her treasure—in a common trinket she wore all the day. I knew I had seen this somewhere before. And where was that? In portraits of the old lady—when I was on the case. She wore it on her breast. I remember it clearly though it was fifteen years ago. Fifteen years! Dear God in heaven, am I not a wonderful man!

MRS. MANNINGHAM: And I had it all the time. I had it all the time.

ROUGH: And all because he could not resist a little common theft along with the big game. . . . Well, it is I who am after the big game now. [*He shows signs of going*]

MRS. MANNINGHAM: Are you going?

ROUGH: Oh, yes. I must certainly go. [*Begins to collect his coat and things*] And very quickly at that.

MRS. MANNINGHAM: Where are you going? Are you going to leave me? What are you going to do?

ROUGH: I am going to move heaven and earth—Mrs. Manningham—and if I have any luck I. . . . [*Looking at his watch*] It's very early yet. What time do *you* think he'll be back?

MRS. MANNINGHAM: I don't know. He's not usually in till eleven.

ROUGH: Yes. So I thought. Let's hope so. That will give me time. Here, give me that. Have you closed it? [*Takes brooch*] We will put it back where we found it. [*He crosses to desk*]

MRS. MANNINGHAM: But what are you going to do?

ROUGH: It's not exactly what I am going to do. It's what the Government is going to do in the person of Sir George Raglan. Yes, ma'am. Sir George Raglan. No one less. The power above all the powers that be. [*Puts brooch in drawer; closes and locks drawer*] He knows I am here tonight, you see. But he didn't know I was going to find what I have found. [*Pause. Looks at broken drawer*] Yes—we've done for that, I'm afraid— Well, we must just risk it, that's all. [*Tries to force broken drawer into place*] Now, Mrs. Manningham, you will serve the ends of justice best by simply going to bed. Do you mind going to bed?

MRS. MANNINGHAM: No. I will go to bed. [*She starts upstairs*]

ROUGH: Good. Go there and stay there. Your headache is worse. Remember, be ill. Be anything. But stay there, you understand. I'll let myself out.

MRS. MANNINGHAM: [*Suddenly. Comes downstairs and crosses to* ROUGH] Don't leave me. Please don't leave me. I have a feeling. . . . Don't leave me.

ROUGH: Feeling? What feeling?

MRS. MANNINGHAM: A feeling that something will happen if you leave me. I'm afraid. I haven't the courage.

ROUGH: Have the goodness to stop making a fool of yourself, Mrs. Manningham. Here's your courage. [*He gives her whiskey, taking it from pocket*] Take some more of it, but don't get tipsy and don't leave it about. Good-by. [*He is at doors, about to exit*]

MRS. MANNINGHAM: Inspector.

ROUGH: [*Turns to her*] Yes.

MRS. MANNINGHAM: [*Summoning courage*] All right. Good-by. [*She starts up the stairs*]

ROUGH: Good-by.

> [*He goes, shutting the doors. Pause, as* MRS. MANNINGHAM *stops on the stairs and glances around the room.* ROUGH *suddenly opens the doors*]

ROUGH: Mrs. Manningham!

MRS. MANNINGHAM: Yes.

> [ROUGH *motions to her to go upstairs. She does so and he watches her*]

ROUGH: Good-by. [*When she is out of sight around the curve on the stairs he exits and closes the doors*]

CURTAIN

ACT THREE

The time is eleven the same night. The room is in darkness, but the doors are open and a dim light in the passage outside can be seen. There is the sound of the front door shutting. Footsteps can be heard, and MANNINGHAM *appears outside. He stops to turn out the light in the passage. He enters the room and goes to the lamp on the center table and turns it up. Then he lights the two brackets and crosses to table up right and puts his hat on it. He goes in a slow and deliberate way over to the bell-cord and pulls it. He is humming to himself as he goes over to the fireplace.*

> NANCY *puts her head round the door. She has only just come in and is dressed for out-of-doors.*

NANCY: Yes, sir. Did you ring, sir?

MR. MANNINGHAM: Yes, Nancy, I did ring. It seems that the entire household has gone to bed without leaving me my milk and without leaving me my biscuits.

NANCY: Oh, I'm sorry, sir. They're only just outside. I'll bring them in! [*Turns to door, then stops*] Mrs. Manningham usually gets them, doesn't she, sir? Cook's in bed and I've only just come in.

MR. MANNINGHAM: Quite, Nancy. Then perhaps you will deputize for Mrs. Manningham, and bring them into the room.

NANCY: Certainly, sir.

MR. MANNINGHAM: And after you do that, Nancy, will you go upstairs and tell Mrs. Manningham that I wish to see her down here.

NANCY: Yes, sir. Certainly, sir. [*She exits*]

[MR. MANNINGHAM *walks into room up right.* NANCY *returns. She has milk in a jug, a glass and biscuits on a tray, and puts them on the table. She goes upstairs. He comes back in and crosses slowly over to desk.* NANCY *comes downstairs and stops at the foot of the stairs*]

MR. MANNINGHAM: Well, Nancy?

NANCY: She says she has a headache, sir, and is trying to sleep.

MR. MANNINGHAM: Oh—she still has a headache, has she?

NANCY: Yes, sir. Is there anything else you want, sir?

MR. MANNINGHAM: Did you ever know a time when Mrs. Manningham did not have a headache, Nancy?

NANCY: No, sir. Hardly ever, sir.

MR. MANNINGHAM: Do you usually perform your domestic tasks in outdoor costume, Nancy?

NANCY: I told you, sir. I've only just come in, and I heard the bell by chance.

MR. MANNINGHAM: Yes, that's just the point.

NANCY: How do you mean, sir?

MR. MANNINGHAM: Will you be so good as to come closer, Nancy, where I can see you. [NANCY *comes closer. They look at each other in a rather strange way*] Have you any idea of the time of the day, or rather night, Nancy?

NANCY: Yes, sir. It's a little after eleven, sir.

MR. MANNINGHAM: Are you aware that you came in half a minute, or even less, before myself?

NANCY: Yes, sir. I thought I saw you, sir.

MR. MANNINGHAM: Oh—you thought you saw me. Well, I certainly saw you.

NANCY: [*Looking away*] Did you, sir?

MR. MANNINGHAM: Have you ever reflected, Nancy, that you are given a great deal of latitude in this house?

NANCY: I don't know, sir. I don't know what latitude means.

MR. MANNINGHAM: Latitude, Nancy, means considerable liberty—liberty to the extent of two nights off a week.

NANCY: [*Pause*] Yes, sir.

MR. MANNINGHAM: Well, that's all very well. It is not so well, however, when you return as late as the master of the house. We ought to keep up some pretenses, you know.

NANCY: Yes, sir. We must. [*She makes to go*]

MR. MANNINGHAM: Nancy.

NANCY: [*Stops*] Yes, sir?

MR. MANNINGHAM: [*In a more human tone*] Where the devil have you been tonight, anyway?

NANCY: [*Pause*] Only with some friends, sir.

MR. MANNINGHAM: You know, Nancy, when you say friends, I have an extraordinary idea that you mean gentlemen friends.

NANCY: [*Looking at him*] Well, sir, possibly I might.

MR. MANNINGHAM: You know, gentlemen friends have been known to take decided liberties with young ladies like yourself. Are you alive to such a possibility?

NANCY: Oh, no, sir. Not with me. I can look after myself.

MR. MANNINGHAM: Are you always so anxious to look after yourself?

NANCY: No, sir, not always, perhaps.

MR. MANNINGHAM: You know, Nancy, pretty as your bonnet is, it is not anything near so pretty as your hair beneath it. Won't you take it off and let me see it?

NANCY: [*As she removes hat*] Very good, sir. It comes off easy enough. There— Is there anything more you want, sir?

MR. MANNINGHAM: Yes. Possibly. Come here, will you, Nancy?

NANCY: [*Pause*] Yes, sir— [*She drops hat on chair. Coming to him*] Is there anything you want, sir?—[*Changing tone as he puts his arms on her shoulders*] What do you want?—eh— What do you want? [MANNINGHAM *kisses* NANCY *in a violent and prolonged manner. There is a pause in which she looks at him, and then she kisses him as violently*] There! Can she do that for you? Can she do that?

MR. MANNINGHAM: Who can you be talking about, Nancy?

NANCY: You know who I mean all right.

MR. MANNINGHAM: You know, Nancy, you are a very remarkable girl in many respects. I believe you are jealous of your mistress.

NANCY: She? She's a poor thing. There's no need to be jealous of her. You want to kiss me again, don't you? Don't you want to kiss me?

    [MANNINGHAM *kisses* NANCY]

There! That's better than a sick headache—ain't it—a sick headache and a pale face all the day.

MR. MANNINGHAM: Why yes, Nancy, I believe it is. I think, however, don't you, that it would be better if you and I met one evening in different surroundings.

NANCY: Yes. Where? I'll meet you when you like. You're mine now—ain't you—'cos you want me. You want me—don't you?

MR. MANNINGHAM: And what of you, Nancy. Do you want me?

NANCY: Oh, yes! I always wanted you, ever since I first clapped eyes on you. I wanted you more than all of them.

MR. MANNINGHAM: Oh—there are plenty of others?

NANCY: Oh, yes—there's plenty of others.

MR. MANNINGHAM: So I rather imagined. And only nineteen.

NANCY: Where can we meet? Where do you want us to meet?

MR. MANNINGHAM: Really, Nancy, you have taken me a little by surprise. I'll let you know tomorrow.

NANCY: How'll you let me know, when she's about?

MR. MANNINGHAM: [*Quietly*] Oh, I'll find a way, Nancy, I don't believe Mrs. Manningham will be here tomorrow.

NANCY: Oh? Not that I care about her. I'd like to kiss you under her very nose. That's what I'd like to do.

MR. MANNINGHAM: All right, Nancy. Now you had better go. I have some work to do.

NANCY: Go? I don't want to go.

MR. MANNINGHAM: There, run along. I have some work to do.

NANCY: Work? What are you going to work at? What are you going to do?

MR. MANNINGHAM: Oh—I'm going to write some letters. Then I—Go along, Nancy, that's a good girl.

NANCY: Oh, very well, sir. You shall be master for a little more. [*Her arms around his neck. Kisses him*] Good night, your lordship. [*She starts to door and picks up her hat on the way*]

MR. MANNINGHAM: Good night.

NANCY: [*At door, stops and turns to him*] When shall you let me know tomorrow?

MR. MANNINGHAM: When I find time, Nancy, when I find time. Good night.

NANCY: Good night! [*She goes out*]

[MANNINGHAM *crosses to the desk and sits down. He rises and crosses to the secretary, gets some papers, crosses back to the desk and sits down again. He takes up the pen and begins to write. He stops and takes out his key ring which is on the other end of his watch chain and unlocks the upstage drawer, then turns to unlock the downstage drawer. He stops as he discovers it has been forced and quickly rises. He turns to the upstage drawer, opens it and rummages through it. He then looks toward the stairs, crosses to the door, hesitates, then turns and goes to the bell cord, pulls it, and goes back to desk and takes a quick look at both drawers, then closes them*]

NANCY: [*Re-enters*] Yes? What is it now?

MR. MANNINGHAM: Nancy, will you please go upstairs and take a message for me to Mrs. Manningham.

NANCY: Yes. What do you want me to say?

MRS. MANNINGHAM: Will you please tell her that she is to come down here this instant, whether she is suffering from a sick headache or any other form of ailment.

NANCY: Just like that, sir?

MR. MANNINGHAM: Just like that, Nancy.

NANCY: With the greatest of pleasure, sir. [*She goes upstairs*]

> [MANNINGHAM *looks at the drawer again carefully. He walks over to the fireplace and stands with his back to it, waiting*]

NANCY: [*Returns*] She won't come. She doesn't mean to come.

MR. MANNINGHAM: [*Steps forward*] What do you mean, Nancy—she won't come?

NANCY: She said she can't come—she's not well enough. She's just shamming, if you ask me.

MR. MANNINGHAM: Really? Then she forces me to be undignified. [*Walking over to the stairs*] All right, Nancy, leave it to me.

NANCY: The door's locked. She's got it locked. I tried it.

MR. MANNINGHAM: Oh—really—the door is locked, is it? Very well. . . . [*He starts up the stairs past her*]

NANCY: She won't let you in. I can tell by her voice. She's got it locked and she won't open it. Are you going to batter it in?

MR. MANNINGHAM: [*Turns, comes down*] No—perhaps you are right, Nancy—let us try more delicate means of attaining our ends. [*He goes to desk, sits, and starts to write*] Perhaps you will take a note to this wretched imbecile and slip it under her door.

NANCY: Yes, I'll do that. [*Coming to desk*] What are you going to write?

MR. MANNINGHAM: Never mind what I am going to write. I'll tell you what you can do though, Nancy.

NANCY: Yes? What?

MR. MANNINGHAM: Just go down to the basement and bring the little dog here, will you?

NANCY: The dog?

MR. MANNINGHAM: The dog, yes.

NANCY: What's the game? What's the idea with the dog?

MR. MANNINGHAM: Never mind. Just go and get it, will you?

NANCY: [*Starts*] All right.

MR. MANNINGHAM: Or on second thought perhaps you need not get the dog. [*She stops. Turns to him*] We will just let it be supposed we have the dog. That will be even more delicate still. Here you are, Nancy. [*She crosses to desk*] Please go and put this under the door.

NANCY: [*Pause*] What's the idea? What have you written in this?

MR. MANNINGHAM: Nothing very much. Just a little smoke for getting rats out of holes. There. Run along.

NANCY: You're a rum beggar, ain't you? [*At stairs*] Can't I look?

MR. MANNINGHAM: Go on, Nancy!

[NANCY *goes up. Left alone,* MANNINGHAM *shuts and locks the top of his desk. Then he comes down and carefully places an armchair facing the fireplace—as though he is staging some ceremony. He looks around the room. Then he takes up his place in front of the fire, and waits.* NANCY *comes downstairs*]

NANCY: She's coming. It's done the trick all right.

MR. MANNINGHAM: Ah—so I thought. Very well, Nancy. Now I shall be obliged if you will go to bed at once.

NANCY: Go on. What's the game? What's the row about?

MR. MANNINGHAM: Nancy, will you please go to bed?

NANCY: [*Coming forward, to him*] All right, I'm going. [*Kisses him*] Good night, old dear. Give her what-for, won't you.

MR. MANNINGHAM: Good night, Nancy.

NANCY: Ta-ta.

[MRS. MANNINGHAM *appears and stands on the stairs.* MRS. MANNINGHAM *says nothing.* NANCY *goes out. After a long pause,* MANNINGHAM *goes to the door, and looks to see that* NANCY *is not there, closes it. He comes back and standing again with his back to the fireplace, looks at her*]

MR. MANNINGHAM: Come and sit down in this chair, please, Bella.

MRS. MANNINGHAM: [*Unmoving*] Where is the dog? Where have you got the dog?

MR. MANNINGHAM: Dog? What dog?

MRS. MANNINGHAM: You said you had the dog. Have you hurt it? Let me have it. Where is it? Have you hurt it again?

MR. MANNINGHAM: Again? This is strange talk, Bella—from you—after what you did to the dog a few weeks ago. Come and sit down here.

MRS. MANNINGHAM: I do not want to speak to you. I am not well. I thought you had the dog and were going—to hurt it. That is why I came down.

MR. MANNINGHAM: The dog, my dear Bella, was merely a ruse to compel you to pay me a visit quietly. Come and sit down where I told you.

MRS. MANNINGHAM: [*Starts upstairs*] No. I want to go.

MR. MANNINGHAM: [*Shouting*] Come and sit down where I told you!

MRS. MANNINGHAM: [*Coming downstage to back of table*] Yes—yes—what do you want?

MR. MANNINGHAM: Quite a good deal, Bella. Sit down and make yourself comfortable. We have plenty of time.

MRS. MANNINGHAM: [*As she crosses back toward stairs*] I want to go. You cannot keep me here. I want to go.

MR. MANNINGHAM: [*Calmly*] Sit down and make yourself comfortable, Bella. We have plenty of time.

MRS. MANNINGHAM: [*Going to chair which he did not indicate and which is nearer the door and sits*] Say what you have to say.

MR. MANNINGHAM: Now you are not sitting in the chair I indicated, Bella.

MRS. MANNINGHAM: What have you to say?

MR. MANNINGHAM: I have to say that you are not sitting in the chair I indicated. Are you afraid of me that you desire to get so near the door?

MRS. MANNINGHAM: No, I am not afraid of you.

MR. MANNINGHAM: No? Then you have a good deal of courage, my dear. However, will you now sit down where I told you?

MRS. MANNINGHAM: Yes. [*She rises and slowly crosses*]

MR. MANNINGHAM: Do you know what you remind me of, Bella, as you walk across the room?

MRS. MANNINGHAM: No. What do I remind you of?

MR. MANNINGHAM: A somnambulist, Bella. Have you ever seen such a person?

MRS. MANNINGHAM: No, I have never seen one.

MR. MANNINGHAM: Haven't you? Not that funny, glazed, dazed look of the wandering mind—the body that acts without the soul to guide it? I have often thought you had that look, but it's never been so strong as tonight.

MRS. MANNINGHAM: [*Sitting in armchair*] My mind is not wandering.

MR. MANNINGHAM: No?—When I came in, Bella, I was told that you had gone to bed.

MRS. MANNINGHAM: Yes. I had gone to bed.

MR. MANNINGHAM: Then may I ask why you are still fully dressed? [*She does not answer*] Did you hear what I said?

MRS. MANNINGHAM: Yes, I heard what you said.

MR. MANNINGHAM: Then will you tell me why, since you had gone to bed, you are still fully dressed?

MRS. MANNINGHAM: I don't know.

MR. MANNINGHAM: You don't know? Do you know anything about anything you do?

MRS. MANNINGHAM: I don't know. I forgot to undress.

MR. MANNINGHAM: You forgot to undress. A curious oversight, if I may say so, Bella. [*Leaning over her*] You know, you give me the appearance of having had a rather exciting time since I last saw you. Almost as though you have been up to something. Have you been up to anything?

MRS. MANNINGHAM: No. I don't know what you mean.

MR. MANNINGHAM: [*Straightens up*] Did you find that bill I told you to find?

MRS. MANNINGHAM: No.

MR. MANNINGHAM: [*Goes to milk on table*] Do you remember what I said would happen to you if you did not find that bill when I returned tonight?

MRS. MANNINGHAM: No.

MR. MANNINGHAM: No? [*Is pouring milk into glass*] No? [*She refuses to answer*] Am I married to a dumb woman, Bella, in addition to all else? The array of your physical and mental deficiencies is growing almost overwhelming. I advise you to answer me.

MRS. MANNINGHAM: What do you want me to say?

MR. MANNINGHAM: I asked you if you remembered something. [*Going back to fireplace with glass of milk*] Go on, Bella—what was it I asked you if you remembered?

MRS. MANNINGHAM: I don't understand your words. You talk round and round. My head is going round and round.

MR. MANNINGHAM: It is not necessary for you to tell me that, Bella. I am just wondering if it might interrupt its gyratory motion for a fraction of a second, and concentrate upon the present conversation. [*Sips milk*] Now please, what was it I a moment ago asked you if you remembered?

MRS. MANNINGHAM: [*Labored*] You asked me if I remembered what you said would happen to me if I did not find that bill.

MR. MANNINGHAM: Admirable, my dear Bella! Admirable! We shall make a great logician of you yet—a Socrates—a John Stuart Mill! You shall go down to history as the shining mind of your day. That is, if your present history does not altogether submerge you—take you away from your fellow creatures. And there is a danger of that, you know, in more ways than one. [*Puts milk on mantel*] Well—what did I say I would do if you did not find that bill?

MRS. MANNINGHAM: [*Choked*] You said you would lock me up.

MR. MANNINGHAM: Yes. And do you believe me to be a man of my word? [*Pause in which she does not answer*] You see, Bella, in a life of considerable and varied experience I have hammered out a few principles of action. In fact, I actually fancy I know how to deal with my fellowmen. I learned it quite early actually—at school in fact. There, you know, there were two ways of getting at what you wanted. One was along an intellectual plane, the other along the physical. If one failed one used the other. I took that lesson into life with me. Hitherto, with you, I have worked with what forbearance and patience I leave you to judge, along the intellectual plane. The time has come now, I believe, to work along the other as well— You will understand that I am a man of some power. . . . [*She suddenly looks at him*] Why do you look at me, Bella? I said I am a man of some power and determination, and as fully capable in one direction as in the other.—I will leave your imagination to work on what I mean.—However, we are really digressing. . . . You did not find the bill I told you to find.

MRS. MANNINGHAM: No.

MR. MANNINGHAM: Did you look for it? [*He moves toward desk*]

MRS. MANNINGHAM: Yes.

MR. MANNINGHAM: Where did you look for it?

MRS. MANNINGHAM: Oh, around the room. . . .

MR. MANNINGHAM: Around the room. *Where* around the room? [*Pause. As he bangs on the desk with his right hand*] In my desk, for instance?

MRS. MANNINGHAM: No—not in your desk.

MR. MANNINGHAM: Why not in my desk?

MRS. MANNINGHAM: Your desk is locked.

MR. MANNINGHAM: Do you imagine you can lie to me?

MRS. MANNINGHAM: I am not lying.

MR. MANNINGHAM: Come here, Bella.

MRS. MANNINGHAM: [*Coming to him*] What do you want?

MR. MANNINGHAM: [*Pause*] Now, listen to me. Your dark, confused, rambling mind has led you into playing some pretty tricks tonight—has it not?

MRS. MANNINGHAM: My mind is tired. [*She starts to stairs*] I want to go to bed.

MR. MANNINGHAM: Your mind indeed is tired! Your mind is so tired that it can no longer work at all. You do not think. You dream. Dream all day long. Dream everything. Dream maliciously and incessantly. Don't you know that by now? [*She starts to give way*] You sleepwalking imbecile, what have you been dreaming tonight—where has your mind wandered— that you have split [*Pounds on desk*] open my desk? What strange diseased dream have you had tonight—eh?

MRS. MANNINGHAM: Dream? Are you saying I have dreamed—Dreamed all that happened?—

MR. MANNINGHAM: All that happened when, Bella? Tonight? Of course you dreamed all that happened—or rather all that didn't happen.

MRS. MANNINGHAM: Dream— Tonight—are you saying I have dreamed? [*Pause*] Oh, God—have I dreamed? Have I dreamed again?—

MR. MANNINGHAM: Have I not told you—?

MRS. MANNINGHAM: [*Storming*] *I haven't dreamed. I haven't! Don't tell me I have dreamed. In the name of God don't tell me that!*

MR. MANNINGHAM: [*Speaking at the same time, and forcing her down into small chair left*] Sit down and be quiet. Sit down! [*More quietly and curiously*] What was this dream of yours, Bella? You interest me.

MRS. MANNINGHAM: I dreamt of a man— [*Hysterical*] I dreamt of a man—

MR. MANNINGHAM: [*Now very curious*] You dreamed of a man, Bella? What man did you dream of, pray?

MRS. MANNINGHAM: A man. A man that came to see me. Let me rest! Let me rest!

MR. MANNINGHAM: Pull yourself together, Bella! What man are you talking about?

MRS. MANNINGHAM: I dreamed a man came in here.

MR. MANNINGHAM: [*As he grasps her neck and slowly raises her*] I know you dreamed it, you gibbering wretch! I want to know more about this man of whom you dreamed. Do you hear! Do you hear me?

MRS. MANNINGHAM: I dreamed—I dreamed—

[*She looks off at door up right, transfixed.* MANNINGHAM *turns and looks as* ROUGH *enters door up right.* MANNINGHAM *releases her and she sinks back into the chair*]

ROUGH: Was I any part of this curious dream of yours, Mrs. Manningham?— Perhaps my presence here will help you to recall it.

MR. MANNINGHAM: [*After pause*] May I ask who the devil you are, and how you got in?

ROUGH: Well, who I am seems a little doubtful. Apparently I am a mere figment of Mrs. Manningham's imagination. As for how I got in, I came in, or rather I came back—or better still, I effected an entrance a few minutes before you, and I have been hidden away ever since.

MR. MANNINGHAM: And would you be kind enough to tell me what you are doing here?

ROUGH: Waiting for some friends, Mr. Manningham, waiting for some friends. Don't you think you had better go up to bed, Mrs. Manningham? You look very tired.

MR. MANNINGHAM: Don't you think you had better explain your business, sir?

ROUGH: Well, as a mere figment, as a mere ghost existing only in your wife's mind, I can hardly be said to have any business. Tell me, Mr. Manningham, can you see me? No doubt your wife can, but it must be difficult for you. Perhaps if she goes to her room I will vanish, and you won't be bothered by me any more.

MR. MANNINGHAM: Bella. Go to your room. [*She rises, staring at both in turn in apprehension and wonderment, goes to the stairs*] I shall find out the meaning of this, and deal with you in due course.

MRS. MANNINGHAM: I—

MR. MANNINGHAM: Go to your room. I will call you down later. I have not finished with you yet, madam.

[MRS. MANNINGHAM *looks at both again, and goes upstairs*]

ROUGH: You know, I believe you're wrong there, Manningham. I believe that is just what you have done.

MR. MANNINGHAM: Done what?

ROUGH: Finished with your wife, my friend. [*He sits down easily in arm-chair*]

MR. MANNINGHAM: Now, sir—will you have the goodness to tell me your name and your business if any?

ROUGH: I have no name, Manningham, in my present capacity. I am, as I have pointed out, a mere spirit. Perhaps a spirit of something that you have evaded all your life—but in any case, only a spirit. Will you have a cigar with a spirit? We may have to wait some time.

MR. MANNINGHAM: Are you going to tell me your business, sir, or am I going to fetch a policeman and have you turned out?

ROUGH: [*Puts cigar back in pocket*] Ah—an admirable idea. I could have thought of nothing better myself. Yes, fetch a policeman, Manningham, and have me turned out— [*Pause*] Why do you wait?

MR. MANNINGHAM: Alternatively, sir, I can turn you out myself.

ROUGH: [*Standing and facing him*] Yes. But why not fetch a policeman?

MR. MANNINGHAM: [*After pause*] You give me the impression, sir, that you have something up your sleeve. Will you go on with what you were saying?

ROUGH: Yes, certainly. Where was I? Yes. [*Pause*] Excuse me, Manningham, but do you get the same impression as myself?

MR. MANNINGHAM: What impression?

ROUGH: An impression that the light is going down in this room?

MR. MANNINGHAM: I have not noticed it.

ROUGH: Yes—surely— There— [*The light goes slowly down. As* ROUGH *moves,* MANNINGHAM *keeps his eyes on him*]—Eerie, isn't it? Now we are almost in the dark— Why do you think that has happened? You don't suppose a light has been put on somewhere else— You don't suppose there are other spirits—fellow spirits of mine—spirits surrounding this house now—spirits of justice, even, which have caught up with you at last, Mr. Manningham?

MR. MANNINGHAM: [*His hand on the back of chair right of table*] Are you off your head, sir?

ROUGH: No, sir. Just an old man seeing ghosts. It must be the atmosphere of this house. [*As he looks about*] I can see them everywhere. It's the oddest thing. Do you know one ghost I can see, Mr. Manningham? You could hardly believe it.

MR. MANNINGHAM: What ghost do you see, pray?

ROUGH: Why, it's the ghost of an old woman, sir—an old woman who once lived in this house, who once lived in this very room. Yes—in this very room. What things I imagine!

MR. MANNINGHAM: What are you saying?

ROUGH: Remarkably clear, sir, I see it— An old woman getting ready to go to bed—here in this very room—an old woman getting ready to go up to bed at the end of the day. Why! There she is. She sits just there. [*Points to chair right of table.* MANNINGHAM *removes his hand from the chair*] And now it seems I see another ghost as well. [*Pause. He is looking at* MANNINGHAM] I see the ghost of a young man, Mr. Manningham—a handsome, tall, well-groomed young man. But this young man has murder in his eyes. Why, God bless my soul, he might be you, Mr. Manningham—he might be you! [*Pause*] The old woman sees him. Don't you see it all? She screams—screams for help—screams before her throat is cut—cut open with a knife. She lies dead on the floor—the floor of this room—of this house. There! [*Pointing to floor in front of table. Pause*] Now I don't see that ghost any more.

MR. MANNINGHAM: What's the game, eh? What's your game?

ROUGH: [*Confronting* MANNINGHAM] But I still see the ghost of the man. I see him, all through the night, as he ransacks the house, hour after hour, room after room, ripping everything up, turning everything out, madly seeking the thing he cannot find. Then years pass and where is he?— Why, sir, is he not back in the same house, the house he ransacked, the house he searched—and does he not now stand before the ghost of the woman he killed—in the room in which he killed her? A methodical man, a patient man, but perhaps he has waited too long. For justice has waited too, and here she is, in my person, to exact her due. And justice found, my friend, in one hour what you sought for fifteen years, and still could not find. See here. Look what she found. [*Goes to desk*] A letter which never reached your wife. Then a brooch which you gave your wife but which she did not appreciate. How wicked of her! But then she didn't know its value. How was she to know that it held the Barlow rubies! There! [*Opening it out*] See. Twelve thousand pounds' worth before your eyes! There you are, sir. You killed one woman for those and tried to drive another out of her mind. And all the time they lay in your own desk, and all they have brought you is a rope around your neck, Mr. Sydney Power!

MR. MANNINGHAM: [*Pause*] You seem, sir, to have some very remarkable information. Do you imagine you are going to leave this room with such information in your possession? [*Going up to doors as though to lock them*]

ROUGH: Do you imagine, sir, that you are going to leave this room without suitable escort?

MR. MANNINGHAM: May I ask what you mean by that?

ROUGH: Only that I have men in the house already. Didn't you realize that they had signaled their arrival from above, your own way in, Mr. Manningham, when the lights went down?

MR. MANNINGHAM: [*Pause. He looks at* ROUGH] Here you— What the devil's this? [*He rushes to the door, where two* POLICEMEN *are standing*] Ah,

Gentlemen— Come in. Come in. Make yourselves at home. Here. [*He makes a plunge. They grab him*] Leave go of me, will you? Here. Leave go of me! Here's a fine way of going on. Here's a fine way!

[A struggle ensues. ROUGH, *seeing help is needed, jerks down the bell cord. With this, they secure* MANNINGHAM. ROUGH *kicks him in the shins. He falls*]

ROUGH: [*Taking paper from his pocket*] Sydney Charles Power, I have a warrant for your arrest for the murder of Alice Barlow. I should warn you that anything you may say now may be taken down in writing and used as evidence at a later date. Will you accompany us to the station in a peaceful manner? You will oblige us all, and serve your own interests best, Power, by coming with us quietly. [MANNINGHAM *renews struggle*] Very well—take him away—

[*They are about to take him away when* MRS. MANNINGHAM *comes down the stairs. There is a silence*]

MRS. MANNINGHAM: Inspector Rough. . . .

[*The two* POLICEMEN *turn so that* MANNINGHAM *faces* MRS. MANNINGHAM]

ROUGH: [*Going to her*] Yes, my dear, now don't you think you'd better—

MRS. MANNINGHAM: [*In a weak voice*] Inspector . . .

ROUGH: Yes?

MRS. MANNINGHAM: I want to speak to my husband.

ROUGH: Now, surely, there's nothing to be—

MRS. MANNINGHAM: I want to speak to my husband.

ROUGH: Very well, my dear, what do you want to say?

MRS. MANNINGHAM: I want to speak to him alone.

ROUGH: Alone?

MRS. MANNINGHAM: Yes, alone. Won't you please let me speak to him alone? I beg of you to allow me. I will not keep him long.

ROUGH: [*Pause*] I don't quite understand. Alone?— [*Pause*] Very well. You may speak to him alone. [*To* POLICEMEN] Very well. Make him fast in this chair. [*He signifies that they are to tie him to chair. They do so and exit*] This is anything but in order—but we will wait outside. [MRS. MANNINGHAM *crosses to desk.* ROUGH *examines fastenings on* MANNINGHAM *and crosses up to door*] I'm afraid you must not be long, Mrs. Manningham.

MRS. MANNINGHAM: I do not want you to listen.

ROUGH: No, I will not listen. [ROUGH *hesitates, then exits*]

[MRS. MANNINGHAM *stands looking at her husband. At last she goes over to door, locks it and then comes to him*]

MRS. MANNINGHAM: Jack! Jack! What have they done to you? What have they done?

MR. MANNINGHAM: [*Struggling at his bonds, half whispering*] It's all right, Bella. You're clever, my darling. Terribly clever. Now get something to cut this. I can get out through the dressing room window and make a jump for it. Can you fetch something?

MRS. MANNINGHAM: [*Hesitating*] Yes—yes. I can get something. What can I get?

MR. MANNINGHAM: I've just remembered— There's a razor in my dressing room. Quick! Can you get it, Bella?

MRS. MANNINGHAM: [*Feverishly*] Razor—yes—I'll get it for you.

MR. MANNINGHAM: Hurry—yes— In my dresser— Hurry—quick and get it.

[*She goes into room up right, talking and mumbling, and comes back with the razor and crosses to desk. As she takes the razor from case, a scrap of paper falls to the floor. She stoops to pick it up, almost unconsciously tidy. She glances at it and a happy smile illuminates her face*]

MRS. MANNINGHAM: [*Joyously*] Jack! Here's the grocery bill! [*She comes to him, the grocery bill in one hand, the razor in the other. She is half-weeping, half-laughing*] You see, dear, I didn't lose it. I told you I didn't!

MR. MANNINGHAM: [*Uncomfortably*] Cut me loose, Bella.

MRS. MANNINGHAM: [*She stares at him for a moment, then at the grocery bill, then back at him*] Jack—how did this get in here? You said that I. . . . [*Her voice trails off, a wild look comes into her eyes*]

MR. MANNINGHAM: [*Trying to placate her with charm*] I must have been mistaken about the bill. Now—quickly, dear, use the razor! Quick!

[*She stares at him for a moment, then moves a step closer. His look falls upon the razor. He glances up at her and a momentary hint of terror comes into his face. He draws back in the chair*]

MRS. MANNINGHAM: Razor? *What* razor? [*She holds it up, under his face*] You are not suggesting that this is a razor I hold in my hand? Have you gone mad, my husband?

MR. MANNINGHAM: Bella, what are you up to?

MRS. MANNINGHAM: [*With deadly rage that is close to insanity*] Or is it I who am mad? [*She hurls the razor across the room*] Yes. That's it. It's *I*. Of course, it *was* a razor. Dear God—I have lost it, haven't I? I am always losing things. And I can never find them. I don't know *where* I put them.

MR. MANNINGHAM: [*Desperately*] Bella!

MRS. MANNINGHAM: I must look for it, mustn't I? Yes—if I don't find it you will lock me in my room—you will lock me in the madhouse for my mischief. [*Her voice is compressed with bitterness and hatred*] Where could it be now? [*Turns and looks around*] Could it be behind the picture? Yes, it must be there! [*She goes to the picture swiftly and takes it down*] No, it's not there—how strange! I must put the picture back. I have taken it down, and I must put it back. There. [*She puts it back askew*] Where now shall I look? [*She is raging like a hunted animal. Turns and sees the desk*] Where shall I look? The desk. Perhaps I put it in the desk. [*Goes to the desk*] No—it is not there—how strange! But here is a letter. Here is a watch. And a bill— See, I've found them at last. [*Going to him*] You see! But they don't help you, do they? And I am trying to help you, aren't I?—to help you escape— But how can a mad woman help her husband to escape? What a pity. . . . [*Getting louder and louder*] If I were not mad I could have helped you—if I were not mad, whatever you had done, I could have pitied and protected you! But because I am mad I have hated you, and because I am mad I am rejoicing in my heart— without a shred of pity—without a shred of regret—watching you go with glory in my heart!

MR. MANNINGHAM: [*Desperately*] Bella!!

MRS. MANNINGHAM: Inspector! Inspector! [*Up to door; pounds on door then flings it open*] Come and take this man away! Come and take this man away! [ROUGH *and the others come in swiftly.* MRS. MANNINGHAM *is completely hysterical*] Come and take this man away!

    [ROUGH *gestures to the men. They remove* MANNINGHAM. MRS. MANNINGHAM *stands apart, trembling with homicidal rage.* ROUGH *takes her by the shoulders sternly. She struggles to get away. He slaps her across the face. She is momentarily stunned.* ELIZABETH *enters, quickly takes in the situation, gets a glass of water from table up right and brings it down to* MRS. MANNINGHAM *and gives her a drink.* ROUGH *stands watching them for a second*]

ROUGH: [*His eyes on* MRS. MANNINGHAM *whose wild fury has resolved in weeping. He leads her to chair*] Now, my dear, come and sit down. You've had a bad time. I came in from nowhere and gave you the most horrible evening of your life. Didn't I? The most horrible evening of anybody's life, I should imagine.

MRS. MANNINGHAM: The most horrible? Oh, no—the most wonderful. Far and away the most wonderful.

CURTAIN

Cactus Flower

ABE BURROWS

Based On A Play by

PIERRE BARILLET AND
JEAN-PIERRE GREDY

ABE BURROWS
PIERRE BARILLET AND
JEAN-PIERRE GREDY

Cactus Flower, Abe Burrows's Americanized treatment of a French comedy, *Fleur de Cactus,* by Pierre Barillet and Jean-Pierre Gredy, ran for 1,234 performances, placing it thirteenth among Broadway's longest-running plays.

A high-spirited and thoroughly delightful comedy in the best tradition of a French farce yet as unmistakable in its New York feeling as the twin towers of the World Trade Center, it provided an ideal vehicle for Lauren Bacall after years in films. It also brought forth bellows of laughter from delighted audiences for three years. According to Richard Watts, Jr., of the *New York Post:* "Mr. Burrows has filled it out with his characteristic freshness of humorous observation, wittiness and brightness of dialogue, and casual, easygoing and captivating charm, with the result that it is steadily entertaining in its appealing fashion."

Its Cinderella theme with its starchy heroine who emerges from her cocoon and reveals herself as a ravishing beauty with hidden wells of pent-up emotion, of course, is universal. As Whitney Bolton wrote in *The Morning Telegraph:* "When it was in rehearsal, Mr. Burrows confided to me, without revealing any secrets at all, that it was a non-nation play that just happened to have been written first in French with a Paris locale. He implied that so universal was the basic theme that it could be done in West Berlin with a German locale, in Vienna as an Austrian play and, probably, with enough professional effort, in Zambia in Central Africa in native Bembe. He made it a New York play, drenched in the gaudy and carnival spirit of Manhattan."

It has been proven on many occasions that most French comedies do not cross the ocean very well and those that have were adapted, rather than merely translated, by skillful American playwrights. As Burrows told a journalist: "Now, as you can imagine, there's a problem in properly translating a French comedy into American. The sense of humor's different. The point of view. Words always mean something else. So I start with a quick, literal translation. Then I *adapt* the dialogue, make it into the American equivalent." One of the theatre's most nimble practitioners of comic pyrotechnics, Burrows continues: "Laughter's a special emotional response. I believe humor's a serious tool you use to deal with serious subjects. My theory is that a laugh from an audience is a bigger reaction than a tear. I say something funny. You laugh, you go hah-hah—and you're defenseless. It means I touched a deep nerve. You recognize a truth. You say, 'Yeah, that's right, my wife's like that!' It may be a cop-out, but when you laugh like that you can release something—and be safe. And laughter is sharing something."

Author-director Abe Burrows was born in New York City on December 18, 1910. Educated at the College of the City of New York and the New York University School of Finance he was propelled, however briefly, into a career of accountancy and brokerage. He began writing for radio in 1938 and remained with the medium for a decade. An amiable raconteur and wit, he also entertained radio listeners as a performer with his ready, rapid patter (and later, television viewers on talk and game shows).

Burrows made his Broadway debut in 1950 as coauthor of the book for *Guys and Dolls,* a reigning smash hit and winner of the New York Drama Critics' Circle Award and the Antoinette Perry (Tony) Award as the year's best musical. Other musicals followed: *Three Wishes for Jamie* (1952, coauthor and director); *Can-Can* (1953, author and director); *Silk Stockings* (1955, coauthor); *Say, Darling* (1958, coauthor and director); *First Impressions* (1959, author and director); and *How to Succeed in Business Without Really Trying* (1961, winner of the Pulitzer Prize and New York Drama Critics' Circle Award for best musical; coauthor and director).

After *Cactus Flower,* Burrows resumed his association with Barillet and Gredy by directing the New York productions of *Forty Carats* (1968) and *Four on a Garden,* which he also adapted (1971).

Pierre Barillet and Jean-Pierre Gredy were both born in the mid-1920s. Their initial collaboration took place in 1949 with the comedy *Le don d'Adèle.* It ran in Paris for almost 2,000 performances and was followed by their equally popular *Ami, Ami.* During their three decades as collaborators, the pair have contributed many successful comedies to the French stage as well as doing adaptations of more than a dozen American plays. Both have also worked extensively in films, including fashioning the scenario with René Clair for the classic *Les belles de nuit.*

Presently, they have two productions running concurrently in Paris: *Le Préféré (The Favorite)* and an adaptation of Leonard Spigelgass' *A Majority of One.*

The movie version of *Cactus Flower*—with Ingrid Bergman, Walter Matthau, and Goldie Hawn (winner of an Academy Award for her supporting performance)—was released in 1969.

CACTUS FLOWER was first produced at the Royale Theatre, New York, on December 8, 1965, by David Merrick. The cast was as follows:

TONI SIMMONS	*Brenda Vaccaro*
IGOR SULLIVAN	*Burt Brinckerhoff*
STEPHANIE DICKINSON	*Lauren Bacall*
MRS. DIXON DURANT	*Eileen Letchworth*
DR. JULIAN WINSTON	*Barry Nelson*
HARVEY GREENFIELD	*Robert Moore*
SEÑOR ARTURO SANCHEZ	*Arny Freeman*
CUSTOMER	*Will Gregory*
WAITER	*Michael Fairman*
BOTICELLI'S SPRINGTIME	*Marjorie Battles*
MUSIC LOVER	*Michael Fairman*

Directed by Abe Burrows
Scenic Production by Oliver Smith
Costumes by Theoni V. Aldredge
Lighting by Martin Aronstein
Associate Producer: Samuel Liff
Produced in Association with Beresford Productions, Ltd.

The action of the play takes place in fifteen scenes scattered around uptown and downtown Manhattan. The time is the present.

ACT ONE

Toni's apartment. This is somewhere in Greenwich Village. It's one of those apartments where everything is visible on entrance: the bed, stove, cooking equipment, and maybe some pieces of "living room" furniture. There should be a door leading to a bathroom and a large window upstage. Beyond it we see a fire escape. The time is around four A.M. The lights in the apartment are off, but dim light filters through the window, revealing TONI. *She is lying on the bed, face down, unconscious, her head hanging off the front of the bed. She's a beautiful girl, wearing an attractive short nightgown. A small radio on the shelf at window is on and rock 'n' roll music is playing. We hear someone pounding at the door.*

IGOR'S VOICE: [*off*] Hey, in there . . . something wrong? [*Another knock on the door*] Hey, I smell gas!

[IGOR *appears on the fire escape. He tries to open the window, can't, then smashes one of the panes, which enables him to open the lock and get in. He's a good looking young fellow. Very athletic and quick in his movements. He is dressed in T-shirt and chino pants. He looks around the apartment quickly, sniffing as he looks. He glances quickly at* TONI *and rushes to the stove, turning on light switch by door as he passes. He turns off the burners, closes oven door, opens window over sink. He then rushes back, turns off radio, turns to* TONI. *He leans over and puts his ear against the upper part of her back in order to listen to her heartbeat. He then makes a move as though to give her artificial respiration while she is still lying face down. He then decides to turn her over, face up. He turns her over, holds her in his arms and gets ready to give her mouth-to-mouth resuscitation. He takes three preparatory deep breaths, then as he leans forward to put his mouth to hers, she kisses him, wiggles her toes. After a moment, her arms go around his neck. He very sensibly holds still for a long kiss. Then he pulls back*]

TONI: [*In a very sleepy voice her arms still around his neck*] Julian. Julian . . .

IGOR: Hey, I'm not Julian . . . Wake up, wake up.

TONI: [*Same sleepy voice*] Julian, kiss me.

IGOR: [*Looking around*] Sorry, Julian, whoever you are.
[*They kiss again*]

TONI: [*Pulling away*] Who are you—what are you doing?

IGOR: Mouth-to-mouth resuscitation.

TONI: You were kissing me.

IGOR: [*Releasing her*] It sort of got away.

TONI: Wait a minute, where am I? I was trying to—

IGOR: Look, I live next door and I smelled gas.

TONI: Gas? I'm alive! I fizzled it! [*She falls back into her former position and bangs on floor*] I fizzled it! Oh boy, I really fizzled it!

IGOR: [*Leaning over her*] Hey, take it easy. Boy, you're lucky I busted in.

TONI: Why did you?

IGOR: I thought you were dying.

TONI: That was the whole *idea!* Why didn't you keep out of it, you snoop?

IGOR: [*Crossing to door*] Sorry. Next time you turn on the gas, leave a "Do Not Disturb."

TONI: [*Throwing pillow at him*] Dammit, you made me fizzle it!

IGOR: It happens you were going about it all wrong. I believe you're supposed to put your head *in* the stove. [*He puts pillow on bed*]

TONI: [*In kneeling position on bed*] It's a second-hand stove. There were no directions.

IGOR: [*Crossing back to her*] Why are you so anxious to shuffle off? Is it Julian?

TONI: How do you know about Julian?

IGOR: You called me that while you were kissing me.

TONI: I wasn't kissing you, you were kissing me. By the way, is that all you did?

IGOR: You'll never know, will you?

TONI: I'm sorry. I guess I should be grateful. What's your name?

IGOR: My name is Igor. . . . Igor Sullivan.

TONI: Igor Sullivan. That's wild.

IGOR: I made it up.

TONI: How come you picked Igor?

IGOR: Igor's my own. I made up the Sullivan.

TONI: Oh.

IGOR: Igor Sullivan is a good strong name for a writer.

TONI: Oh, you're a writer. [*Suddenly recovering some of her strength, kneels*] Oh, you're *the* writer. The one who keeps pounding that typewriter all night. Your typing has been driving me crazy.

IGOR: Oh, it has?

TONI: Yes.

IGOR: Well, it's a lucky thing for you I was in there typing tonight or you'd have been—

TONI: I wish I was. [*Falls back down, her head toward foot of bed*]

IGOR: That's crazy. You should be happy that you're all right. I know *I'm* happy that you're all right. Listen, uh—uh—what's your name?

TONI: [*Mumbles*] Antoinette Simmons.

IGOR: What?

TONI: Antoinette Simmons.

IGOR: Look, Antoinette . . .

TONI: Toni.

IGOR: Look, Toni, what did this Julian do to you?

TONI: Nothing. [*Sits up and starts to put on her slippers*]

IGOR: [*Sits on edge of bed*] He must have done something. Did he cheat on you? [TONI *shakes her head*] Beat you? Is he a drunk? A crook?

TONI: Worse.

IGOR: Oh, he's married.

TONI: For life. He has three kids. I don't know why I'm telling you all this. Like you were my mother.

IGOR: Well, I did snatch you from the Valley of the Shadow.

TONI: Boy, you must be a pretty corny writer.

IGOR: I thought it was rather picturesque.

TONI: But you *did* save my life and I'm beginning to feel better about it. So, anyway, where was I?

IGOR: You just found out that that dirty rat Julian—

TONI: [*Indignant*] He's not a dirty rat, he's a dentist! A fine dentist. [*Crawling over to headboard*] Park Avenue. [*From headboard she picks up a card, hands it to* IGOR *proudly*] Here's his card.

IGOR: [*Looking at it*] Well, let me rephrase my statement. You just found out that Dr. Julian Winston, D.D.S., Park Avenue, has a wife and three children.

TONI: I *didn't* just find it out. Julian told me he was married the first time we met. That's one of the things that attracted me to him. Made me love him more.

IGOR: You go for married men, huh?

TONI: I like honesty. All my life people have lied to me and I can't stand it. Julian had the decency to warn me right away that he had a wife and a family. I was in love with him and I accepted it.

IGOR: So what's the problem?

TONI: I couldn't accept it. At first I thought it was all going to be a carefree, gay fling. Whoopee. Then came all those times when he couldn't see me. Night after night I'd be ready and waiting, then, bang! there'd be a phone call or a note.

IGOR: Tough.

TONI: Boy, I tell you when he cancelled last night, I wanted to . . . [*She rises, makes violent karate-like gestures with her hand*] It was our anniversary. [*She gets robe off hook*]

IGOR: Anniversary of what?

TONI: Julian and I met one year ago at the L.P. That's the record shop where I work.

IGOR: [*Rises*] The Village L.P.? I've been there. I never noticed you. [IGOR *helps her on with robe*]

TONI: Well, Julian did. And I noticed him. And he was charming. A gentleman. Good looking, beautifully dressed. . . . [*A look at* IGOR's *clothes*] No T-shirts.

IGOR: [*Looking at his clothes*] Sorry, I didn't know this suicide was black tie.

TONI: You look all right.

IGOR: But, Toni, after putting up with it for a year, why did you suddenly—?

TONI: I don't know. I became completely unglued. Maybe because it was our anniversary . . . But I suddenly had the sickening feeling I had thrown away my whole life. You know, Igor, I'm twenty-one.

IGOR: You poor old bat.

TONI: You're not a girl.

IGOR: [*Looking at the stove*] Hey, what's this mess all over the stove?

TONI: [*Looking at it*] Chicken cacciatore.

IGOR: Chicken cacciatore?

TONI: Julian is mad about it. His wife won't make it for him. He says she's one of those health nuts.

IGOR: Hey, Toni. The pot boiled over while you were trying to do yourself in, and it blocked up all the burners.

TONI: Hurray!

IGOR: Miss Simmons, it was not the brave Sullivan who saved you, it was chicken cacciatore.

TONI: [*Amused*] You're a very cute youngster. What sort of things do you write.?

IGOR: Plays.

TONI: What kind of plays?

IGOR: Unproduced. I've written eight plays . . . at least I think they're plays. No one else does.

TONI: And you're growing bitter.

IGOR: [*Pacing back and forth*] It's tough sitting there, all alone, typing away, thinking you have talent, thinking you have something to say . . . and nobody cares whether you live or die. You feel rejected by the whole world.

TONI: How do you manage to live?

IGOR: I get an allowance from my father.

TONI: Uh huh.

IGOR: [*Suddenly realizing how it sounds*] Well, you see, when I got out of the Army, he let me have one year to try writing.

TONI: Oh, boy! And I was feeling sorry for you.

IGOR: I can't help it if I'm not poor. Say, Toni, now that you're through with this Julian, how about one of these nights you and me—?

TONI: [*Sudden thought*] Hey, what time is it?

IGOR: [*Looking at his watch with a rueful smile*] Four A.M.

TONI: Four A.M.! Oh, my God!

IGOR: What's the matter?

TONI: I've got to get up and go to work tomorrow. I don't know how I'll do it. [*As she says this, she leaps up, takes off robe, rushes onto the bed*] Go away, I have to sleep. [*She drops her head to the bed as though falling into a deep sleep. She gets right up*] I won't try to work. I'm going to take the day off.

IGOR: Yeah, why kill yourself?

TONI: That's very witty.

IGOR: I'm sorry. Is there anything I can get you?

TONI: [*Making herself comfortable, head on the pillow*] Thanks, I just want to sleep.

IGOR: [*Crossing to door*] Sleep well. If you need me I'll be next door. Just pound on the wall. [*He pounds on wall just left of door*] I'll come right away.

TONI: Thanks, Igor.

IGOR: [*Switching off lights*] Good night.

[*He goes. The lights are now back to the opening dim reading.* TONI *sits bolt upright and screams*]

TONI: Oh, my god, my letter! My letter! [*She runs to wall, pounds on it at same spot as* IGOR *did*] Igor! Hey, Igor!

IGOR: [*Rushing back and throwing lights back on*] What's the matter?

TONI: My letter. I mailed a letter.

IGOR: What letter?

TONI: To Julian. I wrote him a letter telling him what I was going to do.

IGOR: What did you do that for?

TONI: What would be the point of my killing myself if he didn't know about it? But now that I fizzled it, he's got to be told before he reads my letter. Igor, you must call him for me.

IGOR: Why don't you call him yourself?

TONI: First of all, I'll be sleeping. Second of all, I'm through with him and I won't give him the satisfaction of hearing me cry. [*Lying down on the bed*] Besides, he's liable to call the cops or something.

IGOR: [*Giving up*] Okay. Nine A.M.

TONI: [*Getting herself comfortable and covering herself with blanket*] Thanks, Igor, You're sweet. Will you turn on the radio? It's too quiet in here.

IGOR: [*Walking towards radio and looking at card*] Say, what will I tell this guy?

TONI: Just tell him I'm alive.

IGOR: Oh, great. [*Turns on radio. Rock 'n' roll music is heard*] That's all? [*Touches her; she's asleep*] Okay, kid, sleep. You need it. [*Crosses towards door, stops momentarily and pantomimes talking into imaginary telephone*] "Hello, Dr. Winston. I have very upsetting news for you Toni is alive." [*He goes*]

BLACKOUT

SCENE TWO

Dr. Julian Winston's office. Nine o'clock. The main part of the set will be the reception room. Center is the desk of Stephanie Dickinson, Dr. Winston's secretary-assistant. On her desk is a small cactus plant, among the other things that a dentist's assistant might have on her desk. Telephone, etc. Among the details that are planned for the office are a large stereo-hi-fi built into the wall. It's playing music. On the walls are several modern paintings. Upstage right is the door of Dr. Winston's working office or the operating room. Every time the door of this office opens, we will get a strong flare of fluorescent light. STEPHANIE *enters from the operating room.* STEPHANIE *is the completely efficient nurse. She's dressed in a white uniform, low-heeled shoes, very little make up. She walks to the desk and picks up mail, looks through it quickly. Phone rings. She goes to the stereo, turns down the sound. The music keeps playing, but at a much lower level. She crosses back to the phone and picks it up and answers it. When* STEPHANIE *speaks, her voice is soft, soothing, yet impersonal. Her voice, plus the soft music, creates an effect that is supposed to be very soothing for the patients.*

STEPHANIE: Hello, Dr. Winston's office ... Oh, good morning, Mrs. Andrews ... Well, let me see. [*She sits. She riffles the appointment book*] I'm afraid I have nothing open for the next two weeks. I can squeeze you in a week from Thursday, the twenty-seventh, at nine-fifteen, Friday the twenty-eighth at four-thirty, or Monday the thirty-first at ... Oh, well, as long as you're in pain, make it a week from Thursday. That'll be nine-fifteen, and, remember, the doctor insists on punctuality. Thank you. [*Hangs up. Starts going through some mail on her desk. She goes through the letters quickly, comes to one that stops her. She looks at it with interest*] Hhmmmmmmmmmm. "Personal and confidential." [*Phone rings as she says the above. She picks it up*] Hello, Dr. Winston's office. . . . Who's calling? . . . Igor Sullivan? Is it about an appointment? . . . I'm sorry, Mr. Sullivan, you can't talk to the doctor now. He's with a patient. If you'll just give me the message. . . . [*Doorbell chimes*] Well, if you insist on speaking to him personally, you'll have to call back later. [*Doorbell chimes*] I have to go now.

> [*She hangs up, goes to door to admit* MRS. DIXON DURANT, *a society matron. She is carrying a lighted cigarette*]

MRS. DURANT: A caramel. One lousy caramel, and the whole damned filling came out!

STEPHANIE: [*Follows her, picks up ash tray and holds it for* MRS. DURANT'S *ashes*] Mrs. Durant, it was only a temporary filling and you were warned to be careful. Caramels! [*Puts ash tray on desk*]

MRS. DURANT: [*Stamping out cigarette in tray*] Good God, I've given up everything else! Where's the doctor?

STEPHANIE: He'll see you in a moment, Mrs. Durant. Since you were delayed, he gave your time to another patient who was on time.

MRS. DURANT: [*Annoyed*] Just because I'm a minute late—

STEPHANIE: [*Sweetly*] Twenty minutes, Mrs. Durant. [*Indicating waiting room*] Now if you'll just wait out here. . . .

MRS. DURANT: Please hurry the doctor. I must be through in half an hour. Charles will be waiting.

STEPHANIE: Charles?

MRS. DURANT: Mr. Charles. The hairdresser. Today he's taking care of me personally. I can't keep him waiting.

STEPHANIE: Really, Mrs. Durant, your teeth are more important than your hair.

MRS. DURANT: [*Looking at her for a moment*] You really think that, don't you? How sad.

> [*She goes into waiting room.* STEPHANIE *is thrown by this for a moment, reaches up and touches her hair. She closes door, crosses back to desk and sits. The door of the operating room opens. We hear* JULIAN'S VOICE]

JULIAN'S VOICE: That's all for now, Harvey. Get your coat on.

> [JULIAN *enters. He starts making a few notes on a card he takes from his pocket*]

STEPHANIE: Mrs. Durant is here. Ate a caramel, lost her filling.

JULIAN: Serves her right. [*Puts card down*] Mr. Greenfield will be out in a minute. Give him the same appointment next week.

STEPHANIE: [*Crossing to file with card*] Doctor, I've been meaning to speak to you about Mr. Greenfield's bills.

JULIAN: Miss Dickinson, you know he's an old friend of mine.

STEPHANIE: Well, I think he's taking advantage of you.

JULIAN: Miss Dickinson, there are some things a man just can't do. I won't push Harvey for money. I've known him too long. You do it.

STEPHANIE: I'll be happy to. [*Sits at desk*]

>   [HARVEY GREENFIELD *enters from operating room, carrying his jacket. He crosses to* JULIAN]

JULIAN: Well, Harvey, how does your mouth feel?

HARVEY: My mouth feels fine. My teeth hurt.

JULIAN: Oh, that'll go away in three or four days.

HARVEY: [*Putting on jacket*] Thanks, Hey! Been a lot of changes since I was last here. Very classy.

JULIAN: Oh, a few changes. New furniture, sound proofing, a few new paintings.

HARVEY: [*Going to stereo*] What's that? Looks like a jet cockpit.

JULIAN: It's stereo. Music has become a very important part of modern dental therapy. It's very soothing to the dentist.

HARVEY: At your prices you can afford Heifetz in person. [*Reaches up and turns knob on the stereo. Sound blares*]

STEPHANIE: [*Jumping up quickly and turning off stereo*] Mr. Greenfield, that's a very sensitive instrument.

HARVEY: [*Cutting in and retreating a bit*] All right, all right! I hardly touched it. But I do have the right, if I so wish. After all, as a patient I pay for that thing. I really do.

STEPHANIE: You really should. [*Sits*]

HARVEY: Julian, I feel insulted. It isn't as if I'm planning to stick you.

JULIAN: It isn't as if you were planning to *pay* me, either.

HARVEY: Well, I figure you make it up on your other patients.

STEPHANIE: Mrs. Durant is waiting, Doctor.

HARVEY: [*Quickly*] Mrs. Durant?

JULIAN: Mrs. Dixon Durant. Frozen foods.

HARVEY: Boy, I'll bet you soak her plenty!

JULIAN: Ssshhhhh. Even with the sound proofing . . .

STEPHANIE: [*Rising*] Doctor, I don't think you should keep Mrs. Durant waiting. I'll make the room ready.

JULIAN: Good.

STEPHANIE: [*Looking at her watch as she crosses to operating room door*] You're already running very late today. *Very* late. [*She goes into operating room*]

HARVEY: That dame makes me feel like I'm back with the Seabees.

JULIAN: She is very efficient.

HARVEY: [*Tone of disgust*] Come on. I always figured you'd have a nurse who was a . . . *nurse*. You're Julian Winston. Bachelor, connoisseur—

JULIAN: [*Cutting in*] Harvey, Miss Dickinson is my assistant for the very reasons you complain about. She's like a wife, a good wife . . . devoted, efficient, takes care of all my needs . . . during the day! And at night she goes home, to *her* home. And I, with no cares, no problems, go to my girl. My life is arranged the way I like it. [*Sits on desk*]

HARVEY: [*Sudden take, crossing to* JULIAN] Hey, did you say "your girl"?

JULIAN: Yes.

HARVEY: Did you use the singular—?

JULIAN: Yeah.

HARVEY: Girl? One girl?

JULIAN: Didn't I tell you? It's been a year now.

HARVEY: But you— you're Julian Winston. Captain of the basketball team. Track star. A different girl every night. Boy, how we guys on the debating team used to envy you!

JULIAN: You guys talked too much.

HARVEY: All those girls . . . Marie. . . .

JULIAN: Mmmmmm.

HARVEY: Sally . . . Frank—

JULIAN: Frank?

HARVEY: Sally's brother. He nearly killed you. Boy, you managed to duck out on all of them.

JULIAN: [*Rises, puts arm around* HARVEY] Harvey, I find your hero worship very sweet, but Toni has changed all that. I don't want anyone else.

HARVEY: Julian, with a little moral courage, that sort of illness can be fought.

JULIAN: Tried to fight it. Take last night. I cancelled a date with Toni and I deliberately made a date with another girl. An airline stewardess. Spectacular looking. A Swedish blonde. Tall. Built. We went to her place, we had a few drinks . . .

HARVEY: [*Excited*] Yeah?

STEPHANIE: [*Re-enters from operating room*] The room is ready. I'll get Mrs. Durant. [*Starting for waiting room*]

JULIAN: Good. [*He crosses below* STEPHANIE *and starts towards operating room*]

HARVEY: [*Turns, finds himself confronting* STEPHANIE *by mistake*] You can't leave me hanging!

[STEPHANIE *opens door.* MRS. DURANT *hurries in. Her manner in the presence of* DR. WINSTON *is subdued and penitent*]

MRS. DURANT: Dr. Winston, I'm so sorry I was late.

JULIAN: [*A real bedside manner*] Oh, that's all right, dear lady, however . . . [*He takes her hands*] I hear we've been very naughty . . . caramels!

MRS. DURANT: [*Looking accusingly at* STEPHANIE] You told.

STEPHANIE: It's my job.

MRS. DURANT: I only had one.

JULIAN: One too many. You know, Mrs. Durant, outside of the fact that they're bad for your teeth, [*He spreads her arms wide*] think how caramels can hurt those splendid hips.

MRS. DURANT: [*to* HARVEY] Is he your dentist?

HARVEY: [*Nodding*] Great, isn't he?

MRS. DURANT: Great. He's a magnificent dentist, but he would have made a simply marvelous obstetrician.

> [*She goes into operating room, followed by* STEPHANIE. JULIAN *looks back at* HARVEY]

HARVEY: Obstetrician!

JULIAN: [*Rubbing his hands together*] Hot water! Plenty of hot water! [*He starts for the operating room*]

HARVEY: Wait a minute, Julian, you didn't finish with the stewardess. What happened?

JULIAN: [*Stops*] Nothing.

HARVEY: Nothing?

JULIAN: Toni stopped me.

HARVEY: Toni? She showed up?

JULIAN: In my mind. I suddenly thought of her . . . saw her face. . . . I couldn't shake it. . . . I got up and left. Walked out.

HARVEY: You mean you wasted a whole stewardess? With the world full of so many hungry guys?

JULIAN: I'm not going to romance a different girl every night just to make you happy.

HARVEY: You're going to get married.

JULIAN: Married? [*Grabbing him by the lapels*] Who said anything about getting married?

HARVEY: Well, if you feel that way about your girl . . .

JULIAN: I feel that way *because* she's my girl. You'd never catch me feeling that way about a wife. Do you think I'm crazy? I have a wonderful office, a wonderful practice, and a wonderful girl. Marriage would ruin all that.

HARVEY: That's a very healthy outlook. But what about her?

JULIAN: No problem.

HARVEY: Girls want to get . . . [*Does wedding walk across room*]

JULIAN: Not Toni Simmons. She thinks I'm already married.

HARVEY: Julian. You pulled that old stunt on her?

JULIAN: I've never done it before, but this time I had to. When I first set eyes on Toni I knew this was the one. She could make me do anything.

HARVEY: It's scary.

JULIAN: She could change this whole pleasant life of mine. So . . . I told her I had a wife and three children.

HARVEY: The three children is a nice touch.

JULIAN: And I told it to her right away. Five minutes after we met—so that everything between us would be open and aboveboard.

HARVEY: Very good. Very good. It's such a big dirty rotten lie that it has class.

JULIAN: Thanks! [JULIAN *starts for operating room.* HARVEY *stops him*]

HARVEY: By the way, Julian, I too am having trouble with a girl. She's a very beautiful—

STEPHANIE: [*Coming out of operating room, crossing to desk and sitting*] Mrs. Durant is ready for you, Doctor.

JULIAN: See you next week, Harvey.

HARVEY: [*Indignantly, grabbing* JULIAN's *arm, stopping him*] Wait a minute! I listened to you about *your* girl. Let me tell you about *mine.*

STEPHANIE: Doctor—

HARVEY: I need some help.

JULIAN: [*Impatiently*] But, Harvey, I—

HARVEY: [*Going on*] She's beautiful . . . think of Botticelli's Springtime. Great figure—

JULIAN: Uh huh.

HARVEY: Beautiful eyes—

JULIAN: Uh huh. But her teeth need work.

HARVEY: They overlap a little, and I promised her that—

STEPHANIE: Doctor . . . Mrs. Durant—

JULIAN: You've pulled this before.

HARVEY: Julian—

JULIAN: [*Giving up*] Oh, send her around and I'll see what I can do. But don't you know any girls with straight teeth? [*He goes into operating room*]

> [STEPHANIE *is working on her appointment book. She ignores* HARVEY *completely. He turns to her*]

HARVEY: [*Approaching* STEPHANIE *carefully*] Excuse me, Sergeant, uh, Miss Dickinson, Dr. Winston said I was to make an appointment for a lady friend of mine.

STEPHANIE: [*Trying to get rid of him quickly*] How about two weeks from Wednesday at seven A.M.

HARVEY: You're kidding. I'm asleep at seven A.M.

STEPHANIE: I thought the appointment was for a lady.

HARVEY: That's right. We're both asleep at seven A.M. [*He chuckles, then quickly*] I'm sorry. I hope I'm not shocking you.

STEPHANIE: No, but it must be a terrible shock for her. Incidentally, who's paying for the treatment?

HARVEY: [*Picks up hat on seat by door*] Put it on my tab.

STEPHANIE: There's no more room on your tab.

HARVEY: [*Cutting in*] I'll take care of it. It's just that right now I'm between employment.

STEPHANIE: You know, Mr. Greenfield, I've never known what your employment is.

HARVEY: I'm an actor.

STEPHANIE: An actor?

HARVEY: Why do you look so startled? [*Growing a little annoyed, crossing back to* STEPHANIE] Haven't you ever seen me on television?

STEPHANIE: I'm sorry, Mr.—

HARVEY: Come on, Miss Dickinson, you must have seen me.

STEPHANIE: No, I swear it.

HARVEY: [*Refusing to believe*] Everyone has seen my big hit. You know, woman is in the kitchen crying, her washing machine won't work. Then I walk in, carrying a little tool kit, and I say ... [*Commercial voice*] "Madam, your problem is an overabundance of suds. Try Slosho. It contains Hexosloshinol to slosh those suds away." [*Posing as though holding a bottle*] "Slosho." You never saw that?

STEPHANIE: I hate myself for missing it.

HARVEY: What about the appointment for my girl?

STEPHANIE: How about Thursday the fourth and five-thirty in the afternoon? Or is that too early?

HARVEY: We'll set the alarm. [*He goes*]

[JULIAN *enters from operating room, turns and speaks to* MRS. DURANT, *whom we don't see*]

JULIAN: Mrs. Durant, that will be set in a moment. Don't move and please keep your mouth open. [*He goes to* STEPHANIE] Next patient here yet?

STEPHANIE: Not yet. You know, you'll have no time to go out for lunch. So I've prepared something.

JULIAN: Thank you.

STEPHANIE: I made some of your favorite sandwiches—chicken and egg salad.

JULIAN: Again?

STEPHANIE: You always like them.

JULIAN: I guess I do.

STEPHANIE: It's your sister's birthday today. I sent an azalea plant with your card on it.

JULIAN: [*Looks at her*] She likes roses.

STEPHANIE: I know, but they were much too expensive. [*She hands him envelope*] And this came for you—"Personal and Confidential." [JULIAN *walks over, takes letter and starts to open it*] And, Doctor, your tailor has called several times. You simply must find time to get in for fittings.

JULIAN: Okay, okay, okay. I'll try.

STEPHANIE: You always say that. I can't very well go in your place, any more than I can go to the barber for you, which, by the way, you could use as well.

JULIAN: Yes, yes!

STEPHANIE: I'm sorry if I annoy you.

JULIAN: [*As he reads the letter*] Oh God!

STEPHANIE: What's wrong, Doctor?

JULIAN: [*Taking off white coat, he goes into closet*] I have to go out for a moment.

STEPHANIE: [*Rising*] What about Mrs. Durant?

JULIAN: [*Off, his voice rising*] I tell you I have to go!

STEPHANIE: Dr. Winston, please explain it calmly to me.

JULIAN: [*Off*] Miss Dickinson, I have nothing to explain to you.

STEPHANIE: What will I say to the patients?

JULIAN: [*Reappears in suit jacket, heads for door*] Whatever you want. Get out of it somehow. Oh, God, I hope I don't get there too late. [*Hurries to door, followed by* STEPHANIE]

STEPHANIE: Doctor, I know that letter came from a woman. Really, if your girl friends start coming before your patients—

JULIAN: [*Opens door, turns back to her*] Miss Dickinson, shut up!

STEPHANIE: [*Shocked*] Doctor, you've never said that to me before.

JULIAN: Remind me to say it more often. [*He goes*]

STEPHANIE: Doctor— [*She is really shaken. Phone rings. She crosses to desk, picks up phone*] Hello, Dr. Winston's office. . . . No, he's not here. Now look, Mr. Sullivan, if you have a message for the doctor, you had better give it to me. . . . What? Toni is alive? But who is Toni? Hello . . . Hello? . . . [*She hangs up phone*]

> [MRS. DURANT *comes running out of the operating room. She is covered with all the stuff dentists put on you and her mouth is still open, according to the doctor's instructions. Her cheeks are packed with stuff and when she speaks, she speaks through all this. Just sounds come out*]

MRS. DURANT: Where's the doctor?

> [STEPHANIE *waves off* MRS. DURANT. *The music blasts out loudly*]

BLACKOUT

Toni's apartment. We light up on TONI *sitting at the table, eating potato chips, drinking Coke and leafing through a magazine. Rock 'n' roll music is coming from radio. The door bursts open.* JULIAN *enters, doesn't see* TONI.

JULIAN: [*Looking for her*] Toni! Toni! You all right?

TONI: [*Calmly*] I didn't know dentists made house calls.

JULIAN: I knew it, I knew it, I knew it! Anyway, I should have known it. As a matter of fact, I did know it.

TONI: Know what?

JULIAN: That you wouldn't do it. [*He goes to radio, turns it off*]

TONI: I almost did. But then I had somebody phone you and say I didn't.

JULIAN: Nobody phoned me. All I got was the letter. A whole day full of appointments, twenty patients coming, and you send a letter that you're going to kill yourself and then you don't.

TONI: Well, I'm sorry to disappoint you.

JULIAN: The whole thing was a fake, wasn't it?

TONI: Everything's a fake, Julian, including our love affair. There's no room for *me* in your life.

JULIAN: Toni, this doesn't sound like you.

TONI: I know. I must always be sweet ... fun ... accept everything with a smile, even when you break a date at the last minute.

JULIAN: Now we're getting to it. You mean all this is because I broke one lousy little date? It happens I had a meeting last night with a Swedish dentist. We were talking shop. [*He moves to her, tries to take her hands*] Oh, sweetheart, why do we try to hurt each other?

TONI: [*She stops him with a hand gesture*] Don't, Julian, I've made a decision. We're through.

JULIAN: Through? What are you talking about? We're so happy together.

TONI: We are?

JULIAN: Well, I'm happy together.

TONI: [*Rises*] I'm fed up. When I love, it's all or nothing. I want a man of my own. For me alone. [*Going to kitchen cabinet and getting shopping bag*] So here, I packed your pajamas and your cough syrup and your slippers and your robe— [*Throws it at him*]

JULIAN: Stop it, Toni! [*He tosses the bag behind bed. There is a knock on the door*] Here everything was going so smoothly.

[JULIAN *opens the door.* IGOR *stands in the entrance with a paper bag in his hand.* TONI *sits at table again*]

IGOR: I brought Toni some fruit.

JULIAN: [*Taking fruit*] Thanks. [*Starts to close door*]

TONI: Wait a minute, that's Igor.

IGOR: I didn't know you had company.

TONI: It's only Julian.

> [JULIAN *has been looking at him very coldly*]

IGOR: Oh, hello, Dr. Winston. I'm Igor Sullivan. [*Takes back bag of fruit*] I just spoke to your nurse on the telephone.

JULIAN: [*Coldly*] Something wrong with your teeth?

IGOR: [*Smiling*] No, I just called to tell you that Toni was alive and you didn't have to worry about her letter.

JULIAN: [*Stunned*] Alive?

IGOR: Feeling all right, Toni? [*He puts fruit in refrigerator*]

TONI: Oh, fine.

IGOR: I'll stop by later this evening, anyway, just to make sure you've turned off the gas.

JULIAN: [*Startled*] The gas?

IGOR: The gas. [*He goes*]

TONI: The gas.

JULIAN: The gas. [*He has been standing there, feeling miserable*] Toni, I'm a bastard.

TONI: Now, Julian—

JULIAN: [*Sits. Going on*] A real bastard—

TONI: Please—

JULIAN: You really *did* try to kill yourself! And because of me.

TONI: I saw no other way out.

JULIAN: I'm a bastard. The biggest bastard in the whole world.

TONI: Julian, please, you're starting to make it sound like bragging. [*She rises and stands directly behind him*] It wasn't really your fault. I knew what I was getting into. You've always told me the truth.

JULIAN: I should have kept my mouth shut.

TONI: You couldn't, Julian. You're a decent guy. And that's why I've loved you. And now I'm returning you to your wife and children, and I hope you will be very happy. [*Making motion as though hitting him in back of head*]

JULIAN: No, Toni, no! It's going to be all right with us. I'm going to make up for everything.

TONI: Oh, I know how it will be. We'll go to Easthampton for a weekend . . . we'll be happy. [*Sits on bed*] Then I'll get another one of your cancellations and I'll feel worse than before.

JULIAN: [*Rises*] No, Toni, no weekends. I'm talking about a whole lifetime. Toni, I'm going to marry you.

TONI: What do you mean, "marry"?

JULIAN: You know, "Do you? I do. Do I? You do." . . . Marry. Right away.

TONI: What about your wife?

JULIAN: My wife? I'll divorce her.

TONI: What about your children?

JULIAN: I'll divorce them, too.

TONI: Julian, this isn't funny.

JULIAN: I'm very serious. I should've thought of this long ago. Oh, baby, when I think you were ready to die because of me. [*Sits by her on bed*]

TONI: Then you really do love me, Julian?

JULIAN: [*Tenderly*] Are you just now finding it out?

    [*They embrace*]

TONI: [*Pulling away*] Julian, not now.

JULIAN: [*Unhearing*] I'm crazy about you.

TONI: [*Rises*] Not now.

JULIAN: Why not now?

TONI: [*Points*] Igor is right next door . . . he can hear everything.

JULIAN: Igor's been right next door before.

TONI: But I hadn't met him then.

JULIAN: [*Rises*] The sooner we move you out of here, the better. Soon you'll be Mrs. Julian Winston . . . [*Goes to her, puts his arms around her, holds her head against his shoulder with his right hand*] "Mrs. Julian Winston." Imagine that. Me, a married man. [*She is startled and lifts her head. He quickly pushes it back on his shoulder*] I mean, me, married to you.

TONI: [*Breaking loose*] Julian, what will become of her? Your wife.

JULIAN: [*Walking away in annoyance*] Why do we keep talking about my wife?

TONI: You'll have to make some arrangement about her. What do you figure on doing?

JULIAN: Simple. [*Snaps fingers*] Hup. Out!

TONI: Is that what you'll say when you tire of me? [*Snaps fingers*] "Hup. out"?

JULIAN: Toni, this is different. I love you. My wife and I . . . why, I never even knew her.

TONI: How did the three children come, United Parcel?

JULIAN: Well, at the beginning I was polite. [*Sits on bed. Reaches for her hand. She pulls away*] Don't worry about my wife. She'll be taken care of.

TONI: What if she refuses to give you a divorce?

JULIAN: She wouldn't dare. Let's forget her. [*Keeps reaching for her*]

TONI: I can't, I can't. The thought of breaking up a home sort of spoils things.

JULIAN: [*Rising*] I never thought you'd be like this. I think of you as so happy and carefree. [*He does a little happy movement with his hands and feet*]

TONI: [*Imitating his movement*] You don't really know me. I may do a lot of strange things . . . bad things . . . but I have standards.

JULIAN: [*Pacing in thought*] What if . . . Toni, I haven't wanted to go into this, but what if . . . what if, it's my *wife* who wants the divorce?

TONI: Oh, God, you mean she found out about us?

JULIAN: Let's just say she wants the divorce, too.

TONI: [*Thoughtfully*] Well, if that's true. . . .

JULIAN: [*Going to her and taking her hands*] It is! It is!

TONI: [*Looks at him*] Julian, in that case, I'd be proud to marry you.

JULIAN: Oh, darling! [*Embraces her*]

TONI: [*Breaking away*] But there is one thing you've got to do for me.

JULIAN: [*Holding her hands in a wide expansive gesture*] Anything, darling, anything.

TONI: I'd like to meet her.

JULIAN: Who? [*Suddenly*] My wife? [*He starts to pull away.* TONI *hangs onto his left hand. He crosses right, dragging* TONI *with him during the following*]

TONI: Yes. I'd like to get things straight with her.

JULIAN: Oh, come on, Toni.

TONI: [*Doggedly*] I want her to tell me herself that she wants to leave you.

JULIAN: [*Breaking free*] She does! Have I ever lied to you?

TONI: [*Going right on.*] It's very important to me that she doesn't think of me as some evil homewrecker. I don't want to have to hide every time I see her somewhere. [*Sits on bed*] Julian, if I don't meet her, we'll never have a happy day together.

JULIAN: But. . . .

TONI: [*Reaching her hand to him*] Oh, baby—

JULIAN: [*Sits on bed. Melting*] Oh, baby. . . .

[*They embrace*]

TONI: You'll arrange for us to meet, won't you, Julian?

JULIAN: [*Right now he'd promise anything*] Yes, Yes, honey. I'll arrange it.

[*Just before the lights are all out, we hear* TONI]

TONI: [*Very firm again*] Julian . . .

JULIAN: [*Sleepy-sounding*] Yes, Toni, dear.

TONI: [*Deadly sure*] I want to meet her.

JULIAN: Don't worry, You'll meet her.

BLACKOUT

SCENE FOUR

Dr. Winston's office. STEPHANIE *is at her desk. It's the afternoon of the same day.* STEPHANIE *is not at the moment the efficient, hard-working nurse that we saw at the beginning of the play. There are no patients around, no phone calls, her work is evidently all done and she is quite impatient. She sits there tapping a pencil and waiting. The door chime rings. She rises, goes to door and opens it.*

STEPHANIE: Come in, Señor Sanchez.

[SEÑOR ARTURO SANCHEZ *enters. He is a well-dressed South American. He looks tense and worried*]

SANCHEZ: [*His English is fairly good with a pleasant Spanish accent*] The doctor . . . he is waiting?

STEPHANIE: [*Closes door*] I tried to phone you at the U.N. but you had already left.

SANCHEZ: [*The fact is, he's scared*] I was given an appointment for five o'clock.

STEPHANIE: I know, but the doctor had to go out this morning and he hasn't returned. He can't keep the appointment.

SANCHEZ: [*Straightens up and suddenly happy and blooming*] Oh, really. Well, isn't that too bad! [*By now he is positively beaming*]

STEPHANIE: [*The reproving, motherly nurse*] You know, Señor Sanchez, I would say you sound relieved. [*Sanchez chuckles*] You're not afraid of Dr. Winston? He's very gentle.

SANCHEZ: [*Puts down hat, goes to her*] It's funny. . . . I'm not by nature a coward. In my country I'm known as "El Bravo."

STEPHANIE: [*Acting impressed, sits*] "El Bravo"! Wow!

SANCHEZ: I've been through six bloody revolutions. I've played a whole game of polo with a broken leg. I have sat in my seat at the United Nations and, without flinching, I have listened to ten full-length Cuban speeches. But dentists. . . . [*Shakes his head*]

STEPHANIE: [*Soothingly*] I'll give you an appointment for next week.

SANCHEZ: No hurry. [STEPHANIE *looks in appointment book*] You can make it next year. [*Small laugh*] I'm really not a coward. [*He takes her hand*]

STEPHANIE: [*Removes hand*] We all have our little weaknesses.

SANCHEZ: [*Takes her hand again*] I have several *big* ones. [STEPHANIE *looks at him a little startled*] You know, my dear, you're very charming . . . and so easy to talk to.

STEPHANIE: [*Removes hand again, picks up pencil*] Graçias, señor. Now, how about—?

SANCHEZ: [*Taking pencil from her hand*] Miss Dickinson, I've been watching you ever since coming here. You are a very attractive woman and yet you try to conceal it.

STEPHANIE: [*Wryly*] Very successfully, I'd say.

SANCHEZ: That uniform doesn't fool me. We Latins have a great eye for hidden beauty. You see, for centuries our women were all covered up—mantillas, long dresses, veils—so in self-defense Latin men had to develop an instinct for guessing what was underneath. [STEPHANIE *takes another pencil*] You are a woman worth knowing.

STEPHANIE: What about next Thursday?

SANCHEZ: Wonderful! Where shall we meet?

STEPHANIE: This is you and Dr. Winston!

SANCHEZ: Oh. But I'd like for us to have dinner together one of these evenings . . . a small dinner . . . candlelight, guitars—

STEHPANIE: [*With a twinkle*] Will you bring along your wife?

SANCHEZ: [*Dead serious*] My WIFE? You wouldn't like her. Nobody likes her. Now let's make it next Thursday after my appointment.

STEPHANIE: [*A bit more sharply*] Señor Sanchez, I can't. You're a married man.

SANCHEZ: I don't understand. If I'm married, that's *my* problem. What has that got to do with you? I would not be prejudiced if *you* were married. [STEPHANIE *writes in book. He sighs*] Americans. . . . [*He picks up hat on chair, opens door, then stops and turns*] I still think you're very attractive. What is your first name?

STEPHANIE: Stephanie. They call me "La Brava."

SANCHEZ: [*Salutes her*] Hasta la vista, La Brava.

STEPHANIE: Hasta la vista.

[JULIAN *enters suddenly through the door.* SANCHEZ *turns, freezes for a moment in fright at sight of* JULIAN]

JULIAN: [*Indicating operating room*] Señor Sanchez! Come, I can take you now.

SANCHEZ: [*Quickly*] I can't take *you* now. [*He scoots out*]

STEPHANIE: Well, you made him happy.

JULIAN: [*Closes door*] I'm glad. Miss Dickinson, I'm sorry I ran out on you this morning.

STEPHANIE: [*Coldly*] I managed.

JULIAN: I knew you would.

STEPHANIE: [*Irritated*] Oh, you knew I would. Well, I didn't know I would. But I did. Everything got straightened out. I told Mrs. Durant some story about your mother being bitten by a tsetse fly or something. [*Very sarcastic*] And I gave new appointments to all the other patients.

JULIAN: I can always count on you in a jam.

STEPHANIE: Thanks, Doctor. [*Rises*] Now, if you don't need me for anything else tonight— [*Phone rings*] Dr. Winston's office.... Is it about an appointment? ... Oh. [*Hands phone to* JULIAN] It's personal. [*She turns away from him*]

JULIAN: [*Into phone*] Hello. [*Moves away from desk*] I'm busy now.... Don't worry, you'll meet her.... 'Bye. [*Hangs up*]

STEPHANIE: I'll just straighten up inside and leave. [*She starts for operating room*]

JULIAN: Miss Dickinson....

STEPHANIE: [*Stops and turns*] Doctor?

JULIAN: Are you in a hurry this evening?

STEPHANIE: Why, no, Doctor. If there's anything I can do for you, I'd be—

JULIAN: Well—

STEPHANIE: —glad to stay.

JULIAN: I'd like to have a little talk with you.

STEPHANIE: Talk? With me? What about? [*She slowly sits at her desk*]

JULIAN: You know, you and I have worked side by side for years and I've suddenly realized how little I know about you. I really don't know who you are.

STEPHANIE: I'm Stephanie Dickinson. You see me at my desk. I'm out in the open.

JULIAN: But once you leave here at night you ... you do continue to exist? Who is Stephanie Dickinson?

STEPHANIE: Why would you want to know?

JULIAN: Go on. I want to hear. Everything. All about you.

STEPHANIE: This is silly. [*Laughs, pulls dress down*]

JULIAN: No, go ahead.

> [STEPHANIE *thinks for a moment, then begins to talk in the manner of a person discussing something she's never discussed before. Or even thought about. The words will come out fairly slowly and carefully as she goes through her life, item by item*]

STEPHANIE: I live in Jackson Heights.....

JULIAN: Alone?

STEPHANIE: Yes. I mean, no. I live with my mother. We have three rooms, actually three and a half—there's a dining alcove. It's a very big dining alcove so you could really call it four rooms. That's where we keep the television. We like to watch the news when we're eating. I like Walter Cronkite. My mother likes Huntley and Brinkley better. So we don't often watch Walter Cronkite.

> [*There is a long silence.* JULIAN *has been studying her carefully, during this long recital. Now, when the silence happens, he helps her a bit*]

JULIAN: And what do you do after Huntley-Cronkite ... after dinner?

STEPHANIE: I go for a walk with Frieda, my cocker spaniel.

JULIAN: Frieda? That's a hell of a name for a cocker spaniel.

STEPHANIE: Frieda loves it. And some evenings I visit my sister. She and my brother-in-law and I like to play Scrabble.

JULIAN: Scrabble. That's fun.

STEPHANIE: My brother-in-law is very good at it, but he cheats. They have two little boys. I'm very fond of my nephews. On my day off I like to take them to the park or the circus. Other times I go to the movies. I like movies. Foreign movies. Italian. I like Mr. Marcello Mastroianni. He seems very intelligent.

JULIAN: What do you do on your vacation?

STEPHANIE: Ah, that's when I change. I become another person. I saddle up my little MG.

JULIAN: A sports car! Hey!

STEPHANIE: I told you I change in the summer. I break away from everything and go zooming up to Cape Cod.

JULIAN: Alone.

STEPHANIE: No, with my mother. Mother loves the Cape and she's marvelous company. Of course, we also take Frieda.

JULIAN: Naturally.

STEPHANIE: We rent a little cottage by the water. It's part of an artists' colony. Quite Bohemian.

JULIAN: Bohemian! Really wild, huh?

STEPHANIE: Mother wears blue jeans. You ought to see her.

JULIAN: I'd love to. But . . . Miss Dickinson, I've enjoyed hearing about your family and your mother and Frieda. But, what about you . . . your personal life? I mean. . . . [*He gropes for the right word*]

STEPHANIE: [*Calmly*] You mean men?

JULIAN: Yes. What I'd like to know is . . . I don't want to pry. . . . [*A little embarrassed chuckle*]

STEPHANIE: At the moment there are no men in my life.

JULIAN: Ah, you said "at the moment." Then there have been men.

STEPHANIE: Doctor, I'm no sex goddess, but I haven't spent my life in a tree. I was even in love once.

JULIAN: Oh!

STEPHANIE: Astounding, isn't it? But I was. Terribly in love . . . it lasted almost three years. But. . . .

JULIAN: But?

STEPHANIE: He was married.

JULIAN: [*Not thinking*] Him, too?

STEPHANIE: What do you mean, "him, too"?

JULIAN: Nothing. I was thinking of a similar case.

STEPHANIE: [*She looks at him*] Yes, I sent him back to his wife and children. I went out with a couple of other men. Very attractive, but they were married, too. It's strange, Doctor, I seem to be the type that attracts married men. I guess I look safe or something. Frankly, I hadn't planned on being an old maid.

JULIAN: An old maid? You've a long way to go.

STEPHANIE: Yes, but I'm making very fast progress. [*Rises*] Well, I've talked an awful lot, Doctor. I'm afraid I'm going to be late for dinner. [*She starts to go again*]

JULIAN: Miss Dickinson . . .

STEPHANIE: Doctor?

JULIAN: I'm glad we had this little talk. You're a very rare person. Sensitive and generous.

STEPHANIE: [*Modestly*] Oh, I guess I'm all right.

JULIAN: I have a feeling that if I found myself in trouble, I could count on you to be on my side . . . to help me.

STEPHANIE: [*She puts left knee on her chair and very earnestly leans toward* JULIAN] You *know* that's true, Doctor.

JULIAN: But sometimes a problem comes up that's so difficult that. . . . [*He's stuck*]

STEPHANIE: Why don't you try me?

[*He looks into her eyes momentarily, then starts to move away.* STEPHANIE *is watching him intently. Her knee is still on the chair and she's leaning forward on the desk*]

JULIAN: You could do me a great service. Miss Dickinson, I'm greatly in need . . . of a wife.

[*As he says the word "wife,"* STEPHANIE's *chair slides from under her and she falls forward on the desk. This is a quick fall. She catches herself with her arms and recovers quickly*]

STEPHANIE: A wife! Doctor, I . . . [*She is tremendously flustered. She straightens her desk, puts on her glasses*] I . . . this is something I never expected. Wife!

JULIAN: [*Suddenly realizing what she thinks*] Oh, please understand something. . . . I need a wife temporarily . . . fifteen or twenty minutes.

STEPHANIE: [*Dazed*] Fifteen or twenty . . .

JULIAN: I'm telling this all very badly. Miss Dickinson, I want someone to play the part of my wife.

STEPHANIE: [*Suddenly stonefaced*] Someone like me.

JULIAN: [*Going to her*] If you only would. It wouldn't involve any . . . uh . . . All you'd have to do is to tell a certain person that you want a divorce. [*Moving away again*] You see, Miss Dickinson, I've suddenly decided to get married. [*He stops and turns*] Oh, I didn't tell you.

STEPHANIE: [*Quickly*] No, you didn't.

JULIAN: Well, I have.

STEPHANIE: Congratulations.

JULIAN: Thanks. But the girl I want to marry—her name is Toni Simmons—

STEPHANIE: How do you do?

JULIAN: She thinks I'm already married.

STEPHANIE: [*Ironically*] Now, whoever could have told her that?

JULIAN: At the time I had my reasons. I'll straighten it out later on. But right now I've got to dig up a wife. [*Going back to her*]

STEPHANIE: [*Takes glasses off*] Right now stop digging and tell the girl the truth. Good night. [*She starts to go*]

JULIAN: I can't tell her now. She's liable to . . . she's so . . . so young. She has suffered from so many unfortunate episodes. I'm the first decent man she's ever known.

STEPHANIE: Are you quoting her or you?

JULIAN: Toni's a very sensitive girl. Won't marry me till she meets my wife. She doesn't want to be a homewrecker. Isn't that sweet?

STEPHANIE: Just darling.

JULIAN: [*Goes to desk, takes pencil and writes address on a pad*] She works at the Village L.P., and if you'd just go to see her and—

STEPHANIE: I'm sorry, Doctor, but I loathe lies.

JULIAN: No more than I do, Miss Dickinson, no more than I. [*Throws pencil down*] But I don't know how to get out of this one. Miss Dickinson, you hold my happiness in your two hands. [*Extending hands*]

STEPHANIE: [*Extending hands, faces him*] Doctor, for many years these two hands of mine that now hold your happiness, have only handled your surgical instruments and your appointment book. You've managed to handle your happiness without any help from me. Now you want to use me in this disgusting way. You just tricked me into talking about myself so I'd break down and. . . . [*She's getting a little shaky. Takes tissue from box on desk*] What you did wasn't very pretty, Doctor— [*She goes into operating room*]

JULIAN: [*Left alone*] You can't get decent help these days.

BLACKOUT

SCENE FIVE

The L.P. Record Shop in the Village. It's afternoon a few days later. We hear some music playing in the back of the shop. TONI *is putting records on a shelf. Music stops. A* MAN *comes on carrying a few records which he has evidently been trying out.*

MAN: I don't like any of these. [*Hands her the records*]

TONI: Too bad.

MAN: What have you got there?

TONI: Albinoni.

MAN: Oh, I like him. I'll try it. [*Takes record*]

TONI: Hey, you've been playing records all day. Why don't you ever *buy* one?

MAN: I'm a music lover. [*He goes*]

> [TONI *looks at the pile of records with a sigh, starts putting them away on the top shelf.* STEPHANIE *enters from the street door. Actually, it's her first change of clothes in the play. She's wearing a very attractive suit and very smart hat and shoes. She carries gloves and a good looking purse. As she comes in, she spots* TONI *and looks her over*]

TONI: [*From the ladder*] May I help you, Madam?

STEPHANIE: [*Every inch the upper middle class lady*] I'm really not looking for anything in particular. I just thought I'd browse a bit.

TONI: Fine. I'm here if you want me.

STEPHANIE: I've heard there's a marvelous recording of uh . . . [*Trying to think of something*] of Horowitz's last concert. Do you have it?

TONI: Horowitz? We're all out, but I can send it to you.

STEPHANIE: That will be fine. I believe my husband has a charge account here. Send the record to . . . [*Laying it on*] Mrs. . . . Julian . . . Winston.

> [TONI *has been putting records away as she talks. Now when she hears* JULIAN's *name, she misses the shelf with a record and it drops*]

TONI: [*Coming down ladder and crossing to* STEPHANIE] You?

STEPHANIE: [*Nodding*] Me.

TONI: You didn't come on account of Horowitz?

STEPHANIE: No. You see, Miss Simmons—

TONI: Call me Toni.

STEPHANIE: [*Graciously*] Thank you. Toni . . . Dr. Winston, my husband, said that you were most anxious to meet me. Well, here I am. [*She sits and crosses her legs*]

TONI: [*After a moment, a bit impatiently*] Did he . . . did he tell you about his—*our* plans?

STEPHANIE: [*Same gracious smile*] The divorce? Naturally.

TONI: [*After another pause*] Well?

STEPHANIE: Well what?

TONI: You don't mind?

STEPHANIE: My husband and I are in complete agreement about the divorce.

TONI: [*Letting out a sharp breath of relief*] Whew! That makes me very happy!

STEPHANIE: [*As sweetly as possible*] I'm glad.

TONI: You see, Mrs. Winston— [*Sudden thought*] You know, I don't know your first name.

STEPHANIE: [*Thinks for a moment*] Mrs. Winston will do very nicely. Of course, I won't be Mrs. Winston very much longer. [*There is a slight touch of real and fake sadness in that last phrase*]

TONI: [*Suddenly*] Then you *do* mind.

STEPHANIE: Of course I don't. Things between the doctor and me have become . . . impossible.

TONI: I can't tell you how *good* that makes me feel.

STEPHANIE: [*Looking at her with a smile*] I've really made your day.

TONI: It's just that I didn't want to be the cause of your divorce. I never pushed Julian into it. I am no homewrecker.

STEPHANIE: I'll remember that. [*Rises, speaks gravely*] Now, Toni, may I ask you a question?

TONI: Anything.

STEPHANIE: Are you absolutely sure you love Julian?

TONI: You *can't* ask *that!*

STEPHANIE: I just did. Do you love him?

TONI: Madly! Wildly! Desperately!

STEPHANIE: Just so long as you're fond of him. I don't want him to end up unhappy and bitter.

TONI: Oh, I understand, especially after he's just had such a terrible marriage.

STEPHANIE: [*Stiffening*] Not so terrible! Our marriage, after all, lasted ten years and we still have a very deep respect for each other.

TONI: Of course.

STEPHANIE: I've always had to look after Dr. Winston, my husband. You know, aside from his profession, at which he's a master, the doctor is a very vulnerable man. An idealist . . . a child . . . a silly child . . . damned silly child.

TONI: Also an adorable child.

STEPHANIE: I guess you *do* love him. Well, now that you've heard what you wanted to hear, I'll be running along. [*Holds out her hand to* TONI. TONI *takes it*] I do hope you have better luck with Julian than I did.

TONI: Mrs. Winston. . . . What about you? What are you going to do?

STEPHANIE: Forget about me. I'll ride off into the sunset . . . or something.

TONI: It's just that . . . I want to be sure you're all right.

STEPHANIE: I'll write you every day. [*She starts for street door*]

TONI: [*Hurrying after her and stopping her*] Mrs. Winston, who's going to tell the children?

STEPHANIE: [*Stopping dead. No one has told her about this*] The children. The children.

TONI: It's going to be tough explaining such a horrible thing to those three little children.

STEPHANIE: [*Pulling herself together*] Three. We will have to tell the children ... Three. [*Thinking rapidly*] I'll tell them. Julian's no good at that sort of thing.

TONI: How will they take it?

STEPHANIE: Oh, they'll get used to it. At least now I'll be able to devote myself to them full time. I'm afraid, I haven't been a very good mommy because I've spent so much time with Julian, helping him with his work. [*Catches herself*] Of course, he does have a nurse.

TONI: I know. I hear Miss Dickinson is marvelous.

STEPHANIE: She is.

TONI: One of those sterling old maids. Probably madly in love with the boss.

STEPHANIE: Did Julian tell you that?

TONI: No. But the way he described her—

STEPHANIE: How *did* he describe her?

TONI: He didn't really describe her. But once when he was working late, I felt a sudden pang of jealousy about Miss Dickinson, and I told Julian about it and he laughed and laughed. ... [TONI *laughs.* STEPHANIE *responds by laughing rather painfully*] Have you ever been jealous of her?

          [MUSIC BEGINS]

STEPHANIE: No. Besides, any woman who's married to the dashing Dr. Julian Winston had better not be the jealous type. She'd have no time for anything else. I shouldn't be saying this to you.

TONI: It's all right. I know Julian must have played around. But, after all, when a man has a terrible marriage—

STEPANIE: [*Through her teeth*] Don't keep saying that! [*Sudden switch*] I must go. [*She starts*]

TONI: [*Crossing to her and stopping her*] Mrs. Winston, you asked *me* a question about me. Now I want to ask you one ... about you. Are you absolutely sure you don't love him any more?

          [*Music builds*]

STEPHANIE: [*In this speech she gradually works herself into a reverie. She is actually mixed up between fantasy and reality. She speaks softly and dreamily*] Of course, I don't love him any more. But it isn't as simple as that. ... You can't leave a man you've lived with for ten years without a little ... pain. This is a man with whom you've shared all the little things of everyday life ... worrying about his tailor, his barber, making sandwiches for him—he's crazy about chicken and egg salad sandwiches—buy his shirts, shorts, handkerchiefs ... looking after him, thinking for him constantly . . . a man who is all yours. [*Really lost in thought*] Or at least almost all yours. [*Suddenly pulling out of it.*] I don't know what's come over me. I'm talking gibberish. [*Making a joke of it*] It's probably that music. What is it?

TONI: [*She's been caught up in* STEPHANIE'S *recital and now suddenly recovers*] Uh . . . that's Albinoni . . . the adagio.

STEPHANIE: Lovely. I'd like to have it. I'll take it with me now.

TONI: Of course. I have another one up here. [*She hurries up ladder, pulls out the record*] Shall I charge it to Dr. Winston?

STEPHANIE: [*Getting money from purse*] No, I think I'll start paying for things myself.

TONI: I'll give you the same ten percent discount I give Dr. Winston.

STEPHANIE: How nice of you.

TONI: You're entitled to it. That'll be three dollars. Thank you.

STEPHANIE: Thank you, and this time I really must go.

TONI: Mrs. Winston. . . .

STEPHANIE: Yes?

TONI: Mrs. Winston, I want to say . . . well, I can't let you go without telling you that I think you're a gracious, charming, very attractive woman.

STEPHANIE: Thank you, my dear.

BLACKOUT

SCENE SIX

Toni's room. Early evening of the same day. Lights are out. After a beat the door opens. JULIAN *comes bursting through, carrying a bouquet of flowers.*

JULIAN: [*Calling*] Honey . . . Toni. Are you home, baby?

[*There's no answer. He switches on lights. He walks to the kitchen area, looking for something to put the flowers in. He finds a coffee pot and starts stuffing the flowers in. The door opens part way.* IGOR *sticks his head in, then he steps in*]

IGOR: [*Calling out*] Hey, it's me! [*He comes in with no clothes on except for a towel around his middle*] I just wanted to. . . .

[*Stops dead as he sees* JULIAN. *They look at each other for a moment*]

JULIAN: Mr. America?

IGOR: I was runner-up. I'm sorry, sir. I thought I heard Toni come in and . . . I just came in to get my razor. [*Closes door*]

JULIAN: [*Putting flowers on the table*] And why the hell should *your* razor be in here?

IGOR: Toni borrowed it this morning.

JULIAN: Why didn't she use my electric razor? It's here.

IGOR: She's scared of it. And it gives her goose pimples.

JULIAN: You know a lot about Toni, don't you? [*No answer from* IGOR] And why would you come in here looking like that?

IGOR: You want me to get all dressed to shave? Look, sir, I just want to find my razor. I have an early date and I have to shave right away. I'm sorry if I'm annoying you.

JULIAN: How do you expect me to feel towards someone who comes barging in my fiancée's apartment dressed in a loin cloth.

IGOR: [*Bitterly*] Fiancée. Why do you keep kidding her?

JULIAN: Kidding her—?

IGOR: Now look, dentist—

JULIAN: Doctor.

IGOR: Sorry. I know this is none of my business, but why the hell don't you be a sport and get out of the poor little kid's hair? Don't forget, she almost killed herself on account of you. Now you're still feeding her that *fiancée* stuff.

JULIAN: Suppose that fiancée stuff is true?

IGOR: Huh? *Is it?*

JULIAN: [*Nodding*] Toni and I are getting married.

IGOR: [*He is upset and blurts this out*] Why didn't she tell me?

JULIAN: [*Annoyed*] Why should she tell *you?*

[TONI *enters*]

TONI: Hey, Igor. That's a new towel. [*Hangs purse on pole*]

IGOR: [*A bit sullen*] Toni, I just heard the good news. Congratulations.

TONI: Thanks, Igor, but it will take a while yet. [*Looking at* JULIAN] First there's the divorce.

IGOR: [*Perking up a bit*] Oh, so we haven't gotten our divorce yet?

TONI: Well, it's just that—

JULIAN: Toni, this gentleman just came in for his razor. Please get it so we won't have to keep him any longer.

TONI: Oh, sorry, Igor. I should've returned it. [*She hurries into the bath-room*]

IGOR: [*To* JULIAN, *thoughtfully*] So you haven't gotten your divorce yet.

JULIAN: I'd like to have you in my chair for just five minutes.

[TONI *returns, carrying* JULIAN'S *electric razor*]

TONI: I can't find it, Igor.

IGOR: Oh, damn.

TONI: But here's Julian's electric razor. You can use it.

IGOR: I hate electric razors.

JULIAN: Sorry.

IGOR: Automation. [*Makes buzzing sound like a razor. He goes*]

JULIAN: [*To* TONI] While you were at it, why didn't you lend him my toothbrush? By the way, where have you been? It's late.

TONI: [*She hasn't been listening*] Julian, I had a visitor this afternoon.

JULIAN: At the shop?

TONI: [*Nodding*] Your wife.

JULIAN: [*Startled but pleased*] She came?

TONI: You arranged it!

JULIAN: Oh. You see, at first she didn't want to visit you. However, I guess I convinced her. How did it go? All right? [TONI *is silent; she's thinking*] I mean, are you satisfied now?

TONI: Julian, she was magnificent . . . marvelous. Handled herself beautifully. She's a lady.

JULIAN: [*He's been a little puzzled by what he's heard*] Well, I don't marry just anybody . . . Then everything is cleared up?

TONI: [*She lifts her hand to stop him like a traffic cop*] Julian, you've lied to me.

JULIAN: [*Scared*] Never! What did she tell you? I deny it!

TONI: You didn't really lie. Maybe you are unaware of it yourself. Julian, dear, your wife still loves you.

JULIAN: [*After a moment of stunned silence*] Would you mind repeating that?

TONI: I'm telling you your wife still loves you.

JULIAN: [*Shaking his head like a man in shock*] Look, did she or did she not tell you that she agreed to a divorce?

TONI: She did.

JULIAN: [*Satisfied*] There!

TONI: But she'll do anything to make you happy. Julian, she's crazy about you. Anybody can see that.

JULIAN: Toni, let's be calm. Tell me what that damned fool—[*Catching himself. He takes her arms and seats her in chair*] what my wife said.

TONI: It's not what she said, it's what she didn't say.

JULIAN: All right, tell me what she *didn't* say. Word for word.

TONI: It's hard to . . . there was something about her manner . . . for instance, when she talked about you and your barber and your shirts and handkerchiefs . . . I got all choked up. [JULIAN *just stares and shakes his head*] And she talked so sweetly about the chicken and egg salad sandwiches.

JULIAN: She bragged about those goddam sandwiches?

TONI: She didn't brag. She just told me she made them and it sounded as though they were made with love.

JULIAN: They're made with mayonnaise! And too much mayonnaise and the next time she gives me one I'm going to smack her across the mouth with it! [*Sits in chair*]

TONI: [*Rises, crosses to him*] Julian, there's a very cruel streak in you. This fine woman—

JULIAN: [*Cutting in very sharply*] This fine woman! Suddenly you're my wife's lawyer. Look, Toni, I did my part. I did what you asked. You wanted to meet my wife. I arranged it.

TONI: That was a mistake.

JULIAN: That was a mistake, great!

TONI: [*Going on in the same thoughtful fashion, as though she hasn't heard him*] Maybe if I had never met her . . . but I *did* meet her and I liked her. The way you like an older sister. I wanted to protect her . . . especially after I saw her with the children.

JULIAN: [*Startled*] The children. She brought the children?

TONI: [*Indignantly*] Oh, not into the shop. She wouldn't be that indelicate. Julian, you really don't *know* her at all.

JULIAN: Oh boy, that's an understatement.

TONI: [*Crosses to bed, sits*] The children were waiting in the sweet shop across the street. When she left I watched through the window. She bought them each an ice cream cone and then they all left. Incidentally, she didn't bring the little girl, just the two boys.

JULIAN: Two boys. [*Sudden thought*] Must be those damned nephews.

TONI: Nephews? Nonsense! A woman knows when she sees a real mother with her own children. Besides, anyone who sees those kids couldn't doubt that they're yours. [JULIAN *and* TONI *laugh*] It's fantastic how much the older boy looks like you.

JULIAN: Yes, it is fantastic.

TONI: Incidentally, how old is Peter?

JULIAN: Peter?

TONI: [*Persisting teasingly*] Your older boy. That's Peter, isn't it?

JULIAN: Yes, that's Peter, all right. Well, uh . . . let's see, uh . . . how old would he be now? [*Looks at his watch*]

TONI: You told me he was eight.

JULIAN: Well, if I told you he's eight, he's eight. [*Rises*]

TONI: Why do men fib about their children's age? [*Rises, crosses to* JULIAN] Julian, I saw that boy. He looks eleven or twelve.

JULIAN: Well, I guess I'm caught. Peter is eleven or twelve.

TONI: That's very interesting, considering you're married only ten years. [JULIAN *is stuck*] Come on, Julian, the truth.

JULIAN: All right. The truth? Peter was a premature baby. Born before we were married.

TONI: I'm glad. It confirms everything.

JULIAN: How's *that?*

TONI: Don't you see? Here's a woman who gave herself to you before you were married. This was not a marriage of convenience, it was love.

JULIAN: Oh, for God's sake!

TONI: And she still loves you.

JULIAN: Now, Toni—

TONI: And I'd always feel guilty if I did anything to—

JULIAN: [*Interrupting angrily*] Toni! Did it every cross your mind that she wants the divorce as much as I do? And for a very good reason?

TONI: What good reason?

JULIAN: [*He's stuck and he chuckles knowingly*] Oh, boy! Ha! [*Then suddenly*] Another guy! [*He sits and a small look passes over his face. He feels he has come up with a good thought*]

TONI: Your wife? Another man? I'd be very much surprised.

JULIAN: Toni, this is the kind of thing a man with a normal ego wouldn't lie about.

TONI: [*Looking at him seriously*] I guess that's true. [*Suddenly switching to a gayer mood*] Well, why shouldn't she have a boy friend? After all, you have a mistress. [*As she says this last line, she does an imitation of a sexy vamp. Goes to bed and hurls herself on it in a comic movie vamp pose. She holds the pose for a moment*]

JULIAN: You nut.

TONI: [*Getting up on her knees*] You know, Julian, I sort of like it better.

JULIAN: Like what better?

TONI: The fact that you have been cheated upon. Your wife doing that makes it all seem nicer.

JULIAN: [*Getting up and crossing to bed*] If it makes you happy, I'm happy. Now will you please shut up about my wife? [*He holds her face with his hands in a loving gesture*]

TONI: You think he'll marry her?

JULIAN: Huh? Who?

TONI: Her fellow.

JULIAN: [*Continuing to caress her*] I don't know. Maybe. Who cares? I'm not at all interested in him.

TONI: Well, I'm curious. What's he like? What does he do?

JULIAN: I haven't the slightest idea. I don't know him.

TONI: Well, wouldn't you like to *meet* him. Sort of look him over? [JULIAN *stares at her, backs away. She pauses, then with elaborate casualness*] I know I'd like to meet him.

JULIAN: [*Stricken with horror*] No—!

TONI: [*Trying to cut in*] But, Julian—

JULIAN: No, no!

TONI: [*Standing up on bed and bouncing up and down*] Julian, this man may become your children's stepfather. Maybe he'll rob your wife, exploit her, beat her. You have to arrange for us to meet this fellow.

JULIAN: No—

TONI: [*Jumping off bed*] All right, I'll arange it myself. Now that I know your wife, I'll just call her up.

JULIAN: No, no, no! You mustn't!

TONI: All right, Julian. [*He relaxes in relief, goes upstage and leans against the wall above table. This is the wall that* IGOR *uses for his knock signal*] But if you love me—

JULIAN: [*Pounding the wall*] No, no, no, no—

[*As he does, door opens and* IGOR *enters wearing towel and shaving himself with electric razor*]

IGOR: Something wrong, Toni?

BLACKOUT

SCENE SEVEN

DR. WINSTON's *office. The next day. Music fades lower. In the black we hear* STEPHANIE's VOICE.

STEPHANIE's VOICE: No, no, no, no, no, no, no!

[*We light up on her last couple of "no's" and see* STEPHANIE *sitting at her desk.* JULIAN *is standing beside her, buttoning his white jacket*]

JULIAN: But it's such a little thing. We just have to find a man who will pretend to—

STEPHANIE: [*Loudly*] No!

JULIAN: But—

MRS. DURANT: [*Off*] Aaaaahhhh!!

JULIAN: [*Goes up to door and opens it*] I'll be right with you, Mrs. Durant. Just keep your mouth open. [*Closes door. To* STEPHANIE] Look, Miss Dickinson, I'm afraid I threw this boy friend at you too quickly. I'll go get rid of Mrs. Durant, then I'll explain this whole thing to you.

STEPHANIE: It won't do you any good.

JULIAN: Boy, you're getting as prickly as your damn cactus.

STEPHANIE: [*As* JULIAN *exits into operating room*] My cactus and I will be happy to resign. [*She rises, turns off stereo*] I'm beginning to hate him and this whole damn place— [*Phone rings. She picks it up*] Dr. Winston's office. [*Sits*] Oh, yes, Mr. Greenfield. . . . Well, I'm sorry your filling fell out, but the doctor can't see you today. He's completely booked up. . . . It is *not* spite on my part. It's just that . . . please, Mr. Greenfield, you mustn't come up now. I told you the doctor is—[HARVEY *has evidently hung up*] Mr. Greenfield, Mr. Greenfield! [*Hangs up*] Well, let him come. At least he's in pain. That gives me something to look forward to.

    [MRS. DURANT *and* JULIAN *come out of the operating room*]

JULIAN: Sorry I had to hurt you a little.

MRS. DURANT: Well, it happens so rarely. You're probably overtired. You bachelors run around a lot.

JULIAN: Oh, not this bachelor, Mrs. Durant. I'm afraid I live a very regular life. I start work very early in the morning and I have to be in bed very early in the evening. [*Gestures genially towards* STEPHANIE] Miss Dickinson can confirm that.

STEPHANIE: [*She gives him a dirty look, then smiles*] Oh, yes. He's in bed very early.

    [JULIAN *gives her a quick dirty look*]

MRS. DURANT: Well, you might try sleeping! [*She goes*]

JULIAN: [*Turning quickly to* STEPHANIE] You listen to me!

STEPHANIE: No, you listen to me. You asked me to pose as your wife. It was ridiculous but I did it, and I think I did it beautifully.

JULIAN: The trouble was you did it *too* beautifully. Toni thinks you're still in love with me.

STEPHANIE: Me?

JULIAN: Not you, my wife.

STEPHANIE: Where would she get a ridiculous notion like that?

JULIAN: From you.

STEPHANIE: Nonsense. [*Rising, crosses to* JULIAN] My behavior was impeccable. I was a dignified, civilized, willing-to-be-divorced wife. I said nothing that would lead Toni to—

JULIAN: [*Cutting in*] It wasn't what you said, it was what you didn't say.

STEPHANIE: There was *nothing* I didn't say!

JULIAN: Well, you got her all choked up. . . . The way you talked about my shirts and those chicken and egg sandwiches—

STEPHANIE: *I* was playing a part and I wanted to play it right. I couldn't very well take my situation lightly. A divorce is a very serious thing, especially when there are children. [*Sudden switch*] By the way, you might have told me I had children.

JULIAN: [*Starting to bawl her out*] Well, why did you have to bring them along? She saw you with them and that choked her up, too.

STEPHANIE: [*Standing up for her rights*] It was my day off. I always take my nephews out on my day off. There was no necessity for your fiancée to spy on me. And if I can't spend my day off as I see fit, [*Crosses to desk*] Doctor, I'm giving you my two weeks' notice right now. [*Sits*]

JULIAN: Miss Dickinson, you know I can't get along without you.

STEPHANIE: Of course I do.

JULIAN: [*Putting his hands on her shoulders in a friendly way*] You *must* help me. Not only as my dear friend, but as my nurse. It's your professional duty.

STEPHANIE: Professional?

JULIAN: Yes. My problems with Toni are beginning to affect my work. You know what happened in there just now? I *hurt Mrs. Durant*. She felt pain! It's the first time I have ever hurt a patient.

STEPHANIE: [*Smugly*] I've predicted your disintegration.

JULIAN: Miss Dickinson, you played my wife once and I know you enjoyed yourself. [STEPHANIE *shrugs*] The truth, Miss Dickinson. You did enjoy it.

STEPHANIE: It wasn't too bad.

JULIAN: Now, here's your chance to play it again. You don't want to give up that role without one more performance. Why, it's ... it's ... like an actress doing a great Joan of Arc and then playing it for only one night. [STEPHANIE *covers her face with her hands, seems to be sobbing. Her shoulders shake*] What's the matter? Did I upset you?

STEPHANIE: [*Taking her hands away and revealing the fact that she has been laughing. She speaks in a tired, amused voice that conveys the feeling that she has given up fighting*] I'm sorry, no. I was just thinking that between the two roles, Joan of Arc has the happy ending.

JULIAN: [*Pretending to enjoy this*] Ah, very amusing, very amusing. But will you do it for me? [*Bends over her*] Just once more. You'll never have to do it again.

STEPHANIE: [*Shrugging*] Well, so I lose a husband and gain a lover. All right, I'll go see her and tell her I have a boy friend.

JULIAN: No good. She has to see him with you.

STEPHANIE: In the flesh? How are we going to do that?

JULIAN: Don't worry, I'll fix it. Have you a friend you could ask to do this? What about your brother-in-law?

STEPHANIE: Keep my family out of this. Look, Doctor, you want me to play a part, and now you want me to furnish my own props. You want me to have a boy friend? You find me one.

JULIAN: It's not too easy.

STEPHANIE: Oh?

JULIAN: Has to be someone I can trust.

STEPHANIE: [*Rises, gaily making a joke*] Say, what about old Señor Sanchez? He's already asked me for a date.

JULIAN: [*Suddenly severe*] Really? Señor Sanchez made overtures to you?

STEPHANIE: Oh, not overtures. Just a tiny bossa nova.

JULIAN: [*Very coldly*] Miss Dickinson, you know I don't care for that sort of thing in the office. It can lead to—

[*The doorbell chimes*]

STEPHANIE: [*Walking toward the door*] Oh, be quiet, Doctor, and keep working on my boy friend.

[*She opens the door.* HARVEY GREENFIELD *appears in the door*]

HARVEY: Hey, Julian, I have to see you right away.

[STEPHANIE *closes door*]

JULIAN: [*Rushing over*] Harvey! Hello, Harvey—You're the one!

STEPHANIE: No, not him, not him! [*She runs into operating room*]

JULIAN: [*To* STEPHANIE] Why not? You don't have to sleep with him.

HARVEY: Boy, does she hate me!

JULIAN: [*Sitting him in chair*] You're wrong, Harvey. I want to tell you that girl is very interested in you. Now, Harvey, you want your girl friend's teeth fixed. . . .

HARVEY: Free?

BLACKOUT

SCENE EIGHT

A small night spot a few days later. The lighting is very dim. When we first see it, the lighting will be at its dimmest. However, we will come up gradually once the dimness of the nightclub is accepted. At the start of the scene we can pick out HARVEY GREENFIELD *at the table. He is sitting by himself in a banquette. A* WAITER *serves him and goes.* HARVEY *pours some whiskey into his glass, adds some water, tastes the drink, then adds some more whiskey. He takes a drink. From time to time he looks at his watch. He is obviously expecting someone. There is soft music playing in the background, perhaps a single piano.* STEPHANIE'S *silhouette appears. For this scene* STEPHANIE'S *clothes go up another notch. She is wearing a chic dinner dress. Her hair is done smartly and there is further progress in the emergence of* STEPHANIE *as a looker.* HARVEY *spots her as she stands there looking around in the dimness.*

HARVEY: Hey! Over here. [*He goes to meet her*]

STEPHANIE: My God, it's dark!

    [HARVEY *escorts her to banquette*]

HARVEY: Sit down.

STEPHANIE: Where's the chair?

HARVEY: Sit down, it'll be there. [*She sits. He sits right of her*] This is atmosphere. Mood lighting.

STEPHANIE: But you and I are *here* to be *seen.* Why did Dr. Winston pick a place with visibility zero?

HARVEY: *I* picked it.

STEPHANIE: I should have known.

HARVEY: I come here a lot.

STEPHANIE: This can't be much of a place. There's nobody here.

HARVEY: Too early. It's only midnight. This place doesn't come to life until about four in the morning.

STEPHANIE: Four in the. . . . By that time I'll be safely home in my little bed. [*Looks at her watch impatiently*] Where are they?

HARVEY: They'll be here. [*He peers at her a little more closely*] Hey, you know, you look different tonight. Pretty good. All dressed up. When you're in the office you look sort of like a large Band-aid.

STEPHANIE: [*Annoyed*] Mr. Greenfield, your opinion of—

HARVEY: I'm sorry. Here, have a drink. It'll make me look better to you.

STEPHANIE: There isn't that much whiskey in the world. Well. . . .

    [HARVEY *hands her a drink, and raises his glass in a toast*]

HARVEY: To our love affair.

STEPHANIE: [*Raising her glass*] God forbid. [*She drinks*]

HARVEY: I think we're getting off on the wrong foot. I'm your lover! The reason why you're getting a divorce. Let's act a little crazy about me, shall we?

STEPHANIE: When Dr. Winston and Toni get here. Not one moment sooner. In the meantime let me have these few minutes to fight off my revulsion. [*Puts glass down*]

HARVEY: This is going to be a fun evening. Look, as long as we agreed to do this favor for Dr. Winston, we might as well make the best of it and— [*During this speech he has put his hand on her knee*]

STEPHANIE: [*Suddenly*] Your hand.

HARVEY: What about my hand?

STEPHANIE: It's on my knee.

HARVEY: Sorry, I thought it was mine. [*Removes his hand, takes a drink*] Like to dance?

STEPHANIE: I'd rather die.

[TONI *and* JULIAN *appear*]

JULIAN: Let's find a little corner where we can be alone.

TONI: That shouldn't be hard. We're the only ones here. [*They sit in banquette*]

HARVEY: Oh-oh, here they are.

STEPHANIE: Where? I can't see them—I have night blindness. Oh, yes, there they are. [*Getting excited*] Quick!

HARVEY: Quick what?

STEPHANIE: Act natural. Romantic. Flirt with me.

HARVEY: You want me to flirt with you and act natural at the same time?

STEPHANIE: [*She has gone into her romantic act. She smiles sweetly at* HARVEY *and speaks softly*] You really are a louse. [*They hold hands*]

TONI: What made you drag us to this creepy place?

JULIAN: I hear it's one of the new "in" spots. A friend of mine told me about it.

TONI: I never heard of it.

JULIAN: Nobody has. Maybe that's why it's "in."

HARVEY: [*Looks at* TONI. *Confidentially to* STEPHANIE] Hey, the girl's not bad. Good old Julian. He can pick 'em.

STEPHANIE: Don't stare at them. They should be the ones to see us first.

TONI: [*Suddenly stiffening*] Julian!

JULIAN: What? [*Turns head*]

TONI: [*She grabs his face, turns it back*] Don't turn around. It's your wife.

JULIAN: My wife? Nonsense.

TONI: Honest. I recognize her. I'm sure.

JULIAN: [*Pretending to peer in the dark*] Where? Where?

TONI: In the corner. With a man.

JULIAN: [*Looks and shrinks back. Acting all the way*] Say, it *is* my wife. And her boyfriend. Well, well, imagine us all here at once!

[*Slow Fox Trot begins*]

TONI: Oh, this is embarrassing.

JULIAN: You insisted on seeing him.

TONI: But, now I feel like a spy. [*Getting up*] Let's go.

JULIAN: [*Puzzled, rises*] Okay.

TONI: [*Pushes him down*] Well, as long as we're here. . . . [*She looks over at the other table*] How do you know that's her boyfriend?

[HARVEY snuggles his head against STEPHANIE's *shoulder.* STEPHANIE *puts her arm across him and slaps his face rhythmically*]

JULIAN: Who else would it be? And, besides, look at them.

TONI: They seem very affectionate.

JULIAN: I thought she only played Scrabble.

HARVEY: [*Coming out of position, uncomfortably*] How are we doing?

STEPHANIE: [*Looks over at* TONI *and* JULIAN] They don't act as if they noticed us. We'd better push things a little. Let's dance.

HARVEY: But when I asked you before you—

STEPHANIE: Shut up and dance.

[HARVEY *rises and gets to dance floor first.* STEPHANIE *rises and joins him. They start dancing*]

TONI: Come on, Julian, I want to see him a little closer.

[*They rise*]

JULIAN: Hey! She dances! [JULIAN *and* TONI *dance— The* TWO COUPLES *dance a bit, end up bumping into each other They stop dancing,* TONI *and* HARVEY *in center of group*] Why, hello.

STEPHANIE: Hello, Julian. [*Graciously, to* TONI] Good evening.

TONI: Good evening, Mrs. Winston.

JULIAN: What a coincidence.

STEPHANIE: [*Gesturing towards* HARVEY] I'd like you to meet my . . . a. . . .

HARVEY: [*To* TONI] Hi, honey. I'm Harvey Greenfield, the boyfriend.

TONI: Hi.

STEPHANIE: [*Gesturing towards* JULIAN] And . . . uh . . . uh . . . Harvey, this is . . . my . . . husband.

HARVEY: [*They shake hands*] Good to meet you, old man. I've heard a lot about you. As a matter of fact, I—

JULIAN: [*Cutting him off*] Would you care to join us for a drink?

STEPHANIE: [*Hesitantly*] Well— I don't think so.

JULIAN: I know this is a rather unusual situation. But, after all, we're civilized people.

HARVEY: You have a point. [*Puts arm around* STEPHANIE]

JULIAN: Unless, of course, you two would prefer to remain alone.

HARVEY: Christ, no! [*Catching himself*] I mean, we *are* civilized people. [*Moving towards his table*] Here, come to our table. This party's on me.

[HARVEY *beckons to* WAITER. STEPHANIE *walks to banquette, sits and crosses her legs.* HARVEY *sits with her.* TONI *and* JULIAN *follow*]

JULIAN: What do you think of him?

TONI: I don't know yet.

[*They sit at end of banquette, two* GIRLS *in the center. There's an awkward pause.* WAITER *serves them, goes*]

JULIAN: Stephanie, I never thought I'd see you enjoy a night club, my dear. You've turned into quite a swinger.

STEPHANIE: You've never really known me. [*Taps* HARVEY *on shoulder*] Pour me another drink, Harve.

HARVEY: Yes, dear. [*Hands her a drink*]

STEPHANIE: [*To* TONI] You see, Toni, Dr. Winston never realized that I couldn't go out much because of our children. They were too young.

TONI: [*Sympathetically*] Of course. [*Turning quickly to* HARVEY] By the way, Mr. Greenfield. . . .

HARVEY: Yes?

TONI: How do you like children?

HARVEY: Grilled, medium rare. [*He laughs at his own joke, bumps* STEPHANIE *and she uncrosses legs*]

JULIAN: Ha, ha. That's very funny, Mr. Greenfield, but, actually, it's the kind of joke made by a man hiding a profound emotional feeling. [HARVEY *just stares at him*] Deep down I know you love children.

HARVEY: Huh?

STEPHANIE: Deep down.

HARVEY: [*Getting it*] Oh, deep down, yes. Especially yours. I'm nuts about them.

TONI: [*She's been watching* HARVEY *with a jaundiced eye*] Mr. Greenfield, what business are you in?

STEPHANIE: Pour me another drink, Harve.

HARVEY: I was asked a question. I'm not in business, my dear. I'm in television.

JULIAN: Everybody have another drink!

HARVEY: You see, I'm an actor.

TONI: An actor. Isn't that a very insecure profession?

HARVEY: Only financially. Julian, that's quite a girl you have there. I hear it's going to happen very soon between you two.

JULIAN: As soon as we can make it.

TONI: [*Coldly*] Julian, I hardly think this is the moment to discuss things like—

JULIAN: Oh, come on, Toni. We have nothing to hide from these people. It's all sort of family.

HARVEY: Right, Julian. [*Putting his arm around* STEPHANIE] Stephanie and I have nothing to hide, either.

STEPHANIE: [*Pulling away*] Please, let's change the subject.

HARVEY: Look at her blushing. Isn't she cute? [*He kisses her on the neck*]

STEPHANIE: [*Fighting him off*] Really, Harvey!

HARVEY: Come on, Baby, don't play-act with me. [*To* JULIAN] She's kind of cold in public. But, boy, when we're alone together— Wow! [STEPHANIE *is doing everything but crawling under the table*] Of course, I forget, you know her as well as I do. [STEPHANIE *looks up, startled*] She's absolutely—

[STEPHANIE *pokes him in ribs with her elbow.* HARVEY *collapses in pain, all bent over*]

JULIAN: Let's all have another drink.

HARVEY: Yeah, the party's dying.

[*He picks up whiskey glass. A big, handsome brunette appears in entrance and crosses onto center of dance floor. We'll call her* BOTTICELLI'S SPRINGTIME *after* HARVEY's *earlier description of her*]

BOTTICELLI'S SPRINGTIME: Oh, there you are, Harvey. [HARVEY *turns*] Sorry I'm late, honey. Hello, everybody.

[*They all stare at her in dead silence.* HARVEY's *reaction is an interesting one. He also stares in dead, shocked silence*]

STEPHANIE: [*Finally*] Won't you join us?

HARVEY: [*Leaping up*] No, she doesn't want to join us. We have to talk . . . uh . . . business.

BOTTICELLI'S SPRINGTIME: What is this? Did we have a date tonight or didn't we?

HARVEY: [*Pushes her away*] Come, we'll talk at the bar. [*Turning back to group, leaning over banquette*] Please excuse us, folks, this is important. She's the daughter of one of my sponsors. Silly debutante. I'll be right back. [*He rushes to her*]

BOTTICELLI'S SPRINGTIME: All right, Harvey, what are you trying to pull? We had a—

HARVEY: [*Cutting in quietly*] Quiet or you'll be stuck with your old teeth. [*He grabs her arm and escorts her off to the bar*]

STEPHANIE: [*Rises. A moment of humiliation*] Would you excuse me? I think I'll powder my nose or something.

[JULIAN *rises*]

TONI: [*Rises. Sympathetically*] Do you want me to go with you?

STEPHANIE: Thank you, dear. I'll be all right. [*She goes with great dignity*]

TONI: [*Ready to explode*] Well, Julian?

JULIAN: [*Mildly*] What's wrong?

TONI: He's a bum. [*Sits*]

JULIAN: [*Sits*] But he seems pleasant. And my wife loves him.

TONI: Loves him? Didn't you see how humiliated she was?

JULIAN: What the hell do you want me to do?

TONI: We've got to snatch your wife from that man's clutches.

JULIAN: Now, Toni, the guy maybe had a little too much to drink.

TONI: Don't you dare defend him! I'm angry enough because you were so chummy with him. Julian, my respect for you is going down every minute. I see you with different eyes and what I see—

[HARVEY *enters during the above. He now interrupts her*]

HARVEY: Is the party still going on?

JULIAN: [*Rising, crosses to* HARVEY] Not for you, Harvey.

HARVEY: Huh?

JULIAN: [*Grabs* HARVEY'S *arm*] Sir, I don't like the way you treated my wife.

HARVEY: [*Puzzled, starts to move away*] All right, a joke's a joke.

JULIAN: [*Pushing him back again*] I'm not joking! [*Grabbing him by his lapels and pushing him to center of dance floor. He speaks to* HARVEY *very sharply*] Now look, Mr. Greenfield, I don't like the way you behaved toward my wife *or* my girl.

HARVEY: Hey, this is my good suit.

JULIAN: I want you to leave quietly and never see my wife again. Or my children. [*He starts pushing him toward the exit*] If I should ever hear that you bothered Stephanie again, I'll knock all your teeth out. [*He shoves* HARVEY *back*]

HARVEY: [*Beckons to* JULIAN *with his finger.* JULIAN *crosses to him*] What about my temporary filling?

JULIAN: [*Shouts*] Out, out! Out! [HARVEY *goes*] I guess that'll take care of him.

TONI: [*Impressed. Rising*] My goodness. Julian, I've never seen that ferocious side of you. You were beautiful.

JULIAN: [*Modestly*] It was nothing.

TONI: I liked it.

JULIAN: [*He snuggles with her a minute and his voice turns sexy, as it usually does when they snuggle*] Let's go home, Toni. What do you say? Let's go home where we can be alone.

TONI: [*Purring*] I feel that way myself, but . . . [*Suddenly pulls herself away as* STEPHANIE *returns*] Stop it. Here's your wife.

[*Cocktail piano music starts again*]

STEPHANIE: [*To* JULIAN] I just called for a taxi. I'm a little tired and I'd like to go home. I hope you won't mind my leaving so abruptly.

TONI: You're going home alone? Without an escort?

STEPHANIE: [*A little sigh*] Oh, I'm used to that.

TONI: You're really one of the gamest women I know.

STEPHANIE: [*Goes to table for her gloves*] You're sweet, Toni. Well, I'll be going.

TONI: [*Firmly*] No! Julian will drive you. You can't go home alone.

STEPHANIE: Oh—

TONI: It's out of the question. I live right near here. I'll take the taxi.

STEPHANIE: Oh, I couldn't allow that.

TONI: I insist. Believe me, Julian will be happy to do it.

> [JULIAN *doesn't look very happy*]

STEPHANIE: Well, if I thought Julian wouldn't mind. Julian? You wouldn't mind?

JULIAN: Say, I'll tell you what. We'll all go together and I'll drop you off, Stephanie.

STEPHANIE: [*She's enjoying this*] In that case, why don't we drop Toni off first? She lives right near here.

JULIAN: [*Quickly*] No, no, I'll drop you first.

STEPHANIE: What do you think, Toni?

TONI: She's right, Julian. I'm taking the taxi. I'll be all right, don't worry about me.

JULIAN: [*Weakly*] Okay, come on. [*Starts*]

STEPHANIE: Julian dear, don't forget to say good night to Toni? I'll wait for you. [*She moves toward exit. She's out of earshot, but she watches their furtive conversation with a smile*]

JULIAN: [*Keeping his voice down, to* TONI] Thanks a lot. You're a great little fixer. All right, I'll see her home then come right back to your place.

TONI: [*Same voice as* JULIAN's] No, Julian, not tonight. Stay with her.

JULIAN: Are you out of your mind?

TONI: After all she's put up with, we can at least sacrifice one night.

JULIAN: What the hell am I going to do with her?

TONI: You're going to be "very nice."

JULIAN: [*Startled*] Now wait a minute—

TONI: "Very nice." To please me.

> [STEPHANIE *has been putting on her gloves. She's still waiting.* JULIAN *crosses to* STEPHANIE]

JULIAN: [*Grimly*] All right, let's go.

STEPHANIE: [*A small needle*] It's been such a long time, dear, since we've gone home together.

JULIAN: [*Through clenched teeth*] A very long time. Come on. [*He walks out*]

STEPHANIE: Good night, Toni.

TONI: Good night, Stephanie.

STEPHANIE: You've been very thoughtful.

> [JULIAN *reappears in entrance*]

JULIAN: For God's sake, will you come on!

STEPHANIE: [*As though she's afraid*] Oh, I'd better hurry. God knows what he'll do.! [*She goes*]

[*Cocktail piano music swells*]

CURTAIN

ACT TWO

SCENE ONE

The doctor's office, early the next morning. STEPHANIE *enters from supply room with watering can. She waters her cactus plant with can and—believe it or not—*STEPHANIE *is humming. Humming happily. She puts down can, turns on the stereo, picks up can, puts it away in supply room.* JULIAN *enters in his street clothes. He looks fairly grim and low.*

STEPHANIE: [*Cheerily*] Good morning, Doctor. [JULIAN *goes into closet and reappears, putting on his white coat. She goes happily on*] Isn't it a beautiful day? I love days like this. Sunny but not hot. [*She helps him button his white coat*] It was marvelous driving in this morning. Simply wonderful. The air was so fresh and clean, it made me feel so good.

JULIAN: [*Studying her grimly*] What the hell are you so happy about?

STEPHANIE: [*Very casually*] Doctor, is there anything wrong with my being happy?

JULIAN: [*Turns off stereo*] Yes. I don't like it.

STEPHANIE: Now, Doctor, you've been complaining that I'm too grim and efficient. You compared me with my cactus plant. Well, Doctor, every once in a while this prickly little thing— puts forth a lovely flower that some people think—

JULIAN: [*Interrupting sharply*] Cut it out! I know why you're happy. You're happy because last night was a complete and utter disaster.

STEPHANIE: Oh, I don't know. I admit I've had gayer evenings— [*Sits*] but all in all—

JULIAN: [*Cutting her off*] Who's the first patient?

STEPHANIE: Mrs. Durant.

JULIAN: [*Really snappish*] I suppose that old razorback will be late, as usual.

STEPHANIE: My, my! We really feel rotten, don't we?

JULIAN: [*Holding his head*] Yes, we do.

STEPHANIE: Didn't you sleep well?

JULIAN: Nope.

STEPHANIE: It's your nerves. You ought to—

JULIAN: [*Bursting out*] Will you ever stop *mothering* me? Do you want to know why I couldn't sleep? I'll tell you why I couldn't sleep. It's because I hate sleeping alone!—[*Catches himself*] What I mean is ... oh, the hell with it—what I mean is, I hate sleeping alone. [STEPHANIE *starts her happy humming again*] Stop humming!

STEPHANIE: You know, I was sure that as soon as you took me home last night, you would rush right back to your lovely little passion flower.

JULIAN: Well, I didn't.

STEPHANIE: Why not?

JULIAN: Well, Toni thought you were sad and humiliated and she insisted that I should stay with you.

STEPHANIE: Wait a minute—

JULIAN: To comfort you.

STEPHANIE: But you didn't comfort me.

JULIAN: You're damn right I didn't.

STEPHANIE: [*Rises, goes to him*] Look, I'm in this so deep now I just want to get our stories straight as far as Toni's concerned. [*Turns her back to* JULIAN] Did we ... did we spend the night together?

JULIAN: No.

STEPHANIE: Good. I only asked because, with your imagination, I never know what you'll have me doing next.

JULIAN: You'll be happy to know you didn't do *that*.

STEPHANIE: But what about Toni? When she hears that we *didn't*, she's liable to insist that we *do* and ask to come over and watch.

JULIAN: Don't worry about Toni. I'm going to tell her the truth. I thought about it last night as I tossed and turned. Now I'm convinced I have to do it. The whole truth and nothing but the truth.

STEPHANIE: [*Convinced*] Say! I'll bet that makes you feel better.

JULIAN: No, it doesn't. It makes me feel rotten. Toni is liable to do something terrible. And it's all your fault.

STEPHANIE: My fault.

JULIAN: [*Going on*] Yeah. Who the hell asked you to stick your nose in my affairs?

STEPHANIE: [*Furious*] Who the hell? You the hell, that's who the hell! [*Sits*] And I, like a dope, did everything I could to help you.

JULIAN: Plus everything you could to louse me up. Poor Harvey.

STEPHANIE: Poor Harvey!

JULIAN: The terrible things I had to say to him.

STEPHANIE: They couldn't have been terrible enough for that odious man.

JULIAN: Oh, I know Harvey's a fool, but still—

STEPHANIE: [A warning in her voice] Still what?

JULIAN: [Starts out cautiously and builds] You might have been a bit more flexible. You didn't have to convince Toni that you hated him. And you didn't have to put on that big act about being humiliated.

STEPHANIE: [Really sore] I was humiliated, and I did hate him.

JULIAN: [Assuming a psychiatric manner which can be very irritating] Hmmm.

STEPHANIE: What do you mean, "hmmm"?

JULIAN: [Crossing to her and continuing his same manner] I'm curious. Do you hate all men?

STEPHANIE: [A shout] No!

JULIAN: [Takes pencil from desk] How loudly you say that. Perhaps too loudly.

STEPHANIE: Now don't start analyzing—

JULIAN: [Cutting in] I'm not speaking as a layman, you know. At dental school we had a whole year of psychiatry.

STEPHANIE: I'd still only trust you with my teeth and gums.

JULIAN: [Going right on] Miss Dickinson, as a trained observer, I detect in you a strong ambivalence about men.

STEPHANIE: [Another shout] I don't give a damn about men.

JULIAN: Again you're loud . . . and a bit coarse.

STEPHANIE: [A whisper] I don't give a hoot about men.

JULIAN: But you don't hate them.

STEPHANIE: [A shout] No! [Catches herself and whispers] No.

JULIAN: You know, I think I believe you.

STEPHANIE: Thank you very much.

JULIAN: I think you think you're telling the truth. But truth can be very complicated. You see, you hate men—

STEPHANIE: I don't hate men!

JULIAN: Dammit, let me finish. You give the impression you hate men. And why? Because deep down you don't. But you're afraid that you don't so you pretend that you do. But you really never have.

STEPHANIE: A whole year of psychiatry.

JULIAN: [Going on] It's a textbook case. A deep-seated fear that forces you to destroy any possible relationship. That's really what caused you to hate Harvey. [Puts pencil on desk]

STEPHANIE: No one needs a reason for hating Harvey.

JULIAN: [*Ignoring her answer*] Now take what happens here in the office every day. I'm a man. You're very nice to me, you look after me devotedly. But how do you make up for that? By completely defeminizing yourself.

STEPHANIE: Doctor, I don't care what you think of me or the way I look. I'm a nurse, not a geisha girl. [*She reaches for a Kleenex, dabs her nose and eyes*]

[*Door chimes*]

JULIAN: [*Worried he has gone too far*] What I'm trying to say is—

[*Door chimes again.* JULIAN *stops talking.* STEPHANIE *holds the Kleenex.* JULIAN *admits* MRS. DURANT. *He is a bit distraught and* STEPHANIE *is still dabbing at her eyes with tissue. He closes door*]

MRS. DURANT: Sorry I'm late, Doctor, but I— [*Turns*] Is there anything wrong?

JULIAN: No, no. I was . . . was talking to Miss Dickinson about uh . . . uh . . . her cold. [*To* STEPHANIE] How does your cold feel, Miss Dickinson?

STEPHANIE: [*Gives him a dirty look*] What cold?

JULIAN: *Your* cold.

STEPHANIE: Fine. I'll see to the. . . . [*Starts to rise*]

JULIAN: Don't get up. I'll take care of Mrs. . . . uh . . . uh. . . .

MRS. DURANT: What's the matter with you lately?

JULIAN: Nothing, Mrs. . . . uh . . . [*To* STEPHANIE] What's her name, Miss—er?

MRS. DURANT: Last week you nearly drilled the top of my head off. Now you forget my name.

JULIAN: I'm sorry, Mrs. Durant. [*Remembering*] Mrs. Durant! [*Extends hand to her*]

MRS. DURANT: Pleased to meet you. [*They shake hands*] You know, Doctor, I don't think you're up to being a bachelor. Too tough. You see, you're always surrounded by women. Women patients and . . . [*Looks at* STEPHANIE, *then dismisses her with her hand*] Well, anyway, lots of women. And you know that chic white coat gives you a lot of razzamatazz. It must put you under quite a strain. Makes you very nervous.

JULIAN: I—I—I'm not nervous.

MRS. DURANT: Better pay attention to me, Doctor. I know what I'm talking about. I have a great nose for sexual tension. [*She goes into operating room*]

JULIAN: [*Looking at* STEPHANIE] Sexual. . . . [*He starts off, comes back*] This whole place is going to hell. Look, Miss Dickinson, this afternoon I'm going to go see Toni. I'll tell her the truth, she and I will get married and then I can forget her. [*He puts his hands on her shoulders*] After that, you and I will go on working as before. And I know you'll be happy.

STEPHANIE: [*Ironically*] You mean it's my professional duty. Look, Doctor, you've made it very clear what you think of me.

JULIAN: I didn't mean those things. Well, yes, I did.

STEPHANIE: Yes, you did.

JULIAN: Yes I did, you *do* defeminize yourself. And why? Because you're afraid, Miss Dickinson. You're afraid of life, afraid of intimacy, afraid to let yourself go. You're as scared as that cocker spaniel of yours.

STEPHANIE: Frieda has had twenty-two puppies!

BLACKOUT

SCENE TWO

The L.P. Record Shop, that afternoon. TONI *is up on top of the ladder, stacking records on the top shelf.* JULIAN *enters carrying a large box.* TONI *doesn't see him right away.*

JULIAN: Hey!

TONI: [*Turning*] Julian! What are you doing here so early?

JULIAN: Two patients cancelled so I have an hour free. [*Looking at her up on the ladder as she shows a lot of leg*] Say, do you always stand up there like that?

TONI: Like what?

JULIAN: Well, if any customers stand where I'm standing . . . let's just say it's quite an angle.

TONI: [*Shrugs*] Oh, that. Nobody here looks. Most of our customers are *classical.* [*Comes down one step and points to the box*] What's that you're carrying?

JULIAN: Come on down, it's a surprise. [*Puts box on counter*]

TONI: What is it?

JULIAN: I wanted to give it to you for your birthday, but I couldn't wait.

TONI: What could it possibly be? It's such a big box.

JULIAN: Guess.

TONI: Black leather slacks?

JULIAN: [*Amused*] Black leather *slacks?*

TONI: A suede coat?

JULIAN: Can't you think bigger than that?

TONI: [*Jumps down ladder*] What can it be? I've got to see. [*She finally gets the box open. She takes out a card, then a stole*] My God, a mink stole! A mink stole! [TONI's *voice is not that of delight. She is sort of awed and puzzled. The mink stole is all wrong for her]* And a card, too. [*Reading from the card as she crosses to* JULIAN] "As ever, Julian."

JULIAN: I wanted to say: "To my darling, adorable, delicious Toni." But I got it wholesale. From a guy I know, so I—

TONI: [*Nodding*] You had to be discreet.

JULIAN: He's a patient of mine. It still cost me a bundle.

TONI: [*Looking at the fur*] It *must* have.

JULIAN: You haven't yet told me you like it.

TONI: [*Putting it on*] A mink stole! [*Quietly*] A mink stole.... [*Sudden switch*] Julian, are you trying to tell me something?

JULIAN: Huh?

TONI: You've done something bad and you want me to forgive you.

JULIAN: [*Uneasy*] What makes you say that?

TONI: You're not a stingy man, but you're no Diamond Jim spender, either. I don't know, Julian.

JULIAN: Matter of fact, there *was* something I wanted to tell you.

TONI: I thought so.

JULIAN: It's about me and my. . . .

TONI: Your wife.

JULIAN: Yes.

TONI: Don't be nervous. I think I understand.

JULIAN: You do?

TONI: Sure. Last night . . . you and she . . . for old times' sake— [*Shakes tails of stole*]

JULIAN: That's absurd. I—

TONI: Julian, I understand. After all, it was I who told you to be nice to her. Of course, it was up to you to decide *how* nice. [*She takes off stole and replaces it in box*]

JULIAN: Toni, it's nothing like that. Will you please let me talk?

TONI: Okay, Julian, go ahead, talk.

JULIAN: All right. Something has been bugging me for a long time.

TONI: I know, I know. You've been very nervous lately.

JULIAN: I have to get this off my chest. Toni, Stephanie is . . .

TONI: Yes?

MAN: [*Enters shop from street door*] Excuse me, Miss, do you have the Hindemith quartet?

TONI: [*To* JULIAN, *ignoring the* MAN] What were you saying?

MAN: The Hindemith quartet. [*She turns to him, stares*] By Hindemith.

TONI: [*To* MAN] You wouldn't like it. [*To* JULIAN] Go ahead.

MAN: I *love* Hindemith. [*He goes*]

TONI: Pest. Go ahead, sweetheart, Stephanie is . . .

JULIAN: Stephanie is . . .

TONI: Come on, Julian, let's have it. You know me. I can forgive anything except a lie.

JULIAN: Forget it. [*Sits*]

TONI: Oh no, we won't forget it. Let me try to help you. You've got a problem with Stephanie. Right?

JULIAN: Forget it.

TONI: Let's see. She drinks?

JULIAN: No.

TONI: She's a kleptomaniac.

JULIAN: No, no!

TONI: She takes drugs. [JULIAN *shakes his head*] Well, there is only one thing I know of that a husband would really be ashamed to talk about, and Stephanie is no nymphomaniac. [*Turns and looks at him. We see* JULIAN's *face light up for a moment. This nymphomaniac thing hits him as a good possibility and a way out. He quickly reverts to a sad expression*] I guessed it? [JULIAN *nods, one big nod*] And that's what you came here to tell me? [*He nods many times*] Wow! Go ahead, give me all the details. And I promise we'll never talk about her again.

JULIAN: You mean that?

TONI: Absolutely. We're through protecting her.

JULIAN: It's too painful to talk about.

TONI: Yeah, well. . . .

JULIAN: My wife Stephanie is a slave to her desires.

TONI: That's a very sweet way to describe a nympho.

JULIAN: Now you know the truth, Toni. That's why she agreed to a quiet divorce with no publicity.

TONI: Julian, you must get the children out of the house right away.

JULIAN: Why? It's not catching.

TONI: But still, an awful woman like that. . . . An awful woman? What am I saying? She's not an awful woman. She's marvelous. I admire her. [*She gets package of records from shelf*] I was just about to send her these. A couple of records I know she'd love.

JULIAN: Why would you do that?

TONI: Oh, I felt so sorry for her last night. Julian, are you sure that she's really . . . a slave to her desires?

JULIAN: [*Rises. Suddenly hurt and angry*] Look, I'm sick of this! You promised we wouldn't talk about her any more. I've told you the whole ugly story. You can imagine how painful that was and how bad my life has been. [*His voice turns appealing*] Must all your sympathies still be with her? Can't you think of me?

TONI: [*Puts records on desk and goes to him*] You poor dear. I *have* been dopey. [*She embraces him*] Julian, I'm sorry. It's just that all this time I thought she was in love with you and now I see what a miserable life you've had. I'll make it up to you.

JULIAN: [*His sexy voice*] I wish I could stay.

TONI: So do I. But that Hindemith's liable to come back.

JULIAN: [*Kisses her*] I'll come by and pick you up about seven. We'll go out and have some fun. [*He starts to go*]

TONI: Julian . . . . [*He stops*] If you don't mind, I'm still going to send her the records.

JULIAN: You're hopeless. [*Comes back to her*] But I must say, if all women were as sweet and thoughtful as you. . . . [*He kisses her again*]

[IGOR *enters from street, stops dead*]

TONI: Hi, Igor.

JULIAN: [*After a hostile look at* IGOR] I'll see you later, Toni. [*He starts off again*]

IGOR: [*To* JULIAN] Hi, there.

JULIAN: Hi, where? [*He goes*]

IGOR: Guess my timing was off.

TONI: [*Leaning on desk*] What are you doing here?

IGOR: I was just wandering around and thought I'd drop in for a minute.

TONI: Wandering? What about your work? Say! You know, I haven't heard your typewriter pounding lately.

IGOR: That's because I haven't been pounding it. Can't seem to get going.

TONI: Something on your mind? A girl?

IGOR: [*Crossing up and climbing a ladder*] Ahh, I'm fed up with girls and stuff like that. I seem to want . . . to need something else, but I don't know what. I wish these records were breakable. [*Takes album and bends it*]

TONI: [*Thoughtfully*] I know exactly how you feel.

IGOR: Well, you have no problem—you're madly in love.

TONI: [*After a beat*] I guess so.

IGOR: [*Comes down*] You *guess* so!

TONI: Look, Eugene O'Neill, we're not talking about me, we're talking about you. We can't let a great writer go to pieces. What are you doing tonight?

IGOR: I had planned to just stay home and be depressed.

TONI: Nonsense. You'll have dinner with Julian and me.

IGOR: Oh, boy, Julian will love that.

TONI: He'll be very happy to have you. Well, anyway, he'll pay the check. [*She puts on stole*] It's all settled. And after dinner we'll go out dancing. [*Shaking tails of stole at him*]

IGOR: What is that?

TONI: It's mink. From Julian. How do you like it?

IGOR: Turn around. [TONI *turns and models the mink.* IGOR *studies her, then speaks quietly and thoughtfully*] Very nice. You look just like my aunt.

TONI: [*Taking off the mink*] I wanted black leather slacks.

IGOR: Much more tasteful.

TONI: Poor Julian. He thought this would please me.

IGOR: It pleased *him*. That kind of character gets his kicks by draping his women in mink.

TONI: That's very unkind, Igor. Boy, when I think of all the women who would give their souls for this. [*She rolls stole up in a ball*] And here am I, not really wanting it. [*Sudden thought*] Hey! Igor!

IGOR: What?

TONI: Here's my chance to do a good deed. I was going to send his wife these records. [*He looks at her*] I'll send her the mink.

IGOR: Oh, boy.

TONI: What's wrong? She'll love it.

IGOR: [*Tenderly*] Toni, you're the most ridiculous, wonderful kook I ever knew. But Mrs. Winston would never accept a mink stole from you.

TONI: [*Ignoring him*] Where's that card? [*She looks on counter, picks up card, shows it to* IGOR]

IGOR: [*Reading*] "As ever, Julian."

IGOR *and* TONI: Aahhhh!

TONI: Now we're all even. I stole her husband, I give her a *stole*.

[*They both laugh. Music starts*]

BLACKOUT

SCENE THREE

The doctor's office, later that afternoon. STEPHANIE *is at her desk, wearing her glasses.* JULIAN *enters from operating room, hands her small box.*

JULIAN: Miss Dickinson, will you please send this to the lab?

STEPHANIE: Certainly, Doctor. [*He starts for operating room*] Oh, by the way— [*She rises, taking off her glasses*] there was a call from your home a while ago. Seems there was a package there addressed to me. Or, rather, to Mrs. Winston.

JULIAN: Oh?

STEPHANIE: Your maid was puzzled so I just told her to send it along to the office.

JULIAN: Oh, I know what that is. It's for you.

STEPHANIE: But what—?

JULIAN: You'll understand when you get it. Now quickly, please, the lab. [*He goes*]

> [*She hurries to the door of the waiting room as the doorbell chimes. She opens door to admit* SR. SANCHEZ]

STEPHANIE: [*Looking at watch*] Señor Sanchez! You're ten minutes early.

SANCHEZ: Imagine Arturo Sanchez being early for the dentist. It's a different person, eh?

STEPHANIE: Certainly is.

SANCHEZ: Today I *hurried* to get here. And do you know why?

STEPHANIE: El Bravo rides again.

SANCHEZ: Yes! [*Puts hat on chair*] My cowardly fear of dental torture has been overcome by something stronger. The desire to see the lovely, delicious Stephanie. . . . [*Takes her hand and kisses it*]

STEPHANIE: [*Breaking loose*] But first we must see the gentle, painless Doctor Winston. I'll tell him you're here.

SANCHEZ: [*Stopping her*] Wait. Don't call your duenna yet. I have a surprise. [*She comes back toward him*] Stephanie, tonight is the night of the April in Paris Ball. Have you ever been to an April in Paris Ball?

STEPHANIE: I'm afraid not. It's a little out of my—

SANCHEZ: [*Interrupting her and pulling an envelope out of his pocket*] As a diplomat, I have been given an invitation for two. You will do me the honor?

STEPHANIE: What about your wife?

SANCHEZ: Good God! Do we have to take my wife *everywhere?* Besides, she's away. Stephanie, the April in Paris Ball! I hear it will be delightful this year. Very few Frenchmen.

STEPHANIE: [*Chuckling*] Thank you, Señor Sanchez, but I rarely go out during the week and I don't have the clothes for anything like—

SANCHEZ: [*Quickly*] I can buy you anything. In a Swiss bank I have twenty million—

STEPHANIE: [*Sits at desk*] No, thank you.

> [JULIAN *comes out of the door of the operating room. He stands behind* SANCHEZ, *who doesn't see him.* JULIAN *is holding small white towel*]

SANCHEZ: [*To* STEPHANIE *in a very intimate tone*] All right for now, Stephanie. [*Puts invitation on desk*] But let me warn you, the men of my blood are very persistent.

JULIAN: [*A tiny bit annoyed and impatient*] Ready for you, Señor Sanchez.

SANCHEZ: [*Noticing* JULIAN] The firing squad. [*Turns to* JULIAN, *takes towel from his hand*] Please, no blindfold.

[*He goes into the operating room.* JULIAN *stays behind and gives* STEPHANIE *a curious look*]

JULIAN: Was he . . . ? Get me his X-rays. [*He goes*]

STEPHANIE: Yes, Doctor. [*She starts for file but is interrupted by the doorbell chimes.* STEPHANIE *hurries to the door. She opens it and stands there*]

VOICE: [*Off*] Mrs. Winston?

STEPHANIE: Well, yes. Thank you. [*She closes door, crosses to desk, carrying the same box that* JULIAN *brought to* TONI. *She looks at it, puzzled, puts it on her desk, opens it, glances in and gasps, quickly closes box*]

JULIAN: [*Sticking head out the door*] Where are those X-rays?

STEPHANIE: [*Goes to file, gets X-rays, hurries to* JULIAN *who is waiting in the doorway with back to audience*] Here they are, Doctor. [*Gives him the X-rays. He goes. She hurries to desk, takes box to chest, opens box again, takes out card and reads*] "As ever, Julian." Oh my God, how beautiful! [*She seems dazed and a little faint*] For me—for me—from Julian. [*Hugging mink*]

[JULIAN *steps through door of the operating room*]

JULIAN: [*Not looking at her; sharply*] Miss Dickinson, you gave me Harvey Greenfield's X-rays.

STEPHANIE: [*Puts mink in box, crosses to him, still holding card*] Oh, forgive me, Doctor. I was, uh . . . [*She stands there, staggering, as though she is about to faint.* JULIAN *steadies her*]

JULIAN: What's wrong, Miss Dickinson?

STEPHANIE: Nothing, nothing. I felt a little dizzy.

JULIAN: Do you want to go home?

STEPHANIE: No, Doctor, no, I'm fine. It's just that it came and . . . oh, it's too much.

[*This section is staged so that* JULIAN *doesn't see the mink until we want him to*]

JULIAN: What the hell are you talking about? [*Puts* HARVEY'S *X-rays on desk*]

STEPHANIE: The gift. It's overwhelming . . . unbelievable. . . .

JULIAN: Holy smoke, it's not that great a thing. Just a few. . . .

STEPHANIE: [*Raving on*] And your card. How sweet. [*Gives card to him*]

JULIAN: [*Reads*] "As ever, Julian." Well I must say I did spend considerable time trying to pick out the sort of thing you like. After all, you've put up with a lot from me lately.

STEPHANIE: I'll never be able to thank you enough.

JULIAN: I'm glad to have given you so much pleasure. I know you love beautiful music. [*Gives card to her, goes into operating room*]

STEPHANIE: [*Returns to chest*] Music! What a lovely way of describing this. [*She takes the stole from box, puts it on and twirls around. She suddenly rushes to phone and dials. Kneels on chair*] Hello, Mother . . . ? [*Quickly puts down phone as* JULIAN *re-enters*]

JULIAN: Miss Dickinson, we're forgetting Señor Sanchez's X-rays. . . .

[*She starts for file.* JULIAN *starts off, turns back quickly as he spots the stole. He staggers as though about to faint. She rushes toward him*]

STEPHANIE: [*Frightened, grabs him*] What's wrong, Doctor?

JULIAN: Nothing, nothing . . . I felt a little dizzy, too.

SANCHEZ: [*Rushing out of operating room*] What's wrong with my X-rays? You know I'm very nervous!

JULIAN: Nothing, nothing. . . . [*He shoves* SANCHEZ *into operating room ahead of him*]

SANCHEZ: [*Reappears in doorway. Speaks to* STEPHANIE] You look beautiful. [*He disappears into operating room again as* JULIAN *grabs his arm and yanks him off*]

JULIAN: [*To* STEPHANIE] Quick, give me those X-rays.

STEPHANIE: [*Digging them out of file*] Here they are, Doctor. [*She hands them to* JULIAN] It is beautiful, isn't it? [JULIAN *gives a sickly laugh and exits into operating room.* STEPHANIE, *left alone, hurries back to the telephone. Sits—looks at* SANCHEZ's *invitation*] Hello, Mother. . . . Now listen, dear, I want you to do something for me. Call Lucille at her dress shop. She showed me a dress yesterday. It was much too expensive, I can't afford it and I want it. Tell Lucille I'll pick it up on the way home. . . . And, Mother, tell her it's very important because tonight I'm going to the April in Paris Ball. . . . What? Mother, I didn't know you were planning pot roast. . . .

BLACKOUT

SCENE FOUR

The night spot, later that night. In addition to banquettes, there is now a small table and two chairs on upstage portion of dance floor. TONI *and* IGOR *are dancing to rock 'n' roll music.* JULIAN *is seated at a banquette.*

TONI: [*Calling*] Hey, Julian, I think Igor is getting over his depression. [*Music fades*]

JULIAN: He gave it to me.

TONI: [*Stops dancing, goes to him and sits*] Aren't you having fun?

JULIAN: Oh, sure, I love watching you two dance. Very educational.

IGOR: [*Standing near table and fumbling in his pockets*] I need some cigarettes. I'll only be a minute. [*Starts*]

JULIAN: Please hurry back. We'll be lonesome.

IGOR: Ciao. [*He goes*]

TONI: [*To* JULIAN] You're not being a very good host.

JULIAN: Do you expect me to enjoy a whole evening with that character? I wanted us to be alone. Incidentally, why the hell did we come *here?*

TONI: It was the one sure place where we wouldn't run into your wife.

JULIAN: [*Sarcastically*] Why, I thought you'd love seeing your dearest friend. After all, you gave her an expensive mink stole.

TONI: Oh, boy, you're never going to stop talking about that mink. I'm glad Igor's here. At least it stops you from nagging—

JULIAN: [*Going right on*] Imagine giving away such a gift. And putting my card in it.

TONI: She'd never have accepted it from me.

JULIAN: She'd never have *gotten* it from *me.* Have you no idea of the value of money?

[*Slow Fox Trot starts*]

TONI: Boy, you're starting to talk just like a square husband. [IGOR *appears*] Come on, dear, smile and enjoy yourself.

JULIAN: Too late—*he's* back.

[IGOR *comes to banquette*]

IGOR: Want to dance, Toni?

TONI: [*Looking furtively at* JULIAN] Well. . .

JULIAN: [*Sarcastically*] Go on, dance, kiddies. I don't mind sitting here alone. [*She rises, goes to floor*] Oh, by the way, Igor, if you have a minute, will you run out and bring me back a crossword puzzle?

TONI: [*Pulling* IGOR *to the floor*] Come on, Igor. Let's dance.

[*They start dancing.* HARVEY *and his girl friend,* BOTTICELLI'S SPRING-TIME, *appear. They are each holding a glass of whiskey and they both look a little drunk. They cross below dance floor.* HARVEY *in the lead*]

BOTTICELLI'S SPRINGTIME: Harvey, I don't want to sit in here. Let's go back to the bar?

HARVEY: Let's put it this way—shut up! [*He pushes her into banquette and sits*]

[BOTTICELLI'S SPRINGTIME *seats herself sullenly.* JULIAN *has seen* HARVEY *enter. Now, as* TONI's *back is turned to him as she dances, he hurries over to* HARVEY's *table*]

JULIAN: [*Leans over back of banquette*] Hello, Harvey, how are you?

HARVEY: How am I? I'm sore, that's how I am. Good and sore, that's how.

JULIAN: I don't blame you, but I—

HARVEY: Last night you talked to me like *I* was dirt and you were Mister Clean.

JULIAN: Harvey, I'll explain it to you in the office. You know I'd never deliberately offend you.

HARVEY: [*Grudgingly*] Well—

JULIAN: [*Quickly*] Toni's watching. I have to go. [*Hurries back to table*]

BOTTICELLI'S SPRINGTIME: Who's that?

HARVEY: He's going to be your dentist.

BOTTICELLI'S SPRINGTIME: He seems very nervous for a dentist.

HARVEY: He gets bitten a lot.

[*Music stops.* TONI *and* IGOR *come back to the table*]

TONI: [*To* JULIAN] What were you saying to that terrible person?

JULIAN: Oh, just hello.

TONI: [*Sits*] Hello? After what he did to your wife?

[IGOR *sits.* WAITER *comes on, leading* STEPHANIE *and* SANCHEZ. *He seats them at upstage table. She is in a sensational evening gown and she's wearing the mink stole. They are laughing.* SANCHEZ *carries souvenirs from the Ball. She hands stole to* WAITER, *who places it on back of chair*]

SANCHEZ: [*Seats her and looks around*] Interesting. How did you happen to pick this place?

STEPHANIE: It's one of my favorites.

SANCHEZ: [*Sits*] In that case, I like it.

STEPHANIE: [*To* SANCHEZ] That Ball was marvelous.

SANCHEZ: *You* were marvelous.

TONI: [*Stunned*] Well, look at that!

IGOR: Who is that?

TONI: [*Not wanting to take her eyes off* STEPHANIE] Sshhhhh, I'll tell you in a minute.

SANCHEZ: [*Looking fondly at her*] Stephanie, you know, you're amazing.

STEPHANIE: Thank you, Arturo.

[WAITER *enters from bar, puts two drinks on table*]

SANCHEZ: Everyone at the Ball was staring at you. That gown is absolute poetry.

STEPHANIE: Paris. It's a copy, of course, not the original.

SANCHEZ: [*Gallantly*] You should have only originals. [WAITER *exits.* SANCHEZ *kisses her hand again.* STEPHANIE *laughs*] In a Swiss bank, I— [*Hands her a drink; she takes it*]

STEPHANIE: On top of all that champagne?

SANCHEZ: Live!

TONI: [*With awe*] I can hardly believe that's Stephanie.

JULIAN: [*Dolefully*] It is. I recognize the mink.

TONI: [*Staring at the other table*] And she's already found somebody else.

JULIAN: That silly gaucho.

TONI: [*Shaking her head*] She certainly works fast.

IGOR: Toni, would you let me in on this?

TONI: That woman over there—that's Julian's wife.

IGOR: [*Impressed*] Hey, not bad, Julian, not bad at all.

JULIAN: Thank you.

TONI: [*To* IGOR, *confidentially*] Well, get this—she is surrounded by—
[*Pointing to* JULIAN] her husband— [*Pointing to* HARVEY] her ex-boy-friend . . . and her new one.

IGOR: Boy, that lady must like action.

JULIAN: [*Sharply to* IGOR] Never mind that.

IGOR: I meant it as a compliment. She's very beautiful.

TONI: [*To* IGOR] Say, Igor, this is news. You go for the older ones.

IGOR: So do you. [*He gives a quick glance at* JULIAN]

TONI: Sshhhh. [*Smiles at* JULIAN]
   [JULIAN *doesn't like any of this*]

SANCHEZ: [*He suddenly spots* JULIAN] Ho ho. There's Doctor Winston.

STEPHANIE: Oh dear, where? [*She turns, waves at* JULIAN, *who waves back*]
   Never thought I'd see *him* here tonight.

SANCHEZ: Would you rather we leave?

STEPHANIE: No, I don't mind him being here, do you?

SANCHEZ: Not if he didn't bring his drill.

STEPHANIE: Let's ignore him. After all, my evenings are my own.

SANCHEZ: [*Sexy voice again, caressing her hand*] What about your weekends?

STEPHANIE: They belong to my Mom.

SANCHEZ: [*Taking his hand away and speaking a bit coldly*] I see.

STEPHANIE: [*She wants to keep the action going for the benefit of* JULIAN] El
   Bravo, you're not going to give up so easily, are you?

SANCHEZ: Señorita, what kind of game are you playing?

STEPHANIE: Game? [*She laughs coquettishly with an eye on the other table*]

BOTTICELLI'S SPRINGTIME: [*To* HARVEY] Who's that? I know her. Isn't that
   the woman from last night?

HARVEY: Say. I do believe you're right.

BOTTICELLI'S SPRINGTIME: Who is she?

HARVEY: That's the dentist's . . . wife.

BOTTICELLI'S SPRINGTIME: Well, who's that with the dentist?

HARVEY: That's his girl friend.

BOTTICELLI'S SPRINGTIME: He has a wife and a girl friend?

HARVEY: Better than two wives.

BOTTICELLI'S SPRINGTIME: Well, who's that with her?

HARVEY: With who?

BOTTICELLI'S SPRINGTIME: The dentist's wife.

HARVEY: The new boy friend.

BOTTICELLI'S SPRINGTIME: I'm shocked.

HARVEY: Why are you shocked?

BOTTICELLI'S SPRINGTIME: I'm from Philadelphia.

HARVEY: Oh.

> [*Rock 'n' roll music starts playing.* SANCHEZ *stands up, bows to* STEPHANIE. *She rises. They start dancing*]

JULIAN: [*Watching them*] My God, they're dancing!

TONI: So what? Are you jealous?

JULIAN: No, but she shouldn't leave the mink lying around like that. Someone might take it.

TONI: It's now *her* mink.

JULIAN: [*Rising, to* TONI] Come on, let's dance.

TONI: All of a sudden you want to dance.

JULIAN: Are you coming or not? [*He crosses to dance floor*]

TONI: [*Getting up quickly and obediently*] I'm coming, I'm coming. [*She rises, crosses to dance floor. She passes* IGOR, *gives him a look and whispers as though* JULIAN *is a nut*] Boy! [TONI *and* JULIAN *dance near the other couple and they all exchange greetings as they dance*]

STEPHANIE: Good evening. Good evening.

> [JULIAN *mumbles something*]

TONI: Good evening, Stephanie. You look simply marvelous.

STEPHANIE: Thank you, dear, and so do you.

SANCHEZ: Good evening, Doctor.

JULIAN: Good evening, patient.

BOTTICELLI'S SPRINGTIME: [*To* HARVEY] Look at them all being so damned polite. They're all rotten, rotten.

HARVEY: What do you want them to do, start kicking each other?

BOTTICELLI'S SPRINGTIME: Rotten, rotten. . . .

> [*Music swells*]

TONI: [*Doing a swinging new step*] No, Julian, this way.

> [JULIAN *struggles to follow her*]

STEPHANIE: [*Watching the new step*] That must be a new step they're doing. Let's try it.

[*She begins doing what* TONI's *doing.* SANCHEZ *vainly tries to follow her. Finally, the* GIRLS *are doing the step together and the* TWO MEN *join hands and try to imitate it*]

TONI: That's it, Stephanie. It's fun!

STEPHANIE: I've got it!

[*She swings downstage, dancing like mad*]

HARVEY: Hi, Sergeant!

STEPHANIE: Hi, Harve.

TONI: Boy, you're terrific! [*She joins* STEPHANIE]

[*Disgusted,* JULIAN *and* SANCHEZ *go to their separate tables.* TONI *circles* STEPHANIE *once, then calls to* IGOR]

TONI: Hey, Igor. . . .

[IGOR *hurries over and gets between the* GIRLS *and joins them in their step. The* THREE *of them are now doing a body-shaking movement, facing front*]

IGOR: [*As he dances*] Introduce me.

TONI: [*Dancing*] Mrs. Winston, meet Igor Sullivan. He's very depressed.

IGOR: How do you do, Mrs. Winston?

STEPHANIE: [*Still dancing*] How do you do? [*Sudden take*] Igor Sullivan?

IGOR: Yeah. [*He does the Swim*]

STEPHANIE: What's that? Igor Sullivan?

IGOR: The Swim.

JULIAN: I hope he drowns!

[IGOR *does a little bit of the Swim with* STEPHANIE *and* TONI *following him. Then he switches movement*]

IGOR: The backstroke.

[*The* GIRLS *follow that.* STEPHANIE *now changes to a tooth-pulling hand movement*]

IGOR: What's that?

STEPHANIE: A new step.

IGOR: What do you call it?

STEPHANIE: The dentist.

[*They do this for a moment.* TONI *heads for the banquette, dances alone, tries to get* JULIAN's *attention.* STEPHANIE *grabs* IGOR's *necktie and follows* TONI, *pulling* IGOR *along. When they arrive on center platform, the rock 'n' roll music is coming to a finish.* STEPHANIE *starts for table, pulling* IGOR *by his tie*]

TONI: [*To* JULIAN] Are you sulking again? [*Sits*]

JULIAN: If I finally decide to dance, I don't want it to be with Señor Sanchez.

> [*The music segues into a slow, dreamy ballad.* SANCHEZ *rises as though to go. He picks up stole.* STEPHANIE *is stopped by* IGOR *and they both start dancing to the ballad*]

SANCHEZ: [*Looking at* HARVEY] I should have brought my wife. [SANCHEZ *puts stole on* STEPHANIE'S *chair, sits*]

STEPHANIE: [*To* IGOR] I'll bet you feel as though you're dancing with your mother.

IGOR: [*Crisply and firmly*] Be quiet. I'm enjoying this.

STEPHANIE: So am I.

IGOR: Then relax. Let's not get neurotic about age. You're a very sexy lady.

STEPHANIE: Well, I *am* a lot older.

IGOR: Good. Let's run away and live on your Social Security.

> [STEPHANIE *laughs.* IGOR *holds her closer. They keep dancing.* TONI *and* JULIAN *are staring at them and at each other*]

TONI: Quite a sight, eh?

JULIAN: I must say, that Igor of yours is a pretty vulgar dancer.

TONI: What do you mean, Igor? She's the one that's plastering herself against him. That's no lady, that's a barracuda. And when I think of all I've done for her.

> [IGOR *kisses* STEPHANIE *on the neck*]

JULIAN: I don't know what's come over her. Hey, did you see that? He just kissed her on the neck.

> [SANCHEZ *rises*]

TONI: I have a feeling that perhaps we're in the way. Oh boy, Julian, everything you said about Stephanie sure was true.

JULIAN: [*Stunned with surprise*] Yes, it was, wasn't it? Look at them now! Toni, if someone doesn't stop that man, he's going to make love right in the middle of the floor.

TONI: [*Hiding her irritation with nonchalance*] I don't care to watch any more. Let's get out of here.

> [*They rise. Music changes to loud rock 'n' roll again*]

STEPHANIE: [*To* IGOR] Our song! [*They start wild dance*]

TONI: [*Rises*] Julian?

JULIAN: [*Rises*] I don't know. Maybe I shouldn't leave her alone when she's like this.

TONI: [*Shocked*] Leave her alone? That's some talk from a man who's planning a divorce.

JULIAN: Oh, it's just that . . . Hey, look at him now. I don't know why I don't punch him in the nose.

[STEPHANIE *picks up stole. She and* IGOR *start to swing it*]

TONI: I'll tell you why. Because it's none of your business. [*She starts off*]

JULIAN: Toni!

TONI: If you want to stay, stay. I'm going.

> [*She exits.* SANCHEZ *rises, stands at edge of dance floor, arms folded, looking angry*]

JULIAN: Honey! [*He follows her*] Toni! [*As he steps onto dance floor, he grabs mink stole from* IGOR *and* STEPHANIE. *They continue to dance.* JULIAN *rolls it up and throws it to the puzzled* SANCHEZ] Even though I got it wholesale. . . . [*He goes off*]

BOTTICELLI'S SPRINGTIME: They're rotten, rotten!

HARVEY: Rotten, rotten!

BLACKOUT

SCENE FIVE

Doctor's office, the next morning. Stage is empty. There is one interesting change in the office. A special spot is directed at STEPHANIE'S *cactus plant which has blossomed! There is a good-sized, lovely flower. After a moment the rest of the lights come up.* JULIAN *comes out of operating room looking at his watch, pacing back and forth impatiently. Finally sits on seat by door. After a moment,* STEPHANIE *tiptoes in. She doesn't see* JULIAN. *She is still in her evening clothes from the night before, mink stole and everything. She acts a bit guilty. She quietly heads for the supply closet.*

JULIAN: [*Sardonically, closing door*] Good morning.

STEPHANIE: [*Startled, almost to supply room door*] Good morning. I'm afraid I'm a bit late. [*She sees cactus flower*] Hey! [*She hastens to desk, picks up cactus*]

JULIAN: [*Rises*] It's after ten. Two patients have already come and gone. The phone's been ringing . . . and you stroll in here in evening clothes. [*Sudden take*] Evening clothes!

STEPHANIE: I didn't have time to go home and change. It would have made me even later. [*Smells flower on plant*] What a night! What a night!

JULIAN: [*Cutting her off*] I don't care to hear about it. I'd appreciate it if you'd put down that oasis and go change into your uniform.

STEPHANIE: Sorry.

> [*She puts down plant, starts for supply closet.* JULIAN, *after letting her take about three steps, can no longer contain himself*]

JULIAN: [*A real blast*] Where the hell have you been?

STEPHANIE: [*She stops and looks at him. She's enjoying this. Then she speaks in a casual, playgirl manner*] Oh, I don't think it would interest you. Besides, it's all a blur. A beautiful, blurry blur.

JULIAN: When I left the club you were already doing fairly well. I mean, blurry-wise.

STEPHANIE: You shouldn't have gone so soon. Things really started to swing after you left.

JULIAN: I'm sure my departure helped.

STEPHANIE: Maybe. Anyway, the place started to fill up with lovely, noisy people . . . everyone was happy . . . everyone bought everyone else drinks. Say, have you ever had a gin and tonic made with tequila?

JULIAN: No, thank you. [*Raising his eyes to heaven*] Tequila and tonic!

STEPHANIE: No, you substitute the tequila for the tonic.

JULIAN: Gin and tequila?

STEPHANIE: [*Nodding*] It's called a Mexican Missile. They tell me it prevents malaria.

JULIAN: So you stayed there all night, fighting malaria?

STEPHANIE: Oh, not all night. Only until about four-thirty. Then we went uptown. One of the musicians flang a big bash at his place and—

JULIAN: Flang a big bash?

STEPHANIE: A party. There was a great jam session . . . a lot of crazy dancing . . . everyone sat around smoking pot. . .

JULIAN: [*Cutting in*] Pot! [*In his best medical manner*] Do you happen to know that pot is marijuana?

STEPHANIE: No!

JULIAN: You didn't smoke it.

STEPHANIE: Just a puff, to be a sport. [*Puffs imaginary cigarette*]

JULIAN: I've created a monster!

STEPHANIE: No, Dr. Frankensteineo, this was no creation of yours, this was *me*. Me, experiencing some new things . . . things I've never tried before . . . and having a hell of a goddam good time! I'll never forget it. The dancing, the music, the fun. And, best of all, the sunrise on the beach.

JULIAN: The beach?

STEPHANIE: We wanted some fresh air so we took a long drive out to Coney Island. It's lovely at dawn. Nobody there. We sat on the beach and watched the sun come up. [*She shakes her stole vigorously.*]

JULIAN: You sat on the beach in your new mink stole?

STEPHANIE: Oh, a little sand won't hurt it. [*Dragging stole*] Besides, I had to lie on something.

JULIAN: [*Follows her*] You said you were sitting. Were you sitting or lying?

STEPHANIE: I don't remember. I was too busy watching the sun rise. Now, if you'll excuse me, I have to get dressed and take an Alka Seltzer.

JULIAN: Well, I think Señor Sanchez had a hell of a nerve!

STEPHANIE: [*Stops dead*] Oh, my God!

JULIAN: What's the matter?

STEPHANIE: Señor Sanchez! I forgot all about him.

JULIAN: But you were *with* him.

STEPHANIE: No. We must have lost him somewhere along the way. [*Giggles and shakes stole*] We didn't even miss him.

JULIAN: We? Who's we?

STEPHANIE: Igor and me.

JULIAN: You mean this whole night of debauchery was spent with that beatnik?

STEPHANIE: It wasn't debauchery and Igor is not a beatnik. He's just young . . . and sensitive . . . and very poetic.

JULIAN: Poetic? I saw him kiss you on the neck.

STEPHANIE: Well, he's a friendly kid. [*She puts stole on desk*]

JULIAN: [*Shaking his head in disbelief*] So you and this friendly kid ditched poor Señor Sanchez.

STEPHANIE: [*Sarcastically*] Poor Señor Sanchez! He's an old foof.

JULIAN: An old foof?

STEPHANIE: Yes, and a pretty *fresh* old foof.

JULIAN: That old foof is a damn good patient. If I lose him—

STEPHANIE: Oh, he'll come back. You only put in a temporary filling.

JULIAN: Miss Dickinson, I find your behavior, last night and today, completely outrageous. And I won't stand for it.

STEPHANIE: [*Firmly*] Now wait a minute, Doctor, the only crime I've committed as far as you're concerned is that I am one hour late. If you like, you can take it off my salary.

JULIAN: [*Shaking his head as he paces*] It's grotesque, absolutely grotesque. Throwing yourself at that young kid. It certainly looks ridiculous at your age.

STEPHANIE: How about that father-and-daughter thing of yours?

JULIAN: It's different with a man. When a man is with a younger woman, it looks entirely appropriate. But when it's vice versa—

STEPHANIE: Try asking a vice versa about *that* vice versa.

JULIAN: Well, at least I wasn't kissing Toni on the neck. And don't tell me it was just friendly. There is no such thing as a friendly kiss on the neck.

STEPHANIE: You know, Doctor, you were the one who told me I was discouraging men. Stifling my femininity. But the first time a cute, virile, young man holds me a little closely, you go to pieces. If I didn't know better, I'd almost swear you were jealous. [*She sits in desk chair*]

JULIAN: Jealous? Of you? Come now, Miss Dickinson. . . . It's just that I think it in very bad taste when, under my very eyes and the eyes of my fiancée, my wife decides to take part in an indecent, immoral, semipornographic exhibition. That's all I have to say.

STEPHANIE: Well, it isn't all I have to say. Yes, I let him kiss me on the neck, and if you thought I liked it, you were right. I've lost a lot of time. But the world is full of pleasures I can still have, and now I'm going to have them. I'm not going to be afraid of life ... afraid of love—

JULIAN: I should have kept my mouth shut.

STEPHANIE: [*Rises and crosses to him*] You know, it wasn't easy for me to go out with that South American last night. But whenever I felt shaky, I thought of you.

JULIAN: Oh, it was obvious you were thinking of me.

STEPHANIE: I thought of those terrible things you said. And it made me hold my head up. Oh, maybe I overdid things ... I drank too much ... but I'm glad I did. It freed me.

JULIAN: Well, it certainly freed your neck for Igor.

STEPHANIE: [*Sharply*] Never mind Igor. He was fine, warm, sincere, and he thought I was beautiful ... he even said sexy!

JULIAN: [*Tolerantly*] Well, with those dim lights ... and with my mink stole—

STEPHANIE: [*Cutting in*] Charming. Sure, the soft lights helped. But there was something else. There was a spark—electricity ... I could feel it, and it was *my* electricity.

JULIAN: Oh, well, if you brought along your own battery—

STEPHANIE: [*She means this*] Don't joke about this, Doctor. If you do, I'll kick you.

JULIAN: Now, Miss Dickinson, I was just trying to—

STEPHANIE: [*Through clenched teeth as she grabs lapels of his suit*] Drop it, Doctor. I warn you, drop it. [*She gives him a small shove*]

JULIAN: [*He's decided that he's gone too far*] Oh, let's not be angry, Stephanie. You spent a gay, wild evening and it went to your head. I'm sure there's no harm done. After all, it was just a little flirtation. Right?

STEPHANIE: [*She stands there, steaming*] Maybe it was more than that.

JULIAN: All right, it was a mad passion! But at least you didn't ... that is, you didn't. . . ?

STEPHANIE: [*Not looking at him*] You still treat me like an antiseptic spinster. [*Sits and looks at him*] Why don't you just ask me if I went to bed with him?

JULIAN: All right. Did you go to bed with him?

STEPHANIE: It's none of your business.

JULIAN: Now listen, let's have it. What happened out there on my mink stole ... I mean, the beach? [STEPHANIE *ignores him*] You must answer. I insist!

STEPHANIE: By what right?

JULIAN: A husband's right. Let me point out that you're still my wife.

STEPHANIE: [*Rising*] No more! I want a divorce. After the years of misery I've had with you, I no longer—

JULIAN: Years of misery?

STEPHANIE: [*Going on*] All the things I had to put up with! The mysterious phone calls, the pretty patients you treated free, the hairpins I found under the cushions on the sofa. Your handkerchiefs all smeared with lipstick—

JULIAN: Hey, wait a minute—

STEPHANIE: And your wallet.

JULIAN: My wallet?

STEPHANIE: Let's not forget your wallet all stuffed with dirty pictures of girls in bikinis.

JULIAN: [*To the world at large*] She goes through my pockets! [*Turns to her*] You went through my pockets. That's the most immoral thing I ever—

STEPHANIE: Don't talk about morals, you . . . you libertine! With your wild weekends in Easthampton!

JULIAN: How did you know about my wild weekends in Easthampton? You spied on me! You had me followed! All right, you want war. You can have it.

STEPHANIE: Good!

JULIAN: I'll tell the whole world about you. Your drunkenness! Your marijuana parties! Your orgies on the beach! *You* want a divorce. It's *I* who wants a divorce.

[*During this speech,* STEPHANIE *has been gesturing, looking through a spy glass, drinking out of a glass, smoking, etc.*]

STEPHANIE: And you can have it. I'm through as your wife and through as your personal slave. [*As she says this, she crosses to desk, wraps the mink around his neck*] Here, give that to your child concubine. [*She starts for the door*]

JULIAN: [*Tearing off mink and flinging it on floor*] Stephanie, I warn you, if you go out that door don't ever try to come back.

STEPHANIE: [*At door, turns back*] Come back? Do you think I'm a masochist? [*Switches to great dignity*] Don't worry, Dr. Winston, you'll never, never see me again. [*She opens the door, starts through it, stops and turns*] And that goes for the children, too. [*She goes*]

BLACKOUT

SCENE SIX

TONI's *apartment, that evening.* IGOR *is sitting in chair near table and* TONI *is standing next to him.*

IGOR: It's none of your business.

TONI: I have a right to know. She's my fiancé's wife.

IGOR: [*Cutting her off*] Toni, I'd rather not discuss the lady.

TONI: The lady! Well, I don't really have to ask. I happen to know that this particular *lady* swings with anybody.

IGOR: [*Blurts it out as he rises*] Then I guess I'm not anybody!

TONI: [*Giving him a long, puzzled look*] Igor!

IGOR: That's it. Nothing happened.

TONI: She didn't want to, huh?

IGOR: Why do you assume that? Maybe *I* didn't want to.

TONI: I doubt that. I saw you kiss her neck.

IGOR: Maybe I just happen to love necks. Like Dracula.

TONI: But if nothing happened, what were you doing all night?

IGOR: We danced a lot, we drank a lot, and talked a lot.

TONI: About what?

IGOR: Oh, I don't know, we just talked. I enjoyed talking to her about my work . . . about myself . . . it's a rare thrill to find a woman you can talk to.

TONI: Are you implying that you cannot talk to me?

IGOR: [*Sits*] Come to think of it, I can *not*. You're always doing the talking and it's always about your troubles with that ridiculous old decadent dentist.

TONI: Don't you talk that way about Julian. He's a good man.

IGOR: Well, maybe he's good enough for you, but he's sure not good enough for his wife.

TONI: You should know what *I* know.

IGOR: I know what *I* know. She's a hell of a dame, good-looking, smart, warm, and *very appealing*.

TONI: Ahah! Then you did want to.

IGOR: Want to what?

TONI: You know, Igor.

IGOR: Oh, for God's sake, you have an absolutely filthy, juvenile mind.

[*There is a knock on the door.* TONI *opens door and* STEPHANIE *enters*]

TONI: [*After a look at* STEPHANIE] Igor, it's for you.

IGOR: Hi, Stephanie. [*He rises and goes to meet* STEPHANIE]

STEPHANIE: Igor, my favorite debaucherer.

IGOR: How's your head today?

STEPHANIE: I don't know. I just got it back on.

TONI: If you two would prefer, I could go wait in the ice box.

STEPHANIE: Relax. I came to talk to *you*. [*Turns to* IGOR *and indicates door*] Igor, dear, if you don't mind. . . .

IGOR: I don't know. If you two are going to fight over me, I feel I should. . . . [*He trails off as* STEPHANIE *looks at him*] Okay, okay. May the best woman win. [*He goes, closing door*]

TONI: And I used to worry about you.

STEPHANIE: That's what caused all the trouble. Now, Toni, you're probably expecting Julian and I don't want to run into him. So, if you don't mind. . . .

TONI: [*Still on the same subject*] Boy, you and Igor. That child.

STEPHANIE: [*Puts down purse*] Toni, don't make this more difficult for me. Never mind Igor. I'm here to talk about Julian and me.

TONI: He sent you?

STEPHANIE: I'm here on my own. To straighten out this whole mess.

TONI: It's about time. Now, what about Julian? Are you keeping him or not? Do I take him or can't you spare him? I have to know.

STEPHANIE: There's something else you have to know first. [*Puts hand on her shoulder*] Sit down, dearie. You won't have so far to fall.

[TONI *sits on bed.* STEPHANIE *paces a moment*]

TONI: [*A little frightened*] What can it be?

STEPHANIE: I have no patience with people who shilly-shally about these things. I'm going to come straight to the point. Julian and I. . . . [*She stops, turns, looks at* TONI] Oh God, this isn't as easy as I thought.

TONI: [*Sudden thought*] I know what it is. You're pregnant.

STEPHANIE: I don't think so. Where did you ever get a crazy thought like that?

TONI: Crazy? Not for the swinging Mrs. Winston.

STEPHANIE: I'm not Mrs. Winston, I'm *Miss* Dickinson.

TONI: [*Rises*] Miss Dickinson! You, the old maid?

STEPHANIE: That's right.

TONI: That's ridiculous!

STEPHANIE: That's what I think. Toni, I hate to be the one to have to tell you this, but—

TONI: [*Cutting in, goes to* STEPHANIE, *puts arm on her shoulder*] Wait a minute. Let's be calm. Don't get nervous. You're Miss Dickinson, Julian's nurse. Right?

STEPHANIE: Right.

TONI: Then who's Mrs. Winston?

STEPHANIE: That's a very good question. Julian's not married. Never been.

TONI: Wait a minute! This is a trick. You're trying to confuse me so I'll do something and you'll get to keep him for yourself. Along with Harvey and Igor— [*Sudden realization as she sits on bed*] You mean he lied to me? Why?

STEPHANIE: [*Tenderly*] I'm sorry, Toni, this would be a shock to anyone. But I know it's even greater for someone of your youth, your idealism, your—

TONI: [*Quietly*] The dirty son of a bitch!

STEPHANIE: That's one way of looking at it. [*Sits by* TONI, *puts arm around her*] Now look, Toni, I didn't come here to bury Julian. I've always helped him with his problems and I want to help him with this one. He loves you.

TONI: Then why did he lie like that?

STEPHANIE: Dr. Winston is a good man, but I'm afraid he's a bit weak.

TONI: A weak man but a strong liar! [*Rising*] When I think of all those thousands of details . . . the little things he made up about his married life.

STEPHANIE: That's one of his faults. He's a perfectionist. If I told you the work he does on a simple cavity.

TONI: Dammit, I'm a person, not a tooth! I've been swindled.

STEPHANIE: You haven't been swindled.

TONI: Hah!

STEPHANIE: Toni, Julian is *marrying* you. A lot of girls would leap at such a swindle. [*Rises, goes to table and picks up bag*] Now look, Toni, I don't want to run into him, so I really must go.

TONI: How come you suddenly decided to come here and unmess this mess?

STEPHANIE: Let's just say Miss Dickinson is a neat nurse. She likes to leave everything tidy before she goes. Now look, Toni, one of these days Julian will come to you and tell you the truth on his own. When he does, try to help him, accept him. Well, try to.

TONI: A man who lies can not love.

STEPHANIE: That sounds like something out of a fortune cookie. [*She goes, closing door*]

TONI: [*She picks up picture from headboard. To photo*] Dirty married bachelor! [*She crosses to the side wall and knocks on it, goes to door, opens it. Calling*] Igor! Igor!

[*We hear* IGOR's *muffled voice*]

IGOR: [*Off*] What do you want? I'm trying to work.

TONI: Come quickly, I need you right away.

IGOR: [*Off*] Okay.

TONI: You decadent swindler! [*She puts the picture in the icebox, as* IGOR *enters*]

IGOR: Toni . . . [*She kisses him*] Well, what did you want?

TONI: This is what I wanted. [*She kisses him again*]

IGOR: Toni, what's come over you? What about Julian?

TONI: Ha! It serves him right.

IGOR: [*Closes door*] Now wait a minute. Are you using me to punish Julian?

TONI: Never mind that, Igor. Kiss me again.

IGOR: Okay, but after this one I want a complete explanation. [*They kiss. There is a knock at the door. Pulling away*] The door! It must be Julian.

TONI: [*Clutching him again*] So what?

[IGOR *backs up. She clings to him*]

IGOR: You wanted him to catch us. You were using me, you little trollop! I'm getting out of here. [*He starts for the door*]

TONI: [*Putting hand on door and stopping him with a smile*] He's out there. [*Knock on the door again*] There's no way you can go.

IGOR: I'll hide in the bathroom.

TONI: That's going to look worse. Suppose he wants to wash his hands.

IGOR: He's a dentist. They're always clean.

[*He hastens into the bathroom.* TONI *opens the door.* JULIAN *enters*]

JULIAN: I thought you'd never answer. What were you doing?

TONI: I was taking a bath.

JULIAN: But you're all dressed.

TONI: All right. I was sailing my boats.

JULIAN: Please, Toni, not today. Today I need all your help and understanding.

TONI: [*Interested*] What do you mean?

JULIAN: I have something to tell you and it's . . . it's . . . tough.

TONI: You've come to tell me the truth. [*He nods*] Julian, don't worry, darling. If you want to tell me the truth—you *are* here to tell me the truth? [*He nods*] Go ahead, sweetheart. I promise it will be all right. [*She sits*]

JULIAN: Thanks, my love. You're just marvelous. This isn't going to be easy, but . . . here it is. My wife . . . Stephanie . . . She no longer wants a divorce. [TONI *looks at him, doesn't react at all*] Try to be calm, dear, it was a blow to me, too. I'm absolutely sick about it. [*He sits on bed*]

TONI: [*Playing along*] So am I. Oh, you poor man. [*Rises*] Now, let's see if I can get this straight. Your wife has actually changed her mind and now refuses to give you your freedom.

JULIAN: [*Nodding*] Isn't that unbelievable?

TONI: [*Momentarily collapses*] Completely. When did she tell you this?

JULIAN: This morning. Oh, I fought like a tiger. I roared and ranted and raged . . . and then I pleaded. I offered her anything. The apartment, the silver, the furniture, my paintings, more money . . . but she and her lawyer are adamant. No divorce.

 [*During above,* TONI *is making vicious Karate chops at his back*]

TONI: But, say, you can divorce *her*. You have grounds . . . her wild nymphomania, all her lovers. . . . [*She sits next to him*]

JULIAN: Oh, I threatened her with that, but she laughed. She knew I wouldn't use that. All that nasty stuff coming out in the papers. . . . It could ruin me. I'm sorry, baby, the dame has us over a barrel. We're cooked. Our beautiful dream is now just that. A dream.

TONI: Just one thing. What happens to me in all this?

JULIAN: [*He puts his arm around her*] Oh, we'll go right on seeing each other as before.

TONI: Oh, good.

JULIAN: We'll still manage to snatch a few scraps of happiness from life. It's a compromise.

TONI: [*As though she agrees*] Well, dear, if that's the way it has to be. . . .

JULIAN: Oh, baby, how wonderfully well you're taking this. [TONI *makes a face*] You'll see, we'll be even happier than before.

TONI: It really won't be a bad arrangement. And it's fair. You'll still have your wife and me, and I'll still have you and Igor.

JULIAN: Igor? . . . Igor? But you always said he was only a friend . . . the kid next door. Toni! [*Rises*]

TONI: [*Rises*] Julian.

JULIAN: Were you lying to me?

TONI: [*Drops her head*] I'm ashamed to admit it. [*Lifts her head*] I know how you hate the thought of a lie.

JULIAN: Aah, this is just a rib. [*Reaching for her*] Come on, Toni, you're putting me on, aren't you?

TONI: [*Calling*] Igor, come on out. Come out of the bathroom, don't be afraid. [*No response from the bathroom*]

JULIAN: What could there possibly be between you and that dopey kid?

TONI: He's not a dopey kid. He's a writer. He talks to me like a person and he's not married. [*Calls*] Igor!

JULIAN: All right, cut it out, Toni. You know damned well that if I thought for one moment that beatnik was in there, I'd be out of here like a shot.

 [*The bathroom door opens quickly and* IGOR *appears. He's wearing nothing but a towel around his waist.* JULIAN *stares at him;* IGOR *stares back*]

IGOR: Hi, there.

> [JULIAN *gives* TONI *a look, then turns and heads for the door. He opens it*]

TONI: [*Follows him*] Julian, don't feel too bad about this. You'll get over the—

JULIAN: [*Cutting her off with dignity as he turns back*] I'll be fine, Toni. You broke up my home. You took me away from my wife. You alienated me from my children. But, thank God, I still have one thing left ... my integrity.

> [*He goes, leaving the door open.* TONI *closes the door with an attitude of finality. They look at each other.* TONI *gives* IGOR *a salute. He returns it*]

IGOR: I'd better get some clothes on. It's cold. [*He goes into bathroom. From offstage*] Toni, I'm sorry I came out looking like that, but I heard what was being said and I figured I might as well go all the way.... Toni?

TONI: I hear you. Igor?

IGOR: [*Off*] Yeah?

TONI: What are you doing tonight?

IGOR: [*Off*] Nothing.

TONI: How about having dinner together?

IGOR: [*Off*] Great. I'll go out and get some Chinese food.

TONI: Igor?

IGOR: [*Off*] Yeah?

TONI: How would you like some chicken cacciatore?

> [IGOR *comes slowly out of bathroom. They smile at each other and wave, as lights dim slowly*]

BLACKOUT

SCENE SEVEN

In the black we hear phone ringing and the doorbell chiming. On light STEPHANIE *comes out of the supply room, buttoning her uniform and holding her cap, which she puts on desk. She picks up phone.*

STEPHANIE: Hello, Dr. Winston's office. ... No, Mrs. Andrews, the doctor isn't in yet. I'll call you back.

> [*She hangs up. Doorbell chimes again. She goes to door, opens it.* JULIAN *steps in and stands there, looking hung over*]

JULIAN: Excuse me, I thought there was nobody here.

STEPHANIE: Then why were you ringing the bell?

JULIAN: I swallowed my key. Hey, what are *you* doing here? You quit . . . resigned. . . .

STEPHANIE: [*Stubbornly*] When a nurse resigns, it's her duty to stay until an adequate replacement is found. [*Closes door*] It's after ten. Where have you been?

JULIAN: I've been on the Drinking Man's Diet. Lost eighty-five pounds.

STEPHANIE: Everything all right between you and Toni? [*She crosses to file*]

JULIAN: Oh, yes. Things are all straightened out and, I might add, without your help and interference.

STEPHANIE: I'm very happy for you. [*She opens file drawer*]

JULIAN: Thank you. Toni and I are all washed up.

STEPHANIE: [*Turns*] Huh?

JULIAN: I went to see her and told her that you wouldn't agree to a divorce. [STEPHANIE *covers her face and starts laughing*] What the hell's so funny?

STEPHANIE: Nothing. Except I went to see Toni and told her the whole truth. That we weren't married and everything.

JULIAN: [*After reacting to this*] Why the hell did you do that?

STEPHANIE: I thought I'd fix things so that . . . [*Slams drawer*] well, at least somebody'd be happy.

JULIAN: You can't stop making chicken and egg sandwiches.

STEPHANIE: Well, why did you have to go there and lie?

JULIAN: [*He blurts it out*] Because it was the only way I could get out of marrying her. [*Sits*]

STEPHANIE: Don't you *want* to marry her?

JULIAN: It's always been a mistake. And when I finally caught her with Igor, I knew that—

STEPHANIE: Igor? She thinks he's a child.

JULIAN: I know. He was in her bathroom, wearing a diaper. They both made me feel like an idiot and I got out as fast as I could.

STEPHANIE: Now I understand why you went out and got drunk.

JULIAN: No, you don't understand why I got out and went drunk! [*Rises*] When I walked out of there I was angry. Absolutely furious! Homicidal!

STEPHANIE: [*Sits in desk chair*] So that's why you—

JULIAN: Stop interrupting! I was sure as hell sore at Toni. And then all at once . . . it was like magic . . . my anger disappeared, and all I felt was a delicious feeling of relief. Blessed, joyous relief. I never loved Toni and she never loved me. Now I was out of it. I said to myself, "Julian, thank God that's over. Now you can go home to your wife." I scampered down the stairs singing to myself, and then . . . bam! I remembered. I had no wife! When I got home there would be nobody. And when I got to the office, you wouldn't be there either.

STEPHANIE: [*Excited, rises*] So you went out and got drunk.

JULIAN: Stinking!

STEPHANIE: [*Going to him*] That's marvelous, marvelous! [*In her happiness, she puts her arms around him, then quickly takes them away*] That's very nice, Doctor.

JULIAN: [*Grabbing her hand before she can get away and pulling her towards him*] Stephanie?

STEPHANIE: Doctor?

JULIAN: I think I'm going to kiss you.

STEPHANIE: Oh?

JULIAN: Unless you have some objections—

STEPHANIE: None.

    [*He kisses her*]

JULIAN: Well, I kissed you.

STEPHANIE: Yes, you did.

JULIAN: And I'm going to do it often.

STEPHANIE: Me, too. [*She kisses him, then breaks away*]

JULIAN: It's funny. . . .

STEPHANIE: It is, isn't it?

JULIAN: I feel as though you've always been my wife. We don't even need to bother getting married.

STEPHANIE: Well, just as a matter of form.

    [*Phone rings; she crosses to answer it*]

JULIAN: Hey! I'm going to need a new nurse.

STEPHANIE: After all the trouble I went to. I'm not going to give another old maid a crack at you. [*She picks up phone*]

JULIAN: After all the trouble *you*. . . . [*He goes into closet to change into white coat*]

STEPHANIE: [*On phone*] Hello, Dr. Winston's office. Well, the doctor's busy. May I take a message? [*Listens a moment as* JULIAN *re-enters*] I see. One moment, please. [*Doesn't look at* JULIAN. *He is buttoning on his white coat*] It's a young lady. She's a stewardess with Swedish Airlines. She says she's free this evening.

JULIAN: [*Slightly rueful*] Tell her I've been grounded.

STEPHANIE: [*Back to phone*] Hello. I'm sorry, Miss, but Dr. Winston doesn't do that sort of work anymore.

    [*She hangs up, turns on stereo, which plays the "Hallelujah Chorus." She turns slowly and starts to cross to him, as*]

CURTAIN